ISBN 978-1-331-91868-4
PIBN 10253887

This book is a reproduction of an important historical work. Forgotten Books uses
state-of-the-art technology to digitally reconstruct the work, preserving the original format
whilst repairing imperfections present in the aged copy. In rare cases, an imperfection in
the original, such as a blemish or missing page, may be replicated in our edition. We do,
however, repair the vast majority of imperfections successfully; any imperfections that
remain are intentionally left to preserve the state of such historical works.

1 MONTH OF
FREE
READING

at

www.ForgottenBooks.com

By purchasing this book you are eligible for one month membership to ForgottenBooks.com, giving you unlimited access to our entire collection of over 700,000 titles via our web site and mobile apps.

To claim your free month visit:

www.forgottenbooks.com/free253887

English
Français
Deutsche
Italiano
Español
Português

www.forgottenbooks.com

Mythology Photography **Fiction**
Fishing Christianity **Art** Cooking
Essays Buddhism Freemasonry
Medicine **Biology** Music **Ancient**
Egypt Evolution Carpentry Physics
Dance Geology **Mathematics** Fitness
Shakespeare **Folklore** Yoga Marketing
Confidence Immortality Biographies
Poetry **Psychology** Witchcraft
Electronics Chemistry History **Law**
Accounting **Philosophy** Anthropology
Alchemy Drama Quantum Mechanics
Atheism Sexual Health **Ancient History**
Entrepreneurship Languages Sport
Paleontology Needlework Islam
Metaphysics Investment Archaeology
Parenting Statistics Criminology
Motivational

ROAMING THROUGH THE WEST INDIES

BY
HARRY A. FRANCK
Author of "A Vagabond Journey Around the World,"
"Zone Policeman 88," "Vagabonding
Down the Andes," etc., etc.

ILLUSTRATED WITH PHOTOGRAPHS
BY THE AUTHOR

NEW YORK
THE CENTURY CO.
1920

TO

MY WIFE, RACHEL,
WITH WHOM THIS WAS THE BEGINNING
OF A FAR LONGER JOURNEY, AND
TO
MY SON, HARRY,
WHO JOINED US ON THE WAY

FOREWARNING

Some years ago I made a tramping trip around the world for my own pleasure. Friends coaxed me to set it down on paper and new friends were kind enough to read it. Since then they have demanded more — at least so the publishers say — but always specifying that it shall be on foot. Now, I refuse to be dictated to as to how I shall travel; I will not ·be bullied into tramping when I wish to ride. The journey herewith set forth is, therefore, among other things, a physical protest against that attempted coercion, a proof that I do not need to walk unless I choose to do so. To make broken resolutions impossible, I picked out a trip that could not be done on foot. It would be difficult indeed to *walk* through the West Indies. Then, to make doubly sure, I took with me a newly acquired wife — and we brought back a newly acquired son, though that has nothing to do with the present story.

I will not go so far as to say that I abjured footing it entirely. As a further proof of personal liberty I walked when and where the spirit moved me — and the element underfoot was willing. But I wish it distinctly understood from the outset that this is no " walking trip." Once having broken the friends who flatter me with their attention of expecting me to confine myself to the prehistoric form of locomotion — I shall probably take to the road again to relieve a chronic foot-itch.

The following pages do not pretend to " cover " the West Indies. They are made up of the random pickings ·of an eight-months' tour of the Antilles, during which every island of importance was visited, but they are put together rather for the entertainment of the armchair traveler than for the information of the traveler in the flesh. While the latter may find in them some points to jot down in his itinerary, he should depend rather on the several thorough and orderly books that have been written for his special benefit.

HARRY A. FRANCK.

TABLE OF CONTENTS

ix

LIST OF ILLUSTRATIONS

xiv ILLUSTRATIONS

ROAMING THROUGH THE WEST INDIES

ROAMING THROUGH THE WEST INDIES

CHAPTER I

OVERLAND TO THE WEST INDIES

WE concluded that if we were to spend half a year or more rambling through the West Indies we would get sea-water enough without taking to the ships before it was necessary. Our first dream was to wander southward in the sturdy, if middle-aged, gasolene wagon we must otherwise leave behind, abandoning it for what it would bring when the mountains of central Cuba grew too diffi-cult for its waning vigor. But the tales men told of southern highways dampened our ardor for that particular species of adventure. They were probably exaggerated tales. Looking back upon the route from the eminence of automobile-infested Havana, we are of the impression that such a trip would have been marred only by some rather serious jolting in certain parts of the Carolinas and southern Georgia, and a moderately expensive freight-bill from the point where lower Florida turns to swamps and islands. If our people of the South carry out the ambitious highway plans that are now being widely agitated, there is no reason that the West Indian traveler of a year or two hence should hesitate to set forth in his own car.

The rail-routes from the northeastern states are three in number, converging into one at something over five hundred miles from the end of train travel. Those to whom haste is necessary or more agreeable than leisure may cover the distance from our greatest to our southern-most city in forty-eight hours, and be set down in Havana the following dawn. But with a few days to spare the broken journey is well worth the enhanced price and trouble. A truer perspective is gained by following the gradual change that increasing length of summer gives the human race rather than by springing at once from the turmoil of New York to the regions where winter is only a rumor and a hear-say.

In the early days of October the land journey southward is like the running backward of a film depicting nature's processes. The rich

3

autumn colors and the light overcoats of Pennsylvania advance gradually to the browning foliage and the wrapless comfort of the first autumn breezes, then within a few hours to the verdant green and simpler garb of full summer.   There are reservations, however, in the change of human dress, which does not keep pace with that of the landscape.   Our Southerners seem to be ruled in sartorial matters rather by the dictators of New York fashions than by the more fitting criterion of nature, and the glistening new felt fedora persists far beyond the point where the lighter covering would seem more suitable to time and place.

To the Northerner the first item of interest is apt to be the sudden segregation of races in the trains leaving Washington for the South. From the moment he surreptitiously sheds his vest as he rumbles across the Potomac the traveler finds his intercourse with his African fellow-citizens, be they jet black or pale yellow, circumscribed by an impregnable wall that is to persist until all but a narrow strip of his native land has shrunk away behind him.   Only as superior to inferior, as master to servant, or as a curiosity akin to that of the supercilious voyager toward the " natives " of some foreign land, is his contact henceforth with the other race.   Stern placards point out the division that must be maintained in public buildings or conveyances; custom serves as effectually in private establishments; the very city directories fetch up their rear with the " Colored Department."

The tourist's first impression of Richmond will largely depend on whether his train sets him down at the disreputable Main Street station or at the splendid new Union Depot on the heights of Broad Street. Unfortunately, the latter is as yet no more nearly " union " than it is, in spite of a persistent American misnomer, a " depot," and his chances of escaping the medieval landing-place are barely more than " fifty-fifty."   But his second notion of the erstwhile capital of the Confederacy cannot but be favorable, unless his tastes run more to the picturesque than to modern American civilization.   He may at this particular season grumble at a sweltering tropical heat that appears long before he bargained for it, but the hospitable Richmonder quickly appeases his wrath in this regard by explaining that some malignant cause, ranging from the disturbance of the earth's orbit by the war just ended to a boiling Gulf Stream, has given the South the hottest autumn in — I hesitate to say how many decades.   Nor, if he is new to the life below Mason and Dixon's Line, will he escape a certain surprise at finding how green is still the memory of the Confederacy.

The Southerner may have forgiven, but he has not forgotten, nor does he intend that his grandchildren shall do so.

In that endless stretch of sand, cotton, and pine-trees which is locally known as " Nawth Cahlina, sah," there are other ways of passing the time than by watching the endless unrolling of a sometimes monotonous landscape. One can get into conversation, for instance, with the train-crew far more easily than in the more frigid North, and listen for hours to more or less verdant anecdotes, which the inimitable Southern dialect alone makes worth the hearing. Or, if wise enough to abandon the characterless cosmopolitan Pullman for the local atmosphere of the day coach, one may catch such scraps as these — of special interest to big-game hunters — from the lips of fellow-passengers:

" Say, d' you hear about Bud Hampton? "

" What Bud done now? "

" Why, las' week Bud Hampton shot a buck niggah 't weighed ovah *two hunderd* pound! "

This particular species of quarry seemed to grow blacker with each succeeding state. The two urchins in one-piece garments who lugged our hand-bags up the slope in Columbia made coal seem of a pale tint by comparison. At the corner of a main street so business-bent as to require the constant attention of a traffic policeman they steered us toward the door of a somewhat weather-worn establishment.

" This the best hotel? " I queried, a bit suspicious that the weight of their burdens had warped their judgment. " How about that one down the street? " It was a building of very modern aspect, looming ten full stories into the brilliant Southern heavens.

" *Dat* ain' no hotel, sah," cried the two in one breath, rolling their snow-white eyeballs, their black toes seeming to wriggle with pride at the magnificence it presented, " dat 's de *sky-scrapah!* "

It was in Columbia that we felt for the first time irrevocably in the South. Richmond had been merely an American city with a Southern atmosphere; South Carolina's capital was the South itself, despite its considerable veneer of modern Americanism. One must look at three faces to find one indubitably white. Clusters of mahogany-red sugar-canes lolled in shady corners, enticing the black brethren to exercise their powerful white teeth. Goats drowsed in patches of sand protected from the insistent sunshine. Motormen raised their caps with one hand and brought their dashing conveyances to a sudden halt with the other at the very feet of their " lady acquaintances," whose male escorts returned the greeting with equal solemnity.

I puzzled for some time to know what far-distant city this one, with its red soil stretching away to suburban nothingness from the points where the street paving petered out, with its goats and sugar-cane, its variegated complexions, and frank contentment with life, was insistently recalling to memory. Then all at once it came to me. Purged of its considerable American bustle, Columbia would bear a striking resemblance to Asunción, capital of far-off Paraguay. Even the wide-open airiness of its legislative halls, drowsing in the excusable inoccupancy of what was still mid-summer despite the calendar, carried the imagination back to the land of the Guarani.

An un-Northern spaciousness was characteristic of the chief hostelry, with its ample chambers, its broad lounging-room, its generously gaping spitoons, offering not too exacting a target to the inattentive fire of Southern marksmanship. The easy-going temperament of its management came as a relief from the unflinching rule-of-thumb back over the horizon behind us. The reign of the old-fashioned " American plan," synonymous with eating when and what the kitchen dictates rather than leaving the guest a few shreds of initiative, had begun again and was to persist for a thousand miles southward. But can some trustworthy authority tell us what enactment requires that the " choicest room " of the " best hotel" of every American city be placed at the exact junction-point of the most successful attempt to concentrate all its twenty-four hours of uproar? I ask not in wrath, for time and better slumber have assuaged that, but out of mere academic curiosity. In the good, old irresponsible days of my " hobo " youth the " jungle " beyond the railroad yards was far preferable to this aristocratic Bedlam.

The "sky-scrapah " loomed behind us for half an hour or more across the mighty expanse of rolling sand-and-pine-tree world, with its distance-purple tinge and its suggestion of the interior of Brazil, which fled northward on the next lap of our journey. The cotton-fields which interspersed the wilderness might have seemed patches of daisies to the casual glance, rather sparse and thirsty daisies, for this year the great Southern crop had sadly disappointed its sponsors. Powder-dry country roads of reddish sand straggled along through the endless stretches of scrub-pines, carrying here and there the sagging buggy and gaunt and dust-streaked horse of former days. I relegate the equine means of transportation to the past advisedly, for his doom was apparent even in these sparsely cultivated and thinly peopled regions. Before a little unpainted, wooden negro church that drifted by us there clustered twenty-eight automobiles, with a bare half-dozen steeds drooping limply on their weary legs in the patches of shade the machines afforded them. King Cotton, abetted by his royal contemporaries overseas, has drawn no color-line in deluging his favors on his faithful subjects. Forests of more genuine trees replaced the scrub growth for long spaces farther on; here and there compact rectangles of superlatively green sugar-cane contrasted with the dead-brown patches of shriveled corn. In the smoking compartment of the coach placarded "White" shirt-sleeves and open collars were the rule, but the corresponding section of the "Colored" car indulged in no such disheveled comfort. The negroes of the South seem more consistent followers of Beau Brummel than their white neighbors.

We descended at Savannah in a hopeful frame of mind, for a recent report announced it the most nearly reasonable in its food prices of the fifty principal cities of our United States. Georgia's advantage in the contest with starvation was soon apparent. At the desk of the hotel overlooking a semi-tropical plaza the startled newcomer found staring him in the face a dire threat of incarceration, in company with the recipient, if he so far forgot himself as to offer a gratuity. There was something strangely familiar, however, about the manner of the grandson of Africa who hovered about the room to which he had conducted us, flecking away a speck of dust here, raising a curtain and lowering it again to the self-same height over yonder. I had no desire to spend even a short span of my existence in a Southern dungeon, along with this dusky bearer of the white man's burdens. But he would have made a most unsuitable spectator to the imperative task of removing the Georgian grime of travel. Enticing him into a corner out of sight of the key-hole I called his attention to the brilliancy of a silver coin. Instead of springing to a window to shout for the police, he snatched the curiosity in a strangely orthodox manner, flashed upon us a row of dazzlingly white teeth, and wished us a pleasant evening. Possibly I had read the anti-tipping ordinance too hastily; it may merely have forbidden the *public* bestowal of gratuities.

A microscopic examination might possibly have proved that the reckoning which was laid before us at the end of dinner showed some signs of shrinkage; to the naked eye it was quite as robust as its twin brothers to the North. But of course the impossibility of leaving a goodly proportion of the change to be cleared away with the crumbs would account for Savannah's low cost of living. The lengthening of the ebony face at my elbow as I scraped the remnants of my bank-note together might have been due to the exertions of the patent-leather shoes that sustained it to contain more than their fair share of contents. But it seemed best to make sure of the source of dismay; we might have to eat again before we left Savannah.

"I understand you can't accept tips down here in Georgia?" I hazarded, reversing the usual process between money and pocket. The increasing elongation of the waiter's expression branded the notion a calumny even sooner than did his anxious reply:

"*Ah* been taking 'em right along, sah. Yes, sah, thank you, sah. Dey did try to stop us makin' a livin', sah, but none of de *gen'lemans* do'n ferget us."

I can highly commend the anti-tipping law of Georgia; it gives one a doubled sense of adventure, of American freedom from restraint, reminiscent of the super-sweetness of stolen apples in our boyhood days.

We liked Savannah; preferred it, perhaps, to any of the cities of our journey southward. We liked the Southern hospitality of its churches, consistent with their roominess and their wide-open windows. We were particularly taken with the custom of furnishing fans as well as hymn-books, though we may have wondered a bit whether the segregation of the colored people persisted clear beyond St. Peter's gate. We were especially grateful to the genius of Oglethorpe, who had made this a city of un-American spaciousness, with every other cross street an ample boulevard, which gave the lungs and the eyes a sense of having escaped to the open country. Perhaps it was these wooded avenues, more than anything else, that made us feel we were at last approaching the tropics, where life itself is of more real importance than mere labor and business. Had we settled there, we should quickly have attuned ourselves to the domesticity of her business customs,— breakfast at nine, dinner from two to four, giving the mind harrassed with the selling of cotton or the plaints of clients time to compose itself in household quiet, supper when the evening breezes have wiped out the memory of the scorching sun. We liked the atmosphere of genuine companionship between the two sections of the population, despite the line that was sternly drawn between them where social intercourse might otherwise have blended together. The stately tread of the buxom negro women bearing their burdens on heads that seemed designed for no other purpose fitted into the picture our imaginations persisted in painting against the background of the old slave-market, with its barred cells, in defiance of the assertion of inhabitants that not a black man had ever been offered for sale there.

The man who conducted us to the top of Savannah's " sky-scrapah " — for every Southern city we visited boasted one such link between earth and heaven — was still frankly of the " rebel " turn of mind for all his youthfulness. He deplored the abolition of slavery. In the good old days a " niggah " was as valuable as a mule to-day ; no owner, unless he was a fool, would have thought of abusing so costly a possession any more than he would now his automobile. The golden age of the negro was that in which he was inspected daily, as soldiers are, and sternly held to a certain standard of outward appearance and health. To-day not one out of ten of them was fit to come near a white man. Laziness had ruined them ; their native indolence and the familiarity toward them of white men from the North had been their downfall. The South had no fear of race riots, however ; those were things only of the North, thanks to the Northerner's false notion of the " nigger's " human possibilities. Why had the black laborers who had raised this pride of Savannah to its lofty fifteen stories of height always lifted their hats to him, their foreman, and addressed the Northern architects with the disrespect of covered heads ? Wise men from " up east " soon learned the error of their ways in the treatment of the " niggah," after a few weeks or months of Southern residence. Slavery, in principle, was perhaps wrong, but it was the only proper system with negroes. Besides, we should not forget that it was not the South that had introduced slavery into the United States, but New England !

Many things, I knew, were chargeable to our northeastern states, but this particular accusation was new to me. Yet this son of the old South was a modern American in other respects, for all his out-worn point of view. His civic pride, bubbling over in a boasting that was not without a suggestion of crudity, alone proved that. Savannah was destined to become sooner or later the metropolis of America ; it was already second only to New York in the tonnage of its shipping. I cannot recall offhand any American town that is not destined some day, in the opinion of its proudest citizens, to become the leader of our commercial life, nor one which is not already the greatest something or other of the entire country. No doubt this conviction everywhere makes for genuine progress, even though the goal of the imagination is but a will-o'-the-wisp. What breeds regret in my soul, however, is the paucity of our cities that aspire to the place of intellectual leader-

ship, as contrasted with the multitude of those which picture themselve:
the foremost in trade and commerce.

Possibly Savannah will some day outstrip New York, but I hope not
for it has something to-day the loss of which would be an unfortunate
exchange for mere metropolitan uproar and which even its own
leisurely ambitious people might regret when it was too late. This
view from its highest roof, with its chocolate-red river winding away
to the sea sixteen miles distant, and inland to swampy rice-fields and the
abodes of alligators, that can be reached only by "bâteau," with its
palm-flecked open spaces and its freedom from smoke, raised the hope
that it might aspire to remain what it is now incontestably, a "city of
trees" and a pleasant dwelling-place.

There were suggestions in the over-languid manner of some of its
poorer inhabitants that the hookworm was prevalent in Savannah.
Well-informed citizens pooh-poohed the notion, asserting that "hookworm is just a polite Northern word for laziness." The particular
sore spot of the moment was the scarcity of sugar. From Columbia
onward it had been served us in tiny envelopes, as in war-days. That
displayed in store windows was a mere bait, for sale only with a corresponding quantity of groceries. All of which was especially surprising
in a region with its own broad green patches of cane. The unsweetened
inhabitants explained the enigma by a reference to "profiteers," and
pointed out the glaringly new mansions of several of this inevitable
war-time gentry. Others asserted that the ships at the wharves across
the river were at that very moment loading hundreds of tons of sugar
for Europe and furnishing even Germany with an article badly needed
at home. An old darky added another detail that was not without its
significance:

"Dey's plenty of sorghum an' merlasses right now, sah, but de white
folks dey cain't eat nothin' but de pure white."

Men of a more thoughtful class than our guide of the "sky-scrapah"
had a somewhat different view of the glories of the old South.

"Slavery," said one of them, "was our curse and in time would
have been our ruination. Not so much because it was bad for the
negroes, for it wasn't, particularly. But it was ruining the white
man. It made him a haughty, irresponsible loafer, incapable of con-
trolling his temper or his passions, or of soiling his hands with labor.
We have real cause to be grateful that slavery was abolished. But that
does not alter the fact that right was on our side in the war with

the North — the right of each State to dissolve its union with the others if it chose, which was the real question at issue, rather than the question of holding slaves, though I grant that we are better off by sticking to the union. If the South had won, the United States would be to-day a quarrelsome collection of a score of independent countries, unprogressive as the Balkans."

On a certain burning question even the most open-minded sons of the South were of the prevailing opinion.

"Whatever the North may think," said one of this class, "we are forced to hold the fear of lynching constantly over the negro. In the North you are having far more trouble with them than we. And why? Because you depend on the authorities to curb them. Down here a serious crime by a negro is the general, immediate business of every man with a white skin. We cannot have our wives or daughters appearing on the public witness-stand to testify against an attacking negro. The surest, fairest, most effective, and least expensive means of dealing with a black scoundrel is to hang him at once from the nearest limb and go home and forget it. It seems to be the prevailing notion in the North that we are more apt than not to get the wrong man. That does not happen in one case out of a hundred. Our police and our deputy sheriffs know the whole history, the habits, character, and hiding-place of every nigger in their districts. When one of the bad ones commits a serious crime, they know exactly where to look for him, and the citizens who go with them take a rope along. Without lynching we would live in mortal terror day and night. As it is, we have far less trouble with the negroes than you do in the North, and the vast majority of them get along better with us than they do with you."

Good friends squandered a considerable amount of time and gasolene to show us the region round about Savannah. Despite their warning that this floor-flat coast land was not the real Georgia, we found the mile after mile of cream-white roads, built of the oyster-shells that hang like the bluffs of mountain spurs above its coastal waters, teeming with interest to Northern eyes. The endless festoons of Spanish moss alone gave us the sense of having found a new corner of the world. Sturdy live-oaks were untroubled by these draperies of vegetation, though other trees seemed gradually to waste away beneath them. The dead-brown fields of corn had passed the stage where they would have been cut and shocked in the North, and the ears hung limply, awaiting the hand of the picker. Corn-stalks do not tempt

animals that can graze all through the winter. The "crackers" whos
ramshackle abodes broke the semi-wilderness carried the memory bacl
to the peasants of Venezuela or of the Brazilian hinterland; thei
speech and their mode of life were but a degree less primitive, curiou
anachronisms in the bustling, ahead-of-date America of to-day. Her
and there we passed what had once been a great plantation of th
South, productive now chiefly of aggressive weeds. One such bus
estate of slavery days had been revamped and partly restored to it:
pre-war condition. By a new generation of Southern planters? No
indeed! It is to-day the rendezvous of slangy, dollar-worshipping
youths from the North, who bring with them clicking cameras and
pampered movie stars. Thus is the aggressive modern world constantly treading on the heels of the leisurely past.

Through the first hint of the brief southern twilight there came
marching toward us under the festooned trees a long double-column
of negroes, dressed in dingy cotton garments, with broad black-and-
white stripes, clanging chains pending from their waists to their legs,
shovels over their broad shoulders, and flanked by several weather-
browned white men in faded khaki, carrying rifles. To our unaccustomed eyes they seemed a detail of some medieval stage-setting, long
since abolished from the scenes of real life, at least in our western
world. Our hosts, however, accepted the group as a consistent bit of
the landscape, scarcely noticeable until our interest called their attention
to it.

"One of our far-famed Georgia chain-gangs," laughed the man at
the wheel, "which so frequently arouse the wet-eyed pity of your
Northern philanthropists. A little experience with the 'poor victims'
usually shows them that the system is not so satanic as it looks from
the strained perspective of the North. You can take my word for it
that at least half those niggers steal something else as soon as possible,
once they are freed, so they can come back again to this comfortable life
of irresponsibility and three square meals a day."

The scarcity of towns farther south was less surprising within
sight of the soil they must feed on than in the geographies of our
school-days. The region reminded me of tropical Bolivia, with its
thinly wooded pampas alternating with swamps, its reddish, undomesti-
cated-looking cattle grazing through a wilderness scattered with palm-
trees. Gaunt razor-backed hogs foraged savagely for nourishment
among the forest roots about each "cracker's" weather-painted her-

mitage. Other signs of animal life were rare, except the first buzzards of the tropics we were approaching, lazily circling over the tree-tops. The single grass-grown track sped constantly away behind us, as if even this way-station local saw few reasons to halt in so uncultivated a landscape. One of those narrow reddish rivers that seem to form the boundaries between all our southern states rumbled past beneath us, and the endless brown, swampy flat-lands of Florida, punctuated here and there with clusters of small wooden houses, inconspicuous in their drab setting as animals of protective coloring, rolled incessantly away into the north.

Jacksonville, the " gateway to Florida," is not so Southern in aspect as Savannah. The considerable percentage of Northerners among its inhabitants and its bustling pursuit of material fortune give it a " business-first " atmosphere we had not encountered since leaving Richmond. Negroes, too, were scarcer in proportion to white men, and destined to become more so as we proceeded, a phenomenon equally noticeable in Brazil as the traveler approaches the equator. The reason, of course, is plain, and similar in the two countries. In slavery days neither our most southern state nor the region of the Amazon were far enough developed to draw many ship-loads of Africans, and their more recent exploitation has brought an influx of fortune-seekers, chiefly white in color. The creamy shell roads about " Jax," as the tendency to short cuts and brevity has dubbed Florida's most northern city, race smoothly away in all directions through endless vistas of straight yellow pines, interspersed with patches of lilac-hued water hyacinths, and strewn with spider-like undergrowth that quenches its thirst from the humid air. To the casual glance, at least, the sandy soil does not hold great promise, but it is highly productive, for all that. As proof thereof it is sufficient to mention that the saw-mills that furnished lath at a dollar a thousand a few years ago command eight times that in these days of universally bloated prices.

Trainmen in light khaki garb pick up the south-bound express for its long run of more than five hundred miles through the peninsular state. A brick highway, inviting to motorists, parallels the railroad for a considerable distance, and surrenders its task to an efficient, if blacker, route farther on. There are other evidences than this that Florida is more conscious of her appeal to Northern excursionists than are several of her neighbors along the Atlantic seaboard.

St. Augustine is perhaps more attractive, in her own way, than even Savannah, at least to the mere seeker after residential delights. But

she is scarcely a part of the American South, as we of the North pictur
it. The nasal twang of our middle West, or the slurred " r " of Nev
England are far more often heard on her streets and verandas tha1
the leisurely drawl of what was once the Confederacy. Tasks tha
would fall only to the lot of the black man in Georgia or the Carolina:
are here not beneath the dignity of muscular Caucasian youths. Abov‹
all she has a Spanish tinge that marks her as the first connecting-lin1
with the vast Iberian civilization beyond. The massive fortress fronting the sea, the main square that still clings to its ancient name o1
" Plaza de la Constitución," carry the thoughts as quickly back to the
days of buccaneers and the dark shadows of the Inquisition as those
where the Castilian tongue holds supreme sway. Here the very stones
of protective walls and narrow back streets are impregnated with
rousing tales of conscienceless governors from old Spain and revolts
of the despised *criollos* against the exactions of the ruling " Goths."

But St. Augustine is, of course, genuinely American at heart for
all its origin, and even its scattering of negroes are proudly aware of
their nationality.

" Look like dat some ovehseas equipment you got dah, sah," said
the grinning, ink-complexioned youth who carried my *musette* to a
chamber filled with inviting sea breezes.

" Yes, indeed, George. Why, were you over there? "

" Ya-as, sah. Ah sure help run dem or'nry Germans home. Dey
hyeard a-plenty from d' shells *we* sent on fo' dem — from Bohdeoh."

The memory of the war he had waged in Bordeaux caused a broad
streak of ivory to break out across his ebony face as often as he caught
sight of us until the " ovehseas equipment " had again disappeared in
the direction of the station.

Occupation, to St. Augustine, seems to be synonymous with the un-
remitting pursuit of tourists. Her railway gates are the vortex of a
seething whirlpool of hotel-runners and the clamoring jehus of horse
and gasolene conveyances. An undisturbed stroll through her streets
is out of the question, for every few yards the pedestrian is sure to
hear the gentle rumble of wheels behind him and a sugary, " Carriage,
sah? All de sights in town fo' two dollars, sah, or a nice ride out
to ——" and so on for several minutes, until the wheedling voice has
run through the gamut of sanguinity, persuasiveness, and shriveled
hope, and died away in husky disappointment, only to be replaced a
moment later by another driver's honeyed tones.

Ponce de Leon, seeking the fountain of youth, failed to recognize in St. Augustine the object of his quest. Could he return to-day, he would find that at least the immortality of fame has been vouchsafed him, for his name flourishes everywhere, on hotel façades, shop fronts, and cigar-boxes. Perhaps, too, he was near the goal of physical permanence without suspecting it. At least, if assertion be accepted as proof, St. Augustine is without a peer in longevity. "The oldest" is the title of nobility most widely prevalent in all the region. The oldest town, with the oldest house, flanked by the dwelling of the oldest woman, who attends the oldest church, linked to her residence by the oldest street, and visible to possessors of the oldest inducement to human endeavor, leaves the gaping traveler no choice but to accept the assertion of its inhabitants that here is to be found the oldest everything under the sun, or at least in the United States, which is the same thing, for surely no one would be so unpatriotic as to admit that other lands or planets could outdo us in anything we set out to accomplish. Even "old Ponce," dean of the six thousand saurians — count them if you dare to doubt — that sleep through the centuries out at St. Augustine's "Alligator Farm" confesses, through the mouth of his keeper from upstart Italy, to five hundred unbroken summers, and placidly accepts the honor of being "the oldest animal in captivity." One stands enraged at the thought that if "Ponce" cared to open his capacious mouth and speak, he might tell an eager world just what Hernando de Soto wore when his boat glided over his everglade home, or what were the exact words with which his human namesake acknowledged his inability to prolong his butterfly existence by finding the waters of immortality. Small wonder, indeed, that he dares raise his scaly head and yawn in the face even of insurance agents.

The trolley that carries "Ponce's" visitors across the wastes of brackish water and worthless land separating St. Augustine from the open sea is virtually a private car to the rare tourist of October days. This comatose period of the year gives the bather the sense of having leased the whole expanse of the Atlantic as his own bath-tub. For the native Floridans, however widely they may extoll their endless stretch of coast-line, seem to make small use of it themselves.

For hundreds of miles southward the eyes of the traveler weary at the swamp and jungle sameness of the peninsular state. The Gulf Stream and the diligent coral have built extensively, but they have left the job unfinished, in the indifferent tropical way. Grape-fruit farms and orange-groves break forth upon the primeval wilderness here and there, yet only often enough to emphasize its unpeopled immensity. Even Palm Beach has nothing unusual to show until the holidays of mid-winter bring its vast hostelries back to life. One loses little in fleeing all day onward at Southern express speed.

Miami, however, is worth a halt, if only for a glimpse of the United States in full tropical setting. There the refugee from winter will find cocoanuts nodding everywhere above him; there he may pick his morning grape-fruit at the door; and he need be no plutocrat to have his table graced with those aristocratic fruits of the tropics, the papaya and the alligator-pear. He cannot but be amused, too, at the casual Southern manners of the street-cars, the motorman-conductors of which make change with one hand and govern their brakes with the other, or who retire to a seat within the car for a chat with a passenger or the retying of a shoelace, while the conveyance careens madly along the outskirt streets.

Thanks, perhaps, to its sea breezes, Miami seemed no hotter than Richmond, though it was a humid, tropical heat that forced its inhabitants to compromise with Dame Fashion. As far north as Savannah a few eccentric beings ignored her dictates to the extent of fronting the July weather of October in white suits and straw hats, but they had a self-conscious, hunted manner which proved they were aware of their conspicuousness. In southern Florida, however, it was rather those who persisted in dressing by the calendar who attracted attention, and there were men of all occupations who dared to appear in public frankly devoid of the superfluous upper garment of male attire.

Some thirty miles south of Miami the " Dixie Highway," capable and well-kept to the last, disappears for lack of ground to stand on. The soldierly yellow pines give way to scrub jungle, and swamps gain the ascendency over solid earth. Amphibious plants cover the landscape like armies of ungainly crabs or huge spiders. Compact masses of dwarf trees and bristling bushes cluster as tightly together as Italian hill-top villages, as if for mutual protection from the ever-increasing expanses of water. Wherever land wins the constant struggle against the other element, the gray " crabs " of vegetation stretch away in endless vistas on each hand. White herons rise from the everglades at the rumble of the train, and wing their leisurely way into the flat horizon. A constant sea breeze sweeps through the coaches. At rare intervals a little wooden shack or two, sometimes shaded by half a dozen magnificent royal palms, keeps a precarious foothold on the

St. Augustine, Florida, from the old Spanish fortress

A policeman of Havana

Cuba's new presidential palace

shrinking soil; but it is hard to imagine what means of livelihood man finds in these swampy wastes.

The mainland ends at Jewfish, a cluster of three or four yellow wooden cabins, and for more than a hundred miles the traveler experiences the uncouth sensation of making an ocean voyage by rail. Strangely enough, however, there is more dry land for a considerable distance after the continent has been left behind than during the last twenty miles of mainland. The swamps disappear, and the gray coral rock of the chain of islands along which the train speeds steadily onward sustains a more generous vegetation than that of the watery wastes behind. Gradually, however, the grayish shallows on either hand turn to the ultramarine blue of the Caribbean, and the score of island stepping-stones along which the railroad skips grow smaller and more widely separated, with long miles of sea-washed trestles between them. Within an hour these have become so narrow that they are invisible from the car windows, and the train seems to be racing along the surface of the sea itself, out-distancing ocean-liners bound in the same direction. Brazil-like villages of sun-browned shacks surrounded by waving cocoanut palms cluster in the center of the larger keys, as the Anglo-Saxon form of the Spanish *cayo* designates these scattered islets of the Caribbean. The names of the almost unpeopled stations grow more and more Castilian — Key Largo, Islamorada, Matacumbe, Bahia Honda, Boca Chica. In places the water underneath is shallow enough for wading, and shades away from light brown through several tones of pink to the deepest blue. The building of a railroad by boat must have been a task to try at times the stoutest hearts, and the cost thereof suggests that the undertaking was rather a labor of love than a hope of adequate financial return.

The Cuban tinge of the passengers had steadily increased from Jacksonville southward; now the "White" car showed many a complexion that was suspiciously like those in the coach ahead. As with the Mexican passengers of our southwest, however, the "Jim Crow" rules are not too rigorously applied to travelers from the lands beyond. Indeed, the color-line all but fades away during the long run through Florida, partly, perhaps, because of the increasing scarcity of negroes. By the time the traveler has passed Miami, African features become almost conspicuous by their rarity.

Toward the end of the three-hour railway journey by sea, land grows so scarce that platforms are built out upon trestles to sustain the stations. The wreckage of a foundered ship lies strewn here and there along the edge of sandy spits across which we rumble from sea to sea. The pirates of olden days would scarcely believe their eyes could they awake and behold this modern means of trespassing on their retreats. Hundreds of palm-trees uprooted by the hurricane of the month before marked the last stages of the journey, the islands became larger and more closely fitted together, and as the sun was quenching his tropical thirst in the incredibly blue sea to the westward, the long line of a city appeared in the offing and the railroad confessed its inability to compete longer with its rivals in ocean transportation.

Key West, fifteen hundred miles south of New York, is a quaint mixture of American and Latin-American civilization, with about equal parts of each. Its wooden houses of two or three stories, with wide verandas supported by pillars, lend tropical features to our familiar architecture. The Spanish tongue, increasingly prevalent in the streets from St. Augustine southward, is heard here as often as English. The frank staring that characterizes the Americas below the United States, the placid indifference to convenience typified in the failure of its trolley-cars to come anywhere near the railroad station, the tendency to consider loafing before a fruit-store or a hole-in-the-wall grocery a fitting occupation for grown men, mark it as deeply imbued with the Spanish influence. Small as the island is, the town swarms with automobiles, and the chief ambition of its youths seems to be to drowse all day in the front seat of a car and trust to luck and a few passengers at train- or boat-time to give them a livelihood. Doctors and dentists announcing " special lady attendant " show that the Latin-American insistence on chaperonage holds full sway. The names of candidates for municipal offices, from mayor to " sexton of the cemetery," are nearly all Spanish. As in the towns along our Mexican border, the official tongue is bilingual, and Americans from the North are frankly considered foreigners by the Cubanized rank and file of voters. Freight-cars marked " No sirve para azucar " (" Do not use for sugar ") fill the railroad yards; the very motor-men greet their passengers in Spanish.

The resident of the " Island City " does not look forward with dread to his winter coal-bill. Not a house in town boasts a chimney. But this advantage is offset by his year-long contest with mosquitos and the absence of fresh water. The railroad brings long trains of the latter in gigantic casks; the majority of the smaller householders depend upon the rains and their eave-troughs.   As in all tropical America, the scarcity of vegetables restricts the local diet.   Fish, sponges, and mammoth turtles are the chief native products, with the exception, of course, of an industry that has carried the name of Key West to every village of our land.

Of the two principal cigar factories we visited one was managed by a Cuban and the other by an American.   The employees are some seventy per cent. natives of the greatest of the West Indies, and Spanish is the prevailing tongue in the workshops.   There, as in the city itself, the color-line shows no evidence of existence.   Each long table presents the whole gamut of gradations in human complexions. Piece work is the all but invariable rule, and the notion of striking for shorter hours would find no adherents.   The cigar-maker begins his daily task at the hour he chooses and leaves when he has wearied of the uninspiring toil.   This does not mean that the tables are often unoccupied during the daylight hours, for the citizen of Key West, like those in every other corner of this maltreated and war-weary world, finds the ratio between his earnings, whatever his diligence, and the demands made upon them, constantly balancing in the wrong direction, despite a long series of forced wage increases within the last few years. Not only the pianist-fingered men who perform the most obvious operation of cigar-making, that of rolling the weeds together in their final form, but those who separate the leaves into their various grades and colors by spreading them around the cloth-bound edge of a half-barrel, the women who deftly strip them of their central stem, even those who box and label the finished product, all have the fatness of their pay envelope depend on the amount they accomplish.

Cigar-making came to Key West as the most obvious meeting-place of material, maker, and consumer thirty-five years ago.   To-day its factories are almost too numerous for counting.   The largest of them are broad, low, modern structures facing the sea and ventilated by its constant breezes; the smallest are single shanty rooms.   The raw material still comes chiefly from Cuba, but that from our own country, as far away as Connecticut, has its place in even the best establishments.   Though women predominate in several of the processes, the actual making is almost entirely in the hands of men — and their tongues, I might add, for they do not hesitate to lend the assistance of those to the glue with which the consumer's end is bound together. The average workman rolls some two hundred cigars a day.   Men, too, sort the damp and bloated cigars into their respective shades of colors and arrange them in boxes, which are placed under a press. From these they are removed by women and girls, a dozen labels hanging fan-wise from their lower lips, and each cigar is banded and returned to the box in the exact order in which they were taken from it. Stamped with the government revenue label precisely as one affixes the postage to a letter, the boxes are placed in an aging and drying room — theoretically at least, though the present insistency of demand often sends them on their way to the freight-cars the very day of their completion.

The wrapper is of course the most delicate and costly of the materials used, being now commonly grown under cheese-cloth even in sun-drenched Cuba. The by-products from the maker's bench are shipped northward to cigarette factories. Imperfect cigars are culled out before the boxing process and consumed locally, being given out to the " general help " to the extent, in the larger factories, of five or six thousand a month. The workman, however — and here we find the present day tyranny of labor maintained even in this far-flung island of our southern coast — is paid for every cigar he makes, though he may find himself invited to seek employment elsewhere if his average of " culls " is too persistently high. It is said that the makers of candy never taste the stuff they supply a sweet-tooth world; the same may almost be said of the *cigarreros* of Key West. If they smoke at all in the tobacco-laden atmosphere of the factories, they are far more apt to be addicted to the cigarette than to the product of their own handicraft. The smoker, by the way, who visits Key West is doomed to disappointment; cigars are no cheaper there than in the most northwestern corner of our land. Nor should he bring with him the hope of sampling for once the brands beyond his means. The factories treat their swarms of visitors with every courtesy — except that of tucking a cigar, either of the five-cent or the dollar variety, into a receptive vest pocket.

The cigar-makers of Key West have one drain upon their income which is not common to other professions. Each one contributes a small sum weekly to the support of a " reader." A superannuated member of the craft sits on a platform overlooking the long roomful of eagle-taloned manipulators of the weed and reads aloud to them as they work. The custom has all the earmarks of being a direct descendant of the doleful dirge with which negro and Indian laborers, in the Old as well as the New World, are still in some regions urged on to greater exertion. But the reader's calling has lost its romantic tinge of earlier days. Those we heard were not droning the poetry or the colorful tales of the Castilian classics, but read from a morning newspaper printed in Spanish, with special emphasis on the successful struggles of the " working class " against " capitalists " the world over.

The hurricane that vented its chief fury on the Florida keys early in September was still the chief topic of conversation in Key West. For two days the inhabitants had been without electricity, gas, or transportation; in most houses even the bread gave out. The damage was wide-spread, sparing neither the pipe-organs of churches nor the mattresses of family bedrooms. Many a house was reduced to a mere heap of broken boards. Sea-walls of stone were strewn in scattered bits of rock along the water-fronts; the roofs of some of the stanchest buildings bore gaping holes that carried the memory back to Flanders and eastern France.

Two other routes to the Caribbean converge on this one through Key West, those by way of New Orleans and Tampa. The ferry, for it is little more than that, which connects the southernmost of our cities with Havana is the chief drawback of the overland journey. In the first place its rates testify to its freedom from competition, fifteen dollars and tax for a bare ninety miles of travel. It is as if our ocean-liners demanded $500 for the journey to Liverpool, without furnishing food or baths on the way. Then, as though the continued exactions of passport formalities long after any suitable reason for them had passed were not sufficiently troublesome to the harassed passenger, his comfort is everywhere second to that of the steamer personnel, while the outstretched palm invites special contribution for even the most shadowy species of service. But once the door of his breathless state-room is closed behind him, a brief night's sleep, if the inexplicable uproar with which the crew seems to pass its time during the journey permits it, brings him to the metropolis of the West Indies. A glimpse through the port-hole at an unseasonable hour shows the horizon dotted at regular intervals by the arc-lights of Havana's Malecón, and by the time he has reached the deck, these have faded away in the swift tropical dawn, and the steamer is nosing its way through the bottle-mouth of the harbor under the brow of age-and-sea-browned Morro Castle. There ensues the inevitable wait of an hour or two until the haughty port doctor rises and dresses with meticulous care and leisurely sips his morning coffee. When at last he appears, his professional duty does not delay the long file of passengers, for the simple reason that his attention is confined to the incessant smoking of cigarettes behind his morning newspaper. Passports, so sternly required of the departing American, are not even worthy of a glance by the Cuban officials; the custom examination is brief and unexacting. Once he has escaped the aggressive maelstrom of multicolored humanity which welcomes each new-comer with hopeful shrieks of delight, the traveler quickly merges into the heterogeneous multitude that is as characteristic as its Spanish style of architecture of the cosmopolitan capital of *Cuba libre.*

THE AMERICAN WEST INDIES

A CONSTANT procession of Fords, their mufflers wide open, were hiccoughing out the Carlos III Boulevard toward the Havana ball-park. The entrance-gate, at which they brought up with a snort and a sudden, bronco-like halt that all but jerked their passengers to their feet, was a seething hubbub. Ticket-speculators, renters of cushions, venders of everything that can be consumed on a summer afternoon, were bellowing their wares into the ears of the *fanáticos* who scrimmaged about the ticket-window. Men a trifle seedy in appearance wandered back and forth holding up half a dozen tiny envelopes, arranged in fan-shape, which they were evidently trying to sell or rent. The pink *entradas* I finally succeeded in snatching were not, of course, the only tickets needed. That would have been too simple a system for Spanish-America. They carried us as far as the grand stand, where another maelstrom was surging about the chicken-wire wicket behind which a hen-minded youth was dispensing permissions to sit down. He would have been more successful in the undertaking if he had not needed to thumb over a hundred or more seat-coupons reserved for special friends of the management or of himself every time he sought to serve a mere spectator.

We certainly could not complain, however, of the front-row places we obtained except that, in the free-for-all Spanish fashion, all the riffraff of venders crowded the foot-rests that were supposedly reserved for front-row occupants. Nine nimble Cubans were scattered about the flat expanse of Almendares Park, backed by Principe Hill, with its crown of university buildings. Royal palms waved their plumes languidly in the ocean breeze; a huge Cuban flag undulated beyond the outfielders; a score of vultures circled lazily overhead, as if awaiting a chance to pounce upon the " dead ones " which the wrathful " fans " announced every time a player failed to live up to their hopes. On a bench in the shade sat all but one of the invading team, our own " Pirates " from the Smoky City. The missing one was swinging his club alertly at the home plate, his eyes glued on the

Cuban *zurdo,* or "south-paw," who had just begun his contortions in the middle of the diamond. The scene itself was familiar enough, yet it seemed strangely out of place in this tropical setting. It was like coming upon a picture one had known since childhood, to find it inclosed in a brand new frame.

I reached for my kodak, then restrained the impulse. A camera is of little use at a Cuban ball game. Only a recording phonograph could catch its chief novelties. An uproar as incessant as that of a rolling-mill drowned every individual sound. It was not merely the venders of "*El escor oficial,*" of sandwiches, lottery-tickets, cigars, cigarettes, of bottled beer by the basketful, who created the hubbub; the spectators themselves made most of it. The long, two-story grandstand behind us was packed with Cubans of every shade from ebony black to the pasty white of the tropics, and every man of them seemed to be shouting at the top of his well-trained lungs. I say "man" advisedly, for with the exception of my wife there were just three women present, and they had the hangdog air of culprits. Scores of them were on their feet, screaming at their neighbors and waving their hands wildly in the air. An uninformed observer would have supposed that the entire throng was on the verge of a free-for-all fight, instead of enjoying themselves in the Cuban's chief pastime.

"Which do you like best, baseball or bull-fights?" I shouted to my neighbor on the left. He was every inch a Cuban, by birth, environment, point of view, in his very gestures, and he spoke not a word of English. Generations of Spanish ancestry were plainly visible through his grayish features; I happened to know that he had applauded many a *torero* in the days before the rule of Spain and "the bulls" had been banished together. Yet he answered instantly:

"Baseball by far; and so do all Cubans."

But baseball, strictly speaking, is not what the Cuban enjoys most. It is rather the gambling that goes with it. Like every sport of the Spanish-speaking race, with the single exception of bull-fighting, baseball to the great majority is merely a pretext for betting. The throng behind us was everywhere waving handsful of money, real American money, for Cuba has none of her own larger than the silver dollar. Small wonder the bills are always ragged and worn and half obliterated, for they were constantly passing, like crumpled waste-paper, from one sweaty hand to another. The Platt Amendment showed incomplete knowledge of Cuban conditions when it decreed the use of American money on the island; it should have gone further and ordered the bills destined for Cuba to be made of linoleum. Bets passed at the speed of sleight-of-hand performances. The *fanáticos* bet on every swing of the batter's club, on every ball that rose into the air, on whether or not a runner would reach the next base, on how many fouls the inning would produce. Most of the wagers passed so quickly that there was no time for the actual exchange of money. A flip of the fingers or a nod of the head sufficed to arrange the deal. There were no dividing lines either of color or distance. Full-fledged Africans exchanged wagers with men of pure Spanish blood. Cabalistic signs passed between the grand-stand and the sort of royal box high above. Across the field the crowded *sol,* as the Cuban calls the unshaded bleachers, in the vocabulary of the bull-ring, was engaged in the same money-waving turmoil. The curb market of New York is slow, noiseless, and phlegmatic compared with a ball-game in Havana.

Close in front of us other venders of the mysterious little envelopes wandered back and forth, seldom attempting to make themselves heard above the constant din. Here and there a spectator exchanged a crumpled, almost illegible dollar bill for one of the sealed *sobres.* My neighbor on the left bought one and held it for some time between his ringed fingers. When at last a runner reached first base he tore the envelope open. It contained a tiny slip of paper on which was typewritten " *1a base; 1a carrera* " (1st base; 1st run). The purchaser swore in Spanish with artistic fluency. I asked the reason for his wrath. He displayed the typewritten slip and grumbled " *mala suerte* "; then, noting my puzzled expression, explained his " bad luck " in the patient voice of a man who found it strange that an American should not understand his own national game.

" This envelope, which is bought and sold ' blind '— that is, neither I nor the man who sold it to me knew what was in it — is a bet that the first run will be made by a first baseman, of either side. But the man who has just reached first base is the rrri' fiel', and the first baseman is the man who struck out just before him. If he had made the first run I should have won eight dollars. But you see what chance he has now to make the first *carrera.* Cursed bad luck! "

" Rrri' fiel'," however, " died " in a vain attempt to steal third base, and his partner from the opposite corner of the garden was the first man to cross the home-plate. Instantly a cry of " Lef' fiel' " rose above the hubbub and the erstwhile venders of envelopes began paying the winners. A lath-like individual, half Chinaman, half negro, whom the *fanáticos* called " Chino," took charge of the section about us, and handed eight greasy bills to all those whom luck had favored, tucking the winning slips of paper into a pocket of his linen coat. But these simple little wagers were only for " pikers." There were men behind us who, though they looked scarcely capable of paying for their next meal, were stripping twenty and even fifty dollar bills off the rolls clutched in their sweaty hands and distributing them like so many handbills.

The game itself was little different from one at home. The Cuban players varied widely in color, from the jet-black third baseman to a shortstop of rice-powder complexion. Their playing was of high order, quite as " fast " as the average teams of our big leagues. Cubans hold several world championships in sports requiring a high degree of skill and swiftness. The umpire in his protective paraphernalia looked quite like his fellows of the North, yet behind his mask he was a rich mahogany brown. His official speech was English, but when a dispute arose he changed quickly to voluble Spanish. The " bucaneros," as the present-day pirates who had descended upon the Cuban coast were best known locally, won the game on this occasion; but the day before they had not scored a run.

Baseball — commonly pronounced " bahseh-bahl " throughout the island — has won a firm foothold in Cuba. Boys of all colors play it on every vacant lot in Havana; it is the favorite sport of the youthful employees of every sugar estate or tobacco *vega* of the interior. The sporting page is as fixed a feature of the Havana newspapers as of our own dailies. Nor do the Cuban reporters yield to their fellows of the North in the use of base-ball slang. Most of their expressions are direct translations of our own vocabulary of the diamond; some of them are of local concoction. Those familiar with Spanish can find constant amusement in Havana's sporting pages. " Fans " quite unfamiliar with the tongue would experience no great difficulty in catching the drift of the Cuban reporter, though it would be Greek to a Spaniard speaking no baseball, as a brief example will demonstrate:

EL HABANA DEJO EN BLANCO
A LOS PIRATAS
José del Carmen Rodríguez realizó varios doubleplays sensacionales
BRILLANTE PITCHING DE TUERO
El catcher rojo, Miguel Angel González, cerró con doble llave la segunda base
a los corredores americanos
Primer Inning
Bucaneros — Bigbee out en fly al center. Terry, rolling al short, out en primera. Carey struck out. No hit, no run.

Habana — Papo out en fly al catcher. Merito muere en rolling al pitcher. Cueto lo imita.

Segundo Inning

Bucaneros — Nickolson, rolling al tercera, es out al pretender robar la segunda. Cutshaw batea de plancha y es safe en primera. Barber out en rolling á la segunda, adelantando Cutshaw. Carlson out en fly al catcher. No hit, no run.

Habana —— Juan de Angel Aragón out en linea al center. Hungo se pasea. Calvo hit y Hungo va a segunda. Torres se sacrifica. Acosta, con las bases llenas, es transferido y Hungo anota. González out en foul al pitcher. Un hit, una carrera.

Thus the Havanese "reporter de baseball" rattles on, but his reports are not snatched from the hands of newsboys with quite the same eagerness as in the North. For the Cuban *fanático* is not particularly interested in the outcome of the game itself. A bet on that would be too slowly decided for his quick southern temperament. He prefers to set a wager on each swing of the pitcher's arm, and with the last "out" of the ninth inning his interest ceases as abruptly as does the unbroken boiler-factory uproar that rises to the blue tropical heavens from the first to the last swing of the batter's club.

The visitor whose picture of Havana is still that of the drowsy tropical city of our school-books is due for a shock. He will be most surprised, perhaps, to find the place as swarming with automobiles as an open honey-pot with flies. A local paragrapher asserts that "a Havanese would rather die than walk four blocks." There are several perfectly good reasons for this preference. The heat of Cuba is far less oppressive than that of our most northern states in mid-summer. Indeed, it is seldom unpleasant; but the slightest physical exertion quickly bathes the body in perspiration, and nowhere is a wilted collar in worse form than in Havana. Moreover, one must be exceedingly nimble-footed to trust to the prehistoric means of transportation. The custom of always riding has left no rights to the pedestrian in the Cuban capital. The chances of being run down are excellent, and the result is apt to be not merely broken ribs, but a bill for damages to the machine. Hence the expression "cojemos un Ford" is synonymous with going a journey, however short, anywhere within the city. Your Havanese friend never says, "Let's stroll around and see Perez," but always, "Let's catch a Ford," and by the time you have succeeded in slamming the door really shut, there you are at Perez's *zaguan*.

Fords scurry by thousands through the streets of Havana day and night, ever ready to pick up a passenger or two and set them down again in any part of the business section for a mere twenty-cent piece — a *peseta* in Cuban parlance. More expensive cars are now and then seen for hire; by dint of sleuth-like observation I did discover one Ford that was confined to the labor of carrying its owner. But those are the exceptions that prove the rule, and the rule is that the instant you catch sight of the familiar plebeian features of a "flivver" you know, even without waiting to see the hospitable "Se Alquila" ("Rents Itself") on the wind-shield, that you need walk no farther, whatever your sex, complexion, or previous condition of pedestrianism. They are particularly suited to the narrow streets that the Spaniard, in his Arabic avoidance of the sun, bequeathed the Cuban capital. There is many a corner in the business section which larger cars can turn only by backing or by mounting one of the scanty sidewalks. The closed taxi of the North, too, would be as much out of place in Havana as overcoats at a Fourth of July celebration. A few of the horse carriages of olden days still offer their services; but as neither driver, carriage, nor steed seems to have been groomed or fed since the war of independence, even those in no haste are apt to think twice or thrice, and finally put their trust in gasolene. Hence the Ford has taken charge of Havana, like an army of occupation.

Unfortunately, a Ford and a Cuban chauffeur make a bad combination. The native temperament is quick-witted, but it is scantily gifted with patience. In the hands of a seeker after pesetas a "flivver" becomes a prancing, dancing steed, a snorting charger that knows no fear and yields to no rival. Apparently some Cuban Burbank has succeeded in crossing the laggard of our northern highways with the kangaroo. The whisper of your destination in the driver's ear is followed by a leap that leaves the adjoining façades a mere blur upon the retina. A traffic jam ahead lends the snorting beast wings; it has a playful way of alighting on all fours in the very heart of any turmoil. If a pedestrian or a rival peseta-gatherer is crossing the street twenty feet beyond, your time for the next nineteen feet and eleven inches is a small fraction of a second over nothing. Brake linings seem to acquire a strangle hold from the Cuban climate. If the opening ahead is but the breadth of a hand, the Havana Ford has some secret of making itself still more slender. I have never yet seen one of them climb a palm-tree, but there is no reason to suppose that they would hesitate to undertake that simple feat, if a passenger's destination were among the fronds.

The newspapers run a daily column for those who have been "Ford-ed" to hospitals or cemeteries. What are a few casualties a day in a city of nearly half a million, with prolific tendencies? There are voluminous traffic and speed rules, but he would be a friendless fellow who could not find a *compadre* with sufficient political power to "fix it up." Death corners — bill-boards or street-hugging house-walls from behind which he may dart without warning — are the joy of the Cuban chauffeur. Courtesy in personal intercourse stands on a high plane in Havana, but automobile politeness has not yet reached the stage of consideration for others. Traffic policemen, soldierly fellows widely varied in complexion, looking like bandsmen in their blue denim uniforms, are efficient, and accustomed to be obeyed; but they cannot be everywhere at once, and the automobile is. They confine their efforts, therefore, to a few seething corners, and humanity trusts 'to its own lucky star in the no-man's-lands between.

The private machines alone would give Havana a busy appearance. All day long and far into the night the big central plaza is completely fenced in by splendid cars parked compactly ends to curb. Toward sunset, especially on the days when a military band plays the *retreta* in the kiosk facing Morro Castle and the harbor entrance, an endless procession of seven-passenger motors files up and down the wide Prado and along the sea-washed Malecón, two, or at most three, haughty beings, not infrequently with kinky hair, lolling in every capacious tonneau. Liveried chauffeurs are the almost universal rule. The caballero who drives his own car would arouse the wonder, possibly the scorn, of his fellow-citizens; once and once only did we see a woman at the wheel. There is good reason for this. The man who would learn to pilot his own machine through the automobile maelstrom of Havana would have little time or energy left for the pursuit of his profession. Moreover, the Latin-American is seldom mechanic-minded. The cheaper grades of cars are not in favor for private use. Wire wheels are almost universal; luxurious fittings are seldom lacking. Even the unexclusive Ford is certain to be decked out in expensive *vestiduras*,— slip-covers of embossed leather that remind one of a Mexican peon in silver-mounted sombrero.

The cost of a car in Havana is from twenty to thirty per cent. higher than in the States, which supplies virtually all of them. A dollar barely pays for two gallons of gasolene. Licenses are a serious item, particularly to private owners in Havana, for the fee depends on the use to which the car is put. Fords for hire carry a white tag with black figures and pay $12.50 a year. Private cars bear a pink *chapa* at a cost of $62.50. Tags with blue figures announce the occupant a government official or a physician. Then, every driver must be supplied with a personal license, at a cost of $25. In theory that is all, except a day or two of waiting in line at the municipal license bureau. In practice there are many little political wheels to be oiled if one would see the car free to go its way the same year it is purchased.

Once the visitor has learned to distinguish the tag that announces government ownership, he will be astounded to note its extraordinary prevalence in Havana. Even Washington was never like this. Government property means public ownership indeed in Cuba. If one may believe the newspapers of the Liberal party,— the "outs" under the present administration,— the explanation is simple. "Every government employee," they shriek, "down to the last post-office clerk who is in personal favor, has his own private car, free of cost; not only that, but he may use it to give his babies an airing, to carry his cook to market, or to take the future *novio* of his daughter on a joy ride."

The new-comer's impressions of Havana will depend largely upon his previous travels. If this is his first contact with the Iberian or the Latin-American civilization, he will find the Cuban capital of great interest. If he is familiar with the cities of old Spain, particularly if he has already seen her farthest-flung descendants, such as Bogotá, Quito, or La Paz, he will probably call Havana "tame." The most incorrigible traveler will certainly not consider a visit to this most accessible of foreign capitals time wasted. But his chief amusement will be, in all likelihood, that of tracing the curious dovetailing of Spanish and American influences which makes up its present-day aspect.

Both by situation and history the capital of Cuba is a natural place for this intermingling of two essentially different civilizations, but the mixture is more like that of oil and water than of two related elements. The ways of Spain and of America — by which, of course, I mean the United States — are recognizable in every block of Havana, yet there has been but slight blending together, however close the contact. Immigrants from old Spain tramp the streets all day under their strings of garlic, or jingle the cymbals that mean sweetmeats for sale to all Spanish-speaking children. Venders of lottery-tickets sing their numbers in every public gathering-place. On Saturdays a long procession of beggars of both sexes file through the stores and offices demanding almost as a right the cent each which ancient Iberian custom

Vendors of lottery tickets in rural Cuba

The winning numbers of the lottery

Pigeons are kept to clear the tobacco fields of insects

Ploughing for tobacco in the famous Vuelta Abaja district. The large building is a tobacco barn, the small ones are residences of the planters

allots them. The places where men gather are wide-open cafés without front walls, rather than the hidden dens of the North. Havana's cooking, her modes of greeting and parting, her patience with individual nuisance, her very table manners are Spanish. Like all Spanish-America, her sons and daughters are highly proficient in the use of the toothpick; like them they are exceedingly courteous in the forms of social intercourse, irrespective of class. As in Spain, life increases in its intensity with sunset: babies have no fixed hour of retirement; midnight is everywhere the " shank of the evening "; lovers are sternly separated by iron bars, or their soft nothings strictly censored by ever vigilant duennas.

The very Government cannot shake off the habits of its forebears, despite the tutelage of a more practical race. Public office is more apt than not to be considered a legitimate source of personal gain. As in Spain, a general amnesty is ever smiling hopefully at imprisoned malefactors. The Spanish tendency to forgive crime, combined with the interrelationship of miscreants and the powers that be, has not merely abolished, in practice, all capital punishment; it tends to release evil-doers long before they have found time to repent and change their ways. Men who shoot down in cold blood — and this they do even in the heart of Havana — have only to prove that the deed was done " in the heat of the moment " to have their punishment reduced to a mere fraction of that for stealing a mule. The pardoning power is wielded with such Castilian generosity that the genial editor of Havana's American newspaper wrathfully suggests the " loosing of all our distinguished assassins," that the enormous *cárcel* facing the harbor entrance may be replaced by one of the hotels sadly needed to house Havana's " distinguished visitors."

Amid all this the island capital is deeply marked, too, with the influence of what Latin-America calls " the Colossus of the North." One sees it in the strenuous pace of business, in the manners and methods of commerce. The dignified lethargy of Spain has largely given way to the business-first teachings of the Yankee gospel. Billboards are almost as constant eyesores in Havana and her suburbs as in New York; huge electric figures flash the alleged virtues of wares far into the soft summer nights. Blocks of office buildings, modern in every particular, shoulder their way upward into the tropical sky. With few exceptions the sons of proud old Cuban families scorn to dally away their lives, Castilian fashion, on the riches and reputations of their ancestors, but descend into the commercial fray.

One sees the American influence in many amusing little details. The Cuban mail-boxes are exact copies of our own, except that the lettering is Spanish. Postage-stamps may be had in booklet form, which can be said of no other foreign land. Street-car fares are five cents for any distance, with free transfers, rather than varying by zones, as in Europe. Barbers dally over their clients in the private-valet manner of their fellows to the north. Department stores operate as nearly as possible on the American plan, despite the Spanish tendency of their clerks to seek tips. Cuban advertisers struggle to imitate in their newspaper and poster announcements the aggressive, inviting American manner, often with ludicrous results, for they are rarely gifted with what might be called the advertising imagination. In a word, Havana is Spain with a modern American virility, tinged with a generous dash of the tropics.

I have said that the two opposing influences do not mix, and in the main that rule strictly holds. A glance at any detail of the city's life, her customs, appearance, or point of view, suffices to determine whether it is of Castilian or Yankee origin. But here and there a fusing of the two has produced a quaint mongrel of local color. Havana bakes its bread in the long loaves of Europe, but an American squeamishness has evolved a slender paper bag to cover them. The language of gestures makes a crossing of two figures, a hiss at the conductor, and a nod to right or left, sufficient request for a street-car transfer. The man who occupies the center of a baseball diamond may be called either a pitcher or a *lanzador*, but the verb that expresses his activity is *pitchear*. Shoe-shining establishments in the shade of the long, pillared arcades are arranged in Spanish style, yet the methods and the prices of the polishers are American.

Barely had we stepped ashore in Havana when I spied a man in the familiar uniform of the American Army, his upper sleeve decorated with three broad chevrons. I had a hazy notion that our intervention in Cuba had ceased some time before, yet it would have been nothing strange if some of our troops had been left on the island.

"Good morning, Sergeant," I greeted him. "Do you know this town? How do I get to —"

But he was staring at me with a puzzled air, and before I could finish he had sidestepped and hurried on. I must have been dense that morning, after a night of uproar on the steamer from Key West, for a score of his fellows had passed before I awoke to the fact that they were not American soldiers at all. Cuba has copied nothing more exactly than our army uniform. Cotton khaki survives in place of olive drab, of course, as befits the Cuban climate; frequent washings have turned most of the canvas leggings a creamy white. Otherwise there is little to distinguish the Cuban soldier from our own until he opens his mouth in a spurt of fluent Spanish. He wears the same cow-boy sombrero, with similar hat-cords for each branch of the service. He shoulders the same rifle, carries his cartridges in the old familiar web-belt, wears his revolver on the right, as distinct from the left-handed fashion of all the rest of Latin-America. He salutes, mounts guard, drills, stands at attention precisely in the American manner, for his " I. D. R." differs from our own only in tongue. The same chevrons indicate non-commissioned rank, though they have not yet disappeared from the left sleeve. His officers are indistinguishable, at any distance, from our own; they are in many cases graduates of West Point. An angle in their shoulder-bars, with the Cuban seal in bronze above them, and the native coat of arms on their caps in place of the spread eagle, are the only differences that a close inspection of lieutenants or captains brings to light. From majors upward, however, the insignia becomes a series of stars, perhaps because the absence of generals in the Cuban Army leaves no other chance for such ostentation.

The question naturally suggests itself, " Why does Cuba need an army? " The native answer is apt to be the Spanish version of " Huh, we 're a free country, are n't we? Why should n't we have an army, like any other sovereign people? Poor Estrada Palma, our first president, had no army, with the result that the first bunch of hoodlums to start a revolution had him at their mercy."

These are the two reasons why one sees the streets of Havana, and all Cuba, for that matter, khaki-dotted with soldiers. She has no designs on a trembling world, but an army is to her what long trousers are to a youth of sixteen, proof of his manhood; and she has very real need of one to keep the internal peace within the country, particularly under a Government that was not legally elected and which enjoys little popularity.

There were some fourteen thousand " regulars " in the Cuban Army before the European War, a number that was more than tripled under compulsory service after the island republic joined the Allies. To-day, despite posters idealizing the soldier's life and assuring all Cubans that it is their duty to enlist, despite a scale of pay equalling our own, their land force numbers barely five thousand. Many of these are veterans of the great European war,— as fought in Pensacola, Florida. Some wear fifteen to eighteen years' worth of service stripes diagonally across their lower sleeves; a few played their part in the guerilla warfare against the Spaniards before the days of independence, and have many a thrilling anecdote with which to overawe each new group of " rookies." In short, they have nearly everything in common with our own permanent soldiers — except the color-line. I have yet to see a squad of white, or partly white, American soldiers march away to duty under a jet-black corporal, a sight so common-place in Havana as not even to attract a passing attention.

Havana has just celebrated her four-hundredth birthday. She confesses herself the oldest city of European origin in the western hemisphere. Her name was familiar to ocean wayfarers before Cortés penetrated to the Vale of Anáhuac, before Pizarro had heard the first rumors of the mysterious land of the Incas. When the Pilgrim Fathers sighted Plymouth Rock, Havana had begun the second century of her existence. In view of all this, and of the harried career she led clear down to days within the memory of men who still consider themselves youthful, she is somewhat disappointing to the mere tourist for her lack of historical relics. This impression, however, gradually wears off. Her background is certainly not to be compared with that of Cuzco or of the City of Mexico, stretching away into the prehistoric days of legend; yet many reminders of the times that are gone peer through the mantle of modernity in which she has wrapped herself. From the age-worn stones of La Fuerza the bustle of the city of to-day seems a fantasy from dreamland. In the underground passages of old Morro, in the musty dungeons of massive Cabaña, the khaki-clad soldiers of Cuba's new army look as out of place as motor-cars in a Roman arena. The stroller who catches a sudden unexpected glimpse of the cathedral façade is carried back in a twinkling to the days of the Inquisition; Spain herself can show no closer link with the Middle Ages than the venerable stone face of San Francisco de Paula. The ghosts of monks gone to their reward centuries ago hover about the post-office where the modern visitor files his telegram or stamps his picture postals. The British occupied it as a barracks when they captured Havana in the middle of the last century, whereby the ancient monastery was considered desecrated, and has served in turn various government purposes; yet the shades of the past still linger in its flowery patio and flit about the corners of its capacious, leisurely old stairways.

Old Havana may be likened in shape to the head of a bulldog, with the mark of the former city wall, which inclosed it like a muzzle, still visible. The part thus protected in olden days contains most of Havana's antiquity. Beyond it the streets grow wider, the buildings more modern, as one advances to the newer residential suburbs. Amusing contrasts catch the eye at every turn within the muzzled portion. Calle Obispo, still the principal business street, is a scant eighteen feet wide, inclusive of its two pathetically narrow sidewalks. The Spanish builders did not foresee the day when it would be an impassable river of clamoring automobiles. They would be struck dumb with astonishment to see these strange devil-wagons housed in the tiled passageways behind the massive carved or brass-studded doors of the regal mansions of colonial days, as their fair ladies would be horrified to find the family chapels turned into bath-rooms by desecrating barbarians from the North. Office buildings that seem to have been bodily transported from New York shoulder age-crumbled Spanish churches and convents; crowds as business-bent as those of Wall Street hurry through narrow *callejones* that seem still to be thinking of Columbus and the buccaneers of the Spanish main. Long rows of massive pillars upholding projecting second stories and half concealing the den-like shops behind them have a picturesque appearance and afford a needed protection from the Cuban sun, but they are little short of a nuisance under modern traffic conditions. Old Colon market is as dark and unsanitary as when mistresses sent a trusted slave to make the day's purchases. Its long lines of cackling fowls, of meat barely dead, of tropical fruits and strange Cuban vegetables, are still the center of the old bartering hubbub, but beside them are the very latest factory products. One may buy a chicken and have it killed and dressed on the spot for a *real* by deep-eyed old women who seem to have been left behind by a receding generation, or one may carry home canned food which colonial Havana never tasted.

The city is as brilliantly lighted as any of our own, by dusky men who come at sunset, laboriously carrying long ladders, from the tops of which they touch off each gas jet as in the days of Tacón. Ferries as modern as those bridging the Hudson ply between the Muelle de Luz and the fortresses and towns across the harbor; but they still have as competitors the heavy old Havana rowboats, equipped, when the sun is high, with awnings at the rear, and manned by oarsmen as stout-armed and weather-tanned as the gondoliers of Venice. Automobiles of the latest model snort in continual procession around the Malecón on Sunday afternoons, yet here and there a quaint old family carriage, with its liveried footmen, jogs along between them. Many a street has changed its name since the days of independence, but still clings to its old Spanish title in popular parlance. A new system of house numbering, too, has been adopted, but this has not superseded the old; it has merely been superimposed upon it, until it is a wise door indeed that knows its own number. To make things worse for the puzzled stranger, the two sides of the street have nothing in common, so that it is nothing unusual to find house No. 7 opposite No. 114.

Havana is most beautiful at night. Its walls are light in color, yellow, orange, pink, pale-blue, and the like prevailing, and the witchery of moonlight, falling upon them, gives many a quaint corner or narrow street of the old city a resemblance to fairy-land. But when one hurries back to catch them with a kodak in the morning, it is only to find that the chief charm has fled before the grueling light of day.

The architecture of the city is overwhelmingly Spanish, with only here and there a detail brought from the North. The change from the wooden houses of Key West, with their steep shingled roofs, to the plaster-faced edifices of Havana, covered by the flat *azoteas* of Arab-Iberian origin often the family sitting-room after sunset, is sharp and decided. Among them the visitor feels himself in a foreign land indeed, whatever suggestions of his own he may find in the life of the city. The tendency for low structures, the prevalence of sumptuous dwellings of a single story, the preference for the ground floor as a place of residence, show at a glance that this is no American city. Yet the single story is almost as lofty as two of our own; the Cuban insists on high ceilings, and the longest rooms of the average residence would be still longer if they were laid on their sides. To our Northern eyes it is a heavy architecture, but it is a natural development in the Cuban climate. Coolness is the first and prime requisite. Massive outer walls, half their surfaces taken up by immense doors and windows, protected by gratings in every manner of artistic scroll, defy the heat of perpetual summer, and at the same time give free play to the all but constant sea breezes. The openness of living which this style of dwelling brings with it would not appeal to the American sense of privacy in family life. Through the iron-barred *rejas,* flush with the sidewalk, the passer-by may look deep back into the tile-floored parlor, with its forest of chairs, and often into the living-rooms beyond. At midday they look particularly cool and inviting from the sun-drenched street; in the evening the stroller has a sense of sauntering unmolested through the very heart of a hundred family circles.

Old residents tell us that Havana is a far different city from the one from which the Spanish flag was banished twenty years ago. Its best streets, they say, were then mere lanes of mud, or their cobbled pavements so far down beneath the filth of generations that the uncovering of them resembled a mining operation. Along the sea, where a boulevard second only to the peerless Beira Mar of Rio runs to-day, the last century left a stenching city garbage-heap. The broad, laurel-shaded Prado leading from the beautiful central plaza to the headland facing Morro Castle was a labyrinthian cluster of unsavory hovels. All this, if one may be pardoned a suggestion of boasting, was accomplished by the first American governor. But the Cubans themselves have continued the good work. Once cleaned and paved, the streets have remained so. Buildings of which any city might be proud have been erected without foreign assistance. In their sudden spurt of ambition the Cubans have sometimes overreached themselves. A former administration began the erection of a presidential palace destined to rival the best of Europe. About the same time the provincial governor concluded to build himself a simple little marble cabin. Election day came, and the new president, after the spendthrift manner of Latin-American executives, repudiated the undertaking of his predecessor, which lies to-day the abandoned grave of several million *pesos*. The governor of the province was convinced by irrefutable arguments that his half-finished little cabin was out of proportion to his importance, and yielded it to his political superior. It is nearing completion now, a thing of beauty that should, for a time at least, satisfy the artistic longings even of great Cuba. For it has nothing of the inexpensive Jeffersonian simplicity of our own White House, fit only for such plebeian occupants as our Lincolns and Garfields, but is worthy a Cuban president — during the few months of the year when he is not occupying his suburban or his summer palace.

Havana has grown in breadth as well as character since it became the capital of a free country. While the population of the island has nearly doubled, that of the metropolis has trebled. Vibora, Cerro, and Jesús del Monte have changed from outlying country villages of thatched huts to thriving suburbs; Vedado, the abode of a few scattered farmers when the Treaty of Paris was signed, has become a great residential region where sugar-millionaires and successful politicians vie with one another in the erection of private palaces, not to mention the occasional perpetration of architectural monstrosities. Under the impulse of an ever-increasing and ever-wealthier population, abetted by energetic young Cubans who have copied American real-estate methods, Havana is already leaping like a prairie fire to the crests of new fields, which will soon be wholly embraced in the conflagration of prosperity.

One of the purposes of Cuba's revolt against Spain was the suppression of the lottery. For years the new republic sternly frowned down any tendency toward a return of this particular form of vice. To this day it is unlawful to bring the tickets of the Spanish lottery into the island. But blood will tell, and the mere winning of political freedom could not cure the Cuban of his love for gambling. Private games of chance increased in number and spread throughout the island. The Government saw itself losing millions of revenue yearly, while enterprising persons enriched themselves; for to all rulers of Iberian ancestry the exploitation of a people's gambling instinct seems a legitimate source of state income. New palaces and boulevards cost money, independence brings with it unexpected expenditures. By the end of the second intervention the free Cubans were looking with favor upon a system which they had professed to abhor as Spanish subjects. The law of July 7, 1909, decreed a public revenue under the name of " Loteria Nacional," and to-day the lottery is as firmly established a function of the Government as the postal service.

There are two advantages in a state lottery — to t : government. It is not only an unfailing source of revenue; it is a sp. ndid means of rewarding political henchmen. *Colectorias,* the privilege of dispensing lottery-tickets within a given district, are to the Cuban congressman what postmasterships are to our own. The possession of one is a *botella* (bottle), Cuban slang for sinecure; the lucky possessor is called a *botellero.* He in turn distributes his patronage to the lesser fry and becomes a political power within his district. The whole makes a splendidly compact machine that can be turned to any purpose by the chauffeur at the political wheel.

The first and indispensible requisite of a state lottery is that the drawings shall be honest. Your Spanish-minded citizen will no more do without his gambling than he will drink water with his meals; but let him for a moment suspect that " the game is crooked " and he will abandon the purchase of government tickets for some other means of snatching sudden fortune. The drawing of the Cuban lottery is surrounded by every possible check on dishonesty. By no conceivable chance could the inmost circle of the inner lottery councils guess the winning number an instant before it is publicly drawn. But there is another way in which the game is not a " fair shake " to the players, though the simpler type of Cuban does not recognise the unfairness. The average lottery, for instance, offers $420,000 in prizes. The legal price of the tickets is $20, divided into a hundred " pieces " for the convenience of small gamblers, at a *peseta* each. Thirty thousand tickets are sold, of which 30% of the proceeds, or $180,000, goes to the government or its favorite henchmen. That leaves to begin with only fourteen of his twenty cents that can come back to the player. Then the law allows the vendor 5% as his profit, bringing the fractional ticket up to twenty-one cents. If that were all, the players would still have even chances of a reasonable return. But the " pieces " are never sold at that price, despite the law and its threat of dire punishment, printed on the ticket itself. From one end of the island to the other the *billeteros* demand at least $30 a *billete;* in other words the public is taxed one half as much as it puts into the lottery itself to support thousands of utterly useless members of society, the ticket-sellers, and instead of getting two-thirds of its money back it has a chance of rewinning less than half the sum hazarded. The most optimistic negro deckhand on a Missississippi steamboat would hardly enter a crap game in which the " bones " were so palpably " loaded." Yet Cubans of high and low degree, from big merchants to bootblacks, pay their tribute regularly to the *Loteria Nacional.*

Barely had we arrived in Havana when the rumor reached me that the *billeteros* could be compelled to sell their tickets at the legal price, if one " had the nerve " to insist. I abhor a financial dispute, but I have as little use for hearsay evidence. I concluded to test the great question personally. Having purchased two " pieces " at the customary price, to forestall any charge of miserliness, I set out to buy one at the lawful rate. A booth on a busy corner of Calle Obispo, a large choice of numbers fluttering from its ticket-racks, seemed the most promising scene for my nefarious project, because a traffic policeman stood close by. I chose a " piece " and, having tucked it away in a pocket, handed the vender a *peseta*.

" It is *thirty* cents," he announced politely, smiling at what he took to be my American innocence.

" Not at all," I answered, blushing at my own pettiness. " The price is twenty cents; it is printed on the ticket."

" *I* sell them only at thirty," he replied, with a gesture that invited me to return the ticket.

" The legal price is all I pay," I retorted. " If you don't like that, call the policeman," and I strolled slowly on. In an. instant both the vender and the officer were hurrying after me. The latter demanded why I had not paid the amount asked.

" The law sets the price at twenty cents," I explained. " As a guardian of order, you surely do not mean to help this man collect an illegal sum."

The policeman gave me a look of scorn such as he might have turned upon a millionaire caught stealing chickens, and answered with a sneer:

" He is entitled to one cent profit."

" But not to ten cents," I added triumphantly.

The guardian of law and order grunted an unwilling affirmative, casting a pitying glance up and down my person, and turned away with another audible sneer only when I had produced a cent. The vender snatched the coin with an expression of disgust, and retains to this day, I suppose, a much lower opinion of Americans.

This silly ordeal, which I have never since had the courage to repeat, proved the assertion that the Cubans may buy their lottery-tickets at the legal price, but it demonstrated at the same time why few of them do so. Pride is the chief ally of the profiteer. The difference between twenty cents and thirty is not worth a dispute, but the failure of the individual Cuban to insist upon his rights, and of his Government to protect them, constitutes a serious tax upon the nation and enriches many a worthless loafer. With some forty lottery drawings a year, this extra, illegal ten cents a " piece " costs the Cuban people the neat little sum of at least $12,000,000 a year, or four dollars per capita.

The drawings take place every ten days, besides a few *loterias extraordinarias,* with prizes several times larger, on the principal holidays. They are conducted in the old treasury building down near the end of Calle Obispo. We reached there soon after seven of the morning named on our tickets. A crowd of two hundred or more heavy-mouthed negroes, poorly clad *meztizos,* and ragged, emaciated old Chinamen for the most part, were huddled together in the shade at the edge of the porch-like room. A policeman — not the one whose scorn I had aroused — beckoned us to step inside and take one of the seats of honor along the wall, not, evidently, because we were Americans, but because our clothing was not patched or our collars missing. At the back a long table stretched the entire length of the room. A dozen solemn officials, resembling a jury or an election board, lolled in their seats behind it, a huge ledger, a sheath of papers, an ink-well and several pens and pencils before each of them. At the edge of the room, just clear of the standing crowd of hopeful riffraff, was a similar table on which another group of solemn-faced men were busily scribbling in as many large blank-books, with the sophisticated air of court or congressional reporters. Between the tables were two globes of open-work brass, one perhaps six feet in diameter, the other several times smaller. The larger was filled with balls the size of marbles, each engraved with a number; the smaller one contained several thousand others, representing varying sums of money.

Almost at the moment we entered a gong sounded. Four muscular negroes rushed forth from behind the scenes and, grasping two handles projecting at the rear, turned the big globe over and over, its myriad of little balls rattling like a stage wind-storm. At the same time an individual of as certain, if less decided, African ancestry, solemnly shuffled the contents of the smaller sphere in the same manner. Then the interrupted drawing began again. Four boys, averaging eight years of age, stood in pairs at either globe. At intervals of about thirty seconds two of them pulled levers that released one marble from each sphere, and which long brass troughs or runways deposited in cut-glass bowls in front of the other two boys. The urchin on the big globe side snatched up his marble, called out a long number — in most cases running into the tens of thousands — and as his voice ceased, his companion opposite announced the amount of the prize. Then the two balls were spitted side by side on a sort of Chinese reckoning-board manipulated by another solemn-faced adult, who now and again corrected a misreading by the boy calling the numbers.

For the hour we remained this monotonous formality went steadily on, as it does every ten days from seven in the morning until nearly noon, ceasing only when all the balls in the smaller sphere have been withdrawn. Each of these represents a prize, but as considerably more than a thousand of them are of one hundred dollars each — or a dollar a " piece "— the almost constant " con cien pesos " of the prize-boy grew wearisome in the extreme. The men at the reporters' table scribbled every number feverishly with their sputtering steel pens, but the " jury " at the back yielded to the soporific drone of childish voices and dozed half-open-eyed in their chairs — except when one of

the major prizes was announced. Then they sat up alertly at attention, and inscribed one after another on their massive ledgers the number on the ball which an official held before each of their noses in turn,
while the patch-clad gathering outside the room shifted excitedly on
their weary feet and scanned the " pieces " in their sweaty hands with
varying expressions of disgust and disappointment. Now and then the
boys changed places, but only one of them, of dull-brown complexion
and already gifted with the shifty eye of the half-cast, performed his
task to the general satisfaction. The others were frequently interrupted by a protest from one of the recorders, whereupon the number
that had just been called was emphatically reread by an adult, amid
much scratching of pens in the leather-bound ledgers. If the monotony
of the scene was wearisome, its solemnity made it correspondingly
amusing. An uninformed observer would probably have taken it for
at least a presidential election. Rachel asserted that it reminded her
of Alice in Wonderland, but as my education was neglected I cannot
confirm this impression. What aroused my own wonder was the fact
that some two score more-or-less-high officials of a national government should be engaged in so ridiculous a formality, and that a sovereign republic should indulge in the nefarious profession of the book-
maker. But to every people its own customs.

If I had fancied it the fault of my own ear that I had not caught
all the numbers, the impression would have been corrected by the
afternoon papers. All of them carried a column or more of protest
against the " absurd inefficiency " of the boys who had served that
morning; most of them made the complaint the chief subject of their
editorial pages. The *Casa de Beneficencia* — an institution corresponding roughly to our orphan asylums — was solemnly warned that it must
thereafter furnish more capable inmates to *cantar las bolas* (" sing the
balls ") on pain of losing the privilege entirely. Not only had the
" uninstructed urchins " of that morning made mistakes in reading
the numbers — a dastardly thing from the Cuban point of view — but
had pronounced many of them in so slovenly a manner that " our special
reporters were unable to supply our readers with correct information
on a subject of prime importance to the entire republic." Beware that
it never happened again ! It was easy to picture the poor overworked
nuns of the asylum toiling far into the night to impress upon a multi-
complexioned group of fatherless gamins the urgent necessity of learning to read figures quickly and accurately, if they ever hoped to become

normal, full-grown men and perhaps win the big prize some day themselves.

Winning tickets may be cashed at any official *colectoría* at any time within a year, but such delays are rare. Barely is the drawing ended when the venders, armed with the *billetes* of the next *sorteo*, hurry forth over their accustomed beats to pay the winners and establish a reputation not so much for promptitude as for the ability to offer lucky numbers. The capital prize, $100,000 in most cases, is perhaps won now and then by some favorite of fortune, instead of falling to the Government, collector of all unsold winners, though I have never personally known of such a stroke of luck during all my wanderings in lottery-infested lands. Smaller causes for momentary happiness are more frequent, for with 1741 prizes, divisible into a hundred "pieces" each, it would be strange if a persistent player did not now and then "make a killing." But even these must be rare in comparison to the optimistic multitude that pursues the goddess Chance, for on the morning following a drawing the streets of Havana are everywhere littered with worthless *billetes* cast off by wrathy purchasers. Wherefore an incorrigible moralist has deduced a motto that may be worth passing on to future travelers in Cuba:

"Buy a 'piece' or two that you may know the sneer of Fortune, but don't get the habit."

Three days before the wedding of my sister, mama, she and I went to the house of my future brother-in-law to put Alice's things in order. The *novio* was not there. He had discreetly withdrawn to a hotel and only came home now and then for a few moments to give orders to the servants. If he found us there he greeted us in the hall and did not enter the rooms except as we invited him. As there were no women in his family we had to occupy ourselves with all these matters.

"Listen, my daughter," said mama, one night, after the *novio* had gone, "when to-morrow you take leave of your fiancé do not pass beyond the line marked on the floor by the light of the hall lamp." My sister started to protest, "But, mama, what is there wrong in that?" "Nothing, daughter, but it is not proper. Do as I tell you." Alice, though slightly displeased with the order, always obeyed it thereafter.

These two quotations from one of Cuba's latest novels give in a nutshell the position of women in Cuba. Like all Latin-American countries, especially of the tropics, it is essentially a man's country. One of the great surprises of Havana is the scarcity of women on the streets, even at times when they swarm with promenading men. The

Cuban believes as firmly as the old Spaniard that the woman's sphere is strictly behind the grill of the front window, and with few exceptions the women agree with him. The result is that her interest in life beyond her own household is virtually nil. The "Woman Suffrage Party of Cuba" recently issued a pompous manifesto, but it seems to have won about as much support on the island as would a missionary of the prohibition movement. In the words of the militants of the sex in Anglo-Saxon lands, "the Cuban woman has not yet reached emancipation."

The clerks, even in shops that deal only in female apparel, are almost exclusively male. The offices that employ stenographers or assistants from the ranks of the fair sex are rare, and those usually recruit such help in the United States. Except on gala occasions, it is extremely seldom that a Cuban girl of the better class is seen in public, and even then only in company with a duenna or a male member of her immediate family, and few married women consider it proper to appear, unaccompanied by their husbands, despite American example. As another Cuban writer has put it, "One of our greatest defects is the little or entire lack of genuine respect for women. Though we are outwardly extremely gallant in society and sticklers for the finer points of etiquette and courtesy, we almost always look upon a woman merely as a female and our first thought of at least a young and beautiful woman is to imagine all her hidden perfections. The instant a lady comes within sight of the average Cuban gathering all eyes are fixed upon her with a stare that in Anglo-Saxon countries would be more than impertinent, which pretends to be flattering, but which at bottom is truly insulting." He does not add that the women rather invite this attention and feel themselves slighted, their attractions unappreciated, if it is not given. Yet of open offenses against her modesty the Cuban lady is freer than on the streets of our own large cities. Even in restaurants and gatherings where those of the land never appear, an American woman is treated, except in the matter of staring, with genuine courtesy by all classes.

The custom of living almost exclusively in the privacy of her own home has given the Cuban woman a tendency to spend the day in disreputable undress. Their hair dishevelled, their forms loosely enveloped in a *bata* or in a slatternly petticoat and dressing-sack, usually torn and seldom clean, their toes thrust into slippers that slap at every step, they slouch about the house all the endless day. Unless there are guests they never dress for lunch, seldom for dinner, but don instead earrings, necklaces, bracelets, and an astonishing collection of finger rings, powdering their faces rather than washing them.   During meals the favorite topics of conversation are food and digestion; if one of them has had any of the numerous minor ailments natural to a life of non-exertion, it is sure to be the subject of a cacophonous discussion that lasts until the appearance of the inevitable toothpicks. Servants, with whom they associate with a familiarity unknown in Northern homes, are numerous, and leave little occupation for the mothers and daughters.   The women never read, not even the newspapers, and their minds, poorly trained to begin with in the nun-taught " finishing schools," go to seed early, so that by late youth or early middle age their faces show the effects of a selfish, idle existence and a life of continual boredom.   But lest I be accused of being over-critical, let me quote once more the native writer already introduced:

In one of the interior habitations a piano sounded, beaten by a clumsy hand that repeated the same immature exercise without cessation.   There was general discussion in the dining-room at all hours of the day, mingled with the shrieks of a parrot which swung on a perch suspended from the ceiling and the constant disputes of the children, who were snatching playthings from one another, heaping upon each other every class of verbal injury.   The mother sewed and the older children tortured the piano during entire hours, or polished their nails with much care, rubbing them with several kinds of powders.   When they had finished these occupations they slouched from one end of the house to the other, throwing themselves in turn upon all the divans or into the cushioned rocking-chairs and yawning with ennui.   Their skirts fell from their belts, loosened by the languid and lazy gait.   The mother did not want the girls to do anything in the house for fear they would spoil their hands and lose their chances of marriage.   On the other hand, in the afternoon when the hour of visits drew near the time was always too short to distribute harmoniously the color on their cheeks and lips and to take off the little hair papers with which they artificially formed their waves or curls during the day.

This continual hubbub seems to be customary to every household; all intercourse, be it orders to servants or admonitions to the insufferable children, being carried on by yelling.   And there are no worse voices in the world than those of the Cuban women.   Whether it is due to the climate or to the custom of reciting in chorus at school, they have a timbre that tortures the eardrums like the sharpening of a saw, and all day long they exercise them to the full capacity of their lungs. Under no circumstances is one of them given the floor alone, but the slightest morsel of gossip is threshed to bits in a free-for-all whirlwind of incomprehensible shrieking.

On the other hand, the Cuban woman accepts many children willingly, and in accordance with her lights is an excellent wife and mother. Indeed, she is inclined to be over-affectionate, and given to serving her children where they should serve themselves, with a consequent lack of development in their characters. The boys in particular are " spoiled " by being granted every whim. The men are much less often at home than is the case with us, and seldom inclined to exert a masculine influence on their obstreperous sons. The result is a lack of self-control that makes itself felt through all Cuban manhood, a " touchiness," an inclination to stand on their dignity instead of yielding to the dictates of common sense.

But if she is slouchy in the privacy of her own household, the Cuban woman is quite the opposite in public. The grande toilette is essential for the briefest appearance on the streets. American women assert that there is no definite style in feminine garb in Cuba, and I should not dream of questioning such authority, though to the mere masculine eye they always seem " dressed within an inch of their lives " whenever they emerge into the sunlight. But it does not need even the intuition of the sometimes unfair sex to recognise that a life of physical indolence leaves their figures somewhat dumpy and ungraceful, seldom able to appear to advantage even in the best of gowns. Nor is it hard to detect a sense of discomfort in their unaccustomed full dress, which makes them eager to hurry home again to the negligée of bata and slippers.

If the men monopolize other places of public gathering, the churches at least belong to the women. There are few places of worship in Havana, or in all Cuba, for that matter, that merit a visit for their own sake. Though most of them are overfilled with ambitious attempts at decoration, none of these is very successful. A single painting of worth here and there, an occasional side chapel, one or two carved choirstalls, are the only real artistic attractions. But several of them are well worth visiting for the side-lights they throw on Cuban customs. As in Spain, every variety of diseased beggar squats in an appealing attitude against the façades of the more fashionable religious edifices during the hours of general concourse. Luxurious automobiles, with negro chauffeurs in dazzling white liveries, sweep up to the foot of the broad stone steps in as continual procession as the narrow streets permit, but the passengers who alight are overwhelmingly of the gown-clad gender. Within, the perfume of the worshipers drowns out the incense. A glance across the sea of kneeling figures discloses astonish-

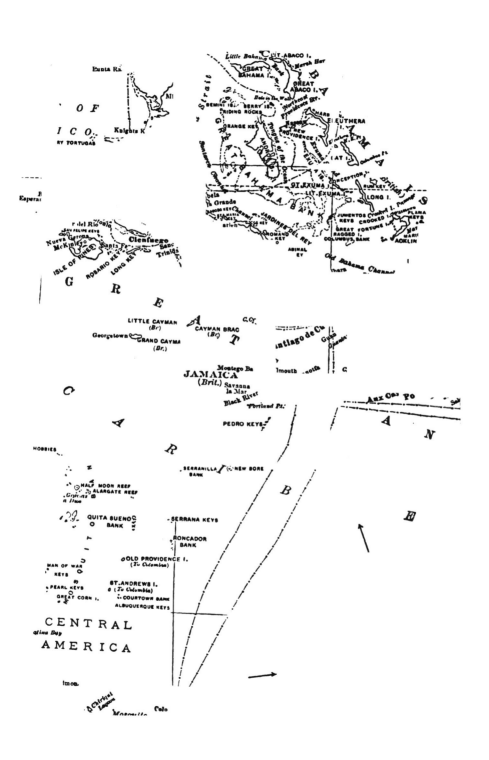

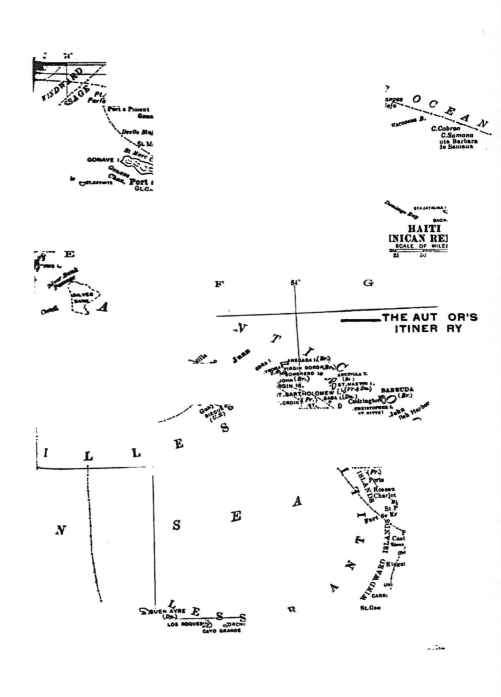

ingly few bare heads. The Cuban men, of course, are "good Catholics," too, but they are apt to confine their church attendance to special personal occasions. The church has no such influence in public affairs in Cuba as in many parts of the continent to the southward; so little indeed, that public religious processions are forbidden by law, though sometimes permitted in practice. If the Jesuits are still a power to be reckoned with, so are *los masones,* and the mere proof of irreligion is no effective bar to governmental or commercial preferment.

A deaf person would probably enjoy Havana far more than those of acute hearing. I have often wondered why nature did not provide us with earlids as well as eyelids. A mere oversight, no doubt, that would not have been made had the Cuban capital existed when the first models of the human being were submitted. Havana may not hold the noise championship of the world, but at least little old New York is silent by comparison. Unmuffled automobiles beyond computation, tramcars that seem far more interested in producing clamor than speed, bellowing venders of everything vendible, are but the background of an unbroken uproar that permeates to every nook and cranny of the city. Honest hotel-keepers tell you frankly that they can offer every comfort except quiet. Even in church you hear little but the tumult outside, broken only at rare intervals by the droning voice of the preacher. It is not simply the day-time uproar of business hours; it increases steadily from nightfall until dawn. In olden days the *sereno,* with his dark lantern, his pike, pistol, bunch of keys, whistle, and rope, wandered through the streets calling out the time and the state of the weather every half-hour. His efforts would be wasted nowadays. The long-seasoned inhabitants seem to have grown callous to the constant turbulence; I have yet to meet a newcomer who confesses to an unbroken hour of sleep. If you move out to one of the pensions of Vedado, the household itself will keep you constantly reminded that you are still in Havana. The Cubans themselves seem to thrive on noise. If they are so unfortunate as to be denied their beloved din, they lose no time in producing another from their own throats. After a week in Havana we took a ferry across the harbor and strolled along the plain behind Cabaña Fortress. For some time we were aware of an indefinable sensation of strangeness amounting almost to discomfort. We had covered a mile or so more before we suddenly discovered that it was due to the unaccustomed silence.

CHAPTER III

CUBA FROM WEST TO EAST

STEAMERS to Havana land the traveler within a block or two of the central railway station, so that, if the capital has no fascination for him, there lies at hand more than four thousand kilometers of track to put him in touch with almost any point of the island. The most feasible way of visiting the interior of Cuba is by rail, unless one has the time and inclination to do it on foot. Automobiles are all very well in the vicinity of Havana, but the Cuban, like most Latin-Americans, is distinctly not a road builder, and there are long stretches of the island where only the single-footing native horses can unquestionably make their way. There is occasional steamer service along the coasts, and with few exceptions the important towns are on the sea, but even to visit all these is scarcely seeing Cuba.

The railroads are several in number and as well equipped as our second-class lines. One ventures as far west as Guane; there is a rather thorough network in the region nearest the capital; or the traveler may enter his sleeping-car at Havana and, if nothing happens, land at Santiago in the distant " Oriente " some thirty-six hours later. Unfortunately something usually happens. The ferry from Key West brings not only passengers, but whole freight trains, and among the curious sights of Cuba are box-cars from as far off as the State of Washington basking in the tropical sunshine or the shade of royal palms hundreds of miles east of Havana. First-class fares are higher than those of our own land, but some eighty per cent. of the traveling public content themselves with the hard wooden benches of what, in spite of the absence of an intervening second, are quite properly called third-class. Freight rates are said to average five times those in the United States. Women of the better class are almost as rarely seen on the trains as on the streets of Havana, with the result that the few first-class coaches are sometimes exclusively filled with men, and all cars are smoking-cars.

There are sights and incidents of interests even in the more commonplace first-class coaches. In the November season, when the mills of the island begin their grinding, they carry many Americans on their way back to the sugar estates, most of them of the highly skilled labor class in speech and point of view. Now and again a well-dressed native shares his seat with his fighting-cock, dropping about the bird's feet the sack in which the rules of the company require it to be carried and occasionally giving it a drink at the passengers' water-tank. At frequent intervals the gamester shrilly challenges the world at large; travelers by Pullman have been known to spend sleepless nights because of a crowing rooster in the next berth. Train-guards in the uniform of American soldiers, an " O. P." on their collars — this being the abbreviation of the Spanish words for " Public Order "— armed with rifle, revolver, and a long sword with an eagle's-head hilt in the beak of which is held the retaining strap, strut back and forth through the train, usually in pairs. Most of them are well-behaved youths, though the wide-spread corps on which the government largely depends to overawe its revolutionarily inclined political opponents is not wholly free from rowdies. The trainboy and the brakemen have the same gift of incomprehensible language as our own, and only a difference in uniform serves in most cases to distinguish the name of the next station from that of some native fruit offered for sale. The wares of the Cuban train vender are more varied than in our own circumspect land. Not only can he furnish the bottles that cheer, in any quantity and degree of strength, but also lottery tickets, cooked food, and oranges deftly pared like an apple, in the native fashion. There is probably no fruit on earth which varies so much in its form of consumption in different countries as the orange.

But it is in third-class that one may find a veritable riot of color. Types and complexions of every degree known to the human race crowd the less comfortable coaches. There are leather-faced Spaniards returning for the *zafra,* fresh, boyish faces of similar origin and destination, Basques in their *boinas* and corduroy clothes, untamed-looking Haitians sputtering their uncouth tongue, more merry negroes from the British West Indies, Chinamen and half-Chinamen, Cuban countrymen in a combination shirt and blouse called a *chamarreta,* men carrying roosters under their arms, men with hunting dogs, negro girls in purple and other screaming colors, including furs dyed in tints unknown to the animal world, and a scattering of Oriental and purely Caucasian features from the opposite ends of the earth. Perhaps one third of the throng would come under the classification of " niggers " in our " Jim Crow " States; Southerners would be, and sometimes

are, horrified to see the blackest and the whitest race sharing the same
seat and even engaged, perhaps, in animated conversation. In a
corner sits, more likely than not, an enormous negro woman with a
big black cigar protruding from her massive lips at an aggressive
angle and a brood of piccaninnies peering out from beneath her voluminous skirts like chicks sheltered from rain by the mother hen. All
the gamut of sophistication is there, from the *guajiro,* or Cuban peasant, of forty who is taking his first train-ride and is waiting in secret
terror for the first station, that he may drop off and walk home, to
others as blasé as the entirely respectable, cosmopolitan, uninteresting
travelers in the chair-car and Pullmans behind.

There are express trains in Cuba, those that make the long journey
between the two principal cities sometimes so heavy with their half
dozen third, their one or two first-class, their Pullman, baggage, express, and mail-cars, that it is small wonder the single engine can keep
abreast of the time-table even when washouts or slippery, grass-brown
rails do not add to its troubles. Section-gangs are conspicuous by
their scarcity, and those who contract to keep the tracks clear of vegetation by a monthly sprinkling of chemicals do not always accomplish
their task. But there is nothing more comfortable than loafing along
in the wicker chairs to be found in one uncrowded end of the first-
class coach, without extra charge, with the immense car-windows wide
open, far enough back to miss the inevitable cinders, through the perpetual, palm-tree-studded summer of the tropics. Even the expresses
are, perhaps unintentionally, sight-seeing trains, though they are frequently more or less exasperating to the hurried business man. But,
then, one has no right to be a hurried business man in the West Indies.

The slower majority of trains dally at each station, according to
its size, just about long enough to "give the town the once over";
or, if it is large enough to be worth a longer visit, one is almost certain
to catch the next train if he sets out for the station as soon as it arrives.
The scene at a Cuban railway station is always interesting. Except
in the largest towns, most of the population comes down to see the train
go through, so that the platform is crowded half an hour before it is
due, which usually means an hour or two before it actually arrives.
The new-comer is apt to conclude that he has little chance of getting a
seat, but he soon learns by experience that few of these platform
loungers are actual travelers. The average station crowd is distinctly

African in complexion, though perhaps a majority show a greater or less percentage of European ancestry. Pompous black dames in gaudy dresses, newly ironed and starched, with big brass ear-rings and huge combs in their frizzled tresses, their fingers heavy with a dozen cheap rings, stand coyly smoking their long black cigars. A man with his best rooster under one arm and his best girl on the other stalks haughtily to and fro among his rivals and admirers. An excited negro with a gamecock in one hand waves it wildly in the air as he argues, or tucks it under an armpit while he wrestles with his baggage. A colored girl in robin's-egg blue madly powders her nose in a corner, using a pocket mirror of the size of a cabinet photograph. *Guajiros* in *chamarretas* with stiffly starched white bosoms which give them a resemblance to dress shirts that have not been tucked into the trousers, a big knife in a sheath half showing below them, the trousers themselves white, or faintly pink, or cream-colored, even of gay plaids in the more African cases, their heads covered with immense straw hats and their feet with noiseless *alpargatas*, gaze about them with the wondering air of peasants the world over. Rural guards of the " O. P." strut hither and yon, making a great show of force both in numbers and weapons. Children of all ages add their falsetto to the constant hubbub of chatter. Here and there a worn-out old Chinaman wanders about offering *dulces* for sale. A negro crone engaged in that unsavory occupation technically known as " shooting snipes " picks up an abandoned cigar or cigarette butt here and there, lighting it from the remnant of another and dropping that into a pocket. The first-class waiting-room is crowded, but the departure of the train will prove that most of the occupants have come merely to show off their finery or examine that of their neighbors. A white-haired old negro man wheels back and forth in the bit of space left to him a white baby resplendent with pink ribbons. When the train creaks in at last; would-be baggage carriers swarm into the coaches or about departing travelers like aggressive mosquitoes. The racial disorderliness of Latin-Americans, and their abhorrence of carrying their own bags, make this latter nuisance universal throughout the length and breadth of the island. It is of no use for the American traveler to assert his own ability to bear his burdens; no one believes him, and they are sure to be snatched out of his hands by some officious ragamuffin before he can escape from the maelstrom. In some stations a massive, self-assertive negro woman " contracts " to see all hand baggage on or off the trains, keeping all the rabble of ragged men and boys, some of them pure white, in her employ and collecting the gratuities herself in a final promenade through the cars.

Sometimes the train stops for a station meal, the mere buffet service on board being uncertain and insufficient. Then it is every one for himself and hunger catch the hindmost, for one has small chance of attracting the attention of the overworked concessionary if the heaping platters with which the common table is crowded are empty before he can lay hand upon them. Then he must trust to the old Chinamen who patiently stand all day along the edge of the platform, or even well into the night, slinking off into the darkness with their lantern-lighted boxes of sweets and biscuits only when the last train has rumbled away to the east or west.

We were invited to spend a Sunday at a big tobacco *finca* in the heart of the far-famed Vuelta Abajo district in Cuba's westernmost province. With the exception of Guanajay the few towns between Havana and Pinar del Rio, capital of the province of the same name, have little importance. The passing impression is of rich red mud, a glaring sunshine, and a wide difference between the rather foppish, over-dressed Havanese and the uncouth countrymen in their *bohios*, huts of palm-leaves and thatch which probably still bear a close resemblance to those in which Columbus found the aborigines living. Then there are of course the royal palms, which grow everywhere in Cuba in even greater profusion than in Brazil. The roads are bordered with them, the fields are striped with their silvery white trunks, their majestic fronds give the finishing touch to every landscape.

Pinar del Rio itself has the same baking-hot, glaring, dusty aspect of almost all towns of the interior in the dry season, the same curious contrasts of snorting automobiles and *guajiros* peddling their milk on horseback, the cans in burlap or leaf-woven saddlebags beneath their crossed or dangling legs. Beyond, the *mixto* wanders along at a jog trot, now and then stopping for a drink or to urge a belligerent bull off the track. Here a peasant picks his way carefully down the car steps, carrying by a string looped over one calloused finger two lordly peacocks craning their plumed heads from the tight palm-leaf wrappings in which their bodies are concealed; there a family climbs aboard with a black nursegirl of ten, whose saucer eyes as she points and exclaims at what no doubt seems to her the swiftly fleeing landscape show that she has never before been on a train. Tobacco is grown in scattered sections all over Cuba, but it is most at home in the gently rolling heart of this western province. Being Sunday, there was little work going on in the fields, but when we passed this way two days later we found them everywhere being plowed with oxen, birds following close on the heels of the plowmen to pick up the bugs and worms, women and children as well as men transplanting the bed-grown seedlings of the size of radish tops. Time was when the narcotic weed had all this region to itself, but the lordly sugar-cane is steadily encroaching upon it now, daring to grow in the very shadow of the old, brown, leaf-built tobacco barns.

Don Jacinto himself did not meet us at the train, but his giant of a son greeted us with an elaborate Castilian courtesy which seemed curiously out of keeping with his fluent English, interlarded with American college slang. How he managed to cramp himself into the driving seat of the bespattered Ford was as much of a mystery as the apparent ease with which it skimmed along the bottomless Cuban country road or swam the bridgeless river. I noted that it bore no license tag and, perhaps unwisely, expressed my surprise aloud, for Don Jacinto's son smiled quizzically and for some time made no other answer. Then he explained, " Those of us who are old residents and large property holders in our communities do not bother to take out licenses; besides, they are only five dollars here in the country, so it is hardly worth the trouble."

Our host, a lordly-mannered old Spaniard who had come to Cuba in his early youth, received us on the broad, breeze-swept veranda of his dwelling. It was a typical Spanish country house of the tropics, low and of a single story, yet capacious, rambling back through a large, wide-open parlor, a dining-room almost as extensive, and a cobbled patio to a smoke-blackened kitchen and the quarters of the dozen black domestics who were tending the pots or responding with alacrity to the slightest hint of a summons from Don Jacinto or his equally imperious son. The living rooms flanked the two larger chambers, and were as tightly closed as the latter were wide open. The guest room opening directly off the parlor contained all the conveniences that American influence has brought to Cuba, without losing a bit of its Castilian architecture. There were of course neither carpets nor rugs in the house, bare wooden floors being not only cooler, but less inviting to the inevitable insects of the tropics. A score of cane rocking-chairs, the same round rattan which formed the rockers curving upward and backward to give the chair its arms, and a bare table, constituted the entire furniture of the parlor. On the unpapered wooden walls hung two framed portraits and a large calendar. Boxes of cigars lay invitingly open in all the three rooms we entered and another decorated the table on the cement-paved veranda.

This last was the principal rendezvous of the household. There a peon dumped a small cartload of mail, made up largely of technical periodicals; there the servants and the overseers came to receive orders. The demeanor of the inferiors before their masters was in perfect keeping with the patriarchal atmosphere of the entire *finca*. Thus, one easily imagined, plantation owners commanded and servants unquestionably obeyed in the days of slavery. There was a certain comradeship, one might almost say democracy, between the two, or the several, social grades, but it was not one which carried with it the slightest suggestion of familiarity on either side.

Luncheon was a ceremonious affair. Rachel, being the only lady present, was given the head of the table, with Don Jacinto on her right. In theory the ladies of the household were indisposed, but it was probably only the presence of strangers, particularly a male stranger, which kept them from appearing, if only in *bata* and curl-papers. Below our host and myself, on opposite sides, the company was ranged down the table in careful gradations of social standing, empty chairs separating those who were too widely different in rank to touch elbows. Thus there was a vacant chair between the son of the house and the head overseer and, farther down, two of them separated the company chemist from a sort of field boss. Conversation was similarly graded. The chief overseer did not hesitate to put in a word or even tell an anecdote whenever guests, father or son were not speaking; the chemist now and then ventured a remark of his own, but the field boss ate in utter silence except when some question from the top of the table brought from him a respectful monosyllabic reply. Of the food served on one mammoth platter after another I will say nothing beyond remarking that two thirds of it was meat, all of it well cooked, and the quantity so great that the whole assembled company scarcely made a noticeable impression upon it. Over the table hung an immense cloth fan like the *punkahs* of India, operated in the same manner by a boy incessantly pulling at a rope over a pulley in the far end of the room. Its purpose, however, was different, as was indicated by its name, *espanto-moscas* (scare-flies), for Cuba's unfailing breeze would have sufficed to keep the air cool; but when the *wallah* suddenly abandoned his task with the appearance

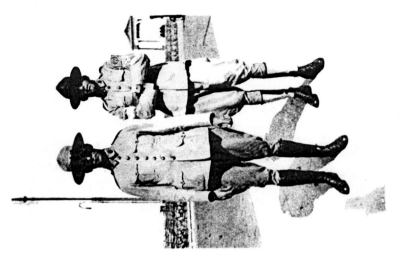

Cuban soldiers

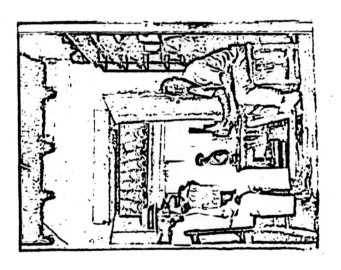

A Cuban shoemaker

Matanzas, with drying sisal fiber in the foreground

The Central Plaza of Cienfuegos

of the coffee the flies quickly settled down upon us in a veritable cloud. It may be that the tobacco fields attract them, for they are ordinarily far less troublesome in the West Indies than during our own summers.

November being merely planting time the *finca* presented a bare appearance compared with what it would be in March, when the tall tobacco plants wave everywhere in the breeze. Behind the house was a dovecote which suggested some immense New York apartment house, so many were its several-storied compartments. A handful of corn brought a fluttering gray and white cloud which almost obscured the sun. Pigeons and chickens are kept in large numbers in the tobacco fields to follow the plows and eat the insects which would otherwise destroy the seeds and the young plants. The supply barn was the chief center of industry at this season, with its plows and watering-pots marshaled in long rows, its tons of fertilizer in sacks, its cords of baled cheese-cloth, its bags of tobacco seed, so microscopic in size that it takes four hundred thousand of them to weigh an ounce. The seed-beds were at some distance. There the seed is sowed like wheat and the plants grow as compactly as grass on a lawn until they are about twenty days old, when they are transferred to the larger fields and given room to expand almost to man's height. For acres upon acres the rolling landscape stood forested with poles on which the cheese-cloth would be hung a few weeks later, the vista recalling the hop-fields of Bavaria in the spring-time. The idea of growing " wrapper " tobacco in the shade, in order to keep the leaves silky and of uniform color, is said to have originated in the United States and to have made its way but slowly in Cuba, where planters long considered a maximum of sunshine requisite to the best quality. To-day it is in general vogue throughout the island.

We whiled away the afternoon on the breezy veranda, where the more important employees of the *finca* and men from the neighboring town came to discuss the crop, to say nothing of helping themselves to the cigars which lay everywhere within easy reach. There was something delightfully Old World about the simplicity of this patriarchal family life, perhaps because it had scarcely a hint of Americanism and its concomitant commercial bustle. Among the visitors was a lottery vender on horseback, who sold Don Jacinto and his son their customary half dozen " strips," these being sheets of twenty or thirty " pieces " of the same number. The company doctor parted with thirty dollars for a " whole ticket." Each had his own little scheme for choosing the numbers, one refusing those in which the same figure was repeated, another insisting that the total of the added figures should be divisible by three, some depending on dreams or fantastic combinations of figures they had seen or heard spoken during the day. The workmen on the estate, as on every one in Cuba, were inveterate gamblers. Not only did they buy as many " pieces " each week as they could pay for, but they all " played terminals," that is, formed pools which were won by the man guessing correctly the last two numbers of the week's winning ticket.

We visited tobacco estates in other parts of Cuba and saw all the process except the cutting and curing before we left the island. At Zaza del Medio, for instance, whole carloads of small plants are handled during November. They are very hardy, living for three or four days after being pulled up by the roots from the seed-beds. Strewn out on the station platform in little leaf-tied bundles, they were counted bunch by bunch and tossed into plaited straw saddlebags, to be transported by pack-animals to fields sometimes more than a day's journey distant. Surrounded on all sides by horizonless seas of sugar-cane, the Zaza del Medio region is conspicuous twenty miles off by its tobacco color, not of course of the plants, but of the rich brown of plowed fields and the aged thatch-built tobacco barns. We rode that way one day, our horses floundering through mammoth mud-holes, stepping gingerly through masses of thorny *aroma,* and fording saddle-deep the Zaza River. Here the small planter system, as distinctive from the big administrative estates of Vuelto Abajo, is in vogue. We found lazy oxen swinging along as if in time to a wedding march, dragging behind them crude wooden plows protected by an iron point. A boy followed each of them, dropping a withered small plant at regular intervals, a man, or sometimes a woman, setting them up behind him. Immense barns made of a pole frame-work covered entirely with brown and shaggy guinea-grass bulked forth against the palm-tree-punctuated horizon. The similarly constructed houses of the planters were minute by comparison. Here, they told us, tobacco grows only waist high, in contrast to the six feet it sometimes attains in Pinar del Rio province. In February or March the plants are cut off at the base and strung on the poles which lie heaped in immense piles, and hung for two months in the airy barns. Then they are wrapped in *yagua* and carried back to the railroad on pack-animals. *Yagua,* by the way, which is constantly intruding upon any description of the West Indies, where it is put to a great variety of uses, is the base of the leaf of the royal palm, the lower one of which drops off regularly about once a month. It is pliable and durable as leather, which it resembles in appearance, though it is several times thicker, and a single leaf supplies a strip a yard long and half as wide.

Rivals, especially Jamaica, assert that the famous tobacco vegas of Cuba are worn out and that Cuban tobacco is now living on its reputation. The statement is scarcely borne out by the aroma of the cigars sold by every shop-keeper on the island, though to tell the truth they do not equal the "Habana" as we know it in the North. This is possibly due to the humidity of the climate. The new-comer is surprised to find how cavalierly the Cuban treats his cigars, or *tobacos,* as he calls them. Even though he squanders *dos reales* each for them he thrusts a handful loosely into an outside coat pocket, as if they were so many strips of wood. For they are so damp and pliable in the humid Cuban atmosphere that they will endure an astonishing amount of mistreatment without coming to grief. Contrary to the assertions of Dame Rumor, Cubans do not smoke cigarettes only; perhaps the majority, of the countrymen at least, confine themselves to cigars.

There are cigar-makers in every town of Cuba, though Havana almost monopolizes the export trade. How long some of the famous factories have been in existence was suggested to us by a grindstone in the patio of the one opposite the new national palace. There the workmen come to whet their knives each morning, and they had worn their way completely through the enormous grindstone in several places around the edge. The methods in Havana cigar factories are of course similar to those of Cayo Hueso, as Cuba calls our southernmost city. In one of them we were shown cigars which "wholesale" at fifteen hundred dollars a thousand, though I got no opportunity of judging whether or not they were worth it, either in tobacco or ostentation. The stems of the tobacco leaves are shipped to New York and made into snuff. An average wage for the cigar makers was said to be five dollars a day. They each paid that many cents a week to the factory reader, who entertains the male workmen with the daily newspapers, and the women, by their own choice of course, with the most sentimental of novels. Girls will be girls the world over.

The dreadful habit of using tobacco has progressed since the day when Columbus discovered the aborigines of the great island of Cubanacan smoking, not Habana cigars, but by using a forked reed two ends of which they put in their nostrils and the other in a heap of burning tobacco leaves.

Neither space nor the reader's patience would hold out if I attempted to do more than " hit the high spots " of our two months of journeying to and fro in Cuba. There is room for a year of constant sight-seeing and material for a fat volume in the largest of the West Indies, though to tell the truth there is a certain sameness of climate, landscape, town, and character which might make that long a stay monotonous despite the glories of at least the first two of these. While he lacks something of that open frankness of intercourse which we are wont to think reaches its height in our own free and easy land, and the exclusiveness of his family life puts him at a disadvantage as an entertainer of guests, the Cuban himself, particularly outside the larger cities, is not inhospitable. But his welcome of visitors from the North is overshadowed by the unbounded hospitality of the American residents of Cuba, whether on the great sugar estates, the fruit farms, in the scattered enterprises of varied nature in all corners of the island, or in the many cities that have become their homes. Merely to enumerate the unexpected welcomes we met with from our own people in all parts of the island would be to fill many pages.

The cities, on the whole, are the least pleasant of Cuba's attractions. Their hotels, and those places with which the traveler is most likely to come in contact, are largely given over to the insular sport of tourist-baiting even before midwinter brings its plethora of cold-fleeing, race-track-following, or prohibition-abhorring visitors from the North. Havana, I take it, would be the last place in the world for the lover of the simplicities of life, as for the man of modest income, in those winter months when its hotels turn away whole droves of would-be guests and its already exorbitant prices climb far out of sight from the topmost rung of the ladder of reason. Incidentally Cuba is in the throes of what might be called a " sugar vs. tourists " controversy. Its merchants would like to draw as many visitors as possible, but even its tourist bureau sees itself obliged to " soft pedal " its appeals. If still more visitors come, where is the island to house them? Time was when her more expensive hotels, especially of Havana, stood well nigh empty through the summer and welcomed the first refugees from Jack Frost with open arms, or at least doors. It is not so to-day. Sugar planters from the interior, who would once have grumbled at paying a dollar for a night's lodging in a back street *fonda*, now demand the most luxurious suites facing the plaza and the Prado, nay, even house their families in them for months at a time, to the dismay of foreign visitors. Stevedores who were once overjoyed to earn two dollars a day sneer

at the fabulous wages offered them now, knowing that a bit of specula-
tion in sugar stocks will bring them many times the amount to be had by
physical exertion. The advice most apropos to the modern visitor to
Cuba whose tastes are simple and whose fortune is limited would be,
perhaps, to come early and avoid the cities.

We found Pinar del Rio town, for instance, far less beguiling than
a journey we made from it over the mountain to the Matahambre mines.
A peon met us with native horses where the hired Ford confessed its
inability to advance farther. Along the narrow trail the vegetation was
dense and tropical. Royal palms waved high along the borders of the
small streams; red-trunked *macicos, yagrumas* with their curious upturned leaves showing their white backs, broke the almost monotony
of the greenery. Here and there we passed a brown grass hut which
seemed to have grown up of itself, a little patch of *malanga, boniato,*
or yuca, the chief native tubers, about it, a dark woman paddling her
wash against the trunk of a palm-tree on the edge of a water-hole,
several babies in single white garments or their own little black skins
scurrying away into the underbrush as we rode down upon them. A
few horsemen passed us, and a pack-train or two; but only one woman
among the score or more we met was mounted. She was a jet-black
lady in a bedraggled skirt and a man's straw hat, who teetered perilously
on her uncomfortable side-saddle, yet who gazed scornfully down her
shaded nose at Rachel, riding far more easily astride. Finally, when the
sun was high and the vegetation scrubby and shadeless, and we had
climbed laboriously up several steep, bare hillsides only to slide down
again into another hollow, a cleft in the hills gave us a sudden panorama
of the sea, and almost sheer below us lay spread out the mining town.
The setting was barren, as is that of most mines, though five years
before it had been covered with a pine forest, until a cyclone came to
sweep it wholly away and leave only here and there a dead, branchless
trunk in a reddish soil that gave every outer indication of being sterile.
A network of red trails linked together the offices, the shafts and the
reduction plant, the red-roofed houses of the American employees, and
the thatched huts of the mine workers.

Mining is not one of Cuba's chief assets, but this particular spot
is producing a high-grade copper. Ore was discovered here by a deer
hunter wandering through the forest of pines, but before he could
make use of his knowledge the region was " denounced " by another
Cuban and still belongs to his family, though there is some bitter-worded
doubt as to which branch of it. It goes without saying that the manager

is an energetic young American. The laborers are chiefly Spaniards, for the Cubans are too superstitious to long endure working underground. The company builds its own roads, and has installed a telegraph and post-office without government aid, yet it pays full rates on its telegrams or letters. We went far down the shaft into the damp blackness of the eighth and tenth levels, hundreds of feet below the surface, following the galleries and " stopes " to where the workmen were piling the bluish rock into the little iron hand-cars, the dull echoing thud of the dynamiting on some other level sending a shudder through the mountain. All night long the mine worked tirelessly on, the suspended ore-cars swinging down their six-mile cables across the gorge to the loading bins on the edge of the sea.

We followed them in a Ford next morning, from the treeless uplands down through an oak-grown strip where half-wild hogs fatten themselves, unwisely, for the plumper of them are sure to grace native boards during the *fiesta* of Noche Buena, then along a strip of palms to the Atlantic. A launch scudded down the coast with us to Esperanza, a long range of mountains, rounded in form, gashed with red wounds here and there, looking lofty only because they were so near at hand, seeming to keep pace with us as if bent on shutting us out of the level country behind them. After luncheon in the " best hotel," with a hen under my chair and a pig under Rachel's, we Forded to Viñales, the road running for miles under the very lee of a sheer mountain wall, trees, especially of the palm variety, rising everywhere out of the crevices of the soft white rock and seeming to keep their foothold by clutching the wall above with their upper branches. Caves with elaborate stalactite and stalagmite formations gaped beneath them, until we rounded the spur and passed through a sort of mountain portal into the familiar, rolling, dense-grown interior again.

We returned to Pinar del Rio by *guagua,* a four-seated mail and passenger auto bus such as ply in many sections of rural Cuba. Its driver was as wild as his brethren of Havana, and the contrivance leaped along over the bad roads like a frolicsome goat. Fortunately the usual crowd had missed their ride that morning and we could stretch our legs at ease. Only a leathery old lady who dickered for a reduction in fare, two or three *guajiros* in their best starched *chamarretas,* a villager's shoes which were to be resoled, and two turkeys in palm-leaf cornucopias made up the passenger list. The shrill whistle in place of a horn warned dawdling countrymen to beware, for our chauffeur had scant respect for his fellow-mortals.

Of the several towns which the traveler in Cuba is more or less sure to visit the first is usually Matanzas, both because it is the first place of any importance on the way eastward and because it boasts two natural phenomena that have been widely reported. The town itself, wrapped around the head of a deeply indented bay, has nothing that may not be found in a dozen other provincial towns, — unpaved streets reeking with mud or dust, according to the weather, a cement-floored central plaza gay with tropical vegetation and flanked by *portales,* or massive arcades, and constant vistas of the more formal hours of family life through the street-toeing window grilles. The pursuit of tourists is among its favorite sports, and not only are the prices and accommodations of hotels infinitely more attractive in the mouths of their runners at the station than at their desks, but the entire town seems to be banded together in a conspiracy to force foreign visitors to hire automobiles. At least we were forced to learn by experience rather than by inquiry that the street-cars carry one two thirds of the way to either of the "sights" for which the place is noted, or that one can stroll the entire distance from the central plaza in half an hour.

The Yumuri valley is, to be sure, well worth seeing. From the hermitage of Montserrat, erected by the Catalans of the island on a slope above the town, the basin-shaped vale has a serene beauty, particularly at sunrise or toward sunset, which draws at least a murmur of pleasure from the beholder. Royal palms, singly and in clumps, dot the whole expanse of plain with their green plumes and silvery trunks and climb the slopes of the encircling hills, which lie like careless grass-grown heaps of cracked stone along the horizon. Even by day the silence is broken only by the distant shouts of a peasant or two struggling with their oxen and plows; the occasional lowing of cattle floats past on the stronger breeze of evening. The Cubans rank this as their most entrancing landscape, but I have seen as pretty views from the abandoned farms of Connecticut. For one thing the colors are not variegated enough in this seasonless land to give such scenes the beauty lent by changing leaves, though much else is made up for by the majesty of the royal palms.

A gentler climb at the other end of town, between broad fields of rope-producing cactus, brings one to a cheap wooden house which might pass unnoticed but for the incongruous rumble of an electric dynamo within it. In sight of the commonplace landscape it is easy to believe the story that the caves of Bellamar remained for centuries unknown until a Chinese coolie extracting limestone for a near-by kiln discovered them by losing his crowbar through a hole he had poked in the earth. To-day they are exploited by the rope-making company which owns the surrounding fields. The main portion of the huge limestone cavern has been fitted with electric lights, which of themselves destroy half the romance of the subterranean chambers; the temperature is that of a Turkish bath, and the stereotyped chatter of the guide grows worse than tiresome. But it would be a pity to let these minor drawbacks repel the traveler from visiting Cuba's weirdest scene. The cave contains more than thirty chambers or halls, the chief of which is the " Gothic Temple," two hundred and fifty by eighty feet in extent, its lofty roof upheld by massive white columns. There are immense natural bath-tubs, forming waterfalls, fantastic grottoes and nature-sculptured figures of all shapes and sizes along the undulating central passageway that stretches far away into the unlighted earth. Mounds that look like snow-banks, towering walls that seem shimmering curtains, white glistening slopes down which one might easily fancy oneself tobogganing, so closely do they resemble our Northern hillsides in mid-winter, resound with the cackling voice of the irrepressible guide. Of stalagmites and stalactites of every possible size there is no end, some of them slowly joining together to form others of those mighty columns which seem to bear aloft the outer earth. The caves are admirably fitted, except in temperature, to serve as setting for the more fantastic of Wagner operas.

If the train is not yet due, it is worth while to visit the rope factory near the station. As they reach full size the lower leaves of the *hene-quen* plants are cut off one by one and carried to the crushing-house on a knoll behind the main establishment. Here they are passed between grooved rollers, the green sap and pulp falling away and leaving bunches of greenish fibers like coarser corn-silk, which shoot down across a little valley on cables to the drying-field. Looped over long rows of poles, they remain here for several days, until the sun has dried and bleached them to the color of new rope. Massive machines tended by women and men weave the fibers together in cords of hundreds of yards long and of the diameter of binding-twine; similar machines twist three of these into the resemblance of clothes-lines, which in their turn are woven together three by three, the process being repeated until great coils of ship's hawsers far larger than the hand can encircle emerge at the far end of the room ready for shipment.

From Matanzas eastward fruit and garden plots, and the more intensive forms of cultivation, die out and the landscape becomes almost

A principal street of Santa Clara

The Central Plaza of Santa Clara

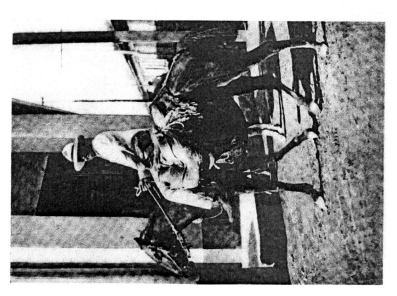

A dairyman, Santa Clara district

Cuban town scenery

unbroken expanses of sugar-cane. The soil is more apt than not to be reddish. Automobiles disappear; in their place are many men on horseback and massive high-wheeled carts drawn by oxen. On the whole the country is flat, uninteresting, with endless stretches of cane-fields, palm-trees, and nothing else. A branch line will carry one to Cárdenas, but it is hot, dusty, and dry, as parched as the Carolinas in early autumn, scarcely worth visiting unless one takes time to push on to its far-famed beach long miles away. Far-famed, that is, in Cuba, where beaches are rare and water sports much less popular than might be expected in a land where the sea is always close at hand and summer reigns the entire twelve-month. Now and again some unheralded scene breaks the cane-green monotony. There is the little town of Colón, for example, intersected by the railroad, which passes along the very edge of its central plaza, decorated with a bronze statue of Columbus discovering his first land — and holding in his left hand a two-ton anchor which he seems on the point of tossing ashore.

The older railroad line ends at Santa Clara, one of the few important towns of Cuba which do not face the sea. But the two daily expresses merely change engines and continue, in due season, to the eastward. An energetic Anglo-Saxon pushed a line through the remaining two thirds of the island within four years after American intervention, without government assistance, without even the privilege of exercising the right of eminent domain, though the Spaniards had been " studying the project " for a half century. There are no osteopaths in Santa Clara. They are not needed; a ride through its incredibly rough and tumble streets serves the same purpose. In Havana it is often impracticable for two persons to pass on the same sidewalk; in many of these provincial towns it is impossible. The people of Santa Clara seem content to make their way through town like mountain goats, leaping from one lofty block of cement to mud-reeking roadway, clambering to another waist-high sidewalk beyond, mounting now and then to the crest of precipices so narrow and precarious that the dizzy stranger feels impelled to clutch the flanking house-wall, only to descend again swiftly to the street level, climbing over on the way perhaps a family or two " taking the air " and greeting them with an inexplicably courteous " Muy buenas noches." The citizens grumble of course at the condition of their streets and make periodical demands upon the federal government to pave them, as in all Latin America. The question often suggests itself, why the dev —, I don't mean to be profane, whatever the provocation,— but why in — er — the world don't you get together and pave them yourselves? But of course any newsboy could give a score of reasons why all such matters as that are exclusive affairs of " the government," and he would pronounce the word as if it were some supernatural power wholly independent of mere human assistance.

In contrast, the central plaza of course is perfectly kept and, though empty by day, is more or less crowded in the evening, particularly when the band plays. Seeing only the crowd which parades under the royal palms in the moonlight, the visitor might come to the false conclusion that the majority of the population is white, and he would make a similar error in the opposite direction if he saw the town only by day. At the evening promenade there is a great feminine display of furs, though it is about cold enough for a silk bathing-suit; the club members have a pleasant custom of gathering in rocking-chairs on the sidewalks before their social meeting-places facing the square. Club life in Cuba follows the lead of family life in the wide-openness of its more public functions, though of course there is more intimate club and family activity far to the rear of the open parlors.

If one is in a lazy mood one rather enjoys Santa Clara, though a hurried mortal would probably curse its leisurely ways, its languid style of shopping, for instance, with chairs for customers, and the invariably male clerks thinking nothing of pausing in the midst of a purchase to discuss the latest cock-fight with a friendly lounger. We voted the place picturesque, yet when we took to wondering what made it so we could specify little more than the crowds of *guajiros* astride their horses, their produce in saddle-sacks beneath their elevated legs, who jogged silently through the muddy streets. Some of these were so superstitious in the matter of photography that they could only be caught by trickery. In the evening hours almost every block resounded with the efforts of amateur pianists. The Cubans are always beating pianos, but they are strangely unmusical. I have been told that a famous Cuban pianist won unstinted applause in New York, but of the hundreds we heard on the island each and all would almost infallibly have won something far less pleasing.

Musically the Cuban is best at the native *danzón,* a refinement of the savage African *rumba.* But every town large or small has its weekly concerts. Perhaps the most amusing one we attended was at the sugar-mill village of Jatibonico. The players were simple youths of the town, as varied in complexion and garb as the invariably tar-brushed promenaders who filed round and round the grass-grown plaza. The instruments were so unorthodox that we paused to make an inventory of them. Besides a cornet played by an energetic youth who now and then made it heard far beyond the reach of the rest of the uproar, there was a trombone and two of what seemed to be half-breeds among horns, the manipulators of which varied the effect by now and then holding their hats over the sound exit. Then there was a cowhorn-shaped gourd which was scraped with a stick, a block of ebony that was periodically pounded by the same man who tortured the bass viol, two kettle-drums which would not be silenced on any pretext, a large metal bowl shaped like a water-jar, that had originally come from Spain filled with butter, in the single opening of which the player alternately blew and sucked, giving a weird, echo-like sound, and, to fill in any possible interstices of sound left, two heathenish rattles. The band had no leader; each played or paused to smoke a cigarette as the spirit moved him, and all played by ear. The unexpected sight of white people among the promenaders caused the entire band to begin a series of monkey-like antics in an endeavor to outdo one another in showing off, until the tomtom effect of the entertainment took on a still more African pandemonium. To this was added the rumble of frequent trains along the near-by track and the vocal uproar of the promenaders, striving to imitate in garb and manner the *retreta* audiences of the larger cities. Long after we had retired a bugle-burst from the enthusiastic cornet-player now and then floated to our ears through the tropical night, for the amateurs had none of the weariness of professional musicians. When the plaza audience deserted them toward midnight, they set out on a serenading party to the by no means most respectable houses. Some of them sang as well as played, in that horrible harmony of Cuba's rural falsetto tenors, only one of whom we ever heard without an all but overwhelming desire to fling the heaviest object within reach.

Cienfuegos, on the seacoast south of Santa Clara, is said to derive its name from the exclamation of a sailor who beheld a hundred Indian fires along the beach. It might easily have won a similar designation from some wrathful description of its climate. The town was laid out a mere century ago by a Frenchman named Déclouet, and many of its streets still have French names. It is reputed to be the richest town per capita on earth, though the uninformed stranger might not suspect that from its appearance. It gives somewhat more attention to pavements than some of its neighbors, to be sure, and has electric street-cars. But ostentation of its wealth is not among the faults of Cienfuegos, perhaps because it takes its cue from its wealthiest citizen, who is said to lead by more than a neck all the millionaires of Cuba. Like Mihanovisch in the Argentine, or the first Astor and Vanderbilt in our own land, this financial nabob of Cuba began at the bottommost rung of the ladder, having arrived from Spain in *alpargatas* and taken to carrying bags of cement on the docks. To-day he is past eighty-five and owns most of the property in Cienfuegos and its vicinity, yet, as one of his fellow-townsmen put it, " if you meet him on the street you want to give him an old suit of clothes." During the war he was placed on the British black-list, and was forced to come often to a certain consulate in an effort to clear himself, yet he invariably came on foot even though Cienfuegos lay prostrate under its skin-scorching summer noonday. He lived across the bay, and while there were millions involved in the business on hand at the consulate, he invariably persisted in leaving in time to catch the twenty-cent public boat, lest he be forced to pay a dollar and a half for a special launch. He abhors modern ways and in particular the automobile, and refuses to do business with any one who arrives at his office in one. The story goes that for a long time after the rest of the island had adopted them Cienfuegos did not dare to import a single automobile for fear of the wrath of its financial czar.

But if the miser of Cienfuegos holds the palm for wealth, one of his near rivals in that regard outdoes him in political power. He, too, is a Spaniard, or, more exactly, a Canary Islander, like many of the wealthiest men of Cuba. To be born in the Canary Islands and to come to Cuba without a *peseta* or even the rudiments of education seems to be the surest road to riches. I could not risk setting down without definite proof to protect me the perfectly well-known stories of how " Pote " got his start in life. Though he owns immense sugar estates and countless other properties of all kind throughout the island, he is rarely to be distinguished from any unshaven peon, and even when a new turn of the political wheel brings him racing to Havana in a powerful automobile he still looks like some third-class Spanish grocer. Not until long years after the island became independent did the government become powerful enough to force " Pote " to remove the Spanish flag from his buildings and locomotives, and the " J. R. L." on the latter still give them the right of way over many a rival cane-grower; for " Pote," whisper the managers of corporation sugar-mills, has ways of getting his product to the market which those who must explain to auditors and directors higher up cannot imitate.

It is not without significance for the future of Cuba that men of this type, uneducated, unscrupulous, utterly without any ideal than the amassing of millions, wholly without vision, have the chief power in its affairs. Politically the island has been freed from Spanish rule, economically it is still paying tribute not merely in material things, but in spiritual, to the most sordid-minded of the grasping *peninsulares*.

One other town and I am done with them, for though Sagua la Grande and Caibarien, Ciego de Avila and picturesque Trinidad, at least, are worthy a passing notice, there is something distinctive about Camagüey, though the difference is after all elusive and baffling. For one thing it is more than four hundred years old; for another it is the largest town in the interior of Cuba. Even it, however, did not shun the coast by choice, but ran away from the northern shore in its early youth to escape the pirates, and, to make doubly sure of concealment, changed its name from Puerto Principe to that of the Indian village in which it resettled. Its antiquity is apparent, appalling, in fact. Projecting wooden window grilles, heavy cornices, aged balconies, also of wood, and tiled roofs hanging well over the street, crumbling masonry, all help to prove the city a genuine antique. Few of its streets are straight, few parallel, few meet at right angles, the result being to give the visitor a curiously shut-in feeling. It is said that this civic helter-skelter is due to the fact that the refugees from the harassed coast staked their claims and built their houses at random in their haste to get under cover, though there is a bon mot to the effect that the streets were purposely made crooked to fool the pirates. The town is noted for its *tinajónes,* in the legitimate sense, that is, for in Spanish the word means not only an immense earthenware jar, but a person with a large capacity for liquid refreshment. Some of these jars would easily contain the largest human *tinajón;* the majority of them are more than a hundred years old; there are said to be none younger than sixty. They serve the same purpose as our cisterns. Several ancient churches lift their weather-dulled gray walls and towers above the mass of old houses. The majority of these are down at heel, their façades battered and cracked, though the patios or small gardens in their rear are gay with flowers and shrubbery. Most of its streets were once paved, but that, too, was long ago, and during the frequent rainy days one must pick one's way across them by the scattered cobbles embedded in mud as over a stream on stepping-stones. The railroad once offered to pave at its own expense the slough bordering the station, but the local politicians would not permit it, for the same reason that Tammany prefers to let its own contracts. Even the social customs of Camagüey are ancient. If " any one who is any one " dies, for instance, as they do not infrequently, " everything " closes and all social functions are abandoned, often to the dismay of hostesses. The town is said to be famed for its beautiful women and its skilled horsemen; its color-line is reputed more strict and its negro population less numerous than in the rest of Cuba, at least three of these things being credited to the fact that the region was long given over to cattle rather than sugar-cane, requiring fewer slaves. The casual visitor, however, sees little to confirm these statements.

To-day even Camagüey province has succumbed to the cane invasion, like all Cuba, and the raising of cattle has become a secondary industry. Droves of the hardy, long-horned, brown breed may still be grazing the savanna lands, searching the valleys for tasty guinea-grass, standing knee-deep in the little rivers, but Cuba now imports meat, in contrast to the days when the exporting of cattle was one of her chief sources of revenue. The climate has had its share in bringing this change. Not only does it cause the milk to deteriorate in quantity and quality within a very few years, but the animals decrease steadily in size from generation to generation. Butter, unless of the imported variety, is as rare in Cuba as in all tropical America, and the invariable custom of boiling milk before using makes it by no means a favorite beverage. Besides, the constant drought in the United States does not extend to Cuba. But all these causes are but slight compared with the sky-rocketing price of sugar, which is swamping all other industries in the island, nay, even its scenery, beneath endless seas of cane.

Our good hosts of Tuinucú varied their hospitality by bearing us off on a two-days' horseback journey into the neighboring mountains. A hand-operated ferry and a road that was little more than a trail, except in width, brought us to the Old World town of Sancti Spíritus, founded in 1514 and rivaling in medieval architecture and atmosphere almost anything Spain has to offer. Here a *práctico,* which corresponds to, but is apt to mean much less than a guide, took the party in charge and trotted away toward the foothills. A group of priests in their somber, flowing gowns and shovel hats grinned offensively at the unwonted sight of ladies riding man-fashion, and the townsmen stared with the customary Latin-American impudence, but the countrymen greeted us with the dignified courtesy of old Castilian grandees. Pack-trains shuffled past in the deep dust now and then, the dozen or more undersized horses tied together from tails to halters. The fact that this left the animals no protection from the vicious flies meant no more to the compassionless *guajiros* than did the raw backs under the heavy, chafing packs. Cuba, like all Latin America, is a bad country in which to be a horse, or any other dumb animal for that matter. Much of the country was uncultivated, though royal palms and guinea-grass testified to its fertility. Big dark-red oxen or bulls were here and there plowing the gentler hillsides, more of them stood or lay at ease under the spreading ceiba trees. The region was once famed for its coffee, but even the few bushes that are left get no care nowadays and the time is already at hand when they are to give way before the militant sugar-cane.

We turned into an old estate where a hundred slaves had once toiled. All but a corner of it was overgrown with bush; the massive old plantation house had lost all its former grandeur except the magnificent views from its verandas. A disheveled family of *guajiros* inhabited it now, its cobbled courtyard seldom resounded to the hoofs of horses bringing guests to its very parlor door, the broad, brick-paved coffee-floor was grass-grown between its joints, the old slave inclosure had been turned over to the pigs, feeding on *palmiche,* the berries of the royal palm. The slattern who thrust her head out of the ruined kitchen building had little claim to propriety of appearance, though she answered a joking question as to whether she, too, would ride astride with a fervent, " Not I, God protect me! "

Reminiscences of slave days brought forth the story of " Old Concha " as we rode onward. She had been a slave on Tuinucú estate as far back as any one could remember, still is, in fact, in her own estimation. No one knows how old she is, except that she was married and had several children when the mother of her present mistress was a child. Her own answer to the question is invariably " thirteen." All day long she potters about the kitchen, though great effort has been made to get her to rest from her labors. She refuses to accept wages, only now and then " borrowing " a *peseta,* the total averaging perhaps five dollars a year, and being mainly spent for tobacco. Whenever any of the modern servants are remiss in their duties or show a suggestion of impudence she warns them that the " master's " whip will soon be tingling their legs, then, recalling herself, sighs for the " good old days " that are gone. She is the chief authority on forgotten family affairs, though incapable of keeping the " in-laws " straight. In her early days Concha accompanied her mistress to the United States. Arrived at the dock in New York, she submitted to her first hat, on the warning that she would be conspicuous without it — and raised it to all white people with whom she spoke. A custom officer questioned her right to bring in the fifty large black cigars which she had first attempted to conceal about her person, doubting that they were for her own use. Concha lighted one forthwith and quickly convinced the skeptic of her ability to consume them. It is useless to try to throw anything away at Tuinucú; Concha is certain to retrieve it and stow it away in her little room, with her " freedom paper " and her souvenir hat.

By sunset we were surrounded by mountains, though perhaps those of central Cuba should rather be called ranges of high hills. The little village of Banao was thrown into a furor of excitement by the arrival of " caballeros," and particularly by the announcement that we planned to camp out on the mountainside. Picnics are as unknown to the Cuban as to the rest of Latin America. Boys swarmed around us and scampered ahead in the swiftly falling darkness to show us a spot well up the slope where water and a bit of open ground were to be found. They told us many lugubrious tales of the dangers of sleeping in the open air and implored us to return instead to the hovels they shared with their pigs and chickens. When it became evident that we were not to be turned from our reasonless and perilous undertaking, they took to warning us at every step against the *guao*, quite fittingly pronounced " wow! " This is a species of glorified poison ivy, equally well named *pica-pica*. Drawbacks of this kind are rare in Cuba, however, where there are few poisonous plants, no venomous snakes, not even potato-bugs! The boys remained with us gladly until the last scraps of the camp-fire meal had disappeared, but fled with gasps of dismay at the suggestion that they spend the night there.

The traveler in the West Indies must learn to rise early if he is to catch the best nature has to offer. Noonday, even when less oppressively hot than our own midsummers, thanks to the unfailing trade-wind, is glaring in its flood of colors, insistent, without subtleties. But dawn and sunrise have a grandeur and at the same time a delicacy, as if the light were filtered through gauze upon the green-bespangled earth, which even the gorgeous sunsets and the evanescent twilight cannot equal. As we watched the new day steal in upon us through the dense foliage, it would have been easy to fancy that we had been transported to some fantastic fairyland in which the very birds were bent on adding to the subtle intoxication of the visitor's senses.

We beat the sun to the grotto of cold, transparent water and by the time it began to express itself in terms of heat were scrambling through the jungle to the nearest summit. Fresh coffee was to be had on many a bush for the picking; and inviting the red berries looked, too, until a taste of them had destroyed the illusion. He who fancies Cuban mountains are not high is due to revise his notions by the time he has dragged himself up the face of one of them through jagged rocks half concealed beneath the matted brush, over veritable hedges of needle-pointed cactus, now and again clutching as the only escape from toppling over backward a treacherous handful of " wow." Our garments were torn, our hands cut and stinging with *pica-pica*, our guide had degenerated from the fearless fellow of the night before to an abject creature who asked nothing better than to be left to die in peace by the time we reached the summit; and even then it was no real summit at all, but only the first of half a dozen knobs which formed a species of giant stairway to some unknown region lost in the clouds. In the light of the struggle it had cost us to cover this infinitesimal portion of the scene before us we seemed mere helpless atoms lost in the midst of a ferocious nature which clothed the pitched and tumbled world far beyond where the eye could see in any direction; or, to put it more succintly in the words of our host, we looked like worn-out fleas caught in the folds of a thick and wrinkled carpet.

The ride homeward was by another road, boasting itself a *camino real,* but little more than a wide trail for all its claim to royalty. Black ranges studded with royal palms cut short the horizon. *Guajiros* slipped past us here and there on little native horses of rocking-chair gait; others rode more slowly by perched on top of their woven-leaf saddle-bags, bulging with produce, a chicken or two usually swinging by the legs from them; all bade us a diffident *" Muy buenas."* Trees worthy of being reproduced in the stained-glass windows of cathedrals etched the sky-line. The stupid peon who posed as guide, flapping his wings with the gait of his horse like a disheveled crow, knew the names of only the most familiar growths, which would not so much have mattered had he not persisted in digging up false ones from the depths of his turbid imagination. Of the flowers, fruit, and strangely tame long-tailed birds he had as little real knowledge, though he had seen them all his life. Nor did he even know the road; I have never met a Latin-American " guide " who did. A negro boy on horseback singing his cows home from pasture; a peasant in the familiar high-crowned, broad-brimmed hat of braided palm-leaves hooking together tufts of grass with a crotched stick and cutting them off with a machete;

children gathering the oily *palmiche* nuts which are the chief delicacy of the Cuban hog, were among the sights of the afternoon. Next to sugar certainly the most prolific crop in Cuba is babies. Black, brown, yellow, and all the varying shades between, they not only swarm in the towns, but cluster in flocks about the smallest country hut, innocent of clothing as of the laws of sanitation, with no other joy in life than to roll about on the ground inside or around their little homes and suck a joint of sugar-cane. The houses of the peasants, still called by the Indian name of *bohío*, owe nothing to the outside world, but are wholly built of materials found on the spot, their very furnishings being woven palm-leaf hammocks, hairy cowhide chairs, pots and dishes made from gourds picked from the trees. The gates to many *fincas*, mildly resembling the entrances to Japanese temples, drew the eyes to more commodious residences as we neared Sancti Spiritus once more, each *casa vivienda* of a single low story covered with a tile roof which projected far out over the earth-floored veranda surrounding it. Nor were these much different from the humbler *bohíos* except in size, and perhaps an occasional newspaper to keep their owners somewhat in touch with the outside world.

The day died out as we were jogging homeward along the dusty flatlands between endless vistas of sugar-cane. But as I have not the courage to try to describe a Cuban sunset I gladly yield the floor to the native novelist known to his fellow-countrymen as the " Zola of the Antilles," who has no fear of so simple a task:

The sun agonized pompously between incendated clouds. Before it opaque mountains raised themselves, their borders dyed purple, orange, and violet. The astra itself was not visible, hidden behind its blood-streaked curtain, but one divined its disk in the great luminous blot which fought to tear asunder the throttling clouds; and on high, light, white cupolas, like immense plumages, were floating, reddened also, like the dispersed birds of a great flock that had been engaged in sanguinary combat. A vast silence had established itself, the solemnity of the evening which was rapidly expiring, with that brevity of the twilight of the tropics, which is similar to a scenic play arranged beforehand. On the blue-gray line of the sea the clouds had floundered in an immense stain of violet color, furrowed with obscure edges which opened themselves like the spokes of a gigantic wheel, in a dress of whitish blue, raising itself to the rest of the heavens. The disk of the sun was no longer evident; but, far off, some separate little clouds seemed to be touched by a lightly purple dyestuff. The picture changed with the celerity of an evening sunset on the stage, visibly obscuring itself, and by degrees, as if in that stage setting some one were shutting off, one after the other, the electric batteries, until the scene had been left in darkness. In a few minutes the great violet stain, formerly full of light, passed through all the tones of color, to convert itself into a great lake, without brilliance, in which swam lead colored flocks of birds dyed with black. The delicate dye-stuff which embroidered for an instant the remote little clouds had suddenly rubbed themselves out. Only an enormous white plume, stretched above the place in which the sun had sepulchered itself, persisted in shining for a long time like a fantastic wreath suspended over the melancholy desolation of the crepuscule. Afterward that went out also.

CHAPTER IV

THE WORLD'S SUGAR BOWL

CUBA produces more sugar than any other country in the world. During the season which had just begun at the time of our visit she expected to furnish four million tons of it. Barely as large as England, being seven hundred and thirty miles long and varying in width from twenty-two to one hundred and twenty miles, the island is favored by the fact that the great majority of her surface is level or slightly rolling, though the Pico de Turquino rises 8320 feet above the sea. Her soil is largely of limestone formation, with very little hard rock. She has considerable deep red earth which, scientists say, is deteriorated limestone without a trace of lime left in it. Fresh limestone brought down from the hills and scattered upon this quickly restores its virgin fertility, and it responds readily to almost any other fertilizers. There are regions in Cuba where this reddish soil permeates all the surrounding landscape, including the faces, garments, and off-spring of the inhabitants, giving its color even to their domestic animals. At least four fifths of the wealth and happiness of her population depends on her chief industry, and it is natural that everything else should take second place in the Cuban mind to the production of sugar.

French colonists running away from their infuriated slaves in Haiti brought with them the succulent cane, and at the same time a certain love of comfort and various agricultural hints which may still be traced on some of the older estates. But the industry has been modernized now to the point where science and large capital completely control its methods and its output. The saying is that wherever the royal palm grows sugar-cane will flourish, while the prevalence of guinea-grass is also considered a favorable sign. As these two growths are well-nigh universal throughout Cuba, it would seem that the island is due to become an even greater leader in sugar production that she is already.

The making of a Cuban sugar plantation is a primitive and, from our Northern point of view, a wasteful process consistent with virgin lands and tropical fecundity. Thus it seems in many parts of the island, particularly in the Oriente, the largest and most-eastern of Cuba's six provinces. Here vast stretches of virgin forest, often three to five thousand acres in extent, are turned into cane-fields in a few months' time. The usual method is to let contracts for the entire process, and to pay fixed sums for completely replacing the forests by growing cane. Bands of laborers under native *capataces* begin by erecting in the edge of the doomed woods their *baracones,* crudely fashioned structures covered with palm-leaves, usually without walls. Here the woodsmen, more often Jamaican or Haitian negroes than Cubans, swing their hammocks side by side the entire length of the building, if the long roof supported by poles may be called that, a few of them indulging in the comfort of a *mosquitero* inclosing their swinging couch, all of them wrapping their worldly possessions in the hammock by day. Then with machetes and axes which to the Northerner would seem extremely crude — though nearly all of them come from our own State of Connecticut — they attack the immense and seemingly impenetrable wilderness.

The underbrush and saplings fall first under the slashing machetes. Next the big trees — and some of these are indeed giants of the forest — succumb before the heavy axes and, denuded of their larger branches, are left where they lie. Behind the black despoilers the dense green woodland turns to the golden brown which in the tropics means death rather than a mere change of season, and day by day this spreads on and on over plain and hillock into regions perhaps never before trodden by man. The easy-going planters of the olden days were apt to spare at least the royal palms and the more magnificent of the great spreading ceibas. But the practical modern world will have none of this compassion for beauty at the expense of utility. As an American sub-manager summed up the point of view of his class, " If you are going to grow cane, grow cane; don't grow royal palms." Everythings falls before the world's demand for sugar, translated by these energetic pioneers from the North to mean the unsparing destruction of all nature's splendors which dare to trespass upon the domain of His Majesty, the sugar-cane. Mahogany and cedar — though occasionally the larger logs of these two most valuable of Cuban woods are carried to the railroad sidings — are as ruthlessly felled as the almost worthless growths which abound in tropical forests. Here and there the contractor leaves an immense *caguarán* standing, in the hope that he may not be compelled to break several axes on a wood far redder than mahogany and harder than any known to our Northern timberlands. But the inspector is almost sure to detect his little ruse and to require that the landscape be denuded even of these resisting growths. Logs of every possible size and of a hundred species cut up the trails over which the sure-footed Cuban horses pick their way when the first inspection parties ride out through the fallen woodland.

The clearing of a Cuban forest has in it little of the danger inherent in similar occupations in other tropical lands. Not only are there no venomous snakes to be feared, but there are few other menaces to the health of the workmen. Now and again a belligerent swarm of bees is encountered, along the coast streams the dreaded *mansanillo* sometimes demands the respect due so dangerous a growth. The sap of the *mansanillo* is said to be so poisonous that to swallow a drop causes certain death; hands and face sprayed with it by a careless blow of the ax swell up beyond all semblance to human form. When one of these rare species is found, the woodsmen carefully " bark " it and leave it for some time before undertaking the actual felling. But with few exceptions this is the only vegetation to be feared in a Cuban wilderness. Even the malarial fevers which follow not the cutting, but the burning, of the woodlands are less malignant than those of other equatorial regions.

The burning usually takes place during the first fortnight of March, at the end of the longest dry season. Indeed, extreme care is exercised that the firing shall not begin prematurely, for the consumption of the lighter growths before the larger ones are dry enough to burn would be little short of a catastrophe for the contractors. When at last the fires are set and sweep across the immense region with all the fury of the element, fuel sufficient to keep an entire Northern city warm during the whole winter is swept away in a single day. At first thought it seems the height of wastfulness not to save these uncounted cords of wood, these most valuable of timbers, but not only would the cost of transportation more than eat up their value before they could reach a market, without this plenitude of fallen forest the burning would not be successful and the fertility of the future plantation would suffer. The time is near, however, scientists tell us, when the Cubans must regulate this wholesale destruction of their forests or see the island suffer from one of those changes of climate which has been the partial ruination of their motherland, Spain.

When the first burning has ended, the larger logs remaining are heaped together and reburned. Some of them, the *júcaro,* for instance, continue to smolder for months, this tree having even been known to burn from top to bottom after catching fire thirty feet from the ground. Though it is usual in the open savannas, plowing is not necessary in these denuded woodlands. Here all that is necessary is to hoe away the grass and the bit of undergrowth that remains. The primitive method of planting in the slave days still survives. In some sections a man sets out along each of the proposed rows carrying in one hand a long sugar-cane and in the other a machete. He jabs the cane into the ground at intervals of about three feet, slashes off the buried end with his cutlass, and marches on, to repeat the process at every step. More often nowadays one man goes ahead to dig holes with a heavy hoe, while another following him drops into each of them a section of cane and covers it with a stamp of his bare heel. Two joints and sometimes three are planted in each hole, to insure the sprouting of at least one of them. There is a more scientific system of planting, in which a rope with knots given distances apart is used, but the first method is more prevalent in the feverish haste of the Oriente. The fact that charred logs and stumps still everywhere litter the ground rather helps than hampers the growth of the cane, for as these rot they add new fertilizer to the already rich soil.

Cane requires some eighteen months to mature in the virgin lands of Cuba, and will produce from twelve to twenty yearly crops without replanting. So prolific is the plant in these newer sections that when a lane several meters wide is left between the rows it is often almost impenetrable a year later. Cane high above the head of a man on horseback is by no means rare in these favored regions. By the beginning of our northern autumn the whole island is inlaid with immense lakes of maturing cane, the same monotonous panorama everywhere stretching to the horizon; the uniformly light green landscape, often spreading for mile after mile without a fold or a knoll, without any other note of color than the darker green of the rare palm-trees that have escaped destruction, grows fatiguing to the sight. Cane-fields without limit on each hand, flashing in the blazing sunshine, have a beauty of their own, though it is not equal to that of a ripening wheat-field with the wind rippling across it. There is less movement, less character; it has a greater likeness to an expressionless human face. Yet toward cutting-time sunrise or sunset across these endless pale green surfaces presents swiftly changing vistas which are worth traveling far to see.

The " dead season," corresponding to the Northern summer, is a time of comparative leisure on the sugar estates. It is then that the higher employees, Americans in the great majority of cases, take their vacations in the North; it is then that the Spanish laborers who come out for each yearly *zafra* return to enjoy their earnings in their own land. Then there is time for *fiestas* among the native workmen and their families and those from the near-by islands, who frequently remain the year round, time for "parties" and dances among the English-speaking residents of the *batey*. The *batey* is the headquarters of the entire *central*, as the sugar estate is called in Cuba. It clusters about the *ingenio*, or mammoth sugar-mill, which stands smokeless and silent through all the "dead season," its towering chimneys looming forth against the cane-green background for miles in every direction. Here the manager has his sumptuous dwelling, his heads of departments their commodious residences, the host of lesser American employees their comfortable screened houses shading away in size and location in the exact gradations of the local social scale. Usually there are company schools, tennis-courts, clubs, stores, hospital, company gardeners to beautify the surrounding landscape. Outside this American town, often with a park or a flower-blooming plaza in its center, are scores of smaller houses, little more than huts as one nears the outskirts, in which live the rank and file of employees of a dozen nationalities. In the olden days, when many slaves were of necessity kept the year round, the *batey* was a scene of activity at all seasons. But the patriarchal plantation life, the enchantment of the old family sugar-mill where each planter ground his own cane, has almost wholly disappeared before these giants of modern industry which swallow in a day the cane that the old-fashioned mill spent a season in reducing to sugar.

With the expiration of slavery the patrician style of sugar raising died out. It became necessary, largely for lack of labor, partly for convenience sake, to separate the agricultural from the other phases of the sugar industry. The more customary method to-day is to divide the estate into a score or more of "colonies," each in charge of, or rented to, a *colono*, who operates almost independently, at least until the cutting season arrives. A few companies are run entirely on the administrative system, directing every operation from planting to grinding from a central office; some own little land themselves, but buy their cane of the independent planters in the surrounding region. But the *colono* system gives promise of surviving longest. For one thing, in case of drought or other disaster, the loss falls in whole or part on the planter instead of being entirely sustained by the company. Even when the land from which they draw their cane is not their own property, the

A Cuban residence in a new clearing

Planting sugar-cane on newly cleared land

Hauling cane to a Cuban sugar mill

A station of a Cuban pack-train

companies keep a force of inspectors who ride day after day through the cane-fields, offering advice to the *colonos* here, ordering them to change their methods there, if they are to remain in the good graces of the central management. The latter keeps in its offices large maps of all the region from which its mill is fed, noting on each plot the condition of the soil, the age of the cane, particularly whether or not it has been burned over, that it may be assigned its proper turn for cutting when the grinding season begins.

Fires are the chief bugaboo of the sugar growers. All the fields are cut up into sections by frequent *guardarayas,* open lanes some fifty yards wide which serve not only as highways, but as a means of confining a conflagration to the plot in which it starts. In many cases there are little watch towers set up on stilts from which to give warning in case of fire, while special employees sometimes patrol the fields during the drier months. Rural guards of the " O. P." corps have orders to be constantly on the lookout for incendiaries; when a fire starts they immediately surround the field, and woe betide the luckless mortal who is caught in it, for all Cuba is banded together to punish the man who wantonly or carelessly brings destruction upon their principal product.

A cane fire is an exciting event, not to say a magnificent sight. Starting in a tiny puff of vapor where some careless smoker has tossed a match, from a passing locomotive, or by intention, it quickly gives warning by the black-brown column of smoke which rises high into the clear tropical heavens. Whistles, bells, anything capable of making a noise, join in the din which summons planters, employees, and neighboring villagers to stem the threatened catastrophe. By the time the bright red flames begin to curl above the cane-tops men and boys of every degree, color, and nationality are racing pell-mell from every direction toward them, *colonos,* overseers, rural guards, Americans, Chinamen, Spaniards, West Indian negroes, Cubans ranging from the village *alcade* to bootblacks. Many of these bring with them machetes, others catch up clubs, handsful of brush, the tops of banana plants, and fall to threshing the flames, which by this time are crackling like the tearing up of thousands of parchments. Men on horseback race up and down the open lanes, directing the fighters, ordering the cutting of a new *guardaraya* there, commanding the lighting of a back-fire yonder. The air is full of black bits of cane leaves, the sun is obscured by the grayish-brown smoke which envelops all the struggling, shouting multitude and covers the field with an immense pall. A gust of wind sends the flames jumping to another plot, whirlwinds caused by the heat catch up the sparks and scatter them at random. New-comers join in the turmoil, indifferent alike to their garments and their skins. Half-asphyxiated men stumble out to the open air, gasp a few lungsful of it, and dash back into the fray; the now immense column of smoke can be seen over half the province. The pungent scent of crude sugar ladens all the air. Bit by bit the leaping flames decrease under the chastisement of hundreds of weapons, or confess their inability to leap across a wider *guardaraya*. The crackling loses its ominous sound, the voices of men are heard more clearly above it, gradually it succumbs to the noise of threshing bushes, the last red glare dies out, and the struggle is over. The motley throng of fighters, smeared, smudged, and torn, emerge into the open lanes, toss away their improvised weapons, and straggle homeward in long streams, while sunset paints the now distant smoke-cloud with brilliant colors, flecked by the little black particles which still float in the air. The burning of a cane-field does not mean the complete loss of its crop. Only the leaves are consumed; the parched canes are still standing. But these must be cut and ground quickly if their juice is to be turned into sugar; the ringing of the heavy cane-knives resounds all through the following day, and by night the field stands forlorn and ugly in its nudity.

One by one during the month of October the mills of the island begin their grinding. The cutting has started two days before, and incessantly through the weeks that follow the massive two-wheeled carts, drawn by four, six, ten, even twelve oxen, drag the canes to the mill, now straddling the charred stumps and logs which litter new fields for years after the first planting, now wallowing in the sloughs into which they have churned the lanes and highways. Or, if the fields are too far away, the ox-carts halt at railway sidings, where immense hooks catch up their entire load and deposit them in cane-cars, long trains of which creak away in the direction of the *ingenio*. The planters are paid on a percentage basis, from five to seven *arrobas* of sugar, or its equivalent in cash at that day's market quotation, for a hundred *arrobas* of cane, a system which gives the *colono* his share in any increase in price. The workmen, more than half of whom are foreigners, are paid by the " task," their earnings depending on their strength and diligence. The natives have a reputation for doing less than their competitors. There are Cubans who work in both the tobacco and sugar *zafras*, but most of them are content to spend from four to six months in the cane-fields earning their five to eight dollars a day, and to loaf and buy lottery tickets the rest of the year. The result is that the entire island has a toilsome, preoccupied air during our winter months and a holiday manner throughout the summer.

Grinding time is the antithesis of the "dead season." Then the dull sullen grumble of the mill never ceases, *fiestas* and "*parties*" are forgotten, all but the higher employees and the field-men alternate in their twelve-hour shifts between night and day, with little time or inclination left for recreation. The chimneys of the *ingenios* belch forth constant columns of smoke, by night their blaze of electric lights makes them visible far off across the country. Once dumped in the chutes the canes have no escape until they have reached the market, or at least the warehouse, in the form of sugar. Rivers of juice run from beneath the rollers to the boiling vats; the centrifugals, most often tended by Chinamen, whirl the thick molasses into grains, great bags of which are stood end up on the necks of burly negroes and trotted away to the *almacen.* The porters must be burly, for Cuba still retains the bag used in slave days, holding thirteen *arrobas,* or two hundred and seventy-five pounds, and the negroes insist they must run with them to keep from falling down. It has more than once been proposed to reduce the size of the bags, but this would require a change all the way back to India, where jute and bags originate.

From the days of the primitive *trapiche,* when two logs turned by an ox or a donkey constituted a Cuban sugar-mill, through the period of individual growing and grinding, when an army of slaves worked under the whip for the benefit of an ignorant and often lazy and licentious owner who considered that work his right, down to the immense *ingenio* and extensive *batey* of modern times, Cuba has been more or less exploited for the benefit of other lands and peoples. Even to-day, when fabulous wages are paid to the men who do the actual toiling under the tropical sun, much of the profit from her soil brings up eventually in the pockets of others. Few are the *centrals* which do not win back a considerable portion of the wages they are forced to pay by maintaining company stores in which the prices are exorbitant, or in selling the right to maintain them. Many an American manager frankly admits the injustice of this, yet all assert themselves unable to remedy it. Of the sums carried off by workmen from other lands the Cubans have no complaint, admitting that they earn their hire. But there is a growing tendency to grumble that the island is being more thoroughly exploited now than in the days of slavery, for it comes to the same thing, they contend, whether the larger portion of their national riches go to Spanish masters or to stockholders who have never set foot on Cuban soil. Notwithstanding that the island claims more wealth per capita than any other land on earth, the inhabitants are not satisfied, either with themselves or with circumstances, as a brief extract from the native novel already several times quoted will indicate:

> They [foreign stock-holders] are the owners of everything, soil and industry. We abandon it to them with good grace so long as they leave to us the politics and public careers, that is, the road of fraud and life with little work. On the other hand they, the producers, profoundly despise us. It is the case of all Latin-America. While we gnaw the bone the true exploiter, who is no Cuban, eats the meat. And if we growl, showing our teeth, all they have to do is to complain to the diplomats. Then they hand us a kick, one on each side, and the matter is settled.

In contrast to the United States, Cuba grows wilder, more pioneer-like, from west to east. The traveler is aware of this increase of wilderness about the time he passes Ciego de Avila and the line of the old *trocha* across the island at the slenderest part of its waist, where are still seen remnants of the long row of forts from sea to sea with which the Spaniards vainly hoped to keep the rebels in the eastern end of the island and save at least the advanced and more populous western half from open rebellion. There are, to be sure, aged towns and *pueblos* on the sunrise side of the *trocha*. Camagüey, for instance, could scarcely be called a parvenu; and Baracoa, on the extreme eastern beach of the island, is Cuba's first settlement. But the fact remains that the traveler feels more and more in touch with primeval nature as he advances to the eastward.

Small as it looks on the map, it is hard to realize that for vast distances the island of Cuba is still the unbroken wilderness of the days of Columbus. Though it is frequently broken by long stretches of civilization, the virgin forest is always near at hand on this eastward journey. There are frequent sugar estates, immense stretches of pale-green cane from horizon to horizon, but they are of the rough, wasteful, unfinished type of all pioneering. Cattle dot the great savannas, sleek, contented-looking cattle of a prevailing reddish tinge, and scarcely bearing out the assertion that the Cuban climate tends to dwarf their size. These unpeopled savannas are often of a velvety brown, now gently rolling, more commonly as flat as the sea itself, and stretching away farther than the eye can follow with the same suggestion of endlessness. Gazing out across them, one likes to let the imagination play on the simpler pre-Columbian days when only the *Siboney* Indians trekked across them in pursuit of the one four-foot game with which nature stocked the island, the diminutive *jutía*.

Of a score of striking trees with which these more open regions are punctuated, the broad-spreading, openwork, lace-like *algarrobo,* thorny and of slight value, is the most conspicuous, almost rivaling the ceiba and the royal palm in the ability to etch the sky-line with its artistic tracery. Stations are far apart and primitive in character in this region. Now and again one of special interest brings the long Habana-Santiago train to a laborious and often lengthy halt. There is Omaja, for example, said to have been settled by immigrants from Nebraska, and laboring under the Cubanization of the name they brought with them. It is the same sun-washed collection of simple dwellings and wide-open pioneer stores as everywhere greets the eye of the Cuban traveler. Yet the American's influence is seen in the immense width of its one street and the more sturdy aspect of its wooden housss, crude, yet not without the simpler comforts. The Americans of Omaja, like several other groups that have settled in Cuba, came to plant fruit, with the accent on the *toronja,* or grape-fruit, so popular on Northern break-fast-tables, yet so scorned by the rural Cuban. But it was their bad luck to strike one of those curious dry spots frequent even in the wettest American tropics, and most of the score who remain have turned their attention to lumber. There are long rows of sturdy fruit-trees, however, as heavy with grape-fruit as a Syrian peddler with his pack, and hundreds of the saffron-yellow spheres lie rotting under the trees. Lack of transportation answers for many incongruities. Some of the orchards have been planted with cane, and only the deep-green crests of the trees gaze out above the pale-verdant immensity. Yet prosperity seems to have come to some of the settlers despite droughts and scarcity of rolling-stock, for in the neighborhood of Omaja are several big farm-houses of the bungalow family which can scarcely be the products of Cuban taste.

Beyond come more miles of the lightly wooded wilderness, everywhere spotted with cattle, here and there a large banana plantation, and frequent half-clearings in the denser forest, heaped with huge logs of red mahogany and other valuable woods. The railroad itself does not hesitate to make ties and trestle beams of the precious *caoba,* the aristocracy of which is much less apparent in its own setting than after the expense of distant transportation has been added to its cost. Then again, like a constant reiteration of the main Cuban motif, come the endless seas of cane, sometimes full-grown and drowning all else except the majestic palms, sometimes just started in a flood of the bluer young plants that cannot yet conceal the burned stumps and charred logs of regions recently deforested.   For a while cultivation disappears entirely, and the dense virgin forest, just as nature meant it to be, impassable, hung with climbing lianas, draped with " Spanish moss," its huger trees bristling with flowerless orchids of green or reddish tint, its countless species of larger vegetation choked by impenetrable undergrowth, shuts in the track for many an uninhabited mile.

But hungry mankind does not long endure this unproductive slovenliness of nature.   Gangs of men as varied in color as the vegetation in species are laying waste new areas of wilderness, and preparing to complete with fire the work of their axes and machetes in taming the unbroken soil for human purposes.   Half-naked families of incredible fecundity swarm to the doors of thatch cabins, to gaze after the fleeing train like wild animals catching their first glimpse of the outside world. It would be easy to imagine that the clearing away of the forest has uncovered these primitive dwellings and their denizens, as it has brought to light the ant-nests in the crotches of the trees.   They seem as little a part of the modern world as the shelter of some prehistoric Robinson Crusoe.

At Cacocúm, the junction for Holguin, up in the hills to the north, the primitive and the latest advances of civilization mingle together. Gaping *guajiros* watch the unloading of apples and grapes, the chief delicacies of Cuban desserts, that were grown in the northwesternmost corner of the United States.   The tougher breeds of automobiles wait to whiz immaculate travelers from distant cities away into the apparently trackless wilderness; inhabitants of those same Robinson Crusoe huts come down to exchange roasted slabs of the half-savage hogs which roam the forests for silver coins and crumpled paper bearing the effigy of American Presidents.

Farther on, we were still more forcibly snatched back to the present and the modern.   The train burst suddenly upon an immense expanse of cane, beyond which a low range of mountains, black-blue with a tropical shower, stretched away with ever-increasing height to the southward.   Almost at the same moment we drew up at the station of Alto Cedro, junction of the line from Nipe Bay, into which a ship direct from New York had steamed that morning.   It had brought one of the first flocks of migratory human birds that annually flee before the Northern winters, made doubly rigorous now by a nationwide drought.   The Cuban passengers of the first-class coach were as suddenly and completely swamped under the aggressive flood of touring Americans as were the native chests and bundles in the baggage-car beneath a mountain of trunks which flaunted the self-importance of their owners. The tales of sad mistakes in picking lottery numbers and debate on the probable *arrobas* of the cane *zafra*, in the softened Spanish of Cuba, turned to chatter of the latest Broadway success and to gurgles of joy at escaping from a coalless winter, in a tongue that sounded as curiously anachronistic in this tropical setting as the heavy overcoats with which the new-comers were laden looked out of place.

The moon was full that evening, and its weird effect was enhanced by a slight accident that left the car without lights. Royal palms, silhouetted against the half-lighted sky, stood out even more strikingly than by day. The moonlight fell with a silvery sheen on the white-clad negroes who lined the way wherever the train halted, casting dense-black shadows behind them. Below San Luis junction, where automobiles offered to carry passengers down to Santiago in less time than the train, the vegetation grew unusually dense, the most genuinely tropical we had ever seen in Cuba. Immense basins filled with magnificent clusters of bamboo, royal palms in irregular, but soldierly, formations along the succeeding crests, masses of perennial foliage heaped up in the spaces between — all shimmered in the moonlight as if the earth had donned her richest ball-dress for some gala occasion. We sped continually downward, snaking swiftly in and out through the hills despite the frequent anxious grinding of the brakes. Here we sank into the trough of one of the few deep railway cuts in Cuba, there we rumbled across viaducts that lifted us up among the fronds of the royal palms. A white roadway darted in and out in a vain attempt to keep pace with us. Now we plunged into tunnels of vegetation, to burst forth a moment later upon a vast rolling plain washed by the intense tropical moonlight, which seemed to fall on the humble thatched roofs scattered about it with a curiously gentle, caressing touch. Our descent grew gradually less swift, the hills diminished and shrank away into the distance, and at length the lights of Santiago, which had flashed at us several times during the last half-hour, spread about us like a surrounding army.

The short stretch between San Luis and Santiago is one of the prettiest in Cuba. Travelers covering it twice would do well to make one trip in automobile. It was our own good fortune to pass four times over it under as many varying conditions. The two-engine climb in the full blaze of day shows the scene in a far different mood than under the flooding moonlight; the ascent at sunset has still another temperament; yet it would be hard to say which of the three journeys more fully emphasizes the beauty of a marvelous bit of landscape. Possibly the trip by road has the greatest appeal, thanks chiefly to an embracing view of Santiago and all its wooded-mountain environment from the crest of a precipitous headland. In the early days of American occupation a splendid highway was built, perhaps in the hope that the Cubans would some day be moved to carry it on across the island to Havana, perhaps that they might have a sample of real roadway to contrast with their own sad trails. But the natives do not seem to have taken the lesson to heart. They call the road " Wood's Folly," and though it still retains some of its former perfection, the condition into which it has already been permitted to lapse does not promise well for the future. To the Cubans, content, apparently, to jounce over all but impassable *caminos,* the building of good highways will probably be long considered a " folly."

Though comparisons are odious, Santiago is the most picturesque city of Cuba, so far as we saw it in two months of rambling to and fro over most of the island. This is due largely to the fact that it is built on and among hills. Seen from the bay, or from several other of the many points of vantage about it, the city lies heaped up like a rock pile, the old cathedral, which some unhappy thought has subjected to a " reforming," crowning the heap, which spreads out at the base as if it had lain too long without being shoveled together again. Several other church-spires protrude above the mass, but none of them is particularly striking. Taken separately, perhaps its houses are little different from prevailing Cuban architecture elsewhere; built as they are on the natural terraces of the hills, they are lifted into plainer view, each standing forth from the throng like the features of persons of varying height in a human crowd. Huge walls from ten to twenty feet high prove to be merely the foundations of the dwellings above, which look out head and shoulders over their next-door neighbors below, to be in turn overshadowed by their companions higher up. Santiago confesses to more than four centuries of age, and proves the assertion by her appearance. The medieval architecture which the conquistadores brought with them direct from Spain has persisted, and has been reproduced in newer structures more consistently than in Havana. The red-tiled roofs curve outwardly far over the street with a curiously Japanese effect. Balconies high above the pedestrian's natural line of vision prove on nearer approach to jut out from the ground floor. Sometimes the steep streets tire with their climbing and break up frankly into broad stairways. In other places they fall away so swiftly that they offer a complete vista of multicolored house-walls, plunging at the end into the dense blue of the landlocked harbor.

Santiago is picturesque because of its quaint old customs, its amusing contrasts, the fantastic colors of its buildings, and the tumbled world that lies about it. All Cuban cities offer a motley of tints, but Santiago outdoes them all in the chaotic jumble of pigments. In a single block we found house walls of lavender, sap green, robin's-egg blue, maize yellow, sky gray, Prussian blue, salmon, tan, vermilion, and purple. This jumble of colors, with never two shades of the same degree, gives the city a kaleidoscopic brilliancy under the tropical sun that is equally entrancing and trying to the eye. Of quaint old customs there is that of setting the entrance-steps sidewise into the wall of the house, so that it must be a sharp-eyed resident who recognizes his own doorway. It is a less open town than others of Cuba, for the steepness of the streets has raised the windows above the level of the eye, and only here and there does the stroller catch that comprehensive glimpse of the interior which elsewhere gives him a sense of intruding upon the family circle. It has, however, those same wide-open, yet exclusive, clubs whose members love to lounge in full sight of their less-favored fellow-citizens. Of contrasts between the old and the new there are many. Pack-trains of mules and asses pass under the very lee of the balcony dining-room overlooking the central plaza, where migratory mortals sup in full-coursed, solemn state. On Saturdays all sorts and conditions of human misery crawl in and out among luxurious automobiles, begging their legitimate weekly pittance. There are few Fords in Santiago; the steepness of her streets make more powerful cars essential to certain progress. On the other hand, the medieval horse-drawn carriage rattles and shakes its palsied way though the narrow *calles* with a musical jangle of its warning bell.

Time was when Santiago was a sink of disease, if not of iniquity. It has largely recovered from that condition, and its hundred thousand inhabitants, tainted in the vast majority of cases with the blood of Africa, no longer live in constant fear of sudden death. The principal streets are well paved; its dwellings and places of public gathering are moderately clean, though in the dry winter season dust swirls high and penetratingly with every gust of wind. The third city of the island in commercial importance — Cienfuegos having outstripped it in this respect — it is the second in political significance. Some rate it first in the latter regard, for it is usually the pot in which is brewed the most serious causes of indigestion for the Central Government at Havana. Santiago has always been noted for an Irish temperament that makes it constitutionally " ag'in' the gover'ment."

Outside the center of town its streets are little more than mountain trails. The houses degenerate to thatched hovels of mud and plaster; full-blooded negroes loll in dingy doorways, which give glimpses of contentment with pathetically few of this world's comforts. Not a few of these outskirts' inhabitants are Jamaicans.. One recognizes them by their ludicrous attempts at aloofness· from the native black Cubans, by their greater circumspection of manner. Here and there a group of them, usually all women, struggle to make some native urchin understand the error of his ways and the reason for their incomprehensible displeasure, and patter off, at least loudly discussing his misbehavior in their heavy, academic English. In these sections the picturesqueness of Santiago is apt to express itself chiefly in the variety and pungency of its odors.

Officially the city is " Santiago de Cuba," so called by its sixteenth-century founders to distinguish it from its namesake, Santiago de Compostella in Spain. Foreigners and even the Cubans of the Western provinces address it familiarly by the first name; the natives of the Oriente dub it " Cuba." Walled on all sides by what to the Cubans are high mountains, it offers a striking panorama from any high point in the city. In places the ranges of big hills, culminating in Pico Turquino, are as brown, bare, and nakedly majestic as the Andes; in others they are half wooded with green scrub forests, above which commonly float patched and irregular cloud canvases on which the tropical sunsets paint their masterpieces with lavish and swift hand.

The city cemetery across the harbor is somehow less gruesome than most Cuban burial-places. For one thing, it is unusually gifted with grass and trees and the aery forms of tropical vegetation, instead of being the bare field of most campos santos in Spanish America. Its graves, however, are family affairs, built of cement and six or eight " stories " deep, so that the coffins are set one above the other, as their time comes, in perfect chronological order. Over the top, commonly a bare three or four feet above the grass, is laid a huge stone slab, preferably of marble, with immense brass or nickeled rings at each corner by which to lift it, and space on its top for a poetic epitaph to each succeeding occupant. As in all Spanish countries, the tombs of all but the wealthiest inmates are rented for a term of years, at the end of which time, if the descendants fail to renew the contract, the bodies are tossed into a common graveyard, to make room for those of greener memory.

Marti, the Cuban "Father of Liberty," is buried here, and Estrada Palma, promoted from humble pedagogue in one of our own schools to first President of Cuba. But neither holds the chief place in the heart of the Cuban masses. That is reserved for Macéo, the negro general killed just before the dawn of independence during a foolhardy scouting expedition in the woods of Cacahual, in company with a bare half-dozen soldiers. The gardeners seemed unusually industrious in the cemetery the day of our visit; it was only next morning that we discovered they were preparing for the Cuban "Memorial day," which is observed throughout the island, with much spouting of poetry and laying on of flowers, on December 7, the anniversary of Macéo's death at the hands of the Spaniards.

San Juan Hill is a mere knoll in comparison with the ranges that surround it on all sides. A street-car sets one down within a few hundred yards of it, or one may stroll out to it within an hour along a very passable highway. The "peace tree," an immense ceiba under which the contending generals came to terms, is peaceful indeed now, with only the twittering of birds to break the whisper of its languid leaves, except when a flock of tourists swirl down upon it in one of Santiago's hired machines and bellow for "Old Jeff" to come and tell them, in the inimical dialect of our Southern "darky," the story of his last battle. From the ugly brick tower which marks the summit of the only Cuban hill known to the average American, El Caney lies embowered in its thick-wooded mountain-slope a few miles away, the same dawdling, sleepy village it was when the Americans stormed it more than twenty years ago.

Morro Castle, unlike its prototype in Havana, is not visible from the city; nor is the Caribbean itself. As one *chugs-chugs* down the land-locked bay, "Cuba" shrinks away, and finally disappears entirely in a fold of the fuzzy hills, before the ancient fortress, framed in the bluest of blue seas, comes into sight. Beyond the point where the *Merrimac* failed in its perilous mission a sheltered cove, with a rusted cannon here and there among the bushes, gives landing-place, and leaves the visitor to scramble upward along an ancient cobbled roadway completely arched over in place with the rampant vegetation. Nature is similarly toiling to conceal the old fortress from modern eyes, and bids fair in time to succeed. The dismal dungeons, the gruesome death-chamber, are still there, but the decay that has let the sunshine filter into them here and there has robbed them of their terror, and left only an imperfect setting for the anecdotes of a bygone age. Lizards and others of their sort are the only inhabitants of El Morro now, and through the huge holes in the outer walls made by American cannon one may gaze out along the Caribbean to the hazy, mountainous shore where still lie some of the skeletons of Cervera's fleet.

Whatever else he misses in Santiago, the traveler should not fail to spend a Sunday evening in the central plaza. It is a small block square, completely paved in asphalt, and furnished with an equal profusion of comfortable benches and tropical vegetation. Any evening, except in the rainy season when the afternoon shower is delayed, will find it a study in human types; but toward sunset on Sunday it becomes the meeting-place par excellence of Santiago's élite. They gather in almost exact order of social rank, the smaller fry first, then the more pompous citizens, until, by seven in this " winter " season, the families that the foreign visitor never sees at any other time of the week stalk past in the continual procession. The men, formed three or four or even six abreast, march on the inside, clock-wise; the women saunter in similar formation around the outer arc of the circle in the opposite direction. A pace of about a mile an hour is a sign of proper social breeding. Negroes are by no means lacking in any Santiago gathering, but they are in the minority at this weekly promenade. The color line is not sharply drawn, but it is approximate, in that each rank or group has its own gradations of tints. The women seldom wear hats; the younger girls tie with a single ribbon the hair that hangs down their backs. Rice powder is in plentiful evidence on every feminine face, very few of which, candor obliges the critical observer to admit, can be called attractive. The men, never robust, more often slender to the point of effeminacy, one and all wear stiff straw hats, tipped back at exactly the angle approved by the Latin-American version of Parisian fashion. A felt hat is prima-facie evidence of a foreigner; a Panama, all but universal in the country towns, is almost never seen. Swarms of children of all sizes and colors, the offshoots of the wealthier families, ludicrously overdressed, scamper in and out with an *abandon* in inverse ratio to the social strata to which they belong. Saucy, rather insolent boys of from twelve to fourteen, dressed like their elders down to the last trousers' crease, swing their diminutive canes and strut along among the men, who treat them with that curious oblivion to their immaturity that is prevalent in all Latin America. Young as they are, they are old enough to ogle the little girls of similar age in the approved fashion, half admiringly, half suggestively, with a cynical shadow of a smile that seems to belie the patent evidence of their age. Nor are the over-dressed little maids behindhand in the game of mutual admiration their elders are playing, and they pass the same quick signs of recognition to their small boy friends as do their older sisters to their own forward admirers.

If the municipal band plays the *retreta*, this inevitable Sunday evening is enlivened, but Santiago comes for its weekly promenade whether there is music or not. By the height of the evening every plaza bench, the entire quadrangle of stone balustrade backed by the low grille inclosing the square, are compactly occupied with admiring citizens or with older promenaders catching their breath after their undue exertions. Seven-passenger cars filled with elaborately upholstered matrons deathly pale with rice powder, with a few elderly, over-slender males tucked in between them, snort round and round the square; the electric lights among the palm-trees disclose a slowly pulsating sea of humanity, chiefly clad in white; the murmur of a thousand low voices resembles the sound of a broken waterfall; the musical tinkle of the steel triangles of sweetmeat-sellers blends harmoniously into the suppressed uproar. "Every one worth knowing" knows every one else in the throng. The straw hats are frequently doffed with elaborate courtesy; gentle little bows pass incessantly between the two opposing columns; the language of fans is constantly in evidence. The requirements of dress are exacting at this general weekly airing. Ladies of Santiago's upper circle must indeed find it a problem not to be detected here too often in the same gown; the men of the town may be seen hurrying homeward every Sunday afternoon from their café lollings or their cock-fights to don their spotless best; negroes of both sexes, starched and ironed to the minute, walk with the circumspection of automatons just removed from excelsior-packed boxes. From our Northern point of view, there is much ill-mannered staring, an ogling of the younger women which, though accepted as complimentary in Cuba, would be nothing short of insulting with us. But with that exception, and a tendency of columns a half-dozen abreast not to give way when courtesy would seem to demand it, there is a general politeness, an evidence of good-breeding in the slight social amenities of daily life, that it would be hard to duplicate in our own brusk-mannered land.

The plaza promenade is a more general gathering-place, a more thorough clearing-house of common acquaintance, than any included in Anglo-Saxon institutions.   Nowhere do the inhabitants of our own cities so thoroughly mingle together irrespective of class.   At the weekly meeting business men make many of their coming engagements — or explain the breaking of one arranged the week before.   Here old friends who find no other chance to get together spend an hour talking over old times; here youth forms new acquaintances, here kindred spirits who might otherwise never have met make enduring friendships.   The exclusiveness of family life wherever Spanish civilization has set its stamp is offset by the intercourse fostered by these Sunday evenings in the public plazas.   There the first tender glances pass between youth and maid, to be followed, with due propriety of delay, by soft words whispered through the *reja* of her prison-like home, and finally by his admittance, under parental supervision, to the chair-forested parlor, whence there is seldom any other escape than past the altar.   There, too, looser characters sometimes form their attachments, but always with due outward propriety.   The best-behaved city of our own land cannot be freer from visible evidence of human perversity than the island of Cuba.

Toward eight the plaza throng begins to thin out.   The more haughty ladies of the *vida social* and their cavaliers stroll away up the laboriously mounting streets toward the better residential districts.   The second social stratum follows their lead in all but direction, descending instead the *calles* that pitch downward toward the harbor.   All but the rattletrap automobiles that ply for hire have snorted away. The average tint of the promenaders grows steadily darker.   Within a half hour the plaza has become plebeian again both in manner and garb; in place of the compact throng their remain only a few scattered groups.   In contrast, the luxurious clubs, facing the square, have taken on new life.   The municipal council meets in its wide-open chamber across the way, a rabble peering in upon it through the heavy iron bars of the *rejas*.   Inside, beneath an elaborate painting of Santiago's first alcade — who was none other than the conquerer of Mexico — taking his first oath of office, politician-faced men of varying degrees of African ancestry slouch down into their seats with the super-bored attitude of legislators the world over.   On a rostrum backed not by likenesses of Cuba's native heroes, but by a portrait of Roosevelt as a young man and another of our own President, a kinky-haired orator begins a peroration that rouses shrill roars of delight from the *reja*-hugging mob far into the moonlighted tropical night.

Cuba's patron saint, though she has never received official papal sanction, is the Virgin of Cobre. The tale of her miraculous appearance is monotonously similar to that with which most Spanish-speaking peoples explain their dedication to some particular enshrined doll. Some three hundred years ago, the legend runs, two men and a negro slave boy from the village of Cobre, not far from Santiago, went to Nipe Bay to gather salt. There they found, floating on the water, an image of the Virgin, bearing the Child on one arm and holding aloft a gold cross. After various vicissitudes which the mere heretic may pass over in silence the image was set up in a shrine on the top of Cobre hill, in a church that had been specially erected for it.

The figure is of wood, about fifteen inches high, and gaudily decorated with the silks and jewels given by the pious believers. If one may accept the testimony of the Cubans of the less-educated class, particularly the fishermen, the *Virgen de Cobre* has performed many astounding miracles. At any rate, her priestly attendants have been richly showered with worldly gifts, and her shrine is surrounded with costly votive offerings — or was, at least, until some one ran away with most of them about the time Spanish rule in Cuba was abolished. Pilgrims still flock to Cobre, especially during the first days of September, and if they do not leave gifts of value, at least they decorate the church with crude and amusing drawings depicting the miracles that have been performed for them, or with wax likenesses of the varying portions of their bodies that have been cured by her intercession. A *guagua* crowded with women of the masses jolts out to Cobre from Santiago even during the off season. Now and then one runs across Cuban women of similar antecedents wearing copper-colored ornaments and even entire costumes of that shade, as signs of having dedicated themselves, in gratitude for her favors, to the Virgin of Cobre. Many a Cuban church displays a replica of the famous image, with a miniature boat, carved from wood and bearing the three salt-gatherers, beneath it.

But the world changes, and the time came when the Virgin entered, in all innocence, into conflict with practical modern forces beyond her control. Copper was discovered in the hill beneath her. An English company contracted to make good any damage their mining operations might cause to the venerated shrine. During their tenure the church suffered no injury. The mine was worked to what was considered the limit of its real productiveness under old methods and was then abandoned. When world conflict suddenly made copper worth increased exertion, Cobre was taken over by an American syndicate. The mine had meanwhile filled with water. When the new company began pumping this out, the old supporting timbers gave way and the church of the Virgin on the hilltop above began to sink. In time it fell completely out of sight. A new shrine, monotonously like the spireless and uninspiring country churches to be found throughout all Cuba, was erected for the Virgin and her pilgrims farther down the valley. The Archbishop of Santiago — for the old Eastern city still remains the religious capital of the island despite Havana's greatness — entered suit against the new company on the strength of the old English agreement. In his innocence of things worldly and geological the ecclesiastic feared that the tricky Yankees were forestalling him by washing out the ore in liquid form. An injunction ordered them to stop pumping, and the mine rapidly filled again with water. At length the prince of the church won his suit, with damages in excess of the value of the mine. The Americans abandoned what had become a more than useless concession, and to-day a mineful of water, colored with copper sulphates and lapping undetermined streaks of ore, remains the property of the Virgin of Cobre.

Daiquiri is not, as Rachel was justified in supposing, a cocktail factory, but an eminently respectable iron mine belonging now to a great American syndicate. It lies a score of miles eastward along the coast from Santiago, and may be reached — when the company chooses it shall be — by a little narrow-gage railroad older than Cuban independence. From a dusty suburb of the eastern metropolis we traveled thither by *cigüena,* as Cubans call a Ford with railroad feet. The halfbreed conveyance roared down a dry and rocky cavern to the coast, bursting out upon the incredibly blue Caribbean beside a forgotten Spanish fortress all but hidden under the rampant vegetation. For a time the line spins along on the very edge of the sea, which lashes constantly at the supporting boulders, and affords the seeker after scenic beauties an entrancing vista of mountain headlands protruding one after another into the hazy distance. This coastal region has little in common with the fertile and richly garbed flatlands of the interior. Jagged coral rock, known as *dientas de perro* (dog's teeth) to the Cubans, spreads away on the left and here and there rises in forbidding cliffs on the right. Vegetation is prolific, as always in the tropics, wherever a suggestion of foothold offers, but it is a dry and thorny

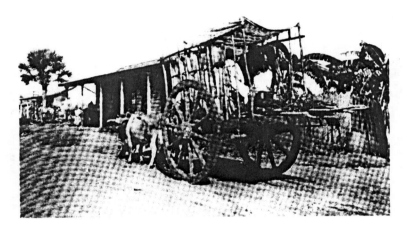

Cuban travelers

A Cuban milkman

Not all Chinamen succeed in Cuba

A street of Santiago de Cuba

growth, a menacing wilderness that invites few inhabitants. Only one abode of man breaks the journey, a cluster of sun-faded huts known as Siboney, on a rock before which stands a monument to the American forces that landed here for the march on Santiago.

Farther on, where the sea hides its beauty behind a widening strip of rocks and bristling vegetation, are a few fertile patches densely covered with cocoanut and banana groves. A cocoanut plantation is the lazy man's ideal investment. Once it is planted, he has only to wait until the nuts drop to have a steady income, taking the trouble to husk them if he cares to save something on transportation, but needing to exert himself no further unless thirst forces him to walk up a tree and cut down one of the green nuts filled with its pint of cool and satisfying beverage. The mountains rose to ever more impressive heights as the tireless Ford screamed onward, their culminating peak exceeded only by the Pico Turquino, peering into the sky from a neighboring range. Half bare, brown of tint, wrinkled as the Andes, they rise majestically into the sky, and if they are not high mountains, as mountains go the world over, they are at least lofty enough to be cloud-capped in the early mornings and now and then during the day. Mining villages, of which there are several besides the "mother mine" of Daiquiri, began to appear, perched on projecting knobs and knolls, long before we drew up at the port where hundreds of tons of ore are dropped every week directly into the ships — when ships can be had.

The mines themselves are laid out in full sight between heaven and earth. For they are open-work mines, each "bench" like the step of a giant stairway, reminding one of the Inca terraces of Peru. Steam-shovels gnaw at the two horseshoe-shaped amphitheaters, frequent explosions rouse the languid mountains to the exertion of sending back a long series of echoes, and the gravity-manipulated ore-buckets spin constantly away across the void to the crushers below. Here, too, the workmen are Spaniards who remain in Cuba only long enough to carry a villager's fortune back to their native land, and their labor in the open air gives them a tint far different from the human moles of most mining communities. Their houses are pitched high on a conical hill far above the mine, the married men living on the topmost summit, the "single village" farther down the slope, no doubt in order to convince the benedicts that they have risen to higher things. A locomotive dragged us up to the bit of a town, whence we rode on horseback to the crest of another foothill, on which stood in splendid isolation the residence of the bachelor manager. Of the veritable botanical and zoölogical gardens with which he had surrounded himself, of the beauty of the scene as the sun sank into the Caribbean far below, the rustling of the cocoanut palms in the steady breeze, and the distant sounds of the mining community settling down for the night I need say nothing except that we regretted we had not a hundred days instead of one to spend there.

The manager had lived through several revolutions, the latest less than three years before, and had grown accustomed to have some brakeman or miner in his employ march into his office at the head of a dozen ragamuffins and announce that he had been made a colonel overnight. Luckily our host was quite plainly liked by all classes of the community, so that such visits were usually mere social calls, and he had only to congratulate the new military genius, give him a drink and smoke a cigarette with him as a sign of equality to have him offer the mine his protection even unto death and stalk merrily away at the head of his "troops." On the mountain-sides across a mighty gully and high above us were still the remnants of old French coffee plantations, with native squatters in the old houses. By daylight the steep slopes stood forth like aged tapestries, golden brown in tinge except where they were dotted with immense mango-trees which looked at this distance like tiny green bushes. There one may find dogs, cats, cattle, guinea-fowls, pigs, and coffee all gone equally wild since the days when the plantation owners fled.

Wedded as it is to its sugar industry, Cuba is nevertheless capable of producing many other things. Of four-footed game there is little, as in all the West Indies. The aborigines must have been mainly vegetarians, for the only animal on the island at the time of the discovery was the *jutía*, which looks like a combination of rat, opossum, and woodchuck, lives in mangroves and hilly places, feeds on the bark of trees, and is so tame and stupid it may be killed with a club. It is still eaten, "its flesh being much esteemed by those who like it," as one description has it, though to the unaccustomed it is oily and insipid. During the last century deer were introduced, which are fairly plentiful in some parts of the island and would be more so if there were game laws and any feasible means of enforcing them. *Jutías* and *boniatos* frequently constituted the entire commissary of the insurgents against the Spaniards. The latter is a tuber so prolific that an acre, free from insects, has been known to produce fifty thousand pounds of it in eighteen months. Its chief rival in the peasant's garden and on most Cuban tables is the *malanga*, the *taro* of the South Seas, easily distinguishable by its large heart-shaped leaves. Of the feathered species there is a larger representation than of quadrupeds. Wild turkeys, called *guanajos*, abound, the flocks of guineas are sometimes so large as to do serious damage to the crops. The indigenous birds are distinguished more by their color than by their ability to sing. The best of them in the latter respect is the *sinsonte*, which not only imitates the songs of other birds, but has been known to learn short pieces of music. Snakes are rare and never venomous, the largest being a species of boa constrictor with a tan-colored skin, so sleepy and harmless that small boys climb the trees in which it sleeps and knock it to the ground with sticks. Cuban oysters are much smaller than ours, though the natives claim they are more succulent and nutritious. There are lobsters also, but the finest of all Cuban sea foods is the *congrejo moro*, a huge crab with a beautiful red and black shell. Little corn is grown, and still less rice, though the latter invariably makes its appearance at the two daily meals. Vegetables, except for the *malanga* and *boniato*, are rare, as in all tropical America; fruit, on the other hand, almost unlimited. There are twenty varieties of bananas, seedy oranges may be had anywhere, the mango, pineapple, *mamey*, *guayaba*, *mamoncillo*, *guanábana*, *chirimoya*, *sapote* or *níspero*, the *papaya*, a tree-grown melon superior to our best canteloupes and with a taste of honeysuckle, and the grape-fruit are among the many island delicacies, but only the pineapple and grape-fruit are cultivated with any attention. Even with all these fruits to choose from the most familiar Cuban dessert is the apple, imported from our Northwestern States and retailing at from twenty to thirty cents each. Unfortunately, though most American fruits arrive in Cuba in perfect condition, few of those grown in Cuba can endure the journey to the United States. Lastly, for the ever-present *palma real* could not be left out of any mention of Cuban products, this most beautiful of the island's trees is as useful as it is incomparable as a landscape decoration. The royal palm has no bark and the trunk is hollow, so that with a very little labor it can be fashioned into waterpipes or split into a rough and ready lumber. The fronds make splendid roofing, light, yet impermeable. The *yagua*, or leaf base, has a score of uses. Pigs prefer the oily little nuts which hang in clusters beneath the leaves to any other food. The branches to which these seeds are attached make good brooms; salt can be had from the roots; the "cabbage" from which the leaves gradually form makes an excellent salad, raw or cooked, and lastly, the lofty tree is peerless as a lightning-rod.

Daiquirí and Cobre by no means exhaust the places of interest in the mammoth eastern province of Cuba. There are branch railroad lines, for instance, to the western, northern, and southern coasts of the province, each several hours from Santiago. On the way to Manzanillo one passes the village in which the " Grito de Yara " began the revolt against Spanish rule, and in the neighborhood of which some of the old revolutionary leaders still live. Antilla, in the north, faces one of the most magnificent bays in the New World; beyond the town of Guantánamo, noteworthy for its unbroken chorus of roosters, two little railways flank the opposite shores of the gulf of the same name, one of them passing through an entrancing little valley. The other wanders across a flat, thorny, and rather arid land to Caimanera, noted for its salt beds and as the nearest place free from the American drought which reigns perpetually over the station of our marines and sailors holding our naval base of Guantánamo Bay.

He who comes to Cuba with the rigid American conception of the gulf separating the African and the Aryan races will find our ward little inclined to follow our lead in that particular matter. In the Havana custom-house his belongings will be examined by a black man. The finest statue in Cuba is that of the negro general, Macéo; had he lived he would in all probability have been the island's first president. One soon becomes accustomed to seeing negroes slap white men on the back with a familiar " Hello, Jim," and be received by an effusive handshake. Sextets gathered for a little banquet at café tables frequently show as many gradations of color, from a native Spaniard to a full African, repulsive perhaps for his diamond rings and over-imitation of Parisian manners, and are served by obsequious white waiters. The majority of Cuban negroes, however, seem less objectionable than those in the lands where the color-line is closely drawn. Accustomed to being treated as equals, many of them have developed a self-respect and a gentlemanliness rare among our own blacks, or even among our working class of Caucasian blood. They have, too, a pride in personal appearance scarcely inferior to that of the sometimes over-dressed white Cubans. Mark Twain once stated that there is much to be said for black or brown as the best tint for human complexions; one is often reminded of the remark in noting how handsome some of these black Cuban dandies look under their stiff straw hats.

Negroes, of course, are by no means in the majority in the largest of the Antilles, though most Cubans probably have African blood in their veins. In the Oriente may still be found traces of the Siboney Indians. Immigrants from all the varied provinces of Spain, African slaves, Chinese coolies, creoles from Haiti, Louisiana, and Florida, and a scattering of many other races have mingled together for generations; and from this blending of east and west, north and south, tempered by the tropical climate, emerges the Cuban. To a certain extent all these types have kept their racial characteristics, but they are only lost under the overwhelming influence of what may be called the national Cuban character, which varies little from that of all Latin-Americans. Like all nations, the islanders have their good and their bad points. The simple amenities of life are more thoroughly cultivated than in our own quick-spoken land. Rudeness is rare; courtesy is wide-spread among all classes. One would scarcely expect to see duplicated in our large cities the action of a mulatto traffic policeman stationed on the busiest corner of Havana's plaza, who waited for a lull in the task assigned him to cross the street and, raising his cap, corrected a direction he had given me a moment before. I have heard a woman tourist who failed to understand one of these immaculate guardians remark petulantly to her companions, "You'd think they'd make them learn English, would n't you?" Our native tongue is often useless in Cuba, to be sure; but how would it be if *they*, whoever they are, required travelers to learn Spanish before entering a Spanish-speaking country? The general courtesy is sometimes tempered by unintentional lapses from what we understand by that word; Cubans call one another, for instance, and try to call Americans, by a hissing "P-s-t," which is not customary in our own good society. They are emotional and excitable; their necessity for gesticulation frequently requires them to put down a telephone receiver in order to use both hands; they have little concentration of attention, and are much given to generalizing from superficial appearances to save themselves the labor of going to the bottom of things. Of quick intelligence, they learn with facility when there is anything to be gained by learning, but memory rather than thought is their dominant faculty. This last is probably due to the antiquated methods of the schools, that make the child a mere parrot and never develop his powers of judgment and comparison, which often remain inactive and dormant throughout life.

His politeness has its natural counterpart of insincerity until, in the perhaps too harsh words of one of his own people, " we cultivate falsehood with a facility which becomes prodigious." This insincerity is perhaps natural in a society that lived for centuries under constant suspicion of infidelity and surrounded by an atmosphere of distrust on the part of the Spanish rulers. Pride, which often reaches the height of a virtue among the Spaniards, is apt to degenerate in the Cuban to mere vanity, making him more susceptible to flattery than to reason. " Our dominating nervous temperament," says the native critic quoted above, " has contributed to make us irritable, sometimes insufferable. On account of this sensitiveness we have more sensations than ideas, more imagination than understanding, with the result that when we turn our attention to anything the pretty is apt to have more importance than the true or useful. We are better path-followers than originators; we prefer to triumph by astuteness rather than by reason ; we are prodigal, and for that reason the thirst for riches is our dominant characteristic. The rascality of our priests, largely from Spain, has made the average Cuban, if not an atheist, at least a skeptic and indifferent in religious matters."

Americans who have lived in Mexico, of whom there are many now in Cuba, all make comparisons unfavorable to the Cubans. We did not meet one of them who was not longing for the day when they, men and women alike, could return to the land of weekly revolutions. " I hear," said a visitor from the North, "that the Cubans are rather slippery in business." " Say rather," replied an old American resident, " that they are good business men, with the accent on the business." This verdict seems to be almost unanimous. The Cuban has a habit of beating himself on the chest and shouting about his *honor* at the very moment when both he and his hearers know he is lying. It is natural, perhaps, that the heat of the tropics should breed hatred for work and cause men to become tricky instead. But this trickery is less conspicuous in business than in politics. The war gave Cuba an enormous commercial impulse, yet there are comparatively few Cubans in commerce. Parents prefer that their sons adopt professions or enter government service. A Cuban congressman ended his appeal for a bill authorizing the government to send a hundred youths abroad each year to study commerce with, " Those who do not succeed in business can become government agents and consuls." The notion of foisting the failures upon the state awakened not a titter of surprise among his hearers; they had long been used to that custom under Spanish rule.

The Cubans are always discussing politics, though the great majority of them have no voice whatever in the government. To an even greater extent than with us the best men shun political office. The few of this class who enter politics soon abandon it in disgust and to an ignorant and avaricious clique are left the spoils. More than one representative has learned to sign his name after being elected. One admitted in public debate that he thought the Amazon was in Europe; another scoffed at the idea that Cuba was entirely surrounded by water. Congressmen go to their sessions armed, and revolvers are frequently drawn during some heated controversy. Some of them have been known to take advantage of the immunity from arrest to refuse to pay their rent and to make attacks upon women. A recent president was elected on a platform of cock-fighting, a national lottery, and *jai alai*, this last being the Basque game of *pelota*, at which gambling flourishes at its best. The president now in power was apparently all that a president should be during the first few months of his term; to-day only those on whom he has showered favors have a good word for him. "The Liberal who ruled before him was a grafter," say natives and foreign residents alike, "but at least he let other people get theirs, while this man grabs everything for himself. In other words he is as Conservative as the other was Liberal." If one is to believe local opinion, Cuba has had but two honest and efficient rulers since her independence, some say in her history,— her first elected president and her first American military governor. Love for the latter is almost universal; one frequently hears the assertion that, if he could run and honest elections could be held, he would be elected president of Cuba by an overwhelming majority, notwithstanding that the average Cuban does not like the average American.

Graft, known in Cuba as "*chivo*," is hereditary in the chief of the West Indies. In olden days Spain looked upon Cuba as a legitimate source of quick and easy gain. Royal grants were bestowed upon favorites; titles and positions were created as a means of securing all the profit possible. The few years of American rule did little to eradicate this point of view, and the old idea still persists. Political positions are treated quite frankly as opportunities for amassing private fortunes, and the man in public life who does not take complete advantage of his position is openly rated a fool. The reign of "*chivo*" is supreme through all the grades of officialdom; it is not necessary to seek examples, they are constantly thrusting themselves upon the attention.

Investigation has shown that half the owners of private automobiles and many liquor dealers have paid no licenses, but have "fixed it up" with the inspectors. During a recent hurricane the new seawall along the Malecón in Havana was totally wrecked, though the portion built during American rule suffered scarcely any damage. The millionaire Spanish contractor had saved on cement by giving part of the sum which should have been spent for it to those whose business it was to pass upon his work. The director of the national lottery made enough in four years to buy one of the largest sugar *centrals* on the island, and his position, you may be sure, did not come to him gratis. A real estate company offered to furnish the oil and tarvia if the government of Havana would pave the streets of a new suburb; one fourth of the material was actually used for that purpose and the rest was sold by the public officials. The church is not behindhand in the pursuit of "*chivo*." Priests demand fabulous sums for marrying, and advise the *guajiros* and laboring classes who cannot pay for the ceremony to go without, as thousands of families have done, many of them having accepted it years later as Christmas presents to themselves and their children from American employers. During the recent census conservative enumerators failed to enroll liberal citizens, thereby depriving them of the right to vote; and if the tables had been turned, the only difference would have been that the other party would have lost their ballots. During the war a chain was lowered each evening across the mouth of Havana harbor as a protection against submarines; an English captain who knew nothing of the new rule against entering the port at night was arrested by a Cuban naval officer and then told that the matter could be "fixed up" for a twenty-dollar bill.

"Concessions" and "permits" are the chief aids of the "*chivo*"-seeker. Each morning six men who have a "concession" netting them a neat little sum for gathering the rubbish floating on the water row across the harbor and back without touching the acres of flotsam, and hurry away to their private jobs early in the day. Havana has several new concrete piers, but they are not used because of "concessions" to the owners of tumbledown wharves. The same is true of a new garbage incinerator; lighterage "concessions" cost fortunes in time and money to ships entering the harbor. Nothing can be built in Cuba without a permit. The man who wishes to erect a house in Havana draws up his plans and submits them to the city architects. As often as he comes to get them, he is informed that " the man who works on these matters is not here now, but "—and if he takes the statement at par, the plans are placed at the bottom of the pile again as he leaves; but if he inadvertently slips a greenback of large denomination among them, the permit is forthcoming within twenty-four hours. One must have a permit to make the slightest alterations in house or office. An American who had secured a permission to paint his house was threatened with arrest for adding a second coat without another permit, and forced to " fix it up." When he tried to erect a fence he found that it could not be constructed of wood, but ten dollars made the inspector so blind that one erected of that material is represented on the city maps as made of cement and iron. The man who examines your baggage upon arrival in Havana will not pass it for hours or even days unless you accept his offer to have it transported to your hotel by draymen of his choosing and at his price, and so on, through all the vicissitudes of life and every branch of daily intercourse. Like the lianas and parasites which cling to the trees of Cuban forests, the productive class of the nation is everywhere supporting these useless hangers-on; and like those giants of the vegetable world the fertility of the island makes it strong enough to bear the burden without any serious impairment of its health and prosperity.

CHAPTER V

WE sailed away from Cuba on the Haitian Navy. It happened that the fleet in question put into Guantánamo Bay to have something done to her alleged engine at a time which happily coincided with our own arrival at the eastern end of the island. Otherwise there is no telling when or how we should have made our second jump down the stepping-stones of the West Indies, for Cuba and Haiti do not seem to be particularly neighborly.

The once proud *Adrea* of the New York Yacht Club is a schooner of almost a hundred tons, and still preserves some of her aristocratic features despite the lowly state to which she has fallen under her new name of *L'Indépendance*. Time was when the fleet of the Black Republic boasted more than twice its present strength; but the larger half of it was sold one day to the " slave trade," as they still call the carrying of negro laborers to the sugar-mills of Cuba, and on the two masts of *L'Indépendance* has fallen the entire burden of preserving the Haitian freedom of the seas.

Eleven wild men, all of them, except one yellow fellow for contrast, blacker than the shades of a rainy-season midnight, made up her crew, and the deep-blue and maroon flag of sovereign Haiti flew at her stern. But there was a lighter tint superimposed upon this dark background both of flag and crew. The former bore the white shield which announces a white man in command, and her three officers, averaging the advanced age of twenty-five, were as Caucasian as a New England village. In real life they were a bo's'n of the American Navy and two enlisted men of our far-flung Marine Corps, hailing from such quaint corners of the world as Cape Cod, Toledo, and Indianapolis; but in that topsyturvy fairy-world of the West Indies they were all first lieutenants of the " Gendarmérie d'Haïti."

By noon of a midsummer day in December *L'Indépendance* was rolling across the Windward Passage in a way out of all proportion to her importance or to the mere playfulness of the Caribbean waves.

When morning broke, the two horns of Haiti loomed far to the rear on each horizon, and we had already covered some two thirds of our journey.

But not so fast, lest the inexperienced reader get too hasty and optimistic a notion of wind-wafted travel. A schooner is a most romantic means of conveyance — when there is something to fill her sails. I can imagine no greater punishment for American impatience than to be sentenced to lie aimlessly tossing through the hereafter in tropical doldrums where even the fish scorn to bite. Evidently the winds within the gaping jaws of Haiti are as erratic as the untamable race that peoples its mountainous shores.

However, let us avoid exaggeration. We did move every now and then, sometimes in the right direction, occasionally at a spanking pace that sent the blue waters foaming in two white furrows along our bows. Yet the mountainous ridges on either hand crept past with incredible leisureliness. All through the second night the tramp of hurrying bare feet and the stentorian " French " of the officers sounded about the deck cots we had preferred to the still luxurious cabins below — and by sunrise we had covered nearly twenty miles since sunset! Gonave Island, with its alligator snout, floated on our starboard all that day with a persistency which suggested we were towing it along with us. Brown and seeming almost bare at this distance, it showed no other signs of life than a few languid patches of smoke, which the mulatto cabin-boy explained as " Burn 'em off an' then make 'em grow." It was well that he had picked up a fair command of English somewhere, for the mere fact that we both prided ourselves on the fluency of our French did not help us in any appreciable degree to carry on conversation with the black crew. The youthful officers, with that quick adaptability which we like to think of as American, had mastered their new calling even to the extent of acquiring that strange series of noises which is dignified in the French West Indies with the name of " creole," but it would never have been recognized even as a foster-child on Parisian boulevards.

The mountainous northern peninsula on our port grew slightly more variegated under an afternoon sun that gave the incredibly blue land-locked sea the suggestion of an over-indigoed tub on wash-day. The peninsula was brown, for the most part, with a wrinkled and folded surface that seemed to fall sheer from the unbroken summit into the placid blue gulf, and only here and there gleamed a little patch of green. Yet it must have been less precipitous than it seemed, for we made out through our glasses more than one clustered village along the hair-line where sea and mountains met, and now and then a fishing smack crawling along it put in at some invisible cove.

Before the third day waned, our goal, Port au Prince, was dimly to be seen with the same assistance, a tiny, whitish, triangular speck which seemed to stand upright at the base of the hazy mountain-wall stretching across the world ahead. The wind, too, took on a new life, but it blew squarely in our faces, as if bent on refusing us admittance to our destination. The shore we were seeking receded into the dusk, and the men of endless patience which sailing-vessels seem to breed settled down to battle through another night, with little hope of doing more than avoid retreat. We were rewarded, however, with another of those marvelous West Indian sunsets which only a super-artist could hope to picture. Ragged handsful of clouds, like the scattered fleece of the golden-brown *vicuña*, hung motionless against the background of a pink-and-blue streaked sky, which faded through all possible shades to the blackening indigo of the once more limitless sea.

How long the winds might have prolonged our journey there is no knowing. Out of the black night behind us there appeared what seemed a pulsating star, which gradually grew to unstar-like size and brilliancy. Excitement broke out among the three white mariners. One of them snatched an electric lamp and flashed a few letters of the Morse code into the darkness. They were answered by similar winkings on the arc of the approaching star. This shifted its course and bore down upon us. The captain caught up a megaphone and bellowed into the howling wind. The answer came back in no celestial tongue, but in a strangely familiar and earthly dialect: "Hello! That you, Louie? Tow? Sure. Got a line, or shall I pass you one?" A search-light suddenly revealed the navy of Haiti like a theatrical star in the center of the tossing stage; a submarine-chaser snorted alongside us with American brevity; our sails dropped with a run, and a few moments later we were scudding through the waves into the very teeth of the gale. When I awoke from my next nap, *L'Indépendance* was asleep at anchor in a placid little cove.

Port au Prince is not, as it appears from far out in the bay, heaped up at the base of a mountain-wall, but stretches leisurely up a gentle, but constant slope that turns mountainous well behind the city. Off and on through the night we had heard the muffled beating of tom-toms, or some equally artistic instrument, and occasionally a care-free burst of laughter, that could come only from negro throats, had floated to us across the water.   The first rays of day showed us a stone's-throw from a shore which the swift tropical dawn disclosed as far denser in greenery than a Cuban coast.   The city lay three miles away across the curving bay.   Two slender wireless poles and the stack of a more distant sugar-mill stood out against the mountain-range behind, while all else still hovered in the haze of night.   Then bit by bit, almost swiftly, the details of the town began to appear, like a photographic plate in the developer.   A cream-colored, two-towered cathedral usurped the center of the picture; whitish, box-like houses spotted the slope irregularly all about it, and the completed development showed scores of little hovels scattered through the dense greenery far up the hillsides and along the curving shore.   Then all at once a bugle sounded, an American bugle playing the old familiar reveille, and full day popped forth as suddenly as if the strident notes had summoned the world to activity.

Two blacks, manning the schooner's tender, set us ashore in the Haitian " navy-yard," a slender wooden pier along which were moored three American submarine-chasers.   An encampment of marines eyed us wonderingly from the doors of their tents and wooden buildings, beyond which a gateway gave us entrance to a thoroughly Haitian scene. A stony country road, flanked by a toy railway line, was thronged with the children of Ham.   Negro women, with huge bundles of every conceivable contents on their heads, pattered past with an easy-going, yet graceful, carriage.   Others sat sidewise on top of assorted loads that half hid the lop-eared donkeys beneath them.   Red bandanas and turbans of other gay colors showed beneath absurdly broad palm-leaf hats.   Black feet, with the remnants of a slipper balancing on the toes of each, waved with the pace of the diminutive animals.   The riders could scarcely have been called well dressed, but they were im-maculate compared with the throngs of foot travelers.   A few scattered patches of rags, dirty beyond description, hung about the black bodies they made no serious effort to conceal.   Men in straggly Napoleon III beards clutched every few steps at the shreds which posed as trousers.   Stark naked urchins pattered along through the dust; more of them scampered about under the palm-trees.   Bare feet were as general as African features.   More than one group sidled crabwise to the edge of the road as we advanced and gazed behind them with a startled expression at the strange sound made by our shod feet. Scores of the most primitive huts imaginable, many of them leaning at what seemed precarious angles, lined the way. Before almost all of them stood a little " shop," a few horizontal sticks raised off the ground by slender poles and shaded by a cluster of brown palm-leaves. Vacant-faced negro men and women, none of them boasting a real garment, tended the establishments squatting or lolling in the patches of shade which the early morning sun cast well out into the roadway. The stock in trade of the best of them would not have filled a market-basket. A cluster of bananas; a few oranges, small, but yellower than those of Cuba; bedraggled-looking alligator-pears; dust-covered loaves of bread, no larger than biscuits, made up the most imposing arrays. Many of the " merchants " had not advanced to the stick-counter stage, but spread their wares on the ground — little handsful of tiny red beans laid at regular intervals along a banana-leaf, similar heaps of unroasted coffee, bundles of fagots, tied with strips of leaf, that could easily have gone into a coat-pocket. Now and again some black ragamuffin paused to open negotiations with the lolling shopkeepers, who carried on the transaction, if possible, from where they lay, rising to their feet only when the heat of the bargaining demanded it. The smallness of each purchase was amusing, as well as indicative of Haitian poverty. One orange, a single banana, a measureful of a coarse, reddish meal tinier than the smallest glass of a bartender's paraphernalia, were the usual amounts, and the pewter coins that exchanged owners were seldom of the value of a whole cent. With rare exceptions the purchasers wolfed at once what they had bought as they pattered on down the road.

Details came so thick and fast that it was impossible to catch them all, even with a kodak. Compared with this, Cuba, after all, had been little more than semi-tropical. Here the vegetation, the odors, the very atmosphere were of the genuine tropics. Breadfruit-trees, with their scolloped leaves, which we had never seen in the larger island to the westward, shouldered their way upward among the cocoanut-palms. Mango-trees, as dense as haystacks, cast their black shadows over the rampant undergrowth. But always the eyes came back to the swarms of black people, with their festoons of rags contrasting with, rather than covering, their coal-tinted bodies. What might have seemed a long walk under a tropical sun became a short stroll amid this first glimpse of an astonishingly primitive humanity.

For all their poverty, the inhabitants seemed to be frankly happy with life. They had the playfulness of children, with frequent howls of full-throated laughter; they seemed no more self-conscious at the super-tattered state of their garments than were the ambling, over-laden donkeys at the ludicrous patchiness of their trappings. That lack of the sense of personal dignity characteristic of the African came to their rescue in the abjectness of their condition. For they *were* African, as thoroughly so as the depths of the Congo. We had strolled for an hour, and reached the very edge of the city itself, before we met not a white man, but the first face that showed any admixture of Caucasian blood. Compared with this callous-footed throng the hodgepodge of Cuban complexions seemed almost European.

As we neared the town, a train as primitive as the scene about us chattered round a bend in the tunnel of vegetation, the front of its first-model engine swinging like the trunk of an excited elephant. The four open, wooden cars that swayed and screamed along behind it were densely packed with passengers, yet even here there was not a white face. The diminutive tender was piled high with cordwood little larger than fagots, and the immense, squatty smokestack was spitting red coals over all the surrounding landscape. As the train passed, the negro women along the road sprang with a flurry of their ragged skirts upon the track and fell to picking up what we took to be coins scattered by some inexplicably generous passenger. Closer investigation showed that they were snatching up live 'coals with which to light the little brown clay pipes which give them a flitting resemblance to Irish peasants.

A lower-class market was in full swing in a dust-carpeted patch of ground on the city water-front. Here the wares were more varied than in the roadside " shops," but sold in the same minute portions. American safety-matches were offered not by the box, but in bundles of six matches each, tied with strips of leaf. Here were " butcher-shops," consisting of a wooden trough full of meat, which owed its preservation to a thorough cooking, and was sold by the shred and consumed on the spot. Scrawny, black hags, who had tramped who knows how many miles over mountain-trails with an ox-load of oranges or coarse tubers on their heads, squatted here all the morning selling a pennyworth of their wares at a time, the whole totaling perhaps forty cents, to be squandered for some product of civilization which they would carry home in the same laborious fashion. The minority of the women venders had come on donkeys and were frank in impressing upon their more lowly sisters the aristocracy which this sign of wealth and leisure conferred upon them. A native gendarme, dressed in a cheap-looking imitation of the uniform of our own marines, but as African

of soul beneath it as the most naked of his fellow-citizens, strutted
back and forth through the throngs of clamorous bargainers. Now
and again, when a group grew too large for his liking, he charged into
it, waving a long stick and striking viciously. at the legs and backs of
all within reach, irrespective of sex or age. Far from fighting back
or even showing resentment, the childlike blacks fled before him, often
with shrieks of laughter. Ours were the only white faces within the
inclosure, yet we were given passage everywhere with an unostentatious
consideration that in less primitive societies would be called extreme
courtesy.

Beggars as inhumanly sunk in degradation as the lowest pariahs of
India shuffled in and out, mutely holding forth filthy tin cups to those
barely a degree above them in want and misery. Near the gate a
seething crowd was collected around a pushcart filled with tin cans of
all sizes, tumbled pellmell together just as they had been slashed open
and tossed aside by a marine mess orderly. An old woman was selling
them to eager purchasers, who looked them over with the deliberate
care one might give an automobile offered for sale, parted at length
with the price agreed upon, after long and vociferous negotiations, and
wandered away gloating over the beauty of their new acquisition, some
of them talking to it in their incomprehensible " French." The prices
varied from " cinq cob " (5 centimes, or 1 cent) for a recent container
of jam or pork and beans to a *gourde* (twenty cents) or more for the
five-gallon gasolene tins that make such splendid water buckets on the
head of the Haitian women. In another corner was arranged in the
dust a display of bottles of every conceivable size, shape, and previous
occupation, from three-sided pickle flasks to empty beer bottles, constituting the entire stock in trade of two incredibly ragged females.
Scarcely a scrap or remnant, even of things which we hire men to
carry to the garbage heap, but had its value to this poverty-stricken
throng. Particularly was anything whatever resembling cloth made
use of to the utmost end of its endurance. One of the best dressed
of the pulsating collection of tatters was a powerful black fellow who
strutted about in a two-piece suit fashioned from unbleached muslin
that had entered upon its second term of servitude. Unlike those of his
fellows, both garments were whole, except for one three-cornered rent
in what, to a less self-confident being, would have been an embarrassing
position. Diagonally across the trousers, just above this vent, blazed
the word " Eventually," and below it the pertinent query, " Why not
now ? "

The entire enlisted personnel of the Haitian Navy

A school in Port au Prince

The Central Square and Cathedral of Port au Prince on Market Day

Looking down upon the market from the Cathedral platform

The American residents of Port au Prince complain that visitors of scribbling propensities have given too much space to its comic-opera aspect. It is hard to avoid temptation. The ridiculous is constantly forcing itself into the foreground, innocently unaware of distracting attention from the more serious background. For there is such a background, one which should in all fairness be sketched into any picture of Haiti which makes a pretense of being true to life. If there has been a constant tendency to leave it out, it is probably due to the fact that the average wanderer over the face of the earth finds most " interesting " the incongruous and the ludicrous.

To close our eyes, then, for the moment to the more obvious details, the capital of the Black Republic is by no means the misplaced African village which common report would indicate. Its principal streets are excellently paved with asphalt; scores of automobiles honk their way through its seething streams of black humanity. Even along the water-front the principles of sanitation are enforced. Barefooted " white wings," distinguished by immense green hats of woven palm-leaves worn on top of their personal headgear, are constantly sweeping the city with their primitive bundle-of-grass brooms. A railroad, incredibly old-fashioned, to be sure, but accommodating a crowded traffic for all that, runs through the heart of the town and connects it with others considerable distances away in both directions. An excellent electric light service covers the city. Its shops make a more or less successful effort to ape their Parisian prototypes; its business offices by no means all succumb to the tropical temptation to sleep through the principal hours of the day. The French left it a legacy of wide streets, though failing, of course, to bequeath it adequate sidewalks. Its architecture is a surprise to the traveler arriving from Cuba; it would be far less so to one who came direct from Key West. Wooden houses with sloping roofs are the general rule, thin-walled structures with huge slatted doors and windows, and built as open as possible to every breeze that blows, as befits the climate. There are neither red tiles, strangely tinted walls, nor Moorish *rejas* and patios to attract the eye. Indeed, there is little or nothing in the average street vista to arouse the admiration, though there is a certain cause for amusement in the strange juxtaposition of the most primitive African reed huts with the attempts of Paris-educated mulattoes to ape, with improvements of their own, their favorite French châteaux.

Only two buildings in Port au Prince — one might perhaps say in all Haiti — boast window-glass. One is the large and rather imposing cathedral, light yellow both outside and within, flooded with the aggressive tropical sunshine in a way that leaves it none of the "dim and mystic light" befitting such places of worship. The other is the unfinished, snow-white presidential palace, larger and more sumptuous than our own White House. The cathedral looks down upon the blue harbor across a great open square unadorned with a single sprig of vegetation; the palace squats in the vast sun-scorched Champs de Mars, equally bare except for a Napoleonic statue of Dessalines, his telltale complexion disguised by the kindly bronze, and attended by a modest and deeply tanned Venus of Melos. The absence of trees in the public squares gives assistance to the wooden houses in proving the city no offshoot of Spanish civilization. The tale runs that the Champs de Mars was once well wooded until a former president ordered it cleared of all possible lurking-places for assassins.

But Port au Prince is by no means unshaded. The better residential part up beyond the glaring parade-ground makes full use of the gorgeous tropical vegetation. Here almost every house is hidden away in its grove of palms, mangos, breadfruit, and a score of other perennial trees, and flowering bushes, ranging all the way from our northern roses to the pale-yellow of blooming cotton-trees and enormous masses of the lavender-purple bougainvillea, crowd their way in between the tree-trunks. Oranges, bananas, and the pear-shaped grape-fruit of Haiti hang almost within reach from one's window; alligator-pears may be had in their season for the flinging of a club; he who cares to climb high enough can quench his thirst with the cool water of the green cocoanut. The dwellings here are spacious and airy, their ceilings almost double the height of our own, and if they lack some of the conveniences considered indispensable in the North, they have instead splendid swimming-pools and, in many cases, such a view of the lower city, the intensely blue bay, and the wrinkled brown ranges of the southern peninsula as would make up for a far greater scarcity of the stereotyped comforts.

It is a leisurely, but constant, climb from the water-front to these forest-embowered dwellings. Port au Prince is not blessed with a street-car system, and its medieval railroad staggers only to the upper edge of the Champs de Mars. Moreover, the painted drygoods-boxes on wheels are invariably so densely crammed with full-scented blacks that not only the white residents, but even the haughty yellow ones, rarely deign to patronize the spark-spitting conveyance. Long-established families have their private carriages; the parvenus from foreign lands own, borrow, or share automobiles; mere clerks and bookkeepers jog homeward on their diminutive Haitian ponies; and chance visitors trust to luck and the oily-cushioned wrecks that ply for hire, finishing the journey on foot from the point where the bony and moth-eaten caricature of a horse refuses longer to respond to the lashings and screams of the tar-complexioned driver. Fortunately, it is perfectly good form to " catch a ride " with any car-owning member of one's own race.

Let me not leave the impression, however, that the majority of those who ascend the city depend on gasolene or horseflesh. At least two thirds of them walk, but it is the two thirds that do not count in polite parlance. All day long, though far more incessantly, of course, in the delightful coolness of early morning or the velvety air of evening, processions of black people of varying degrees of raggedness plod noiselessly up and down the stony streets of the upper town. Noiselessly, that is, only in their barefooted tread; their tongues are rarely silent, and frequent cackles of unrestrained laughter sound from the bundles beneath which their woolly heads are all but invariably buried. For be it large or small, a mahogany chest of drawers or a tin can three inches in diameter, the Haitian always bears his burdens on his head. *Her* head would be more nearly the exact truth of the case, for the women rarely permit their lords and masters to subject themselves to the indignity of toil. But the merest child of the burden-bearing sex is rarely seen abroad except under a load that gives her the appearance of the stem of a toadstool. Some of these uncomplaining females serve the more fortunate residents of the hill; most of them trot to and fro between the market and the tiny thatched cabins sprinkled far up the range behind the city like rice grains on a green banana leaf. Where the streets break up beyond the last man's-size dwellings, narrow trails tunnel on up through the prolific greenery to these scattered huts of the real Haitian, among which it is easy to imagine oneself in the heart of Africa.

Five years ago there were barely a score of white men in Port au Prince, and not many more than that in all Haiti. To-day there are perhaps three hundred American residents, without counting a large force of occupation and their families, and to say nothing of a considerable sprinkling of French, the remnants of what was a flourishing German colony until an epidemic of internment fell upon it, and a scattering of Italian, Syrian, and similar tradesmen. The Americans of the first category are carrying on or opening up new enterprises

that promise to offer Haiti a prosperity not even second to that of
Cuba. No one who has visited the island can question the extraordinary fertility of its soil. The overwhelming portion of it is as virgin
as if the French had never exploited what was once the richest of their
colonies; revolutions have become, by *force majeure*, a thing of the
past. Every new undertaking must, to be sure, be built or rebuilt
from the ground up. During their more than a century of freedom
the negoes have done nothing but destroy. They have not even exercised their one faculty, that of imitation, for they have been too much
shut off from the rest of the world to find anything to imitate. Though
the sugar-cane was introduced into Cuba by the French refugees from
Haiti, the entire country cannot at present compete with the largest
single sugar-mill in the prosperous island to the west. The Haitian
laborer has lost all knowledge of the sugar-making process except his
own primitive method of producing *rapadoue*. He must be taught all
over again, and he is not a particularly apt pupil; moreover, complain
the men who are striving to make Haiti bloom once more with cane,
no sooner is he taught than the Cuban planters entice him across the
Windward Passage with wages ten times as high as he receives at home.
But capital is beginning to recognize that despite its obvious drawbacks Haiti offers a rich future, and several syndicates have already
" got in on the ground floor."

The American residents of Port au Prince, men, women, and children, swear by it. I have yet to meet one who is eager to leave; many
of those who go north for extended vacations cut them short with a
cry of "take me back to Haiti." To the misinformed northerner its
very name is synonymous with revolution and sudden death. Outside
the field of romance there is about as much danger of meeting with
violence from the natives as there is of being boiled in oil at a church
" sociable." There is not a deadly representative of the animal or
vegetable kingdom on the island; except for some malarial regions of
rather mild danger the climate is as healthful as that of the best state
in our union — with due regard, of course, to the invariable rule that
white women should season their residence with an occasional invigorat-
ing breath of the north. The Americans have acquired one by one,
as some yellow politician has lost his grasp on the national treasury,
the grove-hidden houses in the upper town, some of them little short
of palatial. There they live like the potentates of the tropical isles
of romance. The blacks are respectful, childlike in their manner, and
have much of the docility of the negroes of our South before the Civil

War. They work for wages which, as wages go nowadays, are less than a song. House servants receive from five to eight dollars a month, and the one meal a day to which the masses have long been accustomed rarely costs a twenty-cent *gourde*. Families who could scarcely afford the luxury of a single "hired girl" in the land of their birth keep five servants in Haiti, a cook, butler, up-stairs maid, laundress, and yard boy; for the Haitian is strictly limited in his versatility, and the cook could no more serve a dinner than a laundress could give the yard its daily sweeping. They are usually stupid beyond words, with the mentality of an intelligent child of six, but they are sometimes capable of great devotion, with a dog-like quality of faithfulness; and between them all they swathe the existence of their masters in the comfort of an old-time Southern plantation. All this is but half the story of contentment with Haitian residence, for the mere fact that the sun is certain to break forth in all the splendor of a cloudless sky as sure as the morning comes round is sufficient to make the cold and dismal north seem a prison by comparison.

There is a certain amount of friction between the several classes of Americans in Port au Prince, not to mention heroic efforts in "keeping up with Lizzie." Ten-course dinners with all the formality and ostentation which go with them are of daily occurrence; "bridge" flourishes by day and by night, with far from humble stakes, and dances, whether at the American Club or in private houses, are not conspicuous for their simplicity. The two things go together, of course; it is of little use to disagree with a man if you cannot prove yourself his equal by "putting up as good a front" as he does. Roughly speaking, our fellow-countrymen in the Haitian capital may be divided into four classes, though there are further ramifications and certain points of contact. Each class has its own faults and virtues, and comes naturally by them. The half dozen civilian officials who hold the chief offices of our "advisory" share in the civil government have in too many cases been chosen for their political standing rather than for their ability or experience in such tasks as that they are facing. The navy and the marine officers, between whom a rift now and then shows itself, have the characteristics of the military calling the world over. They are by nature direct and autocratic, rather than persuasive and tactful; they have an almost childish petulance at any fancied slight to their rank, which does not make it easy for them to coöperate with the civilian officials. Of their efficiency in their chosen profession there is no question, but our policy of assigning them to administrative posi-

tions simply because they are already on the national pay-roll and expecting them to shine in tasks which call for a lifetime of training
quite opposite to that they have received has its drawbacks. The very
qualities which make for success in pacifying the country hamper them
in dealing with the better class of natives, who are, to be sure, negroes,
yet who have the sensitive French temperament and are much more
amenable to persuasion than to bullying. By chance or design the
great majority of our officers in Haiti are Southerners, and they
naturally shun any but the most unavoidable intercourse with the
natives. This is one of the chief bones of contention between the forces
of occupation and the American civilians engaged in business. The
latter, while still keeping a color-line, contend that the natives of education should be treated more like human beings. They deplore the
narrow viewpoint, the indifference to industrial advancement, the occasional schoolboy priggishness of the officers, and the latter retaliate
by considering the term business man as synonymous with money-
grabbing and willingness to cater to the natives for the sake of trade.
Not that these differences cause open rifts in the American ranks, but
the atmosphere is always more or less charged with them. The native
of education, on his side, resents the whole American attitude on the
race question, and not wholly without reason. The color-line is justifiable in so far as it protects against intermingling of blood, characteristics, and habits, but there is a point beyond which it becomes d — d
foolishness, and that point is sometimes passed by our officers in Haiti.
After all, the Haitians won their independence without our assistance,
and to a certain extent they are entitled to what they call their *dignité
personelle*. The Southerner is famed for his ability to keep the
" nigger " down, but he is less successful in lifting him up, and that is
the task we have taken upon ourselves in Haiti.

As every American should know, but as a great many even of those
who pride themselves on keeping abreast of the times do not, Haiti
has been an American protectorate since the summer of 1915. There
is a native government, to be sure, ranging all the ebony way from
president to village clerks, but if it functions efficiently, and to a certain
degree it does, it is thanks to a few hundred of our own marines and
certain representatives of our navy. How this strange state of affairs,
so contrary to the forgiving spirit of the present administration, came
about is a story brief and interesting enough to be worth the telling.

The Spanish discoverers — for one must be permitted a running start if one is to race through the reeking fields of Haitian history — soon wiped out the native Indian population in their usual genial, but thorough, way. Fields will not plant, or at least cultivate, themselves, however, even in so astonishingly fertile a land as the island that embraces the republics of Haiti and Santo Domingo. Hence the Frenchmen to whom the western end of the island eventually fell, after varying vicissitudes, followed the custom of the time and repopulated the colony with negro slaves. Prosperity reigned for a century or more. There are still jungle-grown ruins of many an old French plantation mansion to be found not merely within the very boundaries of the Port au Prince of to-day, but in regions that have long since reverted to primeval wilderness. Unfortunately, for the French at least, the slave-traders supplied this particular market with members of some of Africa's more warlike tribes, the descendants of whom, taking the theories of the French Revolution *au pied de la lettre,* concluded to abolish their masters. Under a genuine military genius with the blood of African chieftains in his veins, one Toussaint l'Ouverture, and his equally black successor, Dessalines, the slaves defeated what was in those days a large French army, commanded by the brother-in-law of the great Napoleon, and drove the French from the island. New Orleans and Philadelphia received most of the refugees, whose family names are still to be found in the directories of those cities. Except for a few persons the French never returned, and Haiti has been "the Black Republic" since 1804.

The result was about what our Southern statesmen would have prophesied. In theory the government of Haiti is modeled on that of France; in practice it has been the plaything of a long line of military dictators of varying degrees of color and virtually all rising to power and sinking into oblivion — usually of the grave — on the heels of swiftly succeeding revolutions. There have been a few well-meaning men among them, the last of whom, named Leconte, was blown up in 1912, palace and all. Most of them were interested only in playing Cæsar, or, more exactly, Nero, over their black fellow-citizens until the time came to loot the national treasury and flee, a program which was frequently cut short by appalling sudden death. The detailed recital of more than a century of violence, of constant bloody differences between the mulattoes and the genuine blacks, would be a tale too long for the modern reader.

In 1915 the presidency was occupied by a particularly offensive black brother named Guillaume Sam. Though it has not been so recorded,

Sam's middle name was evidently Trouble. Foreign war-ships took to dropping in on Port au Prince and demanding the payments of debts to foreigners. Up in the northern peninsula, as usual in mango-time, when the trees of the island constitute a commissary, revolution broke out, and, to top off his woes, Sam was busy marrying off his daughter and installing her in a new palace. In his wrath at being disturbed at such a time Sam passed the word to his chief jailer to clean out the penitentiary, some of the political prisoners in which were no doubt in sympathy with the revolutionists, but many of whom were there merely because they had aroused the personal enmity of Sam, or some of his cronies. The sentence was carried out more like a rabbit-hunt than an execution. In an orgie in which the primitive instincts of the African had full play the two hundred or more prisoners were butchered in circumstances better imagined than described. Among them were many members of the " best families " of Port au Prince. It is not recorded that any of this class took personal part in the revenge that followed, but they undoubtedly instigated it. The rank and file of the town, those same more or less naked blacks who are ordinarily docile and childlike, surrounded the palace. Sam had taken refuge in the French legation. For the first time even in the turbid history of Haiti, the sanctuary of a foreign ministry was violated by the voodoo-maddened mob. Sam was dragged out, cut to pieces, and tossed into the bay. Then our marines landed and, to use their own words, " the stuff was all over."

American control is due to continue for at least twenty years from that date. A treaty drawn up soon after the landing of our forces, and subsequently renewed, provides for the form under which our " assistance " shall be exercised, as well as specifying the time limit. An American financial adviser, who is far more than that in practice, an American receiver of customs, and heads of the engineering and sanitation departments, are required by the terms thereof, and the final decision in most matters of importance lies with the American minister. Unlike the Republic of Santo Domingo in the eastern end of the island, Haiti still retains her native government, but its acts are subject to a relatively close supervision by the officers above named, despite the pretense that our share is only " advisory."

There are both natives and foreigners who contend that Haiti is fully capable of governing itself if the white man will go away and let the Black Republic alone. The following incident is not without its bearing on the subject:

The Rotary Club of Port-au-Prince decided in the fifth year of American occupation to assess every member five dollars for the purpose of providing a community Christmas for the poor children of the city.   Never had a Christmas-tree been seen in Haiti outside the homes of American or other foreign residents.   The vast majority of Haitians had no conception that so benevolent a being as Santa Claus existed.

The Port au Prince branch of the club had been very recently organized. Its membership included not only the representative business men of all grades in the foreign colony, but it had made a special point of overlooking the color-line and admitting as many Haitians as white men.   A little closer intercourse now and then between the two races, it was felt, would do no one any harm, and the experience of similar clubs in Cuba suggested that it might do considerable good. The military colony, of course, took no part in this flagrant violation of its strict Southern principles beyond granting its official blessing, but the civilians had long contended for a broader-minded attitude.

There was no difficulty in finding representative Haitians of sufficient culture to be worthy a place in such an assembly.   Men educated in Paris, graduates of the best universities in other European capitals, men who spoke the French language as perfectly as the French themselves, men who could give the average American business man cards and spades in any discussion of art, literature, and the finer things of civilization, were to be found in the best Haitian homes.   The native membership as finally constituted included cabinet ministers, former ambassadors to the principal world capitals, lawyers famous for their oratory, and men who had produced volumes on profound subjects, to say nothing of very tolerable examples of lyric poetry.   The club did not, it is true, completely obliterate the color-line.   It merely moved it along.   A complete sweep of the crowded table at the weekly club luncheons, with whites and Haitians nicely alternating, did not disclose a single jet-black face.   But that was not the fault of the club; it was due to the fact that the benefits of higher education have seldom reached the full-blooded Africans of the island, as distinguished from what are known locally as the " men of color."

The wives of the white club members took up the task of providing a suitable Christmas where the men left off, and pushed the matter with American enthusiasm.   They canvassed the white colony for additional funds; they solicited contributions in kind from the merchants of Caucasian blood.   Their evenings they spent in making things that would bring joy to the little black babies, in putting the multifarious gifts in order, in laying new plans to make the affair a success. By day they drove about in their automobiles through all the poorer sections of the city, distributing tickets to the swarms of naked black piccaninnies. Mobs of harmless, clamoring negroes surrounded their cars, holding up whole clusters of babies as proof of their right to share in the extraordinary generosity of the strange white people. Seas of clawing black hands waved about them like some scene from Dante's Inferno in an African setting. A tumult of pleading voices assailed their ears: " Cartes, mamá, donne-moi cartes! Moi deux petits, mamá! Non gagner carte pour petit malade, mamá? "

The " ladies of color " of the other club members formed a committee of their own and lent a certain languid assistance, but the brunt of the work fell on the incomprehensibly generous whites. The men of the yellow features were even more willing · to leave matters to their Caucasian associates. The latter were more experienced in the arrangement of Christmas-trees; moreover, they could descend to vulgar work, which the élite of Port au Prince could not indulge in without losing caste. Curious creatures, these whites, anyway; let them go ahead and spread themselves. The " men of color " were quite willing to sit back and watch *les blancs* run the whole affair — except in one particular, the distribution of tickets. In that they were more than ready to coöperate. They even made the generous offer of attending to all that part of the affair. The minister of public instruction came forward with a plan in keeping with his high rotarian standing. If the bulk of the tickets, say two thirds of them, for instance, were turned over to him, he would personally accept the arduous labor of distributing them to the school-children. Now you must know that the school-children of Port au Prince constitute a very small proportion of the young population, and that they are exactly the class which the sponsors of the Christmas-tree were *not* trying to reach. Furthermore, do not lose sight of the fact that the men of color must be constantly on the *qui vive* to keep their political fences in order. Even the ladies of the Haitian committee advised against the minister's proposition. He, they whispered, would divide the tickets between his favorite teachers, who in turn would distribute them to their pet pupils.

Meanwhile Christmas drew near. A band of black men were sent far up into the mountains to fetch down a pine-tree. They are numerous in some parts of Haiti, occasionally growing side by side with the palms. The blacks could not, of course, understand why they must lug a tree for two or three days over perpendicular trails when trees of a hundred species abounded in the very outskirts of Port au Prince; but this was not the first time they had received absurd orders from the incomprehensible *blancs*. They selected as small a tree as they dared and started down the mountain-side. As the wide-spreading branches hindered their progress, they lopped most of them off. How should they know that the inexplicable white men wanted the branches to hang things on? The gentleman of color, right-hand man of their great national president, who had transmitted the order to them had said nothing about that, nor explained how the branches might be bound close against the trunk by winding a rope around them.

Christmas morning came. Several Americans defied the tropical sun to direct the labors of another band of blacks engaged in planting a diminutive pine-tree with a few scattered twigs at its top, and to hide its nudity beneath another tree of tropical luxuriance, out on the glaringly bare Champs de Mars before the grand stand from which the élite of Port au Prince watches its president decorate its national heroes after a successful revolution. The rotarians of color could not, of course, be expected to appear at such a place in the heat of the day.

The ceremony was set for five o'clock, and was expected to last until nine. The American Electric Light Company had contributed the illumination, and its manager had installed the festoons of colored lamps in person. The American chief of police had assigned a force of native gendarmes to the duty of keeping order. It would be almost their first test of handling a friendly crowd in a friendly manner. Hitherto their task had been to hunt down their *caco* fellows with rifle and revolver, an occupation far better fitted to their temperament and liking. An American of benevolent impulses had consented to play Santa Claus, and give the little black urchins a real Christmas, with all the trimmings.

Poor Santa Claus did not get time even to don his whiskers. By two the crowd began to gather. By three all the populace of Port au Prince's humble sections had massed about the tree which the incomprehensible *blancs* had planted for the occasion instead of performing their strange rites under one of the many live trees with which the city abounded. Word had been sent out that full dress was not essential. Old women who had barely two strips of rag to hang over their dangling breasts, boys whose combined garments did not do the duty of a pair of swimming-trunks, had tramped up from their primitive hovels on the edges of the city. If they were ragged far beyond the northern meaning of that term, at least their strings and tatters were as clean as water and sun-bleaching could make them.   The women and most of the men carried or dragged whole clusters of black babies, most of them as innocent of clothing as a Parisian statue.   As they arrived, the children were herded within the roped inclosure about the tree.   Only adults with infants in arms were permitted inside the ropes; the jet-black sea of small faces was unbroken clear around the wide seething circle.   It was hard to believe that there were so many piccaninnies in the world, to say nothing of the mere half-island of Haiti.   Outside the ropes an immense throng of adults, mingled with better-dressed children without tickets, was shrieking a constant falsetto tumult that made the ear-drums of those in the focus of sound under the tree vibrate as if their ears were being incessantly boxed.   A " conservative estimate " set the number present at ten thousand.

Up to this point the gentlemen of color, even those who had been appointed on the original committee, had kindly refrained from inter-ference with their more Christmas-experienced white associates — ex-cept in the aforementioned matter of tickets.   Now they appeared en masse to give the distinction of their presence and the sanction of their high caste to so praiseworthy an undertaking.   Cabinet ministers, newspaper editors, the bright lights of the Haitian bar, the very presi-dent of the republic, strutted down the human lanes that were opened in their honor and took the chief places of vantage on the distributing platform beneath the tree.   Their dazzling *dernier cri* garments made the simple American committeemen look like the discards of fortune. Their features were wreathed in benign smiles.   They stepped forth to the edges of the platform and waved majestic, benevolent greetings to their applauding constituents outside the ropes.   Some one handed the president a toy horn.   He put it to his lips and blew an imaginary blast to prove what a *bonhomme* he was at heart and how thoroughly he entered into the prevailing spirit.   The other gentlemen of color as-sumed Napoleonic poses; they raised their voices in oratorical cadences, and, when these failed to penetrate the unceasing din, they waved their hands at the heaps of gifts about them with sweeping gestures that said as plainly as if they had spoken in their impeccable French, " See, my beloved people, what *I*, in my bounty, have bestowed upon you!"

Soon after four the minister of public works snatched up a bundle of presents and flung them out into the sweltering sea of upturned little faces.   That was neither the hour nor the manner of distribution that had been agreed upon, but what should a great political genius know of such minor details? Besides, there was no hope of delaying the ceremony much longer. The surging throng was in no mood to watch the absurd antics of the unfathomable white people, with their patched-up tree and their queer ideas of order and equal distribution. What they wanted were the presents, and at once. Those behind were already climbing over those in front in an effort to get at the heaped-up wares. If the original plan of waiting until nightfall and the colored lights had been carried out, the gifts would probably have disappeared in a general mêlée.

The *beau geste* of the Rotary vice-president was a signal for all his yellow confrères to distribute largess to their clamoring constituents. In vain did the white women attempt to exchange gifts for tickets, according to the system they had worked out. Their kinky-haired associates would have no such restrictions. As long as a hand was held out to them they continued to thrust gifts into it, perfectly indifferent to other hands clutching tickets that were being wildly flourished about them. There were presents of every possible usefulness to Haitian poverty — shoes, stockings, hats, shirts, suits, collars, ties, bales of cloth cut in sizes for varying ages of children's garments, candy, toys, food stuffs ranging all the way from cakes to cans of sardines. The plan had been to gage each gift by the appearance of the recipient. There was nothing particularly Santa Claus-like in handing a necktie to a boy who had not shirt enough to which to attach a collar, nor in wishing a pair of stockings off on a youth whose feet had never known the imprisonment of shoes. Stark-naked black babies whose ribs could be counted at a hundred paces were not so much in need of an embroidered sailor-blouse as of a tin of biscuits. But all this meant nothing to the excited Haitians on the platform. They poured out gifts as if the horn of plenty were their own private property. The ministers caught up whole armfuls of presents and flung them clear over the heads of the invited children into the shrieking mobs beyond the ropes. The adults out there were far more likely to vote for them at the next elections than were the half-starved urchins beneath them. One cabinet member was seen to toss bundle after bundle to an extraordinarily tall negro who was known to wield great political power among the masses. Meanwhile the helpless little urchins within the circle rolled their white eyes in despair and frantically waved the tickets clutched in their little black hands, until they went down under the bare feet of those fighting forward behind them.

The native gendarmes in their uniforms so like that of the American marines were preserving order ·much as the pessimists had predicted. One of them, starched and ironed to the minute, approached an American distributor and asked, with the sweet-faced courtesy of a Southern lady of the old school, for one of the riding-whips which some merchant had contributed. " Here's a fine fellow," said the unadorned Santa Claus to himself, " a real soldier. He wants a whip to use on mounted duty, and so gentle-mannered a chap will make only proper use of it." The gendarme accepted the gift with a polite bow and a grateful smile and marched back across the ring — to strike full in the face with all his force a pitiful old black woman who was being forced forward by the crush behind, and to rain blow after blow on her bare head and breast and on the naked infant she had brought on the invitation of the ticket clutched in its tiny hand. What was the good of protesting? ·He had been ordered to hold back the crowd, and as he had been forbidden to use the revolver strapped at his side, how else could he do so? If he had been checked in his onslaught, he would have spent the rest of the afternoon wondering what these strange Americans wanted, anyway.

By dint of superhuman exertions the white distributors succeeded in exchanging something or other for every ticket. But it was a sadly misgifted swarm of children who finally rescued themselves from the maelstrom. Tiny tots who had set their hearts on a cake or a package of candy held up the neckties they knew no use for with a *" Pas bon pour moi! Donne gateau!"* The greatest demand was for shoes. *" Non, non, papa! soulier, soulier!"* came incessant shrieks from the urchins who waved unwelcome gifts before the weary distributors. The gentlemen of color had continued to strew armfuls of presents upon the throng beyond the ropes. The minister with the lanky confederate had tossed him assorted wares enough to break the back of a Haitian donkey — a feat verging on the impossible. When there was nothing else left, he flung him several huge native baskets which a lady of the committee had loaned for the occasion. These he followed with the decorations snatched from the tree. Then he took to unscrewing from their sockets the electric light bulbs belonging to the company that had contributed the useless illuminations. This was too much even for the benevolent-featured man who had been cast for the rôle of Santa Claus. He gathered the slack of the minister's immaculate trousers in one hand and set him down out of reach of further temptation.

The festivities were entirely over by the time the blazing-red tropical sun sank behind the mountainous range to the westward. The throng streamed out across the Champs de Mars like a lake of molten lead that had long been dammed up and had suddenly broken its dikes. Not a scrap even of the tickets that had been canceled by being torn in two remained. In Haiti everything has its commercial value. For days to come little heaps of these bits of cardboard would be offered for sale by the incredibly ragged old women of the more miserable market-places, to be made use of the voodoo gods know how. Among the last of the gentlemen of color to leave the platform was a pompous being resplendent in Port au Prince's most fashionable raiment. He was a graduate of the Sorbonne, a political power in the Black Republic, an officer of the Rotary Club, and the editor of Haiti's principal newspaper. In one hand, which he held half concealed beneath the tails of his frock-coat, he grasped a dozen bright-colored hair-ribbons and several silk handkerchiefs which he had filched from the basket of presents that had been intrusted to him for distribution.

CHAPTER VI

THE DEATH OF CHARLEMAGNE

THE word *caco* first appears in Haitian history in 1867. The men who took to the bush in the insurrection against President Salnave adopted that pseudonym, and nicknamed *zandolite* those who supported the government. The semi-savage insurrectionists, flitting at will through the rugged interior of the country, indifferent alike to the thorny jungle and the precipitous mountains, saw in themselves a likeness to the Haitian bird which flies freely everywhere, and in their opponents a similarity to the helpless caterpillars on which it feeds. The two terms have persisted to this day.

Haiti has never since been entirely free from *cacos*, though there have been occasional short periods when the country has been spared their ravages. Let a new president lose his popularity, however, or some ambitious rascal raise the banner of revolt, and the bandit-revolutionists were quick to flock together, beginning their operations as soon as the mangos were ripe enough to furnish them subsistence. With the exception of a few ephemeral leaders with more or less of the rudiments of education, the *cacos* are a heterogeneous mob of misguided wretches who have been cajoled or forced into revolt by circumstances of coercion. Ragged, penniless, illiterate fellows in the mass, they gather in bands varying from a score to thousands in number, depending on the reputation, persuasiveness, or power of compulsion of their self-appointed leaders. The latter, though in some cases men of standing, are more often as illiterate as their followers. Now and again one of them, usually with some Caucasian blood in his veins, has personal ambitions either of making himself President of Haiti in the long-approved manner, or at least of becoming powerful enough to force the Government to appoint him ruler of a province or of a smaller district. Others are merely the agents of disgruntled politicians or influential " respectable citizens " of Port au Prince or others of the larger cities, who secretly supply funds to the active insurrectionists.

The backwardness and poverty of Haiti are largely due to the con-

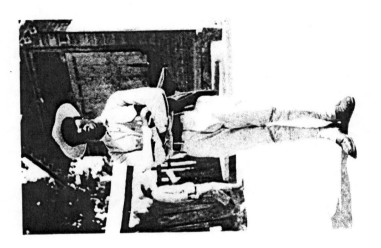

A Haitian gendarme

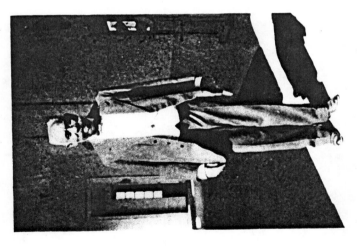

The president of Haiti

A street in Port au Prince

The unfinished presidential palace of Haiti, on New Year's Day, 1920

stant menace of these roving outlaws. Travel has often entirely disappeared from many a trail; more than one fertile region has been left wholly uncultivated and virtually uninhabited because of marauding bands of *cacos*. Cattle, once plentiful throughout the republic, have almost wholly disappeared, thanks to the fact that their flesh furnishes the chief means of livelihood and their hides the one sure source of income for the bandits. The depredations of the *cacos* have cost the Black Republic most of its wealth and the greater share of its worldly troubles.

Some two years after American occupation *cacoism* took on a new life. In perfect frankness it must be admitted that this was partly the fault of the Americans. Next to the cleaning up of Port au Prince the most important job on hand was the building of roads. If Haiti is to take her place even at the tail end of civilization, she must become self-supporting — in other words, able to pay her foreign debts, both public and commercial. The prosperity of French days, when the island exported large quantities of coffee, sugar, and cotton, has as completely disappeared under the anarchy of the blacks as have the old plantations. What little the country might still export, consisting mainly of coffee, could not get down to tide-water for lack of highways, those which the French built having been wholly overgrown by the militant jungle.

In their eagerness to furnish the country with this first obvious step to advancement the forces of occupation resurrected an old French law called the *corvée*. We still have something of the sort in many of our own rural districts — the requirement that every citizen shall work a certain number of days a year on the roads. But there is a wide difference between the public-spirited Americans and the wild black men into which the mass of Haitians has degenerated. Neither they nor their ancestors for several generations have seen the need of roads, at least anything more than trails wide enough along which to chase their donkeys. But they probably would have endured the resurrected *corvée* had it been applied in strict legality, a few days' labor in their own locality, instead of being carried out with too energetic a hand. When they were driven from their huts at the point of a gendarme rifle, transported, on their own bare feet, to distant parts of the country, and forced to labor for weeks under armed guards, it is natural that they should have concluded that these new-coming foreigners with white skins were planning to reduce them again to the slavery they had thrown off more than a century before. The result was that a certain percentage of the forced laborers caught up any weapon at hand and took to the hills as *cacos*. If they have any definite policy, it is to imitate their forefathers and drive the white men from the island. One chief announced the program of killing off the American men and carrying their women off to the hills. The mass of Haitians believe that the world's supply of white men is very limited; it is beyond their conception that there are many fold more of them where these came from. Their ancestors drove out the French, and they not only did not come back, but the blacks were never subjected to any punishment — at least any their simple minds could recognize as such — for their revolt. Why could not a new Toussaint l'Ouverture accomplish the feat over again?

Our mistake in the matter has been corrected. The American officer who countenanced, if he did not sanction, these high-handed methods has gone to new honors on other fields of battle; the young district commanders whose absolute power led them to apply too sternly their orders to build roads have returned to the ranks, and the *corvée* has been abolished. But the scattered revolt persists, and in the opinion of all but a few temperamentally optimistic residents, either Haitian or American, is due to continue for some time to come. That forced labor was not the cause of *cacoism*, for it is in the Haitian blood to turn *caco;* but it made a fertile field of ignorant, disgruntled negroes from which the bandit leaders were able to harvest most of their followers, and it gave added strength to the chief argument of the rascally leaders — the assertion that the Americans had come to take possession of Haiti and reëstablish slavery. To this day even the foreign companies which have no trouble in recruiting labor for other purposes cannot hire the workmen needed to build their roads. The thick-skulled native countrymen see in that particular task the direct route to becoming slaves.

For more than two years courageous young Americans have been chasing *cacos* among the hills of central and northern Haiti, with no other ulterior motive than to give the Black Republic the internal peace it has long lacked and sadly needed. All of them are members of our Marine Corps, though many of them are in addition officers of the Gendarmerie of Haiti, with increased rank and pay. Take care not to confuse these two divisions of pacifiers, for the gendarmerie has a strong *esprit de corps,* and a just pride in its own achievements, in spite of being still marines at heart. For a long time the native gendarmes, of whom twenty-five hundred, officered by marine enlisted men, have been recruited by our forces of occupation, were efficient against the bandits only when personally led by Americans. Merely to shout the word *"Caco!"* has long been sufficient to stampede a Haitian gathering of any size. Bit by bit, however, the gendarmes have been taught by practical demonstration that they are better men than the *cacos,* and the immediate job of hunting down the bandits is gradually being turned over to these native soldiers. American supervision, nevertheless, for years to come will certainly be necessary to eventual success.

Though the world has heard little of it, our *caco*-hunters have performed feats that compare with anything done by their fellows in France. In fact, their work has often required more sustained courage and individual initiative, and has brought with it greater hardships. In the trenches at their worst the warrior had the support and the sense of companionship of his comrades and a more or less certain commissary at the rear; if his opponents were sometimes brutal, they clung to some of the rules of civilized warfare. In Haiti many a young American gendarme officer has set forth on an expedition of long duration through the mountainous wilderness, often wholly alone, except for three or four native gendarmes, cousins to the *cacos* themselves, sleeping on the bare ground when he dared to sleep at all, subsisting on the scanty products of the jungle, his life entirely dependent on his own wits, and his nerves always taut with the knowledge that to be wounded or captured means savage torture and mutilation, to be followed by certain death. Bit by bit the native gendarmes have been trained to fight the *cacos* unassisted, and three or four of them have now reached commissioned rank; but the best of them still require the moral support of a white leader, and the energetic American youths scattered through the " brush " of Haiti have the future peace of the country in their keeping.

It must be admitted that the *cacos* do not constitute a dangerous army in the modern sense of the word. Their discipline is less than embryonic, their weapons seldom better than dangerous playthings. One rifle to five men is the average equipment, and many of these are antiquated pieces captured from the French expeditionary force under Leclerc that was driven from the island more than a century ago. Some of them are of no more use than the *cocomacaque,* or Haitian shillalah, even when their possessors can obtain ammunition. Such cartridges as fall into the hands of the *cacos* are usually wrapped round and round with paper to make them fit the larger bore of their ancient guns, and the

bullet that comes zigzagging down the barrel is seldom deadly beyond
two hundred yards.   But the possession of a rifle, even one worthless
as a firearm, is a sign of leadership that carries with it great personal
pride, and an occasional *caco* owns a high-powered modern carbine.
The mass of them are armed with machetes, rusty swords of the olden
days, or revolvers even more useless than the rifles.

The lesser military ranks are not in favor among the *cacos*.   Every
leader of a band is a general, and usually a major general at that.
Most of them have been commissioned by the *caco*-in-chief — on a slip
of paper scrawled with a rusty pen, or even with a pencil, by the one
man on his staff who can write a more or less legible hand.   These
" commissions " all follow the prescribed form which has been stereotyped in Haiti since the days of Dessalines:

" Liberté   Egalité   Fraternité
                    République d'Haiti

Informé que vous réunissez les conditions et aptitudes voulues —
Informed that you possess the qualifications and aptitude desired, I
hereby appoint you general of division operating against the Americans
and direct that you proceed with your troops to attack " — this or that
hamlet or village in the hills.   The expression " Opérant contre les
américains " is seldom lacking in these scribbled rags, and some of them
raise the holder to higher dignities than were ever reached by mere
field marshals on the battle-grounds of Europe.   The " commission,"
for instance, of the " Chief of Intelligence " of the *caco*-in-chief reads
succinctly, " I name you as chief of the Division of Spies to spy everywhere " — an order that has at least the virtue of leaving the recipient
unhampered with that division of responsibility which has been the
bane of civilized warfare.   Incidentally the intelligence system of the
cacos is their strongest point.   Like most uncivilized tribes the world
over, they have some means of spreading information that makes the
telegraph and even the radio seem slow and inefficient by comparison.
An uninformed stranger, reading these highfalutin' " commissions,"
might easily picture the *caco* " generals " as mightier men than Foch
and Pershing combined, instead of what they really are, stupid, uneducated negroes dressed in the dirty remnants of an undershirt and
cotton trousers, a discard straw or felt hat with a bit of red rag sewed
on it as a sign of rank, and armed with a rusty old saber or a revolver
that has long since lost its power to revolve.

The *cacos* have a mortal fear of white soldiers. Scores of times a single marine or gendarme officer has routed bands of a hundred or more, killing as many as his automatic rifle could reach in the short period between their first glimpse of him and the time it takes the ragged "army" to scatter to the four points of the compass through thorny undergrowth or cactus-hedges which no white man could penetrate though all the forces of evil were pursuing him. The natives cannot "savez" this uncanny prowess of *les blancs,* and commonly attribute it to the sustaining force of some voodoo spirit friendly to the white man. This belief is to a certain extent a boomerang, for the Haitian gendarmes often fancy themselves immune in the presence of a white superior, and more than one of them has bitten the dust because he insisted on calmly standing erect, smoking a cigarette, and placidly handing cartridges to the marine who lay hugging the ground beside him, pumping lead into the fleeing *cacos.* With a white man along how could he be hurt? Up to date at least three thousand bandits have been killed as against four Americans, — a major and a sergeant who were shot from ambush, and two privates who lost their lives by over-confidence.

Captured correspondence shows what a terrible war is this *guerre des cacos:*

"The Americans," reads the report of one *général de division* to his superior, "attacked us in force on the night of the 13–14th. I found myself with a shortage of ammunition, but I succeeded in borrowing ten carbine cartridges and three revolver bullets and was able to hold the situation in hand." As a matter of fact the American "force" consisted on this particular occasion of three marines, and the "general" "held the situation in hand" by scurrying away through the mountains so fast that it was a week or more before he got any considerable number of his band together again.

"I write to tell you," says another great military genius, "that I had a cruel battle before Las Cahobas the other day, with one wounded. I also tell you that I arrested General Ulysses St. Raisin for being drunk and disarmed him and he is under guard in my camp. Also that General Etienne Monbrun Dubuisson had a big battle with the Americans last week and besides having a soldier severely wounded he had one *délégué* taken by the whites."

The Americans who are striving to bring internal peace to Haiti have come to the unanimous conclusion that the mere killing of *cacos* will not wipe out banditism. They have hunted them by every available means, including the use of aëroplanes. The *cacos* show a whole-some terror for the latter, which they call " God's wicked angels " ; they have suffered " cruel " losses before the machine-guns of the deter-mined American youths who are pursuing them, but they continue their *cacoism*. All efforts are now being bent to two ends — to kill off the chiefs and to weed the country of firearms. In the early days of the occupation the native caught in possession of a rifle was given five years at hard labor, and many of them are still serving sentence, though the penalty has recently been reduced to six months. Every report of " jumping " a band or a camp of *cacos* ends now with a regu-lar formula in which only the numbers differ: " Killed 1 general and 2 chiefs; captured 9 rifles, 6 swords, 11 machetes."

The tendency of the *caco* to use his rifle chiefly as ballast to be thrown overboard when the appearance of a white soldier gives his black legs their maximum speed has helped this weeding out of weapons, as the time-honored Haitian custom for opposing warriors to mount a prominent hillock and hurl foul-mouthed defiance at their foes has raised the scores of American marksmen. Recently an intelligent propaganda has been carried on by the gendarmerie to induce the misled rank and file to come in and surrender their arms, receiving in exchange a small cash equivalent and a card attesting them *bons habitants*. This offer of amnesty, which has already shown gratifying results, is brought to the attention of the bandits chiefly through the market-women, who, swarming all over Haiti, have always been the chief channel of infor-mation for the *cacos,* with whom they are in the main friendly despite having frequently been robbed of their wares by some hungry " army." The chief drawback to this plan, however, is a certain lack of team-work between the two corps of caco-hunters. The marines have orders to shoot on sight any native carrying a rifle — a perfectly justifiable command, since there is no other distinguishing mark between a *bon habitant* and a *caco*. But the result is that the chief who has deter-mined that surrender to the nearest gendarme officer is the better part of valor, or the *caco* " volunteer " who has at last succeeded in eluding his own sentries, is forced to wrap his weapon in banana-leaves and sneak up to within a few miles of town, hide his firearm, and apply at the gendarmerie for a native soldier to protect him while he goes to get it.

In most cases the bandits travel in small groups until called together for some projected attack. But more than one permanent camp, veritable towns in some cases, has been found tucked away in some mountainous retreat. The latest of these to be destroyed had seventy-five houses, a headquarters building (with two hundred chairs), a voodoo temple, and a cockpit; for the *caco* remains a true Haitian for all his *cacoism*, and will not be separated from his voodoo rites, his fighting cock, and his women except in case of direst necessity.

Of many courageous feats performed by the American youths in khaki who are roaming the hills of Haiti one stands out as the most spectacular. Indeed, it is fit to rank with any of the stirring warrior tales with which history is seasoned from the days of the Greeks to the recent World War. Hearing it, one might fancy he was listening to a story of the black ages of Haiti when Christophe was ruling his sable brethren with bloody hand, rather than to something accomplished a bare half-year ago by a persevering young American.

Charlemagne Masena Péralte was a member of one of the two families that have long predominated in the village of Hinche. He was what the Haitians call a *griffe*, a three-fourths negro. The French priest with whom he served as choir-boy and acolyte remembers him well as " a boy who was not bad, but haughty and quick to take offense." When he had learned what the thatched schoolhouse of Hinche had to offer, Charlemagne was sent to Port au Prince, where he finished the course given by French ecclesiastics. In other words he was a man of education by Haitian standards. Like many of the sons of the " best families " in Haiti, he decided to go into politics rather than pursue a more orderly profession. But politicians are thicker than mangos in the Black Republic, and for some reason things did not break right for Charlemagne. Wounded in his pride and denied his expected source of easy income, he followed the long-established Haitian custom in such matters. He gathered a band of malcontents and penniless *cacos* about him and marched against the capital. The Government realized the danger and bought Charlemagne off by appointing him commandant of an important district. A few years later, when a new turn of the political wheel left him again among the " outs," he followed the same route to another official position. It got to be a habit with Charlemagne to force each succeeding government to appoint him to office.

Finding himself in disfavor with the American occupation, he set out to work his little scheme once more. It does not seem to have occurred to him that conditions had changed. Captured, and convicted of *cacoism* in October, 1917, by an American court martial sitting in his native town of Hinche, he was sentenced to five years at hard labor.

A year later, while working on the roads in company with other inmates of the departmental prison at Cap Haïtien, he eluded his gendarme guards and escaped. Taking to the bush, he set out to organize a new band of *cacos*. The *corvée*, then at its height, made his task easier. To turn the scales still more in his favor, the large gang working on the highway at Dignon, near his home town, had not been paid in more than three months, thanks to that stagnation of circulation to which quartermaster departments are frequently subject. " Come along," said Charlemagne, " and *I'll* get you your money," and some three hundred disgruntled workmen followed him into the mountains.

Within a few months he was signing himself " Chief of the Revolutionary Forces against the American nation on the soil of Haiti," and had gathered several thousand *cacos* about him. The magic name of General Charlemagne spread throughout the island. Every leader of a collection of lawless ragamuffins sought to be " commissioned " by him. He appointed more generals than ever did a European sovereign. Every lazy black rascal with nothing to lose and everything to gain joined his growing ranks. When the simple countrymen would not follow him by choice, they were recruited by force. He assassinated and punished until his word became law to any one out of reach of gendarme protection. He spread propaganda against the American officers, asserted that they had orders to annex the country, and posed as the savior of Haiti, calling upon the people to help him drive out the white oppressors as their fathers had done more than a century before.

As a matter of fact, the patriotism of Charlemagne, of which he constantly boasted in pompous words, consisted of nothing more or less than an exaggerated ego and an overwhelming desire to advance his own personal interests. He had that in common with all the yellow politicians of Haiti. But he played the patriotic card with unusual success. Disgruntled politicians and men of wealth who had some personal reason for wishing the occupation abolished gave him secret aid. The simple mountain negroes really believed that they were fighting to free Haiti from the white man, and that under the great General Charlemagne the task would soon be accomplished. The *corvée* happened to have been abolished soon after the " general's " escape from prison; he quickly took personal credit for the change and promised the simple Haitians to free them in the same manner of all foreign interference. Before the end of 1918 he attacked his native town with several thousand followers and was not easily repulsed. It was decided to put the marines in the field against him, and for eight months they pursued him in vain. If anything, the *caco* situation was becoming worse instead of better. Despite the " jumping " of many a band and camp by the marines and the gendarmerie, the central portion of the country was becoming more and more bandit-ridden. It became apparent that the pacification of Haiti depended chiefly on the elimination of Charlemagne.

Herman H. Hanneken was a typical young American who had joined the Marine Corps soon after finishing at the preparatory school on the corner of Cass and Twelfth streets in his native town of St. Louis. After taking part in the Vera Cruz demonstration, he was sent to Haiti with the first forces of occupation, in August, 1915. There he reached the rank of sergeant, and in due time became in addition a captain in the Gendarmérie d'Haïti. It was in the latter rather than the former capacity that he took part in the little episode I am attempting to report, which was strictly an affair of the gendarmerie as distinguished from their brotherly rivals in arms, the marines.

In June, 1919, Captain Hanneken was appointed district commander, with headquarters in the old town of Grande Rivière, famous in Haitian military and political annals. A powerful fellow of more than six feet, who had reached the advanced age of twenty-five, he was ideal material for the making of a successful *caco*-hunter. Having recently returned from leave in the States, however, and his former stations having been in peaceful regions, he had little field experience in the extermination of bandits. Moreover, his extreme modesty and inability to blow his own horn had never called him particularly to the attention of the higher officials of the gendarmerie. No one expected him to do more than rule his station with the average high efficiency which is taken for granted in any of the hand-picked marines who are detailed as gendarme officers.

Captain Hanneken, however, had higher ambitions. Having familiarized himself in a month with the routine of his district, he found time weighing heavily on his hands. He turned his attention to the then most pressing duty in Haiti, the elimination of Charlemagne. Unfortunately for his plans, there were almost no *cacos* in the district of Grande Rivière. He could not encroach upon the territory of his fellow-officers ; the only chance of " getting a crack " at the bandits was to import some of them into his own region.

Jean Batiste Conzé, a native of Grande Rivière, was a *griffe*, like Charlemagne; he also belonged to one of the "best families" of his home town.   But there his similarity with the chief of the *cacos* ceased. He had always been a law-abiding citizen, and had once been chief of police on his native heath.   Like all good Haitians, he realized the damage and suffering which the continued depredations of the bandits were causing his country.   Moreover, he was at a low financial ebb; but that is too general a condition in Haiti to call for special comment, beyond stating that a reward of two thousand dollars had been offered for Charlemagne, dead or alive.

One night Captain Hanneken asked Conzé to call upon him at his residence.   When he was certain that the walls had been shorn of their ears, he addressed his visitor in the Haitian "creole," which he had learned to speak like a native:

"Conzé, I want you to go and join the *cacos*."

" 'Aiti, mon capitaine!" cried Conzé, "Moi, toujou' bon habitant, de bonne famille, me faire *caco?*"

"Exactly," replied Hanneken; "I want you to become a *caco* chief. I will furnish you whatever is necessary to gather a good band of them about you, and you can take to the hills and establish a camp of your own."

The conference lasted well into the night, whereupon Conzé consented, and left the captain's residence through the back garden in order to call as little attention as possible to his visit.   A few days later, toward the middle of August, he disappeared from town, carrying with him in all secrecy fifteen rifles that had once been captured from the *cacos*, 150 rounds of ammunition, several swords, and a showy pearl-handled revolver that belonged to Hanneken.   He was well furnished, too, with money and rum, the chief sinews of war among the *cacos*.   With him had gone a personal friend and a trusted native gendarme who was forthwith rated a deserter on the captain's roster.

Conzé took pains to be seen by the worst native element as he was leaving town, among whom he had already spread propaganda calling upon them to join him in a new *caco* enterprise.   On the road he held up the market-women and several travelers, taking nothing from them, but impressing upon them the fact that he had turned bandit.   All this was reported to Captain Hanneken by his secret police.   He told them to keep their ears open, but not to worry, that he would get the rascal all in good season.   One morning a written notice appeared in the market of Grande Rivière. It was signed by Conzé and berated the commander of the district in violent terms, calling upon the inhabitants to join the writer and put an end to his oppression. People recalled that Conzé and the big American ruler of the town had once had words over some small matter. Within three days the talk in all the district was of this member of one of Grande Rivière's most prominent families who had turned *caco*.

Specially favored by his rifles, rum, and apparently unlimited funds, Conzé soon gathered a large band of real *cacos* about him. When questions were asked, he explained that he had captured the weapons from the gendarmerie by a happy fluke, and the wealthy citizens of Grande Rivière, disgusted with the exactions of American rule, were furnishing him with money. The new army established a camp at Fort Capois, at the top of a high hill five hours' walk from Grande Rivière. Now and then they made an attack in the neighborhood, Conzé keeping a secret list of those who suffered serious damage and never allowing his men to give themselves over to the drunken pillaging that is so common to *caco* warfare. The people accounted for this by recalling that Conzé had always been a more kindly man than the average bandit leader. Meanwhile the new chief continued his recruiting propaganda. He made personal appeals to those of lawless tendency, he induced several smaller bands to join him, he sent scurrilous personal attacks on Captain Hanneken to be read in the market-place. The law-abiding citizens of Grande Rivière, well aware of the advantages of American occupation and fearful of a *caco* raid, appealed to the district commander to drive the new band out of the region. Hanneken reassured them in a special meeting of the town notables with the assertion that he already had a scheme on foot that would settle that rascal Conzé.

At the same time he had as many real worries as the good citizens, though of a different nature. The first was a threat by the nearest marine commander to wipe out that camp at Fort Capois if the strangely laggard gendarme officer did not do so. It would have been fatal to Hanneken's plans to take the marines into his confidence; the merest whisper of a rumor travels with lightning speed in Haiti. Besides Conzé and his friend the gendarme " deserter," the only persons whom he had let into the secret were his department commander and the chief of the gendarmerie in Port au Prince. Even his own subordinate officers were kept wholly ignorant of the real state of affairs. In spite of this extreme care, he was annoyed by persistent rumors that the whole thing was a " frame-up." Conzé, ran the market-place gossip, was really a *zandolite,* a "caterpiller" in the pay of the Government and the Americans. General Charlemagne, stationed far off in the district of Mirebalais, had been warned to look out for him, a more or less unnecessary "tip," since it is natural to Haitian chiefs to be suspicious of their fellows. In vain Conzé sent letters written by his secretary, the "deserted" gendarme, in proper *caco* style — most of them dictated by Hanneken — to the big chief, offering the assistance of his growing band. For a month he received no reply whatever. Then Charlemagne wrote back in very courteous terms, lauding Conzé's conversion to the cause of Haitian liberty, but constantly putting him off on one polite pretext or another. These letters, always sent by women of *caco* sympathies, were a week or more old before the replies came back through devious bandit channels, and the situation often changed materially within that length of time, up-setting Hanneken's plans. Meanwhile Conzé cleared the region about him, built houses for his soldiers, and made Fort Capois the talk of all the *cacos.* Each new recruit was given a draft of rum and what seemed to him a generous cash bounty, and better food was served than most of them had tasted in their lives. Still Charlemagne would have nothing to do with him beyond the exchange of polite, non-committal notes.

At length the *caco*-in-chief sent one of his trusted subordinates to report on the situation at Fort Capois. General 'Tijacques marched into Conzé's camp one evening at the head of seventy-five well-armed followers, every man with a shell in his chamber. His air was more than suspicious, and he ended by openly accusing Conzé of being a *zandolite.*

"If I am, go ahead and shoot me!" cried the latter, laying aside his weapons and ordering his men to withdraw. 'Tijacques declined the invitation, but all night long he and his men sat about the fire, their weapons in their hands, while Conzé slept with the apparent innocence of a babe. When morning broke without an attack upon him, 'Tijacques was convinced. He kissed Conzé on both cheeks, complimented him on joining the "army of liberation," and welcomed him as a brother in arms. When Conzé presented him with a badly needed suit of clothes, a still more desired bottle of rum, and money enough to pay his troops a week's salary of ten cents each, he left avowing eternal friendship.

A day or two later Charlemagne sent another of his generals, Papil-

lon, on a secret mission to arrest Conzé and bring him to his own
camp. It was merely a lucky coincidence that Hanneken had decided
on that very night to "attack" Fort Capois, as he had already done
several times before. Conzé, who made three nightly journeys a week
to Grande Rivière on the pretext of getting more money from the inhabitants friendly to his cause, and entered Hanneken's house through
the back garden, was instructed how to conduct himself in the affair
to avoid personal injury. For all that, the American had hard work
to keep his gendarmes from wiping out the camp entirely. In the
midst of the fighting he slipped aside in the bushes and, smearing his
left arm with red ink, wrapped it up in a bandage generously covered
with the same liquid. Then he sounded the retreat, and the gendarmes
fell back pell-mell on Grande Rivière. The next morning the market-
place was agog with the astonishing news. The *cacos* of Fort Capois
had repulsed the gendarmes! Moreover, the great Conzé himself
had wounded the redoubtable American captain! It would not be
long before the bandits descended on Grande Rivière itself! Some of
the frightened inhabitants seized their valuables and fled to Cap Haitien.

For days Captain Hanneken wandered disconsolately about the
town with his arm in a sling. When his own officers or friends joggled
against it by accident, he cried out with pain. His greatest difficulty
was to keep himself from being invalided to the rear, or to keep the
solicitous marine doctor from dressing his wounds. News of the
great battle quickly reached Charlemagne. Meanwhile the agent he
had sent to arrest Conzé met 'Tijacques on the trail.

"You're crazy!" cried the latter when Papillon whispered his orders. "Conzé is as sincere a *caco* as you or I. I will myself return to
Charlemagne and tell him so."

The report of 'Tijacques, added to the news that Conzé had wounded
the accursed American commander, as well as repulsing his force,
won the confidence of Charlemagne — with reservations, of course;
he never put full confidence in any one, being too well versed in Haitian
history. He invited Conzé to visit him at his headquarters. There he
commissioned him "General Jean," thanked him in the name of Haitian
liberty, and promised to coöperate with him. Incidentally, he relieved
him of the pearl-handled revolver that had once belonged to their common enemy, Hanneken. It was too fine a weapon to be carried by
any one but the commander-in-chief, he explained. Before they parted,
he promised the new general to join him some day in Fort Capois.

Meanwhile the "deserted" gendarme had joined Charlemagne's forces and had so completely won his confidence that he was made his private secretary. He found means of reporting conditions and plans now and then to Hanneken. Conzé and Charlemagne entered into correspondence in planning a general attack on Grande Rivière. Here Hanneken well knew that he was playing with fire. If anything went wrong and Grande Rivière was taken, nothing could keep the *cacos* out of Cap Haïtien, the second city of Haiti and the key to all the northern half of the country. Besides, how could he be sure that his agents were not "double-crossing" him instead of Charlemagne?

Negotiations continued all through the month of October. Toward the end of that month Charlemagne, his brother St. Remy Péralte, several other generals, and many chiefs arrived at Fort Capois, bringing with them twelve hundred bandits. In company with "General Jean" they planned a concerted attack on Grande Rivière. At the same time the programs of two other assaults, on the towns of Bahon and Le Trou, were set for the same date. The chief value of the latter was that they would keep the marines busy and leave the larger town to the protection of the gendarmes.

Charlemagne's forces were to approach Grande Rivière from the Fort Capois side and to charge across the river when they received the signal agreed upon. Conzé's men were to descend upon the city from the opposite direction, and "General Jean" was to give the signal himself by firing three shots from an old ruined fortress above the town. As it was well known that Charlemagne never attacked personally with his troops, but hung back safely in the rear, it had been arranged through Conzé that he await events at a place called Mazaire and enter the city in triumph after the news of its capture had been brought to him.

On the night set, the last one of October, Captain Hanneken ordered ten picked gendarmes to report at his residence. With them was his subordinate, Lieutenant William R. Button, who had just been let into the secret. The doors guarded against intrusion, Hanneken told the gendarmes to lay aside their uniforms and put on *caco*-like rags that had been gathered for the occasion. The two Americans dressed themselves in similar garments and rubbed their faces, hands, and such portions of their bodies as showed through the tatters, with cold cream and lamp-black. Then the detail sallied forth one by one, to meet at a place designated, where rifles that had been secretly conveyed there were issued to them.

The pretended *cacos* took up their post at Mazaire behind a bushy hedge along which Charlemagne must pass if he kept his rendezvous. While they lay there, Conzé and his following of real *cacos*, some seven hundred in number, passed close by them on their way to attack Grande Rivière. This had been reinforced with a large number of gendarmes and a machine-gun manned by Americans under the personal command of the Department Commander of the North, all barricaded in the market-place facing the river. Conzé gave the preconcerted signal, and Charlemagne's army dashed out of the foot-hills toward the stream. It was only the over-eagerness of the barricaded force, which failed to hold its fire long enough, that made the *caco* casualties number merely by the dozen rather than by the hundred.

At the height of the battle Charlemagne's private secretary, the " deserted " gendarme, crawled up to Hanneken and informed him that the *caco*-in-chief had changed his mind. With his extraordinary gift of suspicion, he had smelled a rat. He would not come down to Mazaire until the actual winner of the battle came to him to announce the capture of Grande Rivière.

To say that Captain Hanneken received the news quietly is merely another way of stating that he is not a profane man. Here he had planned and toiled for four months to do away with the arch *caco* and break the back of the rebellion that was holding up the advancement of Haiti, only to have all his plans fail through the over-suspicion of the outlaw politician. He had run the risk of having the headquarters of his district captured, with dire, far-reaching results that no one realized better than himself. He had played the part of a dime-novel hero, descended to the rôle of an actor, which his forceful, straightforward nature detested, only to be left the laughing-stock of his fellow-officers of the gendarmerie, to say nothing of the " kidding " Marine Corps, in which he was still a sergeant. Incidentally, he had staked the plan to the extent of eight hundred dollars of his own money, which there was no hope of recovering through the devious channels of official reimbursement if that plan failed, though as a matter of fact this latter detail was the least of his worries. It was not a question of a few paltry dollars, but of success.

If all these thoughts passed through his head as he lay concealed in the bushes with his dozen fake *cacos*, they passed quickly, for his next command came almost instantly. It was by no means the first time in this hide-and-seek game with Charlemagne that he had been forced to change his plans completely on the spur of the moment.

"Button," he whispered, "we will be the successful *caco* detachment that brings the news of the capture of Grande Rivière to Charlemagne."

Led by Jean Edmond François, the "deserted" gendarme and private secretary of the *caco*-in-chief, the little group set out into the mountains. Charlemagne, said the secretary, had come a part of the way down from Fort Capois, but had camped for the night less than halfway to the town. It was nearing midnight. Heavy clouds hung low in the sky, but the stars shone here and there through them. For three hours the detail stumbled upward along a difficult mountain trail. Neither of the Americans knew how soon the gendarmes would lose their nerve and slip off into the night, frightened out of all discipline by the dreaded name of Charlemagne. There was no positive proof that they were not themselves being led into an ambuscade, and they knew only too well the horrible end that would befall two lone Americans captured by the bandits. To make matters worse, Button was suffering from an acute attack of his old malaria, though he was too much a marine and a gendarme officer to let that retard his steps.

The detachment was halted at last by a *caco* sentry, who demanded the countersign. It happened that night to be "General Jean," in honor of Charlemagne's trusted — with reservations — ally, Conzé. François, the "deserted" gendarme, gave it. The sentry recognized him also as the private secretary of the great chief. He advanced him, but declined to let the detail with him pass without specific orders from Charlemagne. The secretary left his companions behind and hurried on.

The disguised gendarmes mingled with the *caco* outpost and announced the capture of Grande Rivière, adding that the population was eagerly waiting to receive the great Charlemagne and his doughty warriors. Shouts of triumph rose and spread away into the night. In all the years of American occupation no town of anything like the size of Grande Rivière had ever been taken by the *cacos*. It was the deathknell of the cursed whites, who would soon be driven from the great Republic of Haiti, as they had been many years before.

Nearly an hour after his departure the secretary returned, to report that Charlemagne had ordered the detachment to come to him immediately with the joyful news.

"But," added François, "there are *six* series of outposts between here and Charlemagne's headquarters. There isn't a chance in the world that we can pass them all without being detected, and *cacos* swarm everywhere along the trail. It is a question of turning back,

A Haitian country home

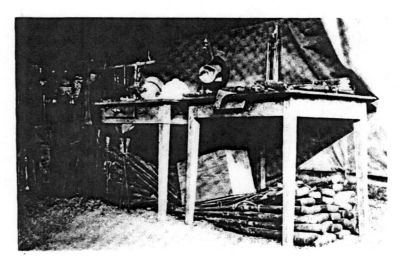

A small portion of one collection of captured *caco* war material

Captain Hanneken and "General Jean" Couze at Christophe's Citadel

The *caco* in the foreground killed an American Marine

mon Capitaine, or of leaving the trail and sneaking up over the mountain through the brush."

" And lose ourselves for good and all," added Hanneken, in his ready " creole." " Nothing doing. Take the lead and keep to the trail."

The first outpost advanced the detachment without question. The score of negroes who made it up seemed to be too excited with the taking of Grande Rivière to be any longer suspicious. Some five minutes later the group was again halted, this time by an outpost of some forty men. Their leader·scrutinized the newcomers carefully one by one as they passed, the latter, in turn, shuffling along with bowed heads, as if they were completely exhausted with the climb from Grande Rivière, which was not far from the truth. Several of the bandits along the way were heard to remark in their slovenly " creole," " *Bon dieu,* but those niggers are sure tired." The third and fourth outposts gave the party no trouble, beyond demanding the countersign, except that casual questions were flung at them by the *cacos* scattered along the trail. These the disguised gendarmes answered without arousing suspicion. Perfectly as he knew " creole," Hanneken avoided speaking whenever possible, and left the word to François, fearful of giving himself away by some hint of a foreign accent or a mischosen word from the southern dialect, with which he was more familiar. No white man, whatever his training, can equal the slovenly, thick-tongued pronunciation of the illiterate Haitian.

At the fifth outpost the leader was a huge, bulking negro as large as Hanneken, and he stood on the alert, revolver half raised, as the detail approached. The giving of the countersign did not seem to satisfy him. He looked Hanneken up and down suspiciously and asked him a question. The captain, pretending he was out of breath, mumbled an answer and stalked on. It happened to be his good luck that he is blessed with high cheek bones and a face that would not be instantly recognized as Caucasian on a dark night. Button, on the other hand, seemed to arouse new suspicion. He was carrying an automatic rifle and, in order to conceal the magazine, bore it vertically across his chest, his arms folded over it. The negro sentry caught the glint of the barrel and snatched Button by the arm.

" Where did you get such a fine-looking rifle? " he demanded.

Hanneken, scenting trouble, had halted several paces beyond, his hands on the butts of the revolver and the automatic which he carried on his respective hips. It would have been easy to kill the suspicious negro, but that would have been the end of his hopes of reaching

Charlemagne — and probably of the two Americans. For though the disguised gendarmes were all armed with carbines, they would have been no match for the swarms of *cacos* about them, even if their taut nerves did not give way in flight under the strain.

Button, however was equal to the occasion.

" Let me go! " he panted, jerking away from the negro leader. " Don't you see that my chief is getting out of sight? "

The black giant, still suspicious, yielded with bad grace, and the Americans hurried on. The sixth outpost was the immediate guard over Charlemagne, about thirty paces from where he had spread his blanket for the night. François gave the countersign, took two or three steps forward, whispered in Hanneken's ear, " he is up there," and slipped away into the bushes. The gendarmes had likewise disappeared. The Americans advanced to within fifteen feet of a faintly blazing camp-fire. On the opposite side of it a man stood erect, his silk shirt gleaming in the flickering light. He was peering suspiciously over the fire, trying to recognize the newcomers. A woman was kneeling beside the heap of fagots, coaxing it to blaze. A hundred or more *cacos* were lined up to the right, at a respectful distance from the peering chief.

Two negroes, armed with rifles, halted the Americans, at the same time cocking their pieces. Hanneken raised his black, invisible automatic and fired at the chief beyond the fire, at the same time shouting, " Let her go, Button! " in an instant the kneeling woman scattered the· fire with a sweeping gesture and plunged the spot in darkness. Button was spraying the line of *cacos* to the right with his machine-gun. The disguised gendarmes came racing up and lent new legs to the fleeing bandits. When a space had been cleared, Hanneken placed his handful of soldiers in a position to offset a counter-attack, and began groping about the extinguished fire. His hands encountered a dead body dressed in a silk shirt. This, however, was no proof that his mission had been accomplished. Some of Charlemagne's staff might have boasted silk shirts, also. He ran his hands down the body to a holster and drew out the pearl-handled revolver which he had loaned to Conzé, and which had been appropriated in turn by Charlemagne. The *caco*-in-chief had been shot squarely through the heart.

When daylight came, the hilltop was found to be strewn with the bodies of nine other bandits, while trails of blood showed that many more had dragged themselves off into the bushes. Among the wounded, it was discovered later, was St. Remy, the brother of Charlemagne, who afterward died of his wounds. The captured booty included nine rifles, three revolvers, two hundred rounds of ammunition, seven swords, fifteen horses and mules, and Charlemagne's voluminous correspondence. This latter was of special value, since it contained the names of the good citizens of Port au Prince and the other larger cities who had been financing the *caco*-in-chief. Most of them are now languishing in prison. But let me yield the floor to Captain Hanneken's official diary of the events that followed. Its succinctness is suggestive of the character of the man:

Nov. 1, 1919.— Killed Charlemagne Péralte, Commander-in-Chief of the bandits. Wounded St. Remy Péralte. Brought Charlemagne's body to Grande Rivière, arriving 9 A. M. Went to Cap Haitien with the body. Received orders to proceed to Fort Capois next morning. Went to Grande Rivière via handcar, arriving 9 P. M. Wrote report re death of Charlemagne. Left Grande Rivière with seven gendarmes, via handcar to Bahon, arriving midnight.

Nov. 2.— Left Bahon 1 A. M. with seven gendarmes. Arrived 200 yards from first outpost of Fort Capois at 5 A. M. Crawled to 150 yards from outpost and remained there until 6:30 A. M., waiting for detachment from Le Trou to attack at daybreak, when six bandits came in our direction. Opened fire, killing three. All bandits in various outposts retreated to main fort. Advanced and captured the first, second, and third outposts. Got within 300 yards of fort when they opened fire from behind a stonewall barricade. They fired a cannon and about 40 rifle shots. Crawled on our stomachs, no cover. Fired the machine gun and ordered the gendarmes to advance 15 yards and open fire. Kept this up until we arrived within 150 yards, when we espied the bandits escaping. Entered fort, burned all huts and outposts. Left Fort Capois at 9 A. M. Arrived in Grande Rivière 2 P. M., very tired.

The most exacting military superior cannot but have excused this last somewhat unmilitary remark. Fatigue does not rest long on Captain Hanneken's broad shoulders, however, and he soon had his district cleared again of the *cacos* he had imported for the occasion. The two-thousand-dollar reward was divided between Conzé and his one civilian assistant. Captain Hanneken, Lieutenant Button, and the gendarmes who accompanied them, were ordered to Port au Prince to be personally thanked by the President of Haiti and decorated with the Haitian *medaille d'honneur,* a ceremony against which the captain protested as a waste of time that he could better employ in hunting *cacos*. At this writing he is engaged again in his favorite sport in another district. His Marine Corps rank has been raised to that of second lieutenant, while Conzé has been appointed to the same grade in the Gendarmérie d'Haïti, with assignment to plain-clothes duty.

The death of Charlemagne has probably broken the back of *cacoism* in Haiti, though it has been by no means wiped out. Papillon, with 'Tijacques and several other rascals as chief assistants, is still roaming at large in the north, and the youthful Bénoit is terrorizing the mountainous region in the neighborhood of Mirebalais and Las Cahobas. But the gendarmerie, assisted by the Marine Corps, may be trusted to bring their troublesome careers to a close all in good season. One of the chief problems of the pacifiers at present is to convince the ignorant *caco* rank and file that the great Charlemagne is dead. His superstitious followers credit him with supernatural powers, and many a captured bandit, when asked who is now his commander-in-chief, still replies with faithful simplicity, " Mais, c'est Charlemagne." The public display of his body at Grande Rivière and Cap Haïtien produced an effect that will not soon be forgotten by those who witnessed it, but even that has not fully convinced the *cacos* hidden far away in the mountains. So great was the veneration, or, more exactly, perhaps, the superstition, in which he was held that it was found necessary to give him five fake funerals in as many different places, as a blind, and to bury his body secretly in the out-of-the-way spot, lest his grave become a shrine of pilgrimage for future *cacos*.

CHAPTER VII

OF many journeys about Haiti, usually by automobile and in the company of gendarme officers, the first was to the *caco*-infested district of Las Cahobas. A marine doctor bound on an inspection trip there had a seat left after his assistant and a native gendarme had been accommodated. Among the four of us there were as many revolvers and three rifles, all ready for instant action. One can, of course, hire private cars for a tour of Haiti, but quite aside from the decided expense, a Haitian chauffeur under military orders is much to be preferred to one who is subject to his own whims; moreover, there is much more to be seen and heard in gendarme company, and, lastly, if one chances to " pop off " a *caco*, there is not even the trouble of explaining, for one's companions will do that in their laconic report to headquarters.

There are few roads in the West Indies as crowded as that broad new highway across the plain which is a continuation of the wide main street of Port au Prince. By it all traffic from the north and west enters the capital. The overwhelming majority of travelers are market-women, most of them barefooted and afoot, but a large number are seated sidewise on their donkeys or small mules, balancing on their toes the slippers, which are never known to fall off under any provocation. Pedestrians carry their invariably heavy and cumbersome loads on their heads, the haughtier class in crude saddle-bags, and the sight of this river of jogging humanity, often completely filling the broad highway as far as it can be seen in the heat-hazy distance, is one of which we never tired as often as we rode out through it.

At the time of the outbreak against the French the population roughly was made up of thirty thousand whites, as many " people of color," and four hundred and fifty thousand blacks. There has been, of course, no census since that time, but signs indicate that Haiti has now two and a half million inhabitants, for however unproductive the semi-savage hordes may be in other ways, they are diligent in the process of multiplication. White people are more rare to-day, even if one count our forces of occupation, than before the revolt, the mixed race has not greatly increased, so that fully nine tenths of the population are full-blooded Africans.   Close observers are convinced that, thanks mainly to the constant revolutions, there are three females to every male, and of the latter a considerable number are now roaming the hills of the interior as *cacos*.   Furthermore, the men take little part in selling the country produce.   The result is that the stream of humanity pouring into the capital is almost entirely made up of jet-black women and girls.

The throng was particularly dense on the morning of our journey to Las Cahobas, for it was Friday, and the great weekly market in Port au Prince begins at dawn on Saturday morning.   An American once stationed himself at the typical negro arch of triumph, straddling the entrance from the Cul-de-Sac to the capital, and counted thirty thousand travelers in an hour, of whom all but about two hundred were market-women.   They were somewhat less multitudinous during our stay in Haiti, for the Americans had recently set a maximum scale of prices for food-stuffs, and many of the women had gone on strike and refused to bring their produce to town.   They had another grievance in the requirement to sell most things by weight.   For generations they had sold only by the " pile," consisting of three articles of such things as eggs, plantains, yams, and the like, or of tiny heaps in the case of grains and similar produce; few of them, moreover, could afford to buy scales, and they resented the right given purchasers to appeal to gendarmes stationed in the market-places for the verifying of weights. But only those who had seen it under still more crowded conditions would have realized that the highway was not thronged to its full density on this particular morning.

Through the main street, out past the only modern sugar-mill in Haiti, for miles across the plain, our constantly honking Ford plowed through this endless procession of black humanity, casting it aside in two turbulent furrows of donkeys, mules, women, and multifarious bundles.   There is nothing more amusing, and pathetic, too, than the behavior of the primitive masses of Haiti before an automobile.   This is scarcely to be wondered at in a country where any wheeled traffic except a very rare ox-cart crawling along on its creaking and wobbling wheels was unknown up to a few years ago, and where the half-dozen automobiles of Port au Prince could not make their way into the country until the Americans had begun the reconstruction of the roads. But it is proof, too, of the close relationship of the Haitians to their savage brethren in central Africa.   Just like this, one can easily imagine, the latter would act at the sudden apparition of a strange machine which the great mass of Haitians firmly believe is run by voodoo spirits devoted to the white man.

The highway, like most of those the Americans have built, is of boulevard width, and there is ample room for even such a throng as this to pass an automobile in safety. But the primitive-minded natives are terror-stricken at sight of one bearing down upon them. The mounted women invariably tumble off their animals and fall to beating, pushing, and dragging them to the extreme edge of the road, at the same time shrieking as if the Grim Reaper had suddenly appeared before them with his sickle poised. The pedestrians succumb to a similar panic, so that the journey out the flat highway presents a constant vista of dismounting women and a turmoil of animals and frightened human beings tumbling over one another in their excited eagerness to get well out of reach of the swiftly approaching demon of destruction. Farther on, where the road begins to wind, and the cuts into the hills are often deep, the scene is still more laughter-provoking, for the startled animals invariably bury their noses in the sheer road-banks and will not, for all the cajolery or threats in the world, swing in sidewise along them. If they are donkeys, the women pick up their hind quarters and lift them out of the way by main force; when they are too large for this courageous treatment, the riders put a shoulder to the quivering rumps, abandon those useless tactics to drag at the halters as the machine draws nearer, and finally bury their faces also in the bank, as if to shut out the horrible experience of seeing their precious animals mutilated beyond recognition.

Still more distracting to drivers is the behavior of persons approached from the rear. A horn is of little use in this case. The Haitian's hearing is acute enough, but his mind does not synchronize in its various faculties; he is aware of a disagreeable noise behind him, but that noise does not register as a warning of danger and a call for action. Then, when at last he realizes that it means something and is addressed to him, or when the bumper or fender touches his ragged coat-tail, he is electrified into record-breaking activity. Unfortunately, his psychology is that of the chicken, and in eight cases out of ten he darts across the road instead of withdrawing to the side of it. This happens even when he is far out of danger at the edge of a wide street or highway, and every automobile trip through the crowded parts of Haiti is a constant succession of interweaving pedestrians bent on getting to the opposite side of the road.

An American estate manager who drives a heavy car at a high rate of speed, yet who is noted for his freedom from accidents, was bowling alone one September afternoon far out in the country. The road was twenty-two feet wide, and he was driving to the right of it, without an animate object in sight except for one ragged countryman plodding along the extreme left in the same direction. Seeing no reason to do so, he did not blow his horn. Suddenly the pedestrian caught sight of the car out of the tail of an eye and darted across the road. The machine struck him squarely and knocked him, as was afterward proved by measurement, fifty-two feet, then ran completely over him. The driver hurried him back to a hospital, where it was found that the only injuries he had sustained were a few minor bruises and a gash on the head. This was treated, and a few days later he was discharged, and returned to his hut, where he died the next week of blood poisoning caused by the native healer whom he insisted on having redress his almost healed wound.

Though somewhat stony and grown with an ugly, thorny vegetation, the great Cul-de-Sac plain is noted for its fertility. Here the aborigines cultivated cotton and tobacco; at the time of French expulsion it had nearly seven thousand plantations, chiefly of sugar-cane, which was brought to Haiti from the Canary Islands early in the sixteenth century. The French had covered it with a thorough irrigation system, with a *grand bassin* in the hills above and streams of water spreading from it like the fingers of the hand to all parts of the plain. There were numerous splendid highways between towns and estates, and the ninety thousand acres were dotted with fine residences, hundreds of sugar-mills, and many coffee, cotton, and indigo works. To-day the roads which our forces of occupation, or the two American companies that are beginning to reclaim some of the plain, have not found time to restore are rutty successions of mud-holes so narrowed by ever-encroaching vegetation as to resemble the trails of blackest Africa, or have disappeared entirely. There are a few rude bridges, usually patched upon the crumbling remains of once fine French structures, but as a rule streams are forded. Except where the newcomers have constructed new ones, the saying in Haiti is, " Never cross a bridge if you can go around it." Many of the former estates are completely overgrown with brush and broken walls, trees rise from former courtyards, the remnants of once sumptuous halls are the haunts of bats, night birds, and lizards. In some of the less dilapidated ruins negro families now cluster; most of them live in shanties patched together of jungle rubbish, their only furnishings a sleeping-net and a German enamelware pot. Whatever else he lacks, the Haitian always has the latter, its holes stopped with corncobs until they become too large, when the pot is filled with earth, planted with flowers, and set up in a conspicuous position about the hovel. Everywhere are to be found reminders of the prosperous days when Haiti was France's richest colony. Large, semispherical iron sugar-kettles, rusted, broken, and full of holes, lie tumbled everywhere along the highway and across the plain. Old French bells bearing pre-Napoleonic dates and quaint inscriptions, ruined stone aqueducts, mammoth grass-grown stairways, rust-eaten machinery, inexplicable stone ruins of all shapes and sizes, are stumbled upon wherever the visitor rambles.

The characteristic sour stench of a dirty little sugar- and rum-mill only rarely assails the nostrils. The natives have lost not only the energy, but almost the knowledge, required for the growing and making of sugar, producing only *rapadoue,* dark-brown lumps of crude, coagulated molasses, which, wrapped in leaves, are to be found in every Haitian market. The American companies found the people so ignorant of agricultural methods that it was impossible to introduce the *colono* system. The men and women who work in the sugar- and cotton-fields of these new enterprises are as patched and ragged a crew as can be found on the earth's surface. The average daily wage for adult male laborers in Haiti is a *gourde,* or twenty cents, a day, women and boys in proportion. The new companies have raised this to thirty cents. In theory the laborers are fed by their employers, but it would be considerable exaggeration to call the one gourdful of rice-and-bean hash which a disheveled, yet dictatorial, old negro woman was dishing out to each of a long line of gaunt and soil-stained workmen on one of the estates at which we stopped one evening the nourishment needed for a long day in the fields. Except for a sugar-cane, a lump of *rapadoue,* or possibly a bit of rice or plantain, which they find for themselves in the morning, this is the only food of the Haitian field laborer. So lazy have they become in their masterless condition that this one meal a day has come to be the habitual diet of the masses and all they expect of their employers; but the impression on both sides that this is all they need is probably costing the companies more in lack of efficient labor than they themselves realize. Only at one season during the year does the average Haitian get more than these slim pickings; that is in mango-time, and then the roads and trails are carpeted with the yellow pits.

Dusty, thorny, and hot, the Cul-de-Sac plain continued as level as the sea at its edge to where we began to climb the steep slope of wrinkled, rusty mountains shutting it off abruptly on the north and offering a panorama of rare beauty from Port au Prince, particularly when sunrise or sunset gives them a dozen swiftly changing colors. As we rose above it, the reedy edged first of two large lakes, one of which stretches on into the Republic of Santo Domingo, broke the red-brown carpet with a contrasting shimmer of blue at the eastern end, and the mountains behind the capital stood forth in silhouette against the transparent tropical sky. The aboriginal name " Haiti " means a high and mountainous land; like its inhabitants, its scenery and vegetation are more savage than those of Cuba. So steep was the new road climbing diagonally up the face of the range that we were twice compelled to dismount and call upon a gang of road laborers· to push the machine over the next stony rise. The stream of market-women continued to pour down this in cascades. Many of the heavy black faces would have made splendid gargoyles. Almost all of the women wore gowns of blue denim; the year before, the driver said, they had all worn purple, but the style had changed only in color. Once we met a lone marine, and higher up paused at a camp where there were several of them. But they were not the spick-and-span " leather-necks " we know taking their shore leave along Broadway. They wore only the indispensable parts of their uniforms, on the faces of those old enough to produce it was a week's growth of beard, and they clutched their rifles with the alert and ready air of expecting to use them at any moment, for we were now entering a region constantly harassed by cacos.

We grasped our own weapons and closely watched the brush-covered banks on each hand, as well as every approaching traveler. There are only two ways of telling a caco from a harmless Haitian; if he is armed or if he runs. Then the orders are to fire, for the " good citizens " do not carry weapons and are very careful to move slowly and be prepared to flourish their bon habitant card at sight of a white face or a gendarme uniform. Several times I fancied for an instant that we had been attacked, until I grew accustomed to the thump of stones with which the road was ever more thickly strewn striking the bottom of the car with reports startlingly like rifle-shots. From the crest of the first range we descended into the Artibonite Valley, remarkable for its colors. A constant series of rusty red humps, more beautiful at a distance, no doubt, than to a hungry marine climbing over them expecting at any moment to run into a caco ambush, patches of scenery almost equal to the Alps in color, slender pines standing out against the red and tumbled background, here and there a clump of palm-trees to give contrast and a suggestion of peaceful tropical languor, spread before us farther than the eye could see.

As far as the marine-garrisoned town of Mirebalais the road was passable, though it had steadily deteriorated from the modern highway of the plain to a road made only by the feet of animals and men. It would have been an exceedingly optimistic stranger, however, who could ever have attempted to drive an automobile over the mountain trail that lay beyond, yet over which the doughty Ford climbed as if military orders forbade it to give up so long as it retained a gasp of life. Here and there we forded a considerable stream, meeting at one of them a group of marines driving pack-laden donkeys and cattle, in some cases astride the latter, more often splashing thigh-deep through the water, and with a score of produce-bearing natives plodding at their heels for protection. Farther on we passed an airplane camp, from which " God's wicked angels," as the natives call them, periodically bombard the retreats of the *cacos*. Rumor has it that these warriors of the air have not always made certain of the character of the gatherings they attack, and the *cacos* once sent a protest to England against the Americans for using a means of warfare which the " Haitians fighting for their liberty " cannot combat or imitate.

The name of Las Cahobas, the old Spanish form of the word for mahogany-trees, is an indication of the fact that it was formerly within the territory of Santo Domingo. It is a miserable little town in which the palm-trunk huts that are the lowest form of dwelling in Cuba are considered residences *de luxe*. A whitewashed jail where the hundred or more black inmates, most simply dressed in two-piece suits of red-and-white striped cotton, seem only too glad to get their three meals a day, two of them with meat rations, was the chief sight of interest. Some of the gendarme guards had become so thoroughly Americanized under their marine officers that they " rolled their own," closed their tobacco-sacks with their teeth, and returned them to hip-pockets exactly as required by our military manuals. It is remarkable what can be done with a backward race under proper guidance. The officers themselves, nearly all enlisted men in the organization from which they had been loaned, were, like most of those I met throughout the country, forceful, energetic, efficient chaps, many of whom spoke the native " creole " as if they had been born in the district. In the North we scarcely think of a corporal or sergeant of marines as standing particularly high in the social scale; in these Haitian villages they have almost the power of absolute monarchs, and are treated with corresponding respect by their native subjects. Even the village accounts are periodically brought to them to be audited. So accustomed do the Haitians become to obeying the commander of the district in which they live that it is difficult to get them to change their allegiance. A marine major who had long reigned in a certain region summoned all the native authorities to meet a newly arrived lieutenant colonel, explaining that the latter was thereafter the commander in chief; yet as long as the major remained, he never broke the natives of the habit of appealing to him first of all whenever any official matter turned up.

On the edge of Las Cahobas, as here and there along the road to it, was a Haitian cemetery. These are invariably bare and sunscorched, the graves covered with vault-shaped structures ranging from heaped-up cobbles to almost elaborate stone and plaster mounds. Without crosses or any other indication of the Christian faith, they seem to be direct importations from the interior of Africa, and though one knows that the stones are piled there primarily to keep the energetic Haitian pigs from rooting up and feasting on the corpses, it is hard to think of them as anything but the African's protection against the voodoo spirits which must be forcibly prevented from escaping out of bodies committed to the earth. The usual Haitian funeral is accompanied with strange rites destined to exorcise these same spirits, after which others of a totally different nature enliven the proceedings, for the corpse is generally carried on the heads of men who dance and sing in a drunken orgy all the way to the burial-ground.

Market-women were still straggling toward town when we returned. The view of the Cul-de-Sac plain toward sunset, carpeted with brown and green vegetation, speckled here and there with little houses, the lakes on the left and the ocean on the right reflecting the colors of the purple and lilac clouds which hung above the mountains, was as striking as any I had seen in many a day. Nearer the capital the road was still almost crowded, while here and there under the trees beside it the women, their big straw hats off now, but still wearing their brilliant bandanas, had camped for the night, and were cooking their humble dinners on fagot fires. Once we found a woman bareheaded, but this was because she was tearing her hair and shrieking in what seemed to be physical agony. As she caught sight of my uniformed companions, she rushed out upon them and reported that she had been robbed by *cacos* of the produce she had expected to spread out in the big market-square before the cathedral by the dawn of Saturday. Such things happen even on the broad highway into Port au Prince, while more often still gendarmes are sent out along the road by some colonel or major whose wife has invited guests, with orders to buy the chickens and turkeys needed before they reach the close competition of the market. In either case the women are deeply disgruntled, for the mere selling is only half their pleasure in offering their wares.

Of the other two highways out of Port au Prince one climbs into the hills to Pétionville, from which a trail leads to cool and refreshing Furcy, among its pine-trees, four thousand feet above the sea. A longer road is that to the southern peninsula. Leaving the capital at the opposite end of the main street from that to the Cul-de-Sac, it passes the "navy yard" and skirts the bay for miles beyond. It, too, is apt to be crowded with market-women, and with donkeys, women, and men carrying rock salt from Léogane. Half-way to that town there is a clearing in the dense woods famed as the scene of frequent voodoo rites, and for a long space the road is bordered by the scraggly tree-bushes of an abandoned castor-bean plantation from which our Government once hoped to produce oil for its airplanes. Léogane is a town of considerable size, the usual grass-grown square of which is faced by a quaint old church of what might almost be called Haitian architecture. Churches were the only buildings spared by the infuriated slaves in their revolt against the French, as the priests were the only white people who escaped attack, but neglect and the tropical climate have in most cases completed the work of destruction. The town and the region about it is one of the few places in Haiti where the malarial mosquito abounds. Here, too, are to be found many bush-grown ruins of French plantations. Far to the westward along the tongue of land forming the southern horn of Haiti, and to be reached only by horse or boat, is the town of Jérémie, near which the elder Dumas was born, the son of a French general and a negro slave.

The gendarme officer with whom I was traveling on this occasion, however, had come to inspect Jacmel, on the southern coast. At two and a half hours by Ford from the capital, the last part of it by a narrow dirt roadway winding through high hills, we changed to moth-eaten native horses and rode away down the River Gauche, which we forded one hundred and eighteen times during the next four hours. The black soil was fertile, and cultivated in scattered patches even to the tops of the hills. Coffee in uncared-for luxuriance often bordering the way showed what this region had been under the French. It was still well populated, for the people of the southern peninsula have never revolted, and *cacos* are unknown, though there is much petty thieving. At every turn of the trail startled, respectful negroes raised their hats as we passed, only a few of them having the half-sullen air of their fellow-countrymen elsewhere at sight of Americans. Their little huts of thatch, or *tache,* as *yagua* is called in Haiti, were everywhere tucked away in the bush, cattle and pigs were numerous, though all animals except the goats had a half-starved appearance. Bananas and oranges grew in profusion; the trail was strewn with the peelings of the native pear-shaped grape-fruit. Frequent patches of Kafir-corn, called *pitimi,* the " creole " abbreviation of *petit maïs,* waved their lofty heads of rice-like grain in the breeze. Immovable donkeys now and then blocked the trail, indifferent alike to the shrieks of their drivers and to the commanding voice of the native gendarme who accompanied us. Here and there washing parties of women were beating their rags on stones at the edge of the stream and spreading them out in the sun to bleach, their almost nude black bodies glistening in the sunshine and their tongues cackling incessantly until a glimpse of us reduced them to sudden silence. Several times we passed voodoo signs — a chicken with its entrails removed hanging by one leg from a pole, the white skull of a horse decorated with bits of red rag set on the top of a cactus-bush. Now and then we came across the most primitive form of cane-crusher except the human teeth. It consisted of a grooved stick driven through a tree or post, with a bit of sapling fastened at one end. While one negro held a sugar-cane, another rolled the sapling back and forth along it, the juice running down the groove into a gourd or pot. Wherever the breeze reached us the weather was agreeable; in the breathless pockets of the hills the humid heat hung about us like a hot wet blanket.

The marine-gendarme commander of Jacmel met us with an automobile farther out along the trail than one had ever been driven before, and the astounded natives fled shrieking before it as if the malignant spirits they fancied they could hear groaning under its hood were visibly pursuing them. In the town itself the people greeted their benevolent despot with just such antics as one might fancy their forefathers performed before their African chiefs. Jacmel, however, has a number of " citizens of color " of education and moderate wealth. The hills about it grow two crops of coffee a year, cotton and cacao alternate all the year round, veritable forests of cotton-trees cover the sites of old

French plantations, and there is considerable shipping, though the bay is deep and dangerous. But its prosperity is mainly due, of course, to its lifelong freedom from *cacos* and revolutions. It is a hilly town of six thousand inhabitants, with sharp lines of caste, more stone buildings than are usual in Haiti, a Protestant as well as a Catholic church, an imposing *hotel de ville,* with the familiar misstatement "Liberté, Egalité, Fraternité" on its façade, "summer" homes in its suburbs, and a tile-roofed market. Strangers but seldom disrupt the languid tenor of its ways, however, and not only is there no hotel, but not even a place to get a cup of coffee and a sandwich, unless one accept the hospitality of marines or gendarme officers. Some years ago a foreign company erected an electric light plant, fitted up all Jacmel with elaborate poles or underground wires, operated for one night, collected their government subsidy and as much as possible from the citizens, and fled. To this day the town continues to worry along with such lights as might be found in an African village. In 1896 it was completely wiped out by fire, the land and sea breeze joining to pile the flames so high that the population was forced to flee to the hills, leaving all their possessions behind.

On our return to Port au Prince the road, particularly from Léogane in, was even more densely thronged than usual; for it was the last day of the year, and New Year's is not only Haiti's day of independence, but the one on which presents are given, after the French custom. Women carrying on their heads heaps of native baskets higher than themselves, others with as disproportionate loads of gourds, donkeys laden to the point of concealment with anything there was any hope of selling for gifts at that evening's big market, filled the tumultuous wake behind us. I called that afternoon on the mulatto President of Haiti in the unfinished palace, and caught him and the minister of finance in the act of shaking and rearranging the rugs in preparation for the coming festivities. No doubt a president whose duties are assumed by men from the outside world must find something to do to pass the time. Next day, however, there was no such informality in his manner as he was driven in silk-hat solemnity to a Te Deum in the cathedral. Four prancing horses drew the presidential carriage, preceded and followed by a company of native horsemen in more than resplendent uniforms and drawn sabers. At the door he was met by the archbishop and all the higher officers of our forces of occupation, who fell in behind the august ruler as he marched down the central aisle, flanked at close intervals by negro firemen in brilliant red shirts of heavy

flannel and shining metal helmets. In their wake came all the élite of
Port au Prince, some in silk hats and full dress, nearly all in brand-
new garb, for New Year's takes the place of Easter in this respect in
Haiti, and so generously perfumed that the clouds of incense arising
about the altar made no impression upon the nostrils. Outside, the
great open square and the adjacent streets were compact seas of upturned black faces. The booming of cannon frequently punctuated the
ceremony, though the beating of tomtoms would have been more in
keeping, and the cost of the powder might then have been spent in
running the trade school which had just been abandoned for lack of
funds. Faces running all the gamut from white to black were to be
seen in the glaringly yellow interior, but none of the former were
Haitian, and the latter were in the decided majority. The clergy were
white, the acolytes black; the formality and solemnity which reigned
could scarcely have been equaled in the elaborate functions in Notre
Dame of Paris.

A Cuban bon mot has it that " The Haitian is the animal which most
nearly resembles man." Without subscribing to so broad a statement,
it must be admitted that they are close to the primitive savage despite a
veneer of civilization which all but hides the African in the upper
class and is so thin upon the masses as to be transparent. Tradition
has it that when the uprising against the French was planned the con-
spirators gave every slave some grains of corn, telling him to throw one
away every day and attack when none remained, for in no other way
could they have known the date. To this day the intelligence of the
masses is of that caliber. Readily capable of imitation, they initiate
nothing, not even the next obvious move in the simplest undertakings.
They have not a trace of gratitude in their make-up, no sexual morality,
unbounded superstition, and no family love. Mothers gladly give away
their children; if they ever see them again there is no evidence of glad-
ness shown on either side. They have a certain naïve simplicity and
some of the unintentional honesty that goes with it; they have of
course their racial cheerfulness, though even that is less in evidence
than among most of their race. A French woman who has spent nearly
all her life in Haiti long tried to discover some symptoms of poetical
fancy or love for the beautiful among the full blacks. One day she
found a servant sitting in the back yard looking up into the tree-tops.
Asked what he was thinking about, he answered, " I am not thinking;
I am listening to the breeze in the cocoanut-palms." That is the sum

Ruins of the old French estates are to be found all over Haiti

A Haitian wayside store

The market women of Haiti sell everything under the sun—A "General Store" in a Haitian market

There are still more primitive sugar mills than these in Haiti

total of sentiment during long years of observation. Family relations are little short of promiscuous. Girls who have reached the age of ten are made to understand that they must be on the lookout for lovers; mothers refuse to support them after they have grown old enough to live with a man. An old maid is considered a freak of nature in Haiti, and such freaks are exceedingly rare in the Black Republic.

More temperamental than our own negroes, the Haitians are incredibly childlike in their mental processes. A certain gendarme officer whose butler was frequently remiss in his duties had him enrolled in the native corps in order to bring military discipline to bear upon him. A few days later the servant requested that he be given the right to carry arms, like other gendarmes. The officer good naturedly gave him a harmless old revolver that had been captured from the *cacos*. A few days later reports began to leak into headquarters that the national force was terrorizing the inhabitants of a certain section of Port au Prince. The detectives got busy, and found that the gendarme-butler, his day's service over, was in the habit of patrolling that part of town in which he was born and where he was well known, strutting back and forth among his awed fellow-citizens during the evening, and from midnight on beating on house doors and commanding the inmates, " in the name of the law," and at the point of his revolver, to come outside and line up " for inspection." He had no designs upon their possessions, but was simply indulging 'his love for display and authority. When his employer took his putative weapon away from him again, he wept like a child of six. His grief, however, was short lived, for when the President called at the home of the officer on New Year's afternoon, he found the butler so dressed up that he inadvertently shook hands with him as one of the guests.

Abuse of authority is a fixed fault in the Haitian character, as with most negroes. Of the several reasons why there are only two or three native lieutenants in the gendarmerie, lack of intelligence and dishonesty are less conspicuous than the inability to wield authority lightly. The Haitians of the masses have only three forms of recreation, dances, cock-fights, and voodooism. They have not even risen to the level of the " movies," for though there are two cinemas in the capital and one in Cap Haïtien, these are too " high brow " for any but the upper class. Of pretty native customs we found only one — that of hanging up little colored-paper churches with candles inside them at Christmas-time. The Haitians are inveterate gamblers, which is only another way of saying that they abhor work. As the negro admires the successful and dominant, so he has supreme contempt for the broken and discredited. The Germans who once ruled the commercial roost in Haiti and who were interned after our entry into the war would find no advantage in returning, even if they were permitted to, for they have lost for life the respect of the natives by allowing themselves to be arrested. The profiteering Syrians who have largely inherited their control of commerce have far more standing to-day despite their slippery methods.

Between the primitive bulk of the population and the slight minority of educated citizens, mainly "people of color," there is a wide gulf. Haiti has no middle class, not even a skilled labor class. Those who have ambition or wealth enough to go in for "higher education" will have nothing to do with anything even suggestive of manual labor. The ability to read, write, and speak French automatically brings with it a contempt for work and workers. As in all Latin America, an agricultural school is worse than useless, because it serves only to spoil what might have been good foremen, and the mere possession of a scrap of paper announcing the holder a graduate of such an institution is prima-facie evidence that he intends to loaf in the shade all the rest of his days. The result is that the population is made up of poverty-stricken, incredibly ignorant laborers and peasants, and of lawyers, "doctors" of this and that, and the political-military class which tyrannizes and fattens on the African masses.

Superficially, the educated class of Haiti is pleasant to meet, though the first impression seldom lasts. It has all the outward manners of the French, with none of their solid basis. In discussions of literature and art these "gens de couleur" could give the average American business man cards and spades; in actually doing or producing something worth while they are completely out of their depth. Once in a blue moon one runs across a full-blooded negro who shows outcroppings of genius. We were invited to meet such a one at the home of a "high yellow" senator on New Year's eve, a pianist who had studied in Paris. I had been told that there were several fine musicians in Haiti, but, in the light of other experiences, had inwardly scoffed at the idea. It required but very little time to be convinced that here at least was one. The man not only played the best classics in a manner that would have been applauded in the highest class of concert halls, but gave several pieces of his own composition which could hold their place in any program. He had played a few times in the United States, but the drawback of color had proved insurmountable, and as there is naturally no income to be derived from such a source in Haiti, Ludovic Lamothe now holds a minor clerkship in the ministry of agriculture! When he had finished, the senator himself sat down at the piano and gave an exhibition which, I have no hesitancy in asserting, could scarcely have been duplicated by any member of our own upper house, and one which reminded us by contrast of the uproarious rag-time that was even at that moment reigning along Broadway. Yet it was such men as these that our marines once evicted from the Haitian senate with, " Come on, you niggers, get out of here! " Even the Southerner who had been induced to come with us, and whose muscles seemed to tense with inward horror as our host greeted him with a handshake and introduced him to the pianist, gradually shrank down into his chair in unconscious acknowledgment of his own ignorance of the higher things of life as compared with these cultured " niggers."

We met a few other men of this type at the yearly " Haitian ball " in the chief native club, which American civilians attend, to the unbounded disgust of the forces of occupation. Yet the primitive African now and then showed itself in the whitest of them. Those who know them well say that even Haiti's élite, educated in Europe or the United States, are apt to forget their Christian faith when troubles assail them and go to a " Papa Loi " for a *wanga*, or charm, and pay for a voodoo ceremony. In Paris lives a certain Mme. Thebes, in high repute among those who believe in sorcery and prophecy. If the stories which gradually leak out from the confidences of returning natives to their friends are trustworthy, she tells all Haitians that they are some day to become president of their country, not a bad guess under old conditions, though the supernatural madame does not seem to have kept up with the times. More than one revolution has been started on the strength of her prophecies. Some of these upper-class " people of color " are descendants of the same families who fled to Philadelphia and New Orleans at the time of the slave revolt. The members who remained behind were or have since become intermixed with the blacks. At least one American connected with the forces of occupation was introduced at a presidential reception to a colored family of the same name, which turned out to be relatives. As the American chanced to be a Southerner, it is easy to imagine whether the discovery brought joy and mutual social calls.

Stories of human sacrifices, cannibalism, and occult poisonings are always going the rounds in Haiti, though it is difficult to find any one of unquestioned integrity who has actually seen such things himself. I met two gendarme officers who asserted they had found the feet of a black baby sticking out of a boiling pot, and there are numbers of well-balanced Americans in Haiti who are firmly convinced that all three of the crimes above mentioned are practised. Certainly many of the natives look hungry enough to eat their own children. The body of a marine was once found in a condition to bear out the charge of cannibalism, but it has never been proved that this was not the work of hogs or dogs. Most frequent of all, say the believers, are the cases of blood-sucking, the victims being preferably virgins. Not long before our occupation a baby in the best district of Port au Prince died for loss of blood, which an old neighbor later confessed to having inflicted while the mother was out of the room. The daughter of a former minister is said to have been similarly treated by her grandmother and a prominent man. The rite over, they pronounced her dead, and she was buried with much pomp, the grandmother, according to the story, replacing with coffee the embalming fluid that was poured down her throat. Five years later a rumor of her existence having reached a priest through the confessional, what is believed to be the same girl was discovered in a hill town. She was wild, unkempt, demented, and had borne three children. The coffin was dug up, and in it was found her wedding dress,— for though she was only eight or nine at the time, it is the custom in Haiti to bury young girls in such garments,— but the autopsy proved the remains to be those of a man, the legs cut off and laid alongside the body. That there are Haitian Obeah practitioners who have so remarkable a knowledge of vegetable poisons that they can destroy their enemies or those of their clients without being detected seems to be generally admitted. Some of these poisons are said to be so subtle that the victims live for years, dying slowly as from some wasting disease, or going insane, deaf, blind, or dumb, with the civilized medical profession helpless to relieve them. Men of undoubted judgment and integrity, some of them Americans, claim to have positive proof of such cases.

The less gruesome forms of Obeah and voodooism are known to be practised in Haiti. The former is a species of witchcraft by men and women who are supposed to possess supernatural powers, and who certainly have far greater sway over the masses of the people than priests or presidents. For a small sum they will undertake to help in business matters, to create love in unresponsive breasts, possibly to put an enemy out of the way, and some of the " stunts " they perform are beyond comprehension. Voodooism, unlike the other, is a form of religion, the deity being an imaginary " great green serpent," with a high priest known as " Papa Loi " and a priestess called " Maman Loi." Chicken snakes and a harmless python are kept as sacred beings in Haiti, and fed by the faithful. In theory the serpent deity demands sacrifices of a " goat without horns "; in other words, a child, preferably white. But there is no positive evidence to prove that anything more than goats, sheep, or roosters are actually sacrificed. These simpler rites are carried on almost openly, and are accompanied by all sorts of childish incantations, with such nonsensical fetishes as red rags, dried snakes and lizards, human bones, or portions of human organs, stolen perhaps from graveyards. The most frequent form of revenge among the Haitian masses is the burying of a bottle filled with " charms " of this nature, over which are recited various incantations at certain phases of the moon, in the hope of bringing destruction or lesser punishment on the object of the enmity. So firm is the belief of the negroes in the power of Obeah that they sometimes succumb to fear and die merely because some one has cast such a spell upon them. A French priest who was traveling through the country called at a cabin one night to ask the occupant to show him the way. The man refused, whereupon the priest, being denied the customary form of expressing displeasure, began to recite a quotation from Ovid. To his surprise the native dashed out of his hut, fell at his feet, and offered to do anything he demanded, if only he would not " put Obeah " on him. Perhaps the most serious result of these practices is the appalling number of children who die under the ministrations of voodoo " doctors."

A group of Americans once offered to pay for a voodoo supper if they were allowed to attend it. White men are seldom admitted to the native ceremonies; some have suffered for their intrusion. In this case there was the added fear that the officials who saw the rites would forbid them thereafter; but a Frenchman finally persuaded the natives that it would be to their advantage to let the Americans see one of their festivities in order to prove that they were harmless. How much was left out because of the guests there is of course no means of knowing.

About seventy dollars was spent for corn-meal, *tafia* (crude native rum), sacrifices, and other things required, and to pay the chief performers their fees. The temple was decorated with flags and various fetishes. The ceremony began with a tom-tom dance by the priests, who were soon joined by the high priestess, wearing a white skirt, a red waist, and a brilliant bandana, and waving spangled flags. Then a goat, scrubbed to spotless white, its horns gilded, and a red bow on its head, was brought in. The priestess danced about it with a snaky motion, holding her shoulders stiffly and giving her waist the maximum of movement. Then she got astride the goat and rode round and round, clinging to its horns. Every few minutes the priests gave her *tafia* until she had worked herself into a real or feigned paroxysm of excitement. To say that she was intoxicated would perhaps be putting it too strongly, for the average Haitian is so soaked in rum from birth that it has little visible effect upon him.

At length a priest caught up a handful of corn-meal and, with what appeared to be two careless gestures, formed a perfect cross with it on the ground. Candles were placed at the ends of the cross, then *tafia* and other liquors were poured along the lines of corn-meal, the priestess meanwhile continuing to ride the goat with hideous contortions. Finally she dismounted, slipped off the white skirt, leaving her entirely clothed in red, and while a priest held the goat by the front feet she pierced a vein in its neck and drank all the blood she could contain. For a time she seemed to be in a stupor; then she began to " prophesy " in loathsome, incomprehensible noises, which a priest " translated," probably in terms of his own choosing. While this pair howled, the goat was prepared and put in caldrons to cook, with rice, beans, *tafia*, salt, pepper, and lard. Old women stirred the contents of these with their bare hands, which had been bleached almost white by frequent emersions in similar boiling messes. When the food was cooked, the priestess came suddenly out of her trance and fell to with all the negroes present, who were still sitting about in a circle eating sacred goat meat and drinking *tafia* when the white spectators finally left.

" The only thing wrong with the Haitians is lack of education," says a recent investigator, which can scarcely be doubted, since it is true of all mankind. By some oversight, perhaps, no mention of schools and courts was made in the treaty under which we are administering the country. The French maintained no schools for the negroes, and it goes without saying that conditions scarcely improved during the century and a quarter of independence. An American superintendent, who is quite properly a Catholic and of Louisiana creole stock, has been appointed, and is in theory directly responsible to the native minister of public instruction. But the higher American civilian officials, clinging perhaps too closely to the letter of the treaty, have not seen fit to assign any great amount of the public revenues of Haiti to this purpose. There are thirteen hundred teachers in the country, probably the majority of whom are in no way qualified for their task, and of the fifty thousand pupils enrolled barely one in three is in regular at-

tendance. In other words, not ten per cent. of the children of school
age get even primary instruction, and less than one per cent. ever reach
the secondary schools. The law school in Port-au-Prince, with thirty
students, is reported to be efficient; the medical school is frankly a farce.
Teaching methods are in all but a few cases primitive, consisting of little
more than monologues by the " teacher," to which the pupils listen only
when nothing else occupies their attention. A thorough reform in this
matter is essential to the task we have undertaken in Haiti, unless we
subscribe as a nation to the old Southern attitude that the negro is
better off without education. The present generation is hopeless in
this as in many other regards; it remains to be seen whether we will and
can lift the next out of the primitive savagery which at present reigns.

The popular language of Haiti bears no very close resemblance to the
tongue from which it is largely descended. The slaves came from
different parts of Africa, in some cases belonging to enemy tribes, and
" creole " is the natural evolution of their desire to talk with one another. The resultant dialect has French as a basis, but it is so abbreviated, condensed, and simplified, and includes so many African
words, that it has become almost a new language. It is quite distinct
from the patois of Canada and even of the French West Indies, though
there are points of resemblance. It has not even the inflection of real
French, and only now and then does one knowing that language catch
an intelligible word. Haitian voices have a softness equal to those of
our Southern darkies, and are in marked contrast to the rasping tones
of Cuba. It is a local form of politeness to use a squeaky falsetto in
greetings, and women of the masses curtsy to one another when they
shake hands, probably a survival from slave days originally adopted as
a sign of their equality to their expelled mistresses. Gender, number,
case, modes, tenses, and articles have almost completely disappeared.
As a rule, only the feminine form of adjectives has survived. Plurality
is indicated, when it is necessary, by a participle. Many words have
been abbreviated almost out of recognition. *Plait-il?* has become
" Aiti ? " The Dominicans over the border are called " Pagno." The
word *bagaille*, probably a corruption of *bagage*, means almost anything;
servants told to " pick up " that *bagaille* grasp whatever is nearest at
hand; *bon bagaille* and *pas bon bagaille* are the usual forms of good
and bad. " Who " has grown to be " Qui monde ça ? " Many words
have changed their meanings entirely; the urchin who approaches you
rubbing his stomach and mumbling " grand gout," wishes to impress
upon you the very probable fact that he has " large hunger." On the

whole, it is probably an advantage, in learning Haitian " creole," not to know real French.

The automobile in which we took our final leave of Port au Prince plowed its way for several miles along the thronged highway across the Cul-de-Sac plain, then turned west through an endless semi-desert bristling with thorny *aroma*. A dead negro lying a few yards from the road on the bare ground awakened no surprise from our native chauffeur or the gendarme in plain clothes beside him. There were no vultures flying about the body. Those natural scavengers were once introduced into Haiti, but the natives killed and ate them. Soon we came out on the edge of the sea, along the foot of those same cliffs we had seen while rolling in the doldrums on the Haitian navy three weeks before. What had then seemed a sheer mountain wall was in reality a flat narrow plain backed by sloping hills. Naked black fisher-men were plying their trade thigh-deep in the blue water. Gonave island and the southern peninsula were almost golden brown under the early sun. For a long time the thorny desert continued, for southern Haiti had for months been suffering from drought. There were several ruins of ox-and-kettle sugar-mills, here and there evidences of former plantation houses; miserable native huts leaning drunkenly against their broken walls. Once we passed a massive old stone aqueduct. The parched and sun-burned landscape was now and then broken by green oases of villages. A little railroad followed us all the way to St. Marc, but there was no sign of trains. The town was carpeted in dust, a ruined stone church towered above the low houses, a dust-and-stone-paved central square had a grandstand and a fountain screaming in the national colors. Down on the edge of the deep bay crooked, reddish logwood dragged in by donkeys was being weighed on large crude wooden scales. This chief product of the region to-day lay in heaps along the dusty road beyond. Cannon bearing the Napoleonic device and date, left by the ill-starred expeditionary force under Leclerc, served as corner-posts of the bridges. The dense green of mango-trees contrasted with the dry mountain-walled plain; nowhere was there a sprig of grass, seldom a sign of water. *Pitimi* grew rather abundantly, however, and there was some cotton. About the mouth of the Artibonite, sometimes called the " Haitian Nile," was a spreading delta of greenery. Miserable thatched huts of mud plastered on reeds were numerous, yet blended so into the dull, dry landscape as scarcely to draw the attention. Negroes carrying huge loads of reed mats now and then jogged past in the hot dust; everywhere was what a native writer calls "l'aridité désolante de la campagne." Yet though the drought occasionally flagellates portions of it, there is scarcely a spot in Haiti which would not produce abundantly under anything like proper cultivation.

Arid hills, with parched, purple-brown scrub forests, shut in the town of Dessalines, with its pathetic little forts that were long ago designed to protect the general of the same name. A small, dust-covered, baking-hot town well back from the sea in a kind of bay of the plain, it was indeed a negro capital. Farther on the dust and aridity largely disappeared. There was considerable cotton showing signs of languid cultivation, some fields were being hoed, others irrigated, as we snaked in and out along the wrinkled skirts of the rocky range on the right. Crippled beggars lined the way even here; in fact, there is a suggestion of India in the numbers of diseased mendicants squatting beside the dusty, sunny roads of Haiti. Women and children were bathing in brackish streams. Then it grew arid again, and we found Gonaïves, more than a hundred miles from the capital, in a very dry setting on the edge of a smaller bay. It claims twenty-five thousand inhabitants, some of whom live in moderate comfort. As in Port au Prince, one was assailed on all sides by the modern Haitian motto, " Gimme fi' cents," which is really not so serious a demand as it sounds, since it only means five centimes. It was in Gonaïves that independence was declared in 1804, and from here Toussaint l'Ouverture was sent to France in chains. The town is engaged chiefly in commerce. From it we turned back north by east into the country. A pathetic little railroad again began to follow us. The first few miles over a range of foot-hills were burned as dry as all the southern slope; then, as we climbed higher, it grew rapidly greener, the dust disappeared, we forded several small rivers many times, and were completely shut in by fresh and verdant vegetation before we reached Ennery.

This is a stony, sleepy little hamlet among the mountains, famed in Haitian history as the place where Toussaint was living when the French general Brunet wrote him, asking for an interview, at which he was traitorously arrested and sent to end his days in a French dungeon. There we left the road to Cap Haïtien and, still fording, rising constantly over long humps of ground, always turning, gradually gained coffee-growing elevation. A fine new road, passing one large marine camp, carried us higher still, until green mountains stood all about us, the air grew pleasant as that of our Northern spring-time, and at length we found ourselves among pine-trees. Just after sun-down, in the soft gray-blue evening of the temperate tropics, we sighted the little white church of St. Michel, beyond which we spun across a floor-level plateau a little farther to the residence of an American estate manager. To say that we had covered a hundred and fifty miles comfortably, with one short and one long stop, between daylight and dark gives some idea of what American occupation has done for Haitian roads.

The great plains, fourteen hundred feet high, were flooded with moonlight all through the night, in which I several times awoke shivering for all my heavy blankets. By day the sea-flat plateau proved to be covered with brown grass beneath which was the blackest of loamy soil. Gasolene tractors were turning this up, working by night as well as by day, and operated by Haitians who had been trained on the spot under American overseers. It was virgin soil, for this region was Spanish territory in the time of the French and had been used only as grazing land. The new company would soon have hundreds of acres planted in cotton, with other crops to follow. Such enterprises, multiplied many fold, are among the most immediate needs of Haiti.

Colonel W—— of the Marine Corps and Major General W——, Chef de la Gendarmérie d'Haiti, who are one and the same person, set out that afternoon on an inspection trip through the heart of Haiti, and invited me to go along. The region being *caco*-infested and a " restricted district " in which white women were not allowed to travel, Rachel was to continue by automobile on the well-guarded highway to Cap Haïtien. The colonel and I left the plantation by car also, skimming for more than an hour across the wonderful grassy plain without any need of a road. Groups of horses were grazing here and there, but there were no cattle. Occasionally we met a lone gendarme plodding along in the shoes to which he was still far from accustomed. An unfinished road carried us on from where the plain began to break up into rolling country, with clusters of trees in the hollows. Now and then the colonel brought down one of the deep-blue wild pigeons which flew frequently past, but the flocks of wild guineas usually found in this region had evidently been warned of his marksmanship. Four-footed game does not exist in Haiti, and even its harmless reptiles are rare; Noah evidently did not touch the West Indies. Gradually the forest appeared, growing thicker and thicker, until we were inclosed in tunnels of vegetation, fording many small rivers. Suddenly a great hubbub ahead caused us to make sure that our rifles were in readiness, but it was only a cock-fight in the woods, the men standing, the women seated on little home-made chairs outside the male circle about the ring, made of barrel staves driven upright into the ground. In the next mile we passed a dozen black men, each with a rooster under one arm, hurrying to the scene of conflict.

At the town of Maissade we halted at a marine camp on a hill overlooking the surrounding country, and commanded by Captain Becker, a famous hunter of *cacos*. His tent was almost filled with captured war material: rifles of every kind in use a century ago corded like so much stove-wood; revolvers and pistols enough to stock a museum devoted to the history and development of that arm; French swords dating back to the seventeenth century; rapiers such as flash through Dumas's stories; heaps of rusted machetes, battered bugles, bamboo musical instruments, and hollow-log tomtoms from voodoo temples; drums abandoned by Leclerc; ragged pieces of uniform decorated with ribbons; dozens of hats and caps of "generals," of felt, cloth, and straw, all more or less ragged, and all bearing such signs of rank as might be adopted by small boy warriors. Then there were beads and charms, Obeah vials found on the bodies of dead *cacos*, mysterious articles of unknown purpose and origin. The captain dissected one of the charms. It consisted of a bullet wrapped in a dirty bit of paper on which were scrawled a few strange characters, the dried foot of a lizard, and what was apparently a powdered insect, all inclosed in a brass cartridge-shell, with a string attached to it long enough to go around the neck of the original owner, whom it was supposed to protect against bullets. The captain had shot him a few days before, and as he fell he cried out in "creole," "O Mama, they've got me!" then died cursing the Obeah man for making an imperfect charm. Some of the *cacos* in the region had recently surrendered, and had been made "division commanders," with the duty of helping to hunt down their former comrades. One of them had showed the marine who shot him the bullet which he had dug out of his flesh with a machete, and now followed him everywhere like a faithful dog.

In the town itself the gendarme detachment was in command of a native lieutenant who was rated an excellent officer, but he had barely a touch of negro blood. Beyond was a road of boulevard width along which we spun at thirty-five miles an hour. Wild pigeons, parrots, and negroes far less ragged than those of Port au Prince enlivened the striking scenery, and at sunset we drew up before the gendarmerie of Hinche, the birthplace of the departed Charlemagne. There was something amusingly anachronistic in the sight of half a hundred marines playing baseball and basketball on the plain about their camp at the edge of town, for Hinche itself had little in common with such scenes.

All Haitian towns have a close family resemblance. There is always a big, brown, bare, dusty central *place,* with a tiny band-stand with steps painted in the national colors and surmounted by a single royal palm-tree, called the "*patrie*." From this radiate wide, right-angled dirt streets lined by low houses, some of plastered mud, a few whitewashed, many of split palm trunks, most of them of *tache,* nearly all with earth floors, all except the few covered with corrugated iron in the center of town being roofed with thatch. Some have narrow sapling-pillared porches paved with little cobblestones, these sometimes also whitewashed; and where houses are missing are broken hedges of organ cactus on which hang drying rags of clothing. Facing the *place* is a more or less ruined church, farther off a large open market-place, with perhaps a few ragged thatch-roof shelters from the sun. Then there is sure to be a spick-and-span gendarmerie, with large numbers of docile prisoners and proud black gendarmes, perhaps a group of marines, or at any rate of their native prototypes, here and there stalking through the dusty streets, ignoring the respectful greetings of the teeming black populace squatted in their doorways or on their dirt floors. Little fagot fires on the ground behind or beside the huts, a well-worn path down to the river, and an indefinable scent of the tropics and black humanity living in primitive conditions complete the picture. Men who have seen both assert that a Congo village is a paradise compared with a Haitian hamlet.

The curate came over to smoke a cigarette and drink a sip of rum with us after supper. He was a large, powerful Frenchman from Brittany, of remarkably fine features, sparkling blue eyes, and no recent hair-cut or shave, dressed in an ecclesiastical bonnet and enormous "congress" shoes run down at heel, and the long black gown which seems so out of place, yet is really very convenient, in the tropics. For twelve years he had shepherded Hinche and the neighboring region, being much of the time the only white man in it. He expected to complete twenty-five years' residence, then go home in retirement. He traveled freely everywhere within his district, *caco* sentinels and the bands themselves hiding when he passed rather than molest him. Cannibalism was certainly practised to this day, in his opinion, especially among the hills, where there were many negroes older than he who had never come to town. There was less superstition in this district, he asserted, because the people came somewhat under the more civilized Dominican influence. While we talked, two former *cacos,* now " division chiefs," came in to report to the efficient young American gendarme commander, simple old souls with childlike eyes and Napoleon III beards whom one would scarcely have suspected of harming a chicken. The day before two native women had brought in a *caco* whom they had cudgeled into submission, and that afternoon an old man, unarmed, had presented the commander with another, leading him by a rope around the neck.

In these circumstances we set out on horseback next morning in no great fear of the bandits, though we· kept our rifles and revolvers handy. With us went a curious dwarf who lived in the next town and who had attached himself to the Americans like a stray mastiff, which he closely resembled in expression and in his devotion to them. He was of full size from the waist upward, but his legs were scarcely a foot long, and his bare feet hardly reached to the edges of the saddle in which he sat, once he had been placed there, with all the assurance of a cow-boy of the plains. Then there was " Jim," looking like the advance agent of a minstrel show. " Jim " was a descendant of American negroes, his grandparents having come from Philadelphia to Samaná, Santo Domingo, where a number of black colonists from our northern states settled at the invitation of the Haitians when they ruled the whole island. He spoke a fluent English, with a mixture of Southern and foreign accent, as well as " creole " and Spanish, and having served the colonel as interpreter years before during the marine advance from Monte Cristi to Santiago, had come to Haiti to join him again when he took charge of the gendarmerie. He had been assigned to plain-clothes duty, but " Jim's " conception of that phrase did not include the adjective, and he had set forth on what promised to be anything but a dressy expedition in a garb well suited for a presidential reception. This was already beginning to show the effects of scrambling through the underbrush in quest of the wild pigeons which had fallen before the colonel's shot-gun.

The mayor of Hinche, a first cousin of Charlemagne, saw us off in person, holding the colonel's stirrup and bidding him farewell with bared head. We forded the Guayamoc River and wound away through foot-hills that soon gave way to a brown, level savanna which two years before had been covered with cattle, now wholly disappeared. Once we climbed over a large hill of oyster-shells, which geologists would no doubt recognise as proof that the region was formerly under the sea; but the French colonists of long ago were probably as fond of oysters as are their fellow-countrymen to-day, and it is worthy of note that these were all half-shells. We passed one small village in a hollow, with a mud hut full of gendarmes; the rest of the morning the dry and arid, yet lightly wooded, country was almost wholly uninhabited. For long spaces the scornful cries of black crows were the only sounds except the constant switching required to keep our thin Haitian horses and mules on the move.

Thomasique, where we halted for lunch at the mud-hut gendarmerie, was a dismal little hamlet of lopsided thatched hove's. The commander of the district had found a new use for captured *caco* rifles, using the barrels as gratings for his outdoor cooking-place. The *juge de paix*, the magistrate, and the richest man of the town, ranging in color from quadroon to *griffe*, called to pay their respects to the general, frankly admitting by their attitude that the young American lieutenant of gendarmes was their superior officer. Under his guidance the revenues of Thomasique had increased five fold in a single month. It was evident from the manner of the judge that he had something on his chest, and at length he unburdened himself. The Government, it seemed, had not paid him his salary — of one dollar a month — for more than half a year, and he respectfully petitioned the general to take the matter up with the president upon his return to Port au Prince. There was probably a connection between his lack of funds and the auditing of the village accounts by the lieutenant.

The country was more broken beyond. Pine-trees of moderate size grew beside girlishly slender little palms with fan-shaped leaves. A high bank of blue gravel along a dry river-bed would probably have attracted the attention of a miner or a geologist. In detail the country was not pretty; in the mass it was vastly so. Brown, reddish, and green hills were heaped up on every hand; the play of colors across them, changing at every hour from dawn through blazing noonday into dusk and finally moonlight, made up for the monotony of the near-by landscape. There were almost no signs of humanity, the silence was sometimes complete, though here and there we passed the evidences of former gardens in dry *arroyos*. Toward sunset we burst suddenly out among banana-groves, starting up a great flock of wild guineas, and at dark rode into Cerca la Source, a more than usually whitewashed little town nestled among real mountains. It was Sunday, and the great weekly cock-fight having just ended at the barrel-stave pit in a corner of the immense open *place*, the hubbub of settling bets had not yet subsided, and for a half hour afterward scores of negroes with pretty game-cocks under their arms wandered about in the moonlight shouting merry challenges to one another for the ensuing Sabbath.

Beyond Cerca la Source a steep mountain trail climbs for hours through the stillness of pine-forests where birds, except the cawing crows, are rare and almost no human habitations break the vista of tumbled world over which even the native horses make their way with difficulty. A telephone wire known among the marines as the "beer-bottle line," those being the only insulators to be had when it was constructed by our forces of occupation, is the one dependable guide through the region. Four hours brought us to a score of sorry huts in a little hollow known as La Miel. Even that had its hilltop gendarmerie and prison, commanded by a native sergeant, who had his force drawn up for inspection when we arrived, though he had no warning of the colonel's approach or any other proof of his official character other than the blouseless uniform he wore. A white rascal owning a marine uniform could play strange tricks in Haiti. Even here there was a big French bell of long ago supported by poles at some distance from the broken-backed church, and Spanish influence of the Dominicans beyond the now not very distant border showed itself in such slight matters as the use of "*yo*" for "*ge*" and "*buen*" instead of "*bon.*" There followed a not very fertile region, with more pine-trees and long, brown, tough grass, with only here and there a *conuco*, shut in by the slanted pole fences native to Santo Domingo, planted with weed-grown *pois Congo, manioc,* and tropical tubers. In mid-afternoon, where the vegetation grew more dense, it began to rain, as we had been warned it would here before our departure from Port au Prince. The first sprinkle increased to a steady downpour by what would probably have been sunset, the trail became toboggans of red mud down which our weary animals skated for long distances, or sloughs so deep and slopes so steep that we were forced to dismount and wade, or climb almost on all fours. Dripping coffee-bushes under higher trees sometimes lined the way, the best information we got from any of the rare passers-by was that our destination was a "little big distance" away. That it remained until we finally slipped and sprawled our way into it.

It rains the year round in the dismal mountain village where we spent the night, until the thatched mud houses are smeared with a reeking slime, and the earth floors are like newly plowed garden patches in the early spring. The place was more than three thousand feet above the

sea, and the cold seemed to penetrate to the very marrow even within
doors. It was ruled with an iron hand by an "old-timer" who had
been so long a sergeant in the Marine Corps that he had come to divide
all the world into exact gradations of rank. My companion he unfailingly addressed as "the General," never by the familiar pronoun
"you," and he took personal charge of everything pertaining to his
comfort, even to removing his wet garments and extracting the bones
from his chosen portions of chicken. Nothing would induce him to eat
before the general had finished or to sit down in his presence. Myself he treated almost as an equal, or as he might have another sergeant
who slightly outranked him in length of service, with now and then a
hint of scorn at my merely civilian standing. He was probably as
small a man as ever broke into our military service, yet the stentorian
voice in which he invariably gave his commands to the great hulking
negro who served as cook in the unsheltered "kitchen" outside and as
general factotum about the hut never failed to cause that person to
prance with fear. The natives he addressed in the same tone, and the
whole town seemed to spring to attention when he opened the door and
bawled out into the night for the mayor to "Report here on the double
quick." How the Haitians managed to understand his English was a
mystery, but they lost no time in obeying every order. After the general had retired, the lieutenant, for such was his rank in the gendarmerie, confided to me that he had several books on "creole" and was
preparing to learn it. As I had been on the lookout for something of
the kind since my arrival in Haiti, hitherto in vain, I expressed a desire
to see them. The lieutenant cast aside a soaked tarpaulin and handed
me half a dozen French grammars such as are used in our own
schools.

The colonel's clothing was dry and newly pressed when we set out
again next morning, though my own was still dripping. "Jim's" plain
clothes were by this time worthy a still more commonplace adjective,
for in addition to the mishaps of the trail, he had spent the night in
them on the bare earth floor of the gendarme barracks. There came a
few more red mud toboggans, then we came out on a vista of half
northern Haiti, to which we descended by a rock trail worn horseback
deep in the mountain-side and so steep that even "Jim" for once
deigned to dismount. The rain ceased a few hundred feet down,
though the sky remained dull and overcast, in striking contrast to the
speckless blue heavens of southern Haiti, for the seasons are reversed
in the two parts of the country. A few hours' jog across another sa-

A corner of Christophe's Citadel. Its situation is such that it could only be well photographed from an airplane

The ruins of Christophe's palace of Sans Souci

Cockfighting is a favorite Haitian sport

The mayor, the judge, and the richest man of a Haitian
town in the bush

vanna of denser vegetation than the plateau of St. Michel brought us to the considerable town of Ouanaminthe, on the Dominican border, where an automobile bore us away to the west. The great Plaine du Nord, once completely covered with sugar-cane and dotted with French plantation houses and mills, was now a wilderness teeming with blue-legged wild guineas, here and there some bush-grown stone ruins, through which a mud road and a single telephone wire forced their way. We passed the populous towns of Terrier Rouge and Le Trou, famed for their *caco* sympathies, and Limonade, in the grass-grown old church of which Christophe, Emperor of northern Haiti, was once stricken with apoplexy, and brought up in the mud and darkness at Cap Haïtien.

Meanwhile Rachel had reached " the Cape," as it is familiarly called, by the usual route. Leaving Ennery, this had begun at once to climb the mountain Puilboreau, winding in and out along its wrinkled face. The vegetation was rather monotonous, with a yellowish tinge to the several shades of green, now and then an orange cactus blossom, a purple morning glory, a pink vine, or the old-gold bark of a tree adding a touch of color. The view back down the valley, with its tiny specks of houses, remained unbroken until they reached the summit three thousand feet above the sea at Bakersville, so called for the marine who had charge of this difficult bit of road building, when there burst forth as far-reaching a scene to the north. The Plaisance Valley lay under the heavy gray veil of a rain-cloud, the harbor of Cap Haïtien visible far below, and far off on the horizon was the faint line of what seemed to be Tortuga, chief of Haiti's " possessions " and once the favorite residence of buccaneers. The change of landscape was abrupt; heavy, dense green vegetation smelling of moisture surrounding the travelers on every hand as they wound down the mountain-side by a mud-coated highway, passing here and there gangs of road laborers. This northern slope was more thickly inhabited, thatched huts conspicuous by their damp brown against the greenery occasionally clustering together into villages in which some of the mud walls were whitewashed or painted. Market-women bound for " the Cape," men grubbing in the fields, women paddling clothes — sometimes those in which they should have been dressed — in the streams, all gave evidence of the slighter dread of *cacos* on this northern slope. Then came another climb and a descent into the valley of the Limbé, some miles along which brought them to the village of the same name and to the greatest difficulty to the automobilist in Haiti.

The fording of the Limbé is certain to be the chief topic of conversation between those who have traveled from Port au Prince to Cap Haïtien. At times it is impassable, and has been known to delay travelers for a week. This time men and women were crossing with bundles on their heads and the water barely up to their armpits. A gang of prisoners was brought from the village gendarmerie, the vitals of the car removed and sent across on their heads, then with the passengers sitting on the back of the back seat, the baggage in their laps, the reunited gang, amid continual shrieks of "*Poussez!*" and an excited jabbering of " creole," eventually dragged and pushed the dismantled automobile to the opposite shore. An hour and a half passed between the time it halted on one bank and started out again from the other, which was close to a record for the crossing. From there on the wide, but muddy, road, now thronged with people returning from market with their purchases or empty baskets, passed many ruins of old plantations, and the crumbling stone and plaster gate-posts which once flanked the only entrances to them.

Cap Haïtien, the second city of Haiti, sometimes called the " capital of the North," is situated on a large open bay in which the winds frequently play havoc. On its outer reef the flagship of Columbus came to grief on Christmas eve, 1492, and the discoverer spent Christmas as the guest of the Indian chief who then ruled the district. The wreckage of the *Santa Maria* was brought ashore near the present fisher village of Petit Anse, and here was erected the first European fort in the New World. In the days of Haiti's prosperity Cap Haïtien was known as the " Paris of America " and rivaled in wealth and culture any other city in the western hemisphere. Then it had an imposing cathedral, several squares and *places* decorated with fountains and statuary, and was noted for its fine residences and urbane society. Old stone ruins still stretch clear out to the lighthouse on a distant point. Destroyed by the revolting blacks, by Christophe in his wars against Pétion, by an earthquake or two, and by more than a century of neglect and tropical decay, it retains little evidence of its former grandeur. Some of its wide streets, however, are still stone-paved, and bear names which carry the imagination back to medieval France. A few of its citizens live in moderate comfort; the overwhelming majority are content to loll out their days in uncouth hovels. It is so populous that it supports a cinema, and some of its business houses are moderately up to date and prosperous, though these are in most cases owned by foreigners. The acrid smell of raw coffee everywhere assails the nostrils; coffee spread out on canvas or on the cement pavement of one of its few remaining squares is constantly being turned over with wooden shovels by bare-footed negroes who think nothing of wading through it; here and there one passes a warehouse in which chattering old women sit thigh-deep in coffee, clawing over the berries with their fleshless black talons. Its market-place is large and presents the usual chaos of wares and hubbub of bargaining; its blue vaulted cathedral easily proves its antiquity, and American marines are everywhere in evidence. On the whole, its populace is somewhat less ragged than that of Port au Prince, but whatever it lacks in picturesqueness is made up for by the view of its surrounding mountains crowned by the great Citadel of Christophe.

Election day came during our stay at "the Cape." In olden times such an event was worth coming far to see, provided one could keep out of the frequent mêlées accompanying it. Under the Americans it is tame in the extreme. To obviate the necessity of counting more votes than there are inhabitants, the marines have introduced a plan charming in its simplicity. As he casts his ballot, each voter is required to dip the end of his right forefinger in a solution of nitrate of silver. The nail of course turns black, for the finger-nails even of a negro are ordinarily light colored,— and remains so until election day is over. Far be it from me to suggest that such a scheme might be adopted to advantage in our own country. A few district commanders, to make doubly sure, use iodine. The rank and file accept this formality as cheerfully as they do every other incomprehensible requirement of their new white rulers, most of them making the sign of the cross with the wet finger. But the haughty "*gens de couleur*" are apt to protest loudly against this "implied insult to my honor," and if they can catch the American official off his guard, are sure to dip in the wrong finger or merely make a false pass over the liquid, meanwhile scowling into silence the low-caste native watchers.

Haiti has long dreamed of some day uniting the several bits of miniature railroad scattered about the country into a single line between the two principal cities. The existing section in the north, twenty odd miles in length, connects Cap Haïtien with Grande Rivière and Bahon. Its fares, like those of the equally primitive lines out of Port au Prince, are so low that for once the assertions of the owners that they lose money on passengers can be accepted without a grin of incredulity. To raise them, however, is not so simple a matter as it may seem, for the Haitian masses are little inclined as it is to part with their rare *gourdes* for the mere privilege of saving their calloused feet. There

were far more travelers along the broad highway out of " the Cape "
than in the little cars themselves in which we followed it through a
region that might have been highly productive had it been as diligently
tended by man as by nature.   The train stopped frequently and long
at forest-choked clusters of negro huts varying only in size.   Such
scenes had grown so commonplace that we found more of interest in the
car itself, particularly among the marines who sprawled over several of
the seats.   The majority of our forces of occupation are so decidedly
a credit to their country that it needed the contrast of such types as
these to explain why the " Gooks," as the natives are popularly known
among their class, generally resent our presence on Haitian soil.   Loud-
mouthed, profane, constantly passing around a grass-bound gallon
bottle of rum, and boasting of their conquests among the negro girls,
they were far less agreeable traveling companions than the blackest of
the natives.   Their " four years' cruise in Hate-eye," one would have
supposed in listening to them, was a constant round of these things and
" fighting chickens," with an occasional opportunity of " putting a lot
of families in mourning " thrown in.   Yet underneath it all they were
good-hearted, cheerful, and generous, despite the notion prevalent
among too many Americans that boisterousness and rowdyism is a
proof of courage and manhood.

Grande Rivière is a town of some consequence in Haiti, prettily situated in a river valley among green hills.   Its grassy *place* and the
unfailing " *patrie* " in its center are decided improvements on most of
those in the republic; the several large church bells under a roof of
their own at some distance from the building itself still retain their
musical French voices.   A dyewood establishment is its chief single industry.   The crooked logwood, carved down to the red heart before it
leaves the forests, is gnawed to bits by a noisy machine, boiled in a succession of vats, the red water running off through sluiceways, and the
waste tossed out to dry and serve as fuel, and the concentrated product,
thick as molasses, is inclosed in barrels for shipment.   Scarcely an hour
passes between the picking up of a log and the rolling away of the
barrel containing its extract.

But of all the sights in any Haitian town the market-place is surest
to attract the idle traveler.   It was Saturday, or beef day, and two
long lines of venders were dispensing mere nibbles of meat to the
clamoring throng of purchasers, no portion of the animal being too
uninviting to escape consumption.   Of a hundred little squares on the
ground dotted with " piles " of miscellaneous wares the inventory we

made of one is characteristic of all, and its sum total of value probably did not reach two dollars. There were long, square strips of yellow soap, brooms and ropes made of jungle plants, castor-beans (the oil from which is used in native lamps), unhulled rice, all kinds of woven things from baskets to saddle-bags, peanuts, green plantains, pitch-pine kindling for torches, huge sheets of cassava bread, folded twice, rock salt, gay calicoes, all tropical fruits, unground pepper, old nails, loose matches, cinnamon bark, peanut and *jijimi* sweets, pewter spoons, scissors, thread, little marbles of blue dye, unassorted buttons, cheap knives, safety-pins, yarn, tiny red clay pipes and the reed stems to go with them, rusted square spikes of the kind used a century ago, shelled corn, ground corn, *pitimi,* several kinds of beans, tiny scraps of leather, four tin cans from a marine messroom, five bottles of as many shapes and sizes, one old shoe, and a handful of red berries used in Haiti as beads.

A bare five days from New York stands the most massive, probably the most impressive single ruin in America. One might go farther and say that there are few man-built structures in Europe that can equal in mightiness and in the extraordinary difficulties overcome in its construction this chief sight of the West Indies. Only the pyramids of Egypt, in at least the familiar regions of the earth, can compare with this gigantic monument to the strength and perseverance of puny man, and the pyramids are built down on the floor of the earth instead of being borne aloft to the tiptop of a mountain. It is curious, yet symbolical of our ignorance of the neighbors of our own hemisphere, that while most Americans know of far less remarkable structures in Europe, not one in a hundred of us has ever hea·d of the great Haitian Citadel of Christophe.

We caught our first view of it from " the Cape." The January day had broken in a flood of tropical sunshine, which brought out every crack and wrinkle of the long mountain-range cutting its jagged outline in the Haitian sky to the southward of the city. On the top of its highest peak, called the " Bishop's Bonnet," stood forth a square-cut summit which only the preinformed could have believed was the work of man. Twenty-five·miles away it looked like an enormous hack in the mountain itself, a curious natural formation which man could never have imitated except on a tiny scale. It is a standing joke in Cap Haïtien to listen in all solemnity to newcomers laughing to scorn the assertions of the residents that this distant mountain summit was fashioned by human hands.

Now and again as we journeyed toward it on the little railroad to Grande Rivière we had a glimpse of the citadel through the dense tropical vegetation, yet so slowly did it increase in size that its massiveness became all the more incredible.   Where we descended at a cross-trail in the forest a group of small Haitian horses was already awaiting us. The gendarme officer in charge of them was a powerful young American beside whom a native of the color known as *griffe*, in civilian garb, looked like a half-grown boy.   For the pilots assigned us on this excursion were none other than Captain Hanneken and Jean Batiste, now Lieutenant, Conzé, the exterminators of Charlemagne.

The trail broke out at length into a wide clearing which stretched away as far as the eye could follow in each direction, its grassy surface cut up by several wandering paths along which plodded a few natives and a donkey or two.   It was once the " royal highway " between Christophe's main palace and Cap Haïtien, outdoing in width the broadest boulevards of Europe.   An hour or more along this brought us to Milot, a small town lined up on each side of the road like people awaiting a procession of royalty.   At the back of it the highway ended at a great crumbling ruin which had about it something suggestive of Versailles.

Christophe's palace of Sans Souci, for such it was, is wholly uninhabitable to-day, yet there is still enough of it standing to indicate that it was once one of the most ornate and commodious structures in the western hemisphere.   Two pairs of mammoth gate-posts, square in form and nearly twenty feet high, guard the entrance to the lower yard-platform, bounded by a heavy stone wall.   On the inside these are hollowed out into unexpected sentry-boxes, for Christophe was a strong believer in many guards.   Higher up, sustained by a still stronger wall, is another grassy platform, from which a stairway as broad and elaborate as any trodden by European sovereigns leads sidewise to a balustraded entrance court, also flanked by sentry-boxes.   Crumbling walls in which many small bushes have found a foothold tower high aloft above this to where they are broken off in jagged irregularity.   The palace was evidently five stories high, built of native brick and plaster, and the architecture is still impressive despite its dilapidated condition and for all its African-minded ostentation.   The roof has completely given way, and in the vast halls of the lower floor grow wild oranges and tropical bush.   Those higher up, of which only the edges of the floors and the walls remain, are said to have included a great ball-room, an immense billiard-hall, separate suites for the emperor and his black consort, and apartments for the immediate royal family. At some distance from the palace proper stand the lower walls of the former lodgings of minor princes, a host of courtiers, the stables, and the caserns. The several *parterres,* once covered with rare flowers watered by irrigating canals, are mere tangles of jungle. The *caimite*-tree under which the black tyrant is said to have sat in judgment on his subjects, after the example of Louis IX of France, still casts its mammoth shade in the back courtyard; a small chapel lower down that was probably used by the lesser nobles serves Milot as a church; with those exceptions there is little left as Christophe saw it. Our forces of occupation are threatening to tear down the walls, which are soon likely to fall of themselves, to clear away the vegetation, and to build barracks of the materials that remain.

The narrow trail that zigzags from the back of the palace up the mountain may not be the one by which those condemned under the *caimite*-tree were carried or dragged to their death before the ramparts of the citadel, but there remain no evidences of any other route. Much of the way it is all but impassable even during a lull in the rainy season, for the dense vegetation shuts out the sun that might otherwise harden the mud in which the hardiest native horses frequently wallow belly-deep and now and then give up in frank despair. For a time it leads through banana- and mango-groves, with huts swarming with negro babies here and there peering forth from the thick undergrowth; higher still there is a bit of coffee, but the last two thirds of the journey upward is wholly uninhabited. Only once or twice in the ascent does one catch a glimpse of the goal until one emerges from a brown jungle of giant grasses, to find its grim gray walls towering sheer overhead.

Before this mammoth structure the memory of Sans Souci sinks into insignificance. As the latter is ornate and cheerful in architecture, the citadel is savage in its unadorned masculine strength. The mighty stone walls, twenty feet thick in many cases, are square-cut and formidable in their great unbroken surfaces. The northern side is red with fungus, the rest merely weather-dulled. Even the cannon of to-day would find them worthy adversaries. Time, which has wrought such havoc on the palace at the mountain's foot, has scarcely made an impression on the exterior of this cyclopean structure, and even within only the wooden portions have given way. Great iron-studded doors groaning on their mammoth hinges give admittance to an endless labyrinth of gloomy chambers, dungeon-like in all but their astonishing size. Cannon of the largest makes known when the fortress was constructed are to be found everywhere, some of them still pointing dizzily out their embrasures, stretching in row after row of superimposed batteries, others lying where the rotting of their heavy wooden supports has left them. Many bear the royal arms of Spain's most famous monarchs, several those of Queen Elizabeth, and the rest evidences of English and French origin. Tradition has it that Christophe mounted three hundred and sixty-five cannon of large caliber in the citadel, and it is small wonder that his successors have not had the courage to attempt to remove them. The imagination grows numb and helpless at the thought of transporting these immense weapons by mere man power to the summit of a steep mountain three thousand feet above the plain below. Yet not only these, but the uncounted mammoth blocks of stone of which the acres of thick walls are constructed, the mortars, the iron chests, the smaller cannon, the heaps of huge iron cannon-supports, the pyramids of cannon-balls that are found wherever the footsteps turn in the clammy chambers or the jungle-grown courtyards, were all brought here by sheer force of human arms.

Higher and higher the visitor mounts by great dank stairways through story after story of immense rooms, the vaulted stone ceilings of a few partly fallen in, most of them wholly intact, all dedicated to the grim business of war, to come out at last in an upper courtyard with the ruins of a chapel and the mammoth stone vault in which Christophe lies buried. Some of the marvels of the place are the stone basins always full of clear running water, the source of which no man has ever been able to discover. Here the group of prisoners whom the captain had sent ahead with the paraphernalia and provisions for an elaborate picnic lunch were shivering in their thin striped garments until their black faces seemed to be blurred of outline. Yet they had less cause to tremble than their fellows of a century ago who were herded in this same inclosure to await their turn for being thrown from the ramparts above. For such was Christophe's favorite method of capital punishment. The throwing-off place is a long stone platform ten feet wide at the very top of the citadel. From its edge the sheer wall drops to a sickening depth before it joins the mountain-slope almost as steep, forming that great hack in the summit which looks from "the Cape" like a natural precipice. Men hurled from this height must have fallen nearly a thousand feet before they struck the bushy boulder-strewn face of the mountain, down which their mutilated remains bounded and slid to where they brought up against a ledge of rock or a larger bush, there to lie until their whitened bones crumbled into dust. Multitudes of his subjects are said to have met this fate under the black tyrant, some in punishment for real crimes, more for having unintentionally aroused his enmity or to satisfy his whims. The story goes that Christophe and his British ambassador once got into a friendly argument on the subject of soldierly discipline. The black emperor contended that there was no order which his troops would not unhesitatingly obey, and to prove his point he led his guest to the top of the citadel, where he set a company to drilling and at a given command caused it to march off the edge of the wall. This particular tale should perhaps be taken with a grain of salt, but there is unquestionable evidence of similar playful acts on the part of the heartless monarch.

Once the visitor can withdraw his eyes from the jagged Golgotha below, the view spread out before him is rivaled by few in the world. All Haiti seems to be visible in every detail: the ocean, the entire course of meandering rivers, high mountains, deep valleys, a sea of greenery, form a circular panorama bounded only by the limitless horizon. Little houses in tiny clearings on the plain below, a dozen towns and villages, " the Cape," Ouanaminthe, even the hills of Santo Domingo, stand forth as clearly as if they were only a bare mile away, some flashing in the tropical sunshine, others dulled by the great cloud shadows crawling languidly across the landscape.

Henri Christophe was a full-blooded negro who passed the early days of his life as the slave of a French planter. When the blacks rose against their masters he led the revolt on his own plantation and quickly avenged his years of bondage. Serving first as a common soldier under Toussaint l'Ouverture, he rose to the rank of general and became one of the chief supporters of Dessalines. The assassination of the latter in 1806 left Christophe commander-in-chief of the Haitian forces and led to his election as the first President of Haiti. His first official act was to protest against the newly adopted constitution on the ground that it did not give him sufficient power. Civil war broke out between him and the mulatto general Pétion, who drove him into the north and became president in his place, leaving Christophe the official ranking of an outlaw. Pétion, however, was never able to conquer his rival. Proclaiming himself president under a new constitution drawn up by an assembly of his own choosing, the rebel took possession of the northern half of the country and ruled it for thirteen long years with one of the bloodiest hands known to history.

In 1811 he proclaimed himself king, honored his black consort with the title of queen, and proceeded to form a Haitian nobility consisting of his own numerous children as "princes of the royal blood," three "princes of the kingdom," eight "dukes," twenty "counts," thirty-seven "barons," and eleven "chevaliers," each and all of them former slaves or the descendants of slaves. These jet-black "nobles," many of whom added to their titles the names of such native towns as Limonade, Marmalade, and the like, soon became the laughing-stock of more advanced civilizations, though candor forces the admission that Christophe was only following the example of those who ennobled the robber barons of Europe in earlier centuries, with the slight difference in the matter of complexions. As "King Henry" he surrounded himself with all the pomp and ceremony of royalty, erected nine palaces, of which Sans Souci was the most magnificent and the only one that has not completely disappeared, built eight royal châteaux, maintained great stables of horses and royal coaches, innumerable retainers and servants, and a tremendous bodyguard. Later, feeling that he had not done himself full honor, he named himself hereditary emperor under the title of "Henri I," and having come within an ace of conquering the entire country, settled down to govern his portion of it in a manner that would have been the envy of Nero.

The name of Christophe, in so far as it is known at all, is synonymous with unbridled brutality. Yet there is a certain violent virtue in the efforts by which the ex-slave sought to force his unprogressive black subjects to climb the slippery ladder of civilization. He founded schools, distributed the estates of the exiled Frenchmen among the veterans of his army, reëstablished commercial relations with England and the United States, created workshops in which the word "can't" was taboo. His methods were simple and direct. Causing a French carriage to be placed at the disposition of his workmen, he ordered them to produce another exactly like it within a fortnight on pain of death. Similar tasks were meted out in all lines of endeavor, the tyrant refusing to admit that what white men could do his black subjects could not do also. His despotism, however, was not bounded by the mere desire for advancement. When he passed, the people were compelled to kneel, and death was the portion of the man who dared look upon his face without permission. Thievery he abhorred, and inflicted capital punishment for the mere stealing of a chicken. It came to be a regular part of his daily life to order men, women, and even children thrown from the summit of the citadel.

Tradition asserts that thirty thousand of his black subjects perished in the building of this chief monument to his ambition. All the French and Belgian architects and the skilled mechanics who worked on it are said to have been assassinated when it was finished. The tale is still going the rounds in Haiti that the emperor once came upon a gang of workmen idling about one of the massive blocks of stone destined for the citadel above, and demanded the reason for their inaction.

"It is too heavy, Sire," replied the workmen; "we cannot carry it to the mountain-top."

"Line up," ordered the tyrant; then turning to his bodyguard, he commanded, "Shoot every fourth man. Perhaps you will feel stronger now," he remarked to the survivors as he rode onward.

On his return, however, the stone was no higher up the hill.

"It is quite impossible, your Majesty," gasped the foreman; "it will not budge."

"Throw that man from the precipice," said the despot, "and repeat the order of this morning."

The remaining workmen, according to the tale, succeeded in carrying the stone to its destination.

Such stories always hover about those mighty monuments that seem impossible without supernatural aid, yet no one who has beheld the success with which the forces of gravity have been derided in this incredible undertaking, incredible even in the enormousness of the structure itself without taking into account its extraordinary situation, will question its cost in such details as a few thousand more or less human lives. Obsessed with the idea that the French would try to reconquer the country, Christophe had resolved to erect a stronghold that would be an impregnable place of resistance against them, or at worst a "nest-egg of liberty," which would afford certain refuge to the *défenseurs de la patrie* until better days dawned for them. There he stored vast quantities of grain and food, of ammunition, flints, bullets, powder, soggy heaps of which are still to be found, clothing, tools, and a gold reserve amounting to more than thirty million dollars. His enemies saw in the citadel only a pretext to indulge his innate barbarism, to decimate his people for the mere pleasure of playing Nero. It may be that this is not a just verdict. Christophe felt that he incarnated the soul of his black brethren and that belief made him wholly insensible to any other consideration. The mere fact that his lack of perspective and his ignorance of such details as the feeding of a long-besieged garrison made his seemingly impregnable fortress an utter waste of effort may speak poorly for the instruction which his French masters gave him, but it does not belittle the actual accomplishment of his superhuman undertaking.

Christophe as violently died as he had lived. Stricken with apoplexy in the church of Limonade, he attempted to cure himself by heroic measures, such as rum and red-pepper baths. Finding this of no avail and refusing to outlive his despotic power over his subjects, he shot himself through the head. Barely was his body cold, if we are to believe current stories, when his officers and retainers sacked the palace of Sans Souci in which it lay, the wealth of many Haitian families of this day being based on the spoils from this and his other royal residences. The corpse was carried to the citadel and covered with quick lime, but tradition asserts that it retained its life-like appearance for many years afterward and was on view to all who cared to peer through the glass heading of the vault until a later ruler decreed this exposition " indecent," and ordered the remains to be covered with earth.

CHAPTER VIII

OUANAMINTHE is the Haitian "creole" name for a town which the Spaniards founded under the more euphonious title of Juana Mendez. It is the eastern frontier station for those who travel overland by the northern route from Haiti to Santo Domingo. We might have been stranded there indefinitely but for the already familiar kindness of our fellow-countrymen in uniform who are scattered throughout the negro republic. Public conveyances are unknown in Ouanaminthe. Strangers are more than rare, and the natives trust to their own broad, hoof-like feet. Walking is all very well for a lone bachelor with no other cares than a half-filled knapsack. But with a wife to consider, the long trail loses something of its primitive simplicity; moreover there sat our baggage staring us in the face with a contrite, don't-abandon-me air. In what would otherwise have been our sad predicament, Captain Verner, commanding the gendarmérie of Ouanaminthe, came to our rescue most delicately with the assertion that he had long been planning to run over to Monte Cristi on a pressing matter of business.

The captain's Ford — his own, be it noted in passing, lest some committee of investigation prick up its ears — was soon swimming the frontier river Massacre with that amphibean ease which the adaptable "flivver" quickly acquires in the often bridgeless West Indies. The change from one civilization to another — or should I call them two attempts toward civilization? — was as sudden, as astonishingly abrupt, as the dash through the apparently unfordable stream. Dajabón, strewn from the sandy crest of the eastern bank to the arid plains beyond, reminded us at once of Cuba; to my own mind it brought back the memory of hundreds of Spanish-American towns scattered down the western hemisphere from the Rio Grande to Patagonia. With one slight exception the island of Santo Domingo is the only one in the New World that is divided between two nationalities; it is the only one on earth, unless my geography be at fault, where the rank and file speak two different languages. Yet the shallow Massacre is as definite a dividing line as though it were a hundred leagues of sea.

Unlike the Haitian shacks behind us, the dwellings of Dajabón were almost habitable, even to the exacting Northern point of view. Instead of tattered and ludicrously patched negroes of bovine temperament lolling in the shade of as ragged hovels of palm-leaves and jungle rubbish, comparatively well-dressed men and women, ranging in complexion from light brown to pale yellow, sat in chairs on projecting verandas or leaned on their elbows in open windows, staring with that fixed attention which makes the most hardened stranger self-conscious in Spanish-America, yet which, contrasted with the vacant black faces of Haiti, was an evidence at least of human intelligence and curiosity. The village girls, decked out in their Sunday-afternoon best, were often attractive in appearance, some undeniably pretty, qualities which only an observer of African ancestry could by any stretch of generosity grant to the belles of the Haitian *bourgs* behind us.

Even the change in landscape was striking. Whether the Spaniard colonized by choice those regions which remind him of the dry and rarely shaded plains of his own Castille and Aragón, or because he makes way with a forest wherever he sees one, he is more apt than not to be surrounded by bare, brown, semi-arid vistas. Haiti had, on the whole, been densely wooded; luxuriant vegetation, plentifully watered, spread away on every hand. The great plain that stretched out before us beyond Dajabón was almost treeless; except for a scattering of withered, thorny bushes, there was scarcely a growing thing. The rainfall that had been so frequent in the land of the blacks behind us seemed not to have crossed the frontier in months. In contrast to *caco*-impoverished Haiti, large herds of cattle wandered about the brown immensity, or huddled in the rare pretenses of shade; but what they found to feed on was a mystery, for there was nothing in the scarce, scanty patches of sun-burned herbage that could have been dignified with the name of grass. Even where something resembling a forest appeared farther on it turned out to be a dismal wilderness of dwarf trees with spiny trunks and savage thorny branches without a suggestion of undergrowth or ground plants beneath them. Dead, flat, monotonous, made doubly mournful by the occasional moan of a wild dove, a more dreary, uninspiring landscape it would be hard to imagine; the vista that spread away as far as the eye could see seemed wholly uninviting to human habitation.

It must be an unpromising region, however, that does not produce at least its crop of mankind. Clusters of thrown-together huts, little less miserable in these rural districts, it must be admitted, than those of Haiti, jolted past us now and then, their swarms of stark-naked children of eight, ten, and even twelve years of age scampering out across the broken, sun-hardened ground to see us pass. Yet in one respect at least even these denizens of the wilderness were superior to their Haitian prototypes — they really spoke their native language. Familiar as we had both been for years with French, it was rare indeed that we got more than the general drift of a conversation in Haitian " creole." The most uneducated *dominicano,* on the other hand, spoke a Spanish almost as clear and precise as that heard in the streets of Madrid. There must be something enduring, something that appeals to the most uncouth tongue, in the Castilian language. Hear it where you will, in all the broad expanse of Central and South America, in the former Spanish colonies of the West Indies, from the lips of Indians, negroes, *mestizos,* or the Jews of the Near East, banished from Spain centuries ago, with minor variations of pronunciation and enrich-. ing of vocabulary from the tongues it has supplanted, it retains almost its original purity. What a hybrid of incomprehensible noises French, on the other hand, becomes in the mouths of slaves and savages we had all too often had impressed upon us in Haiti, and were due to have the lesson repeated in the French islands of the Lesser Antilles. Even our own English cannot stand the wear and tear of isolation and slovenly vocal processes with anything like the success of the Castilian. The speech of Canada and of Barbados, closely as those two lands are linked to the same mother country, seem almost two distinct languages. But if the Dominicans spoke their language more purely, their voices had none of the soft, almost musical tones of the negroes beyond the Massacre. There was a brittle, metallic, nerve-jarring twang to their speech that was almost as unpleasant as the high-pitched chatter of Cuban women.

If we noted all these differences between the two divisions of the island, there was another that impressed us far more forcibly at the moment. In all our jolting over the roads of Haiti, good, bad, and unspeakable, we had never once been delayed by so much as a puncture. In the first mile out of Dajabón we were favored with four separate and distinct blow-outs. The twenty-eight miles between the frontier and Monte Cristi — for it is best to hear the worst at once — netted no fewer than ten!

It was shortly after the fifth, if my memory is not failing, that the open plain gave way to a thorn-bristling wilderness through which had been cut a roadway a generous twenty feet wide — *shortly* after certainly, otherwise the sixth blow-out would have intervened. I use the term roadway advisedly, for road there was really none. The Dominican scorns the building of highways as thoroughly as do any of his cousins of Spanish descent. With American intervention he was forced, much against his will and better judgment, to divert a certain amount of public moneys and labor to making wheeled communication between his various provinces possible. But though you can drive an unbridled horse along any open space, you cannot choose the path he shall make within it. Wide as it was, the roadway was an unbroken expanse of deeply cracked and thoroughly churned brown mud, sun-burned to the consistency of broken rock. Along this the first traveler, after the long forgotten rains, had squirmed and waded his way where the mud was shallowest, with the result that the only semblance to a road wandered back and forth across the misshapen roadway like a Spanish " river " in its ludicrously over-ample bed.

Here and there we were forced to crawl along the extreme edge of one or the other of the bristling walls of vegetation; frequently the only passable trail left the roadway entirely and squirmed off through the spiny forest, the thorny branches whipping us in the faces. Huge clumps of organ cactus and others of the same family forced us to make precarious detours. At the top of a faint rise we sighted the " Morro " of Monte Cristi, a great bulking rectangular hill that guides the mariner both by land and sea to the most western port of Santo Domingo. Our hopes began slowly to revive when — " Groughung! " the sixth mishap befell us — or was it the seventh? I remember that the eighth overtook us at the bottom of the rise, when both daylight and our patches were giving out. The ninth found us in total darkness, and disclosed the fact that there was not a match on board. The lamps of the car had ceased to function months before; one does not. Ford it by night in the island of Santo Domingo except upon extreme provocation. A hut discovered back in the bush was likewise matchless, but the supper fire on the ground beside it still had a few glowing embers. While Rachel held the blaze of one of those dried hollow reeds that do duty as torches in Santo Domingo as near us as was prudent, we improvised a patch that would have caused an experienced chauffeur to gasp with astonishment. Each rustling of the thorny brush about us drew our fixed attention. There are bandits in Santo Domingo as well as in Haiti, and they have far less reputation for making speed to the rear. The captain carried a revolver, an American Marine being equally at home in either of the island republics. But the danger of

The Plaza and clock tower of Monte Cristo, showing its American bullet hole

Railroading in Santo Domingo

The tri-weekly train arrives at Santiago

Dominican guardians

international complications had prevented his black gendarme assistant from bringing with him the rifle that might be badly needed. My visions of losing a congenial companion were vastly enhanced once when a crashing in the bushes caused us to whirl about on the defensive. A stray cow ambled past us and away into the black night.

With the tenth mishap, lightless and patchless, we lost the final remnants of patience and forced our sorry steed to hobble along on three feet. The road had a pleasant little way of eluding us when least expected, and a dozen times within the next hour we brought up against the forest wall, finding our way again only by the sense of touch. Then at last appeared a flicker of light. But it was only the hamlet on the bank of the River Yaque, across which we must be ferried on what looked in the darkness like the top of a soap-box. Fortunately it takes little to float a Ford. Our crippled charger staggered up the steep bank beyond this principal stream of northern Santo Domingo, and a half hour later we rattled into the considerable town of Monte Cristi.

Its streets were as wide as the hilltop roadway behind us, but like it they had only reached the first stage of development. Worst of all we were forced to run the full length of nearly every one of them in the vain quest of some suggestion of hostelry. Our predicament would have been one to bring salt tears to the most hardened eyes but for the saving grace of all the island of Santo Domingo — our own people in uniform. Barely had we discovered the commander-in-chief of Monte Cristi, a Marine captain bearing the name of one of our early and illustrious Presidents, than he broke all records in hospitality within our own experience by turning his entire house over to us. We were never more firmly convinced of the wisdom of American intervention in Santo Domingo than at the end of that explosive day.

The otherwise dark and deserted town was gathered in its best starched attire in the place where any Spanish-American town would naturally be on a Sunday evening — in the central plaza. This, to begin with, was strikingly unlike the bare open squares of Haiti, with their unfailing tribune-and-palm-tree " patrie." First of all, it was well paved, an assertion that could not be made of any other spot in town. An elaborate iron fence surrounded it, comfortable benches were ranged about it, trees and flowering shrubs shaded it by day and decorated it by night, the only public lights in town cast an unwonted brilliancy upon the promenading populace, circling slowly round and round the square, the two sexes in opposite directions, their voices and footsteps half drowning the not too successful efforts of a group of misfitted males in the center of the plaza to produce musical sounds. It was as typically Spanish a scene as the deserted barren *place*, with the weird beating of tomtoms floating across it, is indigenous to the republic of Haiti.

It was not until morning, however,.that we caught full sight of the chief feature of the plaza and the pride of Monte Cristi. By daylight a monument we had only vaguely sensed in the night stood forth in all its dubious beauty. In the center of the now deserted plaza rose a near replica of the Eiffel Tower, its open-work steel frame crowned by a large four-faced clock some fifty feet above our dizzy heads. Well might the Monte Cristians pride themselves on a feature quite unique among the plazas of the world.

From this clock tower hangs a tale that is too suggestive of Dominican character to be passed over in silence. Some years ago, before the intrusive Americans came to put an end to the national sport, a candidate for the Dominican Congress came parading his candidacy about the far corners of the country. In each town he promised, in return for their aid in seating him in the august assembly, that the citizens should have federal funds for whatever was most lacking to their civic happiness. Monte Cristi, being farthest from the cynical capital of any community in Santo Domingo, took the politician seriously. The town put its curly heads together and decided that what it most wanted was — not a real school building to take the place of the rented hut in which its children fail to learn the rudiments of the three R's, nor yet pavements for some of the sandhills that are disguised under the name of streets. What it felt the need of more than anything else was a town clock that would cast envy on all its rivals for many miles around. The politician approved the choice so thoroughly that he advised the opening of negotiations for its purchase at once, without waiting for the mere formality of congressional sanction. In due time the monstrosity was erected. But for some reason the newly elected congressman's influence with his fellow-members was not so paramount as his faithful supporters had been led to believe. Some of them still contend that he did actually introduce a resolution to provide the noble and patriotic pueblo of Monte Cristi with a prime necessity in the shape of a community time-piece; if so the bill died in committee, unattended by priest or physician. For months Monte Cristi bombarded the far-off capital with doleful petitions, until at length, with the sudden coming of the Americans, congress itself succumbed, and the two thousand or so good citizens of the hapless town found themselves face to face with a document — bearing a foreign place of issue at that, caramba! — reading succinctly:

"To one clock and tower, Dr...........$16,000
Please Remit"

To cap the climax, the ridiculous Americans who had taken in charge the revenues of the country brought with them the absurd doctrine that municipalities should pay their bills. Years have passed since the successful politician visited the northwest corner of the country, yet Monte Cristi is only beginning to crawl from beneath its appalling clock tower, financially speaking, and to catch its breath again after relief from so oppressive a burden. Small wonder that her sand-hill streets are unpaved and that her children still crowd into a rented hovel to glean the rudiments of learning.

But the history of the famous clock tower does not end there. Those who glance at the top-heavy structure from the south are struck by a jagged hole just above the face of the dial, midway between the XII and the I. It is so obviously a bullet-hole that the observer could not fail to show surprise were it not that bullet-holes are as universal in Santo Domingo as fighting cocks. Thereby hangs another tale.

In the early days of American occupation the choice of commanders of the *Guardia Nacional* detachment in Monte Cristi was not always happy. It was natural, too, that a group of marine officers, bubbling over with youth, sentenced to pass month after month in a somnolent Dominican village, should have found it difficult to devise fitting amusement for their long leisure hours. Pastimes naturally reduced themselves to the exchange of poker chips and the consumption of certain beverages supposedly taboo in all American circles and doubly so in the Marine Corps. The power of Dominican joy-water to produce hilarity is far-famed. It came to be the custom of the winning card player to express his exuberance by drawing his automatic and firing several shots over his head. This means of expression would have been startling enough to the disarmed Dominicans had the games been played in the open air with the sun above the horizon. But the rendezvous was naturally within doors, usually in the dwelling of the commander, and the climax was commonly reached at an hour when all reputable natives were wrapped in slumber. The sheet-iron roof that sheltered us during our night in Monte Cristi corroborated the testimony of the inhabitants that they had frequently sprung from their beds convinced that yet another revolution was upon them.

One night a difference of opinion arose among the players as to the hour that should be set for the cashing in of chips. The commander offered to settle the problem in an equitable manner. Stepping to the door, he raised his automatic toward the famous $16,000 clock and fired. The decision was made; the game ended at twelve : thirty. It is not particularly strange under the circumstances that the inhabitants of Monte Cristi are not extraordinarily fond of Americans or of marine occupation.

The mail coach — in real life the inevitable Ford — left Monte Cristi the morning after our arrival, obviating the necessity of wiring to Santiago for a private car. The fare was within reason, as such things go in the West Indies — sixteen dollars for a journey of some eighty miles — and despite the pessimistic prophecies of our host we had the back seat to ourselves the entire distance. Our driver, of dull-brown hue, was of the same quick, nervous temperament as his Cuban cousins, and scurried away at thirty miles an hour over " roads " which few American chauffeurs would venture along at ten. Yet he was surprisingly successful in avoiding undue jolts; so often had he driven this incredibly rough-and-tumble route that he knew exactly when and where to slow up for each dry *arroyo*, to dodge protruding boulders or dangerous sand beds, to drop from one level to another without cracking a spring or an axle. The machine was innocent of muffler, hence it needed no horn, and as an official conveyance it yielded the road to no one, except the few placid carts whose safety lay in their massiveness.

Many miles of the journey were sandy barren wastes producing only dismal thorn-bristling dwarf forests. Every now and then we dodged from one wide caricature of a road to another still more choppy and rock-strewn; occasionally we found a mile or two of tolerable highway. The scarcity of travelers was in striking contrast to Haiti. The few people we met were never on foot, but in clumsy carts or astride gaunt, but hardy, little horses. Houses of woven palm-leaves, on bare, reddish, hard soil sheltered the poorer inhabitants; the better-to-do built their dwellings of split palm trunks that had the appearance of clapboards. Villages were rare, and isolated houses wholly lacking. Outdoor mud ovens on stilts, with rude thatched roofs over them, adorned nearly every back or side yard. At each village we halted before a roughly constructed post office to exchange mailbags with a postmaster who in the majority of cases showed no visible negro strain.   Pure white in-habitants were frequent in the larger pueblos; full-blooded African types extremely rare.   Santo Domingo has been called a mulatto coun-try; we found it more nearly a land of quadroons.

What even the sparse population lived on was not apparent, for almost nowhere were people working in the fields, and the towns seemed to be chiefly inhabited by fairly well-dressed loafers, or at best by lolling shop-keepers.   Probably they existed by selling things to one another.   The stocks of the over-numerous shops were amply supplied with bottled goods, but with comparatively little else, and that chiefly tinned · food from the United States.   No old sugar kettles, no ruined French estates, no negro women in broad straw hats or slippers flap-ping with the gait of their donkeys, no improvised markets or clamoring beggars along the way — none of the familiar things of Haiti were in evidence, except the fighting cocks.   Such horsemen as we passed rode in well upholstered saddles, doubly softened by the Spanish-Ameri-can *pellon,* or shaggy saddle rug.   The women accompanying them clung uncomfortably to clumsy side-saddles, and were dressed in far more style than their Haitian prototypes, pink gowns being most in favor, and in place of the loose slippers the majority wore shoes elaborate enough to satisfy a New York shop-girl.   Cemeteries at the edge of each town were forests of wooden crosses, contrasting with the coffin-shaped cement tombs of Haiti.

Guayovin, a town of considerable size and noted for its revolutionary history, the scattered hamlet of Laguna Salada, the larger village of Esperanza, one pueblo after another was the same blurred vista of wide, sandy streets, of open shop fronts and gaping inhabitants.   We soon detected a surly attitude toward Americans, a sullen, passive resentment that recalled the attitude of Colombia as I had known it eight years before.   There was more superficial courtesy than in our own brusk and hurried land; the Dominican, like all our neighbors to the southward, cultivates an exterior polish.   But with the exception of a few who went out of their way to demonstrate their pro-American sentiments, to express themselves as far more pleased with foreign occupation than with the continual threat of revolution, the attitude of silent protest was everywhere in the air.

At the end of fifty kilometers, in which we had forded only one pathetic little stream, the landscape changed somewhat for the better, though at the same time the "road" became even more atrocious. Hitherto the only beauty in the scene had been a pretty little flowering cactus bush, like an inverted candelabra, and the soft velvety colors of the barren brown vistas. Now the thorny vegetation, the chaparral, and the cactus gave way to clumps of bamboo, to towering palms, and other trees of full stature, while corn and beans began to clothe the still deadly-dry soil. High hills had arisen close on the left, higher ones farther off to the right; then ahead appeared beautiful labyrinths of deep-blue mountains, range after range piled up one behind the other in amphitheatrical formation, culminating in the cloud-coiffed peak of Tino, some ten thousand feet above the sea and the highest point in the West Indies.

Navarrete, strung along the beginning of an excellent highway that was to continue, except for two unfinished bridges, to Santiago, boasted real houses, some of palm trunks, most of them of genuine lumber with more corrugated iron than thatched roofs, some of their walls of faded pink, green, or yellow, many of them frankly unpainted. A considerable commercial activity occupied its inhabitants. Beyond, the country grew still greener, with groves of royal palms waving their ostrich plumes with the dignified leisureliness of the tropics, and the highway began to undulate, or, as it seemed to us behind our over-eager chauffeur, to pitch and roll, over low foot-hills. We picked up a rusty little railroad on the left, farther on a power line and a dozen telegraph wires striding over hill and dale, raced at illegal speed through Villa Gonzalez, and entered a still more verdant region of vegetable gardens in fertile black soil. Then all at once we topped a rise from which spread out all the splendid green valley of Yaque, Santiago de los Caballeros piled up a sloping high ground a couple of miles away, with mountains that had grown to imposing height still far distant to the right. A truck-load of marines, monopolizing the right of way in the innocently obstructive manner we had often seen in France, blocked our progress for a time; then we swung past the inevitable shaded plaza of all Spanish-American towns, and drew up with a snort at the Santiago post office just as the cathedral clock was striking the hour of three.

Before we had time even to set foot in Santiago we were greeted by my old friend "Lieutenant Long" of Canal Zone police fame, who had already put the town in a proper mood for our reception. Since the days when we had pursued felons together along the ten-mile strip of Panamanian jungle the erstwhile lieutenant, now more fittingly known as "Big George," had added steadily to his laurels as a good and true servant of mankind. From the defelonized banks of the canal to the command of the sleuths of Porto Rico had been a natural step, and when he had detected everything worth detecting in our West Indian isle, and fathered a company of the 17th Infantry during the late international misunderstanding, " Big George " accepted the Augean task of initiating the Dominicans into the mysteries of their new American-sired land tax.

Considerably more than four hundred years ago, when the redskin north of the Rio Grande had yet to scalp his initial pale face, there was founded in the fertile valley of the Yaque the first of the many Santiagos that to-day dot the map of more than half the western hemisphere. Thirty Spanish gentlemen, as the word was understood in those roistering days, *hidalgos* who had followed on the heels of Columbus, were the original settlers, and because of their noble birth they were permitted by royal decree to call their new home by the name it still officially bears, — Santiago de los Caballeros. Although the present inhabitants of the aristocratic old town by no means all boast themselves "gentlemen" either in the *conquistador* or the modern sense of the term, some of the leading families can trace their ancestry in unbroken line from those old Spanish hidalgos. Many of these descendants of fifteenth century grandees still retain the armor, swords, and other quaint warlike gear of their ancestors. A few have even kept their Caucasian blood pure through all the generations and frequent disasters of that long four hundred years, but the vast majority of them give greater or less evidence of African graftings on the family tree. The Cibao, as the northern half of Santo Domingo is called, is the region in which the Spaniards first found in any quantity the gold they came a-seeking, and gentlemanly Santiago has ever been its principal city.' Twice destroyed by earthquakes, like so many cities of the West Indies, sacked by pirates and invaders more times than it cares to remember, it has persisted through all its mishaps.

But in spite of its flying start Santiago has by no means kept pace with many a parvenu in the New World. Barely can it muster twenty thousand inhabitants, and in progress and industry it has drifted but slowly down the stream of time. Revolutions have been its chief setback, for the innumerable civil wars that have decimated the population of the republic ever since it asserted its freedom from the Spanish crown have almost invariably centered about the city of caballeros. A hundred Spanish-American towns can duplicate its every feature. About the invariable central plaza, with its shaded benches, diagonal

walks, and evening promenaders, stand the bulking, weather-peeled
cathedral with its constantly thumping, tin-voiced bells, the *casa con-
sistorial* where the municipal council dawdles through its weekly meet-
ings, the wide open yet exclusive clubs, and the residences of the most
ancient families, their lower stories occupied by shops and cafés.   In
contrast to this proudly kept square the wide, right-angled streets that
radiate from it are either congenitally innocent of paving or littered
with the remnants of what may long ago have been cobbled driveways.
As in all Spanish-America the lack of civic team-work is shown in the
sidewalks; which are high, low, ludicrously narrow, or lacking entirely,
according to the personal whim of each householder, and rather family
porches than public rights of way.   Its houses, mostly of one story,
never higher than two, are something more than half of wood, the
remainder being adobe or baked-mud structures that some time in the
remote past had their façades daubed with whitewash or scantily painted
in various bright colors.   The cathedral, the municipal building, many
a private residence, our very hotel room were speckled with bullet-holes
more or less diligently patched, corroborating the verbal evidence of
Santiago's revolutionary activities.   There is a faint reminder of the
Moors in the tendency for each trade to monopolize one street to the
exclusion of the others.   A dozen barbershops may be found in a single
block, cafés cluster together, drygoods shops with their languid male
clerks shoulder one another with a certain degree of leisurely, un-
individualistic aggressiveness.   Farther out, the unkempt streets
dwindle away between lop-shouldered little huts that seem to need the
supporting mutual assistance shared by their neighbors nearer the center
of town.

There is not a street car in all the island of Santo Domingo, or Haiti,
as you choose to call it.   Dingy, wretched old carriages, their horses
only a trifle less gaunt and ungroomed than those of Port au Prince,
loiter about a corner of the plaza, behind the cathedral, shrieking their
pleas at every possible fare who passes within their field of vision.
Automobiles are not unknown, but they have not yet invaded Santiago
in force.   The inevitable venders of lottery tickets, which in Santo
Domingo are of municipal rather than national issue and resemble the
hand-bills of some itinerant family of barn-stormers, pester the passer-
by every few yards with spurious promises of sudden fortune.   In the
cathedral the visitor finds himself face to face at every step with admonitions that women must have their heads covered and that worshipers shall not spit on the floor.   The first command is universally recog-

nized, if only by the spreading of a handkerchief over the frizzled tresses, but the latter is by no means so faithfully obeyed. If there is anything whatever individualistic about St. James of the Gentlemen that distinguishes it from its countless cousins below the Rio Grande, it is the stars and stripes that wave above the ancient fortress overlooking the placid River Yaque, and the groups of American marines who come now and then striding down its untended streets.

The average santiagueño reaches the dignity of clothes somewhat late in life. Naked black or brown babies adorn every block, the sight of a plump boy of five taking his constitutional dressed in a pair of sandals, a bright red hat, and a magnificent expression of unconcern attracts the attention of no one except strangers. Girls show the prudery of their sex somewhat earlier in life, but many a boy learns to smoke cigarettes, and even long black cigars, before he submits to the inconvenience of his first garment. It may be this sartorial freedom of his earlier life that makes the Santiago male prone to sport a costume that belies his years. Youths of sixteen, eighteen, and some one might easily suspect of being twenty, display an expanse of brown legs between their tight knee-breeches and short socks that makes their precocious tendency to frequent cafés, consume fiery drinks and man-size cigars, and *enamorar las muchachas* doubly striking. They are intelligent youths, on the whole, compared with their Haitian neighbors, with a quick wit to catch a political argument or the mysteries of a mechanical contrivance, though they have the tendency of all their mixed race to slow down in their mental processes soon after reaching what with us would be early manhood. *La juventud* of Santo Domingo is beginning to look with slightly less scorn upon the use of the hands as a means of livelihood, an improvement which may be largely credited to American occupation, not so much through precept and example as by the reduction in political sinecures and the institution of genuine examinations for candidates to government office.

In character, as in physical aspect, Santiago is true to type. The outward forms of politeness are diligently cultivated; actual, physical consideration for the comfort or convenience of others is conspicuous by its scarcity. The same man who raises his hat to and shakes hands with his neighbor ten times a day shows no hesitancy in maintaining any species of nuisance, from a bevy of fighting cocks to a braying jackass, against the peace and happiness of that same neighbor, nor in hugging a house-wall when it is his place to take to the gutter. A haughtiness of demeanor, an over-developed personal pride that it would be difficult to find real reason for, burden all except the most poverty-stricken class. Amid the medley of tints that make up the population the casual observer might conclude that the existence of a color-line would be out of the question in Santiago. As he dips beneath the surface, however, he finds a very decided one, nay, several, dividing the population not into two, but into three or four social strata, though the lines of demarkation are neither as distinct nor as adamant as with us. Thus one of the tile-floored clubs on the central plaza, the chair-forested parlor of which stands ostensibly wide open, admits no member whose ancestry has not been unbrokenly Caucasian, while another across the square welcomes neither pure whites nor full-blooded Africans. An amusing feature of this club exclusiveness is that the first society, after what is said to have been violent debate, declined to admit American members, as a protest against " the unwarranted interference by superior force in our national affairs." In retaliation, or rather, in supreme indifference to this attitude, the forces of occupation have acquired the premises next door and take no back seat to the Dominicans in the matter of exclusiveness. It may be the merest coincidence that whenever a dance is given in the American clubrooms a still more blatant orchestra, seated close up against the thin partition between the two social rendezvous, furnishes the inspiration for a similar recreation.

The principal business of Santiago, if one may judge by the frequent warehouse doors from which issues the acrid smell of sweating tobacco, is the buying and selling of the narcotic weed. It comes in great bales, wrapped in *yagua*, or the thick, leathern leaf-stem of the royal palm, of which each tree sheds one a month and which is turned to such a variety of uses throughout the West Indies. Women and boys are constantly picking these bales apart and strewing their contents about in various heaps, to just what purpose is not apparent to the layman, for they always end by bundling them up again in the self-same *yagua*, in which dusky draymen carry them off once more to parts unknown. A considerable amount of the stuff is consumed locally, however, for Santiago boasts one large cigar factory and a number of small ones, ranging down to one-room hovels in which the daily output could probably be contained within two boxes — were it not the custom in Santo Domingo simply to tie them in bundles.

The smoker must conduct himself with circumspection in American-governed Santo Domingo. Each and every cigar is wrapped round not only with the usual banded trademark, but also with a revenue stamp. Now beware that you do not indulge that all but universal

American habit of removing the band before lighting the cigar. In Santo Domingo it is unlawful to withdraw this proof of legal origin until the weed has been "partially consumed," and the official expert ruling on that phrase is that the clipping off of the consumer's end does not constitute even partial consumption, which only the burning of a certain portion of the, customarily, opposite extremity, accomplishes. Furthermore, when at last you do venture to remove the decoration, do not on any account fail to mutilate it beyond all semblance to its original state. If you are detected in the perpetration of either of the unlawful acts above specified, no power can save you from falling into the hands of "Mac," who sits in the same office with "Big George"— whenever one or both of them are not pursuing similar malefactors in another corner of the Cibao — facing the charge of unlawfully, wilfully, and maliciously violating Article 12 of the Internal Revenue Law of the sovereign República Dominicana, and there is no more certain road to the prisoner's dock.

But I am getting ahead of my story. "Mac" will make his official entry all in due season. What I started to explain was why one may frequently behold an elephantine Dominican market woman, often with a brood of piccanninies half concealed in the folds of her ample skirt, parading down the street with the air of a New York clubman in spite of the bushel or two of yams or plaintains on her head, puffing haughtily at a cigar the band .of which falsely suggests that she has recently squandered a dollar bill with her tobacconist. Indeed, many an over-cautious Dominican avoids all possibility of falling into the net by smoking serenely on through band, stamp, and all, which, to tell the truth, does not particularly depreciate the aroma of the average native cigar.

There is sound basis for Article 12. In the good old days when there were no battalions of marines to interfere with the national sport of Santo Domingo the stamp tax was already in force, and the consumption of cigars was almost what it is to-day; yet for some occult reason it scarcely produced a tenth of its present revenue. First of all there were the "chivo" cigars, — chivo meaning not merely goat but something corresponding to our word "graft" in the Spanish West Indies — which never made any pretense of bearing a stamp. Some of them were made secretly; a veritable pillar of the social structure of Santo Domingo was discovered to be operating a clandestine cigar-factory long after the Americans took up this particular bit of the white man's burden. Others were privately placed on the market by legitimate manufacturers, who supplied a certain percentage of legal stock also. A third scheme was to fill the pockets of the native inspector with a choice brand and advise him to forget the matter; still another alternative was to buy the stamps at a bargain from some revenue official who was hard pressed for ready cash. But the favorite means of avoiding contributions to the wily politicians in the capital was simplicity itself. A cigar-maker purchased a hundred revenue stamps and wrapped them about his first hundred cigars. His retailer, who might be himself, his wife, his cousin, or at least his *compadre,* greeted the purchaser with a smiling countenance. "Cigars? Why certainly. Try these. *Cómo va la señora hoy? Y los niños?* Curious exhibition that fourth pair of cocks gave on Sunday, *verdad?*" Bargains are not struck hastily in Santo Domingo. By the time the transaction was completed the retailer had ample opportunity idly to slip the bands off the cigars and drop them into his counter drawer. The purchaser made no protest, even if he noticed the manipulation, for he was buying cigars, not revenue stamps. It is vouched for that the same band saw continual service in the old days for a year or two. But it is a careless smoker to-day who ventures to thrust a cigar into his pocket without making sure that its proof of legality is intact.

"Big George" arranged that we should spend the first Sunday after our arrival in the most typical Dominican style of celebration, — the partaking of *lechón asado.* His choice of scene for the celebration, too, was particularly happy. An hour's easy jog from town — easy because the saddle-horses of Santo Domingo, like those of Cuba, are all "gaited," that is, gifted with a singlefoot pace that makes them as comfortable seats as any rocking-chair — brought us to the estate of Jaragua, the exact site of the first founding of Santiago by the Castilian *hidalgos.* It was the first earthquake that caused them to transfer it from this heart of the valley to the bluff overlooking the Yaque. The ruins of an old brick-and-stone church, of a water reservoir or community bath, and long lines of stones embedded in the ground marking the remnants of cobbled streets and house walls, are half covered with the brush and jungle-grass of a modern hog farm. Magnificent royal palms rise from what were once private family nooks; immense tropical trees spread over former parlors more charming roofs than their original coverings of thatch; the pigs frequently root up ancient coins that may long ago have jingled in Columbus' own pocket.

Under the dense, capacious shade of a fatherly old mango-tree sat a negro peon, slowly turning round and round over a fire of specially chosen, aromatic fagots a suckling pig, or *lechón*, spitted on a long bamboo pole.   In the outdoor kitchen of the rambling, one-story, tile-roofed, delightful old Spanish country house a group of ebony servants of both sexes and all ages were preparing a dozen other native dishes the mere aroma of which made a hungry man withdraw to leeward and await the summons with what patience he could muster.   Our host and his family, with just enough African tinge to their ancestry to make their hair curl, hurried hither and yon, striving to minister to our already perfect comfort.   There is no more genuine hospitality than that of the higher class *hacendados* of rural Latin-America, once they have cast aside the mixture of shyness and rather oppressive dignity in which they commonly wrap themselves before strangers.

In due leisurely season the chief victim of the day's feast, his ma-hogany skin crackling from the recent ordeal, bathed in his own tender juices, was slid down the bamboo pole to a giant platter and given the place of honor on the family board.   Flanked on all sides by the results of the kitchen industry, — heaping plates of steamed yuca, mashed yams bristling with native peppers, boiled calabash, plump *boniatos*, golden Spanish chick-peas, even a Brobdingnagian beefsteak — and these in turn by the now thoroughly congenial hosts and guests, a bare-foot, wide-eyed servant behind every other chair, the celebration began. Spanish wines which one would never have credited with finding their way to this far-off corner of the New World turned the big bucolic tumblers red and golden in perhaps too rapid succession.   Dominican tales of the olden times, American pleasantries reclothed in rattling Castilian, reminiscences of Haitian occupation from the still bright-eyed grandmother, all rose in a babel of hilarity that floated away through the immense open doorways on the delightful trade winds that sweep constantly over the West Indies.   But alas for the brevity of human appetite!   Long before the center of attraction had lost his resemblance to the eager little rooter of the day before, while the Gargantuan beef-steak still sat intact, eyeing the circle with a neglected air, one after another of the sated convivialists was beckoning away with a scornful gesture of disinterest the candied and spiced papaya which the servants were bent on setting before him.   What, too, shall I say of the das-tardly conduct of " Big George? "   For with his help the *lechón*, nay, even the neglected beefsteak, might have been reduced to more seemly proportions before they were abandoned to the eager fingers of the gleaming-toothed denizens of the kitchen.   The painful truth is that

the defelonizer of Porto Rico, the erstwhile dread of Canal Zone criminals, the man who had so often given a " summary " to a hapless member of the 17th Infantry for being a moment late at reveille, was absent
without leave. Even " Mac," with his whole family of little Mackites,
their chubby faces giving a touch of old Erin to this Dominican landscape, had arrived on the scene at the crucial moment. What excuse,
then, can one fabricate for an unhampered bachelor whose seven-
league legs might have covered the paltry distance between new and
old Santiago in a twinkling, yet who had chosen to desert his bidden
guests in the heart of a bandit-infested island? Can even poetic license
pardon a man, particularly a man who dents the lintels of half the doors
he passes through, who remains at home to write sonnets when he
might be partaking of *lechón asado?* Certainly the admission of such
irrelevant testimony as the fact that the horse furnished him by an
unobserving Dominican was not capable of lifting clear of the ground
the seven-league legs already stigmatized cannot rank even as extenu-
ating circumstances.

CHAPTER IX

THERE are two railroads in Santo Domingo, confined to the Cibao, or northern half of the Republic, which by their united efforts connect Santiago with the sea in both directions. The more diminutive of them is the Ferrocarril Central Dominicano, covering the hundred kilometers between Moca and Puerto Plata, on the north coast, with the ancient city of the Gentlemen about two thirds of the way inland. It is government owned, but takes its orders from an American manager. It burns soft coal, as the traveler will soon discover to his regret, and, unlike most lines south of the Rio Grande, it has only one class. The result is that the single little passenger train which makes the round trip three times a week and keeps the Sabbath contains a motley throng of voyagers. I say " contains " with hesitation, for that is somewhat straining the truth. The bare statement that its gauge is six inches short of a yard should be sufficient hint to the imaginative reader to indicate the disparity between travelers and cars. In fact, any but the shortest knees are prone to become hopelessly entangled with those of one's companion or in the rattan seat-back ahead, and the fully developed man who would view the passing landscape must needs force his head down somewhere near the pit of his stomach. The train has its virtues, however, for all that. The more than indefinite periods it tarries at each succeeding station give the seeker after local color ample opportunity to make the thorough acquaintance of every town and its inhabitants, particularly as it is the custom of the latter to gather en masse along the platforms.

We made up a party of four for the journey. " Big George," his sonnets safely despatched to his clamoring publisher, was sadly needed to stifle a feud between his two native subordinates in the northern port; the rumor of an illicit still in the same locality had been enough to send " Mac " racing to the station. We wormed our way into one of the two passenger coaches with mixed feelings. For Rachel it was commodious enough. After years of experience with the cramped and weak-jointed furniture of Latin-America I should naturally not be so lacking in foresight as to choose — or be chosen by — a wife who required an undue amount of space. "Mac" and I, too, had been booted about this celestial footstool long enough to accept a certain degree of packing without protest. But if "Big George" stuck doggedly to the platform and gazed pensively along the roofs of the cars ahead to where the wool-pated fireman and engineer were struggling to contain themselves within the same cab, it was not for the sole purpose of gathering inspiration for new sonnets from the fronds of the passing palm trees.

However, I was near forgetting to bring "Mac" in for his formal introduction, and there is no better time to redeem my promise than while we are tearing along at eight miles an hour over a region we have already viewed by Ford. Top sergeant of a troop of American cavalry that won laurels in the Spanish-American war, he had chosen to remain behind in Porto Rico when his "hitch" was ended. There he helped to set our new possession to rights and took unto himself the foundation of a family. With the establishment of American control of customs in Santo Domingo in 1907 he was the first of our fellow-countrymen to accept the dangerous task of patrolling the Haitian-Dominican frontier. Many a party of smugglers did he rout single-handed; times without number he was surrounded by bandits, or threatened with such fate as only the outlaws of savage Haiti and their Dominican confederates can inflict upon helpless white men falling into their hands. "Mac" made it his business never to be helpless. His trusty rifle lost none of the accuracy it had learned on the target-range; the tactics of self-preservation and the will to command he had gained in his long military schooling stood him in increasing good stead. Even when he was shot from ambush and marked for life with two great spreading scars beneath his shirt, he did not lose his soldierly poise, but wreaked a memorable vengeance on his foes before he dragged himself back to safety. "Mac" does not boast of these things; indeed, he rarely speaks of them, except as a background of his witty stories of border control in the old days. But his colleagues of those merry by-gone times still tell of his fearless exploits.

Beyond Navarrete, where the railroad begins to part company with the highway from the west, the train took to climbing in great leisurely curves higher and higher into the northern range of hills. Royal palms stood like markers for steep vistas of denser, but less lofty, vegetation; scattered houses of simple tropical construction squatting here and there on little cleared spaces — cleared even of grass, which the Spanish-

A bread seller of Santo Domingo

Gen. Deciderio Arias, now a cigar maker, whose revolution finally caused American intervention in Santo Domingo

The church within a church of Maca

The "holy place" of Santo Domingo on top of the Santo Cerro where Columbus planted
a cross

American seems ever to abhor — broke the otherwise green and full-wooded landscape. Worn out rails did duty as telegraph poles; the power line that brings Santiago its electric light from Puerto Plata smiled at our pigmy efforts to keep up with it. Higher still the railway banks were lined with the miserable *yagua* and jungle-rubbish shacks of Haitian squatters. An editorial in the least pathetic of Santiago's daily handbills masquerading under the name of newspapers had protested the very day before against this " constant influx of undesirable immigration." Indeed, the American governor had recently been prevailed upon to issue a decree tending to curtail the increase in this sort of population.

Under this new decree all natives of other West Indian islands resident within the Dominican Republic must register within four months and be prepared to leave if their presence is deemed undesirable; those who seek admission in the future must have in their possession at least fifty dollars. " Santo Domingo for the Dominicans " is the slogan of those who have gained the governor's ear. If they are to have immigration, let it be Caucasian, preferably from Latin Europe. This demand sounds well enough in print, but is sadly out of gear with the facts. The Dominican Republic covers two-thirds of the ancient island of Quisqueya, which has an area equal to that of Maine or Ireland. Its more than 28,000 square miles, four times the size of Connecticut and richer in undeveloped resources than any other region of the West Indies, is inhabited by a population scarcely equal to that of Buffalo. Nearly two-thirds of those inhabitants are of the weaker sex; moreover a large percentage of the males are too proud or too habitually fatigued to indulge in manual labor, which is the most crying need of the country. Caucasian settlers would cause it to contribute its fair share to the world's bread-basket, were there any known means of attracting them. But as there seems to be none, its virgin fields must await the importation of labor from its overcrowded island neighbors, particularly from that land of half its size and three times its population which is separated from it only by a knee-deep frontier. Yet what Haitian laborer boasts a fortune of fifty dollars? A black plutocrat of that grade would remain at home to end his days in ease in his jungle palace or finance a revolution. The Dominican is not unjustified in wishing to keep his land free from the semi-savage hordes beyond the Massacre, but a hungry world will not long endure the sight of one of its richest garden spots lying virtually fallow.

Beyond a tunnel at the summit of the line, 1600 feet above the sea, the passengers poured pellmell into a station restaurant. Its long general table was sagging under a half-dozen styles of meat and all the known native vegetables and fruits. But woe betide the traveler who clung to the dignity of good breeding! For he would infallibly be found clamoring in vain for something with which to decorate his second plate when the warning screech of the toy locomotive announced that it was prepared to undertake new feats.

The Atlantic slope of the little mountain range was more unbrokenly green than the interior valley behind, for it has first choice of the rains that sweep in from the northeast. Coffee, corn, shaded patches of cacao, and the giant leaves of the banana clothed the steep hillsides. Cattle grazed here and there beneath the dense foliage. About the Perez sugar-mill horn-yoked oxen butted along the bottomless roads massive two-wheeled carts piled high with cane. Several of the wiser passengers, a woman or two among them, had sought more commodious quarters in the " baggage car " ahead, an open box car in which one might pick a steamer chair or some little less comfortable seat from the luggage piled helterskelter against the two end walls. " Big George " invaded the roof above, where some of us felt impelled to follow, lest his sonnetical abstraction cause him to be left hanging from the telegraph wire that sagged low across the line at frequent intervals. This free-and-easy, take-care-of-yourself-because-we-don't-intend-to manner of operating public utilities is one of the chief charms of the American tropics.

At La Sabana, with its majestic ceiba tree framing the jumping-off place ahead, we halted to change engines. The ten per cent. grade down to the coast had led to the recent introduction of powerful Shea locomotives to take the place of the former rack-rails that lay in tumbled heaps along the edge of the constantly encroaching vegetation. Wrecks of cars, like helpless upturned turtles, rusting away beneath their growing shrouds of greenery below the embankment of several sharp curves, suggested why the change had been made. Trees and bushes completely covered with ivy-like growths as with green clothing hung out in the blazing sunshine to dry lined the way. The widespread view of the foam-edged coast of the blue Atlantic, with the red roofs of Puerto Plata peering through the trees, shrank and faded away as we reached the narrow plain, across which we jolted for ten minutes more through sugar, mango, and banana-bearing fields before the passengers disentangled themselves on the edge of the sea.

The port was somewhat larger, more sanitary and more enterprising than we had expected. Cacao, sugar, and tobacco were being run on mule-drawn hand-cars out to a waiting steamer, though, strictly speaking, the open roadstead can scarcely be called a harbor. The town was pretty, shaded in its outer portions by cocoanut and other seaside tropical trees, and with all the usual Spanish-American features. A church completely covered with sheet iron walled one side of the delightful little plaza, about which were the customary open clubs, one of them occupied by American marines, whose rag-time phonographs and similar pastimes ladened the evening breezes more than all the others. The cemetery on the edge of the sloping hills was agreeably decorated with bushes of velvety, dark red leaves, but I remember it rather because of the name of a marine sergeant on the bulkhead of one of those curious Spanish rows of bureau-drawer graves set into the massive outer wall. Strange final resting-place of an American boy! Nor was he of this new generation of " leather-necks " that has settled down to make Santo Domingo behave itself; he had been left there early in the century, probably from some passing ship. The familiar time-battered carriages with their jangling bells rumbled languidly through the streets; a match factory that lights all the cigars of the revolutionary republic jostled for space among the dwellings; swarms of mosquitoes drove us to take early refuge within our bed-shielding *mosquiteros;* American bugle calls broke now and then on the soft night air, and a large generous bullet-hole gave the final national touch to our weak-showered, tubless hotel bathroom.

Our longer trip eastward from Santiago happily coincided with the monthly inspection tours of their district by " Mac " and " Big George." The run to Moca through a rich, floor-flat valley spreading far away to the southward gave new evidence of the fertility of Santo Domingo. Bananas and cacao, maize and yuca in the same fields, now and then a coffee plantation, constituted the chief cultivation. Tobacco was being transplanted here and there. Frequent villages were hidden away in the greenery ; nowhere was there any evidence of such abject poverty as that of Haiti. A section of the new national highway which, under American incentive, is destined some day to connect Monte Cristi with the far-off capital, followed the railway, but its black loam surface, hardened into enormous cracks and ruts since the end of the last rainy season, made it too venturesome a risk even for the courageous Ford.

A long viaduct lifted the train across what Spanish-Americans call a river, and a moment later we had come to the end of the government railroad.

Moca, famous for its coffee, which is so often taken to be of Arabic origin, is rated a " white town," because of a slightly increased percentage of pure, or nearly pure, descendants of Castilians. Thanks to the coffee-clad foot-hills to the north and the broad, fertile plain to the south and east, it is wealthy above the average, and rumor has it that much gold might be dug up from its back gardens and patios. There is special reason for this, for like its neighbor, Salcedo, it has ever been a center of revolutionists, bandits, and political intrigues. Two presidents have been assassinated in its streets; its hatred of Americans is as deadly as it dares to be under a firm marine commander. An excellent, cement-paved, up-to-date market contrasts with the dusty open spaces, with their squatting, ragged negresses, in Haiti. What was designed to be an imposing stone church, however, has never reached anything like completion. Not long ago the resident padre had the happy thought of instituting a lottery to swell the contributions from his tardy parishioners, and two glaringly new square cement towers are the result of the inspiration. But time moves more swiftly than the best devised schemes; as the towers rise, the already aged stone walls go crumbling away, and the real place of worship consists merely of a ragged thatched roof on stilts covering only a fraction of the half-walled inclosure.

The Ferrocarril de Samaná y Santiago, neither of which towns it actually reaches, connects at Moca with the government line and runs to the port of Sanchez on the east coast, with short branches to La Vega and San Francisco de Macoris. It is popularly known as the " Scotch line," is some thirty years old and still equipped with the original rolling stock, but has a meter gauge, more commodious and better ventilated cars, a more easily riding roadbed, a daily service in both directions except on Sunday, and makes slightly better speed than its rival. The short run to La Vega, with a change of cars at Las Cabullas, is along the same rich valley. Founded by Columbus himself in a slightly different locality, this center of a splendidly fertile cacao and agricultural district is a near replica of Moca, all but surrounded by the river Camú. Rich black mud, as is fitting in a region producing the chocolate-yielding pods, slackens the footsteps of visitor and resident alike in all but the few blocks bordering on the plaza though all its streets were once paved with stone by a Haitian governor.

"Mac" found interest in its distilleries, shops, and revenue office; "Big George" made use of those seven-league legs to set the property valuation of the town in one short day, but our own curiosity centered about the "Holy Hill" and the ruins of the original settlement. To tell the truth the latter does not give the traveler's imagination much to build upon. A few miles from the modern town, along a stone-surfaced section of that national highway-to-be, are the remnants of a few stone walls, a low ancient fortress or two, and slabs of good old Spanish mortar that has outlived the flat, pale-red bricks it once held together, all hidden away in the hot and humid wilderness of a badly tended cacao plantation.

The great place of pilgrimage of the region, indeed, the most venerated spot in all Santo Domingo, is the Santo Cerro, a plump hill surmounted by a massive stone church, a mile or so nearer the town. Now and again some faithful believer still comes from a distant corner of the republic and climbs the long stony slope on his knees, though such medieval piety has all but died out even in Santo Domingo. The church at the summit is in the special keeping of Nuestra Señora de las Mercedes, whose miraculous cures are reputed to have no superior anywhere in the Catholic world. A town of superstitious invalids clusters about the entrance to the inclosure in wretched thatched huts; on certain days of the year the sacred hilltop is crowded with the more modern type of pilgrim, who not infrequently comes by carriage or motor.

The story runs — and up to a certain point at least it is historically accurate — that Columbus and his men had camped on the hill, when they beheld swarming up from the vega below a great horde of Indians, bent on their immediate destruction. The discoverer was equal to the occasion. Ordering his men to cut a branch from an immense *níspero* tree beneath which he had been resting, he fashioned it into a crude cross, and planted it before the advancing enemy. "Then," as the cautious old Italian padre who to-day replaces his illustrious fellow-countryman put it, "I was not present, so I cannot vouch for it, but *they say*"— that the Virgin of Las Mercedes appeared in the sky above and saved the day for the conquistadores. At any rate the Indians were repulsed, and the Spaniards at once set about building La Vega, old La Vega, that is, at the foot of the hill.

The church of pilgrimage is modern, marking the site of the ancient one that was erected over the improvised cross. It, too, is liberally marked with patched bullet-holes, for Dominican revolutionists have no compunction in using even a sacro-sacred edifice as a barricade. Inside, in addition to the richly garbed doll over the altar and the usual gaudy bric-a-brac of such places, there is a square hole in the marble pavement of the principal chapel, filled with yellowish soil. This purports to be the exact spot on which Columbus erected the cross, and the healing properties of the earth within it depend only on the faith of the seeker after health — and certain other indispensable little formalities which are inseparable from all supernatural cures. Pious Dominicans step into the *santo hoyo* barefooted, muttering *promesas,* or promises of reward to the attendant Virgin if their health is restored, and even those who decline to uncover their pedal infirmities in so public a place carry off a pinch or a handful of the sacred earth. Yet the " holy hole " is not the deep well one would fancy four centuries of such excavation must have left it. If anything it is slightly above the level of the ground outside the church. For no matter how much of the yellow soil is carried off during the day, morning always finds the hole filled again by some " miracle "— which somehow brings up visions of a poor old native peon wandering about in the darkest hours of the night with a sack and a shovel.

The original *nispero* stood for more than four hundred years in the identical spot where Columbus found it. Not until the month of May before·our visit did it at length fall down —" *por descuido;* for lack of care," as the present padre put it, sadly. But the pious old Italian has planted in its place a " son " of the historical tree,— a twig that already shows a will to fill the footsteps of its " father "— and from the wood of the latter he has made a boxful of little crosses which he gives away " to true believers as sacred relics; to others as souvenirs " — though there is nothing to hinder the recipient of either class from dropping into the padre's bloodless hand a little remembrance " for my poor."

Even though Columbus had never climbed it nor " miracles " been performed upon it, the holy hilltop would be a place worth coming far to see, or at least to look from. The wonderful floor-flat Vega Real, the most splendid plain in Santo Domingo, if not in the West Indies, is spread out below it in all its entirety. Dense green, palm-dotted above its sea of vegetation, even its cultivated places patches of unbroken greenery, with Moca, Salcedo, far-off " Macoris," and half a dozen other towns plainly visible, a sparkling river gleaming here and there, walled in the vast distance by ranges that rise to pine-clad heights, there are few more extensive, verdant, or entrancing sights in the world than this still more than half virgin vale. Compared with it in any respect the far-famed valley of Yumurí in Cuba is of slight importance.

Several hours' ride across this world's garden of the future, with a change to, and later from, the main line, brought us at nightfall to San Francisco de Macoris. Unlike nearly every other town of Santo Domingo, this one is of modern origin, a mere stripling of less than a century of existence. It lies where the Vega Real begins to slope upward toward the northern range, with extensive cacao estates of rather indolent habits hidden away among the foot-hills behind it. A flat town of tin roofs, its outskirts concealed beneath tropical trees, it offers nothing of special interest to the mere traveler.

A nine-day fiesta in honor of Nuestra Señora de la Altagracia, which had broken out with an uproarious beating of discordant church bells, tinny drums, and home-made fireworks during our day in La Vega raged throughout all our stay in " Macoris." All the population capable of setting one foot before the other joined in the religious processions that frequently wended their funereal way through the half-cobbled streets. We found amusement, too, in a local courtroom, where justice was dispensed by a common-sense old judge in an informal, unbiased way that seemed strange in a Latin-American atmosphere, particularly so in a country where a bare five years before most decisions went to the highest bidder. The improvement suggested that Santo Domingo could be a success so long as some overwhelming power holds it steady by appointing the better class of officials and keeping an exacting eye constantly upon them. A third point of interest which no visitor to the Macoris of the north should neglect is a chat with "old man Castillo." Born in 1834, his mind still extremely active, this grandson of old Spain has been one of the chief sources of information to the wiser Marine commanders of the district. His personal reminiscences of Haitian rule, how as a boy he marvelled at the high hats and gorgeous but often ludicrously patched uniforms of the black troops from the west, make a colorful picture worth beholding, even were he not the only surviving general of the war, contemporary with our own struggle between the north and the south, that brought the final expulsion of Spanish rule from Santo Domingo. His summing up of the present status of the revolutionary republic is that of nearly all the conservative, thoughtful element of the population. For twenty years he had been convinced that intervention would be for the future good of the country; for at least ten he had ardently desired it; he would consider it a national misfortune to have it withdrawn before a new generation has been thoroughly cured of the empleomania and unruliness which had become the curse of Dominican life. Mistakes had been made by the forces of occupation, rather by subordinates than by the higher command, but the whole list of them, he was convinced, had been easier to bear than the least of their constantly recurring revolutions.

The engine that had dragged us up to the edge of the vega had not sufficiently recovered from its exertions to venture down again, and the locomotive from the main line was forced to delay its appointed task to come and get us. It is typical of the easy-going charm of the tropics that the engineer of the day before had profanely declined to exchange his coal-fed steed for that of his colleague from the east, despite telegraphic orders from the master of transportation, duly and officially transmitted through the station agent, hence our not unprecedented delay. Beyond the junction of La Jina the densely green vega changed gradually to broad, brown savannahs not unlike our own Western prairies. These slowly gave place again to *mata,* uncultivated half-wilderness with flat open spaces. Pimentel, a considerable town at which travelers to the more important one of Cotui changed from car seats to saddles, was followed by Villa Riva on the Yuma, the largest river in the West Indies and navigable for small schooners. The landscape grew still more open, with immense trees casting here and there the round shadows of noonday and cacao beans drying on rude raised platforms or on leaf-mats spread frankly upon the ground before every *bohío,* or thatch and palm-trunk dwelling. Royal palm trees stretched in close but broken formation across the flatlands and on up over a high ridge like the soldiers of an arboreal army in disordered rout. Then the train rumbled out across a swampy region where the flanges of the rails were frequently covered by the brackish water and the exhausted engine stumbled into Sanchez only three hours late.

Strewn along the base of a rocky wooded ridge on the inner curve of the great horseshoe bay of Samaná, Sanchez is not much to look at despite its considerable importance, from a Dominican point of view, as the chief northeastern port and the headquarters of the " Scotch line." Several large sheet-iron warehouses and a long wooden pier sprinkled with cacao beans and the plentiful cinders of a switch engine are its chief features. Since the virtual repeal of the export tax on cacao, with "Big George" and the new real estate taxation to take its place, its activity has somewhat increased.

Like many another corner of Santo Domingo, mosquito- and gnat-bitten Sanchez would be a dreary spot indeed but for the presence of our little force of occupation. The natives themselves recognise this, as their constant appeals for medical attention from the uninvited strangers demonstrate. With the possible exception of the capital, the republic is so scantily supplied with physicians that the navy doctors who have the health of the marines in their keeping are permitted to engage in civil practice. Even in Santiago, with its 20,000 inhabitants, the great majority of the population had hitherto no other remedy for their varied ailments than the sticking of a green leaf on each temple. The bright youth of the country saw no reason to submit to the arduous training incident to the medical profession when the study of revolutionary tactics promised so much quicker results. Small wonder the poor ignorant populace, knowing no better course to take, repair in their illness to the Santo Cerro, there to smear themselves with holy dirt in the ardent hope of improvement; and it may be that the simple priests who abet them in those absurd antics are not so rascally as they seem from our loftier point of view, for they too may in their ignorance be more or less sincere believers in this nonsense.

Sanchez saw, though it may not have noted, the breaking up of our congenial quartet. "Mac" had received orders to proceed overland through the bandit-famed province of Seibo to the capital, and accepted my protection and guidance on the journey. That region being a "restricted district" for women, Rachel was forced to submit to the tender mercies of the Clyde Line; while "Big George," whether through devotion to duty, a disparity between his own length and that of his salary, or for a newly developed fear of personal violence, herewith takes his final leave of this unvarnished tale.

Three hours in an open motor-boat manned by Marines, close along an evergreen shore stretching in a low, cocoanut-clad ridge that died away on the eastern horizon, brought the surviving pair of us to Samaná. Tumbled up the slope of the same ridge, with a harbor sheltered by several densely wooded islets, the town was more pleasing than the busier Sanchez. Great patches of the surrounding cocoanut forest were brown with the ravages of a parasitical disease that attacks leaves, branches, and fruit not only of these, but of the cacao plants of the region. Saddle-oxen, once common throughout both divisions of the ancient Quisqueya, ambled through the streets, their heads raised at a disdainful angle by the reins attached to their nose-rings. The soft soil and the frequent rains of the Samaná peninsula account for their survival here in spite of the ascending price of beef and leather. This, too, was a town of bullet-holes, for revolutionists have frequently found its isolation and its custom-house particularly to their liking. It is a rare house that cannot show a scar or two, and both the sheet-iron Methodist churches are patched like the garments of a Haitian pauper.

The existence of two such anomalies in a single town of Catholic Santo Domingo calls the attention to the most interesting feature of Samaná, an American negro colony of some two thousand members scattered about the peninsula. Nearly a century ago, when the black troops from beyond the Massacre had overrun the entire island, the Haitian king, president, or emperor, as he happened at the moment to be called, opened negotiations with an abolition society in the United States with the hope of attracting immigration. Several shiploads of blacks, all Northern negroes who had escaped or bought their freedom, responded to the invitation. Most of them came from Pennsylvania, Ohio, and New Jersey; one of the towns of the peninsula is still known as Bucks County in memory of the exiles from that part of the first-named state. Numbers of the new-comers foiled the purpose of the Haitian ruler by quickly dying of tropical diseases; a very few found their way back to the United States. The survivors settled down on the five acres of land each that had been granted them, the Haitians having frankly ignored all other promises.

Their descendants of the fourth or fifth generation are proud to this day of their " American " origin. They hail one in the streets of Samaná and lose no time in establishing their special identity, in a naïve, respectful manner that has all but disappeared among their brethren in our own land. Scattered over all the Samaná peninsula, some of them have been absorbed by the Dominicans, but a considerable colony has never inter-married with the natives and still retains the speech and customs their ancestors brought with them. The majority are farmers, moderately well-to-do, living miles out in the country and only now and then riding to town on horse- or ox-back. Unlike most of their neighbors they do not live in concubinage, but are married in their own churches. They are not liked by the Dominicans, who seem to resent their superior education and customs, though all admit that they are good citizens and good workers, though not fighters, as Americans on custom border control soon discovered. Bigger men both physically and mentally than the natives, they live in what seem real homes compared with the miserable dirt-floor huts of the Dominicans of the same color. Wherever a glimpse through a doorway shows comfort, cleanliness, and a shelf of books one is almost sure to find English spoken. It is a remarkably pure English, too, for a tongue that has been cut off from its source for nearly a century, far superior to that of the British West Indies, though with certain peculiarities of negro accent. With rare exceptions the "Americans" do not mix in politics, though they were frequently forced to fight on one side or the other during the revolutions, because neutrals, abhorred like a vacuum, lost both liberty and property no matter which side won. In such times no protection was given non-combatants, except to foreigners, and the "American" negroes of Samaná are legally Dominicans despite their protests. One cannot but be proud of the strength of American influence, of the compliment to our civilization which is implied by the insistence of these exiles on keeping a sort of separate nationality, by the strong tendency toward good citizenship they have maintained through all their generations.

In a little parsonage on the edge of town lives the Rev. James, pastor of the A. M. E. church, and temporarily in charge also of the Wesleyan place of worship, locally known as St. Peter's. His bishop, curiously enough, lives in Detroit. Pastor James is a full-blooded negro whose male ancestors have been ministers for generations. Sent to the Northern States for his final schooling, like many children of the colony, he worked his way through Beloit College. His wide fund of information on all subjects would make many of our own ministers seem narrow by comparison; yet he has little of that curious mixture of humility and arrogance which is so common among educated negroes. Even in such minor details as refraining from the use of tobacco his personal habits are a contrast to the often licentious lives of Dominican priests. In his fairly voluminous library so rare in Santo Domingo, such books as "Up from Slavery," "Negro Aspirations," and many other tomes, magazines, and encyclopedias of a serious — and what is more, not merely religious — nature attract the eye.

Each of the churches has some three hundred members, many of whom ride in from miles around on Sundays. Inside the bullet-riddled edifices the un-Catholic pews, the mottoes in English over the pulpits, the old-fashioned organs all add to the American atmosphere.

A third church is maintained in the region, and the colony has several schools of its own.   Among the best American influences the colonists have retained is the un-Dominican tendency to help themselves and not depend upon the government in such matters.   Complete segregation of sexes, from the youngest pupils to the teachers, has been adopted in these schools, where both Spanish and English are taught.   Unlike Haiti, Santo Domingo grants such institutions no government aid. The pastor receives half his salary from mission funds from the United States, and the other half not at all, because local contributions are eaten up by educational requirements.

The Rev. James has a fund of stories, more amusing to the hearer than to the teller, for those who care to listen.   During one of the last revolutions, for instance, the town was attacked during services, and the congregation, putting more faith in self-help than in supernatural aid, stopped in the middle of a prayer to cut a hole through the church floor, and remained on the ground beneath until Monday morning.   The colony, in the opinion of its pastor, is eager to have American occupation continue, or at least to have the United States take possession of the bay of Samaná, as it has that of Guantánamo in Cuba, that forces may be close at hand to curb revolutions.   Influential Dominicans, he is convinced, prefer the present status, with the exception, of course, of the politicians, and even the rank and file are beginning to see the error of their former ways and to wish peace, security, and no more destruction of their farms and herds more than complete national independence.   On the whole it is remarkable how this colony has maintained its customs intact through all the long years since its establishment.   Once given a good start the negro seems to endure the deteriorating influences of the tropics better than the white man.   The Rev. James, four generations removed from the temperate zone, is far more of a credit to civilization than many a Caucasian who has lived a mere twenty years in equatorial lands.

Samaná has a French, or, more exactly, a Haitian colony dating back to the same period, hence many of its inhabitants speak English, Spanish, and " creole."   This portion of the population, living chiefly in the far outskirts, is as much inferior to the Dominicans as the latter are to the " Americans."   Neapolitans and " Turks " monopolize most of the commerce, and as usual do no productive labor.   Coffee was formerly grown in some quantity on the peninsula, but cacao was planted in its place when the latter began to command high prices. Now that the blight has attacked this and there is hardly enough of the former produced for local use, exports are slight. Bananas could be grown in abundance; oranges are so plentiful that the town boys play marbles with them, but there is no market, or rather no transportation for such bulky products, which are sold only in small quantities to passing ships for their own use.

Among the sights of the town is a fine new cockpit as carefully planned as our metropolitan theaters. It resembles a tiny bull-ring. the fighting space surrounded by upright boards painted a bright red. a comfortable gallery rising about the outer circle, ring-side boxes furnished with good cane chairs saving the élite the annoyance of mixing with the collarless rank and file. Cozy little dens for the fighting cocks open directly into the ring; a bright new thatched roof shades spectators and feathered gladiators alike; an outer wall of *yagua* rises just high enough to give the breeze free play, yet at the same time to prevent the tallest citizen from seeing the contest without paying his *peseta* at the neat little ticket window. The " American " residents roll pious eyes at the mention of this nefarious sport. Not merely do they consider it beneath them to attend such exhibitions, but look upon them as a particularly sinful way of losing caste, since they are always held on the " holy Sabbath."

We sailed across the bay on the mailboat *Nereida*, a wretched little single-masted derelict no larger than an average lifeboat. Though its bottom was already heaped with broken rock ballast, an incredible load of American patent medicine, of flour, rum, soap, cigarettes, sprouted onions, cottonseed oil, and sundry odds and ends was tumbled into it before the mails finally put in an appearance an hour after sailing time. Nine passengers and a crew of two, all negroes except " Mac " and myself, crowded the frequently sea-washed deck. What our fate would have been had one of the sudden squalls for which West Indian waters are noted overtaken us it was all too easy to imagine.

A steady wind on the beam carried us diagonally across the gulf in the general direction of our destination without the necessity of tacking. The shore we were leaving was the scene of the first bloodshed between Columbus and the aborigines of the New World, the forerunner of countless massacres. The bay was once offered to the United States by a Dominican president, but a single congressman caused us to decline the honor. Tiny fishing boats with palm-leaf sails ventured a few miles out from the land, then abandoned to us the seascape, which remained unbroken until we neared the southern shore well on in the afternoon. Constant quarrels between the two halves of the crew on the advisability of tacking or not tacking enlivened all our snail-like, zigzag course along the face of the land, and black night had come before we climbed over the water-soaked cargo to the drunken pier of Jovero.

A gawky village of some six hundred inhabitants, boasting only one two-story house, this out-of-the-world place was quickly thrown into a furore of curiosity over its unexpected white visitors. Even the commander of the *guardia* detachment was a native lieutenant; the most nearly Caucasian resident was the town treasurer, a young " Turk " from Tripoli, in the back of whose more than general store we were finally served a much needed meal. With three thousand persons in the region only two copies of a weekly newspaper, according to the post master, brought them the world's news, and that was a pathetic little sheet from across the bay. No wonder false rumors have a free field in such a community. Cattle, pigs, cacao, and an unseasoned tobacco sold in mouldy-scented rolls six feet long, called *andullos,* made up the scanty exports of the district. Barely one per cent. of its territory is under cultivation, for like all the province of Seibo bandits still harass it long after the rest of the republic has been pacified.

Under superior orders the native lieutenant assigned a sergeant and eleven men of the *guardia* to accompany us through the bandit haunts beyond. As they lined up for final inspection they were spick and span out of all parallel in my tropical experience, from newly ironed breeches to oiled rifles; ten minutes later they were marching knee-deep through a river in the well-polished shoes they would gladly have left behind had American discipline permitted it. Their own fault, I mused, for they might have spent some of their ample garrison leisure in building a bridge; but I soon withdrew the mental criticism. A single bridge would not much have improved that route. It consisted of a wide cleared space through the mountainous forest, and nothing more — rather less, in fact, for in many places neither the stumps or the huge felled trunks had been removed. Streams succeeded one another in swift succession; the almost constant rains of this region had made the steep slopes precarious toboggans of red mud, where they were not corduroyed with *camelones,* slippery ridges of earth with deep troughs of muddy water between them. Here and there the guards were forced to climb a slimy bank virtually on their hands and knees; in other places the mud clung to their feet in hundred-weight; with the densest vegetation on either hand cutting off all suggestion of breeze, the sweat dripped from them in streams. Within half an hour the bedraggled, soaked, mud-plastered rifle-bearers staggering before and behind us along the trail showed slight resemblance indeed to the perfectly starched and polished young men who had been drawn up for the lieutenant's inspection.

"Mac" and I on our sorry mounts were not much better off. It was beginning to be apparent why one can get from Santiago to New York more easily and in less time than to the Dominican capital. The ex-"top," as a high government official, had been given Jovero's best mule, but it would be easy to imagine a better one. My own steed had long since become a candidate for the glue factory and his suffering air had already riddled my conscience before a shifting of the saddle-cloth disclosed an open sore on his back larger than my two hands. Santo Domingo needs such a law as that with which we cured the Canal Zone of this heartless Latin-American custom of working their animals in a mutilated condition. But what could one do under the circumstances but urge on the suffering beast? We had come too far for me to turn back in the faint hope of getting another mount; it was as necessary to reach Seibo as it was not to leave "Mac" in the lurch, and even had I taken to my feet along with the mud-caked guards the abandoned animal would have been almost certain to fall into the still less compassionate hands of the bandits.

Precautions against the latter now began to be taken in earnest. We were approaching a labyrinth of sharp gullies and high hills which had always been a favorite lurking-place of the outlaws. Any turn of the now narrow trail would have made a splendid ambush. Drenching showers at frequent intervals made it easy for the ruffians to sneak up through the bush unheard; the heavy humidity of a tropical rainy season deadens sounds even when the sun shines. The sergeant arranged his men in skirmish formation, with strict orders not to "bunch up" under any circumstances. A barefoot native on horseback, who had overtaken us soon after our departure from Jovero, was forbidden to ride ahead of the party. We had no means of knowing whether his assertion that he had hastened to join us for safety's sake, after waiting a fortnight for a chance to make the journey, was truth or pretense. These preparations concluded, we moved forward ready for instant battle.

Nothing of the kind occurred. I might have known it would not; there is no greater Jonah on earth than I for scaring off adventure.

Trails worn deeper than a horseman's head and so narrow as to rub our elbows offered attackers comparative immunity; the dense jungle might easily have concealed a score of men within a yard or two on either side of us; the steepness of the mountain-top, forcing us to dismount and drag our weary, stumbling animals behind us, left us scant breath to spend in physical combat, yet nothing but the deep, oppressive silence of a tropical wilderness enlivened our laborious progress. By the time the summit was reached we were ready to believe that the bandits of Seibo were a myth. An unbroken expanse of vegetation, dark green everywhere, spread away to the limitless southern horizon. Yet the rains ceased abruptly at the crest of the range, and the trail that carried us swiftly downward was as dry as the Sahara.

The sergeant gradually relaxed his vigilance and let his men once more straggle along at will, though he watched closely the rare travelers who began to appear. Several of the guards, I found, as we grouped together again for a rest, spoke to one another in Samaná English rather than Spanish. When I gave a cheering word in the latter tongue to a ragged native civilian who had plodded at my horse's heels since the beginning of the journey, he glanced up at me with an expression of incomprehension and asked the guard behind him to interpret my remark. He was Canadian born, had been seven years in the sugar fields of Cuba without learning a word of Spanish, and had been robbed by Haitian *cacos* of everything except his tattered hat, shirt and trousers. " Nobody told me there were that kind of people in that country," he explained, plaintively, " I never thought such things of people of *my* color." The wisdom gained from that unexpected experience developed a precaution that had held him nearly three weeks in Jovero awaiting a safe opportunity to proceed to the sugar district of southeastern Santo Domingo.

We were soon down on the flatlands again, but it was a long time before the first signs of cultivation broke the dreary wilderness. This was a cacao *canuco,* or tiny plantation, overgrown with brush and weeds and with the scarred ruins of a hut in one corner of it. More of them lined the way for mile after mile, all abandoned for the past three years, fear of the bandits making it impossible even to pick the pods that ripened, rotted, and fell beneath the trees. These endless gardens choked with weeds made this wonderfully fertile valley seem doubly pitiful in its uncultivated immensity. The guards, who, after the fashion of their kind, had made no provision whatever against a

A Dominican switch engine

A Dominican hearse

American Marines on the march

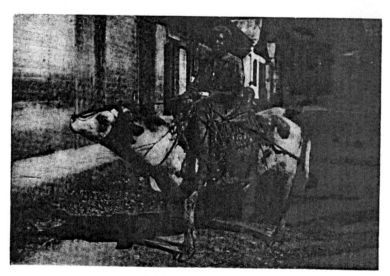

A riding horse of Samariá

long day's hunger, climbed the rotting stick fences and picked half-green bànanas and *papayas*, or *lechosas*, as the Dominican calls them, from the untended plantations. At length huts still standing began to appear, then inhabited ones, occupied almost exclusively by women, showed that we were approaching the safety zone. The creak of guinea hens, like rusty hinges, commenced to break the silence; goats took to capering out of our way; better dressed people of both sexes gradually put in an appearance, crowing cocks challenged one another in ever increasing number, and at sunset the again road-wide trail became the main street of the town of Seibo.

The capital of a province without so much as the pretense of a hotel is a rarity even in backward Santo Domingo. Nothing but the most miserable of thatched huts, with three human nests on legs in one tiny room, and a back-yard reed kitchen attended by a ragged old negro crone, offers accommodation to unbefriended strangers in Seibo. It is perhaps the most out-of-the-way, astonished-at-strangers, unacquainted-with-the-world town of any size that can be found in the West Indies. Though a large detachment of marines camp at its bandit-threatened door, it showed unbounded surprise to see American civilians. Groups of almost foppishly dressed men lounged about its streets, yet the town itself was little short of filthy. A curious old domed church, some of it built four hundred years ago, its original color faded to a spotted pale-blue, and its aged square tower surmounted by a marine wireless apparatus, is the only building of importance. From the top of this, or the one other place in town where one can go upstairs, Seibo is seen to be surrounded by low hills, everywhere wooded, without a hut outside its compact mass, its skirts drawn up like those of a nervous old maid in constant dread of mice. The inevitable fortress that gives Haitian and Dominican villages a likeness to the castle-crowned towns of medieval Italy watches over it from a near-by knoll and houses its *guardia* garrison. Built almost entirely of wood, the low houses of the better class are roofed with sheet-iron, the poorer with palm-leaf thatch. It has no plaza but merely a stony plowed rectangle of unoccupied ground in its center. The public school has no doors between its rooms, hence is a constant uproar of teachers and classes shouting against one another. Seibo bears the reputation of being always " agin' the gover'ment," and it is not strange that we found its people somewhat more surly toward Americans than those of the Cibao.

That did not hinder them from obeying " Mac's " official commands with fitting alacrity, however, whether they were a hint to shop-keepers to display their licenses as the law required or a whisper to his local subordinates to correct their methods. The slip-shod ways of native rule cannot long endure where an exacting American official drops in unexpectedly every now and then to inspect things down to the slightest detail. Such close-rein methods are indispensable to the proper functioning of revenue laws in Santo Domingo. Your Latin-American can seldom rise to the point of impersonal application of governmental decrees; with him it is always a personal matter between official and inhabitant. Checked up in the courteous yet firm manner which " Mac " had learned by long contact with this race, his subordinates had a curious resemblance to backward schoolboys whom a teacher holds up to scratch by frequent kindly assistance with a threat of the switch behind it. The government of occupation has done everything possible to remove temptation from both inspected and inspector in internal revenue matters. Every distillery, for instance, is so constructed that the owner may watch his product behind iron bars as it runs from still to receptacle, yet not a drop can he extract without calling upon the inspector to produce his keys. By such contrivances Santo Domingo is being gradually weaned away from the irregularities that were long the curse of its financial legislation.

An invitation from the major in command caused us to change with alacrity on our second day in Seibo from the "hotel" to a tent in the marine camp on the edge of town, with a far-reaching view, an unfailing breeze, and a "swimming hole" in the river below. Here, by dint of spending most of the day insisting, by offering twice the local rate for good mounts, by promising a peon "guide" a week's pay for a day's work, by seeing that the horses were within the marine corral before going to bed, and by being generally and strictly from Missouri, we succeeded in getting off the next morning at five. The air was damp and fresh. For the first time in five years I beheld the Southern Cross I had once known like the features of an old friend. Endless forests with a level roadway cut through them shut us in all through the morning, only a few *canucos* breaking the perspective of sheer forest walls. As in Haiti, the peasants of Seibo live back out of sight from the main trails, for fear of bandits, as the vicinity of some of our railroads is still shunned out of dread of marauding tramps. At another large marine camp we left the roadway and sagging telegraph wire to La Romana and struck due southward along a half-cleared trail that after an hour or more brought us out upon the sun-toasted advance guard of the cane-fields of the south.   Amid the stumps and logs of immense tropical trees, black with the recent burning, baby sugar-cane was already turning bright green the broad expanse of newly felled forest.   Negroes almost without exception from the French or British West Indies were adding row after row of the virgin fields to the sugar supply of a hungry world.   Farther on, beyond another strip of forest soon due for the same fate, came immense stretches of full-sized cane, then toiling groups of cane-cutters, huge creaking cane-carts, finally a railroad that scorns to carry anything but cane, and by ten we had brought up at the *batey* of Diego, our mounted "guide" straggling in far behind us.

Many of the workmen of the surrounding "colonies" had gone on strike that morning.   The Dominican delegate to the recent labor conference in Washington had brought back with him this new method of bringing to terms the "wicked American and Cuban capitalists who would starve us while carrying off our national wealth."   It was noticeable, however, that only a small fraction of the idle groups crowding the *batey* were natives of the country; the great majority of them grumbled in the easy-going drawl of the British negro.   Small wonder the arguments of the Spanish-speaking manager who harangued them from the door of the office fell chiefly on uncomprehending ears.   Besides, though their own arguments were simpler, they were not easily refuted.   "Wi' rice twenty-fi' cent a pound an' sugah eighteen cent in Macoris town what y'u go'n' a do, mahn, what y'u go'n' a do?   An' de washer lady she ax you a shilling fo' to wash a shirt!   How us can cut a caht-load o' canes fo' seventy cent?   Better fo' we if us detain we at home."

Leaving manager and strikers to settle their differences without our assistance we climbed to the top of a car-load of cane and were soon creaking away across the slightly rolling country.   A train so long that it had to be cut in two at the first suggestion of a grade squirmed away before us like a great green snake.   The land became one vast expanse of sugar-cane, broken only by the clustered buildings of the *bateys* and dotted here and there by a royal palm or ceiba, which the woodsmen had not had the heart to fell.   Branch railroads, like the ribs of a leaf, brought the product of all this down to the main line, whence it poured into the capacious maw of the Central Santa Fé, the tall chimneys of which appeared toward sunset, backed far off by a slightly yellowish Caribbean.

San Pedro de Macoris on the southern coast is a more important town than its near namesake of the Cibao, yet it is disappointing for all its size. With a certain amount of modern bustle, more city features than we had seen since Santiago, a fair percentage of full white inhabitants, and a rather " cocky " air, it exists chiefly because of a bottle-shaped harbor with a dangerously narrow entrance between reefs, while its docks are largely manned by British negroes.

We finally found passengers enough to afford the trip by automobile from Macoris to the capital. With the single exception of the Haitian journey to Las Cahobas, I have never known of a worse road being actually covered by automobile. Sandy or stony beyond words, a constant succession of rocks, stumps, scrub trees, sun-baked mudholes, without a yard of smooth going, it was in fact no road at all, but so often had travelers followed the same general direction that a kind of route had grown up of itself. Several times we came to temporary grief ; once we ran into a tree and smashed a case of Cuban rum that had been tied on the running-board, and as the chauffeur felt impelled to " save " as much of the precious stuff as possible, his driving was far from impeccable during the rest of the journey. One after another we bounced through such towns as La Yeguada, Hato Viejo, Santa Isabela, all spread out carelessly on the flat, dry, prairie-like country peculiar to the coral formation of southern Santo Domingo. In one place the mud was so deep that we were forced to turn aside for a few yards into the private property of a Cuban ex-general, who occupies a wattled hut with his illegitimate brood of mulattoes. This wily individual, in spite of the fact that he draws a generous monthly pension through a foreign bank in the capital, has placed a guard at his gate and collects two dollars from every passing automobile. Then came more sugarcane, another large mill with its creaking ox-carts and striking negroes, and from San Isidro on sixteen kilometers of excellent highway to Duarte, a suburb of the capital, and across the Ozama river into Santo Domingo City. The American governor of the republic had recently made the official announcement that sixty per cent. of the great national highway from the capital to Monte Cristi was already completed! He could scarcely have taken his own words seriously had he been privileged to follow us in the opposite direction.

CHAPTER X

THIS is not the place to recapitulate in detail the busy history of Santo Domingo,— how the island of Quisqueya, or Haïti, was discovered by Columbus on his first voyage and named Hispaniola; how it was gradually settled by the Spaniards, who as usual massacred the aborigines and imported African slaves in their place to cultivate the newly introduced sugarcane; how French buccaneers from Tortuga eventually conquered the western end of the island and were recognized by having a governor sent out from France; how battles raged to and fro between the French and the Spaniards until something like the present frontier between Haiti and Santo Domingo was established; how the English expedition sent out by Cromwell was repulsed and contented themselves with occupying Jamaica instead; how the negroes of Haiti at length rose against their masters and drove the French from the island, then ruled the whole of it for twenty-two years; how the República Dominicana won her independence from Spain, voluntarily surrendered it again, regained it in 1865, and entered into that career of constantly recurring revolutions, in which the winner always became president and his supporters the possessors of the public revenues, that eventually led to the present American occupation. The interest of the modern reader is more apt to begin with this century. In 1906, in order to keep Germany, Belgium, Italy, and several other creditors from landing in Santo Domingo to collect the debts of their nationals, the United States advanced $20,-000,000 and took over the custom houses as security. The following year the United States and the Dominican Republic signed a convention under which the former was to appoint a receiver for bankrupt Santo Domingo, five per cent. of the custom receipts to cover the expenses of the receivership and a certain amount to be set aside to pay off the national debts and provide a sinking fund. The convention further stipulated that Santo Domingo could not contract new public indebtedness without American consent, and that the United States could intervene if conditions within the country threatened to interfere with the collection of the custom duties.

The Dominicans soon broke the former agreement. The government illegally sold revenue stamps at a fraction of their value; *pagarés* were issued at great discounts; goods were purchased in the United States and abroad without being paid for or legally sanctioned. In five years following 1907 there were six presidents, including the Archbishop. In 1911 Cáceres was shot by his own cabinet members because they were not allowed to graft enough. The United States superintended the elections of 1914, with the understanding that all parties should abide by the result. A hard task that for the Dominicans. Within a year another revolution broke out, secretly sponsored either by the president himself for the advantage it would give the government in spending power, or by the opposition party, led by the minister of war. This outbreak was soon suppressed. In 1916 President Jimenez had barely retired to his summer palace when this same Deçiderio Arias, a turbulent *cacique* who had been given the war portfolio in the hope of keeping him quiet, decided that his chief should never return to the capital. Supported by the military forces, with the police split between the two factions, this coup d'état was on the point of winning, when, at the end of April, 1916, the American Minister sent word that there was trouble again in Santo Domingo. Then the United States, which had " offered its good services " many times before and endured Dominican conditions with far too much patience, decided to act. An ultimatum was sent to Arias announcing that the United States would no longer permit the establishment of government by revolution. Marines from Haiti had been landed at Fort San Gerónimo with orders to support the government of Jimenez, and with his clandestine approval, and took the capital with little difficulty. The president publicly repudiated his secret agreement, in spite of having everything in his favor, and announcing in a bombastic *pronunciamento* that his " dignity " would not permit him to endure a foreign military occupation, resigned with all his government. For this the marines were duly thankful; it simplified the whole problem.

Meanwhile a force had landed at Puerto Plata and at Monte Cristi, and fought their way overland, suffering considerably from snipers on the way. Arias, who had escaped with all his supporters from the unprotected side of the city, hurried to the Cibao and attempted to hinder the marine advance, but was forced to surrender with the capture of Santiago. His power was still paramount in the capital, however, and he forced congress to make Hernandez y Carbajal, who had returned from long exile in Cuba, president. The United States refused to recognise this illegal election and declined to let the government have any money, with the result that the country was left without rulers. Finally American military occupation was proclaimed and our forces took over the entire government of Santo Domingo, a status compared with which the mere " advisory " one of our marines in Haiti was far more complicated, and has remained so to this day.

When the Americans took over Santo Domingo the republic was millions in debt — something like $40 per capita, to be exact — completely bankrupt, and the salaries of all but the higher officials were long in arrears. Now, after less than four years of occupation, there is some $4,000,000 in the treasury. The new land tax alone — which it has been impossible to duplicate in Haiti, where laws are still made by a native congress,— has already produced nearly a million. Most of this goes back to the municipalities. The old taxes bore far more on the poor man than on the man of property. Moreover, the government of occupation has collected more than three times as much from these older sources than was the case under native rule, chiefly because there is no tax-gatherer's graft and the friends of the government are no longer let off unpaid. Every disbursement is now paid by check, on voucher in duplicate, and the same man cannot buy and pay. A few American civilians in supervising positions receive their salaries from Dominican funds — and render many times value received. The great bulk of the higher officials are of no expense whatever to the natives, being members of our military forces drawing their pay from the United States treasury.

The sovereignty of the República Dominicana has never ceased. Its functions are merely *administered* by representatives of the United States Navy and Marine Corps, officially called " The Military Government of the United States in Santo Domingo." There is no president or congress. Even the laws are made by the military governor, an American admiral. There have been no elections since our occupation; all officials down to the least important are appointed, directly or indirectly, by the Americans. The latter control all financial matters and exercise supervision over the official acts even of the smallest municipalities. American money, chiefly torn, patched, sewn, dirty, half-illegible bills, constitutes the circulating medium. On the other hand, the republic has its own schools, courts, and minor officials. The Dominican flag flies from all public buildings except American headquarters. In short, in so far as any definite policy has ever been announced, we are in Santo Domingo to do exactly what we did in Cuba.

The Americans found the whole question of land titles one of incredible chaos and fraud. Not only were there few definite deeds in existence, but the country was overrun with what are known as " peso titles." In the old days the King of Spain gave grants of land without any conception of the limits thereof, often supremely ignorant of its whereabouts. Not infrequently the same parcel was given to three or four of his faithful subjects. The grantees, who in many cases had never seen their property, divided their holdings among several children. The latter had no clear idea either of the amount or the location of their property. So they said, " Well, I think it is worth so many pesos," whereupon each child was given his fraction of that amount — on paper — and thus the subdivision went on through many generations. Thousands of these " peso titles " were sold to speculators, or to natives or foreigners who had worse than hazy ideas of their worth. Then on top of this there grew up a big business in fake titles. As many as four thousand have been presented, where fewer than four hundred showed any evidence of being real. Moreover, the real ones, being often hundreds of years old and written by men who could neither spell nor find proper writing materials, were more apt to look spurious than did the false ones. To clear up this intolerable situation the Americans decreed that all land titles not proved up to a certain date reverted to the government. The ruling caused some injustices, but these were unavoidable under the circumstances and as nothing compared with the old order of things. The introduction of a land tax also has caused many who might otherwise have drifted on in the good old tropical way to clear up their titles. A certain amount of litigation between the government and individuals is still going on, but the whole problem is gradually coming to an orderly solution.

Another question which the Americans faced upon their arrival was the disarming of the country. It had long been the custom in Santo Domingo for even the small boys to carry revolvers. Among the weapons were many costly pearl-handled ones; most of them had been manufactured in Springfield, Mass., or Hartford, Conn. A date was set when all firearms must be turned in to the military government. The penalty for non-compliance was at first made very severe. There are men still serving sentence in the road-gangs of Santo Domingo for having guns in their possession three years ago. At present the standard punishment is six months' imprisonment and $300 fine. With the exception of the bandit-infested province of Seibo, the entire country has now been completely cleared of firearms, at least those in actual use. Some, to be sure, are buried or hidden away in the jungle, but time and the rust of tropical climates will soon take care of those. The Americans burned whole roomsful of rifles; more than 200,000 revolvers have been thrown into the sea outside the capital. To-day it is difficult even for provincial officials to get permission to carry a shooting iron.

As in other lands under temporary or permanent American rule, from Haiti to the Philippines, a native constabulary was organized. The *Guardia Nacional* of Santo Domingo, consisting at present of a company of some eighty men in each of the fourteen provinces, has the same organization as the Marine Corps. Its members enlist for three years, and privates get $15 a month. Their uniform lacks only the hat ornament and somewhat more durable dye-stuffs to be an exact copy of that of our " leather-necks." The only difference in equipment is the " Krag Jorgensen " instead of the " Springfield." The officers are marines, usually sergeants, except in the higher commands and a very few natives who have climbed to " shave-tail " rank. All commands are given in English. A " non-com." can put his men through the whole drill in that language, yet if you ask him his name, the answer is almost certain to be *" No hablo Inglés."* Unlike the Gendarmérie of Haiti the Guardia is confined in its duties to matters of national defense; municipal police still keep order in the cities. We got the impression during our short stay that the Guardia officers were not quite the equal of those of the Gendarmérie. For one thing the pay is less attractive, though that of the men is fifty per cent. higher. Recently, too, all marine sergeants holding commissioned rank in the Guardia have unwisely been reduced to privates during their absence from their permanent organizations, with the unfortunate result that the few native lieutenants get more pay than their American captains, unless the latter are also commissioned officers of the Marine Corps. The native rank and file of the Guardia have a cocky, half-insolent air quite foreign to their simpler fellows of Haiti; they look as if they would be better fighters, more clever crooks, and not so easily disciplined.

The *cacos* of Santo Domingo are called *gavilleros, caco* in that country meaning merely thief or burglar. They are usually armed with " pata-mulas " (mule hoofs), which are rifles that have been cut down into revolvers, partly because they are too lazy to carry the whole gun, partly because the abbreviation is easier to conceal. In the olden days any one with a few hundred dollars could raise an " army," especially by making copious promises of government jobs to everyone if — or rather, when — his side won. Not until the Americans came were these anti-governmental groups called bandits; they were dignified with the title of revolutionaries. Santo Domingo had long run more or less wild; many of its men preferred taking to the hills at fifty cents a day with rations and the possibility of loot to doing honest work at a dollar a day. As with all Spanish-sired races, the Dominicans have the gambling instinct well developed. They love the lotteries of life; they would rather take a chance on winning some big prize as bandits or revolutionists to toiling in safety at peaceful occupations. Then, too, many were forced to join these outlaw bands, lest their houses be burned or their families injured. The *gavillero* situation had been bad before the Americans landed. It became worse under the occupation, for reasons that we shall see.

To begin with, Arias released nearly all the criminals in the country during his revolt against the Jimenez government. These quickly turned bandits; later on they pretended to be patriots fighting the American occupation. As a matter of fact the majority of them were fighting for food, rather than for either political or patriotic reasons, but bombast is one of the chief qualities of the Latin-American. The forces of occupation might in some ways have handled this bandit situation better than they did; largely because of ignorance of local customs, partly because of inefficiency and a certain amount of brutality, they made something of a mess of it, or at least let it become more serious than it need have done.

Two regiments of marines are engaged in the occupation of teaching the Dominicans how to live without lawlessness — a scant 5000 of them among a population of 750,000. Unfortunately there are flaws in all organizations. There are marine commanders in Santo Domingo so just and broad-minded that they are almost loved by the naturally hostile population; there were others who have little real conception of their duties. The rascally, brutal, worthless, " Diamond Dick " class of American sometimes gets into the Marine Corps as into everything else and tends to destroy the good name of the majority. Boys brought up on dime novels and the movies saw at last a chance to imitate their favorite heroes and kill people with impunity: some of them, too, were Southerners, to whom the Dominicans after all were only " niggers." The great majority of the forces of occupation were well meaning young fellows who often lacked experience in distinguishing outlaws from honest citizens, with the result that painful injustices were sometimes committed.

These ignorant, or movie-trained, young fellows were sent out into the hills to hunt bandits. They came upon a hut, found it unoccupied, and touched a match to the *nipe* thatch. They probably thought such a hovel was of no importance anyway, even if it were not a bandit haunt, whereas it contained all the earthly possessions of a harmless family. In their ignorance of local customs they could not know that the entire household was out working in their jungle yuca-garden. Or they found only the women and children at home, and burned the house because these could not explain where their man was. Or again, they met a man on the trail and asked him his business, and because he could not understand their atrocious imitation of Spanish, or they his reply, they shot him to be on the safe side. In still other places they burned the houses of innocent accomplices, because bandits had commandeered food and lodging there. If one can believe half the stories that are current in all circles throughout Santo Domingo, the Germans in Belgium had nothing on some of our own " leather-necks."

A parish priest of Seibo, who seemed, if anything, friendly to the occupation, told me of several cases of incredible brutality of which he had personal knowledge. He could not divulge the secrets of the confessional, but he could assure me that many of the victims had been innocent even of hostile thoughts. The Guardia, he asserted, included some of the worst rascals, thieves, and assassins in the country, men far worse than the *gavilleros,* and these often egged the naïve Americans on to vent their own private hates. Scarcely a month before a sad personal experience had befallen him. On Christmas Day he had gone with acolytes to another town to attend a fiesta, when a drunken marine had fired his rifle twice into the wattled hut where it was being held and killed a boy of ten who was at that moment swinging the censer.

I cannot vouch for all the padre's statements, but rumors of this kind were strikingly prevalent among natives and Americans all over Santo Domingo. On the other hand we must remember that the bandit-hunters often have no certain means of telling a *gavillero* from a " good citizen," and they cannot always afford to give a man the benefit of the doubt. One is as apt as the other to look like an honest, simple, harmless fellow, and there have been sad mistakes on the side of leniency also, which have naturally led to over-caution. The Dominican is quite versatile enough to be a bandit one day and to be found scratching the ground of his jungle garden with his machete the next. Captured *gavilleros* have boasted that they hid their guns in a cane-field when a hostile force appeared, came out and helped the marines unsaddle, drank a round with them in the neighboring *licorería*, and recovered their weapons as soon as the hunters had taken to the trail again. The Guardia, too, has not always been free from spies. The difficulties of the situation, and the necessity of a wide knowledge of local customs and conditions on the part of those sent to handle it, is exemplified by the miscarriage of a plan to clear a certain district of Seibo of outlaws. The government of occupation ordered all " good inhabitants " to come into the towns on a certain day, so that the bad ones might be more easily corralled. But the *gavilleros* have a better news service than those who have no particular reason to keep their ears to the ground. The former learned of the order, concealed their weapons, and hastened into the villages, with the result that those who were shot were chiefly honest, simple peasants.

There have been several battles of importance between the marines and the *gavilleros* since the occupation. The latter are more worthy adversaries than the Haitian *cacos,* though the defeat of a band of four hundred by a score of Americans is not considered an extraordinary feat. Thanks either to his Spanish antecedents or to his revolutionary history, the Dominican has a ferocity and a *desprecio* of human life that makes it unwise to be compassionate. More than thirty marines have been killed in Santo Domingo, as against only four in Haiti. One band has announced a determination to completely exterminate the white foreigners, and makes a practice of horribly mutilating the dead and wounded. A persistent rumor has it that one of its leaders is an American.

The story of the killing of the bandit chieftain of Santo Domingo is not so heroic as the extermination of Charlemagne in Haiti — nor as definite. Vicentico and his men had overrun almost the entire province of Seibo. In July, 1917, one account has it, a gunnery sergeant who spoke imperfect Spanish went into his district unarmed and in " civies " and spent a week in winning the chief's confidence. The Americans, he told him, had lost hope of defeating so expert a warrior and would make him a general and chief of the Guardia, with places for the best of his men, if he would disband his forces and support the occupation. Another version is that the real go-between was a " Turk " shopkeeper who had known him in other days.   Questions of individual glory aside, Vicentico at length set out with seventy picked men to report to the marine commander.   On the way he was suddenly startled to hear one of the wild birds of Seibo utter its peculiar shriek in a tree-top above him.

"You are betraying me!" cried the chieftain, whirling upon the "Turk" — or the sergeant — and covering him with his "pata-mulas." "That bird has never failed to warn me of danger."

The emissary, who was evidently gifted with a superhuman tongue, managed to talk his way back into the confidence of the outlaw, and the journey proceeded.   Arrived at the American headquarters, Vicentico marched haughtily in upon the marine colonel, his swarthy face twitching with triumph, and announced himself ready to take over the command of the Guardia.

"You are under arrest," said the colonel, dryly.

"Caramba!" cried the outlaw, while a detachment of marines disarmed his seventy followers, "I *knew* I should have listened to that bird!"

Just what happened after that is not very clear, except that it was nothing of which to be particularly proud.   One version runs that the gunnery sergeant entered the outlaw's cell one night and told him, amid curses and crocodile tears, that his superiors had repudiated their promise, but that he would redeem his own unintentional treachery in the matter by helping the bandit to escape at once — whereupon guards carefully posted outside met him with a volley sanctioned by the *ley de fuga* of his own race.   Another termination of the tale has it that a group of marine officers, "lit up after a big party," staggered to the prison and vindicated the loss of some of their comrades by shooting the outlaw with his handcuffs still on, and without even allowing him time to call a priest.   Just how much truth there is in these varying accounts, or combinations of the two, will probably remain a mystery, but even the marines themselves do not often boast of the killing of Vicentico.

Chronic pessimists and sworn enemies of the occupation assert that the Americans have made ten bandits for every one they have killed. Without taking this statement at par, there is at least a grain of truth in the complementary assertion that the killing of Vicentico made all Seibo turn *gavilleros*.   In some sections only women, children, and old men are seen; the young bucks have all taken to the hills.   The leaders that are left have no confidence in Americans, especially those in a marine uniform, and they will no longer enter into negotiations of any nature. The province wants revenge for what it considers the treacherous betrayal of one of its popular heroes. We should remember the time-honored Spanish attitude towards bandits — something mere warriors, with no time to study history, cannot be expected to know. The government of Spain has always been more or less an oppressor of the common people; those who rise against it, either singly or in groups, are looked upon somewhat as champions of the helpless masses. The favorite heroes of Spanish dramas to this day are *bandidos*, and they are always equally noted for their absolute indifference to personal danger and for their knightly code of honor, to say nothing of their unfailing generosity toward the poor. It is not hard, therefore, to understand why *los Americanos* fell far down the moral scale of Seibo province by their uncaballeresco treatment of Vicentico.

If I may continue this unprejudiced explanation, of things as they seemed to be in Santo Domingo at the beginning of 1920 without giving the false impression that the great majority of our forces of occupation are not a credit to the land of their birth, I would add a word about the effect of personal conduct. A few marines, some officers among them, vary the monotony of their assignment by starting irregular households; a somewhat larger number take undue advantage of their isolation from our new and not too popular constitutional amendment. The former lapse would attract but little attention in Santo Domingo, where it is almost a national custom, were it not an American habit to boast ourselves superior to other races in such matters, at least in view-point. The result is a frequent sneering whisper of "hypocrites." As to the second, like all Latin races the Dominican is seldom a tee-totaler, but he is even more seldom seen under the influence of liquor, at least publicly. In a land where any man of standing loses caste by the slightest evidence of intoxication, the effect on the popular mind of what to their self-appointed rulers is merely a "little celebration" is extremely unfortunate. The result of these things, of a certain amount of crude autocracy, and a tendency to let red tape have the precedence over common sense, is that our forces of occupation are far less popular in Santo Domingo than they could be.

There has been a growing tendency on the part of the Dominicans to show their enmity openly. Several outbreaks at dances and fiestas, ranging from individual encounters to near-riots, have indicated the feeling against Americans. Marine officers dancing with Dominican girls have been subjected to unpleasant scenes. Our men are less often invited to native clubs than formerly. A less serious and more amusing index, almost universal south of the Rio Grande, is the increasing refusal to call us Americans. Several newspapers have permanently adopted the clumsy adjective " Estadunidense." If our Southern neighbors have their way I suppose we shall soon be calling ourselves " Unitedstatians," or, as a fellow-countryman who has lived so long among them as to admit their contention always writes it, " Usians."

What we need in such jobs as that in Santo Domingo are " long time men," soldiers who have learned by experience that the task is rather one of education than of oppression. I should like to see all those removed from our forces of occupation who have not a proper respect for Dominicans; not an unbounded respect — I have n't that myself — but who at least admit that our wards are human beings, with their own rights and customs, and not merely " Spigs " and " niggers." There is too much of that " nigger " attitude among the more ignorant class of Americans, who too often make the color-line a protection against their own shortcomings.

" Mac " — or " Big George," for that matter — is an excellent example of the kind of American we want in such places. An early training that has taught self-control as well as the power to command, a long enough residence to speak Spanish perfectly, with all its local idioms, a bit of Irish blarney, which goes a long way with these simple and really good-hearted people, a due knowledge and regard for their customs and point of view, yet with a sense of humor to see and enjoy, rather than be annoyed by, their ridiculous side — in short, a real American, by which I do not mean the boisterous, bullying fellow who sees no good outside the United States, but one who can adapt himself to all conditions, return courtesy for courtesy, concise and straight-forward, living up to the law in every particular, always giving common sense the right of way over red tape, kindly worded in all his dealings, yet always letting possible recalcitrants sense the revolver loaded and cocked under his — the government's — coat. Such are the men needed for these jobs, not the haughty autocrat nor the ignorant " rough-neck."

The majority of Dominicans object to American occupation for several reasons. A list of the most potent might run something as follows: That of the bad boy made to behave himself; the resentment of politicians who have lost their hold on the public purse; the knowledge that the Americans consider themselves a superior race; the sharpness of the American color-line; the military censorship; "unconstitutional" American military courts; the order against carrying arms; the alleged breaking by the government of occupation of the Dominican law restricting immigration. There are others, but they are unimportant as compared to these.

The first two or three need no explanation. Few Americans realize how irksome is our attitude on the negro question in a country where not one inhabitant in ten can show an unquestionable Caucasian pedigree. Even the Dominicans have a color-line; I have yet to find a country inhabited by negroes that has not; but they see no justice in ranking a well-educated, influential citizen of more than the American average of culture in the same socially impossible category as an illiterate black dock laborer, simply because his hair is curly and his complexion slightly dulled. As to the censorship, the occupation calls it excessively lenient; Dominican writers find it "intolerable." That it is stupid goes without saying; it seems to be a universal rule that a censor must be supremely ignorant of literature and forbidden even to have a speaking acquaintance with the classics. Yet with an uninstructed, inflammable population and a pest of irresponsible, self-seeking scribblers, no military occupation could exist without taking measures to curtail printed sedition. This is a rock on which the rather popular military governor and even the best class of natives have split asunder. The *Comisión Consultiva*, headed by the Archbishop, that was formed to give the admiral unofficial advice on Dominican matters beyond his natural ken, resigned at the beginning of 1920 because the "insupportable" censorship was not wholly abolished, instead of being merely softened.

The *Cortes Prebostales* come in for a large share of Dominican invective. The American military courts, they protest, sometimes try and punish those who have been acquitted by the native courts, and vice versa. It is unconstitutional, they cry. True enough, but so is it unconstitutional to have made it necessary for a foreign military force to assume the government of the country. Courts martial are resorted to only in cases of carrying arms, insurrections, assaults on members of the forces of occupation, and sales of liquor to men in uniform. It takes no great amount of thinking to see how impossible it would be to have such matters passed upon by Dominican judges. For one thing, none of them are covered by the civil laws of Santo Domingo.

It is naturally irksome to a man who has always considered a revolver

Advertising a typical Dominican theatrical performance

A tree to which Columbus tied one of his ships, now on the wharf of Santo Domingo City

The tomb of Columbus in the Cathedral of Santo Domingo City

as a sign of caste, an adornment similar to a diamond ring or a gold-headed cane, to be forced to dispense with this portion of his attire. But not much can be said for the plaintiff in this case.   There is more reason for sympathy with the countrymen who cannot even have a shotgun to kill the crows, woodpeckers, guinea-fowls, and parrots that destroy his crops.   The man, too, is entitled to a hearing who has hundreds of laborers under his command in the wilder sections of the country, or who lives on the edge of the bandit zone, yet who can have nothing better than a machete with which to protect himself or his family.   Our experience of the close resemblance between *gavilleros* and respectable citizens, however, has sadly shattered our confidence, and it is difficult even for native officials whose duties carry them about the country to get permission to dress themselves up in firearms.

I have already spoken of the dog-in-the-manger attitude of the Dominicans on the subject of immigration.   Their complaints on this score have become less acute since the military government promulgated the recent decree of registration and proof of self-support for alien laborers.   There is still some grumbling, however.   Native law forbids the bringing in of negro or Oriental workmen " except in cases of emergency."   The Americans, they assert, have permitted too many blacks from the neighboring islands to take employment in the great cane-fields of the South.   Yet surely the harvesting of sugar is an " emergency " to the unsweetened world of to-day.   Also, the American steamship line that monopolizes the carrying of goods to and from Santo Domingo brings stevedores from Turk's Island and other points to work the cargoes, dropping them again at their homes, and the Dominicans complain that this lowers their standard of living.   The fact is that the native laborers are not merely indolent; they are distressingly independent.   About Thursday a bunch of them get together and say, " We have enough to live on until Tuesday.   Why should we work? "   So off goes the bunch on a dance-fiesta-cockfight spree and the canes wither in the field or cargoes lie untouched in the hold or on the dock.   The workmen of the South, in particular, have the reputation of being the best time-killers in the world.   The great sugar centrals of that region could not exist without the privilege of bringing in Haitian or British West Indian laborers.

Abhorring steady labor as he does, the Dominican has been quick to catch the drift of modern trade unionism in demanding exorbitant wages for indifferent work.   At the recent labor conference in Washington Santo Domingo was represented by the mulatto son of a German, formerly governor of Puerto Plata, and a man who could not but have chuckled at his own humor in addressing the conference as " my fellow workmen." Denied the privilege of holding office in the old style under American rule, these professional politicians are attempting to get a strangle-hold on the public purse by forming labor unions and appealing to the American Federation of Labor to bring its powerful influence to bear on the military government. The parade of a score of *gremios* during our stay in the Dominican capital, nearly all of them formed within six months, shows what success is attending their efforts. The labor dictator of America seems to have fallen into the trap. He requests that the laborers of Santo Domingo be given " full liberty of action," which sounds to those of us who have been there like permission to take a gun and turn bandit. Measured in dollars and cents the wages of the Dominican laborer are not high; balanced against the work he actually accomplishes they show him rather the exploiter than the victim. No one on earth, least of all the occupation, is hindering him from doing a good day's work and getting reasonably well paid for it — except his own indolence, which in the end is apt to leave him swamped beneath foreign immigration in spite of any political manipulations.

Among those I talked with about their country's " wrongs " was Deçiderio Arias, the former war minister who added the last straw to American patience. He runs a pathetic little cigar factory in Santiago now, sleeping on a cot in one corner of it, and professes, I hesitate to report, a great friendship for " Big George." A proud, rather ignorant mulatto, with perhaps a touch of Indian blood, a commanding manner still despite his reverses and the high degree of outward courtesy of all his people, he is, or pretends to be, fairly well satisfied with American occupation. All he wanted, he asserts, was internal peace for his beloved native land, and the marines have brought that, or nearly so, But he regrets that the Americans do not study the customs and " psycholology " of the Dominican people, rather than jumping to the conclusion that what is good for themselves is unquestionably good for all other races.

Then there was Santo Domingo's chief novelist and literary light, the pride of La Vega. He is perhaps the most outspoken opponent of the occupation in the country. " Cuba and Porto Rico have always been colonies," he frothed, " and are used to having a rule of force thrust upon them. But Santo Domingo won her own independence single-handed and what we want, what we must have, is *LIBERTY!*" He did not add that the meaning of the word in this particular case was the right of continual revolution, but it was easy to supply that footnote for him. His wrath was scornful toward those of his fellow-countrymen who had "debased themselves" to accept office under the occupation, and he asserted that all who had done so were "the dregs of our national life." The novelist's testimony was somewhat discounted, however, by "Mac's" characterization of him as a "one-cylinder crook," who had been removed from public office for selling cancelled revenue stamps.

The parish priest of Seibo was far more favorable to the occupation. A native Dominican, without a hint of the asceticism of the French priests in Haiti, with a generous waist-line and the face of one who enjoys to the full all the good things of life, he had the ripe judgment of a man of the world, rather than the view-point of the cloister. All intellectual Dominicans, he explained, are ashamed that it was necessary, yet they know it is for their own good, that the Americans have "annexed" the country. The lesson has been hard to bear, but it was unavoidable, and now they have learned it so well that they "will never do it again" — it sounded like the cry of a bad boy under the paternal strap — if only we will let them govern themselves and still hold a menacing hand over them. It is the old Latin-American cry for protection without responsibility. Every Dominican would bless the United States if the marines were withdrawn and an advisory governor left. They would never again steal public office or government funds. They have been taught that continual revolutions are not a mere pastime, but a crime. The *intellectual* Americans of the occupation had done much good, he asserted, but their works had been largely offset by those of the other class. For all the violence he had reported, he seemed to have no hard feelings against us, but he felt that the time had come for us to go away. He "had heard it said" that the *gavilleros* would return to their *canucos* and settle down again as soon as the Americans leave. Many of them were simple rascals who had no sense of patriotism whatever, but only a desire to live by robbery and plunder. They were as apt to kill their own countrymen as Americans, rather more so, in fact, for the latter went armed and the Dominicans could not. Yet many of them had been driven to the hills by force of circumstances — by threats from the real bandits, by the marines mistaking an innocent family for *gavillero* sympathizers, or a man was falsely given a bad name and dared not come in and give himself up, for fear of suffering the fate of Vicentico. Once these unwilling outlaws abandoned the fight the rest would have no choice but to disband.

It is difficult to admit, however, that Santo Domingo is now ready to govern itself, not because there are no educated and honest men in the country, but because these cannot get into power. Force rules; just elections are impossible. As in all Latin-America, with few exceptions, parties depend upon and take the name of their leader. Principles do not interest the rank and file in the least. In the old days the president always appointed a military man as provincial leader, that his "party" might not assert any signs of independence. Every district had its little local *cacique*, or tribal chief. Elections were two-day affairs. Woolly countrymen were brought in from the hills and voted at once. The *cacique* got them shaved and voted them again; got them a hair-cut and voted them again; gave them a new shirt and voted them again. On the second day a half-dozen more disguises preceded their repeated visits to the polls. It is hard to believe that a bare four years of occupation have completely cured the Dominicans of such habits. The Americans, in fact, have never yet attempted to hold an election, hence there has been no new ideal held up to them in this matter. Under the old régime judges divided fines among themselves, and it cost much effort to get them to give up this privilege. Now they are apt to give ludicrously light fines, because it all goes to the internal revenue, in which they are not personally interested. Like a wayward boy who was never taught to govern himself, but was merely exploited by a heartless stepfather, from whom he finally ran away, Santo Domingo has no real conception of how to conduct itself in political matters, and up to the present occupation no one has ever attempted to teach it what it never learned from Spain or experience.

Some Dominicans would be satisfied with an American protectorate, provided they could have their own congress and a certain show of autonomy. Many thoughtful citizens want us to remain until a new generation has been trained to administer their affairs. So far little such training has been done, and it will take a long time to break them of their "Spig" habits. Cuba and Porto Rico have always been used to obeying the law, yet they have scarcely yet approached proper self-government. Santo Domingo has always run more or less wild; she needs a complete new standard of honor and morals. Among other things this will require at least twenty-five years of good elementary schooling. Nor should it be a hesitant, over-kindly schooling. The text-books adopted should contain such pertinent queries as: " What are the chief faults of Dominicans (of Latin-Americans in general) which it is necessary to correct before they can take their proper place in the modern world? Answer: We must get rid of *Caudillismo,* of personal instead of political parties " — and so on, with what may seem offensive frankness. Not only should Americans remain long enough in Santo Domingo to train a new generation, but we should tell them at once that such is our firm intention. The rumor that our troops are. about to be withdrawn is always going around the country, leaving no one a certain peg on which to hang his hat. Remember how we hate the uncertainty of a presidential year. There should be a proclamation by our own federal government to the effect that we are going to remain for many years — I should say fifty, until all the present generation has disappeared — and that there is no use kicking meanwhile against the inevitable. Instead of that the present governor tells them that he will do all in his power to get them a civil government soon and to have the troops withdrawn, remaining perhaps as a civil governor. I do not believe they are ready for any such move, certainly not to handle their own finances, which is what they wish above all to do. Bit by bit they should be initiated into the mysteries of real self-government, but we should avoid the error we made in Cuba, and to some extent in Porto Rico, of graduating them before they have finished the grammar grades. If the unborn generation can be reared without political pollution from the living, there is promise even in such a race as the Dominican. However, have you ever set out on a journey astride a mongrel native horse and expected him to keep up with a thoroughbred?

The military occupation has made mistakes; all military governments do. But they are by no means so many nor so serious as those the Dominicans made themselves. There have been cases of arbitrariness, snap judgments, and injustice, but on the whole American rule is just, justifiable, and well done. Some of the trouble comes from the fact that navy youths of no experience are given important *secretarías* that require men of exceedingly mature judgment — though, to be sure, the governing of Santo Domingo, with its bare 750,000 inhabitants, is little more than a mayor's job, except in extent of territory. A second drawback is that the most important posts are in the hands of men who know not a word of Spanish and must do all their work through interpreters, usually of the politician stripe, with results easily imagined.

There is no reason whatever why graduates of Annapolis or West Point should not know what has become so important a language to their calling. Did anyone ever hear of a German professional officer who did not speak at least English and French fluently? Some of the time that is now given to " social functions " and the learning of afternoon-tea manners could easily be sacrificed to our new requirements. Lastly, there should be more knowledge and interest in our scattered wards among our higher officials at home. It is not particularly helpful to a naval officer suddenly appointed governor of such a place as Santo Domingo to have the secretary who should outline his policy turn from the map on which he has just looked up that unknown spot and make some such reply as, " Orders? Don't bother me with details. I have more important matters requiring my attention. Go down there and sit on the lid."

As an example of the improvements already accomplished by the occupation there is the matter of marriage. Formerly it was almost impossible for the mass of the people to form legal unions; the cost was too great and the requirements of. birth certificates and other formalities insurmountable. As a result, marriage had come to be looked upon as a superfluous ceremony. This condition, more or less universal throughout the West Indies, is a deliberate legacy of olden times. The exploiters of the islands, particularly the Spaniards, abetted by the church, whose prosperity depended on their prosperity, purposely made marriage difficult among the laboring classes. A married woman and her children could demand support from her husband; a mere consort added to the available labor supply, because she was obliged to earn her livelihood in the fields and to send her children there early in life. Though there were men who treated their irregular families as legal dependents before the Americans came, illegitimate children were frequently abandoned, mistreated, or exploited to a degree that drove many of them to turn bandit. At best they suffered for want of a firm fatherly hand in their early years. The occupation attacked this problem by forcing men to pay for the support and schooling of their " outside " children. As little stigma attaches to this social misbehavior in Santo Domingo, there was seldom any difficulty in establishing the parentage. It was usually common knowledge. Even the priests have families in the majority of cases, many of them frankly acknowledging their sons and daughters. There are men in Santo Domingo, some of them veritable pillars of society, who suddenly saw their burdens increased from two or three children to twenty-five under the new law.   Marriages are now free, and are public ceremonies. They almost always take place at night, and crowds gather outside the wide-open, lighted house.   Members of the family come out and talk with friends in the throng now and then but do not invite them inside. About the parlor table sit the bride and groom, the notary and the priest, surrounded by the standing relatives and intimate *amigos* and *compadres*.   There is much signing of documents and ledgers, each followed by a sort of rapturous sigh from the curious throng in the street, which under no circumstances short of a downpour gives any signs of breaking up until the new couple has retired from the scene.   Most dances, fiestas, and family celebrations are like that in Santo Domingo, where the principal room always faces the street and the heat makes closed doors and windows worse than superfluous.   Sometimes these open, chair-forested parlors are on a level with the sidewalk, sometimes several feet below it, but it is impossible to avoid a peep inside, even if one does not join the crowd.   Besides, there is nothing secretive about such Dominican festivities; the bride who did not see a throng gathered before her door on her wedding night would probably weep her eyes out before morning.

When the Americans arrived there were only 18,000 pupils nominally attending the schools of Santo Domingo.   There were no rural schools whatever.   Many "teachers" never taught at all, but were merely political henchmen who drew salaries, some of them wholly illiterate. Some of them farmed their "pupils" out or worked them in their own fields.   Superintendents and inspectors rarely did either, and kept no records whatever.   Listen to a passage from a novel by a sworn enemy of the occupation:

The average Dominican woman frequented — the word is well chosen — a school of first letters sustained and directed by a priest, where she learned to read and write after a fashion, the barest rudiments of arithmetic and geography, and a world of prayers which the good priest made special effort to teach her.   She had the catechism at her fingers' ends, but except for the forms of devotion she was a complete ignoramus who took seriously any nonsense told her by those who happened, falsely or otherwise, to have her confidence.

There was not even a basis on which to build an educational system. Those charged with the task had to begin from the ground up.   The peculiar status of Santo Domingo gives it an American Minister of Public Instruction and a native superintendent, the reverse of the case in Haiti.   Both are earnest men, but pedagogy is not on the curriculum at Annapolis.   No attempt has been made to Americanize the schools, as in Porto Rico and the Philippines, which is proper enough politically but questionable educationally. Every man has been made personally responsible for the men under him, clear down through the system. The occupation now has 100,000 pupils in the schools, with as many still unprovided for; but many of the former attend only half time for lack of accommodations. Dominican illiteracy still exceeds ninety per cent., and information passes chiefly by word of mouth, with consequent garbling. An attempt is being made to have the university in the capital teach only " practical " subjects, banishing the lofty culture with which the Latin-American loves to flirt. One gets the impression, however, that there is more attention and expense bestowed upon the elaborate educational pamphlets that pour in a constant stream from the government presses than on the adobe school houses and the bare-foot urchins who attend them.

The Dominican of the masses is kindly, hospitable, long-suffering, and hopeful; in spite of having been exploited and mistreated for centuries, despite his tendency to settle things by force of arms and his low value on human life, he is still simple and good-hearted under-neath. Even in the days of revolution lone Americans went in safety where a company of marines now moves with caution. The mothers of American girls married to officers of the occupation would be horri-fied to know that their daughters use murderers from the Guardia prisons as cooks and servants, yet such arrangements scarcely attract a passing comment among the Americans in Santo Domingo. Like all Latin-Americans, the *dominicano* has no compassion, either for animals or his fellow-men. Brave enough in physical combat, he has little moral courage — I have already mentioned the inability of native officials to discipline their own people. Worst of all, he has no idea how to curb his politicians. The best families emigrated to Cuba during the twenty-two years of Haitian rule, and the latter closed the university and many of the schools as superfluous luxuries, which may be among the reasons why the " higher " classes do not measure up cor-respondingly in character with the masses. A rise in the social scale seems frequently to bring a drop in moral standards. As an example: The son of a shoemaker worked his way through school with truly American spirit; he studied medicine in Paris, learned English and French, is a voracious reader of all the literature of his profession in several languages. Yet when a poor countryman with a broken skull was brought in to him by a Guardia detachment, he declined to attend

him, after beginning the operation, because no one could assure him
his $500 fee.

The Dominicans have few strictly native customs, their chief characteristic being their fondness for revolutions. They are gay, vivacious,
and frivolous, fond of music and dancing, and find a great deal of
amusement in the most trivial pastimes. Bull-fights have long since
disappeared, but cock-fighting is the universal male sport, and on Sundays and feast days the cockpit is the center of attraction. Not a city
or village is without its *gallera;* in the country districts there is sure to
be one within easy distance of every collection of thatched huts. On
any holiday the traveler along the principal roads and highways is
certain to meet a cavalcade of horsemen, each carefully carrying in a
sack what the initiated know to be a prize rooster.

The chief *gallera* of Santo Domingo City was just back of our
lodging. On Sunday we were awakened at dawn by its uproar, which
varied in volume but never once ceased entirely until sunset. In the
afternoon I wandered into the enclosure; paid an admission fee of
twenty-five cents, and, climbing the tank-like outer wall, crowded into
a place up near the round sheet-iron roof. The sport is legalized and
a part of the gate-money goes to the municipality, netting some $1,500
a year. This is a mere bagatelle, however, compared to the sums that
change hands among the spectators during a single day's sport. Like
most Spanish games, betting is the chief raison d'être of the cock-fight.
The constant, deafening hubbub recalled the curb market of New York,
as well as the ball games of Havana. Before each separate contest
there were long waits while the shrieking spectators placed their wagers
on the two haughty, gorgeous birds tenderly held by their owners or
hired seconds.

It came as a surprise to find what class of men attend these contests in the capital. The circle of faces rising eight tiers high above
the earth-floored pit were in many cases wholly free from negro strain;
the great majority of the audience was not merely well-dressed, they
showed considerable evidence of moderate affluence. Wealthy merchants and men high in local affairs, two or three ex-ministers, were
pointed out to me as owners of one or several contending cocks.
" Chickens " would be a more exact term, for the fighters, unlike the
spectators, were not confined to one sex. The *toilettes* of the birds
were fantastic in the extreme — each had been clipped, picked, or other-

wise denuded of its feathers on various parts of the body, particularly the thighs and neck, according to the whim or expert opinion of its trainer, and the appearance of its bare skin demonstrated that it was indeed in the " pink " of condition. An invariable formality preceded each contest. On a square board hanging stiffly on poles from the roof was placed a pair of scales in which the two opponents were weighed in their sacks, custom requiring that they balance one another to the fraction of an ounce. Then, when a lull in the betting showed that the spectators had decided their odds, the owner or his agent filled his mouth with rum and water and spurted it in a fine spray over the bird from haughty head to bare legs, and the fight was on.

The first battle after my arrival was between a black hen and a red India rooster. From the moment of release they went straight at it, like professional boxers. Now and then they clinched, but as there was no referee to separate them they eventually broke away themselves. Then the rooster took to running round and round the ring, the hen after him, which a " fan " beside me called clever strategy. During the early part of the fight the favorite changed with every peck, or slash of the spurs. Shouts loud as those at a Thanksgiving football game seemed to set the tin roof above us to vibrating. The shrieks of the bettors were emphasized by waving hands, by jumping up and down, by shaking money in one another's faces and placing wagers at a distance by lightning-quick, cabalistic gestures. Those who hazarded a mere ten dollars a " throw " were the most insignificant of " pikers "; on every side flashed hundred-dollar bills, sometimes two or three of them in the same hand. Screams of ecstasy greeted each clever spur-stroke, awakening a loathsome disgust for one's fellow-men. I found myself wondering how many of these shrieking *fanáticos* had a tenth as much nerve as their gamey chickens. Certainly none of them would have endured ·so much punishment without crying quits. Gradually the bets dropped from even to ten to one. The rooster was getting the worst of it. He had gone stone blind, his head was a mass of blood, he was so groggy on his feet that he fell dizzily on his side now and then, only to struggle up again and fight on, pecking the air at random while his opponent continued a grueling punishment. The owner on the side lines kept shouting frantic advice to him, — " *Anda, cobarde! Pica, gallo!* " A lucky peck or spur-thrust sometimes suddenly gives the battle even to a blind cock, hence there was still hope. Toward the end the rooster frequently lay down from sheer fatigue, his opponent respecting his fallen condition with knightly honor and never once touching him until he had wabbled to his feet again. The exhibition became monotonously disgusting, even some of the " fans " began to protest, and at length the owner stepped into the pit with a deprecating shrug of the shoulders and snatched up the rooster, rudely, in one hand, like some carrion crow. His bleeding head hung as if he were dead. Even when a gamecock wins, it cannot fight again for months; if it loses it means the garbage heap or at best some pauper's pot. A man at the ringside pulled the natural spurs off the defeated bird for use on some other less well-armed fowl, losing bettors began to hunt up the winners and pay their debts, and another throng invaded the ring in preparation for the next disgusting contest.

Santo Domingo City, more often called " La Capital " within the country, is a prettier town than Santiago, and somewhat larger. It is less compact, has more trees and open spaces, and many curious old ruins, — palaces, gates, fortresses, and churches — so many old churches, in fact, that some of them are now used as theaters and government offices. Of the several ancient stone gateways remaining from its former city wall the most curious is the " Puerta de la Independencia," opening on a pretty outer plaza — curious because the Dominicans pretend it is the gate through which the triumphant army entered after driving out the Haitians in 1844, though any street urchin knows the entry was really made by a less ornate gate nearer the sea. Then there is the aged tree down in the custom house compound on the banks of the Ozama river to which Columbus is said to have tied one of his ships. The cathedral on the central plaza is a picturesque pile of old stone, without tower or spire, and noteworthy for the elaborate tomb of the famous Genoese just inside its main portal. Without going into the vexed question of whether the bones it contains are really those of the great discoverer, except to say that Havana, Valladolid, Seville, and Santo Domingo City are all equally certain that they have the genuine remains, one can at least say that the tomb itself is worth visiting. Indeed, though a trifle ornate for American tastes, it is astonishingly artistic to the traveler long familiar with the almost universally ludicrous " art " of Latin-American churches. With its splendid bronze reliefs, its excellent small figures in marble, and its inspiring general form, it might almost rank as the gem of ecclesiastical architecture south of the Rio Grande.

Once in the cathedral there are several other things worth a glance before leaving, though its tiny windows give the interior an eternal twilight. Two or three paintings by Velasquez and Murillo have a genuine value; a picture brought over by Columbus can be seen only by means of the sexton's key; a cross which the discoverer of America is said to have set up nearby is protected by glass doors let into the wall because the faithful and the curious were given to chipping off pieces as sacred relics or souvenirs. The mahogany choir-stalls, the pulpits, and the altars are all of rich-red old woodwork. There is an excellent tomb of the archbishop who was once president. Indeed, it does not seem necessary to be of Columbian stature to be able to sleep one's last sleep beside the doughty old navigator. During our stay in the city the marble floor was opened a few feet from the historic tomb to receive the remains of a Syrian merchant, long resident in " La Capital " but deceased in New York, whose only claim to glory seemed to be a fortune easily won and wisely spent. The interior of the cathedral has been generously " restored " by daubing the walls with gleaming white. It was planned to whitewash the aged outer walls also, but the Pope vetoed the suggestion, for which the Dominicans seem to have a grievance against him.

The government palace, occupied now by Americans in navy and marine uniforms, is full of capacious leather-upholstered chairs, in striking contrast to the average uncomfortable Dominican seat. No wonder they fought one another to become president. Ostentation is more important than real use among the two score or more automobiles with wire wheels and luxurious tonneaux that hover about the central plaza, though there are good macadam roads for 16, 25, and 30 kilometers respectively in as many directions. The theaters are seldom occupied by actors in the flesh, though now and then there is a bit of opera. The only regular attractions are the movies, which begin at nine in theory, nearer ten in practice, and feature the same curly-haired heroes and vapid-faced heroines that nightly decorate the screens in the United States. Like all Latin-Americans, the people of " La Capital " are great lovers of noise. Despite American rule the crack-voiced church bells begin their constant din long before dawn. During the " flu " epidemic, with its endless succession of funerals, they thumped for nine mortal days without a pause, until the marine doctors protested that most of the victims were dying for lack of sleep. Automobiles scorn to use mufflers; carriages are constantly jangling their bells. Every boy in town is an expert whistler, and every passer-by will find some way of making a noise if he has to invent it. The throngs returning from the cinemas habitually make slumber impossible until after midnight. One comes to wonder if it is not this constant lack of sleep that makes the Dominicans so nervous, inattentive, and racially inefficient.

Small as it looks on the map it is not a simple matter to cover all Santo Domingo in a few weeks. Among the parts we missed were the south-western provinces, including the town of Azua, seventy miles from the capital, founded in 1504 by Don Diego Velazquez, who later conquered and settled Cuba. Thereabouts once dwelt many illustrious sons of old Spain, among them Cortés, the conqueror of Mexico, Pizarro, who subjugated Peru, and Balboa, the discoverer of the Pacific. A much shorter route from Port au Prince to the Dominican capital is that through this region, but it is chiefly by water. Lake Azua, partly in Haiti, is fifty-six feet above sea-level, and a paradise for duck-hunters. Lake Enriquillo, only five miles east of the other, and named for the last Indian chief who opposed the Spaniards, is a hundred feet *below* the sea and more salty than the ocean itself. Nor should the traveler to whom time is unlimited fail to visit the high mountain ranges in the center of the country, with their break-neck trails and luxuriant vegetation.

One of the drawbacks of West Indian travel is the lack of shipping between the islands, particularly the larger ones. Only in the ports themselves can one get the slightest data on sailings, and often not even there. This is especially true of Santo Domingo, one of whose chief misfortunes is the American line that holds a virtual monopoly of its sea-going traffic. Not only are its freight and passenger rates exorbitant, its treatment of travelers and shippers worse than autocratic, and some of its steamers so decrepit that they take twenty-six days for the run down from New York, halting every few hours to pump out the vessel or patch something or other essential to her safety, but it keeps a throttle hold on poor Santo Domingo by more or less questionable means. Not long ago another line proposed to establish traffic between the island and New Orleans. One of its steamers put into a Dominican port, offering to take cargo at reasonable rates. Though the warehouses along the wharves were piled high with cacao, not a bag was turned over to the newcomer. Her captain button-holed a shipper and asked for an explanation.

"It's like this," whispered the latter, " we should like to give you our cargo, but if we do, the other line will leave our in-coming goods, on which we are absolutely dependent, lying on the dock in New York until they rot."

The captain visited several other ports of the republic, with the same result, and the proposed line to New Orleans died for lack of nourishment. Disgruntled natives assert that the monopoly keeps its hold because it has a large fund with which to starve out competitors, and because its president is a member of our Shipping Board. The Dominicans, however, are losing patience, and there are signs that the freight that should go in American bottoms will gradually go to British, Dutch, and later to German steamers.

We were spared all this through the kindness of the military governor, who sent us to La Romana on a submarine chaser. Lest some reader be subject to seasickness by suggestion, I shall not say a word about the ability of these otherwise staunch little craft to cut incredible acrobatic capers on a barely rippling sea. The fact that we noted the gaunt old American battleship *Memphis* still sitting bolt upright on the rocks beside the seaside promenade of the capital just where a wave tossed her in September, 1916, the dangerous bottle entrance to the harbor of San Pedro de Macoris, with its wrecked schooner, and the water that spouted a hundred feet into the air through the coral holes along the low rocky coast and hung like mist for minutes before it fell, must be accepted as proof that we are experienced sailors. At length appeared the red roofs of La Romana, with its narrow river harbor, similar to that of the capital, and the Santo Domingo we knew was forever left behind.

Though it is in Dominican territory, La Romana is virtually American, a vast estate belonging to a great sugar company of Porto Rico. Thanks largely to it, sugar is the chief product of Santo Domingo. Here again was one of the huge *centrals* with which we had grown so familiar in Cuba, with its big-business atmosphere, its long rows of excellent dwellings built of light coral rock along the edge of the jagged coast, its own stores, clubs, movies, and its many miles of standard-gauge railroad. We rode about this all the next morning, past immense stretches of cane, most of it recently cut, through bateys of white wooden huts raised on stilts, sidetracked now and again by long trains of cane, hungry bees hovering about them, and finally out upon great fracts where the company is pushing back the forests and the bandits to make way for increased sugar production. La Romana embraces a quarter million acres, of which only 16,000 are under cane, immense as the fields already look. Three fourths of the estate is estimated good cane land, and the foothills make excellent pasture as fast as they are cleared. The felling of these great forests, with what would seem to the uninformed a wanton waste of lumber, has already altered the rainfall of the region. Formerly the rains were regular; this year not a drop fell in January, yet during the forty-eight hours of our visit in early February, the gauges registered more than five inches. The country women were everywhere paddling about under strips of *yagua* in lieu of umbrellas.

The company employs from 7500 to 9000 men, of whom a bare hundred are Americans, most of them dwelling in the great central *batey*. The rest are chiefly Haitians and Porto Ricans, with a large sprinkling of negroes from all the other West Indian islands. English, Porto Rican, and Dominican schools are maintained, the teachers of the two former being paid out of company funds. There are very few Dominican employees, the natives, though good ax-men, being usually " too Castilian to work for a living." Wages range from an average of $1.20 a day for cane-cutters to $4 for mechanics, with twelve-hour shifts and a twenty per cent. bonus for all. The contrast between this productive region and the great virgin wilderness of most of Santo Domingo gave serious meaning to the parting words of the company punster, " What the Dominicans need most is to stop raising Cain and go to raising cane."

We left La Romana and Santo Domingo on one of the two cane boats that ply nightly between this dependency and the mother country. She was the flat-bottomed steamer *Glencadam* from the Great Lakes, flying the British flag and captained by a quaint old Scotchman whose cabin far forward contained almost transatlantic accommodations. Once more I draw the curtain, however, on the merely personal matters of pitch and roll, greatly abetted in this case by the recent rains, which had made it impossible to gather more than half a cargo. The very canes themselves were showing a tendency to waltz before we had passed the mouth of the river and turned our nose toward Porto Rico, already lying cloud-like and phantasmal on the eastern horizon.

CHAPTER XI

"WHEN the queen asked for a description of the island," says an old chronicle, "Columbus crumpled up a sheet of paper and, tossing it upon the table, cried, ' It looks just like that, your Majesty!' "

If we are to believe more modern documents, the intrepid Genoese made that his stock illustration for most of the islands he discovered. Even the firm head of Isabela must have wobbled under its crown as one after another of the misnamed " West Indies " were pictured to her in the same concise fashion, and brushed off into the regal waste-basket. Fortunately, paper was cheaper in those days. Or was it? Perhaps it was the wrath born of seeing her last precious sheet turned into an island that soured the queen's gratitude, and brought the doughty discoverer to dungeons and disgrace.

Questions of wanton waste aside, there could be no more exact description of Porto Rico. The ancient jest about quadrupling the area of a land by flattening it out all but loses its facetiousness when applied to our main West Indian colony. Barely a hundred miles long and forty wide, a celestial rolling-pin would give old Borinquen almost the vast extent of Santo Domingo. Its unbrokenly mountainous character makes any detailed description of its scenic beauties a waste of effort; it could be little more than a constant series of exclamations of delight.

For all its ruggedness, it is as easy to get about the island as it is difficult to cover the larger one to the westward. There is not a spot that cannot be reached from any other point between sunrise and sunset. A railroad encircles the western two thirds of the island, with trains by night as well as by day. When the Americans came, they found a splendidly engineered military road from coast to coast, with branches in several directions. If this sounds strange of a Spanish country, it must be accounted for not by civic pride or necessity, but in the vain hope of defending the island from armed invasion. To-day there are hundreds of miles of excellent highway covering Porto Rico

Ponce de Leon's palace now flies the Stars and Stripes

Thousands of women work in the fields in Porto Rico

A hat seller of Cabo Rajo

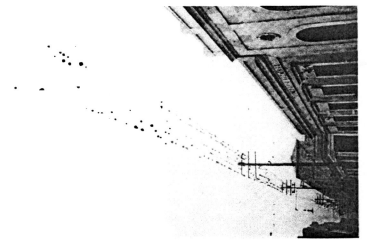

Airplants grow even on the telegraph wires in Ponce

with a network of quick transit that reaches all but the highest peaks of its central range. It is doubtful whether any state of our union can rival this detached bit of American territory in excellence and extent of roads, certainly not in the scenic splendor that so generally flanks them.

Automobiles flash constantly along these labyrinthian *carreteras*, many of them bearing the licenses of "the Mainland." If the visitor has neglected to include his own car among his baggage and trembles at the thought of the truly American bill that awaits the end of a private journey, there are always the *guaguas*, pronounced "wawas" by all but those who take Spanish letters at full English value. Scarcely a road of Borinquen lacks one or two of the public auto-buses each day in either direction, carrying the mails and such travelers as deign to mix with the rank and file of their fellow-citizens of Spanish ancestry. My tastes no doubt are plebeian, but I for one gladly pass up the haughty private conveyance for these rumbling plow-horses of the gasolene world. They have all the charm of the old stage-coaches that prance through the pages of Dickens, except for the change of horses. In them one may strike up conversation with any of the varied types of rural Porto Rico, and the halt at each post-office brings little episodes that the scurrying private tourist never glimpses.

"We divide the people of Porto Rico into four categories for purposes of identification," said the American chief of the Insular Police, "according to the shape of their feet. The minority, mostly town-dwellers, wear shoes. Of the great mass of countrymen, those with broad, flat feet, live in the cane-lands around the coast. The coffee men have over-developed big toes, because they use them in climbing the steep hillsides from bush to bush. In the tobacco districts, where the planting is done with the feet, they are short and stubby. It beats the Bertillon system all hollow."

The man bent on seeing the varying phases of Porto Rican life could not do better than adopt the chief's broad divisions of the population; for our over-crowded little Caribbean isle is a complex community, as complex in its way as its great stepmother-land, and one that defies the pick-things-up-as-you-go method. Small as it is, it contains a diversity of types that emphasizes the influence of occupation, immediate environment, even scenery, on the human family.

San Juan, the capital — to give the shod minority the precedence — is compacted together on a small island of the north coast, attached to the rest of the country only by a broad macadam highway along which stream countless automobiles, and strictly modern street-cars and their rival auto-buses in constant five-cent procession. It was a century old when the Dutch colonized New Amsterdam. Small wonder that it looks upon its scurrying fellow-citizens from " los Estados " as parvenus. Palaces and fortifications that antedate the building of the *Mayflower* still tower above the compact, cream-colored mass, most of them now housing high officials from the North. Casa Blanca, built for Ponce de Leon — the younger, it is true — now resounds to the footsteps of the American colonel commanding the Porto Rican regiment of our regular army. The governor's palace, almost as aged, has an underground passage that carried many a mysterious personage to and from the outer sea-wall in the old Spanish days, and through which more than one American governor is said to have regained his quarters at hours and under conditions which caused him to mumble blessings on Castilian foresight, though it is hard to give credence to this latter tradition, for how could he escape the all-seeing American chief of police who occupies the lower story? The Stars and Stripes still seem a bit incongruous above the inevitable Morro Castle, while the tennis-court in its moat and the golf-links across its grassy parade-ground have almost a suggestion of the sacrilegious. Of the cathedral with its green plaster covering there is little to be said, except that the solemn Spanish dedication over the bones of Ponce de Leon loses something of its solemnity in being signed by Archbishop Monseñor Bill Jones. The mighty sea-wall that holds the sometimes raging Atlantic at bay, and massive San Cristobal fortress at the neck of the town are worth coming far to see, but they have that in common with many a Spanish-American monument.

For after all, San Juan is still a son of Spain, despite the patently American federal building that contains its post-office and custom-house. Its architecture is of the bare, street-toeing façade, interior-patio variety, its sidewalks all but imaginary, its noise unceasing. Beautiful as it looks from across the bay, heaped up on its nose of land, it has little of the pleasant spaciousness of younger cities, and withal no great amount of the Latin charm with which one imbues it from afar. Its Americanization consists chiefly of .frequent " fuentes de soda " in place of its bygone cafés, and a certain reflection of New York ways in its larger stores, whose almost invariably male clerks sometimes know enough English to nod comprehendingly and bring an armful of shirts when one asks for trousers. Something more than that, of course; its dressier men have discarded their mustaches as a sign of their new citizenship, and many a passer-by who knows not a word of English has all the outward appearance of a continental American. Base-ball, too, has come to stay, though the counter influence may be detected in the custom of American schoolmarms of attending the bet-curdling horse races in the outskirts of the capital on Sunday afternoons.

The central plaza on a Sunday evening has a few notes of uniqueness to the sated Latin-American traveler. It is unusually small, a long, narrow rectangle with few trees or benches, cement paved from edge to edge, and burdened with the name of " Plaza Baldorioty." The Porto Rican seems to like free play in his central squares; more than a few of them have been denuded of the royal palms of olden times, and are reduced to the bare hard level of a tennis-court. A few years ago a venturesome American Jew conceived the plan of providing concert-going San Juan with rocking-chairs in place of the uncomfortable iron *sillas* that decorate every other Sunday-evening plaza south of the Rio Grande. Strangely enough, the innovation took. Now one must be an early arrival at the weekly *retreta* if he would exchange his dime for even the last of the rockers that flank the Plaza Baldorioty four rows deep on each side. While the municipal band renders its classical program with a moderate degree of skill, all San Juan rocks in unison with the leader's baton. All San Juan with the color-line drawn, that is; for whether it is true that the well-groomed insular police have secret orders to ask them to move on, or it is merely a time-honored custom, black citizens shun the central square on Sunday evenings, or at most hang about the outskirts. There is no division of sexes, however, another evidence perhaps of American influence. Señoritas sometimes good to look at in spite of their heavy coating of rice powder trip back and forth beside their visibly enamored swains as freely as if the Moorish customs of their neighboring cousins had long since been forgotten. For the time-honored promenade has not succumbed to the rocking-chair. One has only to turn his rented seat face down upon the pavement, like an excited crap-player, to assure his possession of it upon his return from the parading throng, whose shuffling feet and animated chatter drown out the music a few yards away, and no great harm done. In that slow-moving procession one may see the mayor and all the " quality " of San Juan, a generous sprinkling of Yankees, and scores of American soldiers who know barely a

word of English, yet who have a racial politeness and a complete lack
of rowdyism that is seldom attained by other wearers of our military
uniform.   Then suddenly one is aware of a tingling of the blood as the
retreta ends with a number that, far from the indifference or scorn it
evokes in the rest of Latin America, brings all San Juan quickly to its
feet, males uncovered or standing stiffly at salute — the Star-Spangled
Banner.

From the sea-wall one may gaze westward to Cabras Island, with
its leper prisoners, and beyond to Punta Salinas, " poking its rocky nose
into the boiling surf."   Ferries ply frequently across the bay to pretty
Cataño, but it is far more picturesque at a distance.   From San
Juan, too, the tumbled deep-green hills behind the little town have a
Japanese-etching effect in the mists of the rainy season that is gradually lost as one approaches them, as surely as when the sun burns
it away.

But there is more to modern San Juan than this old Spanish city
huddled together on its nose of rock.   It has grown in American
fashion not only by spreading far beyond its original area, but by
boldly embracing far-flung suburbs within the " city limits."   Puerta
de Tierra, once nothing more than the " land gate " its name implies,
is almost a city of itself, a pathetic town of countless shacks built of
tin and dry-goods boxes, spreading down across the railroad to the
swampy edge of the bay, where anemic babies roll squalling and naked
in the dirt, and long lines of hollow-eyed women file by an uninviting
milk-shop, each holding forth a pitifully small tin can.   It is far out
across San Antonio Bridge, however, that the capital has seen most of
its growth under American rule.   More than half of its seventy thousand, which have raised it, perhaps, to second place among West Indian
cities, dwell in capacious, well-shaded Miramar and Santurce.   Time
was when its people were content to make the upper story of the
old town its " residential section," but it is natural that the desire for
open yards and back gardens should have come with American citizenship.

Ponce, on the south coast, gives the false impression of being a larger
city than the capital, loosely strewn as it is over a dusty flat plain and
overflowing in hovels of decreasing size into the low foot-hills behind.
It is the most extensive town in Porto Rico, and, like many of those
around the coast, lies a few miles back from the sea, for fear of pirates

in the olden days, with a street-car service to its shipping suburb of Ponce-Playa. Air-plants festoon its telephone wires, and its mosquitos are so aggressive that to dine in its principal hotel is to wage a constant battle, while to disrobe and enter a bathroom is a perilous undertaking.

It was carnival time when we visited Ponce. By day there was little evidence of it, except for the urchins in colored rags who paraded the streets and the unusual throngs of gaily garbed citizens who crowded the plaza on Sunday afternoon. At night bedlam broke loose, though, to tell the truth, the uproar was chiefly caused by automobile-horns. The medieval gaieties of this season have sadly deteriorated under the staid American influence. What there is left of them takes place chiefly within the native clubs, each of which has its turn in gathering together the élite of the city and such strangers as can establish their ability to conduct themselves with Latin courtesy. We succeeded in imposing ourselves upon the Centro Español. But there were more spectators than spectacle in its flag and flower-festooned interior. Toward ten the throng had thickened to what seemed full capacity, but it was made up chiefly of staid dowagers and solemn *caballeros* whose formal manners would have been equally in place at a funeral. Only a score of girls wore masks, and these confined their festive antics to pushing their way up and down the hall, squeaking in a silly falsetto at the more youthful oglers. Even confetti was strewn sparingly, evidently for lack of spirit of the occasion, for the mere fact that a small bag of it cost $1.50 seemed no drawback to those who would be revelers. At the unseemly hour of eleven the queen at length made her appearance, escorted to her throne by pages, knights and ladies-in-waiting, while courtiers flocked about her with insistent manners that could be called courteous only in Latin-American society. But her beauty was tempered by an expression that suggested bored annoyance, whether for the tightness of her stays or the necessity of avoiding life-long disgrace by choosing one of these pressing suitors before a year had passed there was no polite means of learning. The most aggressive swain led her forth and the dancing began. It differed but slightly from a dance of "high society" in any other part of the world. I wandered into the "bar." But alas! I had forgotten again that I was in my native land. There was something pathetically ludicrous in the sight of the score of thirsty Latin-Americans who gazed pensively at the candy, chewinggum, and "soft drinks" that decorated what had once been so enticing a sideboard, for after

all they were not of a race that had abused the bottled good cheer
that has vanished.

Mayagüez was more like the ghost of a city than a living town.   Its
ugly plaza was a glaring expanse of cracked and wrinkled cement
across which wandered from time to time a ragged, hungry-looking
bootblack or a disheveled old woman, dragging her faded calico train,
and slapping the pavement in languid regularity with her loosè slippers.
On his cracked globe pedestal in the center of the square the statue of
Columbus stood with raised hand and upturned gaze as if he were
thanking heaven that he had not been injured in the catastrophe.   Of
the dozen sculptured women perched on the balustrade around the
place several had lost their lamps entirely; the rest held them at tipsy
angles.   The massive concrete and mother-of-pearl benches were
mostly broken in two or fallen from their supports.   Workmen were
demolishing the ruined cathedral at the end of the square, bringing
down clouds of plaster and broken stone with every blow of their
picks, and now and then a massive beam or heavy, iron-studded door
that suggested the wisdom of seeing the sights elsewhere.   House after
house lay in tumbled heaps of débris as we strolled through the broad,
right-angled streets, along which we met not hundreds, but a scattered
half-dozen passers-by to the block.   The majority of these were
negroes.   The wealthier whites largely abandoned the town after the
disaster.   Spaniards gathered together the remnants of their fortunes
and returned to more solid-footed Spain; Porto Ricans began anew
in other parts of the island.   The sisters of St. Vincent de Paul have
a bare two hundred pupils now where once they had two thousand.
It was hard to believe that this was a city of teeming, over-crowded
Porto Rico.

Eighty years ago earthquakes were so continuous in this western
end of the island that for one notable six months the population ate
its food raw; pots would not sit upon the stoves.   But the new generation had all but forgotten that.   Guide-books of recent date assert in
all sincerity that " Porto Rico is as free from earthquakes as from
venomous snakes."   Then suddenly on the morning of October 11,
1918, a mighty shake came without an instant's warning.   Within
twenty seconds most of Mayagüez fell down.   The sea receded for
several miles, and swept back almost to the heart of the town, tossing
before it cement walls, automobiles, huge iron blocks, débris, and

mutilated bodies. Miraculous escapes are still local topics of conversation. A merchant was thrown a hundred yards — into a boat that set him down at length on his own door-step. A great tiled roof fell upon a gathering of nuns, and left one of them standing unscratched in what had been an opening for a water-pipe. Scientists, corroborated by a cable repair-ship, explain that the sea-floor broke in two some forty miles westward and dropped several hundred fathoms deeper. Lighter quakes have been frequent ever since; half a dozen of them were felt all over Porto Rico during our stay there. The inhabitants of all the western end are still nervous. More than one American teacher in that region has suddenly looked up to find herself in a deserted school-room, the pupils having jumped out the windows at the first suggestion of a tremor.

Mayagüez is slowly rebuilding; of reinforced concrete now, or at least of wood. Little damage was done on that October morning to wooden structures, which is one of the reasons that the crowded hovels along the sea front have none of the deserted air of the city proper. A still more potent reason is that this class of inhabitants had nowhere else to go. By Porto Rican law the entire beach of the island is government property, for sixty feet back of the water's edge. As a consequence, what would in our own land be the choicest residential section is everywhere covered with squatters, who pay no rent, and patch their miserable little shelters together out of tin cans, old boxes, bits of driftwood, and *yagua* or palm-leaves, the interior walls covered, if at all, with picked-up labels and illustrated newspapers.

One can climb quickly into the hills from Mayagüez, with a wonderful view of the bay, the half-ruined city, with its old gray-red tile roofs, rare now in Porto Rico, and seas of cane stretching from the coast to the foot-hills, which spring abruptly into mountains, little huts strewn everywhere over their crinkled and warty surface as far as the eye can see.

Its three principal cities by no means exhaust the list of important towns in Porto Rico. Indeed the number and the surprising size of them cannot but strike the traveler, the extent even of those in the interior astounding the recent visitor to Cuba. There is Arecibo, for instance, a baking-hot, dusty place on a knoll at the edge of the sea, with no real harbor, but a splendid beach — given over to naked urchins and foraging pigs — and a railroad station that avoids the town by a mile or more, as if it were suffering from the plague. San Germán, founded by Diego Columbus in 1512, destroyed times without number by pirates, Indians, all the European rivals of Spain, and even by mosquitos, which forced its founders to rebuild in a new spot, has moved hither and yon about the southwestern corner of the island until it is a wonder its own inhabitants can find it by night. Or there is Cabo Rojo, where hats of more open weave than the Panama are made of the *cogolla* palm-leaf of the palmetto family.

Yauco, a bit farther east, is striking chiefly for the variegated hay-stack of poor man's hovels resembling beehives, that are heaped up the steep hillside in its outskirt and seen from afar off in either direction. Guayama is proud, and justly so, of its bulking new church, which is so up-to-date that it is fitted with Pullman-car soap-spouts for the saving of holy water. Maunabo, among its cane-fields, lies out of reach of buccaneer cannon, hurricanes, and tidal waves, like so many of the " coast " towns of old Borinquen, and does its seaside business through a " Playa " of the same name. It still holds green the memory of the stern but playful young American school-master who first taught its present generation to salute the Stars and Stripes, but though it boasts a faultless cement building now in place of the hovel that posed as *escuela pública* in those pioneer days, it seems not to have learned the American doctrine of quick expansion as well as some of its fellows.

Beyond Maunabo the highway climbs through huts and rocks that look strangely alike as they lie tossed far up the spur of the central range, then past enormous granite boulders that suggest reclining elephants, and out upon an incredible expanse of cane, with pretty Yabucoa planted in its center and Porto Rico's dependent islands of Vieques and Culebra breaking the endless vista of sea to the southward. Humacao and Naguabo have several corners worthy a painter's sketch-book, and soon the coast-line swings us northward again to sugar-choked Fajardo, with its four belching smokestacks, and leaves us no choice but to cease our journeyings by land or return to San Juan. There we may dash across or around the bay to Bayamón, a " whale of a town and a bad one," in the words of the police chief, but also the site of the " City of Puerto Rico " that afterward changed its name and location and became the present capital. Of the towns that dot the mountainous interior the traveler should not miss Caguas and Cayey, Coamo and Comerio, Barranquitas and Juana Diaz, Lares and Utuado, and a half-dozen others that are no mere villages, including Aibonito (Ai! Bonito! — Ah! Pretty!) set more than two thousand feet aloft, and famed for its *fresas*, which in Porto Rico means a fruit that grows on a thorny bush beside the little streams of high altitudes, that looks like a cross between a luscious strawberry and a mammoth raspberry and tastes like neither.

But it is high time now to descend to Coamo Springs for the one unfailingly hot bath in the West Indies — when one can induce the servants to produce the key to it.

Some eighty years ago a man was riding over the breakneck trail from Coamo to Ponce to pay a bill — there is a fishy smell to that last detail, but let it pass — when he lost his way and stumbled by accident upon a hot spring. Making inquiries, he found that the region belonged to a druggist in the southern metropolis and that his own broad acres bounded the property on the left. He called on the druggist and after the lengthy preliminaries incident to any Spanish-American deal, offered to sell his own land to the apothecary.

" It 's of no use to me," he explained, " and as you have the adjoining land — and — and "

" Why," cried the druggist, " my own *finca* is not worth a peseta to *me*! Why on earth should I be buying yours also? "

" Well, then, I 'll buy yours of *you*," suggested the horseman; " there is no sense in having two owners to a tract that really belongs together. Let 's settle the matter and be done with it. I happen to have two thousand dollars with me. I was going to pay a debt with it "— the fishy smell was no olfactory illusion, you see —" but —"

The druggist jumped at the chance, the titles were transferred, and the horseman rode homeward — no doubt giving his creditor a wide berth. He built a shack beside the hot spring, carved out a bath in the rock, invited his friends, who also found the strange custom pleasant, and gradually there grew up around the place a hotel famous for its — gambling. Clients willingly slept in chairs by day, when rooms were full, if only they could lose their money by night. By the time the Americans came Coamo Springs was synonymous with the quick exchange of fortunes. A more modern hotel had been built, with a broad roofed stairway leading down to the baths, and rooms enough to ensure every gambler a morning siesta. Then one day — so the story goes, though I refuse to be haled into court to vouch for it — an American governor who was particularly fond of the attraction of the place, betook too freely of the now forbidden nectars and ended by smashing up most of the furniture within reach, whereupon the proprietor sent him a bill for $1000 damages. Two days later the governor learned officially, to his unbounded surprise, that gambling was going on at Coamo Springs! The place was at once raided, and to-day the most model of old ladies may visit it without the slightest risk of having her sensibilities so much as pin-pricked.

I came near forgetting entirely, however, what is perhaps the most typical town of Porto Rico. Aguadilla, nestling in the curve of a wide bay on the northwest coast, where the foot-hills come almost down to the sea, and with a pretty little isle in the hazy offing, has much the same proportion between its favored few and its poverty-stricken many as the island itself. A monument a mile from town commemor-ates the landing of Columbus in 1493 to obtain water, though Aguada, a bit farther south, also claims that honor. The distinctly Spanish church, too, contains beautiful hand-carved reproductions in wood of Murillo's "Assumption" and "Immaculate Conception," note-worthy as the only unquestionably artistic church decorations in Porto Rico. The merely human traveler, however, will find these things of scant interest compared to the vast honeycomb of hovels that make up all but the heart of Aguadilla.

The hills, as I have said, come close down to the sea here, leaving little room for the pauperous people of all Porto Rican suburbs. Hence those of Aguadilla have stacked their tiny shacks together in the narrow rocky canyons between the mountain-flanking railroad and the sea-level. So closely are these hundreds of human nests crowded that in many places even a thin man can pass between them only by advancing sidewise. Built of weather-blackened bits of boxes, most of them from "the States," with their addresses and trademarks still upon them, and of every conceivable piece of rubbish that can deflect a ray of sunshine or the gaze of passers-by, they look far less like dwellings than abandoned kennels thrown into one great garbage-heap. Of furnishing they have almost none, not even a chair to sit on in many cases. The occupants squat upon the floor, or at best take turns in the "hammock," a ragged gunnysack tied at both ends and stretched from corner to corner of the usually single room. A few have one or two soiled and crippled cots, but never the suggestion of a *mosquitero*, though the mosquitos hold high revel even by day in this breathless amphitheater. For wash-tubs they use a strip of *yagua* pinned together at one end with a sliver and set on the sloping ground beneath the hut to keep the water from running away at the other. The families are usually large, in spite of an appalling infant mortality, and half a dozen children without clothing enough between them to properly cover the smallest are almost certain to be squalling, quarreling, and rolling about the pieced-together floor or on the ground beneath it.

For the hovels are always precariously set up on pillars of broken stone under their four corners, and the earth under them is the family playground and washroom. There is no provision whatever for sewerage; water must be lugged up the steep hillside from the better part of the town below. Break-neck ladder-steps, slippery with mud and with a broken rung or two, connect ground and doorway. The poverty of Haiti, where at least there is spaciousness, seems slight indeed compared to this.

Yet this is no negro quarter. Many of the inhabitants are of pure Caucasian blood, and the majority of them have only a tinge of African color. Features and characteristics that go with diligence and energy, with success in life, are to be seen on every hand. Nor is it a community of alms-seekers. It toils more steadily than you or I to be self-supporting; the difficulty is to find something at which to toil. Scores of the residents own their *solar,* or patch of rock on which their hut stands; many own the hut itself. Others pay their monthly rental, though they live for days on a handful of plantains — pathetic rentals of from twenty to thirty cents a month for the *solar* and as much for the hovel, many of which are owned by proud citizens down in the white-collar part of the town.

For all their abject poverty these hapless people are smiling and cheerful, sorry for their utter want, yet never ashamed of it, convinced that it is due to no fault of their own. That is a pleasing peculiarity of all the huddled masses of Porto Rico. They are quite ready to talk, too, on closely personal subjects that it is difficult to bring up in more urbane circles, and to discuss their condition in a quaintly impersonal manner, with never a hint of whining.

I talked with an old woman who was weaving hats. She lived alone, all her family having died, of under-nourishment, no doubt, though she called it something else. The hat she was at work upon would be sold to the wholesalers for thirty cents; it was almost the equal of the one I wore, which had cost five dollars, — and the material for two of them cost her twenty cents. She could barely make one a day, what with her cooking and housework. Cooking of what, for Heaven's sake? Oh, yams and tubers, now and then a plantain from a kind friend she had. One really required very little for such labor. She smiled upon me as I descended her sagging ladder and wished me much prosperity.

A muscular fellow a bit farther on, white of skin as a Scandinavian, was "a peon by trade," but there was seldom work to be had. He sold things in the streets. It was a lucky day when he made a profit of fifteen cents. His wife made hats, too. With three children there was no help for it, much as he would like to support his family unassisted. The house? No, it was not his — yet; though he owned the *solar*. The house would cost $32; meanwhile he was paying thirty cents a month for it.

A frail little woman in the early thirties looked up from her lace-making as I paused in her doorway. In her lap was a small, round, hard cushion with scores of pins stuck in it, and a wooden bobbin at the end of each white thread. She clicked the bits of wood swiftly as she talked, like one who enjoyed conversation, but could not afford to lose time at it. Yes, she worked all day and usually well into the night — nodding at a wick in a little can of tallow. By doing that she could make a whole yard of lace, and get eighty cents for it. It took a spool and a third of thread — American thread, *mira usted* — at ten cents a spool. Fortunately, she was young and strong, though her eyes hurt sometimes, and people said this work was bad on the lungs. But she had her mother to support, who was too old to do much of anything — the toothless crone, grinning amiably, slouched forward out of the " next house," which was really another room like the incredibly piece-meal shack in which I stood, though with a separate roof. The rent of the two was thirty cents; they were worth thirteen dollars — the lace-maker mentioned that enormous sum with a catch in her breath. Then she had a little girl. There had been four children, but three had died. Her husband was gone, too — Oh, yes, she had been really married. They had paid $3.75 for the ceremony. She had heard that the Protestants did it cheaper, but of course when one is born a Catholic. . . . Some women in the quarter were " only married by God," but that was not their fault. She never had time to go to mass, but she had been to confession four times. There had been no charge for that. Her daughter — the frizzly-headed little tot of six or seven had come in munching a mashed *boniato* in a tiny earthen bowl, with a broken spoon — went to school every day. She hoped for a great future for her. She had gone to school herself, but she " was n't given to learn." She could n't get the child the food the teacher said was good for her. Even rice was sixteen cents a pound, and those — pointing to three or four miserable roots in the burlap " hammock "— cost from one to four cents apiece now.   And clothing!   Would I just feel the miserable stuff her waist was made of — it was miserable indeed, though snowy white.   Then she had to buy a board now and then for two or three cents to patch the house; the owner would never do it.   Once she had tried working in a ware- house down by the wharf.   The Spaniards said they paid a dollar a day for cleaning coffee — because the law would not let them pay less, or work women more than eight hours a day.   Yet the cleaners *must* do two bags a day or they did n't get the dollar, and no woman could do that if she worked ten, or even twelve, hours.   Clever fellows, those *peninsulares!*   The little basket of oranges in the doorway?   Oh, she sold those to people in the gully, when any of them could buy.   Some days she made nothing on them, at other times as much as four cents profit.   But " that goes for my vice, for I smoke cigarettes," she con- cluded, as if confessing to some great extravagance.

Down in the plaza that night a score of ragged men lolled about a cement bench discussing wages and the cost of food.   Beans cost a fortune now; sugar was sixteen cents; coffee, their indispensable coffee, thirty-two.   They did not mention bread; the Porto Rican of the masses seldom indulges in that luxury.   And with the sugar *centrals* in the neighborhood paying scarcely a dollar a day, even when one could find work!   " I tell you, we working-men are too tame," con- cluded one of them; " we should fight, rob. . . ."   But he said it in a half-joking, harmless way that is characteristic of his class through all Porto Rico.

It is time, however, that we leave the towns and get out among the *jíbaros,* as the countrymen are called, from a Spanish word for a domesticated animal that has gone wild again.

The American Railroad of Porto Rico was originally French, as its manager is still.   Though it is narrow-gauge, it has a comfort and *aseo* unknown even in Cuba, a cleanliness combined with all the smaller American conveniences, ice water, sanitary paper cups, blotter-roll towels — prohibition has at least done away with the yelping train- boy and made it possible to drink nature's beverage without exciting comment.   Its fares are higher than in the United States,— three cents a kilometer in first and 2¼ in the plain little second-class coaches with their hard wooden benches that make up most of the train.   The single first-class car is rarely more than half filled, for all its comfortable swivel chairs. Automobiles and the lay of the land, that makes Ponce less than half as far over the mountain as by rail, accounts for this; though by night the sleeping-car at the rear is fully occupied by men, usually men only, who have adopted the American custom of saving their days for business. The sleeping compartments are arranged in ship's-cabin size and run diagonally across the car, to leave room for a passageway within the narrow coach. These two-bunk cabins are furnished with individual toilet facilities, thermos bottles of ice water, and electric lights, and many Porto Ricans have actually learned that an open window does not necessarily mean a slumberer turned to a corpse by morning. The trainmen are polite and obliging in an unostentatious way that make our own seem ogres by comparison. In short, it is a diligent, honest little railroad suiting the size of the country and with no other serious fault than a tendency to stop again at another station almost before it has gotten well under way.

For nearly an hour the train circles San Juan bay, the gleaming, heaped-up capital, or its long line of lights, according to the hour, remaining almost within rifle-shot until the crowded suburbs of Bayamón spring up on each side. Then come broadening expanses of cane, with throngs of men and women working in the fields, interpersed with short stretches of arid sand, or meadows bright with pink morning-glories and dotted with splendid reddish cattle. Beyond comes a fruit district. Under Spanish rule scarcely enough fruit was grown in Porto Rico to supply the local demand. The Americans, struck with the excellency of the wild fruit, particularly of the citrus variety, began to develop this almost unknown industry. But among the pathetic sights of the island is to see acre after acre of grape-fruit, unsurpassed in size and quality, rotting on the trees or on the ground beneath them. While Americans are paying fabulous prices for their favorite breakfast fruit, many a grower in Porto Rico is hiring men to haul away the locally despised *toronjas* and bury them. Lack of transportation is the chief answer — that and a bit of market manipulation. Not long ago the discovery that the bottled juice of grapefruit and pineapple made a splendid beverage led a company to undertake what should be a booming enterprise, with the thirsty mainland as chief consumers. But the promoters quickly struck an unexpected snag. The available supply of bottles, strange to relate, was quickly exhausted, and to-day the company manager gazes pensively from his windows across prolific, yet unproductive, orchards.

The pale-green of cane-fields becomes monotonous; then at length the blue sea breaks again on the horizon. Beyond Arecibo the railroad runs close along the shore, with almost continuous villages of shaggy huts half hidden among the endless cocoanut-grove that girdles Porto Rico, the waves lapping at the roots of the outmost trees. These without exception are encircled by broad bands of tin. During an epidemic of bubonic plague the mongoose was introduced into the island, as into nearly all the West Indies, to exterminate the rats. The rodents developed new habits and took to climbing the slanting cocoanut trees, which afforded both food and a place of refuge. The bands of tin have served their purpose. To-day both rats and snakes are scarce in Porto Rico, but the inhabitants discovered too late that the chicken-loving mongoose may be an even greater pest than those it has replaced. Cocoanuts brought more than one Porto Rican a quick fortune during the war. Now that the gas-mask has degenerated into a mural decoration, however, immense heaps of the fibrous husks lie shriveling away where the armistice overtook them, and even the favorable state of the copra market seems incapable of shaking the growers out of their racial apathy.

Several pretty towns on knolls against a background of sea attract the eye as the train bends southward along the west coast. Below Quebradillas the railroad swings in a great horseshoe curve down into a little sea-level valley, plunges through two tunnels, and crawls along the extreme edge of a bold precipitous coast, past mammoth tumbled rocks, and all but wetting its rails in the dashing surf. A few tobacco patches spring up here, where the mountains crowd the cane-fields out of existence, women and children patiently hoeing, and men plowing the pale-red soil behind brow-yoked oxen. Crippled Mayagüez drags slowly by, new seas of cane appear, then the splendid plain of San Germán, with its vista of grazing cattle and its *pepinos gordos*, reddish calabashes clinging to their climbing vines like huge sausages. Beyond, there is little to see, except canefields and the Caribbean, until we rumble into Ponce, spread away up its foothills like a city laid out in the sun to dry. On the southeastern horizon lies an island the natives call Caja de Muertos —" deadman's box," and it looks indeed like a coffin, with the lighthouse on its highest point resembling a candle set there by some pious mourner. Local tradition has it that this is the original of Stevenson's " Treasure Island."

The train turns back from Ponce, but the railroad does not, and one may rumble on behind a smaller engine to Guayama. Some day the company hopes to get a franchise for the eastern end of the island

and encircle it entirely.   A private railroad covers a third of the remaining distance as it is.   But the traveler bent on circumnavigating all Porto Rico must trust to *guaguas,* an automobile, or his own exertions through this region, and swinging in a great curve around the Luquillo range, with the cloud-capped summit of the island purple and hazy above him, eventually fetches up once more in sea-lashed San Juan.   By this time, I warrant, he will long for other landscapes than spreading canefields.

Sugar was shipped from Porto Rico as early as 1533, but the Spaniards gave it less attention than they did coffee.   For one thing their methods were antiquated.   Two upright wooden rollers under a thatched roof, turned by a yoke or two of oxen, was the customary cane-crusher.   Here and there one of these may be seen to this day. The big open iron kettles in which they boiled the syrup are still strewn around the coast, some of them occupied in the plebeian task of catching rain-water from hovel roofs, many more rusting away like abandoned artillery of a by-gone age.   All the coastal belt is dotted with the ruins of old brick sugar-mills, their stocky square chimneys broken off at varying heights from the ground, like aged tombs of methods that have passed away.   They do not constitute a direct loss, but rather unavoidable sacrifices to the exacting god of modern progress, for barely sixty per cent. of the sugar contents was extracted by the contrivances of those ox-gaited, each-planter-for-himself days.

It is natural that combinations of former estates, with immense central *engenios,* should have followed American possession.   To-day four great companies control the sugar output of Porto Rico, from Guánica on the west to Fajardo in the east.   Like the mammoth *central* of Cuba, they reckon their production in hundreds of thousands of bags and utilize all the aids of modern science in their processes.   Their problem, however, is more complex than that in the almost virgin lands of Cuba and Santo Domingo.   The acreage available for cane production is definitely limited ; virtually all of it has been cultivated for centuries.   Charred stumps and logs of recent deforestation are unknown in Porto Rican canefields.   Instead there is the acrid scent of patent fertilizers and, particularly in the south, elaborate systems of irrigation.   After each cutting the fields must be replanted ; in Cuba and the Dominican Republic they reproduce for eight to twelve years. A few areas never before devoted to cane have recently been planted, but they are chiefly small interior valleys and the loftier foothills well

There are school accommodations for only half the children of our Porto Rico

The home of a lace maker in Aquadillo

The Porto Rican method of making lace

back from the coast. For the Porto Rican sugar producer is forced to encroach upon the mountains in a way that his luckier fellows of the larger islands to the westward would scorn, and his fields of cane are sometimes as billowy as a turbulent Atlantic.

Porto Rico was in the midst of a wide-spread strike among the sugar workers during our stay there. All through this busiest month of February there had been constant parades of strikers along the coast roads by day and thronged *mitines* in the towns each evening. The paraders were with few exceptions law-abiding and peaceful despite the scores of red flags that followed the huge Stars and Stripes at the head of each procession. When the authorities protested, the strike leaders explained that red had long stood as the symbol of the laboring class in Spanish countries. They were astounded to learn that to people beyond the blue sea that surrounds them, the color meant lawlessness and revolt by violence, and they lost no time in adopting instead a green banner. When this in turn was found to have a similar significance in another island somewhere far away, they chose a white flag. It was not a matter of one color or another, they said, but of sufficient food to feed their hungry families.

Negro spell-binders from the cities, evil-faced fellows for the most part, whose soft hands showed no evidence of ever having wielded a cane-knife, harangued the barefoot multitudes in moonlighted town streets. When the head of the movement was taken to task by neutral fellow-citizens for not choosing lieutenants more capable of arousing general public sympathy and confidence, he replied with a fervent, " I wish to God I could! " But the ranks of Porto Rican workmen do not easily yield men of even the modicum of education required to spread-eagle a public meeting. Held down for centuries to almost the level of serfs, they have little notion of how to use that modern double-edged weapon, the strike. They do not put their heads together, formulate their demands, and carry them to their employers. Inert by nature and training, they plod on until some outside agitator comes along and tells them they shall get higher wages if only they will follow his leadership, whisper to one another that it would be nice to have more money, and quit work, with no funds to support themselves in idleness or any other preparation. It is the old irresponsibility, the lack of foreplanning common to the tropics. Then, that they may not be the losers whichever side wins, they strive to keep on good terms with their employers by telling them that only the fear of violence from their fellows keeps them from coming to work, being so docile by nature that they would not hurt even the feelings of their superiors.

This time the strikers had been encouraged by what they mistook to be federal support. The American Federation of Labor had sent down as investigating delegates two men of forceful Irish wit who were naturally appalled to find their new fellow-citizens living under conditions unequalled even among their ancestral peat-bogs. What they did not recognize was that all over Latin-America, even where land is virtually unlimited and there are no corporations to "exploit" the populace, the masses live in much the same thatched-hut degradation. Their familiarity with the Porto Rican environment was as negative as their knowledge of the Spanish language; they made the almost universal American mistake of thinking that what is true of the United States is equally so of all other countries, and their straight-forward national temperament made them no match for the wily, intricate machinations of native politicians.

Porto Rico had not been so lively since the Americans ousted the Spaniards. I had an opportunity of hearing both sides of the case, for with the privilege of the mere observer I was equally welcome — whatever the degree may have been — in the touring car of the delegates and at the dinner-tables of the sugar managers.

"These simple fellows from the States," said the latter, "think they can solve the problem of over-population by giving $2.50 a day to all laborers, good or bad, weak or strong. The result would be to drive the best workmen out of the country, and leave us, our stock-holders, and the consumers, victims of the poorest. Like the labor union movement everywhere, it would give the advantage to the weakling, the scamper, the time-killer. We have men in our fields who earn $3.50 a day, and who will tell you they do not know why on earth they are striking. Men who can cut six tons of cane a day on piece-work will not cut one ton at day wages. Then there are men so full of the hookworm that they haven't the strength to earn *one* dollar a day. We *centrals* insist on keeping the *ajuste* system that has always prevailed in Porto Rico — the letting of work by contract to self-appointed gang leaders; and we will not sign a minimum wage scale because there is no responsible person to see that the terms are carried out on the laborer's side. We refuse to deal with the strikers' committees because we cannot listen to a lot of bakers and barbers from the towns who do not know sugarcane from swamp reeds. There is nothing but politics back of it all any way. This is a presidential year; that explains the sudden interest of politicians in the poor down-trodden laboring class. Our men earn at least $1.75 a day — and they seldom work in the fields after two in the afternoon. Besides that we give every employee a twenty per cent. bonus, a house to live in if he chooses, free medical attention, half-time when they are sick, and the privilege of buying their supplies in our company stores at cost. Cuba pays higher wages, but the companies get most of it back through their stores. We run ours at a loss; I can prove it to you by our books; and we give much to charity. Hungry indeed! Do you know that our biggest sales to our laborers are costly perfumes? They may starve their children, but they can always feed fresh eggs to their fighting-cocks. There is hardly a man of them that is not keeping two or three women. If we paid our men twice what we do, the only result would be that they would lay off every other day. Let them strike! We can always get hillmen from the interior or men from Aguadilla who are only too glad to work for even less than we are paying now."

I found Santiago Iglesias literally up to his ears in work at the headquarters of the Socialist-Labor party, a few doors from the governor's palace. About him swarmed several of the foxy-faced individuals he had himself privately deplored as assistants. A powerful man in the prime of life, of pure Spanish blood, the radical Porto Rican senator was quite ready to recapitulate once more his view of the situation. If he was " playing politics "— and what elective government official is not every time he opens his mouth or turns over in bed? — he gave at least the impression of being genuinely distressed at the condition of Porto Rico's poverty-bred masses. We had conversed for some time in Spanish before he surprised me by breaking forth into a vigorous English, amusing for its curious errors of pronunciation. The minimum wage demanded, for instance, which recurred in almost every sentence, always emerged from his lips with the second f transformed into an s. That is the chief trouble with Santiago, according to his opponents — his methods are " too fisty."

" There has been a vast improvement in personal liberty in Porto Rico under American rule," he began. " But the island has been surrendered to Wall Street, to the heartless corporations that always profit most by American expansion. Moreover, American rule has forced upon us American prices — it always does — without giving our people the corresponding income. Formerly all our wealth went to Spain. Now it goes to the States, but with this difference,— under

Spanish rule wages were low but the employers were paternal; they thought occasionally about their peons. At least the workers got enough to eat. The corporations that have taken their place are utterly impersonal; the workmen who sweat in the sun for them are no more to the far away stock-holders than the canes that pass between the rollers of their sugar-mills. When they get these magnificent returns on their investment do the Americans who hold stocks and bonds in our great *centrals* ever ask themselves how the men who are actually earning them are getting on? No, they sit tight in their comfortable church pews giving thanks to the Lord with a freer conscience than ever did the Spanish conquistadores, for they are too far away ever to see the sufferings of *their* peons.

" The sugar companies can produce sugar at a hundred dollars a ton; they are getting two hundred and forty. The common stock of the four big ones, paid from fifty-six to seventy dollars last year on every hundred dollars invested, not to mention a lot of extra dividends, and their profits for this *zafra* will be far higher. The island is being pumped dry of its resources and nothing is being put back into it. In the States not twenty per cent. of the national income goes out of the country; the rest goes back into reproduction. In Porto Rico seventy per cent. goes to foreigners, and of the thirty left wealthy Porto Ricans spend a large amount abroad. We do not want our land all used to enrich non-resident stock-holders; we need it to feed our own people. There is not corn-meal and beans enough now to go round, because the big sugar *centrals* hold all the fertile soil. They have bought all the land about them, even the foot-hills, so that the people cannot plant anything, but *must* work for the companies. Stock-holders are entitled to a fair profit on the capital actually invested — *actually*, I say — and something for the risk taken — which certainly is not great. But the Porto Ricans, the men, and women, and the scrawny children who do the actual work in the broiling tropical sun should get the rest of it, in wages. We should tax non-resident sugar companies ten per cent. of their income for the improvement of Porto Rico; we should borrow several millions in the States and give our poor people land to cultivate, and pay the loan back out of that tax. But what can we do? The politicians, the high officials are all interested in sugar. They and the corporations form the *invisible* government; they are the law, the police, the rulers, the patriots. Patriots! The instant the Porto Rican income-tax was set at half that in the States the corporations made Porto Rico their legal residence. When the federal government would not stand for the trick and forced them to pay the balance they cried unto high Heaven. Porto Rican law forbids any company or individual to own more than five hundred acres. They get around the law by trickery, by dividing the holdings among the members of the same family, by making fake divisions of company stock. The Secretary of War and other federal officials come down here to 'investigate.' They motor across our beautiful mountains, have two or three banquets in the homes of the rich or the *central* managers, and the newspapers in the States shout 'Great Prosperity in Porto Rico!' I tell you it is the criminal lack of equity, the same old blindness of the landed classes the world over and in all ages that is driving Porto Rico into the camp of the violent radicals.

"You admire our fine roads. All visitors do. You do not realize that they were built because the corporations needed them. And did we pay for them by taxing the corporations? We did not. We paid for them by government bonds — that is, we charged them up to the children of the peons. You have probably found that we have inadequate school facilities. The corporations, the invisible government, do not want the masses educated, because then they would not have left any easily manipulated laboring class. Nor do I take much stock in this over-population idea. At least I should like to see the half million untilled acres turned over to the people before I will believe emigration is necessary. Sixty per cent. of Porto Rico is uncultivated, yet eighty per cent. of the population goes to bed hungry every night in the year. Then there is this cry of hookworm. Do not let the Rockefeller Foundation, a direct descendant of the capitalists, tell you lies about 'anemia.' The anemia of Porto Rico comes from no worm, but from the fact that the people are always hungry. It is the sordid miserliness of corporations, bent on keeping our peons reduced to the level of serfs, in order that they may always have a cheap supply of labor, that is the fundamental cause of the misery of Porto Rico, of the naked, barefoot, hungry, schoolless, homeless desolation of the working classes."

The calm and neutral observer, neither underfed nor blessed with the task of clipping sugar-stock coupons, detects a certain amount of froth on the statements of both parties to the controversy in Porto Rico. But he cannot but wonder why the sweat-stained laborers in the cornfields should be seen wearily tramping homeward to a one-room thatched hovel to share a few boiled roots with a slattern woman and a swarm of thin-shanked children while the Americans who direct them from the armchair comfort of fan-cooled offices stroll toward capacious bungalows, pausing on the way for a game of tennis in the company compound, and sit down to a faultless dinner amid all that appeals to the aesthetic senses. Least of all can he reconcile the vision of other Americans, whose only part in the production of sugar is the collecting of dividends, rolling about the island in luxurious touring cars, with the sight of the toil-worn, ragged workers whose uncouth appearance arouses the haughty travelers to snorts of scorn or falsetto shrieks of "how picturesque."

The problem in Porto Rico, as the reader has long since suspected, is the antithesis of that in Santo Domingo. In the latter island the difficulty is to get laborers enough to develop the country; in the former it is to find labor enough to occupy the swarming population. Barely three-fourths of a million people are scattered through the broad insular wilderness to the westward; the census of 1920 shows little Porto Rico crowded with 1,263,474 inhabitants, that is nearly four hundred persons to the square mile. There are several reasons for this discrepancy; for one thing Santo Domingo has been fighting itself for generations, while Porto Rico has never had a revolution. The obvious solution of the problem has two serious drawbacks. The Dominicans do not welcome immigration; they wish to keep their country to themselves. The Porto Rican is inordinately fond of his birthplace. Send him to the most distant part of the world and he is sure sooner or later to come back to his beloved Borinquen. Emigration from the island can reach even moderate success only when entire families are sent. The letters of Porto Rican soldiers no nearer the front than Florida or Panama were filled with wails of homesickness that would have been pitiful had they not been tinged with what to the unemotional Anglo-Saxon was a suggestion of the ludicrous.

There is a Japanese effect in the density of population of our little West Indian colony. When the traveler has motored for hours without once getting out of sight of human habitations, when he has noted how the unpainted little shacks speckle the steepest hillside, even among the high mountains, when he has seen the endless clusters of hovels that surround every town, whether of the coast or the interior, he will come to realize the crowded condition. If he is a trifle observant, he will also see everywhere signs of the scarcity of work. Men lounging in the doors of their huts in the middle of the day, surrounded by pale women and children sucking a joint of sugar-cane, are not always loafers; in many cases they have nowhere to go and work. While the women toil at making lace, drawn-work, or hats, the males turn their hands to anything that the incessant struggle for livelihood suggests. The man who spends two days in weaving a laundry basket and plods fifteen or twenty miles to sell it for sixty cents is only one of a thousand commonplace sights along the island highways.

A job is a prize in Porto Rico. If one is offered, applicants swarm; many a man " lays off " in order to lend his job to his brother, his cousin, or his *compadre*. Naturally, employers take advantage of this condition. The American labor delegates told the chief of police that he should be the first to lead his men on strike, for certainly he could not keep them honest at forty-five dollars a month.

" Oh, yes, I can," retorted the chief, " for while we have barely eight hundred on the force, there are twelve thousand on the waiting-list, and every policeman knows that if he is fired, he will have to go back to punching bullocks at a third as much." *Mozos* and chambermaids in the best hotels seldom get more than five dollars a month. Street-car men get from sixteen to twenty-five cents an hour, depending on the length of service. In a large clothing factory of Mayagüez, fitted with motor-run sewing-machines, only a few of the women get a dollar a day; the majority average fifty cents. The law, of course, requires that they be paid a minimum wage of a dollar; but what is a mere law among a teeming population which the Spaniards spent four centuries in training to be *manso* and uncomplaining? The favorite trick is to pay the dollar, and then fine the women fifty cents for not having done sufficient work. Among the regrettable sights of the island are groups of callous emissaries frequenting the leading hotels who have been sent down as agents of certain American department stores to reap advantage from the local poverty. These *comisionistas* motor about the island, placing orders with the wretched native women, but by piece-work, you may be sure, to avoid the requirement of paying a dollar a day. American women who are paying several times what they once did for Porto Rican lace, blouses, and drawn-work, may fancy that some of this increase goes to the humble *mujeres* who do the work. Not at all. They are still toiling in their miserable little huts at the same ludicrous prices, while their products are being sold on the " bargain " counters in our large cities, at several hundred per cent. profit. So thoroughly have these touts combed the country that the individual can nowhere buy of the makers; their work has all been contracted far in advance.

CHAPTER XII

THE American who, noting the Stars and Stripes flying everywhere and post-offices selling the old familiar postage-stamps, fancies he is back in his native land again is due for a shock. Though it has been Americanized industrially, Porto Rico has changed but little in its every-day life. Step out of one of the three principal hotels of the capital and you are in a foreign land. Spanish is as necessary to the traveler in Porto Rico who intends to get out of the Condado-Vanderbilt-automobile belt as it is in Cuba, Mexico, or South America. Though it is not quite true that ": base-ball and poker are the only signs of American influence," the other evidences might be counted on the fingers. There is the use of personal checks in place of actual money, for instance; venders of chickens carry them in baskets instead of by the legs. Offenders are tried by a jury of their peers; the native regiment wears the uniform of our regular army; it would take deep reflection to think of many more instances. Only one daily newspaper in Pórto Rico has an English edition. The first American theatrical company to visit the island since the United States took it over was due the week we left. There are barely ten thousand American residents; except in the capital and the heart of two or three other cities one attracts as much gaping attention as in the wilds of Bolivia. In a way this conservatism is one of the charms of the island. The mere traveler is agreeably disappointed to find that it has not been " Americanized " in the unpleasant sense of the word, that it has kept much of its picturesque, old-world atmosphere.

English is little spoken in Porto Rico. That is another of the surprises it has in store for us, at least for those of us old enough to remember what a splurge we made of swamping the island with American teachers soon after we took it over. It is indeed the " official " language, but the officials who speak it are rare, unless they come from the United States, in which case they are almost certain to be equally ignorant of Spanish. The governor never stirs abroad without an interpreter. The chief of police rarely ventures a few words of

Castilian, though there is scarcely a patrolman even in the heart of San Juan who can answer the simplest question in English. Can any one think up a valid reason why a fair command of the official tongue should not be required of natives seeking government employment? Spanish is a delightful language; its own children are no more fond of it than I am. But after all, Porto Rico differs from the rest of Spanish-America, in that it is a part of the United States. She aspires some day to statehood. That day should not come until she knows English; it is not a question of one language in place of another, but of mutual understanding.

To be sure, English is compulsory in all the schools of the island, but few pupils learn it thoroughly enough to retain it through life. Most of them can read it in a parrot-like manner; if they speak it at all, it is to shout some half-intelligible phrase after a passing American. " Aw right " is about the only expression that has been thoroughly Portoricanized. That is not exactly the fault of the pupils. The ear shudders at the " English " spoken even by those teachers who are supposed to be specialists in it; the rest are little short of incomprehensible. Passed on from one such instructor to another, the English that finally comes down to the pupils resembles the original about as much as an oft-repeated bit of gossip resembles the original facts. It might almost be said that there has been no progress made in teaching Porto Rico English in the twenty years of American rule, or at least in the last fifteen of them.

On the whole the state of education in Porto Rico is a disappointment. It is a surprise to the visitor who has thought this essential matter was settled long ago to find sixty per cent. of the population illiterate, few countrymen over thirty who can read, and scarcely a third of the children of school age in school. We had, of course, much to make up. In 1898, after four centuries of ostensibly civilized government, there was but one building on the island specially erected for educational purposes. The total enrollment in the schools, with a population of nearly a million, was 26,000. Three-fourths of the males of voting age were wholly illiterate. Pupils were " farmed out," teachers drew salaries without ever going near a schoolhouse, all the old Spanish tricks were in full swing. But that was twenty years ago. Yet the department of education asks for twenty years more to bring things up to a " reasonable standard." Why? Moreover, at the rate things have been moving it will not nearly do that. The thousand and more school-buildings that have been erected, tropical Spanish in architecture, well lighted and ventilated, of concrete in the towns and wood in the country, their names in English over the entrances, are all very well, but they are far from sufficient. The census taken just before our arrival showed almost a half million children of school age, with 181,716 enrolled, and 146,561 in average attendance. Of the 2984 teachers only 148 were Americans. The only inducement Porto Rico offers to instructors from " the States " is an appeal to the love of adventure. Those who wish to make a trip to the tropics may be sure of a position — at a lower salary than they receive at home, and with the privilege of paying their own passages down and back to profiteering steamship companies. No wonder the " English " of Porto Rico is going to seed.

In the graded school system of the towns all instruction is given in that maltreated tongue except the class in Spanish. In the rural schools all the work is given in Spanish except a class in so-called English as a special subject in all grades above the first. The University of Porto Rico, seventeen years old, has fewer than a thousand students. The Agricultural College in Mayagüez has some two hundred. Private institutions like the Polytechnic Institute of San Germán are doing yoeman service, but why should the education of Porto Rico depend on private enterprise? The natives claim that the trouble is that nearly all the commissioners of education sent down from the United States have been political appointees; the latter lay the blame to the fact that salaries and disbursements are set by the native legislature. Somewhere between the two the education of Porto Rico is suffering.

For all their misfortunes, or perhaps because of them, the Porto Ricans, especially outside the large cities, are hospitable and soft-mannered, characterized by a constant courtesy and a solicitude to please those with whom they come in contact, with little of that bruskness of intercourse for which "the Mainland " is notorious. The island has a less grasping, less materialistic atmosphere than Cuba, it is less sinister, less cynical, more naïve, its people are more primitive and simple, though industrial oppression and American influence are slowly changing them in this regard. Their naïveté is often delightful. It is reported that a company of youthful *jíbaros* drafted into the Federal service during the war waited on their captain one day and asked for their " time," as they did not care for a job in which they had to wear shoes! The children are rarely boisterous, rather well-bred, even where little chance for breeding exists. As a race they have kept many of the peculiarities of their Spanish ancestry. They are still Latin Americans in their over-developed personal pride and their lack of a sense of humor. Moorish seclusion of women still raises its head among the " best- families." The horror in the slightest suggestion of manual labor, of a lowering of caste, still oppresses the " upper " class. Few of them would dream of carrying their own suitcase or a package from a store, even though they must abandon them for lack of a peon. Though they are far more polite than our own club-swingers in super-ficial matters, it has required persistent training to get the insular police to forget their high standing and help across the street women or children of the socially inferior class. Finally, Porto Ricans are little to be depended upon in the matter of time; *mañana* is still their watch-word despite twenty years of Anglo-Saxon bustle. But, for that matter, Americans get hopelessly irresponsible on this same subject after a few years in the tropics.

The unprepared visitor will find Porto Ricans astonishingly white, especially in the interior. There are few full negroes on the island; sixty per cent. of the population have straight hair. Yet there is a motley mixture of races, without rhyme or reason from our point of view. Mulatto estate owners may have pure white peons working for them; a native octoroon is frequently seen ordering about a Gallego serv-ant from Spain. There is still considerable evidence of Indian blood in the Porto Rican physiognomy, for the aborigines, taking refuge in the high mountains, were wiped out only by assimilation. Then there are Japanese or Chinese features peering forth from many a hybrid face. The Spaniards brought in coolies to work on the military roads, and they mixed freely with all the lower ranks of the population. Yet pure-blooded Orientals are conspicuous by their absence; so over-crowded a community does not appeal even to the ubiquitous Chinese laundryman. For the same reason Jews, Syrians, and Armenians have not invaded the island in any great numbers, though one now and then meets an olive-skinned peddler tramping from village to town with a great flat basket filled with bolts of calico and the like on his cylindrical head.

Small commerce is almost entirely in the hands of Spaniards, thanks to whom the mixture of races that made Latin-America a hybrid is still going on — to say nothing of an exploiting of the simple *jíbaros* that would have been scorned by the old straight-forward, sword-brandishing conquistadores. The modern Spaniard, especially the

Canary Islanders, come over as clerks, live like dogs until they have acquired an interest in their master's business, and eventually set up a little store for themselves.   Sharp, thrifty, heartless, utterly devoid of any ideal than the amassing of a fortune, they resort to every species of trickery to increase their already exorbitant profits.   The favorite scheme is to get the naïve countrymen into a gambling game, *manigua*, the native card-game, for instance, and to urge them on after their scanty funds are exhausted with a sweet-voiced " Don't let that worry you, *Chico*, I 'll lend you all you want.   Go ahead and play," until they have a ·mortgage on " Chico's " little farm or have forced him to sign a contract to sell them all his coffee at half the market price.   Then when his fortune is made, the wily Iberian leaves each of his concubines and her half-breed flock of children a little hut, goes back to Spain, marries, and bequeaths his wealth to his legitimate offspring.   Many a little plantation is still encumbered with these " manigua mortgages."

To the casual observer there seems to be no color-line in Porto Rico ; but in home life and social matters there is comparatively little mingling of whites and blacks above the peon class.   In the Agricultural College at Mayagüez, for instance, this question is left entirely to the pupils. The students draw their own color-line.   Clubs are formed that take in only white members, though a few of these might not pass muster among Americans.   The colored boys do not form clubs because they cannot afford to do so.   In the early days the teachers gave a dance to which all students were invited without distinction.   But the darker youths brought up all sorts of female companions from the *playa* hovels, and the experiment was never repeated.   Yet it is no unusual sight to see a white and a mulatto youth sharing a textbook in the shade of a campus mango-tree.

There remain few strictly insular customs to distinguish Porto Rico from the rest of Latin-America.   The native musical instrument is a calabash, or gourd, with a roughened surface over which a steel wire is rubbed, producing a half-mournful, rasping sound almost without cadence.   Thanks perhaps to American influence, the church bells are musical and are rung only by day, in grateful contrast to the incessant, broken-boiler din of other Spanish-settled countries.   The *Rosario,* a kind of native wake, consists of all-night singing by the friends and relatives of the recent dead.   Possibly the most universal local custom is that of using barbed-wire fences as clothes-lines, to the misfortune even of the linen of trustful visitors.   The panacea for all rural ills seems to be the tying of a white cloth about the head.   Doctors seldom go into the country, but let the sick be brought in to them, whatever the stage of their illness. More than ten thousand, chiefly of the hut-dwelling class, died of " flu " during the winter of 1918–19, largely because of this inertia of physicians.

One must not lose sight of their history in judging the present condition of the Porto Rican masses. It is only fifty years since slaves over sixty and under three were liberated, and later still that slavery was entirely abolished. No wonder the owners were glad to be rid of what fast breeding had made a burden, especially with free labor at twenty cents a day. Yet they were indemnified with eight million dollars from the insular revenues. Nor was servitude confined to Africans. Spain long used Porto Rico as a penal colony, and when public works no longer required them, the convicts were turned loose to shift for themselves. Most of them took to the mountains where the " poor white " population is numerous to this day. Yet the later generations are no more criminal than the Australians; if there is much petty thieving, it is natural in a hungry, overcrowded community.

The insular police established by the Americans have an efficiency rare in tropical countries. Their detective force rounds up a larger percentage of law-breakers than almost any other such body in the world. The insular character of their beat is to their advantage, of course; few Porto Ricans can swim. The island has long since been " cleaned up," and the unarmed stranger is safer in its remotest corners than on Broadway. In olden days the Porto Rican was as fond of making himself a walking arsenal as the Dominican; ten thousand revolvers were seized in nine years, and miscellaneous weapons too numerous to count have been confiscated and destroyed. To-day, except in the rare cases when a desperado like " Chuchu " breaks loose, or strikers grow troublesome, the spotlessly uniformed insular force has little to do but to enforce the unpopular laws that have come with American rule.

Porto Rico voted herself dry in 1917. Three varying reasons are given for this unnatural action, according to the point of view of the speaker. Missionaries assert that, thanks largely to their work with the populace, the hungry rank and file determined that *their* children should not grow up under the alcoholic burden that had blasted their own success in life. Scoffers claim the people were misled by psychological suggestion. The majority make the more likely assertion that the result was largely due to a mistake on the part of the ignorant peons. The " dries " chose as their party emblem the green cocoanut, a favorite rural beverage.   Their opponents decorated the head of their ballot with a bottle.   Now, the bottle suggests to the *jíbaros* of the hills the Spaniards who keep the liquor shops, and they hate the Spaniards as fiercely as they are capable of hating anything.   Whatever the workings of their obscure minds, the unshaven countrymen came down out of the mountains to the polls, and next morning Porto Rico woke up to find herself, to her unbounded surprise, " bone-dry."   The mere fact that the politicians and the " influential citizens" almost in a body, and even the American governor, who saw insular revenues cut down when they sadly needed building up, were against the change had nothing to do with the case.   Since then the insular police have confiscated hundreds of home-made stills and thousands of gallons of illicit liquor. It is rumored that they would like to indict the Standard Oil Company as an accessory before the fact, for virtually all the stills that languish in the police museum in San Juan are made of the world-wide five-gallon oil can, some of them ingenious in the extreme.

Cock-fighting was forbidden by American edict soon after we took over the island — and in retaliation the Porto Rican Legislature forbade prize-fighting, even "practice bouts."   But there is no law against keeping fighting-cocks, and where there are game-cocks there is bound to be fighting, at least in Latin-America.   The police are on the constant look-out for clandestine *riñas de gallos.*   One point in favor of the sleuths is that, though they cannot arrest people for harboring prize roosters, they can bring them up on the charge of cruelty to animals if they pick and trim the birds as proper preparation for battle requires.   Americans who have lived long in Porto Rico assert that cock-fighting and the lottery are so indigenous to the island that there is little hope of really stamping them out.   Indeed, even the police are in sympathy with the sport, though they may not let that sympathy interfere with doing their duty.   High American officials sometimes ask what there is wrong in running a lottery, so long as other forms of gambling are permitted, especially as the old government lottery kept up many benevolences.   Why, they ask, should not the poor man be allowed to "take a chance" as well as speculators on the stock exchange?   Roosters and *billetes* are two things that are sure to come back if Porto Rico wins her autonomy during the life of the present inhabitants.   Possibly the next generation will be like-minded; one of the absorbing tasks of the insular police is to keep street urchins from gambling on the numbers of passing automobiles.

It is not surprising that Porto Rico has more than her share of

juvenile offenders.   Sexual morality is on a low plane in the island.
Though there is less public vice than with us, the custom of even the
" best citizens " to establish " outside families " is wide-spread.   Even
the " Washington of Porto Rico," who is pointed out as the model
man of the island, always kept two or three *queridas,* and lost none of
his high standing with the natives for that reason.   Estate owners are
well-nigh as free with the pretty wives of their peons as were old
feudal lords.   Women of this class are often more proud to have a son
by the " señor " than by their own husbands.   The latter are easy-
going to a degree unknown among us; they may be cajoled by presents
or threatened with discharge — and where else ·shall they find a spot
to live on? — or at worst they can seek consolation in the arms of their
own *queridas.*   The men usually acknowledge their illegal children
without hypocrisy, but they frequently abandon them to their own
devices.   Homeless children are one of the problems of all Porto
Rican cities; in San Germán a gang of little ruffians roost in trees by
night.   The cook of an American missionary family openly gave all
her wages, except what went for the rent of her hovel, to her " man,"
who was married to another.   It was not that he demanded it; there
is little of the " white slave " attitude in Porto Rico, but she was proud
to do so and it is *costumbre del país.*   Much as they deplored such an
employee, the missionaries endured her, knowing only too well by
experience that they might look farther and fare worse.   Few Porto
Ricans of the better class permit their women to go to confession, however strictly they keep up the other forms of religion.   Out of church
the priests are frankly men like other men, and seldom have any
hesitancy in admitting it.   One famous for his pulpit eloquence brazenly
boasts himself " the most successful lover in Porto Rico."

It is natural that there should be a certain political unrest in Porto
Rico.   The island does not know, for instance — nor does any one else,
apparently — whether it is a colony or a possession of the United
States, or whether it is an integral part of it.   A bit of history is
required to explain the situation.   The island was under the jurisdiction
of Santo Domingo from its settling to the end of the sixteenth century,
when a royal decree made it an independent colony.   For a long time
it was not self-supporting — thanks, no doubt, largely to the dishonesty
of its governors.   Its government became such a burden that Spain
assigned a certain proportion of the treasure it was drawing from
Mexico to support it.   Incidentally this came near making Porto Rico

British, for ships bringing funds from Mexico were repeatedly made the objects of attack, and the commander of one of these fleets once attempted to occupy the island, but disease among his soldiers forced him to abandon the enterprise, taking with him only such trophies as he could tear from churches and fortresses. When, a hundred years ago, the wave of rebellion swept over all the Spanish colonies, Santo Domingo declared her independence and offered to coöperate with Porto Rico in winning hers also; but a majority of the inhabitants remained loyal to the crown. In 1887 a popular assembly in Ponce, while acknowledging allegiance to Spain, demanded a certain measure of autonomy. There was danger that the Cuban insurgents would send an expedition to Porto Rico to join the malcontents there. Hence on November 28, 1897, Spain granted Porto Rico local government in so far as internal affairs, budgets, customs, and treaties of commerce were concerned. She was to have an elective legislature, an upper house appointed by the governor, and a cabinet composed of residents of the island. The following February such a cabinet was appointed, and on March 27 — note the date — elections were held. In other words Porto Rico had won autonomy without recourse to bloodshed, and was on the eve of exercising it when the *Maine* was blown up. Moreover, she had never in her history asked to be separated from Spain.

When the Americans came, a postal system was organized, the government lottery was suppressed, freedom of speech and of the press was restored, a police force of natives under American officials was established, strict sanitary measures were adopted, free schools were opened, provision was made for the writ of habeas corpus and jury trials, the courts were reorganized, imprisonment for political offenses, chains and solitary confinement were abolished, the foreclosure of mortgages was temporarily suspended, Spanish currency was replaced by American, local officials were elected, and a civil government was established on May 1, 1900. Note, however, that with all this Porto Rico did not get as much autonomy as it had already won from Spain. Gradually the island has almost reached the point politically where the Spanish-American War found it, but meanwhile there had been much discontent. Then along came the "Jones bill." This provides for an elective legislature, extends the appointive judiciary system, admits a delegate to our Congress, and grants American citizenship to Porto Ricans. But the acts of the insular legislature must be approved by the American governor, and six of the heads of departments that make

The place of pilgrimage for pious Porto Ricans

Porto Rican children of the coast lands

The old sugar kettles scattered through the West Indies have many uses

A corner in Aquadillo

up the Executive Council are Americans. The Porto Ricans chafe at citizenship without statehood. The island complains that it is an organized but not an incorporated territory of the United States. Though it enjoys many of the rights of territories, and a larger exemption from federal taxation than ever did any other American territory, it is not politically happy.

There are four political parties in Porto Rico. The Republicans, who have little in common with our " G. O. P.," though they send delegates to its conventions, want immediate statehood. The Unionists, contrary to their title, demand independence. There is a strong socialist and labor party, and a minor group that desires a return to Spanish rule. These divisions are not so definite as they seem, if we may believe an unusually informative native postmaster of the interior.

" The people with small government jobs," he asserted, " many school teachers among them, secretly long for independence, chiefly in the hope of getting more graft. The Spaniards still mix secretly in politics and are really *independentistas,* though pretending to want statehood. Porto Rico would be wholly Americanized now if the governors had not ignorantly put in anti-American *politicos.* There has really been only one competent governor since the Americans took Porto Rico. We are decidedly not yet ready for jury trial; there was one of the most serious mistakes. It was also a mistake to make us American citizens collectively. We should have been given individual choice in the matter. Now if you accuse a man of not acting like an American citizen he cries, ' Pah! They *made* me an American citizen. *I* had nothing to say about it.' The best people think we need twenty years of military rule before we are given even local liberty. A plebiscite would give a false opinion because the politicians and the small-estate owners, who are chiefly Spanish, would send their peons down to vote for independence without any notion of what it means. And the best class would n't vote. Do you think I would have my photograph and thumb-print taken, like a common criminal, in order to cast my ballot? The people do not know how to be free, after centuries of Spanish slavery. If independence were signed at eight o'clock tomorrow morning, I should leave Porto Rico at nine! " he concluded, vehemently.

There is, of course, no more reason why Porto Rico should have her independence than that Florida should. That she is entitled to be made a fully incorporated territory now, and a state in due season, seems the fitting course. But she is decidedly not yet ready for statehood. For one thing she must first know English. The partial autonomy she already enjoys shows her far from prepared for self-rule. Uncle Sam is always in too big a hurry to give his wards local government; also we listen perhaps too much to Latin-American criticism. We are not used to the sob-eloquence of the race, which at bottom means very little. The legislature and native insular officials are by no means free from intrigue, graft, and dishonesty. Towns with $100,000 incomes spend half of it in salaries to the mayor and his colleagues. Teachers were forced to pay ten per cent. of their wages into political funds, and the native court found that " they can do what they wish with their salaries." The great socialist senator himself, rumor has it, bought land in Santurce at a dollar an acre, had public streets put in, and sold out at three dollars, though that, to be sure, might have happened in Trenton or Omaha. Even the post-offices are said to be corrupt with local politics.

So long as there is a great apathetic, illiterate, emotional mass of voters self-government can be no more than a farce, in Porto Rico or elsewhere. No Anglo-Saxon party leader can hope to keep pace with the suave machinations of Spanish-American politicians. They can think of more tricks overnight than he can run to earth in a week. Some years ago a youthful American was approached by a Porto Rican political leader with a request to come and address a public meeting.

" But I don't know a word of Spanish! " he protested.

" All the better," replied the politician; " we want you to speak in English."

" I never made a speech in my life," continued the American.

" Talk about anything whatever," pleaded the other, " the weather, the scenery, baseball."

The youth, who was not averse to a "lark," mounted the platform and began to expound in choppy words the glories of baseball. At the end of each sentence the politician silenced him with a gesture and "interpreted" his statements to the crowded peons, who, to the speaker's astonishment, greeted each well-rounded Spanish phrase with howls of delight. Not until the meeting was over and one of his hearers had addressed him by a name that was not his own, did the youth awaken to the fact that he had been introduced as the son of the governor, and that the Spanish portion of his speech had been an explanation of how anxious his "father" was to have the "interpreter" elected to the office he sought. "*Dice el americano* (the American says)" is still one of the by-words of Porto Rican politics.

But after all one does not visit so beautiful and fascinating a country as Porto Rico to chatter of its problems, but to meet its curious people and to marvel at its glorious scenery. More mountainous than even Haiti and Santo Domingo, the island is such an unbroken labyrinth of hills, ranges, and high peaks, of deep valleys, perpendicular slopes, and precipitous canyons, that its rugged beauty seems never-ending. That beauty, too, is enhanced by the great amount of cultivation, by the character it gains over the often uninhabited island to the westward in being everywhere peopled, by the great variety of colors that decorate it especially in this tropical spring-time of February. Even along the rolling coastal belt the highways are lined with the green- and red-leaved *almendras,* or false almond-trees, which here and there carpet the roads with Turkish rugs of fallen leaves. Higher up comes the *roble,* or flowering laurel, with its masses of delicate pink blossoms, then the *bucaré*-trees, used as coffee shade, daub the precipitous hillsides with splotches of burnt-orange hue; still farther aloft come beautiful tree ferns, symbolical of high tropical altitudes, and everywhere stand the majestic royal palms and the dense, massive mango-trees, in sorrel-colored blossom at this season, to crown the heavy green vegetation that everywhere clothes the island. For although almost every acre of it was denuded of its native forest growth by the tree-hating Spaniards, nature and the necessities of man have replaced its unbroken verdure.

It would be hard to say which of the several splendid roads across the island offers the best glimpse of this scenic fairyland. Some swear by the Ponce-Arecibo route, through the magnificent Utuado valley; others find nothing to compare with the stretch between Comerio and Cayey, the heart of the tobacco district; the most traveled certainly is the great military highway of the Spaniards, from San Juan to Ponce, the first half of it rivalled now by an American-built branch through Barranquitas. Perhaps the most beautiful bit of all is the journey from Guayama up to Cayey, that, too, by a route that antedates our possession. One unconsciously compares these achievements of the old Spanish engineers with our more recent efforts, and the comparison is not always favorable to the Americans. The Spaniard built in that leisurely fashion of European highways, which prefers wide detours to over-steep grades; his successor here and there betrays the impatience of his race by a too abrupt turn or a sharper slope.   Yet the works of both are splendidly engineered, with never a really dangerous spot to a sane driver, for all the hairpin curves, the precipitous mountain walls above and below, the lofty bridges over profound canyons at the bottom of which insignificant brooks meander or roaring torrents tear seaward as if fleeing from the wrath of the towering peaks above, according to the season.   There are reminders of Europe at every turn, — crenelated bridge-parapets, kilometer-posts and white fractions of them at every hundred meters, squatting men wielding their hammers on roadside stone-piles, *caminero* huts every few miles.   It is the latter, in particular, that explain the unfailing near-perfection of Porto Rican highways.   Brick or stone dwellings for the *capataces,* or road foremen, who must proceed at once to any broken roadbed, rain or shine, are interspersed with the too miserable huts of the *peones camineros,* who toil unceasingly day after day in the up-keep of the highways, like scattered railroad section-gangs.   This system, a direct legacy from Spain, would be the answer to our own road troubles, were it possible to find men in our country willing to spend their lives at low wages in such an occupation.

Travel is unceasing along these splendid island roads.   Automobiles, creaking ox-carts and massive tarpaulin-covered freight wagons drawn by several teams of big Missouri mules, mail-busses and crowded *guaguas,* horse carriages and now and then a string of pack-animals to contrast with the flying motors, make endless procession along the way, while countless barefoot pedestrians flank the blurred roadsides. Only the horsemen so frequent elsewhere in Latin-America are conspicuous by their scarcity.   In contrast to carefully tended highways are the constant successions of miserable huts, built of anything that will hold together, some of them so close to the precipitous edge of the road that the front yard sometimes comes tumbling down into it in the rainy season.   Others are pitched up the mountain sides to the clouds above, many of the slopes so sheer that the little garden patches stand almost on end.   A case once actually came to court of a man who sued his neighbor for pushing his cow off his farm, entailing great labor to hoist her up again.   Little American-style schoolhouses, the Stars and Stripes always flying above them, the whole interior from teacher to pupils visible through the wide-open doors, flash past. Lounging men are frequent, women everywhere making lace or drawn-work squat like toads in the doorways of their patched hovels, no one of which is insignificant or inaccessible enough not to have the census-enumerator's tag tacked in plain sight on its bare front wall.

From Guayama almost at sea-level the old Spanish *carretera* climbs quickly into the cooler air, in snaky fashion, the town and the cane-green valley below diminishing to a picture framed by the white beach-line and the fuzzy mountain-slopes, then mounts by tortuous curves and serpentine loops around the brinks of dizzy precipices to a height of three thousand feet. For a time it clings along the cliff of a magnificent little valley, giving an endless succession of vistas, pano-ramas of mountains, ravines, and forested slopes, enhanced by frequent glimpses of the deep-blue Caribbean. No one of these highways is twice alike; morning or evening, under the blazing tropical sun or veiled with mountain showers, there is always a different aspect. Then suddenly it bursts out high above the valley of Cayey, the roof-flecked red of the town surrounded and packed as far as the eye can see with cloth-covered tobacco-fields, the crowning beauty of Porto Rican scenery. As we drop downward by more hairpin curves and climb again into the hills beyond, the steep mountainsides are every-where covered in enormous patches with what look like the snowfields and glaciers of Switzerland, transported to the tropics. All through the region the big unpainted wooden barns of the American Tobacco Company bulk above the shade-grown immensities, as if half buried by drifted snow, until the entranced beholder finds it hard to remember that he is in a land of perpetual summer, despite the royal palms that here and there spring aloft from the white landscape. Elsewhere the unclothed fields are planted in endless rows of tobacco, on, up, and over hill after mountain, some of them so steep as to make cultivation seem impossible, and all looking as if their velvety green fur had been put in order by a gigantic comb.

Here one meets wagon-loads of tobacco plants and men carrying them in baskets on their heads, tiny plants in the transplanting season, great clusters of the full-grown leaves in cutting-time. He is a simple fellow, the stubby-footed toiler of these regions, so naïve that he often tucks away for years the checks with which the company pays for his produce, instead of cashing them. They are always "good," he argues, and easily concealed, and he seems never to have heard of the word interest.

"Where does all this stuff go?" demanded an American tourist who had been motoring for hours through these tropical glaciers, "I have never seen much Porto Rican tobacco in the States."

" Ah, but when it reaches New York it becomes Habana," explained the tobacco agent. " You see, we mix it with the Cuban."

" About one leaf of Habana to a bale of this," suggested the tourist.

" Well, something like that," admitted the tobacco-man.

The holy place of Porto Rico — for it would be a strange Latin-American country without one — is the old church of Hormigueros, a yellow church high on a hill, conspicuous afar off and with the inevitable cane of the coast lands stretching away from it as far as the pilgrim can see.   The pious still climb its great stone stairway on their hands and knees, though rarely now except during the big fiesta in September.   The story is that, some time back in the days of legend, a bull attacked a man in the field below.   The man prayed to the Virgin, promising to do something in her honor if she would save him, and at the very instant his life was about to be gored out the bull dropped dead at his feet.   There is a colored picture of that miracle in the church on the hill, which was built by the grateful man, who also entailed the estate he owned below to support it in perpetuity.   To-day the lands are producing sugar cane for the Guánica *Central*, which pays rent to the church — and which also hastens to contribute when the parish priest suggests that money is needed for a fiesta or for some other purpose.   For if the company does not respond, the priest calls a holiday, digging up some old saint out of the church calendar, and the fields round about go begging for laborers.

There is at least one other " sight " which the visitor to Porto Rico should not miss, for it throws a striking side-light on Latin-American character.   In the hilly little town of Barranquitas is the birth-place of Luis Muñoz Rivera, often called the " George Washington of Porto Rico."   A cheap, thin, little clapboarded building, uninviting by our standards, though almost palatial to the simple country people, it has been turned into a museum to the dead insular hero, such a museum as cannot often be seen elsewhere.   At the back of the house a lean-to garage has been built to accommodate the expensive touring-car in which his remains were carried to the cemetery.   Not that Rivera owned an automobile; he was too honest a servant of his country to have reached that degree of affluence.   It was loaned for the funeral by one of the dead man's admirers, a senator and the owner of a large sugar *central*.   When the mourners returned, it was decided to make a Porto Rican " Mount Vernon " of the humble residence of the departed statesman, to which end the rich senator not only contributed generously in money, but added the improvised funeral-car. There it stands to this day, its brand new tires lifted off the garage floor by wooden horses, the license of four years ago still on its blunt nose, the plank framework that was built out the back of it to hold the coffin still intact. Inside the house is the narrow spring cot on which the hero died, covered with those poetically lettered purple ribbons of which the Latin-American mourner is so fond, and a score of other belongings, similarly decorated. These include a tin bathtub on wheels, a leather valise, the high-hat box indispensable to diplomats, several photographs of the deceased, death-masks of his face and of his hands, his last umbrella — one almost expects to find his last toothbrush, with a purple bow on the handle — all of them more or less covered with cobwebs. On his writing-table lies a specially bound volume of his book of poems, called "Tropicales," and, most striking tribute of all, an elaborate bit of embroidery done in the various shaded hair of his female admirers.

Rivera differed from most politicians in being strictly honest. Not only did he live within his government salary; he gave a large share of it to the poor. Bit by bit hatchet-and-cherry-tree stories are already growing up about his memory. As the leader of the Unionist party he was violently anti-American, went to the United States to fight for the independence of the island — and came back ardently pro-American. His admirers assert that "he would have been the salvation of Porto Rico had he lived," though exactly what they mean by the statement they probably have little notion themselves.

There are two drawbacks to walking in Porto Rico, though the ardent pedestrian will not let them deter him from his favorite sport. For one thing an American attracts attention, and loses the incognito that makes walking in Europe, for instance, so pleasant. Then the roads are too good. The hard macadam surfaces which are the joy of the motorist are not soft underfoot, and the rushing automobiles have small respect for the mere foot-traveler. There are, of course, many unpaved trails in and over the mountains, but they were scarcely passable at the time of our visit, for Porto Rico seems to have no definitely fixed wet and dry season.

I rambled about several sections of the island on foot. There was the trip to and about Lares, for instance, in the heart of the coffee district. The men of the over-developed big toes are less in touch with the outside world than either the cane or tobacco planters. The coffee industry is the only one that suffered by the island's change of sovereignty. Though it was not introduced into Porto Rico until more than two centuries after the sugar-cane, the Arabian berry was the king of the island when General Miles landed the first American troops at Guánica. The loss of their free markets in Spain and Cuba, however, caused the coffee men to succumb under a discouragement from which they have not wholly recovered to this day. It is this, no doubt, which accounts for the careless methods of the *cafetales*, where jungle, weeds, and parasites often choke the bushes, while the berries are dried on half-cured cowhides laid in the open streets or on hut floors, with chickens, dogs, goats, and naked children, to say nothing of pigs, wandering over them at will. Such conditions will of course improve when the United States, the greatest coffee-drinking nation on the globe, finally learns that a berry equal to any in the world can be produced on American soil.

In Lares region the crop is taken a bit more seriously. There are brick coffee-floors in many a yard, and the bushes cover even the crests of the mountains, though the stranger might not suspect it, hidden as they are by the sheltering trees. They are pretty in their white blossoms in the February season, and the *bucaré* trees flame forth everywhere on the steep slopes. The Spaniards, who own many of the estates, pay fifty cents " flat " a day to their peons. The more generous Porto Rican growers, if their own assertions may be taken at par, pay sixty cents, with the right to eat the oranges and *guineos,* or small bananas, that fall from the trees, the rent-free possession of an acre of ground on which to build a hut and graze a cow, a pig, or a few chickens, and plant a garden, and such free firewood as may be picked up on the estate. Formerly they paid thirty cents and gave two meals a day, but the cost of food has caused them to " advance " wages instead. The women and girls of the region spend most of their time making lace or drawn-work, as elsewhere, unless they are attracted to the *cafetales* in picking season by the higher inducement of forty cents a day.

I paused to talk with a youth who kept a roadside " shop." It consisted of a few plantain leaves and pieces of boxes laid together into a kind of shelter and counter. He rarely made a half-dollar daily profit, he admitted, but that was all he could earn in the coffee fields, and there he wore out his shoes, which cost much money. He was an ardent friend of Americans, like many of the country people. Asked to explain his friendship, he based it chiefly on the fact that they required the police to speak politely to everyone, did not allow beating,

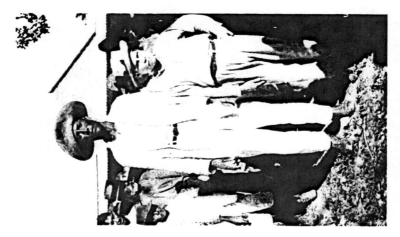

One reason why cane-cutters cannot all be
paid the same wages

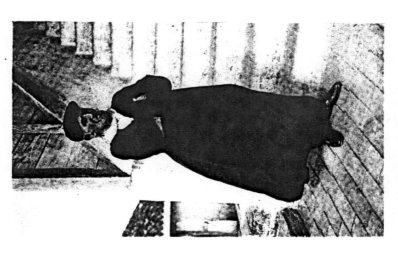

The priest in charge of Porto Rico's place of pilgrimage

A procession of strikers in honor of representatives of the A. F. L.

"How many of you are on strike?" asked Senator Iglesias

and punished their own people as well as Porto Ricans, whereas the Spaniards always used to be let off free. Then the Americans gave free schools. He had gone to one himself, "but he was not given to learn." It is a familiar refrain all over Porto Rico, even from persons who have every outward evidence of being bright as our average. Doctors say there is a special reason for this backwardness.

The peons of the region, silent-footed, listless, are often pure Caucasian in type; indeed their pasty-white complexions frequently contrast with the tanned faces of northern visitors. Now and again one wanders by looking startlingly like a three-day corpse. They are victims of the hookworm. There is more hookworm in Porto Rico, those who should know tell us, than in any other country on the globe, with the possible exception of India and Ceylon. The disease was brought by African slaves — along with most of the troubles of the West Indies — and while it does little harm to negroes, it is often fatal to the whites. The population in the rural areas makes no sanitary provisions, and soil pollution is wide-spread; they invariably go barefooted, with the result to be expected. Ninety per cent. of the laboring class was infected with hookworm when we took over the island. An active campaign was waged at once and had good results, but with partial autonomy the populace has fallen back almost into its first pitiable condition. The Rockefeller Foundation has recently offered three fourths of the preliminary expense of a new attack on the disease, if the insular government will bear the rest. For the cure is simple; it only requires persistence. Drafted soldiers were treated for it, and one may easily detect the superiority in energy of the *camineros* and laborers who are still to be seen in remnants of their old uniforms. In a way it is Porto Rico's most serious problem. Even a light infection causes serious mental retardation, and much money that is spent on schools is lost because of this defective mentality.

The hookworm is troublesome chiefly in the rural districts. The poor of the cities, who are bread eaters, have sprue instead. Of late only certified yeast from the United States has been permitted on the island; moreover, sprue may be cured by vaccination. A more serious thing is the prevalence of " t. b." — which missionaries on the island dub " tin box." Since the Americans came, there has been a constant increase in zinc roofs and sheet-iron houses over the old open-as-wool thatch hovels, and as the countryman persists in closing by night even the single tiny window, like that in the end of a box-car, up under the eaves of his shacks, weak lungs are increasing.

Fruit is abundant along the roads of Porto Rico. Mere bananas are so plentiful that they are often abandoned to the goats and pigs; in Lares a man with a wheelbarrow full of them was selling the largest and best at seven cents a dozen. Wild oranges, sweet, and juicy, for all their seeds, line the highways in what seems quan'ty sufficient to supply the entire demands of the "Mainland." Most of them never reach the market. Here and there one runs across a crude packing-house among the hills, but the fact that a box containing an average of one hundred and fifty oranges, picked, sorted, crated, and hauled to the coast, sells for fifty cents answers the natural query. In the trade these are known as "east-side oranges," and are generally sold by pushcart men in the tenement districts of our large cities — at how many hundred per cent. increase in price purchasers may figure out for themselves.

Vegetable growing has never been favored by the inhabitants of our strictly agricultural little West Indian possession. Like all Latin-Americans, they are content to do as their forefathers have done, and stick to the yams, *yautías*, and *ñames*, a coarse species of sweet potato, which grow almost wild, and will have nothing to do with Yankee innovations, though radishes mature in twelve days, and even Irish potatoes may be grown in the higher altitudes, and the market price of such vegetables is high. Bit by bit the *jíbaros* may be coaxed to improve their opportunities. Clusters of bee-hives are already common sights in the island, which can be said of no other section of tropical America. The Federal Agricultural Experimental Station at Mayagüez is to be thanked for this improvement. The old legend that bees lose their custom of laying up honey after a few seasons in a winterless land was found to be a fallacy, though they mix with the wild black bees of the island and the queens have to be killed and replaced periodically to keep the swarms from following the example of tropical man and refusing duty. Dyewoods, cabinet woods, and timber for building are wholly lacking in Porto Rico. Imported lumber costs $100 a thousand square feet. No wonder huts are made of *yagua*, thatch, and odds and ends. Indeed, the Federal institution mentioned above finds it can get better lumber out of packing-boxes than it can buy on the island. Porto Rico's peculiar condition, a tropical country in which practically all that the people produce is shipped out of the country, and nearly all they consume shipped in, makes eventual improvement of these conditions imperative. It strikes the casual observer as extraordinary, for instance, that there are no large manufacturing industries on the island, with its excellent sources of water-power and its unlimited supply of cheap labor.

I drifted out along the road from Aguadilla southward one day. The first man to arouse my interest was a little *peon caminero* clearing the highway edge of weeds, who was so pretty he would have made a charming bride in proper garments. His wages were $27.60 a month. He rented a "house" at $1.50 monthly, so large a house because he kept his wife's mother and two sisters, "for they have no other shelter." He said it casually, as one speaks of the weather, without the faintest hint of the boasting an American of his class could scarcely divorce from such a statement. A bit farther on a diseased old beggar sat on the edge of the road, the bottom of the dirty old straw hat on the ground before him sprinkled with copper cents — "chavos," they call them in Porto Rico, though the beggars soften their appeal by using the diminutive "chavito." There is a suggestion of India in the island's prevalence of alms-seekers, — blind men led by a boy or a dog, distressing old women publicly displaying their ailments, cripples and monstrosities wailing for sympathy from the passer-by. Scarcity of land and employment, abetted by the bad Latin-American custom of giving alms indiscriminately even to children, has brought a plague of professional beggars. One such fellow in Mayagüez has pleaded himself into possession of a twenty-acre *finca* — and is still begging. A mendicant of San Germán complains that the time-table is so badly arranged that he has to run to meet two trains. An American medical missionary offered to remove the cataracts from his eyes free of charge, but he declined to have his means of livelihood cut off. One of our Porto Rican hosts was responding to the appeal of an old woman for a "chavito" when a boy rushed up and cried, "Don't give her anything, señor, she has a cow!" The crone dashed after the urchin with an astonishing burst of speed, and returned out of breath to wail, "It is true, caballero, I admit it is true. But I have no pasture, and I must beg now to support the cow."

A long row of men were hoeing new sugarcane for the "Central Coloso," the tall stack of which broke the almost flat horizon behind them. They watched my approach, plainly suspicious that any man wearing shoes might be a company spy, and worked with redoubled energy. They were paid $1.50 for a nine-hour day, except two who were "sick" and a boy of seventeen, at two thirds that amount, and the *capataz*, who differed from the others only by the lack of a hoe, at

$1.80. As I turned away, the latter asked in a soft voice if I could tell him the time. Then he drew from his pocket an Ingersoll watch and, apologizing for his *atrevemiento* ("daring"), requested me to show him how to set it, the men under him at the same time protesting that "he should not make so bold with gentlemen." A stout, pure-white peon patching the road farther on, snatched off his hat as I spoke to him. His wages had gone up during the past year — from seventy-three to eighty cents a day! But he could earn little more than half that in the coffee estates at home, so he had been glad to come down to the coast to work. I drifted upon and strolled for a while along the railroad. The section hands were getting a dollar a day, which sets Porto Rico thirty years back in that regard, for I remember that fike wages were paid then on the branch line that passed my birthplace. Perhaps the island's laborers earn no more than they receive; a gang of ten men were loading a cane-cart in a neighboring field a single cane at a time. The two old women who were picking up rubbish beyond them had never been married, but they had three and four children respectively. They had always been paid forty cents a day, but now they had been promised a dollar. Whether or not they would get it only pay-day could tell. They accepted with alacrity the cigarettes I offered. At noon I stepped into a shop-dwelling to ask for food. The lunch that was finally prepared would not have over-fed a field laborer, yet the cost was eighty cents. The family was moderately clean, and energetic above the average. The four children all went to school. On the wall of the poor little hovel, surrounded on all sides by cane-fields, the oldest boy had chalked in English, "We have no sugar because we have sent it all to the poor people of Europe."

Along the soft-dirt private road to the *central* I met an intelligent looking man of thirty or so, capable in appearance as any American mechanic, Caucasian of race, his hair already turning gray. He begged for a *peseta*. I opened my mouth to ask why a big, strong fellow in the prime of life should be asking for alms, when my eyes fell upon his left-leg. It was swollen to the knee with elephantiasis, both the trouser-leg and the skin having burst with the expansion. A year ago, he said, he had been out on a Sunday excursion in the country, and had stopped to wash his feet in a creek. They smarted a bit on the way home, but he thought nothing of it until, some time later, his left foot began to swell. He was a cigar-maker by trade, and the *Sanidad* had refused to let him work in such a condition, yet the government would not take care of him. So he wandered about the country, where the people were more kindly than in the towns. The leg did not exactly hurt any more, but it seemed to drag all his left side down with its weight. He would gladly go and have it cut off, if he could find a place to have it done, though people said even that would not do much good. Tears were near the brim of his eyes, but they did not well over. Hopeless cases of this kind seem much more pitiful when one can talk to the sufferer and find him a rational human being, of some education, than when they are merely the dog-like wretches of India, who seem scarcely capable of thought.

One morning I stepped off the night train to Ponce and struck out across the island by the Utuado road. It was an hour before I had emerged from the populous suburbs of the town. Automobiles snorted past without once offering a "lift." Not that I wanted one, but one gets an impression of selfishness in a community that passes a foot-traveler without a suggestion of help. It was not universal here, how-ever. Before I had climbed a mile into the foot-hills a man in a rattle-trap buggy pulled his packages together in the seat and invited me to jump in. It was hard to explain my refusal. There were many little wayside "restaurants" where one would least expect any demand for such accommodations. But people must win a livelihood somehow, as one of the keepers explained. Then came a string of "villas," of Porto Ricans, Americans, and a few Englishmen, modest little summer homes set where they could look down the valley upon the blue Carib-bean. Here and there were the creeper-grown ruins of old Spanish country houses. Finally — a joke? I hardly think so, for the Latin-American countryman has as little sarcasm as sense of humor — a miserable little tin hut, in the yard of which the owner and his boy were forking manure, was elaborately announced in large letters as " Villa Providencia."

At the first miriametro-post the coffee began, bananas and guayaba-trees shading it. There passed much freight in tarpaulin-covered wagons, the big brakes badly worn. A crowded *guagua* rumbled by, the chauffeur and most of the passengers staring at me with an air that said plainly, " Look at that stingy *americano* saving money by walking!" Staring is universal in Porto Rico, at least outside the larger cities. Even the " schoolmarms," always well-dressed in spot-less but cheap materials, pause in their lessons to gaze at the sight that has drawn the pupils' attention.

Three hours up I had an extended view of the Caribbean, still seem-ing barely a rifle-shot way. A boy of eight, living a few yards from a school, had never attended it, " because he had to take care of a sick mare at home." In the hovel-store where I had lunch three little girls read English to me from their textbooks. I could understand them, but only by giving their curious pronunciation the closest attention. Of the information in their Spanish textbooks they had a moderate knowl- edge for their years. The houses were constant; one was never out of human sight or sound. The scarcity of dogs was in contrast to other Latin-American countries; during an outbreak of bubonic plague some years ago seven thousand were killed in Ponce alone. In a spot where the roadside grew precipitous a sad-eyed peon stood looking at the little garden before his house, which had fallen into the highway, more than fifty feet below, during the night's rain. Higher still the road reached its point of greatest altitude and descended, more or less abruptly, through artistic tree-ferns and clumps of bamboo to Adjuntas. All I remember of the flat little town are the oranges heaped up at the roadside, the drying coffee laid out on burlap sacks before the sleepy little shops, and that " Ponce de Leon Brothers" kept one of the clothing stores.

Many big auto-trucks were carrying bags of coffee in the direction of Ponce, as others like them carry tobacco from the region of tropical glaciers. The road forded a river, but so many stepping-stones had been laid across it that I needed to take off only one shoe. A new highway to Lares chewed its way upward into the almost chalky hills to the left. We certainly build good roads in Porto Rico; the Spanish influence seems to have survived the change of sovereignty. The high- way under my feet followed a rock-tumbled river all the rest of the day. Census-tags decorated every hut. The enumerators did not skip their political opponents, as in Cuba, and though the date had passed after which the tags might be removed, not one of them had been touched. Most of the people could not read the printed permission to do so; besides, they would not dream of meddling in a government matter. Sunset came early between the mountain walls piled high above me on either side. Then fell the quick darkness of the tropics, and there began a constant creaking that suggested young frogs. For an hour I plodded on into the warm night, the road barely visible under a crescent moon, in the faint rays of which the feathery bamboos that lined the highway for a mile or more before reaching Utuado, looked weirdly like faintly moving gigantic fans.

Utuado is a large town for its situation, and piled up the first slopes of the hills about it in a stage-setting effect. Dense masses of fog —

strange sight in the West Indies, where the fog-horn never breaks the slumber of sea passengers — lay in its very streets until the tropical sun wiped them away toward nine. Great precipices of lime-stone on either side, a boiling river below, mountains of bold broken outline ahead, marked the journey onward. The road climbed frequently, even though it followed the growing river. Patches of tobacco, as well as coffee, covered the steep hillsides; vegetation and mankind were everywhere. Here and there the highway clung by its fingernails and eyebrows, as sailors say, along the face of the cliff. Then it regained solid footing and broke out into a broad, flat coastland, hot, dusty, and uninteresting, with cane and smoke-belching sugar-mills, and hurried across it to Atlantic-washed Arecibo.

CHAPTER XIII

IN AND ABOUT OUR VIRGIN ISLANDS

"IT'S all I can do to keep from barking at you," said a passenger on the *Virginia*, as he crawled on hands and knees from one of the four kennels that decorate her afterdeck. As a matter of fact, we all did a certain amount of growling before the voyage was over. Yet the four of us who had won the kennels were lucky dogs compared to the unfortunate dozen or more who had to snatch what sleep they could curled up on the bare deck or in a single sour-smelling cabin below, where neither color, sex nor seasickness knew any distinction.

The weakest link in the shipping chain down the West Indies is that between our own possessions. Once a week a little schooner that was built to defend America's yachting championship, but which never reached the finals, raises its wings in San Juan harbor and, the winds willing, drops a flock of disgruntled passengers, the United States mails, and an assorted cargo in St. Thomas and St. Croix in time to return for a similar venture seven days later. Congressional committees, of course, have their battleships, and the white-uniformed governors of our Virgin Islands their commodious steam-yacht; but the mere garden variety of tax-paying citizen has the privilege of tossing about for several days on the *Virginia*, subsisting on such food as he has had the foresight to bring with him, and drinking such lukewarm water as he can coax from the schooner's cask.

It is nearly fifty miles from Porto Rico to St. Thomas. All day long our racing yacht crawled along the coast, San Juan and the island's culminating peak, El Yunque, equally immovable on the horizon, while the half-grown crew alternated between pumping water from the hold and playfully disobeying the orders of the forceless old mulatto captain. Nine at night found us opposite Fajardo light — more than an hour by automobile from our starting-point! While the crew slept, without so much as posting a lookout, a boy of thirteen sat at the wheel, and the kennelless passengers tossed restlessly on their chosen deck spots. A half-grown pig — the only traveler on board whose ticket specified ship's food — wandered disconsolately fore and aft, now and then

The new church of Guayama, Porto Rico

A Porto Rican ex-soldier working as road peon. He gathers the grass with a wooden
hook and cuts it with a small sickle

Porto Rican tobacco fields

Charlotte Amalia, capital of our Virgin Islands

demanding admission to one or another of the four "cabins." No doubt he recognized them as built for his own, rather than the human, species.

Sunrise overtook us still within sight of Porto Rico, but with her dependencies of Culebra and Vieques abeam, and the hazy mass of the Virgin group visible on the horizon ahead. Brown, rugged, strangely aged-looking, Culebra showed no signs of life except the lighthouse set upon its highest cliff. Vieques, on the other hand, known to English-speaking mariners as "Crab Island," is a diminutive replica of Porto Rico, with four large sugar-mills and a population of some eleven thousand, American citizens all. The Danes once claimed this also, but Spanish buccaneers established the more efficacious right of actual possession, and at length the Porto Rican Government sent an expedition to annex it to the Spanish crown.

With monotonous deliberation the Virgin group grew in size and visibility. St. Thomas and St. John took on individuality amid their flock of rocky keys, and British Tórtola gradually asserted its aloofness from the American islands. Far off on the blue-gray horizon we could even make out St. Croix, like a stain on the inverted bowl of sky. Yet, though the breeze was strong, it was a head wind, and the ocean current sweeping in from the eastward held us all but motionless when we seemed to be cutting swiftly through the light waves. For five profane hours we tacked to and fro within gunshot of a towering white boulder jutting forth from the sea, and fittingly known as Sail Rock, without seeming to advance a mile on our journey.

We turned the isolated precipice at last, and headed in toward mountainous St. Thomas. Neither its scattered keys nor its long broken coast-line showed any evidence of habitation, but at length three white specks appeared on its water's edge, and grew with the afternoon to a semblance of Charlotte Amalie, a city rivaled in its beauty, at a distance, by few others even in the beautiful West Indies. We greeted it with fervent exclamations of delight, piled up white and radiant in the moonlight on its three hills, like occupants of royal boxes at some gala performance in its amphitheatrical harbor. below. Scarcely a sound came from it, however, except the languid swish of the waves on what seemed to be the base of its lower houses, as we dropped anchor near midnight within rowboat distance of the wharves.. It had been an unusually swift voyage, according to the uncommanding captain, a mere two days instead of the four or five it frequently requires.

In due course of time a negro youth rowed out to examine us. He was an exceedingly courteous negro, to be sure, his white uniform was spotless, and his English impeccable; but there was something incongruous in the fact that American citizens must have his permission to be admitted into one American possession from another. The "Grand Hotel," which virtually monopolizes the accommodation of transients in St. Thomas, could not house us, or rather, on second thought, it could, if we would be contented in the "annex" over a barber-shop across the street. Its creaking floors were unbroken expanses of spaciousness, but at least there was a mahogany four-poster in one corner. We sat down on it with a sigh of contentment — and quickly stood up again, under the impression that we had inadvertently sat upon the floor. The Virgin Islands have not yet reached that decadent degree of civilization that requires bed-springs. As to a bath — certainly, it should be brought at once; and a half hour later a loose-kneed negro wandered in and set down on the floor, with the rattle of a hardware-shop in a tornado, a large tin pan, red with rust. All we had to do, explained the ultra-courteous octoroon manager, was to call another negro to bring a pail of water *when* — and the emphasis suggested that the time was still far off — we "desired to perform our ablutions." The tub-bearer was evidently too worn out from his extraordinary exertion to indulge in another before he had taken time to recuperate.

That loose-kneed stroll of the Virgin-Islander is typical of all his processes, mental, moral, or physical. It is not merely slow, rythmical, and dignified; there is in it a suggestion of limitless wealth, an untroubled conscience, and an ancestry devoted to leisurely pursuits for untold generations. In local parlance a "five minutes' walk" means a block. One must not even speak hastily to a native, for the only result is wasted breath and the necessity of repeating the question in more measured cadences. Politeness oozes from his every pore; "at your sarvice, sar," and "only too glad to be of use, ma'am," interlard every conversation; but any attempt, courteous or otherwise, to hurry the Virgin Islander brings a sullen resentment which you will never succeed in smiling away. As the navy men who are governing him put it in the technical vernacular of their calling, he has only two speeds,— "Slow Ahead" and "Stop."

Once the visitor has shaken off the no doubt ridiculous notion that things should be done in a hurry, or done at all, for that matter, he will find our newly adopted children an amusing addition to the family. Like all negroes in contact with civilization, they are fond of four-jointed words where monosyllables would suffice, and of pompous, rounded sentences in place of brief-to-the-point statements. " Presently " means "now "; " He detained from coming " is the local form of " he can't come." Talking is one of the Virgin Islanders' chief recreations. They buttonhole the unknown passerby and unburden themselves to him at endless length, ceaselessly chattering on until he can forge some excuse to tear himself away, when they hasten to ask their friends if they, too, have seen " the stranger with the beard," " the American who arrived last night," " that rich-looking gentleman in a white helmet," that the friends may not lose their chance of waylaying the victim who is already listening to a new monologue around the corner. If they can not find a hearer, they do not for that reason abandon their favorite sport; it is commonplace to meet a pedestrian, particularly a woman, chattering volubly to herself as she shuffles along the street.

Their lack of self-restraint is on a par with their loquacity. When the first navy hydroplanes flew into the harbor, the entire population became a screaming mob of neck-craning, pointing, shoulder-clapping, occupation-forgetting children. The winner of a dollar at the local " horse " races, in which the island donkeys are now and then pitted against one another, may be seen turning somersaults in the midst of the crowd, or throwing himself on the ground, all fours clawing the air, as he shrieks his ecstasies of delight. It is their joy to parade the streets in their gayest costumes on any holiday, American, Danish, or imaginable, that can be dragged into the calendar, dancing and capering with an energy which their work-a-day manner never suggests. Once a month, at full moon, the local band marches through the town playing " Onward, Christian Soldiers," the population trailing en masse behind it, singing, clapping hands, and swaying their rather slender, underfed bodies violently in cadence with the music. They are ardent church-goers in theory, there being six large churches of as many denominations in town — but it takes a rousing round of hymns to bring the majority to indoor services, though boatmen far out in the bay recognize a street meeting of the Salvation Army by the howling chorus of " Lord, ha' mercy on mah sou-ul," which the cliffs echo out to them.

The Sunday evening band concert, on the other hand, is staid enough to make a Spanish-American *retreta* seem uproarious by comparison. It begins at nine, after the last church service of a Britishly dead Sunday. The native band, recruited by the administrative Americans, jet black in features and snow-white in uniform, mounts to the roof of the old red fortress, while outwardly immaculate negroes, stroll rather funereally about little Emancipation Park and along the edge of the quay. The élite of the town sit in their houses, piled steeply up the pyramidal hills, and let the music float up to them on the harbor breeze. Our new fellow-countrymen are ostentatiously patriotic in all that concerns mere formalities. Every morning at eight all St. Thomas becomes static when the marine band plays our national anthem. The market-women on the wharf halt as if suddenly turned to stone, holding whatever posture they happen to be caught in until the last note has died away; the very boatmen in the bay sit with their poised oars motionless. Flags burst forth not merely on our own holidays, but on Danish, on every possible fête day, public or private, even on the birthdays of distant relatives or mere friends. Curious superstitions enliven the quaint local color. The appearance of a lizard in the house is sure proof to the lower classes that there is soon to be an addition to the family. Servant girls cannot be induced to remove their hats, whether cooking, making beds, or waiting on table at the most formal dinner, for fear of sudden death from " dew " falling on their heads — though it be full blazing noonday.

The great majority of the population is undernourished. Even when their earnings are sufficient, most of the money is spent on dress. The chief diet of the rank and file is sugar. A sugar-cane three times a day seems to be enough to keep many of them alive. The morning meal for the rest consists of " tea " only, the local meaning of that word being a cupful of sugar dissolved in warm water. Then along in the middle of the afternoon they indulge in their only real food, and not very real at that. This is a plate of " fungee," a nauseating mixture of fish and corn-meal, which to the local taste is preferable to the most succulent beefsteak. The natural result of the constant consumption of sugar is an early scarcity of teeth. Barely three men in twenty could be enlisted in the native corps, chiefly because of their inability to cope with navy rations.

It goes without saying that such a population does not furnish model workmen. From Friday night to Tuesday morning is apt to be treated as " the Sabbath." The man who works two days a week at eighty cents has enough to provide himself with sugar-cane and " fungee." On the whole, the women are more industrious than the men, perhaps because the great disparity of sexes makes the possession of a " man " something in the nature of a luxury.   Time was when the women of St. Thomas were able to support their husbands in a more fitting manner than at present.   In the good old days hundreds of ships coaled here every month; now many a day passes without one bringing a throng of negresses scampering for the coaling-wharf far out beyond " Bluebeard's Castle."   In a constant stream the soot-draped women jog up the gang-plank, balancing the eighty-pound basket of coal on their heads, often without touching it, thrust out a begrimed hand for the three cents a trip which a local labor leader has won them in place of the original one, drop the coins into a dust-laden pocket, dump their load into the steamer's chute, and trot down again. Sometimes the ship is a man-of-war that unfairly speeds up the pace of coalers by having its band play rousing music on the upper deck. Here and there a man may be made out in the endless chain of black humanity.   At least one of them works with his wife as a " team " — by carrying the empty basket back to be filled while she mounts with the full one.   But most of the males have the point of view of the big " buck nigger " who was lying in the shade of the coal-pile watching the process with an air of languid contentment.   " Why de coalin' is done by women, sah? " he repeated, scratching his head for a reply.   " Why, dat 's woman's work."

The population of our Virgin Islands is overwhelmingly negro. Even Charlotte Amalie cannot muster one white man to ten of African ancestry, and not a fourth of the latter show any Caucasian mixture. Once upon a time the Jews were numerous; there is still a Jewish cemetery, but the synagogue has been abandoned for lack of congregation.   Though the islands were Danish for nearly two and a half centuries, their language has always been English, probably because their business has ever been with ships and men who, though it may not always have been their native tongue, spoke the language of the sea.   Some six years before we purchased the islands the Danes made an attempt to teach Danish in the schools.   But though many little negroes learned to chatter more or less fluently in that tongue, to the detriment of more essential studies, the local environment proved too strong, and the very Danish officials became proficient in English in spite of themselves, though even the British school superintendent was required to write his correspondence and reports in the official tongue.

The only element of the population that has never succumbed to its environment, either racially or linguisticaliy, are the " Chachas."

They are a community of French fishermen, who have themselves lost any certain notion of how they came to be stranded on rocky St. Thomas. Some two hundred of them live in their own village on the outskirts of Charlotte Amalie; others are scattered along the trail to a similar village called Hull, on the opposite side of the island. Intermarriage has given them all a striking family resemblance, and it is hours before the newcomer realizes that it is not the same man he has met over and over again, peddling his fish, his goats, or his crude straw hats in the streets of the town, but a score of more or less close relatives. They have preserved their blood pure from the slightest negro strain; but their aloofness has given them a sort of sick-bed pallor, an anemia both of physique and manner, especially among the women, an almost complete loss of teeth, and little power to resist disease. Yet the men at least have by no means lost their old "pep." They can still fight in a two-fisted manner that is the awe of their negro neighbors, and they venture fearlessly far out to sea in their little narrow-chested fishing boats.

The adults speak a perfectly comprehensible French, but the "creole" of the children is but little improvement on that of Haiti. For many years they had their own school, taught by an old Frenchman who drew the princely salary of five dollars a month. Since his death the children have been attending the English-speaking Catholic school, and some of them already mispronounce a certain amount of that tongue — and can beg as fluently as the little black urchins that swarm about any white stranger. But their aloofness from the colored population remains. The latter scorn them as only a negro can the white man who has fallen socially to his own level, though they take care not to refer to them by the popular nickname within reach of their hardened fists. The term is said to have had its origin in the word *chasser* with which the fishermen interlard their cries. They call themselves *français,* and have a simplicity which suggests they have followed the same calling for many generations. Their houses are mere cabins, with shingled walls and thatched roofs, scattered about the sand knolls at the edge of the bay. These are always floored, decorated with a few chromo prints of a religious nature, and have a better claim to neatness than the hovels of the negroes about them. While the latter loaf, the "Chachas" ply their chosen calling diligently, but on Sunday afternoons they may be found in groups, playing cards in the shade of their date palms, their curious hats of sewn ribbons of straw tossed on the sandy soil about them. They profess complete indifference to their island's change of sovereignty, except to wonder in vague voices if it is this that has brought the appalling increase in the prices of food.

Seen from any of its three hills, Charlotte Amalie looks more like a stage setting than a real town. Its sheet-iron roofs, many of them painted red, seem to be cut out of cardboard, and the steepness of the slopes on which the majority of its houses are built suggests the fantasy of the scene-painter rather than cold practicability. A single long, level street, still known, on its placards at least, as Kronprindsens Gade, runs the length of the town and contains nearly all its commerce. The rest start bravely up the steep hills, but soon tire, like the inhabitants, and leave their task incompleted. On the eastern side, where the storms come from, the houses have glass windows, almost unknown in the larger islands to the westward, and are fitted on all sides with heavy wooden hurricane-shutters. If these are closed in time, the roofs can withstand the frequent high winds that sweep down upon the island, but the local weather prophet has an unenviable task, for to give the signal for closing the shutters when there is no need for it is as reprehensible from the native point of view as to fail to foresee real danger. Bulky stone or brick ovens, separate from the houses, are the only buildings with chimneys, and many of these were mutilated by the hurricane of four years ago. Palm-trees and great masses of red and purple bougainvillea add a crowning beauty to a scene that would be entrancing even without them.

Of a score of solemn old buildings the most imposing is the residence of the governor on the middle of the three hills. Higher still stands a grim tower known as " Blackbeard's Castle," about which cling many legends, but no other certainty than that it was built by a turbulent colonist of long ago, who was credited, justly no doubt, since that clan has not wholly died out in St. Thomas to this day, with being a pirate. But this structure is of slight interest to the average visitor compared to a similar one on the eastern hill, reputed far and wide as the original " Bluebeard's Castle." Just how it gained this reputation is not easily apparent, for its real history is almost an open book. Built by the Danish government in 1700 as a fort, probably to overawe the slaves in the town below, it remained the property of the king until a century ago, when it fell into private hands. If any other proof of its entirely unromantic character is needed, it is sufficient to know that it now belongs to an Episcopal clergyman living in Brooklyn!

With stone walls five feet thick, three rooms one above the other, and all in all a pitiless visage, the tower easily lends itself to the imagination as the scene of marital treachery. The old negro caretaker will assure you that the dreadful crimes took place in it " jes' like de storybook tell." The yarn that has a wider local belief is somewhat different. According to this an old trader married a beautiful girl of Charlotte Amalie and locked her up in the castle while he left the island on business. During his absence she discovered a mysterious old chest in the upper story and finally yielded to the feminine impulse to open it. In it she found letters from a dozen of her husband's discarded sweethearts, all of whom still lived in the town. She invited them to a banquet in the castle — the significant detail of how she got the door open being passed over in silence — and poisoned them. From there on the tale forks. One ending has it that the husband returned, repented, and committed suicide while the beautiful wife was being tried for murder; the other, that he rushed in and carried her off just as she was about to be burned at the stake.

The eyes of the modern visitor are sure to be drawn to what looks like an attempt to pave a large section of the steep hill behind the town. A great triangular patch of cement gleaming in the sun on one of the slopes brings to mind the island's greatest problem. St. Thomas depends entirely upon the rains for her water-supply, for the water to be had by boring is so brackish that it ruins even a steamer's boilers. When renting or buying a house the most important question is to know the size and condition of its cistern and what provision has been made for filling it. In the dry season, which is heartlessly long and appallingly dry, the poorer people wander from house to house begging a " pan " of water, and the word means a receptacle of any size or shape that will hold the precious liquid. The town is convinced that its commercial decline is due to its lack of water, and that it will come into its own again if only Uncle Sam will cover its hillsides with cement or galvanized iron. If they had immense cisterns and a means of filling them, they say, ships would no longer go to Ponce for water, and perhaps pick up their coal in Porto Rico also, but would put in at St. Thomas for all their supplies. To make matters worse, the change of sovereignty has brought with it the inability to furnish other liquids for which sea-faring men have looked to St. Thomas for centuries.

That seemed the last straw, but another has since been added to the already crushing burden. St. Thomas has long been famous for its bay rum. As a matter of fact the bay oil comes from St. John and the rum came from St. Croix, until the colonial council voted the islands " dry " —" as if we were not dry enough already." But the mixture and sale thereof brought many a dollar into local pockets. Soon after the " dry " law went into effect, the natives, to say nothing of our thirsty marines, made the brilliant discovery that the addition of a bit of bay oil to their favorite refreshment left it none the less exhilarating. Banished hilarity returned. The governor was shocked beyond measure, and the sale even of bay rum is now forbidden except on a police permit, issued only on proof that it was not to be used for beverage purposes. It is almost as easy to prove that the moon is made of green cheese. The Virgin Islanders have several grievances against the Americans who have adopted them, the strictness of their color-line, for instance; but the greatest of these is prohibition.

The cluster of islands just east of Porto Rico was discovered by Columbus on his second voyage; anything that escaped him on the first journey seems to enjoy at least that secondary distinction. He named them the Eleven Thousand Virgins; just why, not even his biographers seem to know. It may be that he had just been awakened from a bad dream, or possibly the expression was an old-fashioned Italian form of profanity. It would be easy to think of a more appropriate name, but they have remained the Virgin Islands to this day.

The Spaniards stopped long enough to exterminate the Indians, but it was a long time before any one thought it worth while to settle in such a region. Nothing is more natural than that the name should finally have attracted to it a party of Frenchmen. Evidently they found it disappointing, for they did not increase. Then the Danish West India Company laid claim to St. Thomas and its adjacent islands, and in 1671 a governor was sent out from Denmark, who founded the town of Charlotte Amalie, which he named for the then Danish queen. Of course the British captured the place a few times, and it was often harassed by fires, hurricanes, and slave rebellions, all of which it more or less successfully survived. St. Thomas became a harbor of refuge for pirates, and it frequently became necessary for the English governor of Nevis to raid it — for the British, you remember, did not believe in piracy. When the gentlemen enlisted under the skull-and-cross-bones banner had gone the way of all rascals, the island soon won a place of importance as a distributing center for slaves.

Meanwhile St. Croix, which is neither geographically, geologically, nor historically a bona fide member of the Virgin group, had been having a history of its own. The Knights of Malta colonized it first with three hundred Frenchmen, but these soon decided that Santo Domingo offered better real estate possibilities. Then when the Dutch and the British had concluded that France had a better armed right to it, the latter sold it to the Danish Company for 750,000 livres. Just how much that was in real money I am not in a position to state, beyond the assertion that it would buy far more then than it will nowadays. Thenceforth St. Croix has followed the fate of the other Danish West Indies.

Many of the colonists were disturbers of the peace or agitators, the Bolshevists, in short, of those days, who found it to their advantage to abandon the near-by French and British Leeward Islands. They became too much for the Company, which in 1764 sold the whole collection to the Danish crown. All three of the islands of any importance were long planted in sugar-cane. It covered even the tops of the hills, those of St. Thomas being cultivated by hand in little stone-faced terraces. To-day sugar-cane has completely disappeared from St. Thomas, almost entirely from St. John, and is grown only on the level southern side of St. Croix. Several slave uprisings had been suppressed with more or less bloodshed when Denmark subscribed to the then astounding theory that slavery should be abolished. The agricultural importance of the islands began at once to decline. Free labor was cheap, but it would not labor. Then, too, the competition of sugar grown more economically elsewhere and Napoleon's establishment of a bounty for beet-sugar growers began to make life dreary for all West Indian planters.

However, as their agriculture declined, the importance of the Danish islands as a shipping and distributing center increased, though their days of greatest prosperity were from 1820 to 1830, when the two coincided. St. Thomas harbor was forested with the masts of sailing vessels, carrying goods to and from the four points of the compass. Then along came Robert Fulton with more trouble for the poor harassed islanders. Steam navigation made it easy for the West Indies and South America to import goods direct from Europe, and the Virgin Island merchants began to lose their rake-off. They picked up, however, by establishing a coaling station and making St. Thomas a free port and a general depot of sea-going supplies. Before the World War scores of ships entered the harbor every week; now the pilot often does not drop his feet from his hammock to the floor for several days at a time.

For all this, the islands were a liability rather than an asset to the Danes, and they had long been looking for some kind Samaritan to take them off their hands. Under Lincoln, Secretary Seward negotiated a treaty by which we were to have all the group except St. Croix for $7,500,000. A vote of the population showed them overwhelmingly in favor of the change; the Danish Government was paternal, but it was far away and unprogressive. The treaty was ratified in Denmark. The king issued a manifesto telling his loyal subjects how sorry he was to part with them, but assuring them, as fathers always do, that it was for their own good. He did not mention that he needed the money. Two years later he was forced to admit in another royal document that he was not parting with them, after all. Senator Sumner, chairman of our Foreign Relations Committee, did not walk hand in hand with President Johnson. For two years he kept the treaty in his official pocket, and when it did at length reappear under Grant, it was adversely reported.

In 1902 a better bargain was struck. A new treaty setting the price of the whole group at $5,000,000 was drawn up, and ratified by the American Senate. But this time the Danish Rigsdag turned the tables. Perhaps they had inside information on the future development of American politics. If so it proved trustworthy, for by 1916 we were in the hands of an administration to whom mere money was no object. The Danes quickly caught the idea, the people themselves voted to sell while the selling was good, and on the last day of March, 1917, old Danneborg was hauled down and the Stars and Stripes raised in its place.

I have yet to find any one who knows just why we bought the Virgin Islands, still less why we paid twenty-five millions for them. As a navy man engaged in governing them put it, " They are not worth forty cents to us, or to any one else; though " he added, " it would have been worth a hundred million to keep Germany from getting them." If the loss of the twenty-five millions were an end of the matter, we might forget it; but it is costing us more than half a million a year to support our little black children. Furthermore, the Danes made the most of their ripe opportunity not only in the matter of price, but in an astonishing number of concessions in their favor. Evidently our Government said to them, " Go ahead and write a treaty, and we 'll sign it "; and then in the press of saving the world for democracy we did not have time to glance it over before adding our signature.

If a farmer bought a farm for, say, twenty-five hundred dollars, and found, when he came to take possession of it, that it would cost him fifty dollars a year out of his pocket to run it, that it was inhabited by a happy-go-lucky lot of negroes who expected him to do many things for them, from curing their wide-spread disease to sending them to school; if, furthermore, he discovered that the former owners still held everything on the farm that was worth owning except the title-deed, he would probably give it away to the first unsuspecting tenderfoot who happened along. Unfortunately, governments cannot indulge in that dying-horse method of laying down their burdens. Even had the purchase price of almost three hundred dollars an acre included everything of monetary value on the islands, from the wardrobes of the inhabitants to the last peasant's hut, we should have made a bad bargain. But about all we got for our twenty-five millions is the right to fly our flag over the islands, and half a dozen old forts and government buildings entirely stripped of their furniture. The Danish Government has the reputation of being conservative and economical. It surely is, in more senses than one. By the terms of the treaty " the movables, especially the silver plate and the pictures, remain the property of the Danish Government and shall, as soon as circumstances permit, be removed by it." By virtue of that clause they sold at auction every stick of furniture in the public buildings; they tore the mirrors off the walls; they removed the gilt moldings from them; they tried to tear off the embossed leathery wall-paper, and left the rooms looking as if a party of yeggmen had gutted them; they took down and carried away the rope on the government flagpole! Economy is a splendid trait, but they might have left us a chair in which to mourn the loss of our twenty-five — and more — millions.

Everything worth owning in the islands is still in private, principally Danish, hands. When we planned to erect a naval station on an utterly worthless stony hill on St. Thomas harbor, the owners demanded twenty-five hundred dollars an acre for it. We must maintain all the grants, concessions, and licenses left by the Danish Government. "Det Vestindiske Kompagni" retains most of the harbor privileges; another Danish company, of which the principal share- holder is Prince Axel, cousin of the king, holds the coaling rights, the electric lighting rights, the right to operate a dry-dock. We cannot even use American money in our new possessions. The Danish West Indian bank has the exclusive concession for issuing notes until 1934, paying a ten per cent. tax on profits to the Danish Government, and the good old greenback must be exchanged for the domestic shin- plasters. Naval men stationed in St. Thomas are forced to pay this institution as high as two per cent. discount on their U. S. government pay checks; the yearly budget of our new colony must be made in Danish francs. But though the domestic money is officially in francs and "bits," the people talk in dollars and cents as universally as they speak English instead of Danish. It is difficult to find anything left by the old régime that is not protected by that curiously one- sided treaty. An American remarked casually to an old Danish resident one evening as they were strolling through Emancipation Park:

"I think we'll tear down that old bust of King Christian IX and put one of Lincoln in its place."

"Vat?" shrieked the Dane. "You can't do that. Eet ees in de treaty."

By some oversight the Danes failed to provide for a few of the minor concessions. There were the apothecaries, for instance. Un- der Danish rule one was given exclusive rights in each of the three towns and its contiguous territory. They were inspected often, old drugs being thrown out; and they were not allowed to sell patent medi- cines. Their prices are reasonable as monopolies go, their stores well kept, and their stock ample, within Danish limits. When the islands were sold, the apothecaries complained to the king that they were in danger of being ruined by American competition; whereupon the king, out of the goodness of his heart — and the fullness of the twenty-five million — gave them $30,000 each. Four years have passed since the druggists pocketed this salve to their injured profits, and they are still doing business at the old stands without a rival in sight.

Indeed, there is little evidence of that influx of American business men which was predicted as sure to follow the flag. So far the only one is a young ex-marine who is breaking into the restaurant and soda-fountain business. He has been fought at every step by the local merchants. Living exclusively on trade, with hundred per cent. profits customary from time immemorial, the wealthier class of the islanders have the cuteness of the shopkeeper developed to the nth degree, and they will not readily consent to competition by rank outsiders from the United States.

Among the things which the Danes left behind were their laws, and their own judge to administer them. True, Judge Thiele has become an American citizen, but it is a curious sight to see Americans-born brought into court by negro policemen, to be tried by a man who is still a foreigner in point of view and thinking processes in spite of being no longer officially a subject of the King of Denmark. There are those who claim he sides with the favorites of the old Government to the decided disadvantage of Americans, though there are more who speak well of him. It is enough to know that Americans are being tried in American territory under the Napoleonic code, in that laborious old-fashioned style by which the judge questions the witnesses, dictates their answers in his own more cultured words to a clerk, who writes them all down in laborious longhand in a great ledger, to be sure that a change should be made in the judiciary system of our Virgin Islands.

Having bought them, and being forced to support them for the rest of our natural existence, it might be of interest to make a brief inventory of our new possessions. The total area of the three islands, with their seventeen keys, only three or four of which are inhabited, is about 140 square miles. The census taken soon after the raising of the Stars and Stripes showed something over twenty-six thousand inhabitants, but several signs indicate that these are decreasing. The only real value of the Virgin group proper is the splendid harbor of St. Thomas. St. Croix, forty miles distant from it is considerably larger than all the rest of this group put together, more populous, more fertile, and could easily be made self-supporting governmentally, as it always has been privately, particularly with the introduction of an extensive system of irrigation.

A couple of trails zigzag up the reddish, dry hillside behind Charlotte Amalie, scattering along the way a few hovels. They really lead nowhere, however, for there is no other town than the capital on the island. The hurricane of 1916 blew down most of the farm-houses and many of the trees, and they were never rebuilt or replanted. Once heavily forested, later Nile-green with sugar-cane, St. Thomas is now brown, arid, and dreary, with scarcely a tenth of its acreage under even half-hearted cultivation. Being all " mountain," fifteen hundred feet high in one spot, with buttresses running down to the sea in every direction, it can hardly be expected to compete with modern agricultural methods. Moreover, eight of its ten thousand inhabitants have been drawn into town by the higher wages of harbor work, and though there is now a scarcity of that, they still remain, to the detriment of what might be moderately productive plantations, forcing the island to draw its food from St. John, the British Virgins, or Porto Rico. A journey over the " mountain " brings little reward except some marvelous views and yet another proof of how primitive the human family may become.

A so-called road traverses the island from east to west. In company with a navy doctor I bumped by Ford along the eastern half of this to Water Bay. A cattle-raising estate called " Tatu," with a three-story, red-roofed dwelling, was the only sign of industry along the route. Near the bay we overtook a man on his way — at nine o'clock in the morning — to dig a well for the estate owner, and soon talked him into rowing us across to St. John instead. For the wind was dead ahead, and the old sail in the bottom of his patched and weather-warped dory would have been far more hindrance than help in negotiating the stormy three-mile passage between the islands. Once landed, in Cruz Bay, we rented St. John's only public means of conveyance,— two hard-gaited horses named " Bess " and " Candy Kid " — and rode out into the wilderness.

St. John is little more than that. Its twenty square miles have almost entirely gone back to forest, through which a few trails meander amid a silence as unbroken as that of Robinson Crusoe's place of exile. There is not a wheeled vehicle on the island; one may ride for miles without meeting an inhabitant, and the very birds seem to have abandoned it for more progressive climes. Yet rusted iron kettles and the ruins of stone sugar-mills, scattered here and there in forest and scrub, show that the island was once a place of industry. Sugar and cotton plantations almost completely covered it when, in 1733, a slave rebellion started it on a decline that has never since ceased. The whites quelled the uprising, after a half hundred of them and four times as many blacks had lost their lives, but the negroes won in the end, for the last census showed but four white men on the island. To-day it has barely eight hundred inhabitants, of whom, unlike the other islands, the majority are men. A few mangoes and bananas, yams, okre, and a kind of tropical pumpkin keep its hut-dwellers alive. Here and there is a little patch of cane, from which rum was made before the Americans came to interfere with that; limes are cultivated rather languidly in a few hillside orchards, and the high ridge between Hope and Bordeaux is covered with bay-trees.

These vary in size from mere saplings to trees twenty feet in height. The picking is best done in June, when men and boys break off the smaller branches and carry them to the distilleries. Here the leaves are cooked in sea water in immense brass decanters, from which the bay oil is drawn off, and the leaves tossed out, apparently unchanged except from green to a coppery brown. One hundred and thirty pounds of leaves are required to produce a quart of oil, which sells at present for six dollars, and has long had the reputation of being the best on the market. The bay-tree estates give occasional labor to the inhabitants, but their livelihood depends chiefly on their own little patches of tropical vegetables, their cattle, and their fishing. From the high points of the island one has an embracing view of the British Virgin Islands, separated from our own by only a few miles, and framed in the Caribbean like emeralds of fantastic shape in a setting of translucent blue.

There are no towns on St. John. The nearest semblance to them are a few scattered clusters of huts around the shores, where customs are as backward as those of Africa, or Haiti. A handful of these simple dwellings are rather picturesquely strewn up the steep fish-hook-shaped peninsula that forms the eastern end of the island, connected to the rest by a narrow neck of land. Between this and what might be called the mainland is Coral Bay, a harbor of far greater depth than that of St. Thomas, and so much larger that, experts tell us, the construction of two break-waters would make it a safe anchorage for the largest navy in the world. But what, in the name of Neptune, would the world's largest navy find to do there?

We met all the élite of St. John at the Moravian mission of Emmaus at the head of Coral Bay. The census showed the island inhabited by one Catholic, forty Lutherans, and the rest Moravians, hence there were few local celebrities missing at the annual "show" which happened to coincide with our visit. Negroes dressed in their most solemn garments, the men in staid black, the women in starched white, poured in on horseback and afoot from moonrise until the first of the doleful religious songs and the amusingly stupid dialogues began in the school chapel. There was the black government doctor, the negro

A corner of Charlotte Amalia

Picking sea island cotton, the second of
St. Croix products

A familiar sight in St. Croix, the ruins of an old sugar mill and the stone tower of its cane grinding windmill

A cistern in which rain water is stored for drinking purposes

owners of the two or three farms so large as to be locally known as "estates," the island's few school teachers — its policeman himself might have been there had I not deprived him of the use of his "Candy Kid." To tell the truth they gave a rather good impression, decidedly a better one than the traveler-baiters of St. Thomas. They were almost English in their cold leisurely deportment, yet more volubly courteous, and with few exceptions they frankly looked down upon white men. Many of them had the outward indices of education, speaking with a chosen-worded formality that suggested a national convention of pedagogues; not a hint of hilarity enlivened their intercourse. Perhaps the most amusing part of all was the overdone company-manner in which they treated their wives, those same wives who no doubt would take up the chief family burdens again, once the night had separated the gathering into its natural component parts.

We found Carl Francis more nearly what it is to be hoped our new wards can all gradually be brought to resemble. A member of the Colonial Council, notorious throughout the colony as the man who dared tell the congressional committee in public session that the chief trouble with the Virgin Islands is the laziness of their inhabitants, he would outrank many a politician of our own land in public spirit, for all his ebony skin. He confirmed the famous statement above mentioned, but added that there were other things which St. John needed for its advancement. It needs a mail service, for instance, such as it had under the Danes, instead of being obliged to go to Charlotte Amalie to post or receive its letters. It needs more schools, so that its children shall not have to walk miles over the mountains morning and evening. It must have something in the nature of an agricultural bank to lend the inhabitants wherewithal to replant the old estates, if St. John is to regain under the American flag something of its eighteenth century prosperity.

If the *Virginia* was unworthy of her calling, what shall I say of the *Creole*, which carried me from St. Thomas to St. Croix? A battered old sloop of a type so ancient that her massive wooden rail resembled that of a colonial veranda, barely fifty feet long, and nearly as wide, her bottom so covered with barnacles that she did little more than creep in the strongest breeze, she represented the last stage in ocean-going traffic. Not only were there no other whites on board, but not even a mulatto. The passenger-list was made up chiefly of a batch of criminals and insane who were being sent to their respective institutions in St. Croix. Most of them wore handcuffs and leg-irons, and the rattle of chains and the shrieks of their wearers suggested the slave-ships of olden days. One of the mad women screamed for unbroken hours in the lingo of the Dutch West Indies; another conducted single-handed an entire church service, hymns, sermon, prayers, and all.

Yet the crew were at least grown men, and if they were monkey-like in their playful moods, they had real discipline and a sense of responsibility when the time came for it that was a welcome contrast to the surly indifference with which the boys on the *Virginia* carried out their orders. The captain was a black man of the coast fisherman type, but the most entertaining part of the voyage was the unfailing " sir " with which the mate, a cadaverous old negro who wore a heavy wool skating-cap and a sort of trench-coat fit for the Arctic even at high noon, ended his careful repetition of the skipper's every command. Moreover,— for we are all apt to judge things from our own petty personal-comfort angle — the captain and most of his men treated a white man as if he were of royal blood. Not only did he find me a canvas steamer-chair, but he refused any of the other passengers admittance to the three-berth cabin, lest they should "disturb de gen'le-man." If only he had been able to adjourn the church service and the other uproar beyond the bulkhead, I might have had a real night's sleep.

We left at five in the evening, and by sunrise had covered the forty miles,— though not, unfortunately, in the right direction. Had our destination been Fredriksted at the west end of the island, we should have landed early. But the *Creole's* contract calls for a service between St. Thomas and Christiansted, the two capitals of our Virgin group, and all day long we wallowed eastward under the lee of St. Croix's mountainous northern coast, while " de lepards," as the sane passengers called their unsound sisters below, shrieked their maudlin complaints and the church service began over and over again with a " Brethren, let us pray for her."

Christiansted is prettily situated amid cocoanut-palms and sloping cane-fields at the back of a wide bay, but a long reef with an exceedingly narrow entrance gives it a poor harbor. Its white or cream-colored houses, with here and there a red roof, lend it a touch that is lacking in the half-dozen rather grim-faced villages and estates that may be seen scattered to right and left along the rugged coast. The town has wide, rather well-kept streets, many stone houses, an imposing government building, and climbs away up the stony slope behind as if it had once planned to grow, but had changed its mind. Old-fashioned chain pumps supply it with water, from wells rather than from cisterns; a big Catholic church is barely outrivaled in size by the Anglican; on the whole, it seems better swept than more populous Charlotte Amalie. Its people are simple-mannered, rather "gawky," in fact, with a tendency to stare strangers out of countenance, and have a leisureliness that shows even in the long-drawn "Good ahftehnoon, sar," with which they greet passers-by.

Christiansted, and all St. Croix, has a special grievance against the Americans. Under the Danes the governor spent half the year in this second capital. Now the ruler of the islands only occasionally runs over from St. Thomas in his private yacht, often returning the same day, and the Croixians feel slighted. When the admiral and his aides land, it is mildly like the arrival of royalty. A band or two and most of the population are drawn up in the sanded space facing the wharf, whence all proceed to a meeting of the Colonial Council in the old government building.

Across the street from this is a shop in which Alexander Hamilton once clerked. His mother, born in St. Croix, married a man named Levine, who abused her, whereupon she went to live with a Scotchman named Hamilton in the neighboring British island of Nevis. There Alexander was born, but when his father went to seek his fortune else-where, the mother returned to her native island. While clerking in the Christiansted shop, the son wrote his father a letter describing a hurricane that had swept St. Croix, the father showed it to influential friends, with the result that Alexander was sent to King's College (now Columbia University), and, thanks partly to Aaron Burr, never returned to the West Indies. Meanwhile his mother remained in St. Croix until her death, and was buried on a knoll a few miles west of Christiansted. It is a pleasant burial place, with constant shade and a never-failing trade wind fanning the flowers above it, a quaint old homestead behind it, and a modern monument erected by an American woman, inscribed:

Rachael Fawcett Levine

1736–1768

She was the Mother of Alexander Hamilton

St. Croix is far more of a real country than all the other islands of the group put together. Not only is it much larger, being twenty miles long and five wide, but is much more extensively cultivated. Three splendid roads run nearly the length of the island, with numerous cross roads in good condition. Only the rocky eastern end is a wilderness to which deer, brought into St. Croix by the British when they controlled it during the Napoleonic wars, go to hide after the cane-fields are cut, such a wilderness that hunters rarely succeed in stalking the wary animals in the dense undergrowth. There are far more signs of industry in St. Croix than in St. Thomas; its estate-owners are on the whole an intelligent, progressive class, with a social life quite different from that on the more primitive islands. When one has seen St. Croix, the twenty-five million does not seem quite so complete and irreparable a loss.

I took the "King's Road" through the middle of the island. It runs for fourteen miles, from Christiansted, the capital, to Frederiksted, its rival. These names being too much effort for the negro tongue, the towns are known locally as "Boss End" (either a corruption of the French *Bassin* or an acknowledgement that the "bosses" of the island always lived in the capital) and "West End." The northern side is abrupt, with deep water close to the shore, its highest peak, Mount Eagle, rising 1180 feet. South of this range are undulating, fertile valleys and broad, rolling plains not even suggested along the northern coast, and the land slopes away in shoals and coral ledges for several miles from the beach. The highways are maintained by the owners of the estates through which they run; therefore they follow a somewhat roundabout course through the cane-fields, that the expense of maintenance may be more evenly divided. They are busy roads, dotted with automobiles, of which there are more than one hundred on the island, many donkeys, heavy two-wheeled carts hauled by neck-yoked oxen, a kind of jaunting car of the conservative gentry, and inumerable black pedestrians. The island is everywhere punctuated with picturesque old stone windmill towers that once ground cane, their flailing arms long since departed, and gray old chimneys of abandoned sugar-mills break the sky-line on every hand. Some of these dull-white heaps of buildings on their hill-tops look like aged Norman castles; there is something grim and northern about them that does not fit at all with the tropics. They suggest instead the diligence and foresightedness of the temperate zone. Old human tread-mills may still be found among them, and slave-house villages that in some cases are inhabited by the laborers of to-day. Rusted sugar-kettles, such as are strewn through the West Indies from eastern Haiti to southern Trinidad, lie abandoned here and there throughout the island.

Sugar-cane once covered even the tops of the hills, but to-day only the flatter lands are planted, though there are splendid stretches of cane-green valleys. The names of estates are amusing, and range all the way from cynicism to youthful hopefulness,—"Golden Grove," "Work and Rest," "Hope and Blessing," "Whim," "Slob," "Judith's Fancy," "Barren Spot," "Adventure." The ceiba, or "silk-cotton tree," beautiful specimens of the royal palm, the tibet-tree, full of rustling pods that give it the name of "women's-tongues" in all the English-speaking West Indies, everywhere beautify the landscape. Ruins of the slave rebellion, of the earthquake of 1848, of the disastrous hurricane of 1916, are still to be found here and there. There is a marvelous view from King's Hill, with its old Danish gendarmérie, now a police station, from which the central highway, lined by palms and undulating through great valleys of cane, may be seen to where it descends to "West End" and the Caribbean. In the center of the picture sits Bethlehem, the largest sugar-mill on the island, with its cane railway and up-to-date methods. For the modern process of centralization is already spreading in St. Croix; the small independent mills are disappearing, and with them much of the picturesquesness of the island. These big mills, as well as most of the small, are owned by Danes, half the stock of the largest being held by the Danish government. Unfortunately St. Croix has put all its eggs in one basket, or at most, two, sugar and sea-island cotton.

There is not a thatched roof on the island. The people live in moderate comfort, as comfort goes in the West Indies. Toward sunset the roads are lined with women cane-cutters in knee-length skirts, with footless woolen stockings that suggest the tights of ballet-dancers, to protect their legs in the fields, pattering homeward, with their big cane-knives lying flat on the tops of their heads. Bits of colored rags sewed on the hatbands of the men indicate that they are members of the newly organized labor-union. They still bow and raise their hats to passing white men, yet one feels something of that bolshevistic atmosphere which their black leaders are fostering among them. The King's Road passes a large distillery, which prohibition has closed. Formerly St. Croix made much rum; now it is giving its attention rather to syrup than to sugar, as there is more money in the former; but estate-owners are threatening to give up cane-growing and turn

their fields into cattle pastures, so greatly have the wages of field laborers increased in the last two years — from twenty-five cents to a
dollar a day.   For St. Croix is one of the few islands in the West
Indies where " task work " has never taken the place of a fixed daily
wage.   Cattle are plentiful on the island, from which they are sent to
Porto Rico in tug-towed open barges.   Some of them are so wild that
they are brought down to the coast in cages on wheels, and all of them
are roped and swung on board with little regard to their bodily comfort.

Fredriksted, the third and last town of our Virgin Islands, is a
quaint, " Dutchy " place some five blocks wide and seven long, with
wide sanded streets, two-storied for the most part and boasting no real
public sidewalks; for though what look like them run beneath the
arcades that uphold the upper-story verandas, they are rather family
porches, shut off by stairways or barricades, which force the pedestrian
to take constantly to the sun-scorched streets.   The town has only an
open roadstead; indeed, there is not a good harbor in the island.   A
native band recruited by the American navy breaks the monotony of
life by playing here once a week, as it does daily in Christiansted.
The cable company is required by law to furnish the world's news to
the press, but as the pathetic little newspapers are so small that they
can publish only a few items at a time, the despatches are habitually
some two weeks old, each taking its chronological turn irrespective of
importance.

I visited several schools in the Virgin Islands.   When an American
school director arrived early in 1918 he found no records either of
schools, pupils, or parents.   By dint of going out and hunting them up,
he discovered nineteen educational buildings on the three islands.
Ninety per cent. of the population can read and write after a fashion,
but the majority usually have their letters written by the public scribe,
of whom there is one in each of the three towns, in a set form that
gives all epistles a strong family resemblance.   The school system
was honeycombed with all sorts of petty graft.   A man who received
three dollars a month for keeping a certain school clean had not seen
the building in years.   The town clock of Christiansted has not run for
five years, yet another favored person received a monthly stipend
for keeping it in order.   The new director and his two American
assistants have still to contend with many difficulties.   There are

no white teachers; those now employed were trained either in Denmark or in the Moravian schools, and the "English" of most of them almost deserves to be ranked as an independent dialect. The highest teacher's salary is seventy-five, the average twenty-four dollars a month. Boys of sixteen, drawing the regal income of ten dollars monthly, conduct many of the classes. Those who served a certain number of years under the Danes receive a pension from the famous twenty-five millions. They are small pensions, like those that went to all the small government employees whom the Danes left behind, and those who still hold their places protest against telling their new employer how much they draw from Copenhagen, fancying it may result in a corresponding loss in the increase they fondly hope for under American rule. Lack of funds has forced the director to maintain many of the incompetents in office. One rural school we visited is still taught by the local butcher, whose inefficiency is on a par with his custom of neglecting his educational duties for his more natural calling. But as the island budget does not permit an increase of his monthly thirty-five dollars,— and in every case it is merely Danish, not American, dollars,— no more competent substitute has yet appeared to claim the butcher's ferule.

The country schools have few desks; the children sit on backless benches, their feet usually high off the floor. The tops of the desks are in many cases painted black and used as blackboards. A rusty tin cup was found doing service for all the thirsty; when the Americans attempted to improve this condition by introducing a long-handled dipper with an edge cut in repeated V shape, the teachers bent the sharp points back and returned to the old dip-your-hand-in method. Lessons are often done on slates or pieces of slate, which the teacher periodically sprinkles with water from a bay-rum bottle, then requires the sums to be erased in rhythmical unison. Formerly the teachers sat in the middle of one large room, surrounded by eight different grades, and the resultant hubbub may be imagined. The Americans put in partitions, and the uproar is now somewhat less incoherent. In some of the larger schools there were half-height partitions, with little sliding-doors, through which the principal could peer without leaving his central "office." Loud protests have been heard because the Americans nailed these up, forcing upon the sedentary gentlemen in charge the exertion of walking around to the several doors. The teaching methods were, and in many cases still are, of that tropically medieval type in which the instructor asks long questions that require a single-word answer, even that being chiefly suggested by the questioner.

"What is the longest river in America? Now, then, Miss-Mississi —"

The answer "pi!" by some unusually bright pupil, is followed by exclamations of praise from the teacher. Like most negroes, the Virgin Islanders have tolerable memories, but little ability to apply what they learn. Not the least of the difficulties confronting the new director was the reform of the Catholic schools, which had long put great emphasis on matters of religion and treated other subjects with scant attention. The attempt to better matters sent shrieks of protest to Washington, whence the director's hands were more or less tied by misinformed coreligionists. Bit by bit the Virgin Island schools are being improved, however, a decree permitting superintendents to fine the parents of pupils absent without due cause, simply by sending a policeman to collect the sum assessed, without any troublesome process of law, having given a badly needed weapon against the once widespread inattendance. Parents who decline, or are unable to pay the fines, are required to work one day on the roads for every dollar unpaid.

There is no agriculture worth mentioning in St. Thomas and no employing class in St. John, hence labor troubles have been chiefly confined to St. Croix. The present leaders of the movement in the larger island are three negroes, all of them agitators of the more or less violent type, differing only in degree, and all more or less consciously doing their best to stir up those of their own color. The one considered the most radical is the least troublesome, as he can readily be bought off. Another, a man of some education, runs a newspaper advocating civil government,— that is, negro government, — preaching that the white man is the enemy of the black, that St. Croix belongs by right to the latter, and openly accusing the white officials of incompetency and dishonesty. In addition to this, he publishes secretly a scurrilous sheet that is doing much to inflame the primitive minds of the masses. The third announced in a public meeting that "if the governor don't do what we want, we 'll take him out in the bay and send him back where he come from."

"Since the Americans came, it is all for the niggers," said an old English estate-owner. "The niggers even steal our fruit and vegetables, carrying them to town a bit at a time in their clothes, for the policemen are all friendly or related to them.   Let those black agitators go on a bit longer, and we whites will have to leave the island."

There are signs that the whites are in peril of losing the upper hand in the island, particularly with the methods of the present governor, who caters to the negroes with un-American eagerness.   As an example, though his private yacht may be on the point of steaming from St. Thomas to St. Croix or vice versa, even American white women are left to the mercies of the filthy *Creole,* lest the local merchants complain that trade is being taken away from them.   Yet native negro girls are readily carried back and forth, because they happen to be the daughters, relatives, or dependents of members of the colonial council, or of some other local officials of the islands we are paying taxes to support.

The negro newspaper man sees much " social injustice " in St. Croix, of which certainly a customary amount exists; but he seems incapable of noting the great disinclination to work and the fact that the " paltry dollar a day " buys scarcely one tenth the amount of labor which constitutes a day's work in the white man's countries with which he strives to compare his own.   In 1916 he went to Denmark and raised funds to establish several labor-union estates on the island, where the negroes might raise cattle, cane, and the like, each to get permanent possession of the piece of land on which he was working as soon as he had paid off the mortgage.   But the farms are already, after a bare two years in the hands of the union, largely over-grown with weeds, bush, and miserable shacks, and about the only result of the move has been the loss of more land to world production, and the infliction of the sponsor with an exaggerated self-importance that has made him lose the one virtue of the Virgin-Islander — his courtesy.

On the other hand, the employing class is by no means immune to criticism.   The larger sugar companies were paying cane-growers from six to seven cents Danish for sugar at the same time that they were selling it for from twelve to fourteen cents in American money.   The diligent Yankee who controls the lighterage, wharfage, and many other monopolies at " West End," as well as sharing with the newspaper man the political control of the island, cannot be acquitted of the native charge of exorbitance.   A Danish company whose profits in 1919 were more than a million sent all its gains to Copenhagen, instead of helping to stabilize the exchange by depositing them in New York.

Among the troubles of St. Croix is the problem of what to do with the " immigration fund."   Sugar production requires much labor; ever since slavery was abolished St. Croix has been constantly faced with the difficulty of getting enough of it. A large percentage of the negroes would rather become public charges than work more than a few days a week. In 1854 the planters voluntarily assessed themselves ten cents an acre to establish an immigration fund, the Government making up the deficit. Laborers were brought from the other West Indian islands, particularly from Barbados. Therein lies another grievance of the planters, who assert that though Barbados implored the Government of St. Croix to relieve the former island of some of its over-population, when the request was granted, the Barbadian authorities emptied the jails and sent out all their riff-raff. With the establishment of American rule, it became illegal to bring in contract labor, and though the immigration fund now consists of more than seventy thousand dollars, it is impossible to use it as originally intended. Does the money belong to the planters, to the United States, or to the Danish Government? The Croixians are still heatedly debating the question, and at the same time are complaining of the scarcity and high price of willing labor.

Politically, St. Thomas and St. John, with their numerous neighboring keys and islets, constitute one municipality, and St. Croix another. Under the Danes the executive power was vested in a colonial governor appointed by the crown; the legislative authority being held by a colonial council in each municipality, some of the members likewise crown appointments, some elected. With an American admiral as governor, and naval officers as secretaries and heads of departments, this system has continued, and will continue until our busy Congress finds time to establish another form of government. Though the navy men explain to them that they are virtually under a civil government without the necessity of supporting it themselves, the natives are not satisfied. Among other things the labor leader elected to the colonial council of St. Croix demands the jury trial and " suffrage based on manhood." The vote is at present extended to males over twenty-five having a personal income of three hundred dollars a year or owning property yielding five dollars a month. Moreover — and this, I believe, is more than we demand even in the United States — the voters must be of " unblemished character." Thus the Danes sought to insure the ballot only to men of responsibility and there was good reason for the limitation. To the casual observer it seems that the growing tendency to give the natives the universal franchise should be combated, unless the islands are to become Haitian.

Last year one of the agitators went to the United States on the hopeful mission of getting all the offices filled by natives — that is, negroes. Luckily, his demands were not granted. Civil service already applies; there is nothing to prevent a native from holding any but the higher offices if he is fitted for the task; but native ability is not yet high enough, nor insular morals stanch enough, to give any hope that a native government would work efficiently without white supervision.

There is more justice in the plea for a homestead act that will turn the uncultivated land over to the people, though even that should be framed with care. One of the chief troubles with nearly all the West Indies is the ease with which lazy negroes may squat on public land. The islanders have one real kick, however, on the state of their postal service. Under the Danes there were mail-carriers in the towns, there were country post-offices, and a certain amount of rural delivery; all school-teachers sold stamps, and mail was sent by any safe conveyance that appeared. To-day there are only three post-offices and no mail delivery, the country people must carry their own letters to and from one of the three towns, those living on St. John being obliged to bring and fetch theirs from Charlotte Amalie, and though a dozen steamers may make the crossing during the week, the mails must wait for the languid and uncertain *Virginia* or *Creole*. There are only four postal employees in St. Thomas, in addition to the postmaster, a deserving Democrat from Virginia who, in the local parlance, " does nothing but play tennis and crank a motor-boat." When one of the mail-schooners comes in, the population crowds into the post-office in quest of its mail, disrupting the service, each hopeful citizen coming back again every half-hour or so until he finds that the expected letter has not come. Yet carriers were paid only thirty-five dollars Danish under the Danes, and three or four of them obviated all this chaotic confusion.

Roughly speaking, the St. Thomas division does not want civil government, feeling it cannot pay for it, and St. Croix does, though her colonial council has asked that no change be made for the present and has implied that it expects the expense of government to be chiefly maintained by congressional appropriation even after the change is made. But this same body demands full jurisdiction over all taxation, the one thing it is least competent to handle properly, for it would result in the powerful and influential and their friends escaping their just share of the burden. There are queer quirks in the taxation system left by the Danes. Buildings, for instance, are taxed by the ell, or two square feet, with the result that old tumble-downs often pay more than smaller modern and useful structures. There is a tax on wheels, so that the largest automobile pays five dollars a year, as does the poor man's donkey-cart. Moreover, this money does not go to the maintenance of roads, but into the colonial treasury, as does every other cent of revenue. Under the Danes, even with lottery taxes yielding a hundred thousand dollars a year, and a large income from liquor taxes, the islands were never self-supporting. Our income tax in place of these amounts to little, especially as many find ways to get out of paying it. The public revenues of the islands are barely a quarter million a year. We contribute an equal amount directly, and three hundred thousand dollars a year in navy salaries besides, for the governor and his assistants get no other recompense than their regular pay as naval officers. There are a few persons, not Virgin-Islanders of course, who advocate annexing the group to Porto Rico. Theoretically, this plan would greatly simplify matters; in practice there would be certain decided objections to it, though the scheme might be feasible if worked out with care. Two things are indispensable, however, that during the life of the present generation the islands be given no more autonomy than they have at present, and above all that they be taxed by disinterested outsiders.

A new code of laws, based on those of Alaska and reputed to contain all the latest improvements in government, has recently been drawn up for the Virgin Islands. Unfortunately, the colonial council can reject that code if they see fit; that is another weakness in the treaty. Already they have marked for the pruning-knife every clause designed to improve the insular morals. The marriage ceremony, for instance, has never been taken very seriously by the natives. Unions by mutual consent are so numerous that our census-takers were forced to include a fifth class in their returns — the " consentually married." Illegitimacy runs close to eighty per cent., far out-distancing even Porto Rico. In fact, the mass of the islanders have no morality whatever in that particular matter. Girls of fourteen not only have children, but boast of it. The Danes are largely to blame for this state of affairs, for there were few of them who did not leave " gutter children " behind, though it must be admitted that our own marines and sailors are not setting a much better example. The negro, being imitative, is particularly quick to copy any easy-going ways of his superiors; hence there is almost a complete absence of public sentiment against such unions among the blacks. Formerly a special excuse was found in the high cost of legal and church marriages, the fees for which were virtually prohibitive to the poorer classes. To-day they are only nominal, and many an old couple has been married in the presence of their grandchildren. The Danish laws compel the father to contribute two dollars a month to the support of his illegal children, but though the man seldom denies his possible parentage, the woman has frequently no unquestionable proof of it. The new code would force men to marry the mothers of their children.

"But how can we do that?" cried a member of the colonial council, often referred to as "the best native on the island," yet who makes no secret of having his progeny scattered far and wide. "Most of us are married already; besides, we would have to legalize polygamy to carry out this proposed law. We are quite willing to continue the two dollars a month to our outside children, but how can we marry their mothers? They are not even of our own class!"

Illegitimacy gives rise to another problem. By the Danish laws still in force every minor must have a guardian, and that guardian cannot be a woman, even though she be the mother. Her older brother, her father, or some more distant relative, slightly interested in his task, commonly becomes the legal sponsor for her fatherless offspring. The duties of a guardian are, succintly, to "take charge of the minor's property," with the resultant abuse to be expected. Policemen are now and then appointed the legal guardians of a dozen or more young rascals, and it goes without saying that they do not lie awake nights worrying about the moral and material advancement of their wards.

Another clause that is not likely to escape the blue pencil of the councils is that giving the authorities the right to search the persons and carts of those carrying produce and to demand proof of its legal possession. Yet without some such law there is slight hope of stamping out the wide-spread larceny of growing crops.

One of our most serious problems in the Virgin Islands is to combat disease. The Danes had only three doctors on the islands; now sixteen navy physicians are busy all the time. Their fees are turned into the colonial treasury, an arrangement nowhere else in force in American territory. Half the children die as a natural course, though the islands are really very healthful, and no white child born under proper conditions has died since American occupation. There is no hookworm and little malaria; but much pellagra and "big leg," or elephantiasis. Tuberculosis is common, and tests indicate that eighty per cent of the population is infected with a hereditary blood disease. There is a leper colony in St. Croix. The present generation, in the opinion of the navy men, is hopeless. In the improvement of the next they are hampered by the ignorance, indifference, and superstition of the parents. The doctors of " West End" found nothing unusual in the case of a baby that was brought to the hospital already dead because the father had taken it first to a native healer, who put "chibble" (pot herbs) under its nose to cure it of acute indigestion.

But there is a worse problem than that facing us in the Virgin Islands — the elimination of the habit of trying to live off the exertions of others. Thanks to their race, history, and situation, the islanders are inveterate, almost unconscious, beggars. Young or old, black or white — for environment has given even those of Caucasian ancestry almost the same habits and " ideals " as the negro — they are all gifted with the extended palm. If they do not all beg individually, they do so collectively, in a frank, shameless assertion that they cannot support themselves. The Danes left a " rum fund " that is designed to aid all those who " have seen better days," and to judge by the applicants the entire population ranks itself in that category. The native woman clerk at the " West End " police station does not hesitate to give any one, even the four-dollars-a-day sugar-porters on the wharves, a certificate that he is unable to pay for medical attention, though the navy doctors' fees are nominal and, even when they are paid, go into the colonial treasury. The admiral-governor gave a reception to the natives. Food was provided for five hundred — and was carried off by the first hundred street women and urchins who surged through the door. Next day a large crowd came to demand their share, saying they had got nothing the day before. One of the " labor leaders " told the negroes of St. Croix to hide their mahogany bedsteads and phonographs and sleep on drygoods boxes while the congressional committee was scheduled to visit the island. Of the entire crowd appearing before that committee not one had the general good of the islands on his lips, but all came with some petty personal complaint or request.

In short our new wards want all they can get out of us. They want Uncle Sam to provide them with schools, with sanitation, with irrigation, with galvanized hill-sides, with roads — even in St. Croix, which has better highways than almost any State in the Union — with public markets, with libraries, with means of public transportation, with anything else which, in his unsophisticated generosity, he chooses to give, so long as he does not require them to contribute their own means and labor to that end. The colonial council of St. Croix " hopes means will be found to get Congress to appropriate a half million a year, a sum far beyond our own means, so that we can live up to the high ideals of our great American nation." It never seems to occur to them that the schools, libraries, and streets in our cities are paid for by the inhabitants thereof; they have the popular view of Uncle Sam as the world's Santa Claus. Yet many of the very members of that council have made fortunes in St. Croix and probably could themselves pay a large part of the sum demanded without any more difficulty than the average American finds in paying his taxes. Naïve as they are, the Virgin Islanders can scarcely expect Americans to adopt them and never let them work or want again, yet they talk as if they had some such thought in mind. Or, as a congressman put it during a public hearing, "I doubt whether the farmers of my State of Kansas will be willing to get up at four all summer and pay money into the federal treasury so that you can sleep until nine in the morning and stroll in the park the rest of the day."

There is no reason why the Virgin-Islanders should not be sufficiently taxed to support their own schools and other requirements. Even if St. Thomas is now largely barren, many of its shopkeepers are steadily growing wealthy. The Danish planters of St. Croix send fortunes home to Denmark every year; at the present price of sugar they alone should be able easily to contribute a sum equal to that they are demanding from Congress. Should not even dollar-a-day negroes pay something in taxes? It might develop their civic spirit. The Virgin-Islanders need many things, it is true; but there are millions living in, and paying taxes to, the United States who have by no means what almost every Virgin-Islander has, or could have for a little exertion. The future of the islands depends largely on whether or not we succumb to our national tendency to make our wards mendicants for life, or give them a start and let them work their own way through the college of civilization.

Whenever I look back upon our new possessions I remember a significant little episode that took place during our first day in St. Thomas. A negro woman was sitting a short way up one of the great street stairways that climb the hills of Charlotte Amalie. A descending friend paused to ask her what was the matter, and she replied in that slow, whining singsong peculiar to the community:

"Me knees jes wilfully refuse to carry me up dem steps."

That is the trouble with most of the Virgin-Islanders. Their own knees jes wilfully refuse to carry them up the stairway of civilization. They will have to be lifted — or booted.

THE BRITISH WEST INDIES

CHAPTER XIV

THE CARIBBEE ISLANDS

ONCE he has reached our Virgin Islands, the traveler down the stepping-stones of the West Indies has left his worst experiences behind him. For while connections are rare and precarious between the large islands of the north Caribbean, the tiny ones forming its eastern boundary are favored with frequent and comfortable intercommunication. Several steamship lines from the north make St. Thomas their first stop, and pausing a day or two in every island of any importance beyond, give the through traveler all the time he can spend to advantage in all but three or four of the Lesser Antilles. In these he can drop off for a more extended exploration and catch the next steamer a week or two later.

A twelve-hour run from St. Croix, with a glimpse of the tiny Dutch islands of Saba and St. Eustatius, peering above the sea like drowning volcanoes, brought us to what the British so familiarly call St. Kitts. Columbus named it St. Christopher, one legend having it that he discovered it on his own patron saint's day, another that he saw in its form a resemblance to that worthy carrying in his arms the infant Jesus. The resemblance is not apparent to the critical eye, but the admirals of those days, you recall, were not compelled to take their grape-juice unfermented. Besides, we must not be too hard upon the busy " old man " of the caravel fleet. With a sailor thrusting his head into the cabin every hour or so to say, " Another island, *vuestra merced;* what shall we call it?" it was natural that the Genoese, having no modern novels at hand, should curse his gout and hobble across to the saints' calendar on the opposite bulkhead.

St. Kitts has more nearly the form of a heaping plate of curry and rice — curious this should not have occurred to the galley-fed seaman — culminating in Mt. Misery, four thousand and some feet high, with an eight hundred foot crater nicely proportioned to hold the curry and still steaming with clouds of vapor that habitually conceal its summit. From the shores to the steeper heights of the mountain the swiftly sloping island is covered with sugar-cane; above that the woods are said to be full of monkeys, descendants of the pets which British soldiers brought with them when St. Kitts was a bone of contention between the French and the English. With one slight exception, this and the neighboring island of Nevis are the only West Indies inhabited by our racial ancestors, which are so troublesome that their direct descendants below have given up trying to plant their gardens more than half-way up the mountains.

Though St. Kitts was the first island of the West Indies to be settled by the English, antedating even ultra-British Barbados in that regard by nearly two years, its capital bears the French name of Basse Terre. It is an uninteresting town of some seven thousand inhabitants, scarcely one in a hundred of whom boast of a family tree wholly free from African graftings, and most of them living in unpainted, weather-blackened, shingle cabins hidden away in the forests of cocoanut palms. Even the larger houses in the center of town are chiefly built of clapboards or shingles, painted only by the elements, and with narrow little eaves that give them the air of wearing hats several sizes too small for them. The sums that are uselessly squandered on window-glass would easily suffice to give the entire town a sadly needed coating of paint, were it not that all such improvements are taxed out of existence, as in most of the British West Indies. The only pleasant spot in town is a kind of Spanish plaza run wild, generously shaded with royal palms and spreading tropical trees, beneath which the grass stands ankle-high and hens pilot their broods about among the brown windrows of fallen leaves. Its unshaven condition rather enhances a certain rustic beauty that is not marred by an unexpectedly artistic old stone fountain in its center. Beyond the last lopsided negro hovels Basse Terre is surrounded by cane-fields, with Mt. Misery piled into the sky close behind them.

We had the misfortune to first land in British territory on a Sunday. Basse Terre was as dead as if a general funeral were just over. It was not simply that we bemoaned with the tourist-minded fellow-countrymen from the steamer the fact that every " Liquor Store " was tight and genuinely closed; the dreary lifelessness of the whole place got on our nerves. The very trade wind seemed to refrain from any unnecessary exertion; the citizens appeared to have given even their minds a holiday and replied to the simplest questions with a vacant stare. It was a " holy day " as truly as a French or Spanish Sunday is a " day of feast," or " festival." I imagine heaven is much like an English community on a Sunday — so piously dull that a new inmate would soon be on his knees imploring the gatekeeper to let him go to the only other available place.

At eleven o'clock four species of church service broke out, the Anglican, Catholic, Moravian, and what a black policeman in a white blouse and helmet and the deliberate airs of a London " bobby " referred to in a Sunday whisper as the " Whistling." We went. One was forced to, in self-defense and for the utter absence of any other form of amusement. Then we understood why the community could endure the apparent lack of recreation and exercise of its deadly Sabbath. Negroes striving to maintain the cold, calm, rather bored English manner from opening hymn to benediction supplied the former, and the ups and downs of the Anglican service furnished the latter.

We found St. Kitts more down-at-heel, more indolent, less self-relying than even our Virgin Islands. The shingle shacks of Basse Terre were more miserable than those of St. Thomas; the swarms of negroes loafing under the palm trees about them were as ragged as they were lazy and insolent. Conrad's " Nigger of the Narcissus," you may recall, came from St. Kitts. His replica, except in the genuineness of his ailment, could be seen in any patch of shade. A white stranger strolling through the poorer section was the constant target of foul language and even more loathsome annoyances from both sexes and all ages; in the center of town his footsteps were constantly dogged by clamoring urchins who replied to the slightest protest with streams of curses even in the presence of white residents and the serenely unconscious negro policemen. The inhabitants were incorrigible beggars, from street loafers to church wardens; even the island postmaster begged, under the pretense of selling a historical pamphlet; the country people left their " work " in the fields to shout for alms from the passer-by.

A highway encircles the island, which is twenty-three miles long and five wide. It flanks Brimstone Hill, sometimes called the " Gibraltar of the West Indies " in memory of the part it played in the wars between the French and English for the control of the Caribbean. Cane-fields spread with monotonous sameness on either side of the moderately well-kept roads, with here and there an old stone tower that was once a windmill and what seems many chimneys to one who recalls how seldom two are seen in the same horizon in Cuba. On the whole, the island is not to be compared with St. Croix; despite its abundance of sugar it has a poverty-stricken air, for St. Kitts seems to have lost its " pep," if ever it had any.

It took two days to unload our one-day's cargo in the harbor of Basse Terre. The local stevedores were on strike and their places had been taken by less experienced men from the neighboring island of Nevis. This had magnified the constant enmity between the St. Kittens — or whatever is the proper term — and the inhabitants of "that other country," as they called it; but it was an enmity without violence, except of words, torrents of words in what. close observers assert are two distinct dialects, though the islands are separated only by a narrow channel. The strikers, to all appearances, felt they had won their chief aim by being allowed to lie on their backs in the shade of the cocoanut palms.

The steamer's loss was my gain, for the delay gave me time to visit the island Columbus named " Nieve " from the snow-like clouds hovering about it. Open sailing scows, perhaps three times the size of a lifeboat, were constantly plying across the bay between the two capitals. The wind was on the beam in both directions, and a dozen times I was convinced that the waves that splashed continuously over the leeward gunwale of the creaking old tub would fill her at the next squall sweeping through the deep channel between the islands. But each time the simple son of Nevis at the tiller met my questioning gaze with " Not blow too bad to-day, boss," now and then adding the reassuring information that several boats were lost here every year. High on the windward gunwale the plunging of the crude vessel was exhilarating in spite of the apparent danger, but the negro women in their flashy dresses, tin bracelets, and much cheap jewelry, who sprawled together in the bottom of the boat in supreme indifference to the bilge-water and filth that sloshed back and forth over them seemed to find nothing agreeable in the experience.

The craft half righted herself at length under the lee of the island, heaped up into the clouds in similar but more abrupt and compact form than St. Kitts. One scarcely needed to go ashore to see the place, so nicely were its sights spread out on the steeply tilted landscape. Like its neighbor it was but slightly wooded on its lower slopes, but made up for this by the dense vegetation of its monkey-infested heights. One made out a few groves of cocoanuts, patches of cotton, and green stretches of sugar-cane, with here and there a windmill tower, one of which still survived, its slowly turning arms giving a mild suggestion of the Azores. Charlestown soon appeared out on the end of a low point, a modest little town with a few red roofs peering through the cocoanut trees. Gingertown, five miles in the interior, and the village of Newcastle farther down the coast are the only other places of any size, though the island is everywhere well populated. Time was when Nevis was a famous watering place for Europe and America, with thermal baths and medicinal waters, and an important capital named Jamestown, from which all this region of the Caribbean was ruled. But the city was destroyed one day by an earthquake and submerged beneath the sea, where some of its coral-encrusted ruins can still be seen not far from the shore. Natural causes led to the island's gradual isolation, and to-day, though its hot baths are exploited by an American owned hotel, it becomes highly excited at the arrival of a stranger from the outside world.

Charlestown had little of the insolence of St. Kitts, though it was by no means free from beggars. Its masses were more naïve in manner, even more ragged of garb. Nine pence a day is the average adult male wage of even those who succeed in finding work. *Obeah,* or African witchcraft, seemed still to maintain a hold, for even the native bank clerk who piloted me about town acknowledged a belief in certain forms of it. Two or three blocks from the little triangular park that marks the center of town are the ruins of a gray stone building in which Alexander Hamilton is reputed to have been born. British visitors are more interested in the house where Nelson lived and the little church in which he was married to the widow Nisbet, two miles up the sloping hillside. Love for England does not greatly flourish in Nevis, if one may take surface indications as evidence.

"We are ruled over by an autocrat, a white Barbadian magistrate," complained an islander of the better class, while the group about him nodded approval. "England takes everything from us and does nothing for us. If it were not for the prohibition that would come with it, we would be glad to see the island under American rule."

A forty-mile run during the night brought us to Antigua. Steamers anchor so far off shore that a government launch is required to do the work performed in most of the Lesser Antilles by rowboats. For though there is a splendid double harbor on the opposite side of the island, the English cling to their invariable Caribbean rule of building the capital and only city on the leeward shore. Two pretty headlands are passed on the way in, the more prominent of them occupied by a leper asylum; both are crowned by fortresses dating back to the days when England fought to maintain her hold on the West Indies. From the bay St. John's presents an agreeable picture in the morning sunlight, an ancient two-towered cathedral bulking above the greenery constituting the most conspicuous landmark. It is much more of a town than Basse Terre, though with the same wooden, shingled, often unpainted houses, and wide, unattractive, right-angled streets. What energy it may once have had seems largely to have departed, and for all its size it has the air of a half-forgotten village. Its shops open at seven, close from nine to ten for breakfast, and put up their shutters for the day at four. On closer inspection the cathedral proves to be two churches, one of wood enclosed within another of stone, as a protection against earthquakes. The negro women of the market-place are given to the display of brilliant calicos, but the population as a whole has little of the color, — except in complexion — the dignity, and that suggestion of Gallic grace of the French islanders.

Antigua, thirteen by nine miles, is lower and less mountainous than St. Kitts, being of limestone rather than volcanic formation, with less luxuriant vegetation, having been almost wholly denuded of its forests. In consequence, it suffers somewhat for lack of rainfall, though it is almost everywhere cultivated, and offers many a pretty vista of rolling landscape, usually with a patch of sea at the end of it. Sugar-cane is by far its most important product, though corn-fields here and there break the lighter green monotony, and limes and onions are piled high in crates on St. John's water-front. The island roads are tolerable. Automobiles, mainly of the Ford variety, make it possible for the traveler to see its "sights" in a few hours with less damage to the exchequer than in many of the West Indies. Women in rather graceless colored turbans are more numerous than men in the cane-fields, where wages average 4½ pence per hundred holes of cane, whether for planting, hoeing, or cutting, making the daily wage of the majority about fifteen cents. What they do with all that money is a problem we found no time to solve, thought there were evidences that a fair proportion of it is invested in native rum. Like all the world, Antigua has had her share of labor troubles during the past few years. Two seasons ago much cane was burned by the incensed workers, but the killing of several and the wounding of some thirty more by government troops has settled the wage problem on its old basis. Though many abandoned estates, with the familiar square brick chimneys and armless windmill towers, dot the landscape, two sugar factories to-day consume virtually all the cane. They are rather old-fashioned institutions, with no such pretty, well-planned *bateys* and comfortable employee-houses as are to be found in Cuba and Porto Rico. The hauling is chiefly done by tippy two-wheeled carts, drawn by mules in tandem, occasionally by oxen, specially designed, it would seem, to spill their loads each time an automobile forces them to the edge of the road. Mangos and bamboo, in certain sections clumps of cactus and patches of that troublesome thorny vegetation which the Cubans call *aroma,* are the chief landscape decorations, except on the tops of the scrub-fuzzy, rather than forested hills. Shacks covered with shingles from mudsill to roof-tree, interspersed with fewer thatched and once whitewashed huts, all of them somewhat less miserable than those of St. Kitts, house the country people in scattered formation or occasional clusters bearing such misnomers as All Saints' Village. Like most of the Lesser Antilles, Antigua was once French, but it has retained less of the patois than the other islands of similar history.

The goal of most mere visitors to Antigua is English Harbor on the windward coast, two almost landlocked blue basins in which Nelson re-fitted his fleet in preparation for the battle of Trafalgar. Here stand several massive stone buildings, occupied now only by the negro care-taker and his family. In the great stone barracks is a patch of wall decorated by the none too artistic hand of the present King George, then a sub-lieutenant in the British navy, wishing in vari-colored large letters "A Merry Christmas 2 You All," the space being reverently covered now by a padlocked pair of shutters. More popular with the romantic-minded is the immense anchor serving as gravestone of one, Lieutenant Peterson. The lieutenant, runs the story, was the rival of his commanding officer for the hand of the island belle. On the eve of a naval ball he was ordered not to offer the young lady his escort. He appeared with her at the height of the festivities, however, she having declined in his favor the attentions of the commander, whereupon the latter shot the lieutenant for disobeying orders and caused him to be buried that same night in the barracks compound.

Patriotism for the empire to which they belong is not one of the chief characteristics of the Antiguans. Indeed, there is "no love whatever" for England, if we are to believe most of those with whom I talked on the subject.

"There never was any, even in the old days," asserted a man whose parents emigrated from England half a century ago. "Before the war," he continued, "England would not buy her sugar in the West Indies because she could get it cheaper from the beet-growers in Ger-many and Austria, thanks to their government bounty. The sugar we sent to England often lay on the wharves over there for months, until we had to send money to pay wharfage and storage, and feed our sugar to the hogs here at home. Once we enjoyed home rule; now our laws are made by the Secretary for the West Indies in London, who thinks we wear breech-clouts and speak some African dialect. They take everything from us in taxes and do nothing for us in return. Our governor thinks his only duty is to hold us down. He tries to be a little tin god, permits no one else to ride in the public launch with him when he goes out to a ship, and all that sort of thing. He came here two years ago from a similar position in one of our African colonies, where he was accustomed to see everyone bring him gifts and bow their heads in the sand whenever he passed. He got a surprise when he landed here. Except for a few nigger policemen, no one paid him any attention whatever, except that the drunken fellows shouted after him in the streets and called him foul names. We had no conscription here, yet we sent a large contingent. The well-to-do whites paid their way home to enlist; the poor ones went over with the niggers and were slowly picked out after they got over there. And England has not done a thing for a man of them. The blacks are angry because they got no promotion and all the dirtiest jobs. Mighty few of us would go again to fight for the blooming Empire."

Antigua is the capital of what the British call, for political purposes, the Leeward Islands, comprising all their holdings between Santa Cruz and Martinique. Geographically this is a misnomer, the real leeward islands being the Greater Antilles, from Cuba to Porto Rico inclusive, and all the Lesser Antilles the windward islands, as the Spaniards recognized and still maintain. But the unnatural division serves the purpose for which it was made. St. John's is the seat of the governor and the archbishop of all the group, with the principal prison and asylum. Anguilla, far to the north, near the Dutch-French island of St. Martin, is of coral formation, comparatively low and flat. The same may be said of Barbuda, large as Antigua and reputed to have gone back to nature under the improvident descendants of the slaves of the Codrington family that long reigned supreme upon it. Montserrat, on the other hand, is very mountainous, a flat-topped, pyramidal fragment of earth thirty-five square miles in extent, its lower slopes planted with limes and cacao, its upper reaches forest-clad. White ribbons of roads set forth from Plymouth, the capital, in what looks like a determined effort to scale the precipitous heights, but soon give up the attempt. The population of the island is mainly negro-Irish, it having been settled by emigrants from the " Old Sod," so that to this day Irish names predominate, freckled red-heads with African features are numerous, and the inhabitants are noted throughout the West Indies for their brogue and their gift of blarney.

Dominica, the southernmost and largest of the misnamed Leeward Islands, is also entitled to several other superlatives. Most of the West Indies boast themselves the "Queen of the Antilles," but none with more justice than this tiny Porto Rico isolated between the two principal islands of "French America." It is the highest of the Lesser Antilles, Mt. Diablotin stretching 5314 feet into the tropical sky; the wettest, being habitually surrounded by blue-black clouds that pour forth their deluges by night or by day, in or out of season, even when all the sky about it is translucent blue; and the world's greatest enemy of the scurvy, for it produces most of that fruit which has given the British sailor the nickname of "limy." Incidentally, it is the most difficult of the West Indies in which to travel.

Roseau, the capital, sits right out on the Caribbean, the mountains climbing directly, without an instant's hesitation, into the sky behind it. They are as sheer beneath water as above it and the steamer anchors within an easy stone's throw of the wharves. Boatmen in curious little board canoes, showing their wooden ribs within and bearing such French names as "Dieu Donne," quickly surround the new arrival, some of them bent on carrying her passengers ashore at a shilling a head, others to dive for pennies thrown into this deepest-blue of seas, which is yet so transparent that both coin and swimmer can be perfectly seen as far down as lungs will carry them. Boats of the same quaint structure and only slightly larger jockey for position along the ship's side to receive the cargo from her hatches. They are unreliable and poorly adapted for the purpose, but their owners stick together in protecting their monopoly and every modern lighter brought to Dominica has invariably been scuttled within a week. Almost within the shadow of the steamer other men are standing stiffly erect in the extreme stern of their fishing canoes, steering them by almost imperceptible movements of their single crude paddle, while their companions cast their nets or throw stones within them to lure the fish to the surface. Immense hauls they make, too, without going a hundred yards from the shore. How many fish there must be in the sea when thousands of fishermen can ply their trade about each of these West Indian stepping-stones the year round and come home every day laden to the gunwales with their catches!

Roseau is scarcely more than a village. It is so small that all its business is carried on within plain sight from the steamer's deck, though it strives to look very important with its few two-story stone buildings, like a Briton in foreign parts aware that he must uphold the national dignity unassisted. It is less given to wooden structures than many of its rivals, and has a more aged, solid air, at least along the water-front. An age-softened gray stone church that looks almost Spanish, with an extraordinary width within, like a market-hall filled with pews, and bilingual signs above the confessionals bearing the names of French priests, seems conscious of its mastery over the few small Protestant chapels. Higher still is one of the most magnificent little botanical gardens in the world, with hundreds of tropical specimens arranged with the unobtrusive orderliness of an English park.

I visited Dominica twice, and on the second occasion, having from early morning until midnight, hired a horse to ride across the island. Roseau Valley, a great sloping glen like a cleft in the mountains, climbs swiftly upward to the clouds behind the town, a rock-boiling river, surprisingly large for so small an island, pouring down it. At the bridge across the stream on the edge of town is what claims to be the greatest lime-juice factory on earth. I use both words with misgiving, for it is no more a factory in our sense of the term than the white lumps it ships away to a scurvy-dreading world are juice. Toward this a constant stream of limes, which we would be more apt to call lemons, is descending. Women and girls come trotting down out of the mountains with bushel baskets of them, now and then sitting down on a boulder to rest but never troubling to take the incredible load off their heads. Donkeys with enormous straw saddle-bags heaped high with limes pick their way more cautiously down the steep slope. Occasionally even a man deigns to jog to town with a load of the fruit. They lie everywhere in great yellow heaps under the low trees; they weigh down the usually rain-dripping branches. Yet when they have been grown and picked and carried all the way to town, they sell for a mere seven shillings a barrel! Small wonder the human pack-horses and even the growers are more extraordinarily ragged than any other West Indians outside of Haiti.

Cacao plants, too, are piled up the steeps on either side of the roaring river, for Dominica has that constant humidity and more than frequent rainfall they love so well. The unbroken density of the greenery is one, perhaps the chief, charm of the valley, as of all the island. No-where in all the climb does the eye make out the suggestion of a clearing. Where man has not pitched his lime or cacao orchards, or planted his tiny garden patch, nature forces the fertile black soil to produce to its utmost capacity. It is an un-American density, as of an Oriental jungle, all but completely concealing the miserable little huts tucked away in it all over the lower hillsides; it makes up for the constant succession of heavy showers that belie the sunny promises of the town and harbor below. For the mountains of Dominica have an annual rainfall of three hundred inches, twenty-five feet of water a year!

There are forty automobiles on the island of lemons, but they do not venture far from home. The highway up the valley lasts a bare three miles before it dwindles to a mountain trail that struggles constantly upward, now steeply along the brink of the river far below, now in stony zig-zags that make no real progress, for all their pretense, except in altitude. One has a curiously shut-in feeling, as if there were no escape from the mighty ravine except by the narrow, slippery path underfoot, which is, indeed, the case. Not even the jet black inhabitants inured to mountain-climbing from birth, have attempted to scale the heights by more direct paths than this zigzag trail up the roof-steep bottom of the gorge. They speak among themselves a "creole" as incomprehensible, even to one familiar with French, as that of Haiti, though they babbled a bit of English that seemed to grow less fluent and extensive with every mile away from the capital. There the white stranger was subjected to an insolence and clamoring at his heels inferior only in volume to that of St. Kitts; up here in the mountains the passers-by yielded the trail and raised their ragged headgear with a rustic politeness that would have been more charming had it not almost invariably been followed by "A penny, please, sir" from both sexes and all ages. For all their mountaineer diffidence, they are so given to stealing one another's crops that shops throughout the island are "Licensed to Sell Protected Produce," that the police may have a means of detecting contraband. Perhaps they are scarcely to be blamed for their light-fingered habits, with wages that rarely reach the lofty height of a shilling a day.

The horse had leisurely English manners and the deliberate, loose-kneed action of a St. Thomas waiter, so that we made far less progress than his rangy form had promised. He showed, too, little of that endurance and mountain wisdom for which the far smaller animals of tropical America are noted. We reached the crest of the island at last, however, and paused on the edge of a small fresh-water lake said to fill the crater of an extinct volcano. Sedge-grass surrounded it and dense vegetation framed it on every side, but there was nothing remarkable about it, except, perhaps, to the Dominicans. But the wealth of flora was well worth the excursion. Tree-ferns, ferns large and small, wild bananas, lime-trees, clumps of bamboo, and a score of other plants and trees which only a botanist with tropical experience could name, completely concealed the earth, as the trunks of all the larger species were hidden under climbing parasites with immense leaves, and even the sheer banks were covered with densest vegetation.

A fog, white and luminous, yet impenetrable to the eye at more than twenty yards, covered all the island top. I urged the animal down a far steeper, more stony, trail than that we had climbed, cut deeper than a horseman's head into the red-black mountainside and pitching head-long downward into the foggy void. A half hour of utter stillness, broken now and then by the brief song of the solitaire and the constant stumbling of the horse's hoofs over the stones, brought us suddenly to the edge of the cloud, with a magnificent view of the jagged northern coast edged by the white breakers of the Atlantic. A few negroes again appeared, climbing easily upward, carrying their shoes on their heads, an excellent place to wear them at present prices. Now and then an aged, carelessly constructed hut peered out from the teeming wilderness, but the sense of the primeval, the uninhabited, the un-known to man, brooded over all the scene despite these and the stony trail underfoot.

Halfway down I met two Carib Indians, easily distinguishable from the bulk of the inhabitants by their features and color. They were short and muscular, with more of the aggressive air of the Mexican highlander than the slinking demeanor of the South American aborig-ines. They carried their home-made baskets full of some native produce on their shoulders, rather than on their heads, and apparently spoke but little English. They came from the Carib reservation on the north coast, the only one now left in all the West Indies over which, except for the four larger islands, their man-eating ancestors ruled supreme until long after the discovery. When at length, after long warfare, England entered into a treaty with them, they were given two patches of territory for their own. But the eruption of Soufrière in St. Vincent in 1902 destroyed the colony on that island, and to-day the three hundred of Dominica are the only ones left, and barely forty of these, it is said, are of pure blood. They live at peace with their neigh-bors, make baskets, catch fish, and are noted for their industry, as wild tribes go, in agriculture.

More than halfway down to sea-level huts began to grow frequent again, most of them completely covered with shingles and all of them devoid of any but the scantiest home-made furniture. Ragged, useless-looking inhabitants stood in the doorways staring at the extraordinary apparition of a white man, many of them calling out in cheerful voices for alms as I passed. Dominica is evidently an island without time-pieces; almost everyone I met wanted to know the hour, just why was not apparent, since time seemed to have less than no value to them. My watch having been stolen in Havana and I having declined to tempt West Indians again by buying another, I could not satisfy their curiosity. Besides, the Caribbean is no place in which to worry about time; the fact that the sun rises and sets is all the division of eternity needed in such an African Eden.

At Rosalie, an old-fashioned sugar-mill and a scattering of huts on the north coast, I made a calculation. The sun was high overhead; it could not be later than two; the map in my hand showed the distance around the eastern end of the island to be less than twice that over the mountain; a coast road would be comparatively level and much to be preferred to another climb of 2500 feet on a jaded horse. Besides, I have a strong antipathy to returning the same way I have come. I made a few inquiries. The childlike inhabitants on this coast spoke almost no English and nothing that could easily be recognized as French, but they seemed to understand both tongues readily enough. I had only to ask if it were about four hours ride to the capital to be assured that such was the case. It was not until too late that I realized they were giving me the answer they thought would please me best, like most uncivilized tribes, with perfect indifference to the facts of the case. Any distance I chose to assume in my question was invariably the exact distance; when I awoke to my error and took to asking direct instead of leading questions, the reply was invariably a soft " Yes, sir," with an instant readiness to change to " No, sir," if anything in my manner suggested that I preferred a negative answer. But by this time I was too far along the coast-road to turn back.

I had only myself to blame for what soon promised to be a pretty predicament. Certainly I had traveled enough in uncivilized countries to know such people cannot be depended upon for even approximate accuracy in matters of distance or time. I surely was mountain-experienced enough to realize that an island as small and as lofty as Dominica could have but little level land, even along the coast. As a matter of fact it had virtually none at all. Never did the atrocious trail find a hundred yards of flat going. One after another, in dogged, insistent, disheartening succession, the great forest-clad buttresses of the island plunged steeply down to the sea, forcing the stony path to claw its way upward or make enormous detours around the intervening hollows, only to pitch instantly down again from each hard-earned height into a mighty ravine, beyond which another appalling mountain-wall blocked the horizon immediately ahead. To make matters worse, the horse began to show all too evident signs of giving out. In vain did I lash him with such weapons as I could snatch from the jungle-wall alongside, not daring to take time to dismount and seek a better cudgel. Steadily, inevitably, his pace, none too good at the best, decreased. By what I took to be four o'clock he could not be urged out of a slow walk, even on the rare bits of level going; by five he was merely crawling, his knees visibly trembling, coming every few yards to a complete halt from which he could be driven only by all the punishment I could inflict upon him. His condition was one to draw tears, but it was no time to be compassionate. The steamer was sailing at midnight. It would be the last one in that direction for two weeks. Rachel was waiting to join me on it at Martinique and continue to Barbados. No one on board knew I had gone on an excursion into the hills, nor even that I had left the steamer. My possessions would be found scattered about my stateroom; by the time the ship reached Martinique it would be assumed that I had fallen overboard or suffered some equally pleasant fate. I had barely the equivalent of five dollars on my person, not an extra pair of socks, not even a tooth-brush — and the Dominica cable was broken. Clearly it was no time to spare the cudgel.

But it was of no use. Near sunset the horse took to stumbling to his knees at every step. For long minutes he stood doggedly in his tracks, trembling from head to foot. The sweat of fatigue, as well as heat, ran in rivulets down his flanks. I tumbled off and tried to lead him. We were climbing another of those incessant, interminable buttresses. With all my strength I could only drag him a few creeping steps at a time. After each short advance he sat down lifelessly on his haunches. If I abandoned him in the trail there was no knowing whether the owners would ever see him again; certainly they would not the saddle and bridle, and the owners were a simple mulatto family of Roseau who could ill bear such a loss. But I could scarcely risk further delay. The sun was drowning in the Caribbean; the hazy form of Martinique thirty miles away was still on my port bow, so

Roseau, capital of beautiful Dominica

A woman of Dominica bringing a load of limes down from the mountain

Kingston, capital of St. Vincent

Trafalgar Square, Bridgetown, Barbados, with its statue of Nelson

to speak, showing that I had not yet turned the point of the island, that I was not yet halfway to Roseau. It was stupid of me not to have realized before that Dominica, for all its scant 35,000 ignorant inhabitants, was almost as large as the French island in the offing, and that to encircle one end of it was a stiff all-day job.

I was on the point of abandoning the animal when I caught sight of a man climbing the trail far ahead of us, the first person I had seen in more than an hour. I shouted, and for some time fancied he had dashed off into the wilderness out of fear. Then a break in the vegetation showed him again, and this time he halted. We reached him at last, a stodgy negro youth in the remnants of hat, shirt, and trousers who stood at attention, like a soldier, at the extreme edge of the trail, an expression between fear and respectful attention on his stupid black countenance.

" How far is it to Roseau? " I panted.

" Yes, sir," he replied, seeming to poise himself for a dive into the jungle void behind him.

" How many miles to Roseau? " I repeated, " five or ten or — "

" Yes, sir," he reiterated, shifting his mammoth bare feet uneasily.

" I want to know the distance to the city," I cried, unwisely raising my voice in my haste and thereby all but causing him to bolt. " Can I make it in six hours? "

" Yes, sir," he answered, quickly. Then, evidently seeing that I was not pleased with the answer, he added hastily, " N — No, sir."

"Est-ce qu' on peut le faire en six heures?" I hazarded, but he seemed to understand French even less than English and stared at me mutely. The brilliant idea of wasting no more time passed through the place my mind should have been. I snatched out my note-book and pencil.

" What 's your name? " I asked. " Can you write? "

He could, to the extent of laboriously and all but illegibly penciling his name, to which I added his address, a tiny hamlet up in the mountains. I explained the situation to him briefly in words of one syllable. He seemed to follow me. At least he answered " Yes, sir " at the end of each sentence.

" You will take the horse to the police-station in Grand Bay," I specified, having gathered from my map and his monosyllables that this was the next town. " I will tell the police there what to do with him, and I will leave five shillings with them to give you if you bring horse, saddle and bridle, and do not try to ride him on the way."

" Yes sir," he replied, taking the reins I held out to him, and I turned and fled into the swiftly descending night.

I have climbed many mountains in my day, but none that were as wearying as that endless succession of lofty ridges up the stony sides of which I stumbled hour after hour in a darkness as black as the bottom of a well, only to plunge instantly down again into another mighty, invisible ravine. Several times I lost the trail; how I kept it at all is a mystery. As I strained forward with every ounce of strength within me I caught myself thanking fortune, or whoever has my particular case on his books, that I had been a tramp all my days and had kept myself fit for such an ordeal. Now and then I passed through a " town," that is, what voices told me was a scattered collection of huts hidden in the vegetation and the night on either side of the trail, for a hundred yards or two, along which a few ghostlike figures of negroes in white garments dodged aside at sound of my shod footsteps, each time soon giving way again to the deep stillness of an uninhabited wilderness, broken only by the monotonous chorus of jungle insects. Which of these places was Grand Bay I had no time to inquire, much less batter my head against the native stupidity for sufficient time to find the police-station and make known my case to slow-witted black officials. I would think up some other way of meeting my obligations when I had accomplished the more pressing mission on hand.

Once the trail came out on the very edge of the sea, crawling along under the face of a sheer towering cliff, the spray dashing up to my very feet; a dozen times it climbed what seemed almost perpendicularly into the invisible, starless sky above for what appeared to my wasting strength to be hours. I had eaten a hasty breakfast on board early that morning. Four bananas was the sum total of food I had been able to get along the way. My thighs trembled like the legs of a foundering horse; more than once my wobbling knees seemed on the very point of giving way beneath me. The rain had kindly held off all afternoon, an unusual boon in Dominica, but the pace I was forced to set had so drenched me in perspiration that it dripped in almost a stream from the end of my leather belt.

Then all at once, at the top of an ascent I had told myself a score of times I could never make, the lights of Roseau burst upon me, far below yet seemingly no great distance away. There were a few lights in what seemed to be the harbor, but not enough of them to be sure they were those of a passenger-steamer. Yet hope suddenly stiffened my legs as starch does a wilted collar. The town quickly disappeared again as I plunged down a stony but wide highway that had suddenly grown up under my feet. Several times I was convinced it led somewhere else than where I hoped, so incredibly interminable was the descent to the town that had seemed so near. Even when I caught sight of it again, where the road grew suddenly level, it lay far down the coast, as far, it seemed, as it had been from the top of the range. But the steamer was still there. I broke into a feeble run, for it could not possibly have been much short of midnight, but fell back into a walk when my legs had all but crumpled under me. Never had a small town seemed so interminably long. Once I passed a " nighthawk " and shouted a question at him over my shoulder. " About twelve," he replied, little suspecting the surge of despair his words sent through me. As luck would have it, one boatman had remained at the wharf in hope of a belated shilling. He got two. I had just begun to wring the perspiration out of my coat into my cabin washstand when a long blast of the siren and the chugging of the engines told me that we had gotten under way.

Lest some ungentle reader carry away the impression that I had increased the slight disrepute in which Americans are held in Dominica — for our tourists land there frequently — may I add that I settled in full all my obligations there through the purser of the steamer on its return voyage? But to drop painful subjects and hark back to that other visit to Dominica. Then we left at noon, and Roseau settled back into another week's sleep. There were several pretty villages tucked away in the greenery along the shore, some of them with wide cobbled streets, though hardly a yard of level ground, and each with a church just peering above the fronds of the cocoanuts. A highway crawled as far as it was able along the coast beside us, but soon gave it up where the steep hills, looking like green plush, became precipitous mountains falling sheer into the sea, yet with low forests clinging everywhere to the face of them. Bit by bit the loveliest of the Caribbees, the most unbrokenly mountainous of the West Indies, shrunk away behind us. Tiny fishing boats with ludicrous little pocket-handkerchief sails ventured far out, now standing forth against the horizon on the crest of a wave, now completely lost from sight in a trough of the sea. But by this time Martinique was looming large on the port bow, and we were straining our eyes for the first glimpse of ruined St. Pierre.

St. Lucia, largest of the British Windward Islands and a bare twenty-five miles south of Martinique, is the only one of the Lesser Antilles where the steamer ties up at the wharf. Castries, the capital, is situated on the edge of what was once a volcano crater, but presents little else of interest to those who have seen its replica in several of the other islands. Like all the group to which it belongs politically, it was once French and still speaks a "creole" jargon in preference to English. It, too, is mountainous, with a Soufrière that rises four thousand feet into the sky, and despite its thirty-five by twelve miles of extent, its population is as scanty and as unprogressive as that of Dominica. The most striking of its sights are the two pitons at the southern end of the island, cone-shaped peaks rising more than 2500 feet sheer out of the sea, as if they were the surviving summits of a Himalayan range that sank beneath the waves before the dawn of recorded history.

The next of the stepping-stones is St. Vincent, for though Barbados, a hundred miles due east of it, intervenes in the steamer's itinerary, it is neither geographically, geologically, nor politically a member of the Windward group. St. Vincent was the last of the West Indies to come into possession of the white man, for here the fierce Caribs offered their last resistance and were conquered only by being literally driven into the sea. It is ruggedly mountainous and unbrokenly green with rampant vegetation, its jagged range cutting the sky-line like the teeth of a gigantic saw. It, too, has its Soufrière, which erupted on the afternoon before Pélée in Martinique, killing more than fifteen hundred and devastating one end of the island. Rain falls easily on St. Vincent, and even the capital is habitually humid and drenched with frequent showers. This is named Kingstown, and lies scattered along the shore at the foot of a wide valley sloping quickly upward to the jagged labyrinth of peaks about which black clouds playfully chase one another the year round. It is a gawky, ragged, rather insolent place of unenterprising negroes, with a few scrawny leather-skinned poor whites scattered among them. Some of these are of Portuguese origin, and there is a scattering of East Indians. So colorless is the place, except in scenic beauty, that the appearance of a woman of Martinique in full native regalia in its streets resembles a loud noise in a deep silence. Even the sea comes in with a slow, lazy *swo-ow* among the weather-blackened fishing boats that lie scattered along its beach. So quiet and peaceful is it everywhere out of sound of the clamoring market-place that it would seem an ideal spot in which to engage in intellectual labors, but there is no evidence that St. Vincent has ever enriched the world's art.

Roads climb away from the capital into the pretty, steep hills that surround it, among which are tucked red-roofed estates and negro cabins. The island looks more prosperous in the country than in the town. Its cotton is said to be unsurpassed for the making of lace, and was selling at the time of our visit, for $2 a pound. In addition, it produces cotton-seed oil, arrow-root, cacao, and, above all, nutmegs. The nutmeg grows on a tree not unlike the plum in appearance — residents of Vermont have no doubt seen it often — the fruit resembling a small apricot. Inside this is a large nut prettily veined with the red mace that is another of the island's exports, and the nut being cracked discloses a kernel which, dried and cured, is carried down from the hills in baskets on the heads of negroes and shipped to the outside world as the nutmeg of commerce. The natives, if the swarthy West Indians of to-day are entitled to that term, make also pretty little covered baskets in all sizes, which sell for far less after the steamer has blown her warning whistle than when she has just arrived.

The eight-hour run from St. Vincent to Grenada, capital of the Windward group, is close to the leeward of a scattered string of islands called the Grenadines, some of them comparatively large, mountainous in their small way, others mere jagged bits of rock strewn at random along the edge of the Caribbean, all of them looking more or less dry and sterile. Grenada is rugged and beautiful, though it does not rival Dominica in either respect. It has variously been called the " Isle of Spices," the " Planter's Paradise," and the " Island of Nutmegs." What claims to be the largest nutmeg plantation on earth — the West Indians have something of our own tendency for superlatives — lies among its labyrinth of hills; it produces also cinnamon, cloves, ginger, and cacao. Though it is admittedly far more prosperous than St. Vincent, it shows few signs of cultivation from the sea, for none of its principal products in their growing state can be recognized from the forest and brush that cover many an uncleared West Indian isle. The high prices paid for nutmegs during the war, particularly by fruit preservers in the United States, has brought fortunes to many of its planters, despite the fact that the tree takes seven years to mature. Many of the negroes, too, own their small estates and increase their incomes by making jelly from the nutmeg fruit. Yet from the sea all this is hidden under a dense foliage that completely covers the nowhere level island. Along the geometrical white line of the beach are several villages; higher up are seen only scattered huts and a few larger buildings, except where the two considerable towns of Goyave and Victoria break the pretty green monotony.

But if Grenada must yield the palm for beauty to some of its neighbors, St. Georges, the capital, unquestionably presents the loveliest picture from the sea of any port in the Lesser Antilles, if not of the West Indies. Nestled among and piled up the green hills that terminate in a jagged series of peaks above, its often three-story houses pitched in stages one above the other, larger buildings crowning here and there a loftier eminence, the whole delightfully irregular and individualistic, it rouses even the jaded traveler to exclamations of pleasure. The steamer chugs placidly by, as if it had suddenly decided not to call, passes a massive old fortress, then suddenly swings inshore as though it had forgotten its limitation and aspires to climb the mountain heights. A narrow break in the rock wall opens before it, and it slides calmly into a magnificent little blue harbor and drops anchor so close to the shore that one can talk to the people on it in a conversational tone. Why the vessel does not tie up to the wharf and have done with it is difficult to understand, for the blue water seems fathoms deep up to the very edge of the quay. Strictly speaking, it is not a wharf at all, but one of the principal streets of the town, and passengers in their state-rooms have a sense of having moved into an apartment just across the way from the negro families who lean out of their windows watching with cheerful curiosity the activity on the decks below.

The sun was just setting in a cloudless sky when we landed in St. Georges, yet we saw enough of it before darkness came to veil the now all too familiar negro slovenliness, though it could not disguise the concomitant odors. The same incessant cries for alms, the same heel-treading throngs of guides marked our progress, until we had shaken them off in a long tunnel through a mountain spur that connects the two sections of the water-front. For despite its distant loveliness, the town was overrun by the half-insolent, half-cringing black creatures who so mar all the Caribbean wonderland, until one is ready to curse the men of long ago who exterminated the aborigines and brought in their place this lowest species of the human family. On shore St. Georges was different only in its steep, cobbled streets and its rows of houses piled sheer one above another. Every other shop announced itself a " Dealer in Cacao and Nutmegs." In the clamoring throngs of venders squatted along the curb the only unfamiliar sight was the blue " parrot-fish," with so striking a resemblance to the talkative bird as to be mistaken for it at first glance. But even here there were evidences of Grenada's greater prosperity. White men were a trifle more numerous; numbers of private automobiles climbed away into the hills by what at least began as excellent highways; a telephone line on which we counted seventy-six wires disappeared into the interior over the first crest behind the town. Then a full moon came up over the fuzzy hills, lending a false beauty to many a commonplace old house-wall, restoring the romance to the heaped-up town, and flooding the world with a silver sheen long after we had steamed away in the direction of Trinidad.

CHAPTER XV

THE " Ancient and Loyal Colony of Barbados " lies so far out to sea that it requires a real ocean voyage to reach it. Low and uninteresting at first glance, compared to many of the West Indies, it is by no means so flat as most descriptions lead one to suppose. Seen from the sea it stretches up to a fairly lofty central ridge that is regular from end to end, except for being a trifle serrated or ragged in the center of the island. Dutch looking windmills, the only survivors of the cane-crushers that have fallen into disuse and left only the vine-grown ruins of their stone towers in all the rest of the Lesser Antilles, are slowly turning here and there on the even sky-line. Though the island is entirely of coral and limestone formation, glaringly yellow-white under the blazing sunshine at close range, there is a suggestion of England in the velvety slopes of its varied-green fields as seen from far out in the bay. First settled by the English in 1624, it boasts itself the oldest British colony that has remained unceasingly loyal to the crown and accepts with pride the pseudonym of " Little England."

Barbados has come nearer than any other land to solving the vexing " negro problem." Cultivated in all its extent, with a population of 140,000 negroes and 20,000 whites on a little patch of earth twenty-one miles long and fifteen wide, or 1200 human beings to the square mile, without an acre of " bush " on which the liberated slaves could squat, the struggle for existence is so intense that the black man displays here an energy and initiative unusual to his race. The traveler hears rumours of the Barbadian's un-African activity long before he reaches the island; he sees evidences of it before his ship comes to anchor in Carlisle Bay. Not only is the harbor more active, more crowded with shipping than any other in the Lesser Antilles, but it has every air of a place that is " up on its toes." All the languor, the don't-care-whether-I-work-or-not of nature's favored spots are here replaced by a feverish anxiety to please, an eager energy to snap up any job that promises to turn a nimble shilling. Scores of rowboats surround the steamer in a clamoring multitude, their occupants holding aloft boards on which are printed the names of their craft — unromantic, unimaginative names compared to those of the islands that were once or are still French, such as " Maggie," " Bridget," " Lillie White," " Daisy," " Tiger." In face of the fierce competition the boatmen strive their utmost to win a promise from a passenger leaning over the rail, to impress the name of their craft on his memory so that he will call for it when he descends the gangway, to win his good-will by flattery, by some crude witticism,—" Remember the ' Maggie,' mistress; Captain Snowball "; " The ' Lillie White,' my lady; upholstered in and out! " " The ' Daisy,' my gentleman; rowboat extraordinary to His Majesty! " Meanwhile the divers for pennies, a few girls among them, are besieging the passengers from their curious little flat-bottomed boats of double wedge shape to toss their odd coins into the water and " see the human porpoises " display their prowess. Yet, unlike the pandemonium in the other islands, there is no scramble of venders and beggars up the gangway to the discomfiture of descending pas-sengers; no crowding of boatmen about it fighting with one another for each possible fare, to the not infrequent disaster of the latter. A bull-voiced negro police sergeant, in a uniform that suggests he has been loaned from the cast of " Pinafore," keeps perfect order from the top of the gangway, permitting boats to draw near only when they are called by name and ruling the clamoring situation with an iron hand. For there is this difference between the harbor police of Barbados and those of all the other ports, that they speak to be obeyed, permit no argument, and if they are not respected, they are at least duly feared.

Bridgetown was static. The entire population was massed about the inner harbor; beyond the bridge that gives the town its name stood an immense new arch with the words " Welcome to Barbados " em-blazoned upon it. We thought it very kind of them to give us such unexpected attention, until we discovered they were not waiting for us at all, but for one whom some loyal but not too well schooled Bar-badian had named in chalk on a nearby wall the " Prints of Whales." This was the first time in half a century, it seems, that a member of the royal family to which the " ancient and loyal " little colony has shown unbroken allegiance had come to visit it. The black multitude was agog with poorly suppressed excitement: white natives were squirming nervously: even the few Englishmen in the crowd were so thawed by the " epoch-making event " that they actually spoke to strangers. The harbor officer was so eager to lose none of it that he let us pass without examination; an enterprising black youth won a sixpence by finding us a place on a crowded barge a few yards from the royal landing-stage. The tramways had been stopped; black troops lined the vacant expanse of white main street that stretched away toward the government house. Nelson's one-armed statue in Trafalgar Square had been given an oil bath; buildings were half hidden behind the fluttering flags of all the Allies — the Stars and Stripes rarest among them. Even nature had contributed to the occasion by sending an unexpected little shower to lay the white limestone dust that habitually rouses the ire of new arrivals. The island newspaper announced a special holiday in honor of "the Prince, who will confer upon the loyal inhabitants of this ancient colony the privilege of receiving a message from his august father"; it still carried the advertisements of the closed shops, imploring the citizens not only to buy flags and decorations but to "get new clothes in honor of our royal visitor."

He landed twenty minutes after us. A salvo of twenty-two guns from his battleship in the bay sent as many gasps of excitement and delight through the eager multitude. The subconscious thought came to us that it might be better to pay outstanding war debts than to squander so much powder and coal, but it ill behooves an American of these days to criticize our neighbors for squandering public funds. Besides, it is no easy matter to keep up this loyalty-to-the-king business nowadays, though England, surely, need have no fear of changes. Then a white launch dashed up the cheering inner harbor, a curiously boyish-faced young man in a gleaming white helmet stepped briskly out on the landing-stage into a group of black policemen in speckless girlish sailor suits, who seemed to lack an ostrich feather on their round white straw hats, the governor in full-dress uniform and the lord mayor in purple and red robes bowed low over the hand that was proffered, and the prince and his suite were whisked away.

Black as it was, we were struck by the orderliness of the throng — what a pandemonium such an event would have caused in the temperamental French islands! — and its politeness, compared to the other British West Indies. But if the excitement was suppressed with British sternness, it was not voiceless. The brief glimpse of the fêted youth had aroused a thousand exclamations like that of the ragged old negro woman behind us, "Oh, my God! Dat's he himself! Oh Christ!" On the outskirts of the crowd another who had been so far away as to have caught, at best, a glimpse of the top of the royal helmet was still confiding to her surroundings, " My Jesus, but him good lookin'!" An old negro in a battered derby through which his whitening wool peered here and there elbowed his way through the dispersing crowd mumbling to himself, " No use talkin', it's de British flag *nowadays!*" Farther on a breathless market-woman was asking with the anxious tone of a master of ceremonies who had missed his train and feared the worst, " Has my gentleman landed yet?" But the enthusiasm was not unanimous, for still another woman, who fell in with us down the street, asserted, " Even if de prince landing, it all de same for we workin' people. De Prince Albert him landed fifty year ago, an' de school-girls dat fall wid de grandstand still hobblin' about on dey broken legs."

The prince spent a whole day in the ancient and loyal colony before continuing his journey to Australia, most of it in the isolation of the governor's residence, but if he carried away an imperfect picture of this isolated fragment of the empire, he could at least report to his " august father" that it still retains its extraordinary loyalty to the crown.

Bridgetown is very English, despite its complexion and dazzling sunshine. Broken bottles embedded in the tops of plaster walls, which everywhere shut in private property, shows that this, too, is an over-crowded country where the few who have must take stern precautions against the many who have not. The streets bear such ultra-English names as " Cheapside," " Philadelphia Lane," " Literary Row," " Lightfoot's Passage," " Whitepark Road." The very signboards carry the mind back to England —" Grog Shop — The Rose of Devon," " Coals for Sale," " Try Ward's Influenza Rum — Best Tonic "; the tin placard of some " Assurance Company" decorates every other façade. Even the little shingle shacks in the far outskirts bear some un-romantic name painted above their doors; shopkeepers are as insistent in giving their full qualifications as the clamoring boatmen in the bay. " O. B. Lawless — American Tailor — Late of Panama " announces a tiny one-room hovel. There is a British orderliness of public demeanor even among the naturally disorderly negroes; the women have neither the color sense nor the dignified carriage of their sisters of Martinique, rather the gracelessness of the English women of the lower classes. Yet in one thing Barbados is not English. It is hospitable, quite ready to enter into conversation even with strangers.

When it is not silent and deserted under the spell of a holiday or its deadly Sabbath, Bridgetown pulsates with life. Its wharves are as busy as all those of the rest of the Lesser Antilles put together, as busy as our St. Thomas was before Barbados became the focal point of the eastern Caribbean. Bales and bundles and barrels and boatloads of produce pour into it as continuously as if every one of its 160,000 were wealthy consumers of everything the world has to offer. Its own product is constantly being trundled down to waiting lighters — great hogsheads of sugar or molasses carried on specially designed iron frames on wheels, each operated by three negroes who have not lost the amusing childishness of their race for all their competition-bred industry, for they invariably take turns in riding the contrivance back to the warehouse, though the clinging to it must require far more physical exertion than walking. Steamers, schooners, lighters, rowboats, mule-trucks, auto-" lorries " are incessantly carrying the world's goods to and fro. Innumerable horse-carriages, scores of automobiles, ply for hire. Excellent electric-lights banish the darkness from all but the poorer class of houses. Yet despite the constant struggle for livelihood,— or perhaps because of it,— Bridgetown has little of the insolence of the other British West Indies. Applicants for odd jobs swarm and beggars are plentiful, but the latter are unoffensive and the former approach each possible client with a " Do you want me, my gentleman? " so courteous that one feels inclined to think up some imaginary errand on which to send them. They seem to recognize that politeness is an important asset in their constant battle against hunger, which gives them also a responsibility, a reliability in any task assigned them, and a moderation in their demands that is attained by few other West Indians.

Barbados has a tramway and a railroad, the only ones between Porto Rico and Trinidad. True, they are modest little affairs, the tramcars being drawn by mules. Yet the latter step along so lively, the employees and most of the passengers are so courteous, and overcrowding is so sternly forbidden that one comes to like them, especially those lines which rumble along the edge of the sea in the never-failing breeze, above all in the delightfully soft air of morning or evening. It would be difficult in these modern days of indifferent labor to find more courtesy, more earnest efficiency, and stricter living up to the rules than among Bridgetown's tram-drivers and conductors, yet their highest wage is sixty-four cents a day. But for the war, the system would long since have been electrified; the new rails have already arrived. There is no real reason, except civic pride, however, that the mule-cars should be abolished. They are more reliable than many an electric-line in larger cities; they are a pleasant change to the speed-weary traveler; and the perfection with which their extra mule is hitched on at the bottom of the one hill in town and unhitched again at its summit without the loss of a single trot is a never-ending source of amusement.

Sojourners in Barbados are certain to make the acquaintance of at least the long tram-line to St. Lawrence. There are plenty of hotels in the town proper, but they are habitually crowded with gentlemen of color. White visitors dwell out Hastings way, some two miles from Trafalgar Square. Unlike the French and Spanish towns of tropical America, the downtown section of the Barbadian capital is almost wholly given over to business — and negroes. The numerous white inhabitants and most of the darker ones of any standing dwell in the outskirts. There one may find parks shaded by mahogany and palm-trees, splendid avenues lined by one or both of these species, comfortable residences ranging all the way from tiny "villas" draped with an ivy-like vine or gorgeous masses of the bougainvillea to luxurious estates in their own private parks. Even the poorer classes in another stratum still farther from the center of town dwell in neat little toy-houses of real comfort, compared with the huts of the masses of Haiti or Porto Rico. For miles along the sea beside this longest tram-line one passes a constant succession of comfortable, light-colored houses with boxed verandas, wooden shutters that raise from the bottom, and a sort of cap visor over the windows. In many cases these boast tropically unnecessary panes of glass through which one can make out of an evening interiors of perfect neatness, homelike, well lighted, furnished and decorated in taste, with none of the gaudy and crowded bric-a-brac to be seen behind Spanish *rejas* in the larger islands.

The night life of Bridgetown is worth a ride behind the now weary mules, if only to see a negro urchin diligently striving to light a candle in a tin box on the end of his soap-box cart, lest he be hauled up for violation of the ordinance forbidding vehicles to circulate after dark without lamps. Promptly at sunset the black policemen have changed their white helmets and jackets for German looking caps and capes. On the way downtown one passes half a dozen wide-open churches and chapels in which black preachers are vociferously exhorting their nightly congregations to "walk in de way of de Lard"; one is certain to rumble past the shrieking hubbub of a Salvation Army meeting or two. There are crowds of loafers on many a corner — jolly, in-offensive, black idlers with the spirit of rollicking fun in their ebony faces, bursting into howls of laughter at the slightest incident that seems comical to their primitive minds. The filthy street-habits of the French and Spanish islands are little in evidence, for the police of Barbados are as vigilant as they are heavy-handed.

Downtown the activities of the day have departed. The larger stores have closed at four, the small shops at sundown. Only a scattered score of negro women squat in Trafalgar Square before their little trays of peanuts, bananas, and home-made sweets, a wick torch burning on a corner of them whether they are deposited on the ground or are seeking lack of competition elsewhere on top of their owners' heads. There is no theater in Bridgetown; the cinema is as sad a parody on amusement as it is everywhere, but the audience is worth seeing, once. The negroes sit in the " pit," the élite, chiefly yellow of tint, in a kind of church gallery. Shouts, screams, roof-raising roars of primitive laughter, deafening applause whenever the frock-coated villain is undone, mark the unwinding of the film from beginning to end; it is a scene far different from the comparative dignity of a black French audience. In the French and Spanish West Indies the cinemas begin after nine and end around midnight; in Barbados they start sharply at seven and terminate at ten with a rush for the last mule-cars, with all but the swift out of luck, and Bridgetown settles down to deathly Sunday stillness while the weary mules are still crawl-ing toward the end of their laborious day.

Or, if the visitor does not care to break up his evening by descend-ing into town, there are few more ideal spots in which to hear a band concert than the little park known as Hastings Rocks, on the very edge of the sea, especially under a full moon. I am an inveterate concert-goer; one naturally becomes so in tropical America, where other music is so rare, and I must confess a preference for the Spanish-American type of concert over the Anglo-Saxon, for the gay throngs of promenaders about the sometimes not too successful attempts to render a classical program over the staid gatherings that listen mo-tionless to an uproar of " popular " music. But even this serves to while away an evening and seldom fails to offer a touch of local color. Thus in negro-teeming Barbados there is scarcely a suggestion of African parentage to be seen at this stately entertainment on Hastings Rocks. It is partly the sixpence admission that keeps the negroes outside, but not entirely. Struck by the fact that there was only one mulatto boy and two light-yellow girls, all very staid and quiet, on the seaside benches, I sought information of the negro gate-keeper. Yes, indeed, he refused admittance to most of those of his own color, and to some white people, too.

" You see," he explained, " it is like this. Perhaps last night you might go with a girl downtown, and then you come here to-night with your wife; and if that girl allowed to come in here she might want to get familiar and gossip with you. Or she might giggle at you. We can't have *that*," he added, in a tone that reminded one that the Briton, even when his skin is black, is first cousin to Mrs. Grundy. The English sense of dignified orderliness and the negro's natural gaiety, his tendency to " giggle " at inopportune moments, do not mix well, and the Hasting Rocks concert is one of those places where African hilarity must be ruthlessly suppressed.

Besides Bridgetown, with its 35,000 or more inhabitants, Barbados has a number of what might best be called large collections of houses, such as Speightstown, Holetown — popularly known as " the Hole "— and the like, but its population, surpassed in density, if at all, only by China, a density compared to which that of Porto Rico seems slight indeed, is spread so evenly over all the island that it is hard to tell where a town begins or ends. The island is one of the most remarkable instances of coral formation. Comparatively flat, when likened to most of the West Indies, it consists of a number of stages or platforms that have been built one after the other as the island rose slowly and gradually from the sea to a height, at one point, of nearly 1200 feet. When first discovered it was surrounded by mangrove swamps and tangled, rotting vegetation, but all this has since turned to solid ground. The coral of which it is built contains some ninety per cent. of lime, so that almost the whole island might be reduced to powder in a lime-kiln. The rest of it consists of a species of sandstone known as " Scotland rock," which comes to the surface in the northwestern part of the island.

Thanks to its geological formation, the close network of roads which reaches every corner of Barbados, as well as all its bare open spaces, are glaringly white and hard on the eyes, especially, if one may judge by the prevalence of glasses among them, those of the white and " high yellow " inhabitants. Yet, for the same reason, it is perhaps the most healthful of the West Indies. It has no swamps to breed malaria; the trade winds from the open ocean sweep incessantly across it. Once it was troubled with typhoid, but the establishment of a single unpolluted water supply for the whole island has done away with this danger. There is great equability of temperature day or night the year round. The wet season, from June to October, is less so than in most tropical lands; though visitors and European inhabitants complain of the midday heat, except in December and January, it is always cool compared to midsummer in the United States. Fresh, dry, and constantly laden with ocean ozone, it is a climate that makes little demand upon the strength and vital powers. All indications point to the fact, however, that it is no place for white women as permanent residents, for virtually without exception they grow scrawny, nervous, and weak-eyed, their pasty complexions sprayed with freckles under their veils.

All roads lead to Bridgetown, but to follow them in the opposite direction to any chosen point is not so simple a matter. Signboards are almost unknown, no doubt being considered a superfluity in so small and crowded a community. The country people, though willing enough, are often too stupid to give intelligible directions, though they make up for this by a persistency in showing one the way in person which no amount of protest can overcome. Ask a question or give them any other slightest excuse to do so, and they will cling to the white pedestrian's heels for miles in the hope of picking up a penny or a " bit," always taking their leave with, " I beg you for a cent, sir." Indeed, that is the constant refrain everywhere along the dazzling but excellent highways. Women and men shout it from the doors of their little cabins; children scamper after one, the black babies are egged on by their elders as soon as they can toddle, each shrieking the invariable demand in a tone of voice which suggests that refusal is impossible. They seem to fancy that white strangers cross the island for no other purpose than to distribute a cartload of English coppers along the way. Almost as incessant are the demands upon the kodak-carrier to " Make me photo, sir," or, " Draw me portrait, master."

On week-days the highways of Barbados are as crowded as city streets. Heavy draft horses and mules, auto-trucks large and small, are constantly descending to Bridgetown with the cumbersome hogsheads of sugar and molasses, or returning with supplies for the estates. There is an endless procession of almost toy-like carts, each drawn by a single small donkey, the two wheels habitually wobbly, the name, address, and license number of the owner in crude letters on the front of the diminutive box. The donkey is the invariable beast

The Prince of Wales lands in Barbados

The principal street of Bridgetown, decorated in honor of its royal visitor

Barbadian porters loading hogsheads of sugar always take turns riding back to the warehouse

There is an Anglican Church of this style in each of the eleven parishes of Barbados

of burden of the Barbadian of the masses. He carries to town the products of little gardens; he brings the supplies of the innumerable small shops throughout the island; the country youth takes his "girl" riding in his donkey-cart; in later years the whole ebony family packs into it for a jolt across the country. Unlike the rest of tropical America, Barbados does not ride its donkeys or use them as pack-animals; nor, to all appearances, are they abused. Centuries of British training seems to have given the black islanders a compassion rare among their neighbors. Horesmen and pack-mules are likewise unknown along the white highways; oxen are rare; pedestrians are much less numerous than one would expect in so populous a community, while bicycles are as widely in use as in England.

There is a curiously English homelikeness about the landscape, which, if it is seldom rugged, is by no means monotonous. Every acre of ground is utilized; forbidding stone-and-mud walls topped by spikes or broken glass line the roads for long distances; villages, or at least houses, are so continuous that one is almost never out of human sight or sound. Coral is so abundant and wood so expensive that immense limestone steps often lead up to tiny wooden shacks, as out of proportion to their foundations as statues to their pedestals. The majority of the rather well-kept little negro cabins, however, are simply set up on small blocks of coral at the four corners. More than one band of hilarious sailors from visiting battleships have amused themselves by removing one of these props and tumbling a Barbadian family out of their beds in the small hours of the night.

Shopkeeping might almost be called the favorite sport of the "Badeyan"; the lack of jobs enough to go round has led so many to adopt this means of winning a possible livelihood that the island has been called "Over-shopped Barbados." Everywhere wayside shanties bear the familiar black sign with white letters, varying only in name and number: "Percival Brathwaite — Licensed Seller of Liquors — No. 765." Inside, perhaps behind a counter contrived from a single precious board, are a few crude shelves stocked mainly with bottles of rum or with cheap "soft drinks," a few shillings' worth of uninviting foodstuffs flanking them. The Barbadians have long been known as the "Yankees of the West Indies." They are far more diligent merchants than most natives of tropical America, so much so that neither the Chinese, Jews, Portuguese, nor Syrians, so numerous in the other islands, can compete with them to advantage. But their knowledge of book-keeping is scanty, and it is often only the visible end of his light resources that convinces the petty shopkeeper that he is losing, rather than gaining at the popular pastime.

Every little way along the island roads other shanties bear the sign of this or that " Friendly Society." These are a species of local insurance company or mutual benefit association. The negroes pay into them from three pence to a shilling a week,— some of the poorer neighbors nothing at all,— and receive in return sickness or accident benefits, or have their funeral expenses paid in case of death. But they are typically tropical or African in their indifference to a more distant to-morrow, for at the end of each year the remaining funds are divided among those members who have not drawn out more than they paid in, and with perhaps as much as five dollars each in their pockets the society indulges in a hilarious " blow-out." Equally numerous are the signboards of " agents " of the undertakers of Bridgetown. They do not believe in waiting for the sickle of Father Time, those death-bed functionaries of the capital, but drum up trade with Barbadian energy. The island's newspaper habitually carries their enticing pleas for clients:

" OUR DEAD MUST BE BURIED," begins one of these appeals. " In the SAD HOUR why trouble yourself over the Dead when you can see E. T. ARCHER GITTENS, the up-to-date and experienced UNDERTAKER face to face? Look for the Hearse with the GOLDEN ANGEL!" There follows a "poem" of twenty-four verses setting forth the advantages of being buried by Gittens and ending with the touching appeal:

> Just take a ride to Tweedside Stable
> And you 'll see that this is no Fable.
> Phone 281 night or day
> And you 'll hear what Gittens has to say.
> He and his staff are always on hand
> To accommodate any class of man.
> " All orders will be promptly executed at MODERATE PRICES.
> A TRIAL WILL CONVINCE."

No doubt it would.

The Barbados government railway — one could not call it a railroad in so English a community — is an amusing little thing twenty years old and some two hours long, though that does not mean as much in miles as one might expect. On week-days its passenger-train sometimes makes a one-way journey, at a cost of four shillings and sixpence for first and two shillings for second-class travelers, but on Sundays it indulges in the whole round trip. From the station near the famous bridge from which the capital takes its name, the little train tears away as if excited at its own importance, through slightly rolling cane-fields, rocky white coral gullies, past frequent Dutchy windmills flailing their shadows on the ground. Vistas as broad as if it were crossing a continent instead of a tiny parcel of land flung far out into the ocean, spread on either hand, that to the right flat and almost desertlike in its aridity, the north broken in rugged low ridges, with many scattered villages and gray heaps of sugar-mills on their crests. The soil is so thin one marvels that it will grow anything, yet every acre of it shows signs of constant cultivation, the long expanses of cane broken here and there by small patches of corn, cassava, yams, and the sweet potatoes on which the mass of the population depends for nourishment. Every few minutes the train halts at a station seething with cheerful black faces; everywhere it crosses white coral roads, some of them cut deep down through the limestone ridges. Trees are almost plentiful, but they all show evidence of having been planted. The Spanish discoverers, it is said, gave the island its present name because its forests were bearded (*barbudos*) with what is known in our southern states as "Spanish moss," but this, like the original woods, has long since disappeared.

Sunday is as dead as it can only be in a British community. The cattle and mules stand in the corrals eating dry cane-tops; the square brick chimneys of the boiling-houses emit not a fleck of smoke. Only in rare cases even are the windmills allowed to work, though for some reason nature does not shut off the bracing trade-wind. This is so constant that it forces all the branches of the trees to the southwest, until even the royal palms seem to be wearing their hair on one side. Fields brown with cut cane-tops contrast with the pale green of those still unharvested; the general sun-flooded whiteness of the landscape is painful to the eyes. Here and there is a patch of blackish soil, but it has the vigorless air of having long been overworked, a looseness as of volcanic lava.

In less than an hour the Atlantic spreads out on the horizon ahead. Rusty limestone cliffs, a jagged coral coast against which the sea dashes itself as if angry at the first resistance it encounters since passing the Cape Verde Islands many hundred miles away, stretch out to the north and south. We come out to the edge of it, fifty feet above, then descend to a track so close to the surf that the right of way must be braced up with old rails. It is a dreary, barren-dry, brown-yellow coast, yet of a beauty all its own, with its chaotic jumble of huge rocks among which hundreds of negroes are bathing stark naked and spouting holes out of which the thundering surf dashes high into the air. Farther north the landscape grows almost mountainous, but we have already reached Bathsheba, where Sunday travelers habitually disembark, leaving the train to crawl on alone to a few tiny oil-wells around the next rugged promontory.

I climbed the sheer cliff a thousand feet high above Bathsheba, its face covered with brown grasses, ferns, creeping plants, and the smaller species of palm that cling to each projecting rock as if their available nourishment were as scanty and precious as that of the teeming human population. The view from the summit forever banishes the notion that Barbados is flat. All " Scotland," as the northern end of the island is called, is laid out before you, broken and pitched and jumbled until it resembles the Andes in miniature. White ribbons of roads and a network of trails are carelessly strewn away across it, hundreds of huts are scattered over its chaotic surface, and an immense building stands forth on the summit of its highest hill. Jagged, gray-black sandstone boulders of gigantic size contrast with the white limestone to give the tumbled scene the aspect of having been left unfinished by the Builder of the western hemisphere in his hurry to cross the Atlantic. Below, this scene spreads away to infinity, its scalloped, foam-lashed shore clear-cut in the dry, luminous atmosphere as far as the eye can see in either direction. Behind, the picture is tamer, though by no means level. Rolling cane-fields, with here and there a royal palm, numerous clusters of huts, and the ubiquitous chimneys and windmills of sugar-factories breaking the skyline, stretch endlessly away to the yellow-brown horizon.

I returned to Bridgetown on foot — he who still fancies the island is level and tiny should walk across it on a blazing Sunday afternoon — passing not more than a score of travelers on the way. Once I paused to chat with a group of " poor whites," as they call themselves, or what their black neighbors refer to as " poor buckras " or " red legs." These reminders of our own " crackers " are numerous in Barbados, especially in the " Scotland " district. They are descendants of the convicts or prisoners taken in the civil wars of England during the Commonwealth or the Duke of Monmouth's rebellion. Chiefly Scotch and Irish, some of them royalists of the nobility, they were sent to the island by Cromwell between 1650 and 1660 and sold to the planters for 1500 pounds of sugar a head. It is doubtful whether any of them would be worth that now. Branded and mutilated to prevent their escape, treated more brutally than the blacks by whom they are held in contempt to this day, they steadily declined in health and spirits until their present descendants, with the exception of the few who rose to be planters, are listless and poverty-stricken, degenerate victims of the hookworm and of intermarriage. The original prisoners wore kilts; hence the tropical sun soon won them the nickname of " red legs," which has persisted to this day, perhaps because their bare feet have still a distinctly ruddy tinge. But their faces are corpselike in color and their bodies thin and anemic. Of the adults in this group, not one had more than a half dozen crumbling fangs in the way of teeth.

Yet they seemed moderately well-informed and of far quicker intelligence than the sturdier blacks who so despise them. Their air of honest simplicity acquitted them of any suggestion of boasting when they asserted that the " poor whites " never steal cane and other growing crops, the theft of which by the negroes, despite heavy penalties, is one of the curses of the island. The chief topic of conversation, nevertheless, was that inevitable post-war one the world over, the high cost of food. Coffee, their principal nourishment, they took nowadays without sugar, and though it had sold at sixteen cents a pound when the war ended, it was now forty. Rice, sweet potatoes, meal, even breadfruit, " the staff of Barbados," had trebled in price. Their " spots," as they call their gardens, were constantly being robbed by the negroes. It was no use trying to keep a goat or a sheep; some black thief was sure to carry it off.

I succeeded at length in bringing up the matter of education. They sent their boys to the public schools, but it was not safe to send the girls. There were elementary schools in every parish, where each pupil paid a penny a week. The teachers were nearly all men and all were colored. In the higher public schools, which an average tuition of $72 a year put out of reach for most of them, the teachers were usually Englishmen; but the color-line was drawn only in the private schools, of which there were plenty for those who could afford them. While they talked I noted that the enmity between the two races was camouflaged under an outward friendliness; the greetings between the group of " red legs " and the black passers-by had a heartiness of tone that might easily have deceived an unenquiring observer.

One of the sights of Barbados is the large, old, gray stone Anglican church in each of the eleven parishes. Their erection was decreed way back in the days when the Earl of Carlisle, having a superior "pull" with the King of England, ousted Sir William Courteen as founder of the colony. They are as English in their sturdy bulkiness, with their heavy crenelated stone towers and the replica of an English country churchyard about each of them, despite the difficulty of digging graves in hard limestone, as the English sparrows which flock about the neighboring cane-fields. The Anglicans, having gotten in on the ground floor, have almost a monopoly in the island, though other denominations have no great difficulty in establishing their claims to endowments. The Catholics, of whom there are barely a thousand, have only one small church. Even the shouting sects seem to have less popularity among the Barbadians than in most negro communities. Religion is reputed the true bulwark of the social order in Barbados, but it is rather because the long established churches serve to maintain the class distinctions on which this is based than because they succeed in holding the negroes up to any particularly high standard of morals. Mrs. Grundy is strongly entrenched in all the British West Indies, but her influence is rather superficial among the black masses, who have a considerable amount of what other races call the "hypocrisy" of the Anglo-Saxon.

But Sunday is no time to see Barbados. I walked entirely across the island without meeting one donkey-cart, so numerous on week-days. There was scarcely a wheeled vehicle in all the long white vista of highways, except a rare bicycle and the occasional automobile of a party of American tourists. Pedestrians were as rare; the people were everywhere shut in behind their tight-closed wooden shutters, a few of them singing hymns, most of them sleeping in their air-tight cabins. The few I roused, out of mere curiosity, treated the annoyance as something bordering on the sacrilegious. Nowhere was there a group under the trees; never a picnic party; not a sign of any one enjoying life. Bridgetown itself, compared to the swarming uproar of the "prince's day," was as a graveyard to carnival time.

With the dawn of Monday, however, the island awakens again to its feverish activity, and one may easily catch an auto-truck across the floor-flat, dusty plain stretching some five miles inland from the capital and drop off on the breezy higher shelves of the island. Something of interest is sure to turn up within the next mile or two.

The Barbadian, for instance, digs his wells not to get water, but to get rid of it. They are to be found everywhere, often at the very edge of the highway and always open and unprotected. They are big round holes cut far down into the jagged coral rock, splendid places, it would seem, into which to throw something or somebody for which one has no use. This is exactly their purpose, for they are designed to carry off the floods of the rainy season. Barbados has no rivers and no lakes, or rather, these are all underground, some of them in immense caverns. In former days the mass of the population depended for its water supply on shallow, intermittent ponds, the better class on private arrangements. Now two central pumping stations and more than a hundred miles of underground pipe furnish the entire island with excellent, if luke-warm, water from the unseen rivers. Instead of the roadside shrines of the French islands, the limestone embankments of Barbadian highways have faucets at frequent intervals. Water is free to those who fetch it from these. The better class residents are everywhere supplied by private pipes at a nominal sum per house. Business places pay thirty cents per thousand gallons, which is considered so expensive that only one estate on the island is irrigated though drought is frequently disastrous in the west and south.

The stodgy windmills everywhere fanning the air are used exclusively for the grinding of cane. It is a rare patch of landscape that does not show at least half a dozen of these toiling away six days of the week. The fact that they have survived in Barbados, of all the West Indies, may be as much due to its unfailing trade wind as to the crowded conditions which make the innovation of labor-saving devices so unpopular. Methods long since abandoned elsewhere are still in vogue in Barbadian sugar-mills. The cane is passed by hand between the iron rollers in the stone windmill tower. The big hilltop yard about this is covered with drying *bagasse*, or cane pulp, which is finally heaped up about the boiling-house in which it serves as fuel. The juice runs in open troughs from the windmill to this latter building, where it is strained and left to settle until the scum rises to the surface. Then, this being skimmed off, it is boiled in open copper kettles. A negro watches each of them, dipping out the froth now and then with a huge soup-ladle and tossing the boiling liquid into the air when it shows signs of burning. Toward the end of the process the "sugar-master" is constantly trying the syrup between a finger and thumb, in order to tell when the crystals are forming and when to "strike" the contents of the kettle, which must be done at the right moment if the sugar is to be worth shipping. From beginning to end the work is done by hand, and a Barbadian sugar-mill has little resemblance, except in its pungently sweet odor, to the immense *centrals* of Cuba.

In the early days the sugarmen had much trouble in transporting their product because of the deep gullies and bad roads. Once upon a time camels were used, but though they answered the purpose splendidly, being very sure-footed and capable of carrying the price of a " red leg " each, they died for lack of a proper diet. To this day Barbadian sugar or molasses is shipped in the cumbersome 110-gallon hogsheads which were adopted in the days of camels, though the hauling is now done on mule or auto-trucks.

With an unlimited supply of cheap labor, it is natural that the Barbadian planters should cling to the old processes. Indeed, the estate owner who attempts to bring in new machinery is heartily criticized by his competitors, while the establishment of new mills is out of the question, there being already too many factories for the available acreage. The sugar planters, nine out of ten of whom are as white as the Anglo-Saxon can be after many generations of tropical residence, hold all Barados, leaving only the steeper hillsides and the less fertile patches as " spots " on which the " red legs " and the negroes plant their yams, arrowroot, sweet potatoes, and cassava. They live in luxurious old manor houses, usually on high knolls overlooking their not particularly broad acres, half-hidden in groves of mahogany-trees, which are protected by law from destruction. With few exceptions they are the descendants of English colonists, and still keep the British qualities their ancestors brought with them, keep them so tenaciously that in some ways they are more English than the modern Englishman himself. There are suggestions that they are as short-sighted as most conservatives in taking the last ounce of advantage of the crowded conditions to keep the laboring masses at ludicrously low wages. Molasses, which the Barbadians call " syrup," has advanced from seven cents to a dollar a gallon in the past few years, yet the planters are still paying about a shilling per hundred " holes " of cane, making it impossible for the hardest workers to earn more than "two and six " a day, though the prices, even of the foodstuffs grown on the island, have nearly all trebled. The pessimists foresee trouble and cite the continual presence of a battleship in Barbadian waters as proof that even the government fears it. But though they constitute only one eighth of the population and the percentage is steadily decreasing, the whites have always ruled in Barbados. As early as 1649 the slaves planned to kill them all off, and kept the secret of the conspiracy so well that it would probably have succeeded but for a servant who gave the planters warning on the eve of the attack. In 1816 there came another fierce negro rebellion, which was put down with an iron hand. Since then the blacks have been given little real voice in the government, despite their overwhelming majority, and the traveler of to-day finds Barbados the one island of the British West Indies in which the negroes are not beginning to "feel their oats."

Some attribute the patent difference between the Barbadian and other negroes of the western hemisphere to his origin in Sierra Leone, while the rest came from the Kru or the Slave Coast, but there is little historical evidence to support this contention. Still others credit his superior energy and initiative to the absence of malaria in the island. Most observers see in those qualities merely a proof that the negro develops most nearly into a creditable member of society under physical conditions which require him either to work or starve. Whoever is right, the fact remains that Barbados is one of the few places where emancipation was not disastrous, and that the Barbadians are probably, on the whole, the most pleasant mannered people in the West Indies, if not in the western hemisphere. Except for rare cases of rowdyism, they are always courteous, yet without cringing. Even those in positions bringing them into official contact with the public are, as is too often the reverse in many another country, extremely obliging, cheerful, yet never patronizing, rarely brusk, yet efficient and prompt, fairly true to their promises, for a tropical country, and have little of that aggressive insolence which is becoming so wide-spread among the negroes in our own country and the other British West Indies. The crowded condition of the country evidently makes the constant meeting of people a reason to cut down friction to the minimum, while the necessity of earning a livelihood where work is scarce leads them to be careful not to antagonize any one.

That they are amusing goes without saying. The magnificent black "bobby" in his white blouse and helmet, for instance, does not reply to your query about the next tramway with, "Goin' to Hastings? Better geta move on then," but with a mellifluous, "Ah, your destination is Hastings? Then you will be obliged to proceed very rapidly; otherwise you are in danger of being detained a half-hour until the next car departs." Yet they are not a people that grows upon one. As with all negroes, there is a shallowness back of their politeness, a something which reminds you every now and then that they have no history, no traditions, no ancient culture — such as that which is apparent, for instance, in the most ragged Hindu coolie — behind them.

Small as it is, there are many more points of interest in Barbados. There is Speightstown, for example, where whaling is still sometimes carried on; Holetown, with its monument to the first English colonists; a marvelous view of all the ragged Atlantic coast from the parish churchyard of St. John's, in which lies buried a descendant of the Greek emperors who was long its sexton; Mt. Hillaby, the highest point of the island, from which one may look down upon all the chaotic jumble of hills in St. Andrew's Parish, better known as " Scotland," or in the south the broad, parched flatlands of Christ Church, the only one of the eleven parishes not named for some saint of the Anglican calendar.   Or there is amusement, at least, among the huts tucked away into every jagged coral ravine, in noting the curious subterfuges adopted to wrest a livelihood from an overburdened and rather unwilling soil. Every acre of the island being under cultivation, there is, of course, no hunting; wild animals are unknown, except for a few monkeys in Turner's Woods.   These are rarely seen, for so human have they become in their own struggle for existence that they post a guard whenever they engage in their forays and flee at his first intimation of danger.   Negro boys earn a penny or two a day for keeping the monkeys off the cane-fields.   There being no streams or lakes, the island has no disciples of Isaac Walton, but the Barbadians are inveterate fishermen, for all that.   Time was when the little boats which are constantly pushing out to sea in water so clear that one may see every crevice of the coral bottom sixty feet below brought back more fish than the island could consume.   Then one might buy a hundred flying-fish for a penny; to-day these favorites of the Barbadian table cost as high as two pence each, while the equally familiar dolphins cost twice that a pound.   " Sea eggs," which are nothing more or less than the sea-urchin of northern waters, are a standard dish in this crowded community, for the same reason, perhaps, that the French have discovered the edible qualities of snails.

Barbados is the only foreign land ever visited by the father of our country.   In the winter of 1751–52, nearly a quarter of a century before the Revolution, Captain George Washington, then adjutant general of Virginia at one hundred and fifty pounds a year, accompanied his brother on a journey in quest of his health.   Major Lawrence

Washington of the British army, owner of Mt. Vernon, fourteen years older than George, had been suffering from consumption since he served in the expedition against Cartagena in South America. They sailed direct to Barbados, then a famous health resort, by schooner. The skipper must have been weak on navigation, for, says George's journal, " We were awakened one morning by a cry of land, when by our reckonings there should have been none within 150 leagues of us. If we had been a bit to one side or the other we would never have noticed the island and would have run on down to ——" the future father of our country does not seem to have a very clear idea just where. In fact, school-marms who have been holding up the hatchet-wielder as a model for their pupils — unless some millionaire movie hero has taken his place in the hearts of our young countrymen nowadays — will no doubt be horrified to learn that George was not only weak in geography, but even in spelling. He frequently speaks of " fields of cain," for instance, and sometimes calls his distressing means of conveyance a " scooner," or a " chooner." But let him speak for himself:

Nov. 4, 1751 — This morning received a card from Major Clark welcoming us to Barbadoes, with an invitation to breakfast and dine with him. We went — myself with some reluctance, as the small pox was in the family. Mrs. Clark was so much *indisposed* [the italics are mine] by it that we had not the pleasure of her company. Spent next few days writ⁰ letters to be carried by the Chooner Fredericksburg to Virginia.

Thursday 8th. Came Capt⁰ Crofton with his proposals which tho extravagantly dear my Brother was obliged to give. £15 pr Month is his charge exclusive of Liquors & washings which we find. In the evening we remov'd some of our things up and ourselves; it's pleasantly situated pretty near the sea and ab⁰ a mile from the Town, the prospective agreable by Land and pleasant by Sea as we command the prospect of Carlyle Bay & all the shipping in such a manner that none can go in or out with out being open to our view.

The Washingtons evidently lived near the same spot now inhabited by American tourists, any two of whom would be only too happy nowadays to pay forty-three dollars a month for board and lodging, " Liquor " or no liquor. Capt. Crofton, the rascally profiteer, must have made a small fortune out of his " paying guests," for they were always being invited out to meals at the " Beefstake & Tripe Club " or elsewhere. Church members, however, will be glad to see the next entry, despite of that unhappy break about the " Liquor ":

Sunday 11th. Dressed in order for Church but got to Town too Late. [What man ever kept his sense of time in the tropics?] Went to Evening Service.

Thursday 15th. Was treated with a play ticket to see the Tragedy of George Barnwell acted. [George, you see, was no money-strewing tourist. But then, he was not an American in those days.]

Saturday 17th. Was strongly attacked with the small Pox sent for Dr. Lanahan whose attendance was very constant till my recovery and going out which was not 'till thursday the 12th December.

December 12th. Went to Town visited Maj. Clarke (who kindly visited me in my illness and contributed all he cou'd in send'g me the necessary's required by ye disorder).

Kind of him, surely, after his other little contribution to " ye disorder " in the shape of that first invitation. The only real result of the Washingtons' trip to Barbados was that our first President was pockmarked for life, for Lawrence got no good out of the trip. George went back to Virginia and Lawrence to Bermuda, where he grew steadily worse, and finally went home to die at Mt. Vernon the following summer bequeathing the estate to his younger brother.

Washington speaks constantly in his journal of the hospitality of Barbados. That characteristic remains to this day, where it is carried to an extreme unknown in England and rarely in the United States. Of all the Lesser Antilles, one leaves Barbados, perhaps, with most regret.

CHAPTER XVI

AS his steamer drops anchor far out in the immense shallow of the Gulf of Paria, the traveler cannot but realize that at last he has come to the end of the West Indies and is encroaching upon the South American continent. The "Trinity" of fuzzy hills, to-day called the "Three Sisters," for which Columbus named the island have quite another aspect than the precipitous volcanic peaks of the Lesser Antilles. Plump, placid, their vegetation tanned a light brown by the now truly tropical sun, they have a strong family resemblance to the mountains of Venezuela hazily looming into the sky back across the Bocas. Fog, unknown among the stepping-stones to the north, hangs like wet wool over all the lowlands, along the edge of the bay. The trade wind that has never failed on the long journey south has given place to an enervating breathlessness; by seven in the morning the sun is already cruelly beating down; instead of the clear blue waters of the Caribbean, the vast expanse of harbor has the drab, lifeless color of a faded brown carpet. Sail-boats, their sails limply aslack as they await the signal to come and carry off the steamer's cargo, give the scene a half-Oriental aspect that recalls the southern coast of China.

· There is little, indeed, to excite the senses as the crowded launch plows for half an hour toward the uninviting shore. Seen from the harbor, Port of Spain, with its long straight line of wharves and warehouses, looks dismal in the extreme, especially to those who have left beautiful St. Georges of Grenada the evening before. Yet from the moment of landing one has the feeling of having gotten somewhere at last. The second in size and the most prosperous of the British West Indies may be less beautiful than the scattered toy-lands bordering the Caribbean, but a glance suffices to prove it far more progressive. Deceived by its featureless appearance from the sea, the traveler is little short of astounded to find Port of Spain an extensive city, the first real city south of Porto Rico, with a beauty of its own unsuggested from the harbor. Spread over an immense plain sloping

381

ever so slightly toward the sea, with wide, right-angled, perfect asphalt streets, electric-cars as up-to-date as those of any American city covering it in every direction, and having most of the conveniences of modern times, it bears little resemblance to the backward, if more picturesque, " capitals " of the string of tiny islands to the north.   The insignificant " Puerto de los Españoles," which the English found here when they captured the island a mere century and a quarter ago, was burned to the ground in 1808; another conflagration swept it in 1895, so that the city of to-day has a sprightly, new-built aspect, despite the comparative flimsiness of its mainly wooden buildings.   There are numerous imposing structures of brick and stone, too, along its broad streets, and many splendid residences in the suburbs stretching from the bright and ample business section to the foot of the encircling hills.

Long before he reaches these, however, the visitor is sure to be struck by the astonishing variety of types that make up the population. Unlike that of the smaller islands, the development of Trinidad came mainly after African slavery was beginning to be frowned upon, and though the negro element of its population is large, the monotony of flat noses and black skins is broken by an equal number of other racial characteristics.   Large numbers of Chinese workmen were imported in the middle of the last century; Hindu coolies, indentured for five years, were introduced in 1839, and though the Government of India has recently forbidden this species of servitude, fully one third of the inhabitants are East Indians or their more or less full-blooded descendants.   Toward the end of the eighteenth century large numbers of French refugees took up their residence in Trinidad, and the island to-day has more inhabitants of this race than any of the West Indies not under French rule.   Many of the plantation-owners are of this stock, improvident fellows, if one may believe the rumors afloat, who mortgage their estates when times are hard.   Then, instead of paying their debts when the price of sugar and cacao make them temporarily rich, they go to Europe " on a tear."   Martinique and Guadeloupe have also sent their share of laborers, and there are sections of Trinidad in which the negroes are as apt to speak French as English.   Portuguese, fleeing persecution in Madeira, added to this heterogeneous throng, while Venezuelans are constantly drifting across the Bocas to increase the helter-skelter of races that makes up the island's present population.

All this mixture may be seen in a single block of Port of Spain.

Here the stroller passes a wide-open, unfurnished room where tur-banned Hindus squat on their heels on the bare floor, some with long shovel-beards through which they run their thin, oily fingers, some in the act of getting their peculiar hair-cuts, nearly all of them smoking their curious tree-shaped pipes, all of them chattering their dialects in the rather effeminate voices of their race. On the sidewalk outside are their women, in gold nose-rings varying in size from mere buttons to hoops which flap against a cheek as they walk, silver bracelets from wrists to elbows, anklets clinking above their bare feet, the lobes of their ears loaded down with several chain-links, as well as earrings, their bare upper arms protruding from the colorful cheap shrouds in which they wrap themselves, a corner of it thrown over their bare heads. There are wide diversities of type, even of this one race. Here a group of Madrassis, several degrees blacker than the others, is stretched out on another unswept floor, there a Bengalee squats in a doorway arranging his straight black hair with a wooden comb. Mo-hammedans and Brahmins, sworn enemies throughout the island as at home, pass each other without a sign of recognition. Men of different castes mingle but slightly, despite the broadening influence of foreign travel; they have one and all lost caste by crossing the sea, but all in equal proportion, so that their relative standing remains the same. The influence of their new environment has affected them in varying degrees. Two men alike enough in features to be brothers, the one in an elaborate turban, loose silky blouse, and a flowing white mass of cloth hitched together between his legs in lieu of trousers, the other in a khaki suit and a Wild West felt hat, stand talking together in Hindustanee. Women in nose-rings, bracelets, and massive silver necklaces weighing several pounds are sometimes garbed in hat, shirt-waist, and skirt, some-times even in low shoes with silver anklets above them.

Next door to these groups, or alternating between them, is a family of the same slovenly, thick-tongued, jolly negroes who overrun all the West Indies. The difference in color between these and the Hindus, even the swarthy Madrassis, is striking; the one is done in charcoal, the other in oil colors. As great is the contrast between the coarse features of the Africans and those of the East Indians, so finely modeled that they might be taken for Caucasians, except for their mahogany complexions. Even in manners the two races are widely separated. While the negro is forward, fawningly aggressive, occasionally insolent, the Hindus have a detached air which causes them never to intrude upon the passer-by, even to the extent of a glance. They might be blind in so far as any evidence of attention to the other races about them goes. Abutting the negro residence is perhaps a two-story house with a long perpendicular signboard in Chinese characters, a shop below, a residence above, with many curious Celestial touches. Then comes a building placarded in Spanish, " Venezuelans very welcome," where not a word of English is spoken by the whole swarming family. On down the street stretch all manner of queer mixtures of customs, costumes, races, language, and names. Sing How Can keeps a provision shop next to Diogenes Brathwaite's " Rum Parlor," flanked on the other side by Rahman Singh, the barber, who in his turn is shut in by the leather sandal factory of Pedro Vialva. Women in the striking costume of the French islands stroll past with a graceful, dignified carriage; a man in a red fez pauses to talk to a man with a veritable clothshop wound about his head. Negro Beau Brummels speaking a laboriously learned English with an amusing accent, stately black policemen in spotless white jackets and helmets and those enormous shoes, shining like the proverbial " nigger's heel," worn by all British negroes in uniform, solemnly swinging their swagger-sticks with what suggests the wisdom of the ages until a chance question discloses how stupid they are under their impressive and patronizingly polite manner; now and then a disgruntled Venezuelan general whom Castro or Gomez has forced to seek an asylum under the Union Jack; a pair of sallow shop-keepers sputtering their nasal Portuguese — all mingle together in the passing throng. Then there are intermixtures of all these divergent elements, mainly of the younger generation — a negro boy with almond eyes, a youth who looks like a Hindu and a Chinaman, but is really neither, a flock of children with unusually coarse East Indian features and woolly hair playing about a one-room shop-residence the walls of which are papered negro-fashion with clippings from illustrated newspapers; farther on a Portuguese rum-seller with a mulatto baby on his knee; a few types who look like conglomerations of all the other races, until their family trees must sound like cocktail recipes. Both the Chinese and the Hindu residents of Trinidad are thrifty; many of them are well-to-do, for the former have indefatigable diligence in their favor, and the latter, who neither gamble nor steal, have no very serious faults, except the tendency to carve up their unfaithful wives. But there are failures among both races, even in this virgin island. Outcasts who were once Hindu or Chinese, sunk now to indescribable filth and raggedness, slink about with an eye open for a stray crust or cigarette butt. Under the *saman* trees in Marine Square East Indian

The turn-out of most Barbadians

Two Hindus of Trinidad

A Barbadian windmill

derelicts dressed in nothing but a clout, a ragged jacket sometimes dropped in a vermin-infested heap beside them, are sleeping soundly on the stone pavement upon which white men, sipping their cocktails in the Union Club, look down as placidly as if they were gazing out the windows along Piccadilly.

Modern street-cars carry this racial hash, or as much of it as can afford to ride, about the well-paved city and its shady suburbs. Single car-tickets cost six cents, but a strip of six may be had for a shilling. So many citizens are unable to invest this latter sum all at once, however, that numerous shopkeepers add to their profits by selling the strip tickets at five cents each. Port of Spain has perhaps the finest pair of lungs of any city of its size in the world. Beyond the business section is an immense savanna, smooth as a billiard-table — magnificent, indeed, it seems to the traveler who has seen no really level open ground for weeks — called Queen's Park. Here graze large herds of cattle, half Oriental, too, like the people. There is ample playground left, too, for all the city's population. In the afternoon, particularly of a Saturday, it presents a vast expanse of pastimes seldom seen in the tropics. The warning cry of " Fore! " frequently startles the mere stroller, only to have his changed course bring him into a cluster of schoolboys shrilly cheering the prowess of their respective teams. The game which outdoes all others in popularity is that to the American incredibly stupid one of cricket, which rages — or should one say languishes? — on every hand, notwithstanding the fact that Trinidad is within ten degrees of the equator. Nor is it monopolized by the better classes, for every group of ragged urchins who can scrape together enough to get balls, wickets, and that canoe-paddle the English call a " bat " takes turns in loping back and forth across the grass, to what end the scorer knows. If there is a color-line on the savanna, it is between the few pure whites, many of them Englishmen who have " come out " within the present century and brought all the unconscious snobbishness of their own island with them, and the *olla podrida* of all the other races. Among the latter the lines are social, rather than racial, so that Hindu-mulatto-Chinese youths, leaning on their canes, gaze with scornful indifference upon other youths of similar labyrinthian parentage whom chance has not raised to the dignity of annexing collars to their shirts. But there is room enough for all on the immense savanna.

Here and there it is dotted with huge, spreading trees, which grow more thickly in the residential section surrounding it. The original inhabitants called the island " Iēre," or " Caīri," meaning the " land of humming-birds." It is still.that, but it is also the land of magnificent trees and the land of asphalt. One may doubt whether any fragment of the globe has so high a percentage of perfect streets and roads — no wonder, surely, when it may have its asphalt in unlimited quantities for the mere digging — and the giants of the forest which everywhere spread their canopies give its rather placid landscape a beauty which makes up for its lack of ruggedness. Behind Queen's Park is a delightfully informal botanical garden in the middle of which sits the massive stone residence of the governor. Several times a week a band concert is given on his front lawn, a formality bearing slight resemblance to the Sunday-night gathering in a Spanish-American plaza. It takes place in the afternoon and is attended only by the élite, though this does not by any means confine it to Caucasian residents, for there are many others, at least of the island-born Chinese and Hindus and their intermixtures, who count themselves in this category, while negro and East Indian nursemaids are constantly pursuing their overdressed charges across the noiseless greensward. Any evidence of human interest is sternly suppressed in the staid and orderly gathering. They sit like automatons on their scattered chairs and benches, no one ever committing the faux pas of speaking above a whisper. Woe betide the mere American who dares address himself to a stranger, for British snobbery reaches its zenith in Trinidad, and the open-handed hospitality of Barbados is painfully conspicuous by its absence.

Trim lawns bordered with roses, hibiscus, poinsettia, variegated crotons, and a host of other brilliant-foliaged plants surround the homelike, though sometimes overdecorated, residences of the generously shaded suburbs. Over the verandas hang mantles of pink coronella, violet thumbergia, red bougainvillea, often interlacing, always a mass of bloom, at least in this summer month of April. Maidenhair ferns line the steps leading to the portico, rare orchids cling to the mammoth branches of the spreading trees, the air is sweetly fragrant with the odors of cape jasmine and the persistent patchouli. With sunset cigales, tree-toads, and a host of tropical insects begin to chirrup their nightly chorus — an improvement on the flocks of crowing roosters that make the whole night hideous in the town itself, not only in Port of Spain, but throughout the West Indies.

A magistrate's court is an amusing scene in any of the Antilles; it is doubly so in the racial whirlpool of Trinidad. An English " leftenant," assigned the task of prosecuting for the crown, but who never once opened his mouth, was the only white man present on the morning I visited this farcical melodrama. A mulatto magistrate whose offensive pride of position stuck out on him like a sore thumb held the center of the spotlight. Never did he let pass an opportunity to inflict the crudest of witticisms, the most stupid of sarcasm on prisoners and witnesses alike. In the language of English courts he was known as " Your Worship," a title by which even white men are frequently compelled to address those of his class in the British West Indies, where the law knows no color-line. A group of colored reporters sat below him in the customary railed enclosure, jotting down his every burst of alleged wit for the delectation of their next morning's readers, who would be regaled with such extraordinary moral truths as " His Worship told the defendant that instead of living off his mother and sister he should go and do some honest work to support them and himself," or " His Worship remarked that the witness seemed to be afflicted with a clogging of his usually no doubt brilliant mental processes." Beyond the rail was packed the black audience that is never lacking at these popular entertainments in the British West Indies.

The prisoners and the two pedestal-shod black policemen on either side of them, stood stiffly at attention just outside the rail during all the trial. Witnesses assumed a similar posture in a kind of pulpit, took the oath by kissing a dirty dog-eared Bible — even though they were Hindus or Chinese — and submitted themselves to " His Worship's " caustic sarcasm. The mere fact that the majority of them were patently and clumsily lying from beginning to end of their testimony did not appear to arouse a flicker of surprise in the minds of magistrate, the lawyers of like color, or the open-mouthed audience. The testimony in each case was laboriously written down in longhand by a dashingly attired mulatto clerk, though evidently not word for word, for these fell too fast and furiously to be caught in full. The accused was always given permission to cross-examine the witnesses, with the result that a vociferous quarrel frequently enlivened the proceedings. The majority of cases were petty in the extreme, matters which in most countries would have been settled out of court with a slap or a swift kick. But nothing so pleases the British West Indian, at least of the masses, as a chance to appear in the conspicuous rôle of plaintiff, or even as witness. One black fellow had charged another with calling his wife a " cat." " His Worship " found the case a source of unlimited platitudes before he dismissed it by adding five shillings to the crown's resources. A fat negress accused a long and scrawny one of offering to " box me face," and as British West Indian law takes account of threats, the lanky defendant was separated from her week's earnings, though she scored high with the audience by proving that the accuser had also used threatening language, thereby subjecting her to a similar financial disaster.

Corporal punishment is still in vogue in the British Antilles. Two negro boys had been playing marbles, when one struck the other with a stick. " His Worship " ordered the defendant to receive ten strokes with a tamarind rod, to be administered by a member of the police force. The order was immediately executed in a back room to which casual spectators were not admitted. To judge from the shrieks that arose from it, the punishment was genuine, but they were probably designed to reach the magistrate's ear, for when I put an inquiry to the big black chastiser some time later, he replied with a grin, " Oh, not too hard ; perhaps a tingle or two at the end jes' to make him remember." Even adults are not always spared bodily reminders. A vicious look-ing negro with a hint of Chinese ancestry who was convicted for the fourth time of thieving was sentenced to one year at hard labor and six lashes with the " cat." But as this punishment was inflicted at the general prison, there was no means of learning how thoroughly the implement was wielded.

Though a Chinese and a Hindu interpreter were present, all the wit-nesses, happening to be youthful and evidently born in the colony, spoke perfect English — as it is spoken in Trinidad. It was somehow incon-gruous to hear a Hindu woman in her silken shroud and a small cart-load of jewelry burst forth, as soon as she had kissed the unsavory Bible with apparent fervor, in the negro-British dialect and contradict the assertions of the accused with some such rejoinder as " Whatyer tahlk, mahn, whatcher tahlk? " Those surprises are constantly being sprung on the visitor to Trinidad, however, for notwithstanding the composite of races and the fact that English was not introduced into the island until 1815, it is decidedly the prevailing language. It is a common experience to hear a group that is chattering in Hindustanee suddenly change to British slang, or to turn and find that the discussion of the latest cricket match in the broad-vowelled jargon of the British West Indian negro is between a Chinese and a Hindu youth, both dressed in the latest European fashion. Natives of the islands assert that " the English of a typical Trinidadian is probably as strongly in contrast to that of a typical Barbadian as the language of any two parts of the British Empire." But to the casual visitor they sound much alike, and far removed from our own tongue. We might readily understand the expression " I well glad de young mahn acquit," but few of us would recognize that " Don't let he break me, sir," means " Do not give him a job after refusing it to me." An incensed motorman cried out to a Chinese-Hindu negro hackman who was impeding his progress, " Why y'u don' go home wid dis cyart ef y'u can' drive et ? " to which came the placid reply, " Why you vex, mahn ? Every victoria follow he own wheels." As in the French islands, a banana is called a " fig " in Trinidad, while walls are everywhere decorated with the warning " Stick no Bills."

Speaking of bills of another sort, those of the smaller denominations are badly needed in the British islands. With the exception of Jamaica, they reckon their money in dollars and cents, but they are West Indian dollars, worth four shillings and two pence each and following the English pound in its rise or fall. Notes of five dollars are issued by the Colonial Bank and the Royal Bank of Canada, but with the exception of Trinidad and its dependency, Tobago, the government of which issues one- and two-dollar bills, there is no local small change, and the already overburdened visitor to these tropical climes must load himself down with a double handful of English silver and mammoth coppers each time he breaks a five-dollar bill. To add to his struggles with the clumsy British monetary system, prices are given in cents, when there are no cents. Small articles in the shops are tagged 24c, 48c, 72c, and so on, never 25c, 50c, or 75c, which is easy enough, for those are the local terms for one, two, or three shillings. But it is not so simple for the heated and hurried stranger to calculate that the euphonism " thirty-nine cents " means a shilling, a sixpence, a penny, and a " ha'-penny," and to find the real significance of a demand for $5.35 requires either a pencil and paper or long practice in mental arithmetic. Perhaps the least fatiguing method is to spread on the counter the whole contents of one bulging pocket and trust to the clerk's honesty — except that he, too, even if he is trustworthy, is apt to be weak in mental arithmetic. The fall in the value of the pound sterling following the war forced the Trinidad government to enact a new ordinance forbidding " the melting down of silver coins current in the colony, the keeping possession of more silver than is needed for current expenses, or the buying or offering to buy silver coins at more than their face value." The drop in exchange had given the metal more worth than the coins themselves, and the Hindu custom of turning the family wealth into bracelets and anklets for the women was threatening to make small financial transactions impossible.

Marital felicity is by no means universal in Trinidad, if one may judge from the columns of warnings to the public in its newspapers. In a single issue may be found a score of insertions testifying to this impression and to the mixture of races:

The Public is hereby notified that I will not be responsible for any debt or debts contracted by my wife, Daisy Benjamin, she having left my house and protection.

> IZAKIAH BENJAMIN,
> Petit Valley, Diego Martin.

The Public is hereby notified that I will not hold myself responsible for any debts contracted by my wife Eparaih, she being no longer under my protection and care.

> His
> RAMDOW X
> Mark
> Bejucal, Caroni.

Witness to Mark: SANTIAGO WILSON.

The Public is hereby notified that I will no longer be responsible for the debts of my wife, Yew Chin, she having left my house and protection without any just cause.

> LEE WO SING,
> Rock River Road, Penal.

Occasionally the other side of the house is heard from:

The Public are hereby warned that the undersigned will not be responsible for any debts contracted by my husband, Emmanuel Paul, as we are no longer associated as husband and wife.

> MARGARET PAUL,
> Lance Noir, Toco.

The Spanish influence may be seen in the custom of doctors and dentists advertising " Lady in Attendance," to add reassurance to their female clientele.

The Government of Trinidad runs an excellent railway and coast steamer service. The cars are of three classes, with cross-seats, as in Europe, though with a few compartment partitions. Shades resembling cap-visors project over the windows, and the trains are as clean and orderly as those of Porto Rico. First class is small and exclusive, occupying only one third of a coach, and the rare traveler in it is apt

to be taken for an important government official and saluted by all
railway employees and stared at with envy and astonishment by the
"garden" variety of voyagers.   Even the few white citizens usually
travel second-class, though this is by no means free from African and
Asiatic mixtures.   The bulk of the train is made up of third-class
coaches, their hard wooden benches crowded with every possible combination of negro, Hindu, Chinese, Venezuelan, Portuguese, and French
blood, with an occasional poor white, and presents a truly cosmopolitan
conglomeration of garb and tongue.   Employees are as varied in origin.
A big-bearded "collector," or station-agent, with Hindu features which
seem strangely out of place under his placarded cap, rebukes a Chinese-
Hindu passenger in the amusing "English" of the West Indies, then
slaps a jet black "head guard" on the back with a "How goes?" and
gets the reply, "Oh, getting on poc' á poc'." In addition to these
vigilant ticket-seekers, there are inspectors whose official caps read
"Head Examiner," a title which more than one stranger has miscon-
strued.

Trains are frequent.   They are drawn by large oil-burning Montreal
engines with white "drivers" and set forth from Port of Spain, like
our own fliers, over a roadbed in excellent condition for the first
twenty miles or more.   Beyond that, as the line breaks up into its
several branches, the engines get smaller and smaller; the engineers
become mulattoes, then blacks, with only a tropical sense of the value of
time; the tracks are more and more congested with train-loads of cane
in the cutting season, with the result that a well-arranged time-table
is often disrupted.   Swampy stretches of mangroves to the right and
left flank the first few miles.   Groups of prisoners, in yellow, white, or
orange-colored caps, according to whether they are misdemeanants,
felons, or "long-timers," are turning some of these into solid ground.
Cocoanut plantations soon supersede the swamps, to be in turn replaced
by cane, as flat lands spread farther and farther away on the left
to the base of high hills or low mountains rather arid in appearance,
despite the density of their brush and forest, red trails here and there
climbing their wooded flanks.

Ten minutes out the considerable town of San Juan imposes the first
halt, its platform seething with a multi-colored throng struggling with
every manner of queer luggage.   A few miles farther on, at the base
of El Tucuche, the highest peak of Trinidad, is the old Spanish capital
of the island, San José de Oruña, now called St. Joseph.   Unlike the
British, the conquistadores preferred to build their principal towns

some miles back from the sea. It did them little good in this case, however, for St. Joseph was burned to the ground by that prince of buccaneers, Sir Walter Raleigh, and here the Spanish governor, Chacón, surrendered the island to a superior British force in 1797 without a fight, which may be one of the reasons why a street of the old capital is named for him. St. Joseph lies a bit up hill from the station, with a magnificent view of the vast Caroni plain, a floor-flat *vega* dense with vegetation, dotted with villages, and here and there the stacks of sugar-mills, called *usines* in Trinidad. Scattered, somewhat hilly, with the languid, capacious air of a village, the old capital is interesting to-day for its flora and its historical reminiscences. Veritable grand-fathers of trees, with long beards, their immense branches thickly grown with orchids and other flowering parasites, shade it at every hour of the day. Humming-birds flit in and out among its masses of red and purple bougainvillea. The trade wind, which seldom reaches Port of Spain, sweeps down through a break in the brownish-green hills which hem the former capital in; if it is uncomfortably hot at noonday, it is because all Trinidad is aware of its proximity to the equator. Of Spanish ruins it has none, but there are numerous Vene-zuelan inhabitants, and the Castilian tongue and customs have to some extent survived. Here, too, are strange interminglings of races and tongues — "El Toro Store" on Piccadilly Street; a rum-shop called "The Trinidadians' Delight" on Buena Vista Street. In its dry and stony cemetery are monuments with Chinese, Spanish, Hindu, French and English names, some of the last all too evidently those of negroes.

The newspapers of Trinidad announced a "Big Field Day and Race meeting" at Tunapuna, a few miles beyond St. Joseph, on Easter Monday. Having lived through five British holidays in the brief ten days since our landing in Barbados, we ventured to hope that here might be something less deadly dull. Had we paused to reflect, we should have known that white people did not attend these popular festivities. The horror on the face of an English native to whom we mentioned our destination might have given us the same information, had we not taken it to be an expression of pain at being addressed without a formal introduction.

Tunapuna is as Hindu as St. Joseph is Spanish. The domes, or, more exactly, spheres of a white Brahmin temple bulk high above its low houses. These are little mud-plastered houses, for the most part, with dents poked in their walls before they have dried, by way of decoration, which seem to be direct importations from India. The broad asphalt highway bisecting the town was as seething a stream of humanity as the Great Trunk Road. Hindus in their anklets and toe-rings, their clanking bracelets and light-colored flowing garments, made up the bulk of the throng, with here and there a Venezuelan driving a pack-laden donkey to give contrast to the picture. If the place had a European section, it eluded our attention; it looked like a village of India in which a few African settlers had taken up their residence.

The "field day" was held on a broad level space in the center of town. Constant streams of vari-colored Trinidadians, all clad in their most gasp-provoking holiday attire, poured into it from special trains that arrived in close succession. A bandstand covered with palm-leaves had been erected for the higher social orders, but even this was no place for a white spectator who did not care to arouse conspicuous attention. There were perhaps half a dozen white men, all British soldiers, scattered through the hilarious throng, but not a woman of her own race to keep Rachel in countenance. Of near-whites there was no scarcity, all of them affecting the haughty English manner in the vain hope of concealing the African in their family wood-pile. Some of the mixtures of race, language, and custom were incredible. Next to us sat a woman who appeared to be half Hindu and half English, who spoke Spanish, and who carried a quadroon baby with straw-colored hair and almond-shaped blue eyes. We awarded her the palm for human conglomeration, but there were many more who could have run her a close race.

The contests consisted mainly of bicycle races, an uproarious hubbub invariably breaking out among the motley judges and officials after each of them, causing great delay before the shotgun which served as starting pistol set the stage for a new controversy. In view of the fact that the contestants were vari-colored youths who probably lived in unpainted shanties and wore shoes only on Sundays, the tableful of prizes beside us was amusing. Among them we noted a gold-plated jewel-box, a cut-glass fruit-dish, an ice-cream freezer, a gold-scrolled liqueur set, a hatstand of gilt-tipped ox-horns, two manicure sets, a pair of marble horses, and several overdecorated small clocks. One of the many dandies who were continually displaying their graces to the feminine portion of the stand, under the pretense of finding the open space before it more comfortable than the chairs, protested that the prizes " lacked show." Up to that moment that had seemed to us the one thing they did not lack. This particular individual, a mulatto with a touch of Chinese, wore a tweed coat and white flannel trousers, an artificial daisy in his buttonhole, a brown necktie embroidered at the top with flowers and at the bottom with the word " Peace " in large letters, and carried a riding-crop. Those of his companions who were not armed with this latter sign of field-officer rank all bore canes. One of them flaunted a cravat decorated with the flags of all the Allies. The majority frequently removed their hats, regardless of the blazing sunshine, quite evidently for the purpose of showing that their hair was not curly, an improvement for which several quite evidently had to thank " Mme. Walker's Peerless Remedies." An inattentive spectator might have concluded from the wagers shouted back and forth among them at the beginning of each race that they were persons of unlimited wealth, but it was noticeable that very little money actually changed hands. Here, too, the lines of demarcation were social, rather than racial. A Hindu youth dressed in the latest imitation of London fashion might call across the compound to his equally ornate Chinese friend, " Heh, Lee! Come down, mahn! " but he gave no sign of seeing the East Indian in khaki and a battered felt hat who sold peanuts in tiny measures cleverly arranged so that most of the nuts stuck to the bottom when they were upturned in the purchaser's hand.

Beyond Tunapuna next day other Hindus in the loose garb of their homeland were clawing about the rice blades in their little paddy-fields, cut up into small squares by low dikes. Wattled huts, with East Indians squatted on their heels in the bare, hard-trodden spaces before them, intermingled with wooden shanties, sometimes with lace curtains at the glassless windows, shanties fairly bursting with their swarming negro families. Tall, slender flagpoles from which flew little red flags, some of them already bleached white, showed where goats had been sacrificed in the frequent ceremonies of the Brahmin inhabitants. Little white Hindu temples alternated with small negro churches. Through Tacarigua, with its clusters of buildings flung far up the red-scarred hillsides, Arouca, Dabadie, the procession of huts and cabins continued. Almost without exception they were unpainted and unadorned with anything but the barest necessities, for Trinidad, too, labors under the discouraging " improvement tax."

Arima, the last settlement of the aborigines before they disappeared from the island as a race, spreads over a slightly elevated plateau, its wide streets and well separated houses giving an impression of unlimited elbow-room, its huge trees and flowery shrubbery making up for its dry-goods-box style of architecture. Here is Trinidad's chief race-track, enclosing a grassy playground that almost rivals Port of Spain's savanna, but the incessant staring of the inhabitants suggests that white men are ordinarily rare sights in this important cacao center, as they are in many sections of the island.

Beyond Arima the hills die out and for miles the track is walled by uncultivated brush or virgin forests, with only a rare frontier-like village and a few young cacao plantations sheltered from the sun by the *bois immortel,* or what Spaniards call *madre del cacao*. Hindus are more numerous in this region than negroes. The railway ends at the thriving town of Sangre Grande, though it hopes soon to push on to the east coast. Chinese merchants and the resultant half-breeds are unusually numerous; Hindu women in full metallic regalia, sitting in buggies like farmers' wives in our western prairie towns, some of them smoking little Irish-looking clay pipes, and silversmiths of the same race, naked but for a clout, plying their trade in back alleys, are among the sights of the place.

The Ford mail-and-passenger bus in which I continued my journey was driven by a youth, whose grandparents were respectively Chinese, Hindu, negro, and white. The first had given him an emotionless countenance and a strict attention to business, the second a slender, almost girlish form and a silky complexion, the third wavy hair and an explosive laughter, and the last frequent attacks of that haughty surliness so common to mulattoes or quadroons. Among the passengers was a Hindu girl of striking beauty. She spoke excellent English with a strong West Indian accent, was tastefully and specklessly dressed in a Caucasian waist, black silk skirt, and kid shoes, wore her silky black hair done up in European fashion, and had the manners of an English débutante of the sheltered class. Yet in her nose she wore two gold rings, her arms gleamed with silver bracelets from wrists to elbows, about her neck was a string of heavy gold coins, and a flowered silk wrap was flung about her shoulders and head. Beside her sat a youth of the same race, completely Europeanized in garb and manner. In front, separated from this pair by one of the slow-witted, scornful negroes who filled most of the two seats, was an East Indian in full white Hindu regalia, — a simple, faintly purple turban, white caste marks across his forehead and in front of his ears, and a string of black, seed-like beads about his neck. Not once during the journey did he give a sign of recognition to his Anglicized compatriots.

We snorted away along an asphalt highway bordered by large cacao estates, passing many automobiles, some of them driven by Chinese and

Hindus, even through a great forest with many immense trees, their branches laden with orchids and climbing vines. Except for one low ridge the country was flat, with not even a suggestion of the rugged scenery of most West Indian islands. Long hedges of hibiscus in full red bloom lined the way through the considerable town of Matura, where negroes far outranked the Hindus in numbers and Chinamen kept virtually all the shops. Soon the landscape turned to cocoanut plantations, the now narrow road mounted somewhat, and the Atlantic spread out before us. But it was shallow and yellowish, not at all like the sea-lashed east coasts of Barbados or Dominica, the shores of its many bays and indentations low and heavily wooded, a hazy clump of hills stretching far away into the south. Then came a cluster of ridges and mounds of earth covered with primeval forest, only little patches of which had been cleared to give place to the most primitive, weather-beaten thatched huts. These were scattered at long intervals along the way and all inhabited by negroes, the other races evidently finding the region too undeveloped for their more civilized taste. Nineteen miles from Sangre Grande the bus halted at a cluster of hovels on Balandra Bay, the road, which pushes on to the northeast point of the island, being impassable for vehicles.

From that point one may see the important island of Tobago, the chief of Trinidad's dependencies and the most recent of England's possessions in the West Indies. It is reputed to have been the most fiercely contested bit of ground in the western hemisphere, having been constantly disputed by the French, Spanish, and English, until it finally fell to the latter in 1803. To this day it is surrounded by the ruins of old forts. French names still survive in its capital, Scarborough, and the splendid system of roads it once boasted have been allowed to go back to bush under British rule. In 1889 it was annexed to Trinidad, though it retains its own elective financial board. Like many of the British West Indies, Tobago has seen the insolence and aggressiveness of its negroes greatly increased by the example of those who were debauched in France, and was forced to suppress one riot with considerable bloodshed. The island may be reached weekly by government steamer from Port of Spain.

At St. Joseph the more important branch of the railway turns south and, sending an offshoot through a fertile cacao district and the oil regions about Tabaquite to Rio Claro, follows the coast of the Gulf of Paria to the edge of the southern chain of hills. A so-called express train connects the capital with the metropolis of the south once a week, but on account of the English "staff system" in vogue, its speed is frequently checked and sophisticated passengers get on or off as it slows up at each station to exchange the iron hoop which is the engineer's passport for the ensuing section. Broad, flat *vegas* spread on either hand beyond the old Spanish capital, the northern range of hills withdrawing to the edge of the horizon. Great pastures with huge spreading trees, some of them gay with blossoms, and thick clumps of bamboo alternate with extensive cane-fields, most of them covered with the young shoots after the recent cutting in this April season. Here and there stands a large *usine*, or sugar-mill, with long rows of coolie dwellings, some housing a dozen families side by side, while outside the estate are crowded together the tin-roofed shacks of the negro and Hindu workmen who prefer to house themselves, rather than submit to the exacting sanitary rules of the company. The fields that are still uncut have those fat yellow canes with long joints that are the joy of the sugar grower, for the Caroni plain is famed for its fertility. Humped Indian bulls and their tropic-defying offspring dot the pastures and corrals. From Canupia a road leads to Alligator Village, where Hindus may be seen standing naked and motionless on their flimsy little rafts made of woven palm-fronds catching *cascadura*, the choicest delicacy of Trinidad. The natives have a saying that whoever tastes the flesh of this cross between a turtle and a lizard must return to end his days in the island.

Cacao plantations, shaded by forests of high trees, gradually replace the cane-fields as the train speeds southward. Parasites and climbing lianas, that death-dealing vine called *matapalo* by the Spaniards and " Scotch attorney " by the Trinidadians, which finally chokes to death the tree that sustains it, usurping its heritage of nourishment, give the forest wall the appearance of a great carelessly woven tapestry. Wattled huts as primitive as those of Haiti, many of them of spreading cone shape, thrust their thatched roofs above the vegetation, giving many a vista a touch that carries the mind back to India. Chaguanas, Carapichaima, Couva — the towns nearly all bear Spanish names — are populous, though California has a mere handful of hovels. Near the last the low wooded foothills of the central range begin to peer above the flat cane and cacao lands to the left; then the train bursts suddenly out on the edge of the gulf amid a flurry of cocoanut palms.

Claxton's Bay and Point-à-Pierre again recall Trinidad's mixture of tongues, and at length the staff-hampered "express" staggers into San Fernando.

The second city of Trinidad has but ten thousand inhabitants. It is strewn over a clump of wooded knolls at the base of Naparima Hill, rising six hundred feet above it. Its population is so overwhelmingly East Indian that even the English residents are forced to learn Hindustanee. "His Worship," the mayor, is a Hindu; on certain days of the week the visitor who strolls through its wide, asphalted streets might easily fancy himself in a market city of central India. Such signs as "Sultan Khan, Pawn Broker," "Samaroo, Barber," or "Jagai, Licensed to Deal in Cacao and Licenseable Produce" are triply as numerous as the shops bearing such patently negro mottoes as "To Trust is to Burst."

A toy train runs from San Fernando through rolling fields of cane to Prince's Town, which name it adopted in honor of a visit long years ago by the present king and his brother. The "staffs" in this case are human. Every mile or less the engineer halts to take on board from a kind of sentry-box a uniformed negro wearing a bright red cap — which, no doubt, makes it possible to reduce his wages by half — stenciled with the number of the section for which he is responsible. Prince's Town lies in the Naparima plain, the second of Trinidad's great fertile *vegas;* or one may visit another portion of it by continuing to the end of the main line. On the way are Débé, almost wholly a Hindu town, with a stream of many castes pouring down its highway, and Peñal, with its miles of Hindu vegetable gardens and its mud-and-reed huts that seem to have been transported direct from India. Then comes a long run through an almost uninhabited wilderness, though with considerable cacao on its low, jungle-like hills, and finally Siparia, a rapidly growing frontier village where busses and automobiles are waiting to carry travelers to the slightly developed southern side of the island.

As we raced back down the hill again my hitherto private first-class compartment — no, I shall not divulge the secret of why I chanced to be displaying this sign of opulence and snobbishness — was invaded by the first American I had met in Trinidad outside the capital. He was an oil-driller from one of the newly developed fields. But though he had been drawing three times the salary of a college professor, he had "threw up the job because me an' that there field-man did n't hitch. He's only a Britisher, anyway." What might have been a pleasant

conversation was disrupted by my new companion with such remarks as
" Panama? Where's that? Up towards New Orleans?" "Hindus?
Is them Hindus with rings in their noses? I thought them was East
Indians." There is a saying in Trinidad, as in many other parts of the
world, that only fools or Americans ride first-class. This man was
both, for he was "afraid to go second for fear my friends 'll see me
an' think I'm goin' broke" — an impression that would not have been
at fault, as he had "blowed" his princely wages as fast as he earned
them.

The favorite excursion from Port of Spain is that by government
steamer through the Bocas Islands, which are scattered along the northwestern horn of Trinidad. First comes a cluster of jagged rocks
with a few large trees, called Five Islands, government-owned and
occupied by from one to three houses each, which may be rented by
the week when they are not in use as quarantine stations. On one of
them is the principal prison of the colony, and convicts in charge of a
guard row out for the supplies and mail from town. Indeed, the
journey is a constant succession of rowboat parties, not to say mishaps,
for it is frequently blowing a gale about the Bocas, and as the steamer
nowhere ventures close to shore, passengers and groceries are often
subjected to thorough duckings, if nothing worse. The larger islands
are privately owned, and dotted with pretentious "summer" homes
of those who cannot spend the hottest months in Grenada or Barbados.
An entire bay of one of them belongs to the son of the inventor of one
of Trinidad's most famous products, "Angostura Bitters." I am not
in a position to divulge the secret of its manufacture, beyond stating
that it contains rum, mace, nutmeg, and powdered orange skins, which
latter detail accounts for the fact that the market-women of Port of
Spain pare their oranges as we do an apple and that the stone fences
of the town are always littered with orange-peelings drying in the
sun.

Monos Island lies beyond the mainland, and between that and the
last and largest, rejoicing in the name of Chacachacare, are several
bocas, or channels, through which pass steamers touching at Trinidad.
The colony was in an uproar at the time of our visit because the
government had proposed to turn Chaca — but why repeat it all? —
over to the lepers. Thanks largely to its Hindu population, Trinidad
has more than its share of these sufferers, and though they are "isolated" in an asylum on the mainland or in their own homes, they are

frequently found mingling with holiday throngs. Trinidadians protested against advertising the prevalence of leprosy by housing the invalids on the most conspicuous part of the colony, and the charge of graft was as freely bantered back and forth as in our own merry land under similar conditions. From Chacachacare one may see a great stretch of Venezuela across the straits, the spur of the Andes on which sits Caracas rising higher and higher into the sky and disappearing at length in the direction of lofty Bogotá.

But to most strangers Trinidad has little meaning except as the home of the " asphalt lake." Strictly speaking, it is neither the one nor the other, being rather a pitch deposit, but it would be foolish to quibble over mere words. It is sufficient to know that the spot furnishes most of the asphalt for the western hemisphere.

To reach it one must return to San Fernando by train and continue by government steamer. This frequently flees before the ebbing tide and anchors far out in the shallow, yellowish gulf until its passengers have been rowed aboard, then turns southwest along a flat, uninteresting coast. The pea-soup-colored sea swarms with jelly-fish that resemble huge acorns in shape and color and on which whales come to feed at certain seasons. Among them floats another species with long tendrils, a mere touch of which leaves a sharply stinging sensation for hours afterward. The steamer touches at half a dozen villages down the long southern prong of Trinidad, rounding the point twice a week to Icacos, reputed the largest cocoanut plantation in the world. It is owned by an old Corsican who " came out " in his youth as a porter, and who, in the words of the captain, " is of no class at all," yet he has a mansion in Port of Spain, several daughters married to French counts, and so much money " he does n't know arithmetic enough to count it."

But our interests are in the first port of call out of San Fernando. A bit beyond the reddish town of La Brea (the Spanish word for pitch) a very long pier with an ocean steamer at the far end of it and iron buckets flying back and forth between it and the land, like a procession of sea-gulls feeding their young, juts out into the gulf. Not so many years ago all the population of this spot, called Brighton, lived on the pier, the shore being famous for a fever that brought almost certain death within two days. This completely disappeared, however, when American concessionists turned the jungle into pasture land. The air is full of pelicans, clumsily diving for fish or awaiting their turn for a seat on the protruding jib boom of a wrecked schooner, along which

Trinidad has many Hindu temples

Very much of a lodge

At the "Asphalt Lake"

There is water, too, in the crevices of the asphalt field

others sat as tightly crowded together as subway passengers in the evening rush-hour.

We landed with misgiving, having often heard of " that terrible walk " from the pier to the " lake." No doubt it seems so to many a tourist, being nearly ten minutes long up a very gentle slope by a perfect macadam highway. Beside it buckets are constantly roaring past on elevated cables, carrying pitch to the ship or returning for a new load with an almost human air of preoccupation. The highway leads to the gate of a yard with a mine-like reduction plant peopled with tar-smeared negroes, immediately behind which opens out the " lake."

The far-famed deposit is not much to look at. It is a slightly concave, black patch of a hundred acres, with as definite shores as a lake of water, surrounded by a Venezuelan landscape of scanty brush and low, thirsty palms. To the left the black towers of half a dozen oil-wells break the otherwise featureless horizon. About the surface of the hollow several groups of negroes work leisurely. One in each group turns up with every blow of his pick a black, porous lump of pitch averaging the size of a market-basket; the others bear these away on their heads to small cars on narrow tracks, along which they are pushed by hand to the " factory." That is all there is to it; an easier job for all concerned would be hard to find. A trade wind sweeps almost constantly across the field, the pitch is so light that the largest lump is hardly a burden, from the nature of the case the pace is not fast, and the workers are so constantly in sight that an overseer is hardly needed, nor piece-work required. The men are paid eighty cents a day of ten hours, which seems much to them and little to their employers, producing mutual satisfaction. The work calls for no skill whatever; it is carried on in the open air, with women venders of food and drink free to come and go; on the side of the concessionists the deposit offers not even the difficulty of transportation, being barely a mile from the ship, furnishing its own material for the necessary roads, and virtually inexhaustible. The holes dug during the day fill imperceptibly and are gone by morning, the deepest one ever excavated having disappeared in three days. Only a small fraction of the field is exploited; it could easily keep all the ships of the world busy. Should it ever be exhausted, there is a still larger deposit just across the bay in Venezuela. In the slang of financial circles, " it is like finding it."

The lake is soft underfoot, like a tar sidewalk in midsummer, the heels sinking out of sight in a minute or two, and has a faint smell of sulphur.   In a few places it is not solid enough to sustain a man's weight, though children and the barefooted workmen scamper across it anywhere at sight of a white visitor for the inevitable British West Indian purpose of demanding " a penny, please, sir." A crease remains around each hole as it refills, some of these rolling under like the edge of a rising mass of dough, and in these crevices, the rain gathers in puddles of clear, though black-looking, water in which the surrounding families do their washing.   Only negroes are employed as laborers; the twenty-five white men in the higher positions are nearly all Americans, those with families housed in company bungalows on the slope above the gulf, the bachelors in a company hotel.   Most of the pitch goes directly to the steamer, but as it is one-third water, and royalties, duties, and transportation are paid by weight, a certain proportion is boiled in vats in the " factory " and shipped in barrels constructed on the spot.   From the vat-platforms spreads out a vast panorama, with San Fernando at the base of its lonely hill, Port of Spain on its gently sloping plain, the entire Gulf of Paria, the Bocas Islands, and the mountains of eastern Venezuela all in plain sight.

The pitch lake was known even in the days of Sir Walter Raleigh, who " payed " his vessels here during lulls in buccaneering, but it has been exploited only during the last few decades.   Three hundred thousands tons have been shipped during a single year, the revenue to the Government of Trinidad in 1912 being £63,453.   Indeed, one of the main reasons why the island has a much more prosperous air than its neighbors is that millions have been paid into its treasury in royalties and duties from its only " lake."   When a steamer is loading, buckets and negroes toil all through the night in the glare of electric-lights. The barrels of the refined product were first stowed on their sides, but as they flattened out into a four hundred pound cube that could neither be rolled nor lifted, they are now stood on end, tier after tier.   The crude pitch becomes a solid mass during the journey north, and must be dug up again with picks when it reaches Perth Amboy.

CHAPTER XVII

AFRICAN JAMAICA

IT may be that our affection for Jamaica is tempered by the difficulties we had in reaching it. Lying well inside the curve described by the other West Indies, the scarcity of shipping caused by the World War has left it almost unattainable from any of the other islands and hardly to be reached, except directly from New York or Panama. We first attempted to visit it from Santiago de Cuba, early in our journey. But as this would have meant spending an interminable twenty-four hours, and perhaps much more, on a little coasting-steamer not even fit for the " slave traffic " in which it is chiefly engaged, at a fare equal to that from St. Thomas to Barbados in an ocean liner, the depositing of an equal amount to pay the expenses of a very probable quarantine of a week because of a few scattered cases of small-pox in Cuba, and the unwinding of a formidable mesh of red tape, we decided to defer our call and pick up the island on the way home. That surely would be easy, we concluded, for traffic certainly should be frequent between the two largest of the British West Indies. Arrived in Trinidad, however, we found that island as completely cut off from Jamaica as if they belonged to two enemy powers. We at length succeeded in coaxing the captain of a British freighter — the most pleasant craft, by the way, of all our journey — touching at every port on the north coast of South America and spending three weeks on the way, to carry us to Panama, whence another steamer bore us back again to several Colombian ports and eventually landed us in Jamaica seven weeks after leaving Trinidad. Had we not set our hearts on making our tour of the West Indies complete, we should have long since invited the principal British island to withdraw to a sphere where the temperature is reputed to be more than tropical.

The first view of Jamaica and of its capital is pleasing. A mountainous mass, gradually developing on the horizon, grows into a series of ranges which promise to rival the beauty of Porto Rico. Beyond a long, low, narrow, sand-reef lies an immense harbor, on the further shore of which Kingston is suspected, rather than seen, only a few wharves and one domed building rising above the wooded plain on which the low city stands.   The hills behind it tumble into a disordered heap culminating in the cloud-swathed peak of what are most fittingly called the Blue Mountains.   On this strip of sand, known as the Palisadoes, lies buried the famous buccaneer, Sir Henry Morgan, once governor of Jamaica, and at the extreme end of it stands the remnant of the old capital, Port Royal.   In the good old days of pirates, who made it their headquarters, the depository of their loot, and the scene of their debauchery, this was the most important town in the West Indies, some say the richest and most wicked spot on earth.   One must be chary, however, of too hastily granting such superlatives.   An earthquake befell it one day, sinking all but a fragment of the town beneath the sea, and a new capital, named Kingston, was founded on what promised to be safer ground across the bay.   A later century brought regret that a still more distant site had not been chosen.   To-day Port Royal consists of a quarantine station and a small village so isolated from the mainland that servant women brought from it to the capital have been known to shriek with dismay at sight of their first cow. Ships circling the reef on their way in or out of the harbor sail over the very spot where pirates once held their revels, and negro boatmen still assert that on stormy evenings one may hear the tolling of Port Royal's cathedral bell, lying fathoms deep beneath the waves.

One's first impression of the Jamaicans, as they lounge about the wharf eyeing each trunk or bundle several minutes before summoning up the energy to tackle it, is that they are far less courageous in the face of work than their cousins, the Barbadians.   This is closely followed by the discovery that Kingston is the most disappointing town in the West Indies.   With the exception of a few bright yellow public buildings and a scattered block or two of new business houses, it is a negro slum, spreading for miles over a dusty plain.   Scarcely a street has even the pretense of a pavement; the few sidewalks that exist are blocked by stairways, posts, and the trash of a disorderly population, or degenerate every few yards into stretches of loose stones and earth. The only building worth crossing the street to see is that domed structure sighted from the bay, the Catholic cathedral.   To be sure, the earthquake wrought great havoc, but that was thirteen years ago, time enough, surely, in which to have made a much farther advance toward recovery.

The insolence of nearly all the British West Indies reaches its zenith in Kingston.   Even in the main street clamoring black urchins and no small number of adults trail the white visitor, heaping upon him foul-mouthed taunts, all but snatching his possessions out of his hands in broad daylight; diseased beggars plod beside him in bare feet that seem never to have known the luxury of a scrubbing, scattering their germs in 'a fine gray limestone dust that swirls in blinding clouds which envelop everything in a yellowish veil whenever a breath of wind stirs or a street-car sweeps past. Loose-mannered black females ply their trade with perfect impunity, shrieking worse than indecencies at unresponsive passers-by; assaults and robbery are frequent even by day. One must be vaccinated and often quarantined before entering Jamaica, yet it is doubtful whether any island of the West Indies has more evidence of disease than Kingston itself. Those who carry firearms must deposit them at the custom house, yet with the possible exception of Hispaniola, a revolver is more often needed in the Jamaican capital than anywhere in the Caribbean, as several harmless Chinese merchants learned to their sorrow during our brief stay there. The town is dismal, disageeable, and unsafe for self-respecting white women at any hour; by night it is virtually abandoned to the lawless black hordes that infest it. Weak gas-lights give it scarcely a suggestion of illumination; swarms of negroes shuffle through the hot dust, cackling their silly laughter, shouting their obscenity, heckling, if not attacking, the rare white men who venture abroad, love-making in perfect indifference to the proximity of other human beings, while the pompous black policemen look on without the slightest attempt to quell the disorder.

The white residents of Kingston seem to live in fear of the black multitude that make up the great bulk of the population. When hoodlums and rowdies jostle them on the street, they shift aside with a slinking air; even when black hooligans cling to the outside of street-cars pouring out obscene language, the white men do not shield their wives and daughters beside them by so much as raising their voices in protest. When cursing, filthy market women pile their baskets and unwashed produce in upon them and crowd their own women out of their places, they bear it all with humble resignation, as if they were the last survivors of the civilized race wholly disheartened by an invasion of barbarian tribes. The visitor who flees all this and retires is lucky to catch half an hour of unbroken sleep amid the endless uproar of shouting negroes, the barking of innumerable dogs, and the crowing of more cocks than even a Latin-American city can muster. It would be difficult, indeed, to say anything bad enough of Kingston to give the full, hot, dusty, insolent, half-ruined picture. The traveler will see all he wants and more of the capital in the time he is forced to remain there on the way to or from his ship without including a stay in his itinerary. Port au Prince is clean and gentlemanly in comparison.

The electric street-cars, manned by ill-mannered crews and rocking like ships in a storm over the earthquake-undulated ground, run far out of town. They must, in order to reach anywhere worth going. Beyond Half Way Tree the sloping Liguanea plain grows green and the rain that seems never to descend to Kingston gives the vegetation a fresher coat, yet the way is still lined for a long distance by negro shacks.   Only when one reaches the open meadows of Constant Spring or the residence section served by another branch of the line does anything approaching comfort, cleanliness, and peace appear.   Yet even the boasted Hope Gardens, set far back at the base of the Blue Mountain range, have little of the open, breezy beauty of the Queen's Park in Trinidad.   Until he has drifted farther afield, the stranger will not cease to wonder what charms bring Jamaica its large colony of winter tourists.   Even then he must conclude that the prevalence of a tongue closely enough resembling English to be sometimes comprehensible and the legal existence of John Barleycorn give the island its handicap over Porto Rico.

Unlike the other British West Indies, Jamaica clings to the English monetary system.   The two colonial banks issue pound notes and higher, which are easily mistaken for those in dollars from the other islands, as more than one new cashier has discovered too late to rescue his first month's salary.   The word "dollar" is frequently heard, but it is merely a popular euphonism for four shillings.   Then there are local pennies and half-pennies of nickel alloy that are not readily distinguished from the English shilling and two-shilling pieces.   Jamaica belongs to the postal union, but, unlike the other colonies of the empire, she does not subscribe to the British postal convention with the United States, with the result that visitors commonly find their letters taxed three pence extra postage, to the continual advantage of the local government.

This latter gives the impression of being both backward and clumsy. A governor and a privy council of not more than eight members are appointed by the crown.   The legislative body is presided over by the former and consists of five of the latter, ten other crown appointees, and a *custos,* elected by the people, from each of the fourteen parishes. British male subjects of twenty-one who occupy house property and pay taxes of thirty shillings, or who receive a nominal salary of fifty shillings a year, are qualified voters. A recent enactment gives the few women possessing certain qualifications a limited right to vote. Parish boards can recommend legislation, but only the high colonial officials can actually make laws or pay out money. No bills involving questions of finance are passed if opposed by nine elective members, yet those same *custodes* cannot initiate legislation. Moreover, the king may disallow any law within two years of its passing. The result is a division of responsibility from power and frequent deadlocks that make the apparent autonomy of the island a continual process of "standing pat."

The few white officials are slow, antiquated, precedence-ridden, in striking contrast to the young and bustling, if sometimes poorly informed rulers of our own dependencies. Indeed, a journey to the West Indies is apt to cause the American to rearrange his notions of the relative efficiency of the English, and the French or ourselves, as colonizers. We are sadly in need of a Colonial Office and a corps of trained officials to administer what we dislike to call our colonies, but even our deserving Democrats, or Republicans, as the case may be, scarcely hamper the development of our dependencies as thoroughly as do its medieval-minded rulers that of Jamaica. An example or two will suffice to illustrate the point. The government railway was lifted out of its slough of despond and rehabilitated by an experienced administrator. When he found, however, that his £1000 a year did not suffice to keep him in shoes, the insular powers let him go rather than increase his pittance. Back in the Middle Ages that was a generous stipend for railway managers. By a recent law the Government of Jamaica has decided to take over the making, and later the distribution, of rum. At the time of our departure it was advertising for "an experienced superintendent" at the breath-taking salary of £2000 a year! No doubt there was a rush of managers of Cuban sugar *centrals* contending for this noble prize.

It may be of interest to know that Jamaica is livid with fear that she, too, may be struck by prohibition, and is hastily erecting all manner of protective lightning-rods. Her newspapers carry columns of arguments pro and con, most of them clinched with quotations from the Bible, as if that had anything to do with the case. Reading the impassioned utterances of the "wets," one might suppose that the United States is in the act of organizing a great army of grape-juicers to descend upon Jamaica and wrest from her all bottled joy in life, while the casual observer gets the impression that the great majority of the islanders would rather die at the doors of their rum distilleries and liquor shops than suffer that ignominious fate.

With the exception of Barbados, where special conditions exist, Jamaica has remained a possession of the British crown longer than any other land, and the influence of the English on the African race can perhaps nowhere be better studied. It is not particularly flattering. The Jamaican has all the faults of his rulers and his own negro delinquencies to boot. He is slow-witted, inhospitable, arrogant when he dares to be, cringing when he feels that to be to his advantage. The illegitimate birth-rate is exceedingly high, sexual morality extremely shaky among the masses. Though the country people are sometimes pleasing in their simplicity, they quickly take on the unpleasant characteristics of the town dwellers when they come in contact with them, the most conspicuous being an unbridled insolence and a constant desire to annoy what may quite justly be called their betters. Part of this rudeness is due, no doubt, to the same cause as that of our laboring classes — a misguided attempt to prove their equality by scorning the amenities of social intercourse. A large percentage of it, however, is easily recognizable as native African barbarism, which increases by leaps and bounds as the suppression of former days weakens. If he is working for you or selling you something, the Jamaican can be softly courteous; when he has no such reasons to repress his natural brutality his impudence is colossal.

Even more than in the other British islands the masses of Jamaica have been " spoiled " by the war. Official reports credit the " B. W. I." regiments with " excelling in many acts of bravery "; private information, even from some of the very men who dictated the official reports, has a different tenor. According to this they were useless in actual warfare, not a man of them having died facing the enemy; even as labor battalions they were not worth their keep, and their conduct was such that both the French and the Italians protested against their being stationed within reach of the civil population. Whichever of these reports is more trustworthy, there is no doubt that the hospitality shown these crude-minded blacks by a certain class of European women, and the fuss made over them upon their return, have given their rulers a problem which will scarcely be solved during the present generation.

Those who have spent their lives with the Jamaica negro — and to a certain extent he is typical of his race in all the British West Indies — agree in the main with the casual observer in the summing up of his characteristics. He is apt to take little pride in his work and to meet any criticism with "Cho, too much boderation; can't do better." He sees little immorality in lying, and the man who expects truth from him according to the Anglo-Saxon standard will be grievously disappointed. Exactness in such matters as age, distance, names, and the like means nothing to him. His answer to a roadside inquiry is almost certain to be "not too far," and his age may change by ten years or more within the space of two sentences. He has the child's tendency to exaggeration and the building up of stories out of whole cloth, yet he can scarcely plead the same excuse as the child, for his imagination is, at best, in a comatose state. Gratitude seems to have been completely left out of his make-up. He dearly loves a bargain or a dispute; the shop-keeper who has only one price arouses his hostility, and to appear in court either as plaintiff, defendant, or witness is one of his favorite forms of amusement.

"Like the Irish," as one English Jamaican puts it, "he does himself more credit abroad than at home; like them he is quite ready to emigrate and goes where the dollar calls, rather than aping the Englishman, who prefers a competency under the Union Jack to possible riches under another flag. If there is one thing he dislikes more than another," continues this authority, "it is sarcasm. He will stand any amount of 'cussing,' but he keenly resents ridicule of any kind." What this critic does not add is that the sarcasm must be extremely broad if the average Jamaican is to recognize it as such.

The lower classes are much given to "teefing" small articles, particularly food. One might almost say that the chief curse of the island is "praedial larceny," as they still spell it in Jamaica, which means the stealing of growing crops. Newspapers, public reports, and private conversations contain constant references to this crime, prosecutions for which nearly doubled in the year following the war. Many people no longer take the trouble to plant a crop of ground provisions, knowing that they will almost certainly be stolen by black loafers before the owners themselves can gather them. The main faults of the masses, — insolence, lying, illegitimacy, slackness in work, and thieving,— can scarcely be laid to drink; for though Jamaica rum is famous and drunkenness is on the increase, the women, who drink comparatively little, are as bad as the men in all these matters.

Prisons and penal institutions are more in evidence in Jamaica than schools. While the latter are small and inconspicuous, the prison in Kingston is larger than Sing Sing, in Spanish Town there is another almost as large, and many more scattered throughout the island. The police, who are virtually all jet black, are poorly disciplined and much inclined to look misdemeanors, indecency, and even crime in the face without being moved to action. Pompously proud and inclined to insolence, also, they seldom fail to take advantage of their power over white men whenever it seems safe to do so. For there is little color-line in legal matters, and not only can whites be arrested by black officers, but they run a splendid chance of being tried by colored magistrates. The tendency to give the higher positions of responsibility in the police force to young Englishmen who have been decorated in the war or who have influential friends, yet who are more noted for their card playing and dancing than for ability or diligence in their new calling, has enhanced a situation which the better class of Jamaicans view with alarm. There are one hundred and sixteen constabulary stations on the island and a force of a thousand regular constables, supplemented by almost as many district deputies, yet Jamaica is by no means so well policed as Porto Rico with its insular force of scarcely eight hundred.

Even the friendly critic already quoted finds little to praise in the Jamaican except his cheerfulness, his loyalty, within limits, to those he serves, and his kindness to his own people, and he admits that the first of these qualities is often based on lack of ambition, " though it is nevertheless pleasant to live with." On the other hand, lack of equal opportunity is not without its effect on the negro character. Jamaica suffers from the same big estate and primogeniture troubles that hamper the masses in England. Slightly larger than Porto Rico, with five hundred thousand acres still held by the crown and with only half of the remainder under cultivation, the rest being wooded or " ruinate," as they call it in Jamaica, the island is principally in the hands of the whites. These strive to keep their estates intact and hold the negro in economic subjection.

" Negroes who come back from Panama or Cuba with in some cases hundreds of pounds are seldom able to buy property," complained one of their sponsors. " It is only when the white man becomes very poor or the negro very rich that he can get a chunk of some big estate. The big owners too often pasture, rather than plant, their best land and rent out the worst to the small peasants, at one pound an acre a year. If the rented land turns out to be too stony or otherwise useless, that is the peasant's loss and the owner's gain." One difficulty in bettering this condition, however, is the disinclination of the peasantry to pay regularly. On the whole, the planters show little generosity toward their laborers, thereby increasing the feeling between the two races.

Though it is the most populous of the British West Indies, and the
largest, unless one follows the English habit of including British Guiana,
Jamaica is much less densely inhabited than Porto Rico, for it is natural
that two islands so nearly alike in size, situation, and formation should
constantly suggest comparison. When the British took Jamaica from
the Spaniards in 1655, it had but 4200 inhabitants. Half a century
later the population was more than two thirds negro. In 1842, four
years after the abolition of slavery, the first shipload of indentured East
Indians arrived, but this practice had almost ceased long before the
Indian Government recently put a legal end to it. The Chinese coolies
were tried for a time, but only in small numbers, and their descendants
now confine themselves almost entirely to keeping what we would call
" grocery stores." Both the Hindus and the Chinese, and for that
matter the native whites, speak the slovenly Jamaican dialect, and there
remains little of the Oriental garb and racial mixture so conspicuous in
Trinidad.

" On my arrival in Jamaica in 1795," says one of its governors, " I
found a vast assembly of French emigrants of all ranks, qualities and
colors, who had fled from the horrors of Santo Domingo " — by which,
of course, he meant Haiti. Many Cubans came also when their island
was under Spanish rule. But all these elements scarcely moderate
Jamaica's distinctly African complexion. The visitor is apt to be
astounded by the blackness of the great bulk of the population. The
percentage of full blacks is in striking contrast to the mulatto majority
in the French islands, where the mixture of races is not very sternly
frowned upon, and still more so to the Spanish-American tropics, where
micegenation is so common that nearly everyone is a " colored person."
By her last census, which is nearly ten years old, Jamaica claims 831,383
inhabitants, of whom 15,605 were white, 17,380 Hindus, and 2,111
Chinese. The fact that she has barely two hundred to the square
mile, as compared to twelve hundred in Barbados, is probably not
without its bearing in the visible difference of energy between the two
islands.

The color-line in Jamaica, and it is more or less typical of that in
all the British West Indies, falls somewhere between our own and
the rather hazy one in vogue in the French islands.

" I think the English individually," said a Jamaican *sambo*, that
is a three fourths negro, who had worked on the Canal Zone, " like us

black people still less than you Americans do; but governmentally
they treat us as equals, and you do not. Yet in some ways I prefer
the American system. An Englishman says you are his equal, but
you had better not act as if you were. The American says, 'You're
a damned nigger and you know it,' and there is no hypocrisy in the
matter."

Strictly speaking, there are two color-lines in the British West Indies. Unlike the United States, where "black" and "colored" are
synonomous terms when applied to the negro race, there is a middle
class of "colored people," as there are Eurasians in India, though
actual membership in it implies a certain degree of education, culture,
wealth, or influence. There are "colored" men who rank themselves
and are ranked as negroes, working shoulder to shoulder with them in
the fields; there are others who sit side by side with their white
brethren on the judicial bench and reach high rank in church, politics,
medicine, law, and commerce. Color may almost be said to be no
bar to promotion in official life, within limits. This middle set is extremely assertive in its pride and, on the whole, is more disliked by
the negroes than are the whites themselves.

On a Jamaican train one day I fell into conversation with an octa-
roon school-teacher. He was a forcible fellow who had evidently retained most of the qualities of his white ancestors. For some time I
avoided any reference to the matter of human complexions, having no
desire to offend him. Before long, however, he began to expatiate on
the necessity of keeping the "niggers" in their place.

"Hoho," said I to myself, "so you consider yourself a white
man?"

But he did not, for soon he began to explain the position of "us
colored people." He often met fellow-teachers who were negroes, he
said, but no negro ever entered his house, nor had he ever introduced
his daughter to one of them.

"The nigger," he went on, "always gets cocky when he is given
either authority or encouragement. If I invite a negro to my house,
the next thing I know he is proposing to my daughter and I have to kick
him out, for in Jamaica the colored girl forever loses caste by marrying a black man. I would rather die than marry a negro woman,
yet I would no sooner marry a white woman, because it would be hell
in a few years. At the same time I know that a white man would
have the same fear, if I were his guest. So I do not go to his house,
even if I am asked, for he would be patronizing; and I do not invite

a white man to my house because I know he would feel he was doing me a favor and an honor.

" By the way," he asked later, "how would I get on in the United States? How did you know I am colored? My hair is pretty good." He smiled rather pathetically, passing a hand over it.

It was straight as my own, and his skin was no darker than that of many a Spaniard. Yet, though he might not have been suspected in Paris, or possibly even in London, any American would have recognized him as a negro at a glance. I told him so frankly, and he accepted the statement with consummate good sense. Thanks to the point of view he had expressed, there is little further mixture of races going on in the British West Indies, with the possible exception of Trinidad, and the three castes will probably remain intact and will each have to work out its own destiny.

Included in the government of Jamaica are the Turks and Caicos Islands, which belong geographically to the Bahamas, as they once did officially. Transportation between them and the mother island is worse than uncertain, and they depend chiefly on their salt beds and emigration for their livelihood. There are a few small islands scattered close along the coast of Jamaica, but none of them is of any importance.

The Jamaica Government Railway is one of the oldest in the world, having been first opened to traffic in 1845. It is almost two hundred miles long, running diagonally across the island from Kingston to Montego Bay, and north and eastward to Port Antonio, with two small branches. The fares are high, being about seven cents a mile first-class and half as much for second. The latter is really third-class in all but name, with hard wooden benches and scanty accommodations, and carries virtually all the traveling population. In it one will find the poorer whites, such as ministers with their thin, hungry-looking wives, and other poverty-stricken mortals, contrasting strongly with the " husky," broad-shouldered negroes with their velvety black skins, beautiful as mere types of the animal kingdom. Here and there, perhaps, sits a young Chinaman, inscrutable, seeing and thinking of it all, no doubt, yet never giving a hint of his thoughts, a Celestial still though born on the island. Then there is a scattering of all grades of yellow, some of them so much so that they try to smile one into the belief that they are white. In a corner of one of these coaches is a negro in a wire cage, the railway post-office. First-class consists of a little eight-seat compartment in the end of one, or at most two, coaches, stiff-backed, hot, dusty, commonly filled with tobacco-smoke and scarcely a fit place for a white woman. Occasionally it is crowded with Chinese shopkeepers and the bundles of wares they would not find room for in the other class, but more often it, too, is distinctly African in tinge. For like the island, the " J. G. R." is overwhelmingly negro. All the trainmen are full blacks, as are virtually all the passengers. The " trainboy " is a haughty negro woman in near-silk garb, enormous earrings, and a white, nurse-like cap, who sells chiefly beer and never calls out her wares. In the island dialect a local train is a " walkin' train," and all Jamaican trains fall into this category, as do all those in the West Indies except in Cuba and, to a slight degree, Trinidad. There are no train manners. In a Spanish country if you put so much as a cane in a seat your possession of it is assured and respected to the end of the journey. Put all your baggage, and your coat and hat in addition, into a Jamaican train-seat and you will probably come back to find your possessions tossed on the floor and some impudent black wench occupying your place. Why the " J. G. R." is so ungodly as to run Sunday trains on its Port Antonio branch, I do not know. They are about the only things that do move in the British West Indies on the Sabbath.

From Kingston the train jolts away through the swirling dust across a flat, Arizona-like plain studded with cactus, though moderately green. Soon come broad stretches of banana fields, bananas planted in endless rows down which one can look as through archways, many of the plants heavy with their bunches nearing maturity, others showing little more than the big purple flower shaped like a swollen, unhusked ear of corn, along the stem of which a miniature bunch is just starting. Between these are other fields, with trees girdled and blackened where some forest is being killed to make way for more bananas. Negro women with oval market baskets on their heads tramp energetically along the white highway; now and then the refined features of a Hindu break the monotony of brutal negro faces, though he has lost his distinctive garb. Then comes the prison farm of St. Catherine's Parish, with its green gardens, its irrigation ditches filled with clear water, and its horde of prison laborers. But the train is already coming to a screeching halt in the former capital of the island, twelve miles from Kingston.

As in Trinidad the Spaniards preferred an inland site for their principal city, and this Villa de la Vega was founded by Columbus's son Diego after they had abandoned their first capital of Sevilla Nueva on the north coast. The English, being a maritime people before all else, first set up their government in Port Royal, but even they could not endure a capital that had sunk beneath the sea, and returned to the old Spanish headquarters. This had come to be called St. Jago de la Vega, a name still to be found on ancient mile-posts along the roads of the vicinity, but that was too much of an effort for the thick negro tongues and the place was rechristened Spanish Town. It remained the capital of the island until 1870, and still retains the records' office. Set in a flat plain half covered with bushy trees, it is but a very trifle cooler and not much more pleasant than Kingston. There are still many Spanish names and features in Spanish Town, but only one family which speaks that language, and very few Catholics. An old red brick cathedral recently restored is said to be the oldest in the British colonies, Anglican now, of course, and open only during services. Spanish Town has scarcely ten thousand inhabitants, though it disputes with Montego Bay and Port Antonio the second place among towns of the island. In its center is still a kind of Spanish plaza, with only its grass and trees left, and surrounded by old yellow brick government buildings — all of which, one learns with surprise, were built by the English. Under the portico of one of these is a statue of Rodney, who raised the Union Jack over the French in the West Indies, dressed in that glorified undershirt or incomplete Roman toga worn no doubt by all British admirals in those heated days. The old capital has an open market which is a trifle better dressed, though more bestial and insolent than those of Haiti, and its only hotel is a negro joint overrun with plate-licking cats and setting hens, which masquerades under the name of " Marble Hall."

Though it was for a century and a half under Spanish rule, Jamaica shows few signs of Iberian influence, except in its geographical names. Some of these remain pure, but the majority of them have been corrupted by the thick-tongued negroes into something only faintly resembling the original. Thus Managua has become Moneague, Agua Alta is now Wag Water, a place once noted for its *manteca*, or lard, is Montego Bay, and Boca del Agua has adopted the alias of Bog Walk. When England wrested Jamaica from Spain the property which the Spaniards could not take with them they largely destroyed, so that no real Spanish building has remained intact. Unlike Trinidad the Spanish tongue is almost never heard in Jamaica.

The train continues across the flat plain, everywhere thinly covered with big bushy trees. Indeed one of the stations is called Bushy

Park, where an old brick aqueduct which looks Spanish, though it probably is not, still carries water across the cane-fields. Muscular negro youths in rags, either without the possibility or the desire to earn better garments, swarm about the stations and into the cars, pouncing upon the luggage of any traveler who shows the slightest sign of descending. An hour and a half from Kingston, beyond the station for Old Harbour, the land begins slowly and gradually to rise, and one is soon overlooking a vast tree-bushy rather than forested country. Broad fields of *henequen,* jute sisal, or rope-cactus, as you choose to call it, are planted in rows on rather arid looking ground completely covered with high brown grass. The first suggestion of beauty in the landscape appears near May Pen. A " pen " in the Jamaica dialect means a grassy field or a pasture, and " pen keeping " is the local term for breeding and raising cattle. Here and there the inevitable old square brick chimneys of sugarmills dot the ever descending plain, which at length begins to be hidden by low foothills. Sapling-like forests spring up along the way, and the logwood that grows in scattered quantities all over the island lies piled at the railway stations, the outer layer of wood roughly hacked away, leaving only the reddish heart. Schooners carry north many cargoes of these crooked logs and the still more awkward stumps, while several mills on the island turn it into an extract that is shipped in barrels to color our garments dark-blue or black. Jamaica produces also a certain amount of fustic, a smooth, straight tree which gives a khaki color.

Soon the soil, or " sile," as they call it in Jamaica, turns reddish and clearings and habitations become rare. By this time we were the only white persons on the train and shortly after that the only passengers in the first-class coach. A larger engine took us in tow and we climbed 865 feet in the next six miles. Dense, almost unpopulated forests, like some sections of eastern Cuba, covered the ever more rugged landscape; but if the scenery flanking Jamaica's railway is more striking than that visible from the trains in Porto Rico, it is because it passes through rather than around the island, for on the whole our own West Indian colony is more beautiful. The train continues to climb until it attains an altitude of 1680 feet at Green Vale, then descends steadily past several villages of no great importance, through numerous " tubes," as Jamaicans call a tunnel, now and then past long stretches of bananas, otherwise through almost a wilderness broken only by tiny corn or cane-fields about the rare negro shacks. At Catadupa it breaks out upon a vast vista of wooded valley, and sinks at

As I passed this group on a Jamaican highway, the woman
reading the Bible was saying, "So I ax de
Lard what I shall do"

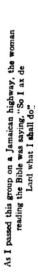

"Draw me portrait please, sir." The load consists of school books and a pair
of hobnail shoes

A very frequent sight along the roads of Jamaica

Our baggage following us ashore in one of the French islands

length into a square mile of sugar-cane beyond which lies Montego Bay on the northern coast.

But we had long since left it, to drive by " buggy "—our American term for a country carriage has somehow become acclimated in Jamaica — into the Manchester hills. The trip from Kingston to Mandeville, 2200 feet above the sea, is like one from down-town New York to the Berkshires in July. Indeed the visitor to Manchester Parish might almost fancy himself in Connecticut, in spite of the prevalence of negroes. The gray stone fences, with big horses ankle-deep in the grassy pastures behind them, the rolling stretches of corn, the very birds bear out the illusion. Even the clumps of bamboo seem to be growing on Connecticut hillsides; the orchids and treeferns contrast strangely with a weather and landscape of the temperate zone; Mandeville itself, long famous as a health resort for the residents of the sweltering coast lands, has that air of calm repose of some old New England village.

Carriage driving has more nearly survived modern invention in Jamaica than in any other of the West Indies, perhaps for the double reason of the high price of " gas " and the existence of good horses. The Jamaican horses are famed throughout the Caribbean for their size and endurance — also for their hard gait as riding animals. They are not handsome, being usually lank and goose-rumped, but they are so docile they may sometimes be driven without being broken and they retain the size of their English ancestors instead of degenerating into the runts of most tropical America, and they are unusually free from disease. Breeders claim that they remain so sound in spite of the enervating climate largely because of the limestone formation of the island and the recuperative effects of its high altitudes. At any rate there are few places where a negro-driven buggy and pair cannot be had on short notice. Many splendid draft mules are also bred on the island.

I preferred, however, to set out on foot from Mandeville for a jaunt diagonally across the island. Walking is not a favorite recreation among either the white or the " colored " castes, though there is no good reason other than inertia why it should not be in the temperate highlands. Jamaica has more than two thousand miles of good roads, far outdoing those of Porto Rico in extent, though they are narrower and sometimes poorly kept, partly because many of them are parochial roads, unknown in the neighboring island. " Fingerboards " point the way everywhere. The high altitudes of Manchester, as of several other parishes, lack only the shade-grown tobacco fields and the variegated tints of intensive cultivation to rival in beauty our own West Indian colony. Birds are always singing, scattered little white houses speckle the immense green hillsides, the road banks are often carpeted with " wandering Jew " enough to make the fortune of an American florist, or they are hung with tapestries of what look like daisies, while other flowers bloom on every hand. In a climate pleasant even at noonday one would scarcely recognize the Berkshire landscape as tropical but for a banana, a giant fern, or a palm tree here and there in the foreground.

Ltttle stone and brick coffee floors, called " barbecues " in Jamaica, frequently flank the roadway. Manchester parish grows much coffee, though it rarely reaches the American market, for England consumes all the island produces. Here the bushes are usually unshaded, protecting trees being unnecessary, if not harmful, at such an altitude. Instead of the little toy donkey-carts of Barbados there are big rattling mule wagons. Donkeys are sometimes ridden, occasionally used as pack-animals. The peasants have little of the insolence of the towns, but greet the traveler with a kind of military salute and a gentle " Good day, sah." Most of them wear caps, as in Barbados, though the similar head-gear of the women in that island is here replaced by bandannas, usually red and never topped off with a hat as in Haiti. The men, and many of the women, smoke home-made pipes with long curved stems, buying their tobacco in long coils called " jackass rope," which the war forced to the painful price of a shilling a yard, though it was once but two pence. Fully developed girls of twelve eye the passer-by with crudely coquettish airs. Information as to distance is given in " chains " if at all, the customary answer being a non-committal " not too far, sah." The great bulk of the country population is jet black, though in the towns there are all grades of yellow, from the impudent slight-cast down to mulattoes.

It was in the cabin of one of the latter that I took shelter from the afternoon shower, in a region rejoicing in the name of Split Virgin. He was perhaps two thirds Irish and one third negro, but always referred to his black neighbors as " niggers." On the walls of his unpainted board parlor hung framed chromo portraits of his white ancestors. The inevitable topic of conversation of course was the high cost of living — where can one escape it? A " head " of sugar had advanced from a " gill " (three farthings) to six pence; corn cost more than the chickens to which it was fed increased in worth; wild nuts were more expensive than the flesh they added to his hogs. Calico, put in his wife, all cloth in fact, was getting impossible. Soon they would have to go naked — which reminded me that one never sees naked children in Jamaica, unlike most of the Caribbean islands. A man could not even grow his own food any more; three fourths of his yam holes were robbed at night by the thieving " niggers." The war and the travel and experience that went with it had debauched even the better class of them, until they were slothful, proud, insolent, and wasteful.

I stopped that night in a mulatto house that took in lodgers, the only point of interest being the dug-out log that served as bath-tub. The invariable Jamaican question in making new acquaintances is " Please, sah, who you is; y'u' name, please sah?" Once they know your name they seem to feel that everything is all right. But you must have a name, with a mister in front of it. You never say your name is Smith. Your name is *Mr.* Smith. I tremble to think what might befall a stranger in rural Jamaica who did not happen to have a name, and a mister to prefix to it.

Over the top of the island range at Coleyville, with its wireless station, I passed a Jamaica sugarmill with a daily capacity of one gross " heads." It consisted of two upright wooden rollers turned by a donkey, an oval iron kettle set into the top of a mud furnace, and a score of little tin cups in which are hardened the one-pound dark-brown lumps of crude sugar that are called " heads " and which form a principal article of diet among the country people. Long-tailed hummingbirds shimmered among the flowers at the roadside. Broad green vistas of banana plants, their broad leaves whipped to ribbons by the trade wind, filled many a valley, sometimes climbing part way up the surrounding slopes. Road gangs, usually of two men, were frequent; negro women young and old, sometimes in long groups, sometimes quite alone, were to be found in every mile, sitting on stone piles and wielding their hammers. They are paid a shilling a " box " for breaking up the stones, which they must hunt for in the fields and carry to the roadside, earning an average, if they told the truth, of nine pence a day. It was planting time for ginger, which grows in little patches on the steep red hillsides. The plant, which is pulled in February or March, somewhat resembles a currant-bush and only the root is valuable, the bushes being broken up and used in the following May or June as seed. With good luck a Jamaica peasant may get 2000 pounds of cured ginger to the acre. Wages varied in this region from " one and six " to " two and six," one of the workmen told me, adding regretfully " de cultivators in de hills can't afford de dollar " (four shillings) " dat am payin' now de sugar estates." Shingle and wood houses were the rule here, and they were better than the rural hovels of Porto Rico, perhaps because the material is more plentiful.

Each morning I met flocks of black children, carrying their slates and their few books on their heads, hurrying to school, usually in the church, from which a chorus of hymns invariably arose as soon as the pupils were gathered. In the early days the government of Jamaica did little toward educating the populace, but left it to the denominational schools. Only a few years ago was the penny a week, still required of pupils in most of the British West Indies, abolished, and though there are public schools now in every parish, the Moravians, Anglicans, Catholics, Presbyterians, the Church of Scotland, the Baptists, the Wesleyans, and the Church of Jamaica get government subsidies for educational purposes. England's school record in Jamaica is as low as our own in Porto Rico. Slightly more than half the children of school age are enrolled, and the attendance of these is fitful. There is compulsory attendance only in Kingston and two or three other towns. Only three out of every hundred pupils reach the sixth grade, and in all the island fewer than three thousand continue in school after the age of fourteen. School inspectors play an important part in the social life, each having about seventy schools in his charge, which he must visit twice a year. The Jamaica government has often been warned against the danger of teaching her democracy to read unless she also taught it to think, but the warning has never been taken very seriously.

The country churches of Jamaica are small and unimposing compared with those of Barbados, though they are more numerous and often conspicuous in their prominent settings on the green hillsides. The sects seem to run in streaks. In this ginger region — most fittingly perhaps — the Church of Scotland holds sway, the ministers receiving their stipends and their instructions from the land of heather. Farther on the Baptists prevailed, and every little negro urchin I questioned announced himself a faithful follower of that sect. On a high hilltop they had built a stone church as high as the eaves, then suddenly abandoned it, apparently because it had occurred to them that there was no water available at that height. The Jamaicans are much given to religious expression. It is nothing rare to hear them " callin' on de Lawd " as they tramp along the roads, and their antics sometimes reach the height of religious insanity. Such seemed to be the case of a ragged old woman I passed during my second day's tramp, or else she was pretending the power of prophecy for the benefit of the score of wide-eyed negroes squatting on the ground about her as she marched back and forth preaching with all the inflections of a negro minister and ending each exhortation with a " Bless de Lawd, Oh, mah soul! " which echoed back from the neighboring hills. Tombstones are less numerous in Jamaican churchyards than one would expect, perhaps because of the custom of burying people on their own property. One often comes upon a little cluster of graves in a lonely bit of woods, or beside a country hut, some of them dating from the slave days. Most of them are covered by a mound of stone and cement, without crosses or other upright monument, some are large vaults, all are well kept and usually freshly whitewashed. Strangely enough the negroes do not seem to be in any way superstitious about them.

Annotto and pimento are two important products of the Jamaican hills that are sure to draw the pedestrian's attention. The former is a reddish berry in a kind of chestnut-burr pod, which grows on a spreading bush and, being boiled, gives an oily extract that is used as a dye. Pimento is what we know as allspice, and is the only Jamaican export indigenous to the island. The tree grows some thirty feet high and its greenish-gray bark and glossy green leaves cause it to stand out conspicuously from the surrounding forest. When crushed in the hand the leaves emit a strong aromatic odor, but they have no commercial value. The berry, of the size of a currant, grows in clusters, is glossy black when ripe and very pleasant to the taste. But it must be gathered before that, and has then a peppery, astringent quality. They are picked by sending a small boy up the tree to break off the ends of all the branches he can reach and throw them to the ground, where the berries are gathered by women and children and carried to the " barbecues," where they are dried like coffee.

Irish potatoes can be grown in the highlands of Jamaica; there are some nutmegs; the oranges are green in color and of poor quality; there are *sapotes* (which are here called naseberries, a corruption of the West Indian Spanish *níspero*), grapefruit, shadducks (a pear-shaped grapefruit with a reddish pulp), the *chocho,* and a dozen other purely tropical fruits and vegetables. But with the single exception of the pimento all these products have been imported, though many of them have fervently adopted their new home. In 1793, for instance, when a famine was ravaging the island, William Bligh brought the breadfruit tree from the South Seas, and to-day it is as familiar a sight as African faces.

A furzy, almost treeless, red soil region surrounded me on my second afternoon. I was flanking the famous cockpit country, made up of numerous basins in close proximity and densely wooded from top to bottom, wilder forms of what are known in Minnesota as " sink-holes." In these the Maroons took refuge in their wars with the English. The Maroons (an abbreviation of cimaroon, said to be derived from the Spanish *cima,* or mountain top) were originally slaves of the Spanish, who took to the cockpit country after England captured Jamaica, where they were joined from time to time by runaway slaves of the newcomers. England won her title to the island almost without a struggle, but it took two regiments to keep the Maroons from recapturing it. For nearly two hundred years they lived in wild freedom in the mountain recesses, frequently descending to harry the lowlands and carry off the cattle. The government at length entered into a treaty with them, granting them 2500 acres of land, and getting in turn their assistance in quelling uprisings of the slaves or repelling foreign invasion. They were a bold, hardy lot of men, holding the servile peasant population in great contempt, knowing every inch of the hills and forests, and were great hunters, either of human or four-footed game. In warfare they dressed themselves in green leaves which caused them to blend invisibly into the landscape. It has always been the policy of the Government to keep the Maroons at odds with the rest of the population, England's familiar old scheme for dominion, like the accentuation of caste lines in India. To-day, though there are several so-called Maroon towns in the cockpit country and another in the northeastern parish, there are said to be almost no " pure blooded " Maroons left. They still exist in name, however, and have their own chiefs, churches, and schools, and once a year they are paid an official visit by the *custos* of the parish, when they " dress up in leaves and similar rubbish and go through a lot of childish hocuspocus." In theory at least they are more independent than the other negroes — which is strong language indeed — but though every little while some black countryman bullies his neighbors by claiming to be a Maroon, there is nothing by which to distinguish the present decendants of the war-like slaves from those whose ancestors peacefully awaited emancipation.

Wayside shops are somewhat less numerous in Jamaica than in Barbados, and it is significant of a larger American influence here that they are called stores. The best of them, virtually all the provision shops in fact, are kept by Chinamen, unknown in "Little England." Even in the most remote corners of the mountainous interior one comes upon Celestials plying their chosen trade, most of them of the younger generation, born in Jamaica and speaking the same slovenly tongue as their negro clients, yet retaining all their native attributes, sphinx-like, taciturn, unflaggingly diligent, apparently wholly devoid of curiosity, only rarely succumbing to the native influence to the extent of mumbling an indifferent "Where y'u go?" or "What y'u name?" In striking contrast to Barbados, too, are the stocks of imported canned and salt fish, even in stores on the edge of the sea. Every scattered collection of huts has its post office, always bearing the blue sign "Quinine for Sale." Single pills of the febrifuge are sold in printed envelopes at a farthing each, though there are few coins of that size in circulation, and he who buys a penny-worth gets his four pills in as many separate envelopes. The favorite native occupation seems to be the patching of shoes. It is a rare mile that does not have at least one "shoemaker" seated in the door of his tiny shanty or single room, striving to make both ends meet with a few scraps of leather and a handful of nails. Almost the only native manufacture, however, is the weaving of "jippi jappa" hats, a very coarse, poor imitation of the Panama, though the country people make all shapes and sizes of baskets.

The language of Jamaica is at best curious; that spoken in the hills seems almost a foreign dialect, and the stranger must listen attentively and usually have phrases repeated before he understands them. He is unlikely to catch more than the general drift of a conversation between the natives. Yet few African words remain; what seem such to the stranger turn out upon inquiry to be mutilated forms of English. "No, please" and "Oh, yes, please, sah" are the habitual negative and affirmative of the rural districts when addressing white persons. Now and then the greeting of the older people is "Good mawnin', dear massa," or "I tell you good evenin', mistress." It is always "I could n't tell you," never "I don't know." A white baby is a "bukra pickney" to the country people; smile at any of their childish antics and they are flattered into confiding to one another " De bukra him laugh." African languages consist largely of gesture. With the learning of English from the stolid Anglo-Saxon this has in great measure disappeared. It is much more prevalent in the country than in the towns, and much more marked when they are talking to one another than when addressing a white man. The negro-English of the masses is no more intelligible to the newcomer than real English is to the rural population, and most planters save themselves time and trouble by addressing their laborers in their own dialect. The Jamaican negro is much given to talking things over with himself, his brain evidently refusing to work silently, and it is the rule rather than the exception to hear those one meets along the roads engaged in a soliloquy. In slavery days queer terms were used for money and they are still heard in the rural districts and in town markets. I found a Chinaman spending his spare time between customers in wrapping up tiny packages of sugar and asked him if they were a penny-worth, which seemed small enough indeed at present prices. No, they are sold at a " gill," or three farthings. Two " gills," or three " ha'p'nnies," is a " quattie." A shilling used to be a " macaroni," three pence was for some reason called " fip-pence," and to this day one occasionally hears the equivalent of thirty West Indian cents referred to as " a mac an' fippence." The ejacu-latory " I mean to say " is as frequent in the speech of even the peasants as it is in England.

What may be called proverbs for lack of a more exact name are numerous among the masses of Jamaica. Let me quote a few, leav-ing the reader to catch what meaning he can out of them:

" Better fe water trow 'way dan gourd fe bruck."
" Black man tief, him tief half a bit; bukra tief, him tief whole a estate."
" Cock crow 'trongest 'pon him own dung'll."
" Cedar board laugh after dead man."
" Don' cry oveh milk wha' trow 'way a'ready."
" Dog hab too much owner him sleep widout supper."
" Ebery dog tink himself lion in him massa yard."
" Ebery John Crow tink him pickney white."
" Ebery man know where him house a leak."
" Follow fashin mek monkey cut him tail."
" Get a quattie better dan a kick."

" Larn te dance a home befo' y'u go outside."

" Man no done grow mus'n laugh afteh short man."

" Man get in trouble pickney breeches fit he."

" Runnin' 'bout too much de ruin ob woman an' fowl."

" Same ting sweet mout' hu't belly."

" Sometime high standin' collar stan' top a empty belly."

" Too much cousin broke shop."

" When y'u hab bad husban' don' mek y'u sweethea't ca' y'u half way."

" Man run too fast run two time."

" Ebery jackass tink him pickney a race horse."

Folk lore shows evidence of English and African mixture. Here is a story as it was told by our son's Jamaican nursemaid, without the inimitable pronunciation:

" One day a gentleman and lady have two girl. And they sent them out to look for them granny. When them got in the thick wood and them meet with a *orangootang*. The orangootang axed them where are them going to. ' I am going to look for my granny.' And said, ' Here is my granny.' And them said, ' No, you is not my granny. My granny got a mark right on her mout'.' And he went in the thick wood took a knife scrape off his mout' and come out and said, ' Here is your granny now.' And he took dem and carry dem in his house and just half cook de food dat carry for dem granny. And when night come him eat off de middle of de biggest one and lef' only de hand and de head and de feet. And de little one said, ' Granny, let I go outside.' And he said go and de smallest one run home and can't talk till three days. And de father get twelve men and gone look for de orangootang. And when he going six mont' he catch de orangootang and put him into de cage and when six mont' come he throw kerosene oil on him and light him a fire."

Tenses mean nothing to the uneducated Jamaican, and the subjective and objective pronouns are more likely to be reversed than not. Between the plural and singular of either verb or noun he shows an engaging impartiality, while the double negative is to him a form of emphasis.

Beyond Ulster Spring, a scattered town in a kind of cockpit so full of mist in the early morning as to seem a lake, my road dropped rapidly down a beautiful narrow valley, the high, ragged hills on both sides tree-clothed in all but the barest white sheer spots. Little wooden houses were pitched on wooded knolls and jutting places that seemed almost inaccessible. Here and there the ancient stone road-parapet had fallen away, giving splendid opportunities for far swifter descent on a dark night. Through the canyon echoed the voice of a negro woman, singing hymns as she walked. Birds sang continually; from the inaccessible little houses came the occasional bleating of goats. Dry River Lake, evidently in the bottom of a prehistoric crater, shimmered far below me, surrounded by the densest vegetation, and utter silence. Jamaica has many rivers that disappear and reappear at random throughout their course. Negro men on their way to work on the jungled hillsides carried their machetes in one hand and a smouldering block of wood in the other, to smoke out the mosquitos. Some bore in addition a blackened five-gallon oil tin of water on their heads. The day did not grow unpleasantly warm until I had passed Sawyer's Market and entered a long fertile plain, completely uncultivated, almost uninhabited, studded with great clumps of bamboo. Dolphin Head, the highest peak in western Jamaica, peered above the landscape to the left. Then bit by bit the negroes grew numerous and impudent again, and I knew that the sugar-bearing coastlands were at hand.

Negroes so black and ox-like that they seemed scarcely human plodded past, never giving greeting as in the hills, though sometimes shouting an obscene jest. Children ran at sight of me, as those of Italy, for instance, do at sight of a negro. Ragged old women were hoeing cane in the fields. They earned five shillings a week; the strongest men three a day, at "task-work," laboring from Monday to Friday. Here and there was an old-fashioned rum-mill, recognisable by its stench as well as by its old brick chimney and the heaps of rotting cane-pulp about it. The cane-carts were hauled by three or four pairs of oxen, a dozen men shrieking about them to urge them up the slopes of the soft fields. Like most of those in Jamaica they were crosses between English and East Indian cattle, particularly the Mysore breed. Though inferior from the butcher's point of view, these cross-breeds are noted for their quickness and endurance under the yoke, and they have a black, sun-resistant skin even when outwardly light-colored or white. Once I passed a ruined old windmill tower, capped with ivy, but they are rare in Jamaica. The thick, hot air hung motionless after the afternoon shower. Rocky, bush-grown hills intruded again where one expected flat, fertile coastlands, sugar-cane died out once more, and with it the negroes.

Then suddenly the Caribbean appeared through a break in the hills, so high and dark-blue that it seemed at first a new mountain range, and on the edge of it I caught a glimpse of Falmouth, not to be seen again until I was treading its very streets. Many old stone ruins, especially the foundations and steps of what had evidently been big plantation houses, peered forth from the bush. There were other signs that large estates had once flourished where all was not " ruinate." Dreary, silent, dismal, swarming with mosquitoes, the last few miles led through an unbroken mangrove swamp. Myriads of landcrabs of all sizes and colors, some huge as small turtles, others no larger than flies, with green, red, cream-colored, and multi-colored backs, scuttled into their holes as I passed. Falmouth had little to recommend it, either as a place of abode or of sojourn. Sweltering even at midnight, its streets impudent with lounging negroes, it recalled by contrast the cool and simple little villages in the hills. I found lodging in a room strewn with the greasy paraphernalia of a negro dentist and which had not known the luxury of a broom or a dust-cloth in weeks, though the mulatto house-owner complained that she " can't get no work to do." A Salvation Army street meeting which erupted a few doors away was the nearest replica of a Central African tomtom dance, with clothes on and smeared with a thin English veneer, that it has ever been my luck to behold in an ostensibly civilized country.

I had not intended to walk the twenty-two miles along the coast from Falmouth to Montego Bay, but as the mail bus left at three in the morning and private automobiles demanded three shillings a mile, I changed my plans. Groups of ragged negro women came down out of the hills singing, their dinner in a rag or a pail on their heads, and fell to work in newly cleared cane-fields. Pedestrians were constantly beating off the mosquitoes with leafy branches. Once there had been big stone houses here also, now there were only miserable negro shacks scattered among the cocoanut groves. The sea breeze was nearly always cut off by these or mangrove jungles. The only noise except occasional shrieking negroes was the cry of mourning doves and the equally mournful " sough " of the slow breakers on the reefs far out from shore. Fishermen were rare. Now and then the swamps disappeared and the road plodded endlessly onward at the very edge of the unruffled inner lagoons. I passed only one shop on the journey, kept of course by a Jamaica-born Chinaman. Drinking water was not to be had; the June sun beat down like a red-hot ingot; the incredibly stupid watchmen, most of whom were females, could not be induced to sell a single one of the green cocanuts under their charge. I adopted the Jamaican custom of praedial larceny and, picking a plump green nut now and then from the low young trees, jabbed a hole in it on a sharp fencepost and quenched a raging thirst that returned again within a half mile. Noisome carrion crows, with red heads instead of black, unlike those of Trinidad, and called "johncrow" by the natives, moved lazily aside as I advanced.

Midway between the two towns I passed a three-story mansion set somewhat back from the sea on what was once one of the finest estates in Jamaica. To-day it is closed and abandoned, yet needs no watchman, for the negroes are convinced that it is haunted. Rose Hall it is called, and its story has long been familiar throughout Jamaica. Here, runs the yarn, lived a pretty Mrs. Palmer, who was so eccentric that she caused the house to be built according to the divisions of time,— 365 windows, 52 doors, 24 rooms, 12 of this, 7 of that, and so on. But eccentricity seems to have been the least of her faults, for in this very house, the tale goes on, she killed four husbands and was on the point of sending the fifth to join them when he turned the tables.

At length the featureless road swung inland along the edge of an immense bay, across which stood forth the wooded hills of Hanover parish. Its waters were glass-smooth, but the seawall smashed for long distances recalled that the Caribbean does not always lie so peaceful and enticing. Cottages with bathing-suits hung over the veranda rails began to appear, then white men, of whom I had seen but one in three days, and he with a negro wife. Montego Bay aspires to be a tourists' winter paradise, but unfortunately the town lies around behind a hill that cuts off that life-saving trade wind which Jamaicans call "the doctor" and in its place comes only the fitful land breeze known as "the undertaker." Then, too, it is short of water. Most of Jamaica is, for unlike Barbados, which has not a tithe as many sources of supply, the island depends chiefly on what it can catch from the rains. The result is frequently to deprive the perspiring visitor of his bath. Tourist literature would have us believe that "the band of the Montego Bay Citizens' Association performs in the Parade" — most Jamaican towns have a dusty central square known by that name — "in the evenings, and greatly adds to the pleasure of the visitor." "Perform" it does indeed, and none can deny that it adds to the risibility of nations; but let no music lover be misled by this particular abuse of the maltreated word "pleasure."

Of the many other beauties of Jamaica space precludes anything more than brief mention. There are the cane-fields of Westmoreland parish, for instance, the tobacco growing hills of St. Elizabeth, the journey up the gorge to Bog Walk, St. Ann's parish with its newly born lake of Moneague, its many pimento trees, its beguiling Fern Gully, where are to be found innumerable species of the plants that give the ravine its name, from the maidenhair to the treefern, known locally as the " rattadrum." Here, too, are Roaring River Falls and the scene of Columbus' longest residence in the West Indies, for he lay a twelve-month with his worm-eaten vessels in what is now called Dry Harbor.

But it would never do to leave Jamaica without getting a " close-up " of her banana industry, and to do this to best advantage one should go to Port Antonio. Above Bog Walk on the way there is Natural Bridge, where the river cuts a great archway through the rocky hills, the highway crossing it far above, recalling famous Rumichaca on the boundary of Colombia and Ecuador, to say nothing of one of our own scenic beauties. Here is a splendid place to end a Sunday stroll, for there is a magnificent bath awaiting one amid the boulders over which the river pours with a constant subway roar and, if one can elude the gaping negroes who are otherwise sure to follow, no other observers than the hundreds of little swallows always flitting in and out of their nests in the rock cliffs. Then when the sun has lost its youthful ardor one may climb again to the village and catch the afternoon train over the mountains to the north coast. The region about Highgate almost rivals the beauty of Porto Rico. Cacao, cocoanuts, clumps of bamboo, the spreading breadfruit-trees, whole valleys full of bananas, some of which climb far up the surrounding slopes, decorate the rugged land-scape. One looks almost in vain, however, as in all Jamaica, for the queen of tropical vegetation, the royal — or, as the English unimagina-tively call it, the cabbage-palm. Then the train descends quickly through tunnels and across lofty viaducts to Anotta Bay, a large col-lection of wooden shanties noted for its mosquitoes, but with the blue Caribbean stretching away beyond it to the horizon.

Along the edge of this the railway squirms through a wide fringe of cocoanuts for two hours more. The frequent stations swarm with female negro food-venders. Hindus are somewhat more numerous and though even the women nearly all wear Jamaican dress their Aryan features and unobtrusive manner distinguish them as quickly as their nose-rings and massive necklaces from the African bulk of the population.   At length comes Port Antonio, with its twin harbors, embowered in hills half wooded with cocoanuts, an unexpectedly delightful place to the traveler who has known other Jamaican coast towns.   Here the trade wind, unknown in Kingston, blows unceasingly, and that alone doubles the worth of any West Indian spot.   Irregular and more compact than the two rivals it has probably outdistanced since the last census, Port Antonio has a more thriving, sanitary, comfort-loving air, thanks perhaps to the American influence of its banana trade.

Jamaica claims advantages over all the rest of the world for banana cultivation.   The vast tracts of virgin land in Central America and Colombia are two days farther from the principal market.   Costa Rica is hampered by frequent droughts at the very season when the fruit most needs rain; for the great game in banana growing is to have them ready to cut at the time when other fruit is scarce in the north.   Cuba is a trifle too near the north pole, it is wedded to its sugar industry, and its labor is several times more expensive than that of Jamaica. Bananas demand heat, moisture, and a good fat soil, and all these may be had in the largest of the British West Indies, particularly in the northeastern parish of Portland, for the Blue Mountains which deny Kingston and its vicinity the rainfall it needs precipitate most of it here.   What was then a little known fruit in American markets was first planted on a large scale in this very parish a half century ago. By 1894 it had become the most important export of the island, outdistancing both products of the sugarcane, and twenty years later it constituted sixty per cent. of Jamaica's contribution to the world's larder.   The war, abetted by three consecutive hurricanes, the banana's greatest enemy, reversed this condition, but the sugar-men themselves do not long hope to hold their new lead.

I chanced to reach Port Antonio at the very height of a banana war. The two powerful older companies had determined to annihilate a new one by that simple little method of starving it to death.   Before the World War a bunch of bananas seldom sold for more than two shillings and six pence in Jamaica, but the competition of the newcomers had gradually forced this up to four shillings.   In the single day of my visit it advanced hourly by leaps and bounds, — five shillings, five shillings and three pence commission, six shillings, six and six, seven shillings, with a six pence commission if need be, and free transportation to the port — as often as the interlopers covered their bids the imperturbable managers of the powerful companies sent out new inducements over their private telephone system, until the joyful planters of some sections were pocketing eleven shillings for every bunch of bananas they could lay down at the roadside bordering their fields. The fruit poured into Port Antonio in an endless stream, by motor-truck, by wagon, pack-donkey, on the heads of men and women, for even the negroes who had but a single bunch worth cutting hastened to part with it at this unprecedented price.

But let us watch the process from the ground up, for the benefit of those who know the banana only as it appears on the fruit-seller's stand. We have only to catch one of the mammoth trucks thundering away empty into the hills in the direction of Mooretown, once a settlement of Maroons. Every little while along the way, jolly, muscular negro laborers swing up over the tail-board until by the time we have reached Golden Vale, said to be the oldest export banana farm in the world, there are enough of them to load the truck in a bare twenty minutes. It is scarcely necessary to say, I suppose, that bananas grow on a species of mammoth weed rather than a tree, that each produces a single bunch, that this grows " upside down " from our fruitstand point of view, and that they must be cut before they are ripe. Golden Vale looks like an immense green lake surrounded by mountains, up the lower slopes of which the bananas climb for a considerable distance. Close overhead sits Blue Mountain Peak, coiffed in blue-black clouds. Hindu men, whom the overseers invariably address as " Babu," do most of the cutting, while the more powerful but less careful negroes do the handling. The " Babus " wander in and out through the green archways, giving a glance at each hanging bunch. When they see one which has reached the proper stage of development, they grasp it by the protruding stem, to which the big blue flower usually still clings, and pull down " tree " and all with a savage jerk. A machete, called a cutlass in Jamaica, flashes, a negro catches the bunch as it falls, another slash severs the flower-bearing stem a few inches from the top-most bananas, a third leaves the " tree " a mere stump, shoulder-high, and the cutters continue their search. Days later, when its sap has run back into the roots, the stump is cut off at the ground and a new shoot springs up to produce next year's bunch. The bunches that have been gathered are wrapped in dry brown banana leaves, and carried to the roadside, along which other brown heaps lie everywhere as we hurry down to the port, the loaders dropping off one by one at their shanties or the frequent rum-shops along the way. Quick handling is an absolute requisite in the banana business, and many a planter has come to grief by not giving sufficient attention to the question of transportation.

Arrived at the wharves the truck is as quickly unloaded, and an end-less chain of negroes, nearly all women, take up the task of distribution, according to size and destination. For there are " English " and " American " bananas, grown in the same field and differing not at all in species but by about ten days in their cutting time, so that the former are lean and the latter fat. Moreover, a bunch is not by any means always a bunch in the language of the banana companies. In the first place they are more often called " stems," and a " stem " must have at least ni .e " hands " of fruit (the latter average a dozen bananas each) if it is to be paid for as a full bunch. If it has more than that well and good ; that is the company's gain and no one's loss. But if there are but eight " hands " it is rated two thirds of a " stem," if seven, one half, if six, one fourth, if less than that the planter might better have fed it to his hogs or his laborers, for the buyers will have none of it. This rating is less unjust than it appears, for the fewer the " hands " the smaller and fewer are the bananas.

The slouching negroes who make up the endless chain, are not re-quired to tax their minds with these problems of size and nationality. They use their heads, to be sure, but only in the manner that seems best fitted to the race — as common carriers. Two men snatch up the bunches one by one, casting aside the brown leaf wrappers, and lay each one flat on a passing head, the owner of which shuffles away as if it were burdened with nothing but a hat instead of an average weight of eighty pounds. At the edge of the shed in which the bananas are piled to await prompt shipment stands a high desk with three men, usually quadroons or lighter, standing about it. The oldest, most intelligent, and most experienced looking of these casts what seems to be a careless glance at each " stem " and mumbles in a weary monotone, " English, eight," " American, nine," " English, seven," or some other of the combinations; his most youthful companion makes a pencil mark on the ledger before him, the least lively looking of the trio hands a metal or cardboard disk to the carrier, who drops it into a pocket and slouches on to the particular pile to which her burden has been assigned. On the way she passes a negro armed with a cutlass, who lops off the protruding ends of the stem in front of her nose and behind her ears as she walks without so much as arousing a flicker of her drowsy, black eyelids.

When the ship comes in, which must be that night or at latest next day, a similar endless chain of negroes, more nearly male in sex, carry the bananas on board, a tally-clerk ringing the bell of an auto-

Private graveyards are to be found all over Jamaica

A street of Basse Terre, capital of Guadeloupe

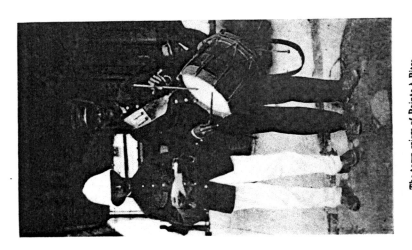

The town criers of Pointe à Pitre

A woman of Guadeloupe

matic counter in his hand as each "stem" passes. In some ports a wide leather belt takes the place of this human chain. But a large gang is required for all that, and when the last pile has disappeared from the wharf the carriers strew themselves about it and sleep soundly on the hard planks until the next load arrives. Its quota supplied, the steamer's hatches are quickly battened down, icy air is turned in upon the perishable cargo, and the vessel rushes full speed ahead for the United States or England, where the fruit begins to rattle away in other trucks before the mere human passengers have leave to descend the gangway. Not until it has reached the retailer does it take on that golden yellow hue that is familiar to the ultimate consumer.

I dropped off at Buff Bay station on the return journey for a jaunt over the Blue Mountain range. The "finger-boards" announced the distance to Kingston as forty-three miles, but there are many short-cuts and an average pedestrian can make the journey in a single day. It is a pleasant walk despite the fact that the first sixteen miles impose a climb of 4080 feet to Hardware Gap. For the foothills begin at once, and the road, narrow and grass-grown from disuse except near the coast, climbs in almost constant shade along the bank of Buff Bay river, and the trade wind sweeps incessantly up the valley. Jamaica is noted for its birds, of which there are said to be more than forty varieties peculiar to the island, and the majority of them seem to make this region their chief rendezvous. Perpendicular banana fields cover the hillsides here and there as high as they can endure the altitude. Masses of bamboos lend a needed touch of daintiness to the dense greenery, as a red-brown tree now and then speckling the steep slopes adds contrast to what would be an almost monotonous color. Then there are the akee-trees, numerous throughout Jamaica, with their bright red, pear-shaped fruit, a favorite food among the negroes, though it is deadly poison except at certain stages of its growth, and even then is reputed the cause of the vomiting sickness that is prevalent among the masses.

Higher up every turn of the road brings to view a new waterfall, standing out against the greenery in flashing whiteness. No wonder the aborigines called the island Xamayca, the land of springs and water; and how one regrets that those same red men do not inhabit it still, if only to give relief from the monotony of black, brutal faces that in time grow almost intolerable to the traveler in the West Indies, until there come moments when he would give all he possesses to see these gems of the Caribbean as they were before they became mere hives of African slovenliness.   But the only Arawaks left in the Jamaica of to-day are those which uphold the arms of the colony on its shield. Here indeed the ancient saying that "every prospect pleases and only man is vile" reaches its full meaning.

I grew weary at length of the incessant negro impudence along the way, which ranged from foul-mouthed shouts to more or less innocent demands of "Heh, bukra, what you sell?"   It is a ridiculous failing, no doubt, but I detest being taken for a peddler.   I took to shouting back, "I am selling something to make niggers white.   Want some?" But, alas, sarcasm seldom penetrates the African skull.   Far from resenting my rudeness, the simple-minded souls greeted it with roars of laughter or took it seriously, more often the latter.   Dozens called after me to know the price of this desirable remedy; several followed me up the road offering to purchase; one old woman pursued me for nearly half a mile; one group sent a boy running after me, clamoring to know the cost of my wares.   "A thousand pounds," I called back over my shoulder, which being duly reported in all solemnity to the group, brought forth a chorus of giggles and a regretful-toned, "Ah, him humbug we!"

The last two hours, from Jiggerfoot Market to the summit, was a laborious climb, but unlike many such it was lightened by frequent streams of clear, cold water.   Then all at once I found myself at the gap, or *abra,* as the Spaniards would call it, and upon me burst a view worth many times the exertion.   All the Liguanea plain from St. Thomas parish to Spanish Town and beyond, far beyond, into the far-thermost hills of St. Catherine's lay spread out like a colored map on a draughtsman's table, Kingston in full sight from the scattered rocks far outside its harbor, with the sea breaking white upon them, to its last suburbs among the foothills, the sand reef called the Palisadoes curving like a fishhook about the harbor, the remnants of what once boasted itself the most wicked town on earth at its point, the water about it so clear that one might easily have fancied he saw the sunken city of the buccaneers.   There is spring water at the very edge of the gap and if one has thought to bring a pocket lunch there is nothing to hinder a long contemplation of this marvelous panorama, except the gradually penetrating cold of the mountains, which seems indeed an anachronism within plain sight of sweltering Kingston.

This sent me striding downward again sooner than I had expected. A hill covered with an abandoned cluster of big barracks soon cut off

Kingston and most of the plain, and left the eyes to contemplate a nearer scene. Ahead, the road, leisurely and still grassy, had clawed itself a foothold in the rocky hillside, sheer and wooded with scrub growth everywhere except where landslides had scratched a white line down its face. Birds sang lustily, as if tuning up their voices for a later public appearance; human kind was pleasantly conspicuous by its absence. Beyond, on the steep flank of Catherine's Peak, the soldier town of Newcastle, where British "Tommies" live in an agreeable climate and still keep an eye on Kingston, went down like a giant's stairway into the gorge, an immense gorge always at my very feet, with little strings of roads winding in and out along its bottom as if in vain quest of an exit. And though the plain below had been faintly hazy and there were banks of clouds in the sky high above, the twin peaks of Blue Mountain range, 7360 higher than the sea, stood out as plainly as though one might have thrown a stone over them.

Five miles constantly downward by a mountain trail, though it is twice that by the highway, brings one from Newcastle to Gordontown, a somnolent hamlet closely shut in by high hills and noisy with the little river which furnishes Kingston its water. Down the bank of this I hurried on to the plain of Liguanea, where rocking street-cars carry one quickly into the insolent capital, for the mangoes were already ripening and it was high time we sailed away from the island Columbus called Santa Gloria.

THE FRENCH WEST INDIES
AND THE OTHERS

CHAPTER XVIII

THERE is a suggestion of the pathetic in the name by which the French call their possessions in the New World — " L'Amérique Française." It recalls the days when the territory they held on the western hemisphere was really worth that title, when Canada and Louisiana promised to grow into a great French empire in the west, and nothing suggested that a brief century would see their holdings reduced to a few fragments wedged into the string of British islands that form the eastern boundary of the Caribbean. The " French America " of to-day, except for Cayenne, a mere penal colony backed by a tiny slice of unexplored South American wilderness, consists of the minor islands of Guadeloupe and Martinique, and half a dozen islets dependent on the former. It is far better entitled to the more modest official name of " French Antilles."

Guadeloupe — if I may be allowed an unpleasant comparison — is shaped like a pair of lungs, the left one flat and low, the other expanded into splendid mountain heights. They are really two islands separated by the short Salt River, across which is flung a single wooden bridge, and by some geographical oversight, their names have been twisted. The lowland to the east masquerades under the false title of Grande Terre, while the truly great land of magnificent heights and mighty ravines to the south and west is miscalled Basse Terre. The misnomers suggest that they were named by some bureaucrat seated before a map, rather than by explorers on the spot.

Columbus landed on what the natives called Turukéra or Karnkéra on his second voyage — a busy time, indeed, he must have had keeping his log on that journey — and recalled the promise he had made to the monks of Nuestra Señora de Guadeloupe in Estremadura to name an island in honor of their patron Lady. He found human flesh cooking in pots on the beach and knew that he had discovered at last a land of the Caribs, the warlike cannibals of whom he had heard in Hispaniola. Among other things he saw here his first pineapple — and no doubt, like all newcomers, was surprised to find they do not grow on trees. Ubiquitous old Ponce de Leon attempted to colonize the island in 1515, but was driven out by the imminent danger of being served up in a native barbecue.   The first French to land were some missionaries who brought the aborigines bodily nourishment instead of the spiritual provender they had planned.   It was not until the days of Richelieu that letters patent were issued giving a private company a monopoly of the island, which was gradually covered with French colonists and sugar-cane.   African slavery followed as a matter of course, with its concomitant slave revolts, one of which came near to turning Guadeloupe into another Haiti, and for almost two centuries the history of the island was a constant succession of attempts on the part of England to add it to her possessions, as she did most of the French Antilles. Then in 1814 a treaty left it definitely French, slavery was abolished in 1848, and since that day Guadeloupe has followed the political reverses and successes of *la mère patrie*.

Basse Terre, the capital, is a modest little town on the southwest corner of the mountainous half of the island bearing the same name. Dating from the early days of French colonization, it once enjoyed a considerable importance, most of which disappeared with the founding of Pointe-à-Pitre, in a similar corner of the flat and more productive Grande Terre.   The rape of its commerce by the parvenu has left it merely the seat of government, the Washington of the colony, more subservient to its business-bent metropolis than it likes to admit.   This French custom of endowing their islands with separate official and commercial capitals has its advantages over the British scheme of collecting all the eggs in one basket.   Martinique would have been left in a far sadder state had the destruction of St. Pierre wiped out its governmental as well as its business center.   But there are also certain drawbacks to this more thoughtful plan; the traveler, for instance, who had hoped to find certain sources of information in Basse Terre is likely to learn that they live at " la Pointe," and vice versa.

Built in the form of a spreading amphitheater and climbing a little way up the surge of ground that culminates in the volcano Soufrière, rival of Pélée in all but its destructiveness, a scant ten miles behind it, the official capital is half hidden under a smothering foliage of trees, which stretch away in a vast carpet of verdure into the mountains beyond.   Its open roadstead is commonly an unbroken expanse of Caribbean blue, often without even a schooner riding at anchor to suggest the olden days of maritime industry.   Though the French mail-packets make this their last port of call before turning their prows into the Atlantic, or the first on the outward journey, they usually come and are gone in the night, with few inhabitants the wiser. The latter seem to worry little at this comparative slight, and dawdle on through a provincial life as if they had lost all hope or desire to wrest from "the Point" its frequent communion with the outside world. An old fort half covered with vegetation, a rambling government building constructed in the comfort-scorning, built-to-stay style of most French official structures of bygone centuries, are almost the only signs to distinguish it from half a dozen mere *bourgs* scattered about the edge of the island. A governor sent out from France dwells in a villa up in the hills; his few white assistants are bureaucrats tossed at random about the French colonies from Madagascar to Cayenne by a stroke of the pen in Paris, and they have little in common with the racial mulattoes who dwell in their uninviting, chiefly wooden houses lining the few long and rather unkempt streets of the drowsy capital, except an ardent, almost unquestioning patriotism for *la France*.

Good highways, with automobiles scattered along them, climb into the hills, especially to St. Claude, with its suburban dwellings, its big hospital, where boarders in the soundest of health are accepted, and its embracing view of the Caribbean already far below, and the dome of Soufrière almost sheer overhead. Higher still lies Matoubá, where one may bathe in icy streams within half an hour of the tropic and enervating sea-coast. But there the highways cease, dwindling away into trails through coffee-groves and verdure-vaulted footpaths which are gradually lost in the great mountain wilderness, so primitive and unexplored that even the map in the governor's office below shows only a blank space for all the heart of Basse Terre, the inaccessibility of which is typified in the name of its central peak, Mt. Sans Toucher. Other highways partly encircle the rugged half-island, clinging close to the shore, but feasible communication ceases everywhere within a few kilometers of the coast. Thus, though Basse Terre is virgin fertile in almost all its extent, and generously watered by countless springs and many rivers, it produces little for the outside world except a few tons of vanilla.

Like all the West Indies, it has almost no four-footed wild life. The *agouti*, of about the size of a rabbit and much prized for its savory flesh, is the only indigenous quadruped. The raccoon, brought from our own land long ago, has become acclimated and numerous; the island is infested with an enormous toad that was introduced to kill the rats, but which has prodigiously spread without doing much damage to the rodents. Martinique and Guadeloupe mutually accuse each other of harboring the deadly fer de lance, but neither seems to be able to produce unquestionable proof either of its own innocence or of its rival's guilt.

There are *guaguas* also in the French islands, where they are called *autos de poste*. But there is little room in them compared with the demand for places, and a curt *" Pas de place "* is almost certain to be the greeting of the would-be traveler who does not buy his ticket at least the day before. Moreover, ticket or no ticket, it behooves him to be on hand at the back of the post-office well before the starting-hour set unless he would see his reserved *place* squeezed out of existence before he has occupied it or the conveyance gone before he arrives. For the public means of transport in the French West Indies have a mania for starting ahead of time that is little less disconcerting than the *mañana* temperament of their Spanish neighbors, particularly as their favorite official hour of departure is daybreak.

Once upon a time the governor of Guadeloupe invited the officials of Pointe-à-Pitre to a ball at the capital. They left on a sailboat, the ladies in evening dress. In theory it is a journey of only a few hours, even in a sailing vessel. But this time the wind turned contrary, after the custom of winds, the boat was forced to put to sea, and it turned up six days afterward — in St. Thomas! These unhappy experiences are no longer required of the residents of the two capitals, for to-day a highway equal, except in spots, to those of France connects the two towns, nearly fifty miles apart, and an *auto de poste* makes the round trip daily. Then, too, as in all the Antilles, there are automobiles for hire to those whose income is not particularly limited.

The tropical night showed no sign of fading when the postal omnibus, its five cross seats packed with travelers of both sexes until its sides groaned, its every available space of running-boards, mud-guards, and bumper piled high with mail-sacks and baggage, rumbled away from the angry group of unsuccessful passengers gathered before the Basse Terre post-office. As we chugged out through the old fortress gate, a thin streak of light suddenly developed on the eastern horizon, widened with the rapidity of a stage effect too quickly timed, wiped out the blue-black dome of sky overhead, and sent the last remnants of night scurrying from their lurking-places like thieves before the gigantic flashlight that sprang above the rim of the earth to the east with un-natural, theatrical swiftness. In the darkness I had taken several of my fellow-passengers to be white. The same slanting sunshine that threw far to the westward the disheveled shadows of the cocoanut-palms betrayed the tell-tale African features of the lightest of them. Behind us spread a fairy panorama as we climbed to Gourbeyre, beyond which another opened out as we descended again through Dolé, with its " summer" homes and its steaming hot-water falls at the very edge of the road. Having cut off the southern nose of the island and regained the coast once more at Trois Rivières, we clung close to this all the rest of the journey, as if any further encroachment upon the rugged domain of Soufrière, its head wrapped in a purple-black mantle of clouds above us, might rouse the slumbering giant to vent his wrath upon puny mankind.

The "Rue Gerville-Réache" in which we halted a moment to exchange mail-sacks recalled the fact that the native of Guadeloupe best known to the outside world is a woman, as is the case with Martinique. Villas hidden away in the dense greenery gave way to little bay-like cane-fields, some of them so large as to boast tiny railroads, while here and there a buttress of the volcano above forced us out to the edge of the surf. In the offing Guadeloupe's smallest dependencies, a cluster of islands named Les Saintes because Columbus discovered them on All Saints' Day, stood forth from the sea like the domes of Oriental fantasy. Now and again the chauffeur or his assistant snatched at a letter held out by some countryman, indifferent to his shout of protest if they missed it, for they deigned to stop only before the town post-offices. The demand for seats was continuous, but those who had won them showed no inclination to descend. A score of times we sped past some lady of color all dressed up in her most resplendent turban, *foulard,* and ample, flower-printed calico gown, who had hoped to go to town that day, the chauffeur indicating by a disdainful wave of the hand across his body that there was "nothing doing." Veritable riots of words assailed him at each halt, as if he might have produced new seats, magician-like, from his sleeve. One by one several male passengers took to displaying their fancied knowledge of English for my benefit; once a burly schooner-captain with just enough negro blood in his veins to make his hair curl, next a darker pair of graduates of the Sorbonne, who, once having impressed their fellow-passengers with their extraordinary learning, dropped back into French again, a French more precise and chosen than that of Paris, as soon as they found I understood it.

Even in the thatched huts along the way there was considerable more *commodité* than in those of Haiti. The old semispherical sugar-kettles one finds scattered throughout the West Indies were here enclosed in stones and mortar and used as outdoor ovens.   At Petit Bourg we came out, on the edge of the open sea again, with a view across the bay to Pointe-à-Pitre, and behind it flat, unscenic Grande Terre, without even a hill to enliven its horizon.   Soon we dropped down into a dreary level country utterly unlike the rolling cane-covered land swelling into mountains behind us, and sped through mangrove swamps that burdened the air with their rotting, salty smell, rumbled across the stagnant Rivière Salée, six miles long and some fifteen feet deep, which divides Guadeloupe into two islands, and turned into a broad, white, dusty road that not long after became the main street of " La Pointe."

Point-à-Pitre is said to have taken its name from the fact that the " point " on which it was founded a century later than Basse Terre belonged to a Dutchman named Peters.   Many refugees of this nationality settled in the French islands after the Portuguese drove them out of Brazil.   The commercial capital is situated at the mouth of the Salt River, in one of the hottest and most uninviting spots in the West Indies. Across the bay Guadeloupe proper, piled up in its labyrinth of mountains veiled in the blue haze of distance, seems to invite the perspiring inhabitants to cease their bargainings and retire to the cool heights. Young as it is, " the Point " has long since outgrown Basse Terre in size and importance.   It is a deadly flat town, with wide, right-angled streets, fairly well paved in a kind of crude concrete, with here and there a corner that recalls Paris, as do the street names.   Its gray plaster houses have heavy wooden shutters and door-sized blinds that give them a curiously furtive air.   Except for the turbans and calicos of the negresses, and the gamut of complexions, it is rather a colorless town, even the " cathedral " being of the prevailing gray, unpainted tint, though set off by a slight square tower in flaming red.   The narrow entrance to its capacious bay is flanked by cocoanut-palms that stretch far around and finally envelop it, the view from the sea having little to attract the eye.   The central square pulsates from dawn until the sun is high overhead with ceaselessly chattering market-women dressed in the hectic cotton garb peculiar to the French islands.   Down by the wharves surges another market where fishermen in immense round hats come with their boatloads of fish and sundry sea-foods, including the *langouste*, a clawless lobster unsurpassed for quality and quantity of flesh and selling for the equivalent of a quarter.

There are suggestions of Parisian street life in Pointe-à-Pitre, interlarded with tropical touches of its own.   Frenchmen whose faces give evidence that they have not left their cuisine and wine-cellars behind cling tenaciously to those white pith helmets without which no man of their race thinks he can endure the tropics. Soldiers and ex-soldiers with varying degrees of African complexions stalk about in their horizon-blue or colonial khaki, a string of medals gleaming on their chests. Negroes in Napoleon III beards stroll along the shaded edge of the streets with a certain Latin dignity befitting such adornment, even when it is accompanied by bare feet. Humped oxen, yoked sometimes on the neck, more often on the horns, saunter through town with their cumbersome carts. The town-criers, two men in uniform, the one beating a drum and the other reading aloud an official notice on each corner, carry the thoughts back to medieval France. Cafés with awning-shaded tables, monopolizing the sidewalks, notices exceedingly French not only in wording, but in general appearance, posted on house and shop walls, even the rather run-down aspect of the buildings, give the place a decidedly French atmosphere. If other proof of its nationality were needed, there are the crowds of wilted, yet patient, people packed about the wickets of post-office, telegraph station, and all other points where the public and the ambitionless, red-tape-ridden mortals whom France appoints to minor government office come into contact.

In the large, rather pleasantly unkempt park, shaded with veritable grandfathers among trees, lepers, victims of the "big leg," and other loathsome ailments were cutting the grass with crude shears and little toy hoes. In the outskirts, to say nothing of suspicious odors in the heart of town, stood stagnant ditches of unassorted garbage. Venders of indecent photographs marched brazenly about town, buttonholing the male tourist at every opportunity. The children did less open begging than those in the British islands, but there were white boys and girls among them whose manners and appearance showed them in a little less degraded condition than the blacks. What a place Pointe-à-Pitre alone would be to "clean up" to something approaching our standards of sanitation and domestic morals, were we so foolish as to follow a recent suggestion and purchase the French Antilles.

We drifted into a courtroom during a civil trial. The room itself appeared not to have been swept or dusted for years except in those conspicuous central portions where it was unavoidable; cobwebs festooned every corner; little heaps of debris lay under nearly every bench. Yet there were numerous statues in and about the building. The court consisted of three judges, a white man in the middle, flanked by two mulattos, all of them, as well as the more or less negro lawyers, dressed in black robes trimmed with " ermine "; that is, with moth-eaten rabbit-skin cuffs and lapels.   On their heads were curious skull-caps, and beneath their robes unpressed white or khaki trousers of a cheap material, which suggested that the high cost of clothing burdened even these lofty officials.   A lawyer was ranting monotonously, the gist of his remarks being that while all Guadeloupe knew that it was the desire of a gentleman recently deceased to leave his fortune to the plaintiff, it was quite impossible to carry out his desires because he had neglected to decorate his will with the required government stamp.   Laboriously a yellow clerk, also in a robe, sat slowly scratching away with an old-fashioned steel pen, adding to the stacks of dog-eared hand-written papers that already filled a musty room next door almost to over-flowing.   Surely there was no doubt about Pointe-à-Pitre being French despite the un-Parisian complexions of its inhabitants.

If it is less beautiful than the mountainous half of Guadeloupe, Grande Terre had a materialistic advantage over the misnamed highland to the west.   Its flatness makes it everywhere accessible by a network of good highways.   A broad, white road stretches out along the coast through the mangroves that surround the commercial capital, and pushes on to the considerable towns of Ste. Anne, St. François, and Le Moule, while other highways crisscross the island, giving easy communication for all the sugar-mills scattered about it.   More exactly they are rum-mills, for the French islanders give far more attention to their far-famed liquor, and the cane-fields that all but cover Grande Terre serve almost exclusively for filling casks and bottles.   Their processes are still rather primitive, but fortunes have been won during the war, for all that.   Once out upon this half of the island, the traveler finds it has a few low hills and ridges, but they are so slight that a bicycle affords easy means of communication, which can be said of few West Indian islands.   Along the mangrove-lined coast are many shacks almost as carelessly thrown together as those of Haiti, yet all over Guadeloupe there is patent evidence that the negro is a far different fellow when directed by the white man than when running wild.   The song of the jungle by night is broken by the constant roar of distant breakers and the noisy, merry negro voices and primitive laughter that explode now and then in the tropical darkness, while fireflies swarm so thickly that they look to the wanderer along the coast roads like the electric-lights of a large city.

All the scattered islets of the French West Indies are dependencies of Guadeloupe, being geographically nearer that island, leaving Martinique to concern herself with strictly domestic affairs. The most important of these is Marie Galante, six leagues south of Grande Terre, with fifteen thousand inhabitants and several *usines* to turn her canefields into rum. Les Saintes, Petite Terre, and Désirade, the latter the first landfall of Columbus on his second voyage, and owing its name to that circumstance, lie somewhat nearer the mother island. Far to the north is St. Martin, the possession of which France also shares with Holland despite its barely forty square miles of extent, making it the smallest territory in the world with two nationalities. No less interesting, though still more tiny, is the neighboring isle of St. Barthélemy, colloquially called "St. Barts." The inhabitants are chiefly white, and among them one finds the physiognomy, traditions, and customs of their Norman ancestors. Yet though they speak French, it is only badly, the prevailing language being English, or at least the caricature of that tongue which many decades of isolation have developed.

The history of "St. Barts" recalls another nation that once had West Indian ambitions. In 1784 Louis XVI ceded the island to Sweden in return for the right to establish at Gothenburg a depot for French merchandise. But its isolation and distance from its homeland made it a burden to the Swedes, and in 1877, after all but one of its 351 inhabitants had voted in favor of a return to French nationality, it was handed back free of charge, King Oscar II making a gift to the inhabitants of the eighty thousand francs' worth of crown property on the island. Since then the people seem again to have changed their minds, due probably to their subjection to the colored politicians of Guadeloupe. A few months ago, when the Crown Prince of Sweden called at "St. Barts" on his way to a hunting expedition in South America, he was received with open arms, and left with what the natives took to be a promise to assist them to transfer their allegiance to England or the United States, preferably the latter. Under the Stars and Stripes, they argue, their "great resources" would be fittingly developed. The island was once noted for its pineapples, but the tendency of shipping to strike farther southward and, touch Barbados instead has ruined this, as it has the tree-cotton industry. Of volcanic formation, the island suffers for lack of trees and water, being forced to hoard its rainfall in large cisterns, like St. Thomas. Gustavia, the capital, was once rich and prosperous, being a depot of French and British corsairs who carried on trade with the Spanish colonies. There are still immense cellars built to hold the booty and merchandise, and zinc and lead mines that lie unexploited for lack of capital.   To-day the inhabitants live for the most part in abject poverty, getting most of their sustenance from the neighboring islands and emigrating to Guadeloupe, where they are noted for their excellency as servants, despite their unfamiliarity with the native " creole."

In the outskirts of Guadeloupe's commercial capital

Port de France, capital of Martinique

The savane of Fort de France, with the Statue of Josephine, once Empress of the French

CHAPTER XIX

RAMBLES IN MARTINIQUE

MARTINIQUE, though considerably smaller than Guadeloupe, from which it is separated by the British island of Dominica, probably means more to the average American, possibly because within the memory of the present generation it was the scene of the greatest catastrophe in the recorded history of the Western hemisphere. Some forty miles long and averaging about half of that in width, it is essentially volcanic in origin, untold centuries of eruptions having given it an almost unbrokenly mountainous character, heaping up those many *mornes* and *pitons*, as its large and small cone-shaped peaks are called, which stretch from its one end to the other. Its latest census, now ten years old, credited it with 184,000 inhabitants, ten thousand of whom consider themselves pure white. Martinique is fond of calling herself the " Queen of the French Antilles," a title not wholly without justification, and to cite the fact that Cayenne and Guadeloupe are subservient to her in certain governmental matters as proof that she is the favorite American child of the mother country.

The traveler who disembarks in the harbor of Fort de France, capital of Martinique since 1680, is sure to have impressed upon him the fact that the negro with French training is even more inefficient under excitement than the excitable Gaul himself. Barely has the steamer come to anchor when her gangway becomes a shrieking, struggling, all but immovable mass of barefoot boatmen, of more or less negro policemen, custom employees, hotel runners, porters, ships' agents, embarking and disembarking passengers, and venders of minor local products, all ignorant of that sophomoric law of physics that descending and ascending bodies cannot occupy the same place at the same time. Bags, bundles, crates, valises, and trunks are dragged helter-skelter down this seething sloping bedlam, one of the latter now and then eluding the grasp of the struggling boatman, who is forced to dedicate one hand to his own safety, and splashing into the sea, there to float serenely about for some moments until it is rescued single-handed by the same hare-brained individual. For the *bateliers* of the French Antilles do not believe in mutual coöperation. Three trunks suffered this particular fate during our landing, but our own luck was less trying, the only mishap being that the boat loaded with all our worldly baggage, forced beyond the grasp of its owner by his clamoring rivals, began to float serenely out to sea.

By some stroke of genius, indispensable to those who have been denied the lesser gift of common sense, the fellow succeeded in rescuing his craft before the swift tropical night had completely blotted it out, and a quarter of an hour later we scrambled up the end of a long, slender, not to say drunken and decrepit, wooden pier all but invisible in the thick darkness. A youth beside whom Rachel looked tall required assistance in placing the trunk on his head, but once under it he requested that the valises be piled on top of it and scurried away as if he had nothing on his mind but the aged felt hat that served him as a pad. The *douane* was dirty, ramshackle, and lighted only with a pair of weak oil torches, but its officials were so courteous that we were not even required to lower our possessions from the bearer's head to the floor. A hotel facing the savanna resembled the hang-outs of Parisian *apaches,* but it was in some ways preferable to spending the night in the park. Luckily the "choice room" into which we were shown was only dimly lighted by a flickering candle.

"Et le bain?" I queried, as the chambermaid was hurrying away to resume her rôle as waitress.

"Bath?" she murmured reminiscently, thrusting her turban-crowned African face back into the room. "Oh, yes, there is a tub below but — but it does n't function."

"No water?"

"Plenty of water, monsieur, but the stopper has been lost."

"What do people do?"

"When *messieurs les clients* wish to bathe, they sit in the tub and pour water on themselves, but — "

"Generally they don't wish to?" I concluded caustically, but the intended sarcasm was completely lost on the femme-de-chambre, who replied with fetching simplicity, "No, usually not, monsieur."

Luckily, the departure of a flock of tourists next day gave us admittance to the one tolerable hotel in the French West Indies.

A few weak electric-light bulbs scattered here and there in the dense humid darkness did not give the town a particularly inviting aspect. On the broad grassy *savane* there was scarcely light enough to see where one was going, which made progress perilous, for the habits of personal sanitation of the French islanders are not merely bad; some of them are incredible. The French themselves being none too careful in such matters, it is hardly to be expected that their negro subjects would develop high standards. Few streets are well paved, most of them have open gutters down each side, but the slope of the town is fortunately sufficient to keep the running water clear except at about eight in the morning, which is the hour chosen by householders to get rid of their accumulated garbage.

Though it was merely Friday evening, a band was playing, and playing well, a classical program in the savanna kiosk. Frenchmen, in huge pith helmets that gave them the aspect of wandering toadstools, were strolling under the big trees of the immense, grassy square. With them mingled, apparently on terms of complete equality, their colored compatriots, the women in Parisian hats or the chic little turban, with its single protruding donkey-ear, peculiar to Martinique, according to their social standing, the men in the drab garb of the mere male the world over. There was not exactly a boisterousness, but a French freedom from restraint which gave the gathering an atmosphere quite different from similar ones in the more solemn British West Indies. Among the most interesting features of the Antilles is to note how closely the imitative negroes resemble in manner, customs, and temperament their ruling nations. Yet one conspicuous feature of French night life was absent from that of Fort de France — the aggressively amorous female of the species.

By day we found the center of the *savane* occupied by the white marble statue of the most famous native of Martinique, the Empress Josephine. Surrounded by a quadrangle of magnificent royal palms, a bas relief of her crowning by Napoleon set into the pedestal, a medallion portrait of her imperial husband in one hand, she gazes away toward her birthplace across the bay with an expression which in certain lights suggests a wistful regret for ever having left it. But it is a flitting expression; most of the time she is visibly the proud Empress of the French, and still the idol of her native Martinique, for all her checkered story. Of other statues the most conspicuous is that of Schoelcher, the Senator from the Antilles who fathered the emancipation of the slaves, decorating the untended little plot before the Palais de Justice.

In the sunlight Fort de France has a cheerful aspect. About the edge of the savanna are several open-air cafés, some of them housed in tents, none of them free from clients even in the busiest hours of the day. The town swarms with women in that gay costume of Martinique, which suggests moving-picture actresses, dressed for their appearance before the camera, rather than staid housewives and market-women engaged in their unromantic daily tasks; some of its buildings rival them in the African gorgeousness of their multicolored walls. Almost wholly destroyed by fire thirty years ago, it has nothing of the ancient air to be found in many West Indian cities, though some of its comparatively modern structures are already sadly down at heel.   Once it was of secondary importance, a mere capital, like Basse Terre in Guadeloupe, but the destruction of St. Pierre increased its commercial prosperity, and its twenty-seven thousand inhabitants of ten years ago have considerably increased since then.   The decrepit horse-carriages of the last decade have almost wholly given way to automobiles, American in make by virtue of the war, and aware of their importance in an island with neither tramways nor railroads.   Window glass, uncalled for in the tropics, is almost unknown, wooden jalousies taking the place of it when the blazing sunlight or a driving storm demands the closing of its habitually wide-open houses.

Its " best families," few of them free from a touch of the tar-brush, have the customs of family isolation of the France of a century ago; its mulatto rank and file have the negro's indifference to publicity in the most intimate of domestic affairs.   If one may judge by the prevalence of ugly French *pince-nez,* the whites and " high yellows " find the glaring sunlight and light-colored streets trying to the eyes.   Seen from any of the several hills high above, the town is dull-red in tint, flat and all but treeless, except for its green rectangular *savane,* only the openwork red spire of the cathedral protruding above the mass.   Yet when the sun plays its cloud shadows across it, and the musical bells of its single church are tolling through one of the interminable funerals, the Fort Royal of olden days is well worth the stiff climb an embracing view of it requires.

The cathedral is modern, decidedly French in atmosphere despite strong negro leanings.   Some of its stained-glass windows depict the native types, mulatto acolytes attending a white bishop, backed by the well-done likenesses of worshipers in the striking female costume of the island, with a male in solemn Sunday dress thrown in between for contrast.   One wonders why the Spanish-Americans have not also adopted so effective a form of decoration instead of clinging tenaciously to the medieval types.   In the congregation few pure whites are to be seen, except for the priests, and the nuns who herd their scores of girl orphans in brown ginghams and purple turbans into the gallery pews. The collection is taken up by a black priest — who gives change to those who have not come supplied with the customary small coin — but the officiating curates are wholly French. The lives they lead, if one may judge from certain indications, are more of a credit to their church than those of their colleagues in the Spanish tropics.

Sunday in Fort de France is not the deadly dull Sabbath of the British West Indies. The market and many of the shops are open in the morning; the cooler hours of the afternoon find the town enlivened with strollers, from the ramparts of grim old Fort St. Louis to the banks of the Rivière Madame, lined by vari-colored boats drawn up out of the water, with whole jungles of nets hung out to dry, with carelessly constructed little houses, in the shadows of which squat chattering, boisterously laughing negroes. The evening is one of the three during the week on which the movies function. We attempted one night to attend the largest of these. A long line of automobiles was disgorging noisy, overdressed natives of all colors except pure white. About the doors squatted scores of turbaned women, each waiting patiently for some admirer to supply her with a ticket; a swarm of ragged young black rascals blocked the entries, casting insolent glances, if not audible remarks, at the more attractive women, particularly if they chanced to be white. Black policemen garbed in resplendent white uniforms for once in the week, stood gossiping in groups, waving to their friends, doing everything except making any attempt to keep order. Then, if further proof of the genuine Frenchness of Fort de France were needed, there was a clawing, shrieking mob wedged in an impenetrable mass about a wicket six inches square and waist-high, in which one negro kept his face plastered for ten minutes, trying in vain to agree with whomever was behind it on the purchase of a paper ticket. The French have many fine qualities, but public orderliness is not one of them, particularly when African blood runs in their veins.

The great covered market of Fort de France is daily the scene of a similar uproar. By day it presents a kaleidoscopic panorama of venders and buyers in every known shade of garb and complexion; by dark, when it remains open that late, it suggests some drunken inferno. Bargaining is one of the chief amusements of the West Indian negro; when he has been reared in a French environment he seems to find double joy in it. Every purchase is the occasion for an extended quarrel which stops short of nothing but actual fisticuffs. A slice of meat tossed from the scales into a purchaser's basket invariably brings a shriek of protest from the seller. The buyer has " short-changed " him! Buyers always do, unless they are the despised tourists who always foolishly pay the first price demanded. A mighty shouting arises over the scene of contention; it increases to an uproar that is almost audible above the general hubbub. The meat and the money are snatched back and forth a score of times; foul names are seen, if not heard, on the thick lips of the shrieking opponents; a copper is added to the handful of now bloody coins, withdrawn again as the seller slashes a match-sized strip off the maltreated slice of meat; copper and strip are once more conceded, the screams grow deafening, until at length a bargain is struck, and the two part company with friendly nods that are mutual promises to engage in similar entertainment on the morrow. The tiny portions of Haitian markets are not found in those of the French Antilles. Whole boxes of matches, entire yams, sometimes as many as two or three bananas change hands in one single transaction. Many a matron whose purchases do not sum up to more than three or four pounds is followed by a porter, who gathers them into his basket. A few of these burden-bearers are white men, beings sunk so low that they slink about among the haughty and more muscular negroes like creatures who are only permitted to live on suffrance; for both the French islands have dwarfish types of similar history to the " Chachas " of St. Thomas.

The traveler in the Lesser Antilles finds himself almost wholly cut off from the world's news. It is a rare cable that has not been broken for months, if not for years, and the local newspapers are faintly printed little rags through which one may search in vain for a hint of the happenings outside the particular island on which one chances to be marooned. Instead of news, the front pages are taken up with local political squabbles, and, in the French islands, with challenges to duels, set in the largest type available. Let it not be supposed, however, that these lead to any great amount of bloodshed. In virtually all cases the long series of letters exchanged between the contestants, or, more exactly, between their seconds, and set down at full length in the public prints, end on some such tone as:

Messieurs Pinville and Larcher, representing M. Marc Larcher, and MM. Binet and Hantoni, representing M. Louis Percin, having met in the city hall in the matter of a demand for satisfaction from M. Marc Larcher by M. Persin, on account of an article in the " Democratic Coloniale " of March 20th, came to an agreement that there was a misunderstanding between M. Percin and M. Marc

Larcher, neither the one nor the other having ever had the intention of making any allegations which should encroach upon the private life of either.

In consequence, they declare the incident irrevocably closed.

Done in duplicate at Fort de France, March 23, 1920,

and signed by the pacifiers. Thus the principals have impressed upon their fellow-citizens their chivalrous code of honor and undaunted courage, the seconds have won a bit of personal publicity, and no harm has been done. In a way the Martinique system has its advantages over the more direct American method of a pair of black eyes.

A coast steamer leaves Fort de France every morning at peep of dawn for what was once the larger city of St. Pierre. For three hours it chugs northwestward along the coast, dotted with little fisher villages half hidden behind cocoanut-palms and the long lines of pole-supported nets drying beneath them. Here and there it halts to pick up or discharge passengers in rowboats, and to take on the capital's daily supply of milk — in five-gallon Standard Oil tins corked with handfuls of of leaves. The sea is usually pond-smooth here under the lee of the island. Many sandstone cliffs as absolutely sheer as if they had been cut with a gigantic knife line the way, with little shrines at the foot of most of them to keep them from falling into the sea. Behind, the verdant mountains climb steeply into the sky, as if, the island being a bare twenty miles wide, they must make the most of the space allotted them. The coast is speckled with fishermen in broad, trapezoidal straw hats, standing erect in their precarious little boats or setting their nets for the day's catch. Their method is simple. Half a dozen of them fence in a great oval stretch of water near the shore with a single net hundreds of yards long and weighted on one side. Then, when only the floating support blocks remain above the surface, they proceed to throw stones into the enclosure, to pound the water with their paddles, to splash about like men gone suddenly mad. Apparently the fish rise to see what all the commotion is about, for half an hour later the fishermen begin to drag their net inshore, and the haul is seldom less than several boatloads of the finny tribe, of every size from the *coli roux*, resembling the sardine, to mammoth fish that must be quickly clubbed to death for safety sake, and of every variety known to the tropical seas. Already the inhabitants of the neighboring villages are trooping down to the shore with their native baskets and makeshift receptacles, and by the time the net is stretched out on its poles to dry the last of the catch has been sold and carried away.

But we are nearing St. Pierre.   Carbet, the last stop, where Columbus landed just four centuries before the great catastrophe, is falling astern, and as we round its protecting nose of land the flanks of Pélée rise before us, broken and wrinkled and cracked and heaped up in scorched brown slopes that end in blue-black clouds clinging tenaciously about the volcano's head, as if to shield the murderous old rascal from detection.   This same steamer, one of the crew who served in the same capacity in those days tells us, barely escaped from the disaster that overwhelmed the chief city of the Lesser Antilles.   She had left St. Pierre at daybreak — for her itinerary was reversed when the capital played second fiddle to her commercial rival — and was entering the harbor of Fort de France when two mighty explosions that seemed to shake all Martinique " set us praying for our friends in St. Pierre." Next day she returned, only to find — but just here our informant was called away to help in the landing, and left us to picture for ourselves the sight that met his eyes as he steamed into this open roadstead on that memorable morning.

Ships no longer anchor off St. Pierre.   For one thing, a shelf of the sea floor was broken off during the eruption, and left the harbor all but unfathomable.   Besides, the world's shipping passes ruined St. Pierre by now, and only this little coaster comes daily to tie up to a tiny pier where once stretched long and busy wharves.   At the end of it one is confronted by a statue, a nude female figure which is meant to be symbolical of the ruined city in the day of its agony. But the effect is unfortunate.   For the thing is so inartistically done that it suggests a lady of limited intelligence crawling out of her bathroom after having inadvertently blown out the gas — and the ludicrous seems out of place in one's first pilgrimage to the American Pompeii.

The St. Pierre of the beginning of this century was the most important city of the French West Indies.   More than that, it was noted throughout the Caribbean for its beauty, gaiety, and commercial activity.   It was a stone city, of real cut stone, built in a perfect amphitheater sloping gently down to the deeply blue sea, and cut sharply off at the rear by sheer hills that spring quickly into mountains.   White *pirogues* and the pleasure boats of its wealthier inhabitants balanced themselves in its bay among steamers and sailing vessels from all parts of the world.   Its boulevards were lined with splendid shade trees; its Jardin des Plantes ranked among the world's best botanical collections; it had electric lights and the only tramways in the Lesser Antilles; its bourse was as busy in its way as our own Wall Street.

Masses of gorgeous flamboyants, of red and purple bougainvillea, decorated its open *places* and its commodious residences, which stretched away into flowery suburbs with half a dozen pretty French names. In a way it had copied Paris too closely, for its night life was hectic with "sadly famous" casinos, with gaiety unconfined; it felt a certain pride in hearing itself called the "naughtiest city in the West Indies."

St. Pierre was proud of the old volcano that seemed to watch with a fatherly care over the destinies of the city at its feet. Never within the memory of the living generation had it given a sign of wrath. A pretty little lake filled its crater, with *fougères* and begonias and soft velvety moss growing about its shores. To the Pierrotins it had long been the chosen place for picnics and Sunday excursions.

Yet never was a people given fuller warning of impending disaster. As early as February in their final year of 1902 the inhabitants commenced to complain of a sulphurous odor from the mountain. During the following month dense clouds began to rise about its summit. "Old Pélée is smoking again," the people told one another, laughingly; but not a man of them dreamed that their old playmate meant them any harm. On April 22 a light earthquake broke the cable to Dominica. On the twenty-fourth a rain of cinders fell on all the northern part of the island. The Sunday following saw many pleasure parties mounting to the crater-lake to watch the playfulness of "old Pélée" at close range. On the twenty-eighth great growlings were heard, as if some mammoth bear were struggling to escape from his prison in the bowels of the earth. From the beginning of May cinders fell almost daily over all Martinique. Steam rose from the crater; bursts of fire, like magnified lightning flashes, played about the volcano's summit; the clouds grew so dense that the days were a perpetual twilight, the water-supply was half-ruined by the soot it carried. On the fifth a great deluge of boiling mud swept down the River Blanche, completely submerging a large sugar-factory on the edge of St. Pierre and killing several persons. Great rocks came rolling down the mountainside; the cable between Fort de France and Santo Domingo parted; rivers were everywhere overflowing their banks; cinders fell continuously; the vegetables which the market-women brought down from the hills were covered with ashes.

St. Pierre began to lose its nerve. But the optimists asserted that the worst was over. A decrease in the fall of cinders on the following day seemed to bear out their assertions, though trees were breaking under the weight of ashes, and the cable to St. Lucia was disrupted, completely cutting Martinique off from the outside world. The men of St. Pierre felt that they could not abandon their affairs for a mere display of gigantic fireworks; their families refused to leave husbands and fathers for their own selfish safety's sake; no doubt pride kept many of the inhabitants from fleeing. A scientific commission in the capital assured the frightened city that it was in no danger whatever — scientists have been known to make serious mistakes on similar occasions. The governor and his wife came to St. Pierre to lend the reassurance of their presence, and the city took on a calmer demeanor and went on about its business.

On the night of May 7 a torrential rain, accompanied by unprecedented thunder and lightning, swept over the island. That, the people told themselves, was a sign that the danger was over. The eighth dawned fresh and clear. The vapors from the crater went straight up and floated away on the trade-wind. The inhabitants forgot their fears and began to prepare for a *jour de grande fête*, for it was Ascension Day. Then suddenly, at eight o'clock, two mighty explosions that were heard as far off as Dominica and St. Lucia had barely subsided when an enormous black cloud with bright streaks in it rolled down from the crater at express speed, enveloped St. Pierre, halted abruptly a few hundred yards north of the neighboring village of Carbet, and floated slowly away before the wind. The pride of the French West Indies, with its twenty-eight thousand inhabitants, had been completely wiped out in the space of forty-five seconds.

That night the wreck of a steamer, its superstructureless deck strewn with a score of charred and dismembered bodies, crawled into the harbor of St. Lucia.

" Who are you? " shouted the crowd gathered on the wharves, " and where do you come from? "

" We come from hell," shouted back the only surviving officer. " You can cable the world that St. Pierre no longer exists."

Eighteen years have passed since the destruction of St. Pierre, and it is still little more than a fishing village. From the waterfront one gets an impression of partial recovery; once landed, one finds only a fringe of houses along the sea, frail wooden houses with little resemblance to the old stone city. Sloping wharves of stone, strewn with broken and rusted lamp-posts, with worthless iron safes, and the twisted remnants of anchor chains, accommodate only a few fishing canoes instead of their former bustling ocean-going traffic. Back of the one partly restored street lies a labyrinth of old, gray cut-stone ruins choked with the rampant vegetation which does its concealing work quickly and well in the tropics. From the beach to the sheer green mountain wall behind, a dark-gray lava dust everywhere covers the natural soil, and from this fertile humus a veritable jungle has sprung up. Former parlors are filled with growing tobacco; banana plants wave their huge leaves from out what were once secluded family residences; one can get lost in the hills of lava, so overgrown are they with forests of brush, of manioc, hedgewood, and thorny brambles. The remnants of stone walls ready to fall down at the least tremor of the earth force the cautious visitor to make many a detour. Here are great stone stairways that lead nowhere; there massive buttresses upholding nothing. Ivy and climbing plants drape the low jagged walls of former rollicking clubs and solemn government buildings. Narrow paths squirm through the thorny brush where once were crowded city streets. Of the five large churches that adorned St. Pierre, only a piece of the tower, a fagment of the curved apse, and a bit of the façade of the great stone cathedral, once among the most important in the West Indies, peer above the surrounding vegetation. The entrance hall and the tiles of the main aisle lead now to a tiny wood-and-tin church built in the center of the former structure. Rusted iron pillars, hanging awry or completely fallen, help the brush to choke up the interior; a pathetic old iron saint, without head, arms, or feet, leans against the outer wall as if he were still dazed by the fall from his niche above. Gaunt black pigs roam everywhere through the ruins, the silence of which is seldom broken except by the wind whispering through the leaves and the murmur of the running water with which the ghost of a city is still abundantly supplied.

A marvelous view of the whole scene may be had from a hill to the south of the amphitheater, where the stone bases of what were evidently once splendid suburban residences are also choked with brush and brambles. From this height the sea is of so transparent a blue that one seems to see on its bottom the reflection of the fishing canoes scattered about the bay. The single restored street, once the main artery, cuts the ruined city in two with a heavy gray line. On either side of this is a broken row of houses, some roofed with somber tin, others with red tiles that are already beginning to take on the brownish tint of age. But these few colors, as well as the rare human noises that ascend on the breeze, are but slight contrast to the gray lifelessness of all the valley, so funereal in its general aspect that the gaily blossoming trees seem strangely out of place in it.   There is a mild suggestion of Machu Picchu, the lost city of the Peruvian highlands, in this view of ruined St. Pierre, with its countless gray stone walls and gables standing forth above the deep green of the vegetation that covers all else.   The gables stand in almost perfect rows, like the headstones of an immense graveyard, so that the little, bare, lava-covered cemetery with its tiny white wooden crosses back near the foot of the mountain-wall has a pathetic, almost ludicrous aspect, like the pretense of cement-made " rustic " furniture, for the whole town is one vast cemetery.

On closer inspection one finds more inhabitants than are suggested by the first glimpse.   Dozens of drygoods-box shacks are hidden away in the lee of towering stone walls that seem on the very point of toppling over.   Hovels of grass and thatch come suddenly to light as one scrambles through the jungles of former palace courtyards and lava-razed fortresses.   The buoyant faith and trust of humanity laughs in the end at such catastrophes even as that of St. Pierre.   We halted to talk with some of the denizens of these improvised homes among the ruins.   An old negro and his wife in one of them had lost their four children in the disaster.   The woman had been sent by her mistress on an errand into the country an hour before it occurred; the man had seen a long row of peasants bound for market killed up to within a few feet of where he was working on the roadside, and a stone had fallen upon his back, crippling him for life.   Yet a few years later they had returned to build their shelter on the very spot where their children had fallen.

" We could n't stand it in Fort de France," explained the old man. " It was always raining, stinking, full of mud and fever."   As a matter of fact, there is scarcely an iota of difference in climate between the two cities, but homesickness easily gives false impressions.

If St. Pierre is not yet rebuilt, it is not because of fear, but by reason of the fact that only a scattered handful of its inhabitants were left alive.   In the city itself there was one survivor, a negro prisoner confined in a deep dungeon from which he was rescued four days later. Only those who chanced to be away from home or in the far outskirts outlived that fateful May morning.   Yet already it has several distilleries, half a dozen schools, a post-office and telephone station, a gendarmerie, and two or three makeshift hotels.   The inhabitants are more kindly, soft-mannered beings than those of the capital, as if the disaster had tamed their souls. But even they are beginning to demand the restoration of their city to the rank of a municipality. At present it is not even a commune, but a suburban dependency of the neighboring village of Carbet. Its streets are unlighted at night; five hundred market women crowd the little Place Bertin daily in blazing sunshine or drenching rain, for lack of a covered market. Only by its re-creation into a separate municipality, insist its inhabitants, will these things and many like them be remedied; and once they are, St. Pierre will begin to take on its old importance and grow rich and prosperous once more. Meanwhile old Pélée, cold and inexorable, sloping majestically upward from the blue Caribbean in broken, wrinkled, treeless, brown grandeur, seems to look down upon the optimistic little creatures at his feet with a grim, sardonic smile.

I set out to climb the volcano that afternoon, halting at Morne Rouge for the night. From St. Pierre a good highway climbs abruptly into the hills, along the lava cliffs of the Rivière Blanche, once seething with boiling mud, now glass-clear again, with washerwomen toiling here and there along its banks. During the eruption, the first visitors after it ceased assure us, blocks of lava a hundred cubic meters in size were thrown out by the monster, and the tropical rains falling on these red-hot ingots produced all manner of violent phenomena. To-day these giant blocks are broken up into far smaller masses, or have disintegrated entirely into lava soil of great fertility. Forty square miles were utterly devastated on that May morning, not a living thing remaining within that area. But if nature destroys in one swift flare, it also reconstructs quickly in these tropical regions. Lava valleys full of waving bamboos, cliffs lined with splendid tree-ferns, patches of sugar-cane stretching up the steep slopes seemed to belie the story of destruction, while swarms of children about the frequent huts, many of the boys in *poilu* caps, the gay little girls with frizzled tresses, sometimes covered with replica of their mothers' gay turbans, showed that even mankind was recovering from the devastation. For the "race suicide" of continental France is not duplicated in her West Indian colonies.

Morne Rouge sits on a ridge of one of the great buttresses that uphold Pélée, towering 4429 feet above the Caribbean, with dimensions not unsimilar to those of Vesuvius. It, too, was destroyed, though some months later than St. Pierre, but many of its inhabitants took warning in time and have returned to reconstruct the place to almost what it was before. By some miracle, according to the French parish priest with whom I spent the night, its huge church all but escaped damage, and only the cross on its spire, still tipsy after eighteen years, recalls the ordeal through which it passed. Wild begonias and many flowering shrubs give the scattered town the air of a semi-tropical garden, and the spreading view of the Caribbean, already far below, enhances the beauty of its situation.

The ascent of Pélée is neither dangerous nor particularly difficult for an experienced pedestrian. If I accepted the guidance of " Patrice," at the curate's suggestion, it was rather because of the weather than for any other reason. The morning was gloomy, with heavy, intermittent showers, and the dense clouds that covered all the upper half of the volcano made it unlikely that a stranger could follow unassisted the path to the summit, though on a clear day there would have been no difficulty. It was so cold that I shivered visibly in my summer garb. Negroes in bare feet but wrapped to the ears in heavy *poilu* overcoats, squatted in the doors of their huts along the highway we followed for several miles farther. Then we struck upward through steeply sloping fields, already soaked from hat to shoes by the drenching downpours that soon became one continual deluge. As a matter of fact, " Patrice " did not boast the latter article of dress, which made it easier for him to cling to the narrow path down which poured a veritable brook. But he was more than once for turning back, and only the fear of what my host of the night might say if he abandoned a " helpless stranger who had been put in his special charge " urged him on. " Patrice " was three-fourths negro,— what the Haitians call a *griffe* and the Martiniquais a *capre*,— but somehow one did not think of his color, possibly because, like many of the French islanders, he seemed to be almost unconscious of it himself, and he had not a trace of that mixture of aggressiveness and obsequiousness of our own and the British blacks. His mind was a curious conglomeration of learning, picked up heaven knows where, and patches of the most astonishing ignorance, but he knew Pélée as a child knows its own back-yard.

This was fortunate, for it was a day in which it would have been more than easy to go astray. Only once or twice in the ascent did the fog lift, giving a glimpse of both the Atlantic and the Caribbean, of Morne Rouge half hidden in its verdure, and the green-gray site of what was once St. Pierre. Great fields of tree-ferns, whole mountainsides of them, showed in these brief intervals of visibility, with deeply wooded valleys and steep peaks and ridges entirely covered with vegetation; nowhere the bare rocks and patches of lava I had expected. Mountain " raspberries," the same inviting but rather tasteless fruit which the Porto Ricans miscall *fresas,* lined the way almost to the summit, enticing us to halt and eat regardless of the downpour. Once during the last sheer miles we had a brief view of the rim of the crater, like the edge of a world broken off by some cataclysm of the solar system. But when we had surmounted this and paused on the brink, there was nothing to be seen except an immense void filled with swirling white mist.

" Patrice " knew the value of patience, however, and for a long shivering hour we waited. Then all at once the cloud-curtain was snatched away for the briefest instant, and at our feet lay, not the quarry-like crater of the imagination, but a great valley filled with a scrub vegetation which might have been duplicated in the highlands of Scotland. Across it, like a mammoth monument, the " needle " that marks the summit, in the new form which the latest eruption left it, stood out against the sky a mere rifle-shot away. Then the mists swept in again, as if nature were some busy caretaker who had little time to waste on mere sight-seers, and left us to find our way as best we could out of the little cell-like chamber of fog in which we were inclosed.

We descended by a path that " Patrice " knew, even in the clouds, to the bottom of the crater. Gigantic rocks of every possible form lay tumbled everywhere, but so completely were they covered with light vegetation that only this closer view revealed their existence. Here and there was a *fumerole,* or smoke-hole, from which issued light clouds of vapor indistinguishable, except in temperature, from the swirling mists in which they were quickly merged. We crawled into one of these, half-covered with a hoodlike boulder, and at once lost the chill that had pervaded our very bones. The vent was like some mammoth chimney-corner, with a damp, sulphurous heat which quickly induced sleepiness and a desire to stretch out and let the world below go hang. That and the bottle of syrupy Martinique rum which " Patrice " had been foresighted enough to bring with him allayed any fear of mishap from exposure, and we ate our lunch in as homelike comfort as if the wintry winds and pouring rain outside were a thousand leagues distant.

The descent was swifter than we would have had it, thanks to the rain-soaked slopes, and almost before I realized it we were down in

the brilliant tropical sunshine again, great clumps of bamboos casting
a welcome shade over the ever more level trail and the mountainside
of tree-ferns again high above us.   At Ajoupa Bouillon (*ajoupa*, a hastily constructed shelter, is one of the few Carib words which has survived) we rejoined the highway and parted company, " Patrice " dubious of a " helpless stranger's " ability to find his way, even along a
public road.   But as I showed no inclination to add another five-franc
note to his unusual day's income for being piloted to the north coast,
he took his leave with a doleful countenance and pattered away in the
direction of Morne Rouge.

Everything I wore or carried was still dripping wet.   I turned
aside into the first open meadow and spread out all of which I could
in decency divest myself, the blazing sunshine drying it with magical
rapidity.   One felt immensely more of a sense of civilization here than
in Haiti.   There a lone white man would have hesitated to lie down
beside the highway, even had there been one.   Here one seemed as
secure as in the heart of France.   Yet there was little outward difference between the Haitians and the simple, kindly country-people
who plodded constantly past, the women carrying big bundles on their
heads.   The hats they secured by laying the load over one rim flapping
behind them, balancing their burdens with a cadenced swing of the
hips, their legs bare to the knees.   The men were fewer and seldom
carried anything.   In the fields were flocks of cattle; the little houses
were all built close to the road, for *cacos* are unknown in Martinique.
Vehicles were few despite the excellence of the leisurely French highway.   The great mass of the islanders do their traveling on foot, the
wealthy by automobile; but the latter are not numerous enough to give
the pedestrian much annoyance.

As I neared the coast, the rolling hills turned to cane-fields, stretching clear down to the edge of the Atlantic.   Compared with Cuba or
Porto Rico, the methods were primitive, or more exactly, diminutive.
Children, women, and old men picked up the cut canes, one by one, tied
them in bundles with the top leaves, and slowly carried them to small
ox-carts in which they were laboriously stood on end, bundle by bundle.
These workers received two francs a day — fifteen cents at the then rate
of exchange.   Men in the prime of life were paid four francs fifty
centimes for such work as hoeing or transferring the ox-cart loads into
the little four-wheeled railroad cars which bore them away to the fac-

A principal street of Port de France with its Cathedral

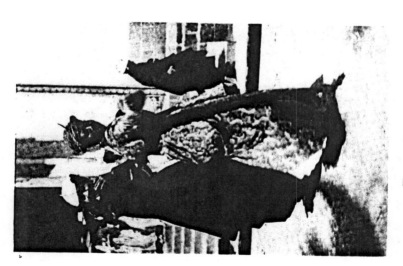

Women of Martinique

The shops of Martinique are sometimes as gaily garbed as the women

Empress Josephine was born where this house stands

tory. Cane-cutters, however, working by the *tache,* earned as much as twelve francs a day.

Unlike the smaller British islands, the French Antilles have not put all their faith in sugar. Cane products, however, form by far the most important industry. If their exports of sugar decreased by half during the war, it is because the making of rum proved more advantageous, especially as France requisitioned their sugar at less than half the price in the open market. In the very years when the United States was adopting its prohibition amendment, Martinque and Guadeloupe increased their rum production by some forty per cent. The present almost unprecedented prosperity of the islands is mainly due to the distilled cane juice they sent overseas while their sons were battling at the front. But here, too, there are loud protests at the inequality of distribution of that prosperity. Three-fourths of the island, the Martiniquais complain, belongs to five families, of pure French blood, who intermarry among themselves, keeping the estates and the chief *usines* in a sort of closed corporation. If a bit of land is offered for sale, the complaint continues, these families bid it in at any price demanded in order to freeze out " les petits." The fact that the latter may also be white men does not alter the attitude of the monopolists. Moreover, the small planter is ruthlessly exploited by the large distillers, who pay him fifty to sixty francs a ton for his cane and sell their rum at seven francs a liter. One finds, therefore, among the middle-class whites a considerable number of still patriotic but disgruntled citizens.

A little story which was going the rounds during our stay in Martinique shows that the game of " high finance " can be played even on a twenty by forty mile island. A " high yellow " native who had never been credited with extraordinary intelligence " cleaned up " three million francs during the last year of the war by the following simple little scheme. France decreed that the freight rate between Martinique and French ports should be three hundred francs a ton. The ships secretly refused space at that price. The " high yellow " individual entered into a private agreement with the steamship companies to pay the price asked, 1200 francs a ton. While his competitors were complaining that they could not ship, this man's rum was being carried to Europe, where it was sold at a high price, but not one at which, his rivals pointed out to one another, he could make any profit at such exorbitant freight rates. The man persisted, however, paying for each shipment by check as soon as it was landed. With the last barrels he, too, went to France. There he wrote a polite note to the steamship company, requesting that he be refunded the nine hundred francs a ton he had paid over the legal rate. The company laughed loudly at his colonial naïveté. He put his check stubs in the hands of a lawyer, and, to cut short the story, the company suddenly recognized the bitter truth in the assertion that he who laughs last shows superior mirth.

I halted that night in Lorrain, on the edge of a small bay with precipitous shores into which the Atlantic threshed constantly, and next morning caught the lumbering *auto de poste,* having had the foresight to reserve a *place* in it some days earlier. Even though we clung to the coast, the road climbed continuously over the buttresses of the central mountain chain, for these smaller West Indian islands have virtually no real flat lands. From the tops of the higher ridges we could plainly make out Dominica on the horizon behind us. Some of the hillsides were built up in terraced gardens, though without stone facings, in which grew among other favorite native vegetables, *gnome,* as Martinique calls the *malanga* of Cuba or the *poi* or *taro* of the South Seas. The chauffeur had small respect for any possible nerves among the passengers, and tore about the constant curves and incessant ups and downs of the ridge-braced coast as if speed were far more essential than ultimate arrival. The coast-line, ragged as a shattered panel, with pretty, old-as-France towns nestled in each scolloped bay, presented many a beautiful vista. Here and there we crossed a little cane railroad, some of the fields that fed them so precipitous that the bundles of cane were shot down across the ravines on wire trolleys. At Trinité, with its long peninsula stretching far out into the Atlantic, we turned inland and climbed quickly into the hills. Here there were a few Chinese and Hindu features, but the overwhelming majority were negroes, though full-blooded Africans were almost rare. The Frenchman is inclined to overlook the matter of color in his attachments, with the result that mulattoes are much more numerous in the French than in the British islands. There is a great difference, too, in what might be called public discipline. To cite one of many examples: one of our fellow-passengers crowded into the coach with an immense plate-glass mirror without a frame. A mishap at any of the sharp turns or steep descents might easily have shattered it and seriously injured the score of persons huddled within the vehicle. But though the one white traveler besides myself kept repeating during all the rest of the journey, " *Mais c'est* excessivement *dangereux,*" the mirror remained. In the British islands the mere attempt to enter a public vehicle with such an object would probably have resulted in a solemn case in a magistrate's court that same morning. Near Gros Morne were several hills completely covered with pineapples, the cultivators climbing along the rows as up and down a ladder. Then suddenly we came out high above the great bay of Fort de France, the square chimneys of a dozen rum *usines* dotting the almost flat lands about it, and descended quickly through ever more populous villages to the capital.

I returned to St. Pierre one morning for a walk through the heart of the island. An excellent road in rather bad repair unites the ruined city and the capital, a distance of twenty-five miles. It climbs quickly into beautiful, cool, green mountains. When one says mountains in the West Indies the word must be taken with a rather diminutive meaning, for though they are real mountains in formation, and sometimes in massiveness, the greater part of them is under water. Old sugar estates dating from the high-priced Napoleonic days, with half perpendicular cane-fields, surrounded the first few steep kilometers. Then the ascent grew more leisurely, though it mounted steadily for some three hours up the valley of the Carbet. If one was to believe the French guidebook in my pocket, I was engaged in a perilous undertaking.

"One must remember," it warned, "that Martinique is a tropical country, and the act of exposing oneself to climbing a slope on foot or of blowing up a bicycle tire, even in the shade "— the paragraph was addressed to cyclists, for the writer would never have suspected a visitor to Martinique of deliberately turning pedestrian —" is dangerous. A tropical helmet," he asserted on another page, "and a flannel stomach-band are indispensable." How I have succeeded in covering many thousand miles of the tropics on foot without harnessing myself up in those indispensable contrivances is, no doubt, a mystery. As a matter of fact, the chatter of sedentary imaginations aside, tramping is no more risky in the West Indies than in the midsummer Catskills.

During the first few miles I met many fierce-looking mulattoes in flaring piratical mustaches and kinky Napoleon III beards, carrying in their hands big, sharp-pointed cane-knives, but every passer-by bade me a soft, kindly, respectful "Bonjour, monsieur"; they had not even the hypocritical obsequiousness or the occasional insolence of the British negro.   Beyond Fond St. Denis the way descended somewhat along another beautiful valley, its slopes densely wooded, a small river boiling over the rocks at its bottom.   The *Pitons du Carbet* bulked majestically into the sky overhead; a lower peak between them was completely covered with tree-ferns.   Then the highway began to mount again, disclosing magnificent new panoramas at every turn.   It was a soft-footed road, and in these higher reaches almost entirely untraveled. The rich center of the island was surprisingly uninhabited.   The unfailing trade-wind swept down through the mountain passes to the left; hurrying clouds broke the fury of the tropical sun; there was splendid drinking water everywhere, usually carried out to the edge of the road in bamboo troughs stuck into the sheer mountain-side.   The climb ended at two huts and a shrine, dignified with the name of Deux Choux, whence another highway descended to Robert, on the Atlantic. My own paused for a marvelous view back down the dense green valley to cloud-capped Pélée and a broad stretch of the Caribbean beyond St. Pierre, then came out on a tiny meadow with grazing cattle, a lonely little hut, and a temperate climate.   A wonderfully symmetrical green peak stood directly overhead, with another, its summit lost in the clouds, breaking the horizon beyond.   Martinique, one was forced to admit, was as beautiful in its small way as Porto Rico, even though it lacks the red-leafed *bucaré,* the color-splashes of orange-trees, and the snow-like tobacco-fields.   A deep stillness reigned, emphasized rather than broken by the murmur of some distant little stream, the creaking of an insect far off in the wilderness, now and then a gust of wind which set the ferns and the bamboo plumes to whispering together.   Once I thought I heard a groan, but it proved to be only the native *boute* I was smoking, struggling for air.   Little wooden shrines were here and there set into the mountain walls, the garments of the dolls they inclosed tattered and weather-rotted.

Some eight miles from the capital a gap in the hills gave a wide-spreading view of the Atlantic, the Caribbean, and all the southern half of Martinique, tumbled, mottled by sunshine and cloud shadows, more brown than this central region, the three little islands that mark the birthplace of a French empress dotting the dense-blue bay.   Houses and people began to appear again, happy-go-lucky little huts, though with far more pride in their appearance than those of Haiti; then came the " summer villas " of the wealthier citizens of Fort de France, until the road became one long suburb.   A branch to the right descended to the hot baths of Absalon; farther on another pitched downward to those of Didier, both at the bottom of an immense cleft in the hills, and an hour later I was plodding through the hot, dusty, crowded streets of gaily-turbanned Fort de France.

The people of the French Antilles have many of the characteristics of the continental Frenchman. His faults and his virtues are theirs, the former magnified, the latter shrunken, as is the way with the negro. In outward demeanor they have little in common with the British West Indian, still less perhaps with our own blacks. They are much less given to outbursts of insolence and are more courteous. But, like the Frenchman, they are impulsive and individualistic, hence one cannot generalize too broadly. I have met some of the most genuinely courteous persons in " French America," mulattoes, *capres,* and even full negroes, with the outward evidences of a culture superior to that of any but our best class; I have met others who made me temporarily a firm believer in the righteousness of Judge Lynch. The former were decidedly in the majority; there were many who were rather over polite. But, like that of the French, their politeness is individual, never collective. After being treated with incredible courtesy by the few with whom one has come into personal contact, one is astounded to find the crowds almost brutal. The country people are, of course, more courteous than the corresponding classes in the capital; the women are, on the whole, less so than the men, another direct legacy from the French. The islanders have, too, something of that French custom of not showing surprise at strange sights or personal idiosyncrasies, that same quality that makes it so easy to live in Paris. A white man on foot, for instance, rarely seems to attract even a passing attention; in the British islands he is the constant butt of inquiry, comment, and crude attempts at ridicule, though he is an equally unusual sight in either group of islands. All these things are visibly the result of environment and the negro's monkey-like faculty for imitation. From the *capre* up he takes on certain other qualities from his white parents, though they seldom equal the original. The one pleasant trait native to the negro — his gaiety and lack of gloom — is tempered in the French islands by a sort of Latin pensiveness, while his sense of personal dignity is distinctly higher than that among the former British slaves.

His superiority to the Haitian is ample proof of the advantage of having the negro ruled over by whites, even though that rule be faulty, instead of letting him run wild. He has more sense of responsibility, more industry, and a civic spirit which the Haitian has almost completely lost. All this tends to make him comparatively law-abiding. There are few country police in the French islands, and they are not numerous in the towns, yet the stranger may wander at will and rarely meet even with annoyance. Barrels of rum are left unguarded for weeks in the streets or on the wharves of Guadeloupe or Martinique, and the case is almost unknown of their being broached or in any way molested. Even our own land scarcely aspires to that high standard. White women may go freely anywhere with far less likelihood of meeting with disrespect than in many Caucasian lands.

The French negro's superiority of deportment is partly due, no doubt, to the higher sense of equality he enjoys under the tricolor. The color line exists, but it is less direct, less tangible, more hidden than with us. When the white inhabitants speak of it at all it is apt to be in whispers. "Creoles" shake hands with, and show all the outward signs of friendship to their colored neighbors; bi-colored functions, business partnerships between the two races are common, yet the whites avoid social mixture as far as they dare. I say "dare" because that is exactly the word which seems to fit the case. The French appear to have a certain fear of their negroes, if not actual physical fear, at least a disinclination to show them discourtesy by referring to the matter of color. In fact, the colored population may be said to have the upper hand. The laws of the islands are made in France, but each of them sends a senator and two deputies to Paris, and equal suffrage gives the whites small chance of winning these offices; they have still less of being elected to municipal and colonial councils.

"It was a great mistake to give the negroes the vote," more than one white islander assured me, in an undertone, "for it leaves us whites swamped beneath them. With negroes voting, justice goes almost invariably to the man who is a friend of the *député*, and the latter is never white."

"Our colored population should be handled with a firm hand," said a white colonial from the island of St. Martin, "but of course you cannot expect the French to do that."

Fortunately for the whites, there is a considerable amount of friction between the negroes and the "*gens de couleur*," and the blacks are often more friendly to the Caucasian element than to those partly of their own race.

Even the "creole" of the islands under French rule is more orderly than that of Haiti. A knowledge of French is sufficient to carry on conversation with all classes, though the language of the masses falls far short of Parisian perfection. Curious local expressions are numerous. "*Li*" means either *il y a* or *il est;* the banana we know is a "*gro' femme*," the tiny ones which seldom reach our markets are "*figues naines*"— literally "dwarf figs." "Who" becomes "*Qui monde*," an improvement at least over the "*Qui monde ça*" of Haiti. Innumerable localisms of this kind, added to a slovenly pronunciation, make the popular tongue difficult for the stranger, but at least he is not called upon to guess the meaning of scores of terms from the African dialects such as pepper the Haitian jargon.

Though French money is current, Guadeloupe and Martinique issue notes of their own of from five francs upward. As these look exactly alike, except for the name of the island printed upon them, yet are not mutually accepted, the inexperienced traveler is sometimes put to considerable annoyance. Nominally, prices are now almost as high as in the United States, but the present low rate of exchange makes living agreeably low for the foreigner. "Telegrams" turned in at a post-office are telephoned to any part of the island in which they originate, with un-Latin despatch, at the slight cost of fifty centimes (four cents at the present exchange) for twenty words. There is no cable service, however, between the two islands, which have less intercourse with each other than with the mother country.

Schools are closely centralized, as in France, and not particularly numerous or effective, though there is less illiteracy than the census of the French islanders who helped to dig the Panama Canal seemed to indicate. Among the surprises in store for the visitor is the profound patriotism of almost all classes. Twenty thousand Martiniquais went to France as conscripts, while the British West Indies sent only volunteers, yet only one British island can in any way compare with their French neighbors in loyalty to the homeland. Thus is France rewarded for the comparative equality which she grants her subjects, irrespective of color. While the British segregated their West Indian troops into the separate regiments, with white officers over them and only the non-commissioned ranks open to soldiers of color, France mixed hers in with the poilus, and gave them equal chances of promotion. More than one black French colonel held important posts during the war. Incidentally, by this intermingling she got considerable fight out of her black troops, which can scarcely be said of the "B. W. I." regiments. This policy, carried out with what to us would be too thorough an indifference to the racial problem, has at least given her "American" subjects a great loyalty and love for France.

The nearest approach to a railroad station in Martinique is a street beside the post-office in the capital.   There, at half-past two each after-noon, three *autos de poste* set out for as many extremities of the island. A throng of would-be travelers, several times larger than the snort-ing old busses can accommodate, forms a whirlpool of gay calicos, multifarious bundles, and sputtering *patois*, in which a lone white man seems strangely out of place.   The distribution of tickets is somewhat disorderly, as one might expect, and when the vehicles chug away with their full, cramped quota, they are followed by angry shrieks and gestures from the disappointed.   The wealthy few of these hurry out to the edge of the *savane* to bargain for private cars, while the majority trudge homeward, hoping that the morrow will bring better luck, or wrathfully set out on foot for their destinations.

I won a place one afternoon in the bus for Ste. Anne, thirty-five miles away on the southern point of the island.   The region proved more rolling, less broken by abrupt hills, than the central portion. Old kettles scattered here and there, the ruins of a few windmill-towers and ivy-grown brick chimneys showed that Martinique, too, had gone through a certain process of centralization in her principal industry.   The sense of smell demonstrated that the larger and rarer *usines* we passed gave their attention rather to rum than to sugar. Beyond Petit Bourg the plains bordering Fort de France Bay gave way to a wilder landscape, with a rich red soil and many by no means perfect roads in every direction.   The turban-coiffed women and bare-foot countrymen tramping them had no such fear of the automobile as their Haitian cousins, but yielded the road to it with a sort of lofty disdain.   Everywhere men and women were working side by side in the cane-fields, which filled each suggestion of valley and cov-ered the lower slopes about it.   The appearance of the soil and the short joints of the canes suggested that this southern region needed irrigation.   Farther on came several precipices and immense ravines, the mountains sprinkled far and wide with huts and little cultivated fields which the irregularity of the ground gave every conceivable shape.   Many of the mountaineers, according to a fellow-passenger, own their farms, those far back in the hills being mainly engaged in the cultivation of cacao.   We passed half a dozen populous towns on the way, that of Rivière Pilote in a setting of enormous black boulders which carried the mind back to Namur in Belgium.   A thorny, half-arid vegetation stretched from there all the way to the petrified forest and salt ponds on the southernmost point of the island.

The St. Pierre of today with Pelée in the background

The Cathedral of St. Pierre

The present residents of St. Pierre tuck their houses into the corners of old stone ruins

Ste. Anne is a thatch-roofed little village of perhaps a hundred inhabitants, yet these included at least four *grands blessés,* cripples from the far off battle-line in France. One blind youth, whose *poilu* cap looked pale above his ebony face, sat playing a broken violin behind the little hut in which he was born. Yet he would gladly go again, he asserted, if " our dear France " needed him. Another wore the khaki overseas cap marked " 321 U. S." he had picked up on the battlefield the day he lost his leg. The policeman who gave me a shake-down in the hut from which he ruled the community insisted on showing me all six of the scars which decorated his black body, while his female companion displayed the fragments of shrapnel that had inflicted them, precious relics which she kept in a broken pitcher. He was still fighting the war over again when I fell asleep. Simple-hearted, obliging negroes, the citizens of Ste. Anne evidently saw a white man so seldom that they were scarcely aware of the existence of the troublesome " color line."

On my return, I dropped off at Petit Bourg and walked out to the village of Trois Islets. A mile beyond it, back in a pretty little hollow in the hills, are the ruins of the overseer's house in which Josephine, once Empress of the French, was born. The walls of the stone building where her parents lived until a hurricane destroyed it just before her birth, can still be traced: the kitchen behind it serves to this day the mulatto family that has built a smaller dwelling on the same site. Farther back in the valley, half hidden by tropical brush and clumps of bamboo, are the roofless remains of her father's sugar-mill — or, more likely, rum plant — where she lived until the age of fifteen. Its square brick chimney still peers above the encroaching vegetation. A long line of women were hoeing the cane on a steep hillside across the brook, their multicolored garments standing out against the Nile-green background, snatches of the falsetto song with which they cheer one another on at their labors drifting by on the trade wind — just such a scene, perhaps, as Josephine herself had known so well in her girlhood.

Marie Joséphine Rose Tascher de la Pagerie was first married to the Vicomte de Beauharnais, son of a governor of Martinique. Her mother lies buried in the parish church of Trois Islets, on a little knoll overlooking the three tiny islands which give the place its name. A stone set into the interior wall of the modest plaster and red-tiled building informs all who care to read:

Ci Git
L'Auguste Madame
Rose Claire Duverger de Sanois
Veuve de Messire J. G. Tascher
de LA PAGERIE
Mère de SA MAJESTÈ
L'IMPERATRICE
des FRANÇAIS
Décédée le 2 Juin 1807
a l'age de 71 ans
Munie des sacrements de
L'EGLISE

But neither the old municipal secretary who takes it upon himself to have a lunch prepared in the municipal building for all " distinguished visitors "— thereby adding generously to his stipend — nor the dwarfish priest in his garden-framed residence behind the church was interested in Napoleonic history. Their problems were more modern.

" How can a man live," they condoled with each other, while I studied the decorations of the priestly parlor, " with rum advanced from fifty centimes to *six francs* a liter? "

Women carrying sewer-pipes and bricks on their heads had loaded the " canoe " which carries the mails daily from Trois Islets to the capital across the bay until its gunwales were barely visible above the water. When a dozen negro passengers and sailors had added their weight to this imminent possibility of disaster, we were rowed out beyond the islets, where the captain of the trusting contrivance stood for some time at the bow blowing on a conch-shell for the wind that at length saw fit to waft us safely across to Fort de France.

CHAPTER XX

THE Dutch possessions in the West Indies consist of six islands in two widely separated groups. Curaçao, Bonaire, and Aruba lie just off the coast of Venezuela; Saba, St. Eustatius, and St. Martin are scattered among the British islands hundreds of miles to the north. A colonial government for all of them sits in Willemsted, chief and only city of Curaçao, and spreads its feelers of red tape to each small dependency and back to the Netherlands. Fifty-seven thousand people live in the four hundred square miles of these little dots on the blue sea, but there is a sharp line of demarkation between the two groups, Dutch though they both are in nationality. The inhabitants of the southern islands are mainly Venezuelan in origin and Roman Catholic in faith; they speak a manufactured language called Papiamento, without syntax or grammar, and made up of Spanish, Dutch, English, and African words, an unintelligible jargon with a teasing way of now and then throwing in a recognizable word or phrase. Those of the northern group are English-speaking and overwhelmingly Protestant. Of them all Curaçao is by far the most important, and the oldest of Holland's present colonies. But the mother country rates her scattered islands in the Caribbean of slight importance in comparison with her newer and far larger possessions in the East, Java, Sumatra, and Borneo; while even Surinam on the coast of Brazil, with its extensive river system, its gold, and its fertile soil, means more to the Dutchman than all the rest of his colonies in the New World.

We sailed for Curaçao late in April. The Caribbean was glaringly blue under the brilliant sun, the trade-wind persistently astern. On the way we passed not only Bonaire and Aruba, dismal-looking mounds of earth partly covered with half-hearted vegetation, with Margarita, jagged-topped and sand-bordered, surrounded by a strip of light turquoise water which seemed to add attraction to its name and typify its tropicality, and Tortuga, low and featureless, melting into the distant horizon. These last two belong to Venezuela, the fifth and last of the nations with possessions in the Caribbean. Early next morning we were awakened by the blowing of the steamer's siren as a signal to Curaçao to open the pontoon bridge across its narrow entrance, and, gliding into the bluest of lagoons, wound a mile or more up into the country before turning around and returning to the dock. As in Barbados, one was struck by the brilliancy of the atmosphere, the lack of restful shade. What trees there were looked dry and scraggly, the country-side was everywhere dead brown, arid, and bare, except for great clumps of organ cactus. A road or two wandered away over the little hills, only one of which could be called so much as a peak, a telegraph line of several wires following the best of them, though there is no other town than the capital on the island. One wondered why this barren reef is so thickly peopled, or inhabited at all, how even the few goats in sight find sustenance. Here and there were a few windmills, behaving with strict Dutch propriety for all the brisk trade-wind. These, and the irrigation they supply, accounted for the few tiny oases one could make out in the dreary landscape. Yet the island is unusually healthful; with ten days' rain a year few microbes can live, and the constant breeze relieves in a measure the heat of the equatorial sun.

Ships tie up to the docks in Willemsted, which is more often known by the name of the island itself, yet such is the formation of these that one must take a punt ashore, or save ten Dutch cents by swinging down the rope ladder. Negroes were languidly sculling about the densely blue harbor, using the Dutch canalboat style of a single heavy oar over the stern of the boat, and swaying their bodies as slowly back and forth as if their vocabularies did not include the word for haste. The town crowds eagerly about the harbor entrance, looking almost miniature from the deck of the towering British freighter. The houses, distinctly Dutch in architecture despite their patently tropical aspect, are well built, rarely of wood, most of them being faced with cement or plaster, all brightly colored, with red or reddish-brown tile roofs, and cornices of contrasting shades, causing them to stand out across the indigo lagoon like the figures on stained glass windows. Now and again the bridge connecting the two halves of the town broke in twain and left a motley throng gathered at each of its entrances. When it was joined together again the procession across it formed a veritable chain of human beings. The one thing that can induce the people of Curaçao to hurry is the signal for the opening of its bridge. Then from both directions comes the scurrying of mainly bare feet, jet-black women with great baskets on their heads dart in and out among those racing from the opposite shore, automobiles honk their way even faster, scattering the pedestrians in two furrows on each side, despite the warning placard in Dutch and Papiamento to " Zeer Langsam Ryden " or " Kore Poko Poko." One may, to be sure, take a punt across, but that costs ten cents, whereas the bridge fare is one cent if barefoot, two if shod, all of course in Dutch currency, and the whistle of an arriving or departing steamer is sure to cause a portion of the population momentarily to throw off its lethargy.

The people of Curaçao are less annoying than the majority of those in the smaller islands of the Caribbean. It may be the proverbial Dutch thrift which keeps the town cleaner and more orderly. The children do not beg, the adults appear occupied with their own affairs, and though the population is overwhelmingly negro, the impudence frequently met with elsewhere is not much in evidence. They are amusingly stolid negroes, with staid Dutch airs, as solemn the week round as their British brethren on the Sabbath, without a suggestion of the chic air of the French islanders. Unshaved Hollanders, with faces like yellow old parchment, wearing the heavy uniforms of their homeland and carrying short swords, mingle with the black throng, but are rarely called upon to exercise their authority. Dutch high officials, in more resplendent uniforms, dash by in fine automobiles as if bent on running down the people they have been sent to govern.

Curaçao is a free port, though this does not tend to lower its prices, and trade is its chief, almost its only, *raison d'être*. The clerks in the stores glibly quote American prices to American travelers, but they are soon out of their depth in English. Many of them can converse fluently in Spanish, but the rank and file knows nothing but Papiamento, and is astoundingly voluble in that. Or it may be that the chattering sounded more noisy because it was unintelligible, for though any one knowing Spanish can catch the drift·of a conversation in the native jargon, it is quite another matter to understand it. The men coaling ship were constantly singsonging it, but little more than the rhythm was comprehensible, though now and then a familiar word burst out clearly, like the face of a friend in a strange crowd. Old women seated in their doorways or on the ground in a patch of shade, weaving coarse hats from the bundles of Venezuelan " straw " which small boys brought them on their heads, chattered ceaselessly in Papiamento even in the hottest hours of the day. Stolid Dutchmen spoke it with accustomed ease. There were few signs in the dialect, for it is rather a spoken than a written language, though there is one tiny weekly printed in Papiamento, and two or three books in it may be had in the shops.

The names over the latter are mainly Spanish and Dutch, occasionally French or English; street names are in Dutch. The daily newspaper is in Spanish, with some of its notices and advertisements in Dutch or English. The official bulletin is of course in the official language, as are the placards in government offices. Why a few signs about town are also in Papiamento is a mystery, for the educated natives all read Dutch, and the others rarely read anything at all.

There are only ten cities in the West Indies which have tramways, and of them all that of Curaçao is the most amusing. For it is single and alone, a crude little car with an automobile engine, which makes the horseshoe-shaped journey around the bay and back every half hour. Even in the suburbs the houses are tile-roofed and plaster-faced, gay and cleanly without, though with the same newspapered interiors of most negro shacks in the West Indies. The streets of the town, following the contours of the bay, are seldom straight, and the vista down any of them gives curiously mixed reminiscences of Holland and at the same time of tropical cities.

We took the unescapable Ford out past the bulking, cream-colored Catholic church, with its glaring whitewashed cemetery of cement tombs decorated with tin flowers rattling in the breeze and a few withered plants, to an ostrich farm in the interior. A hundred or more of the mammoth birds, if one count the gray, disheveled chicks, live in pairs or groups in bare corrals walled with woven reeds, and furnish their Teutonic owner a steady and appreciable income. A dozen American windmills clustered together in a little hollow irrigate space enough to grow the alfalfa and other green stuff needed for their nourishment. Yet even this strange industry looks out of place in so arid a land, and as one scurries over the tolerable roads which cover the island, past occasional make-shift shanties, jolting mule-carts, and an endless vista of bare, parched ground scattered with repulsive forms of thorny vegetation, the wonder comes again that this desert-faced coral reef should have succeeded in attracting human inhabitants.

Of the unimportant islets, keys, and rocks which we did not visit for lack of time, transportation, or inclination, we passed by with most regret the three Dutch islands of the north, for, this being a strictly West Indian journey, we did not pretend to touch that collection of countless small and smaller bits of land, all British, known as the Bahamas. Saba we saw, clear cut against the sunrise, as we steamed lazily on into St. Kitts. It is only a mountain-top, towering three thousand feet above the Caribbean, and extending who knows how far below its surface, for the water is very deep all about this tiny patch of five square miles. Cone-shaped, of volcanic formation, it rises abruptly from the sea to the clouds, and, one thousand feet up, in what must once have been a crater, is the only town, aptly named " The Bottom." Here live some fifteen hundred inhabitants; another five hundred are scattered about in tiny hamlets called " districts." The people are mainly white, descendants of Dutch settlers, though English is the prevailing language. Some legends have it that the Sabans are really English, descended from the Devonshire exiles of the Monmouth Rebellion, but with the mixture that has gone on for many generations it is difficult to confirm this tradition. There is no real harbor; indeed, no sign of " The Bottom " and its people can be seen except from the eastern side. There the " Ladder " of eight hundred steps leads from the difficult landing to the town. Almost every one lives high up on the cone, raising Irish potatoes, onions, and other northern vegetables in the coolness of the heights. One fantastic tale has it that supplies from the outer world and the inhabitants returning with them are hauled up the slope in baskets attached to a cable anchored in the town; the unromantic truth is that the former are carried up on the heads of the latter, or on the little horses which are equally skilful in climbing the rock-cut " Ladder." Strangely enough, Saba is famed for the boats it builds, which are constructed not at the water's edge, but in " The Bottom." If he is set on remaining in Dutch territory, there could be no finer place in which to house the war lord of the twentieth century than the island of Saba.

St. Eustatius, or " 'Statia," as it is familiarly called, is another single mountain near St. Kitts, an extinct volcano with its top cut off and rising from the sea in magnificent white cliffs. Six other islands and all the eight square miles of 'Statia can be seen from its summit. Its anchorage is safe, and a steep path cut in the face of the cliff leads to Orangested, the capital, its old fort now used as court house, post-office, and prison, and the Dutch Reformed church rising above its ancient vaults. Once upon a time 'Statia was a rich and coveted prize, and many nations strove for possession of the " Golden Rock." First colonized by the Dutch, it was successively seized by the English, the French, then went on round the circle again, finally reverting to Holland. Today its glory is faded and gone, and with its deterioration its allegiance has become a bit unsteady. Emigration to the United States is unceasing, that to Holland is slight. The proportion of whites is small, though the local government is well organized under a governor-general from Holland. Several large dilapidated graveyards testify to its one-time grandeur and activity, that of the Jews being long unused, if any other proof of 'Statia's decline were needed. The limited rains and consequent lack of water are largely to blame for its rapid depopulation. The 'Statians drink rain-water, gathered from the roofs and gutters and hoarded in cisterns, their animals the salty stuff from wells. A few vegetables, more tropical than those of Saba, are grown: yams, cassava, arrow-root, sweet-potatoes, also a bit of sisal and sea-island cotton. Once St. Eustatius was a port of call for South American whalers, but even that glory is gradually being wrested from it.

The island of St. Martin is only forty square miles in extent, yet it has been a colony of two great European nations since 1648. The French and Dutch are reported to have landed simultaneously. Said they, "Let's not fight in such a climate over such a bagatelle; we 'll let two men start together and walk around the island, and from here to where they meet shall be the boundary." But the Frenchman was tall and the Dutchman short, so the latter demanded the right to choose the direction. This granted, he set out to the south, where the ground was level and fertile. Possibly he stopped now and then for a drink with the Indians. At any rate, the Frenchman won two thirds of the island. A treaty was signed, and the larger portion of the island long flourished under a private company, which eventually gave it to the French crown. It was several times taken by the English, who, if unable to retain possession, at least left it their language. Finally, at the end of the eighteenth century, Victor Hugues again won it for France and divided it along a rugged range of hills, giving Holland the southern third once more, and annexing the French part to the island of Guadeloupe. The terms of the original treaty remain in force to this day, and the two communities carry on their tiny share of the world's affairs and their common salt industry in perfect amity, despite their two faiths, two sets of laws, and two official languages.

Rather because it has long been an habitual pastime than in the hope of seeing the quest greatly rewarded, I kept a constant lookout for native literature during our journey through the West Indies. Four sections in the Biblioteca Nacional of Havana are devoted to Cuban writers, totaling perhaps five hundred volumes. With the exception of

The harbor of Curaçao

A woman of Curaçao

The principal Dutch island is not noted for its verdure

A Curaçao landscape

about a score of these, however, the collection is made up of ponderous tomes of what might be called history were they not filled with long-winded political squabbles completely devoid of interest to the general reader, and of slender volumes of the lyric poetry which pours forth in a constant stream in all Latin-American communities. The latter, unfortunately, with their inevitable verses on the Niagara Falls, the details of feminine charms, and the horrors of unrequited love, are much more noted for their mellifluous flow of language than for original thought or imagery. Of the twenty left, possibly five would hold the interest of American readers beyond the first few pages. As " every one " writes poetry, no matter what his more useful occupation, there is comparatively little work done in imaginative prose. Nor is there any great demand for such works; the majority of Cubans never open a book, and those who do are apt to turn to translations of the trashier French novels. For, like all Latin-America, the island takes its intellectual cue from France; the " Collection of American Authors " in the Cuban library contains the name of no man born north of the Rio Grande. The natives themselves vote " Cecilia Valdés " their best work of fiction, though many years have passed since its writing. To-day three or four residents of the island are producing occasional volumes of the usual Spanish-American type of novel, over-florid in description, heavy with details, and intimate beyond the point of decency according to our standards, yet with a nicety of style seldom attained by our own present-day novelists and now and then catching a true reflection of a tropical landscape or a native idiosyncrasy. Nothing that Cuba has produced, however, stands out in full world's stature, such as " Maria " in Colombia or " Innocencia " in Brazil.

In Haiti little or nothing of an original nature has been written. We found one small volume in the native jargon, its name, " Cric-Crac," quite aptly describing its contents. In Santo Domingo there are literary aspirations similar to those of Cuba, and as constant, if less voluminous, a flow of " poetry." But while several so-called novels have been, and still are, produced, they are worth reading only because of their scattered pages of often unintentional local color. Porto Rico is a disappointment in a literary way, as in some others. Though the island teems to-day, as it has for centuries, with rich material ready for the picking by the writer of fiction, we found nothing unquestionably indigenous of an imaginative character except a collection of " Cuentos Populares " and the inevitable, almost maudlin, verses of scattered parentage natural to all Spanish-American communities.

A very readable little book called " Phases of Barbadian Life," written, however, by a native of British Guiana, and two pamphlet novels on Trinidad, were the total reward of our quest in the smaller English islands.   One of the latter, " Rupert Gray," by name, is worth perusal for the amusing side-lights it throws on the lucubrations of the African mind, by which it was conceived and brought into being.   There is an added interest in reading these books, slight as is their literary merit, arising from the suspense in guessing whether the heroine is black, " colored," or white, and the uncertainty as to the degree of sympathy which should accordingly be shown for her mishaps.   In Jamaica a man who styles himself a " writer of novels " rather than a novelist has produced several modern tales in which the island life, traditions, and the character of the masses is portrayed with a facile touch in as readable a style of the King's English as may be found anywhere.   Of them all perhaps " Susan Proudleigh " and " Jane " are the most nearly excellent.

In a bit of a shop entitled " Au Bon Livre " in Martinique we picked up a small novel based on the disaster of St. Pierre, called " Cœurs Martiniquais," a simply told, vivid little story.   In the French islands we found also a book in the native patois entitled " Extraits des Bambous," but to all outward appearances it was little more than a translation or an adaptation from La Fontaine's fables.   The French and British islands are much less given to perpetrating poetry than those in which the Spanish tongue is spoken, and show an equal disinclination to producing the heavy volumes on subjects too ponderous for the authors themselves which burden the dusty book-shelves of Ibero-American lands.   On the whole, the West Indies are a virgin field for the literary artist who cares to turn his attention to them.

At various periods during the last hundred years " feelers " have been thrown out from one side or the other to sound the attitude toward the purchase of the British, French, and possibly the Dutch, West Indies by the United States.   The more than attractive price which we squandered for the Virgin Islands, together with the recent suggestions of certain European statesmen that this would be an easy way for England and France to wipe out some of their crushing war debts, has revived the question, and we found it everywhere a topic of conversation in the smaller Antilles.   That the mother countries themselves would consent to such a bargain, if the price corresponded to the one we recently paid for vastly less valuable possessions, is probable, despite the soothing platitudes of princes and ministers, to the general effect that "a mother does not sell her children." What the islands themselves have to say on the subject is perhaps more to the point in these modern days of alleged " self-determination "; and they are backward in expressing themselves.

" In a way we should like to join America," said a white resident of one of the first British islands we visited, " but we have not been entirely pleased with the way America has treated her new West Indian colonies. St. Thomas was too harshly handled; you should have broken them in gradually and left a good impression on the rest of us." (All West Indians apparently labor under the impression that the United States is eager to add them to our population if only the mother countries and they themselves will consent.) " Then, too, we would never stand for prohibition. The negroes would burn every field of sugar-cane on the islands if they were denied their rum. You would have to kill them all off. A man, even a woman, must have his liquor in the tropics. Three or four cock-tails or whiskies a day take the place of the bracing cold of the North. Without it the nerves go bad. We are much more in touch with, I might even say we have more sympathy for, the United States than for England, but for those two reasons we might hesitate to advocate American ownership. Then, many of the blacks are against it because they feel that the United States has never treated the negro fairly."

" We are doing no business except in the absolute necessities," added another white colonial, a man with a string of twenty-six stores throughout the Lesser Antilles. " With so bad an exchange we can't buy in the United States; England has never shipped us the goods we want at prices we can pay; we must wait until Germany gets back into the market. I am almost the only merchant in this island in favor of transferring our allegiance to America. The rest have a ridiculous sentimentality for England or are too conservative to know what is for their own good. Our prosperity would increase by leaps and bounds under the American flag. Look at the prosperity of Cuba and Porto Rico. The preferential tariff has increased their sugar output eight times over. Yet British Guiana alone could produce more sugar than Cuba under a government that would develop her resources."

The other side of the case was most vehemently espoused by a mulatto journalist of Guadeloupe. His editorials accused the " materialistic Yankees " of " wishing to buy the rest of the world cheap," and cited the drop in value of the franc and the pound sterling as proof of their nefarious projects; for it is a general impression in the West

Indies that the rate of exchange is set by American capitalists quite at will. In private conversation he was more courteous, though none the less insistent.

"We are quite ready to admit," he asserted, "that the United States would give us more material advancement in two years than France has in two centuries. We are friendly to Americans, grateful to them; America was the first to give after the Pélée disaster; we might even fight for America; but we feel a love for France as for a mother. We are French and we wish to remain French; we wish to keep our French liberty, which is liberty as we understand it. From our point of view the United States is the greatest autocracy in the world; it has no real republican form of government, no real freedom of the people. Take your white slave law and the prohibition amendment, for example; they are abhorrent to our idea of liberty. The idea of a great federal government chasing a pair of lovers because they happen to cross a state-line, or putting a free citizen in jail merely for selling a bottle of wine, a perfectly legitimate action in any part of the world since the dawn of history! C'est fantastique. The Americans violate our very conception of civil liberty. In Panama and Haiti they come into a house and break up household utensils, throw disinfectants about. We grant that our health might improve under such drastic sanitary measures, but the suffering to our pride would far more than offset that advantage. And above all," he concluded, "under French rule we people of color have what America never has and never will give us, equality of opportunity and standing with the whites."

These two views are typical of a hundred we heard on the subject, and form the boundaries of opinion among West Indians. Roughly speaking, the French islands and Barbados, possibly Trinidad, are decidedly against changing their allegiance, and the rest of the British West Indies looks rather favorably upon the idea. When a rumor came to Martinique soon after the armistice that France was contemplating such a move, frantic cables were sent to Paris, and mobs gathered before the American consulate. "Have we not fought and died for France, not to be thus treacherously abandoned?" demanded the enraged citizens. In Barbados the people froth at the mouth at the mere suggestion of losing their British standing. "Little England" has always been proud of her loyalty; when Charles I was beheaded, the island was so strongly royalist that it immediately declared allegiance to Charles II. Trinidad is farther away and has a prosperity of her own, which may be why the problem is not taken very seriously there. In the other British colonies it is largely an economic question, with no great amount of patriotism or sentiment entering into the matter. Scores of Jamaican negroes replied to the query of whether they had heard of the proposed change with, " Oh, we all wishin' dat hard, sir." Even Englishmen living in Jamaica expressed themselves as feeling it would be better for the island, much as they would regret it from a sentimental point of view. " The trouble with the English," said a Jamaican of standing, " is that if they have a dollar, they put it in the bank and sit on it, whereas the American makes it get out and work for him. We are backward because England will not spend the money to develop our resources. The men who work for the big American companies here on the island get three or four times the salaries of those employed by British corporations."

There are exceptions to the rule in both groups of islands. Thus the working classes are more apt to favor the proposed change than are business men or employers. They feel that the interests of their group are more generously considered under the Stars and Stripes. The poorer white people of the French Antilles are like-minded for another reason: they chafe under the overwhelming political power of the great colored mass of the population. Then there are further ramifications. Many working-men who would otherwise be decided advocates of the transfer stick at the American conception of the color-line. Strangely enough, prohibition is the hardest pill for many to contemplate swallowing, which perhaps is not so strange, after all, in countries where the making of rum is one of the chief industries.

That there would be certain advantages to the United States in acquiring possession of, or political control over, all the islands on our southeastern seaboard goes without saying. Politicians of " imperialistic " tendencies will in all probability explain them to us in detail from time to time as the years roll by. But there is little doubt that they are outweighed by the disadvantages, at least all those of a material nature. Sentimentally it would be pleasant to see our flag flying over all the Caribbean; it would be still more so to feel that no European nation has a foothold on the western hemisphere. That day is in all probability coming, though it is still perhaps far off. As a merely financial proposition, Holland, France, and even England could afford to pay us for taking their possessions in tropical America off their hands. But with the Virgin Islands as an example, we would be paying dearly long after we had parted with any acceptable price which would bring the European West Indies under our flag. Merely to raise them to the American standard in sanitation would be a colossal task, to say nothing of adding materially to our already troublesome " color question."   As some joker has put it, " We could well afford to buy all the West Indies on the basis of the price paid to Denmark, if the sellers would agree to remove all the population "; any other arrangement would probably prove a poor bargain.

CPSIA information can be obtained
at www.ICGtesting.com
Printed in the USA
LVOW10s0306240617
539231LV00035B/1592/P